A Good Golf Course (What Is It?)

How does one define what a "good" golf course really is? It means different things to different people. One definition might be that a "good", or successful, golf course is one that creates a desire in the golfer to return and play it again and again. He might not be able to explain why the attraction exists—it just feels good!

A good golf course is one that the real estate developer, municipality, daily fee operator, resort, or private club can afford to maintain. A golf course might be very dramatic, picturesque, and striking in its visual effect, but if it is too difficult to play, the average golfer, after playing it once or twice, will decide that he is not enjoying it and will never go back again. Income from green fees will diminish and the quality of maintenance will suffer. Poor maintenance will cause a further reduction in rounds of golf played. Also, because of excessively steep mounding and other design features, maintenance costs may be higher than usual. Can this be called a "good" golf course since it is not producing the results expected of it? Anticipated costs of maintenance must be considered during the design phase of the facility.

The design relationship between the parking area, the pro shop, the practice tee and green, the first and 10th tees, and the 9th and 18th greens is very important. This involves walking from the automobile to the pro shop, reaching the practice areas, starting and completing the 18 holes, and returning to the automobile. First and last impressions of the facility are developed during this process.

The design of a good 18-hole golf course first involves the development of a routing plan which takes advantage of existing topography. The goal is to have an interesting rotation of par for the course in which each hole would be followed by one of a different par, such as 4-5-4-3-4-5-4-3-4 for each nine holes. This example is not often possible because of topography and property boundary restrictions (I think it has happened to me twice in the last thirty years!), but an attempt must be made to achieve as much as possible in this regard.

Taking advantage of existing topography means using all the interesting features existing on the land in our design. Where nature has not provided interesting contours or other features, we must attempt to match nature's theme and make it appear that only clearing, floating, and planting was required to develop the golf course.

iv A Good Golf Course (What Is It?)

A good golf course is interesting and challenging, but not impossible or unfair, for all types of golfers, including low, middle, and high handicapper and, very importantly, the ladies. This is done mostly by having multiple tee locations, and positioning hazards so that the longer hitter is faced with the need for accuracy, while the others are provided with much more space at their drive landing area. In short, the farther one hits the ball, the more accurate he must be.

The practice fairway should face toward the north, with a southerly direction being the second choice. The first several holes on the first nine should not require hitting toward the rising sun, and the final holes on the back nine should not aim toward the west.

Each individual hole should be a complete picture within itself, with each area of the hole being a unified part of the total effect. Tee design, contouring throughout the entire length of the hole; mowing patterns at tee, fairway, and green; tree types and location; water courses and lakes; and perhaps the most important part of the whole picture, the individual design of each green, together with locations of those seemingly necessary, but oh, so troublesome cart paths; all are part of the picture to be developed.

If possible, each hole should be aimed in a somewhat different direction than the previous hole, to prevent monotony of the view from the several holes as play progresses. If it is necessary at times to have a succession of parallel holes, they should individually be of different lengths and character.

This is only a short summary of some of the items involved in designing and developing a "good" golf course. The profession of Golf Course Architecture, created out of necessity as a result of the development of the game in Scotland, requires a lifetime of study and practice. It overlaps, and requires knowledge of other fields, such as agronomy, hydrology, land surveying, civil engineering, landscape architecture, arboriculture, site planning, golf course maintenance, heavy equipment operation, and others.

The education process never ends.

— Arthur Jack Snyder
    Former President
    Golf Course Architects Association

Guide Notes

The royal and ancient game of golf is the leading participatory sport in the United States. According to the National Golf Foundation, there are more than 20 million golfers in America. Until now there has not been a comprehensive guide to this nation's public golf courses.

In this Guide we strive to acquaint you with over 14,000 public courses. Of necessity their descriptions are chip shot descriptions: that is, very brief, just enough to give you the basics and tempt you into a pleasant yet challenging round. The listed green and cart fees are based on current information supplied to us by the course's staff. Naturally, prices are always subject to change, and fees often vary with season and time of day, so be sure to confirm policies and prices when you telephone to book your tee time. Many courses have less play in the afternoon, and you're more likely to be at the top of the starter's list if you're willing to tee off later in the day. Also, high handicappers will feel less pressure starting a round after mid-day. You can enjoy a more leisurely game without the long hitters breathing down your back.

Consider the pro shop personnel your best friends. They will help you with rentals, replenish your tee supply and advise you of fast greens and unmarked hazards. And if you don't have a partner ask the fellow at the pro shop to arrange a game when he gives you a starting time. We've found it to be a fantastic way to make new friends. If you prefer a caddie to a cart, ask if they're available when you make your initial inquiries. Most public courses don't offer caddie services, but often the pro can round up one if he has adequate advance notice.

We hope you enjoy using this Guide. If we've missed any of your favorite courses, please send us their names and addresses on our Reader Comment form in the back of the Guide. We welcome your input, and we would like to hear from you.

Straight shooting!

— J. C. Wright
 Petaluma
 September 1996

How This Guide Is Organized

This guide is organized alphabetically by state, and within each state, alphabetically by city or town. Featured courses appear in the front of the Guide. There are additional public courses in our supplementary list at the back of the Guide.

Reservations

Each featured listing includes reservation policy information. We strongly recommend that you call ahead to reserve a tee time. If the course is in a popular resort area, or is highly touted, consider an advance telephone call to confirm your arrangements.

USGA Rating

Most of the listed courses show the USGA rating for the course at the men's white tees.

Restaurant, Bar and Pro Shop

We note these amenities, knowing that golfers enjoy relaxing at the 19th hole.

Green Fees and Rates

The prices shown are intended to give you an idea of the cost of play for one golfer. Prices are always subject to change, and should be verified when you book your tee time. Cart rentals generally refer to the whole cart. The fee can then be split between you and your partner.

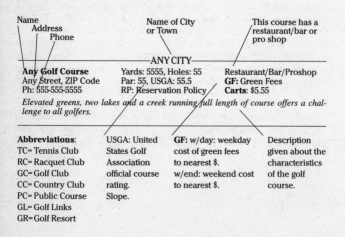

Name
 Address
  Phone

Name of City
or Town

This course has a
restaurant/bar or
pro shop

—————————————ANY CITY—————————————

Any Golf Course   Yards: 5555, Holes: 55   Restaurant/Bar/Proshop
Any Street, ZIP Code   Par: 55, USGA: 55.5   **GF:** Green Fees
Ph: 555-555-5555   RP: Reservation Policy   **Carts:** $5.55

Elevated greens, two lakes and a creek running full length of course offers a challenge to all golfers.

——————————————————————————————————————

Abbreviations: USGA: United   **GF:** w/day: weekday   Description
TC= Tennis Club   States Golf   cost of green fees   given about the
RC= Racquet Club   Association   to nearest $.   characteristics
GC= Golf Club   official course   w/end: weekend cost   of the golf
CC= Country Club   rating.   to nearest $.   course.
PC= Public Course   Slope.
GL= Golf Links
GR= Golf Resort

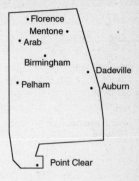

ALABAMA

---ARAB---

Twin Lakes GC
201 13th Ave. N.E.,
35016
Ph: 205-586-3269

Yards: 6800, Holes: 18
Par: 72, USGA: 69.3
RP: Reserve on
weekends only

Restaurant/Proshop
GF: w/day $9.00
Carts: $14.00

Twin Lakes features tree lined fairways, small greens, and nine lakes placed to compliment each hole. Our eleventh hole is a short par 3 with water from tee to green. It will reward good play but will penalize irreverent shots.

---AUBURN---

Auburn Links GC
826 Shell Toomer Kky.,
36830
Ph: 205-887-5151

Yards: 6465, Holes: 18
Par: 72

A narrow, and heavily treed course that is fairly long. There's lots of water on this beautiful course. You'll definitely find a challenge here.

---AUBURN---

Pin Oaks GC
P.O. Box 1792, I-85/US
29 So., 36830
Ph: 205-821-0893

Yards: 6208, Holes: 18
Par: 72, USGA: 72.0
RP: Starting time not
required

Restaurant/Bar/Proshop
GF: w/day $10.00
Carts: $8.00

Fairways lined with pine and oak trees with rolling fairways. Front side championship with lots of dogleg holes. Crossing lake on 3 holes. Back side fun, short and challenging. Lots of doglegs. All four 5 pars great holes.

---BESSEMER---

Bent Brook GC
7900 Dickey Springs
Rd., 35023
Ph: 205-428-9600

Yards: 6824, Holes: 27
Par: 72

Bar
GF: w/day $18.00

Three set of 9-hole courses that can be played in different combinations. The course is very open and you'll enjoy the rolling terrain.

Enter your favorite resort in our "Golf Resort of The Year" contest (entry form is in the back of the book).

─────────────── BIRMINGHAM ───────────────

Eagle Point GC
4500 Eagle Point Dr.,
35223
Ph: 205-991-9070

Yards: 5783, Holes: 18
Par: 71

Elevated tees, short and narrow with lots of water and sand. Your irons will bet a workout.

─────────────── BIRMINGHAM ───────────────

**North Birmingham
Muni GC**
2120 36th Ave. N,
35207
Ph: 205-326-2445

Yards: 5383, Holes: 9
Par: 70, USGA: 65.4

Proshop
GF: w/day $6.00
Carts: $6.00

Our course is the oldest in Birmingham with a beautiful overview of downtown from our #2 & #3 holes. We have nine greens with front nine and back nine tee boxes making our course play like the toughest 18 hole course in the southeast.

─────────────── BIRMINGHAM ───────────────

**Oxmoor Valley
(Valley Course) GC**
100 Sunbelt Parkway,
35211
Ph: 205-290-0940

Yards: 6587, Holes: 18
Par: 72

Designed by Robert Trent Jones, Sr., you know you're going to be in for a terrific round of golf.

─────────────── BIRMINGHAM ───────────────

**Oxmoor Valley GC -
Ridge Course**
100 Sunbelt Parkway,
35211
Ph: 205-290-0940

Yards: 6527, Holes: 18
Par: 72

36-holes of golf, one of them an 18-holes executive type, and the other a Robert Trent Jones, Sr. design. A real championship course with one hole that has something unusual to offer.

─────────────── CAMDEN ───────────────

**Roland Cooper State
Park**
49 Deer Run Dr., 36726
Ph: 205-682-4838

Yards: 6480, Holes: 9
Par: 70

Proshop
GF: w/day $9.00

A perfect course for walking with many chances to see the wildlife of the area. The course is somewhat hilly and there are many beautiful pines to shade your walk.

─────────────── CHOCOLOCCO ───────────────

Pine Hill CC
Chocolocco Rd., 36254
Ph: 205-237-2633

Yards: 6191, Holes: 18
Par: 72

Restaurant
GF: w/day $12.00

A course with a nice setting with mountains as a background. A course that will offer a moderate challenge, with a lot of water and some hillside lies.

Plan ahead! Reserve tee time well in advance, and while you're doing so, confirm rates and services.

──────────────DADEVILLE──────────────

Still Waters GC
1000 Still Waters Dr.,
36853
Ph: 205-825-7887

Yards: 5903, Holes: 18
Par: 72, USGA: 69.1

Restaurant/Bar/Proshop
GF: w/day $20.00
Carts: $8.00

Birdies abound at our 6,500-yard course. Not because famed golf architect George Cobb designed it to be overly easy, but because he created it to be very fair. What's more, Cobb, who has seen more than his share of woods, calls those at Still Waters best.

──────────────DECATUR──────────────

Point Mallard Park GC
3109 8th St., 35601
Ph: 205-351-7776

Yards: 6790, Holes: 18
Par: 72

Restaurant/Proshop
GF: w/day $10.00, w/end
$12.00
Carts: $14.00

A public course near the Tennessee River. Lots of water on this long and straight course. A challenge for most golfers.

──────────────DOTHAN──────────────

Olympia Resorts
P.O. Box 6108, 36302
Ph: 205-677-3321

Yards: 6560, Holes: 18
Par: 72, USGA: 72.0
RP: Tee times required

Restaurant/Bar/Proshop
GF: w/day $12.71, w/end
$15.54
Carts: $8.00

A very long course on which your driving skills will get a severe test. Set on rolling terrain with tree-lined fairways.

──────────────EUFAULA──────────────

Lakepoint State Resort Park GC
Rt.2 Box 94, 36027
Ph: 334-687-6677

Yards: 6531, Holes: 18
Par: 72, USGA: 71.4
Slope: 121
RP: Weekends only

Proshop
GF: w/day $12.00, w/end
$12.00
Carts: $17.00

A warm and hospitable resort that offers wonderful golf. There's plenty of water and sand and some rolling lies. The back nine is tighter than the front and has more trees.

──────────────FLORENCE──────────────

McFarland Park GC
200 McFarland Dr.,
35630
Ph: 205-760-6428

Yards: 6660, Holes: 18
Par: 72, USGA: 69.7
RP: Call for weekend &
holidays

Proshop
GF: w/day $8.00
Carts: $12.00

Located on the banks of the Tennessee River you will find 18 challenging holes with pine trees lining the fairways. As you approach the greens be prepared to bring those short-game skills into play because you'll need a special touch around the 18th.

──────────────FLORENCE──────────────

New Sky Park GC
Rt. 7, Box 327, 35630
Ph: 205-757-4911

Yards: 5900, Holes: 9
Par: 72, USGA: 69.5

Proshop
GF: w/day $3.00
Carts: $8.00

This sporty 9 hole course plays from two sets of tees for greater variety. Rolling fairways and small lush greens demand a variety of shots to score well.

────────────────────FOLEY────────────────────

Lakeview GC
9530 Clubhouse Dr.,
36535
Ph: 205-943-8000

Yards: 6635, Holes: 18
Par: 71

Restaurant/Bar
GF: w/day $29.00, w/end
$33.00

The back nine is the more difficult here, it's somewhat hilly, while the front has narrow fairways and is flat.

────────────────────GULF SHORES────────────────────

Cotton Creek GC
County Rd 4, Cotton
Creek Blvd., Ph: 205-
968-7766

Yards: 6032, Holes: 18
Par: 72

With water and trees in abundance, you're going to find a lot to test your skills. The holes all have a very different personality.

────────────────────GULF SHORES────────────────────

Gulf State Park GC
HC 70 Box 9, 36542
Ph: 205-948-4653

Yards: 6171, Holes: 18
Par: 72

A course that will let you get away with some mistakes, it has wide fairways and large greens. A very popular layout.

────────────────────GUNTERSVILLE────────────────────

**Lake Guntersville
GC**
7966 Alabama Hwy
Box 227, 35976
Ph: 205-582-0379

Yards: 6258, Holes: 18
Par: 72, USGA: 68.8
Slope: 123

GF: w/day $14.00, w/end
$14.00
Carts: $18.00

This state park course has many challenging lies for the unwary. The views and wildlife will also make for an interesting round of golf.

────────────────────HUNTSVILLE────────────────────

Huntsville Muni GC
151 Airport Rd., 35805
Ph: 205-883-3647

Yards: 6407, Holes: 18
Par: 72

Restaurant
GF: w/day $10.00

Bunkers are going to be the main difficulty on this course. Even though the course may appear short, you'll be giving your driver plenty of work.

────────────────────MENTONE────────────────────

Saddle Rock GC
Cloudmont Resort,
P.O. Box 435, 35984
Ph: 205-634-4344

Yards: 2181, Holes: 9
Par: 31, USGA: 70.0
RP: Call for tee times

Restaurant/Bar/Proshop
GF: w/day $6.50, w/end
$8.50
Carts: $8.00

Our first tee is located on top of a thirty foot rock. While up there you can see across the entire course. Executive length course with rolling greens, lakes, tight fairways and an all round challenge.

────────────────────MOBILE────────────────────

Azalea City GC
1000 Gaillard Dr.,
36608
Ph: 205-342-4221

Yards: 6842, Holes: 18
Par: 72

Restaurant
GF: w/day $10.00

The features here are open fairways and large greens, with a bit of water and lots of bunkers. One side is hilly, and the other is fairly flat.

─────────────────── MONTGOMERY ───────────────────

Lagoon Park GC
2855 Lagoon Park Dr.,
36109
Ph: 205-271-7000

Yards: 6773, Holes: 18
Par: 72, USGA: 70.3
RP: Weekends &
holidays

Proshop
GF: w/day $10.00, w/end
$12.00
Carts: $12.00

Set in a park, this layout has a wonderful variety of mature trees. The par-4s are very long and difficult on this course. Lots of water here will be an added challenge to this top-flight course.

─────────────────── MONTGOMERY ───────────────────

Oak Hills GC
7160 Byron Nelson
Blvd, 36116
Ph: 205-281-3344

Yards: 7115, Holes: 18
Par: 72

Bar
GF: w/day $15.00

Designed by Byron Nelson, the course is long and open. The greens are large and towering trees abound. There is water on seven holes and numerous nasty doglegs.

─────────────────── OPELIKA ───────────────────

Grand National GC
3000 Sun Belt Pkwy,
Ph: 205-749-9042

Yards: 5948, Holes: 36
Par: 72

Three 18-holes courses, one of them an executive type. This is a beautiful Robert Trent Jones Sr. design, and is a very scenic and challenging course with trees that are beautiful in every season.

─────────────────── PELHAM ───────────────────

**Oak Mountain State
Park GC**
P.O. Box 278, 35124
Ph: 205-663-6731

Yards: 6423, Holes: 18
Par: 72, USGA: 68.9
RP: Earliest is 6 days in
advance

Restaurant/Bar/Proshop
GF: w/day $8.00, w/end
$10.00
Carts: $10.00

Scenic view—this course sets in the valley of Oak Mountain and Double Oak Mountains. Flat fairways with some elevated greens. Long par 3's and dogleg par 4's and 5's.

─────────────────── POINT CLEAR ───────────────────

**Marriott's Grand
Hotel - Dogwood GC**
Scenic Highway 98,
36564
Ph: 334-990-6312

Yards: 6331, Holes: 18
Par: 71, USGA: 70.5
Slope: 121
RP: Must be guest of
hotel

GF: w/day $65.00, w/end
$65.00
Carts: $Included

The courses here are very hilly with an overabundance of sand. While most of the greens are very small targets, there is also an island green. The beautiful, mature live oaks on the course are an additional hazard that can often come into play.

─────────────────── SIMS ───────────────────

Magnolia Grove GC
7000 Lamplighter Dr,
36575
Ph: 205-645-0075

Yards: 6021, Holes: 36
Par: 72

Two 18-hole course are located here. The courses take advantage of their setting. Robert Trent Jones, Sr. was the designer. An 18-hole executive type course is all available.

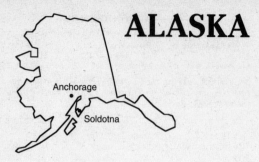

ALASKA

Anchorage •

Soldotna

─────── ANCHORAGE ───────

Anchorage GC
3651 O'Malley Rd.,
99516
Ph: 907-522-3322

Yards: 6115, Holes: 18
Par: 72, USGA: 69.2
RP: One week ahead

Restaurant/Bar/Proshop
GF: w/day $21.00, w/end
$21.00
Carts: $20.00

You start out with a spectacular view of Anchorage and Mt. McKinley in the background. The front is very tight with a little water. A back nine of rolling fairways and mountain view.

─────── ANCHORAGE ───────

Eagle Glen GC-
Military
21CSG/SSRG Bldg 23-
100 Elmendorf, 99506
Ph: 907-552-3821

Yards: 6084, Holes: 18
Par: 72, USGA: 68.6
RP: Week-1 day
advance; weekend-3
day advance

Bar/Proshop
GF: w/day $25.00
Carts: $18.00

The course has water coming into play on 4 holes, and makes the 18th hole especially difficult. There are beautiful tree-lined wide fairways. Wild life is present in the form of eagles to give you an air show.

─────── FAIRBANKS ───────

Chena Bend GC-
Military
APVR-FW-PAD Ft.
Wainwright, 99703
Ph: 907-353-7830

Yards: 6648, Holes: 9
Par: 36, USGA: 12.8

GF: w/day $10.00, w/end
$14.00
Carts: $12.00

Chena Bend is located at Ft. Wainwright. A nine hole course near the Chena River.

─────── FT. RICHARDSON ───────

Moose Run GC
Golf Course Grounds,
99505
Ph: 907-428-0056

Yards: 6429, Holes: 18
Par: 71, USGA: 69.8

Restaurant/Bar
GF: w/day $22.00
Carts: $14.00

This course has a truly magnificent setting.

--------------------------------KENAI--------------------------------

Kenai GC   Holes: 18   **GF:** w/day $12.00, w/end
1420 Lawton Avenue,   USGA: 72.1 $15.00
99611   **Carts:** $15.00
Ph: Dick Morgan

Plenty of water on the course to keep it interesting. Most of the greens are well trapped, with trees as well as sand. Your choice of clubs will make a big difference here, with lots of tough doglegs. A beautiful natural setting.

--------------------------------KODIAK--------------------------------

Bear Valley GC   Yards: 2861, Holes: 9
PO Box 27, 99516   Par: 36
Ph: 907-522-3363

A long 9 hole course located on Kodiak Island.

--------------------------------PALMER--------------------------------

Palmer GC   Yards: 6585, Holes: 18   **GF:** w/day $20.00
1000 Lepak Avenue,   USGA: 72.1   **Carts:** $15.00
99645
Ph: 907-745-4653

A very challenging municipal course with plenty of water. There are a lot of long holes and well trapped greens to keep the challenge going. A very scenic course located on the Matanuska River with The Talkeetna, Chugach Mountains, and Knik Glacier.

--------------------------------SOLDOTNA--------------------------------

Birch Ridge GC   Yards: 3106, Holes: 9   Restaurant/Bar/Proshop
Box 828, 99669   Par: 35   **GF:** w/day $7.00
Ph: 907-262-5270   **Carts:** $1.00

Not a long course, but tree-lined on all fairways with small elevated greens. You will enjoy the mountain views and perhaps the local wildlife, because around here "Moose and other wild critters have the right-of-way."

--------------------------------SOLODOTNA--------------------------------

Shoreline Par 3 GC   Holes: 9   **GF:** w/day $4.00
56910 East Road,   Par: 27

A nice little pitch-and-putt type course. Give it a try twice around, as it really is different from the second tees.

--------------------------------WASILLA--------------------------------

Settlers Bay GC   Ph: 907-376-5466   USGA: 72.0
PO Box 877509, 99687

This course has many elevated tees, with many long holes. The last hole will give you a real test of your golfing skills. A putting green and driving range will give you an opportunity for a little practice, if you desire.

--------------------------------WASILLA--------------------------------

Sleepy Hollow GC   Holes: 9   **GF:** w/day $8.00
HC-33 Box 3056, 99654 Par: 27
Ph: 907-376-5948

Sleepy Hollow is in a very scenic setting, with mountains and a river. Play the 9 holes twice and get a bargain rate.

◄◄◄◄◄◄◄◄◄● ►►►►►►►►►►

ARIZONA

─────────── CAREFREE ───────────

Boulders GC-Private
34636 N. Tom
Darlington, 85377
Ph: 602-488-9028

Yards: 6926, Holes: 36
Par: 71, USGA: 72.6
Slope: 137
RP: Resort and Private
Club

Restaurant/Bar
GF: w/day $115.00, w/end
$115.00
Carts: $Included

Considered one of the top resort layouts. Both courses play tough with the desert intruding, quite often, into the fairways. You never know which course will be available to resort use, so you might want to check ahead if you have a preference.

─────────── CASA GRANDE ───────────

**Francisco Grande
GC**
26000 Gila Bend Hwy.,
85222
Ph: 602-836-6444

Yards: 6451, Holes: 18
Par: 72, USGA: 69.5
Slope: 114

Restaurant/Bar
GF: w/day $20.00, w/end
$25.00

Fast green and lots of length on the course will make this a really challenging round of golf. A favorite tournament course, so be sure to book ahead.

─────────── CAVE CREEK ───────────

**Golf Club at Rancho
Manana**
5734 East Rancho
Manana Blvd., 85331
Ph: 602-488-0398

Yards: 5910, Holes: 18
Par: 72, USGA: 69.1

Restaurant/Bar/Proshop
GF: w/day $70.00, w/end
$70.00
Carts: $Included

Rancho Manana will demand that you pay attention today, or you're sure to have some very difficult golfing lies.

─────────── CAVE CREEK ───────────

Tatum Ranch GC
29888 N. Tatum Ranch
Rd., 85331
Ph: 602-252-1230

Yards: 6870, Holes: 18
Par: 72, USGA: 72.8

Restaurant/Bar
GF: w/day $33.00

The course at Tatum Ranch uses the natural terrain to very good advantage. You'll find this a peaceful and challenging course that will provide a memorable round of golf.

───────────────────CHANDLER───────────────────

Ocotillo GC
3751 South Clubhouse
Dr., 85248
Ph: 602-275-4355

Yards: 6729, Holes: 27
Par: 72, USGA: 70.6

Restaurant
GF: w/day $29.00
Carts: $Included

As you initiate your takeaway, envision the ball strategically sailing over a waterfall, and watch out for the bunkers on the fairways and green. Lakes cover 90 acres, with 14 miles of shoreline, lush, sloping fairways and spectacular waterfalls.

───────────────────CHANDLER───────────────────

**Ocotillo GC - Blue/
Gold**
3751 South Clubhouse
Dr., 85248
Ph: 602-275-4355

Yards: 6729, Holes: 27
Par: 71, USGA: 70.6

Restaurant
GF: w/day $75.00
Carts: $Included

As you initiate your takeaway, envision the ball strategically sailing over a waterfall, and watch out for the bunkers on the fairways and green, reaching out like fingers guarding pin placement. Lakes cover 90 acres, with 14 miles of shoreline.

───────────────────CHANDLER───────────────────

San Marcos GC
100 N. Dakota St.,
85224
Ph: 602-963-3358

Yards: 6117, Holes: 18
Par: 72, USGA: 67.5
RP: Three days in
advance

Restaurant/Bar/Proshop
GF: w/day $23.00
Carts: $10.00

Golf has been a tradition at the San Marcos since 1913. Today, those traditions are being renewed, and we invite you to play golf on our historic PGA championship course. Lined by stately palms, eucalyptus and tamarisk, the 6,500 yards of greens.

───────────────────CHANDLER───────────────────

**Sunbird Golf
Community**
1661 East Riggs Rd.,
85249
Ph: 602-732-1000

Yards: 4131, Holes: 18
Par: 65, USGA: 58.7

Bar/Proshop
GF: w/day $16.00
Carts: $7.00

You start out on the short, but tight and well bunkered front nine, with five shimmering lakes. The tough back nine overlooks the San Tan Mountains, where the par 5 16th has six bunkers strategically placed with a huge lake bordering the right side.

───────────────────DEWEY───────────────────

Prescott CC
1030 Prescott Country
Club Rd., 86327
Ph: 602-772-8984

Yards: 6420, Holes: 18
Par: 72, USGA: 69.6
RP: 3 days in advance

Restaurant/Bar/Proshop
GF: w/day $15.00
Carts: $8.00

Prescott Country Club is surrounded by the beautiful rolling hills, and clear blue skies of Northern Arizona. The course is set for an excellent test of golf. From the elevated tees to the slick bent greens, a round you'll want to remember.

Our listings—supplied by the management—are as complete as possible. Many of the courses have more features than we list. Be sure to inquire when you book your tee time.

DOUGLAS

Douglas GC
N 7/10 Mi Leslie, P.O.
Box 1220, 85608
Ph: 602-364-3722

Yards: 3093, Holes: 9
Par: 35, USGA: 67.5

Bar/Proshop
GF: w/day $6.00, w/end
$9.00
Carts: $9.00

The course is a beautiful desert scene surrounded by mountains. Golf is played the year around. We are in the process of expanding our RV park to accommodate 48 full hook-ups with TV. Within the next 2 years we plan to expand the course to a full 18 hole.

GILBERT

El Dorado Lakes GC
1800 West Guadalupe,
85233
Ph: 602-926-3437

Yards: 6228, Holes: 18
Par: 72, USGA: 70.1
Slope: 128

GF: w/day $65.00, w/end
$65.00
Carts: $Included

Lots and lots of water, and the rolling terrain will keep you on your toes. Elevated tees and green will demand your accuracy to keep out of the water.

GLENDALE

Arrowhead CC
19888 North 73rd Ave.,
85308
Ph: 602-561-9625

Yards: 7001, Holes: 18
Par: 72, USGA: 73.3

Restaurant/Bar
GF: w/day $50.00
Carts: $Included

We asked Arnold Palmer to design the golf course of his dreams. This is it. It will also be the golf course of your dreams, with its breathtaking vistas and challenges for the most experienced pros as well as the most basic beginners.

GLENDALE

Legend GC
21025 N. 67th Ave.,
85308
Ph: 602-561-1902

Yards: 7005, Holes: 18
Par: 72, USGA: 73.0
Slope: 124

GF: w/day $59.00, w/end
$79.00
Carts: $Included

Well bunkered green are the rule on this beautifully designed Arnold Palmer course. Water can play a very real part in your game here. A well maintained layout that is host to many tournaments.

GLOBE

Cobre Valley CC
Box 2629, Apache
Trail, 85502
Ph: 602-473-2542

Yards: 3320, Holes: 9
Par: 36, USGA: 69.9

Restaurant/Bar/Proshop
GF: w/day $15.00
Carts: $12.60

Lush greens enhance the enjoyment of our fine golf course but watch out for the subtle breaks and slopes or there may be a few three putts.

GOLD CANYON

Gold Canyon GC
6100 S. Kings Ranch
Rd., 85219
Ph: 602-982-9449

Yards: 6004, Holes: 18
Par: 71, USGA: 68.0
Slope: 129

Restaurant/Bar
GF: w/day $89.00, w/end
$99.00
Carts: $Included

A tight, well constructed course with small greens and an overabundance of water, this is the desert? The views from here are truly spectacular. A terrific place to stay if you'd enjoy a little privacy and you can even have a private spa.

──────────── GOODYEAR ────────────

Eagle's Nest CC
3639 Clubhouse Dr.,
85338
Ph: 602-935-6750

Yards: 6226, Holes: 18
Par: 72, USGA: 69.4
Slope: 118

Restaurant/Bar/Proshop
GF: w/day $45.00, w/end
$45.00
Carts: $Included

None of the holes have shots over the water, but the doglegs, and rolling greens with strategic bunkering will give you a real challenge.

──────────── GREEN VALLEY ────────────

Canoa Hills GC
1401 W. Calle Urbano,
85614
Ph: 602-648-1880

Yards: 6077, Holes: 18
Par: 72, USGA: 68.2
RP: Two days in
advance

Restaurant/Bar/Proshop
GF: w/day $26.00
Carts: $Included

Canoa Hills is a beautiful, well manicured desert golf course set in the Santa Cruz Valley offering large undulating bent grass greens, rolling fairways and panoramic tees. Course has tight fairways with natural desert surroundings.

──────────── LAKE HAVASU ────────────

Nautical Inn GC
1000 McCulloch Blvd.,
86403
Ph: 602-855-2131

Yards: 4012, Holes: 18
Par: 61, USGA: 57.4
RP: 24 hrs. in advance

Restaurant/Bar/Proshop
GF: w/day $18.00
Carts: $12.00

Our two most famous holes are No.'s 14-15. Both par 3's, #14 is 170 yards from the men's tee and #15 is 190 yards. Both holes require a carry over part of beautiful Lake Havasu. The lake view from both holes is breathtaking.

──────────── LAKE HAVASU ────────────

Queens Bay GC
1480 Queens Bay,
86403
Ph: 602-855-4777

Yards: 1560, Holes: 9
Par: 27, USGA: 52.2
RP: 1 week in advance

Bar/Proshop
GF: w/day $7.50
Carts: $5.00

Erratic tee shots on any of our nine holes could produce high numbers on your score card. The course was built on the natural terrain of the desert, which engulfs all fairways.

──────────── LAKE MONTEZUMA ────────────

Beaver Creek Golf Resort
Montezuma &
Lakeshore, 86342
Ph: 602-567-4487

Yards: 6054, Holes: 18
Par: 71, USGA: 68.0
RP: 48 hours in
advance

Restaurant/Bar/Proshop
GF: w/day $18.00, w/end
$18.00
Carts: $7.00

Rushing waters of Beaver Creek echo softly against craggy cliffs that cradle the lush fairways and bent grass greens of Beaver Creek Golf Resort. Many an Arizonan has claimed Beaver Creek Golf Resort as their personal retreat.

──────────── LITCHFIELD PARK ────────────

Wigwam Golf & CC-Private
4344 N. Litchfield Rd.,
85340
Ph: 602-935-9414

Yards: 6504, Holes: 18
Par: 72, USGA: 71.7

Restaurant/Bar/Proshop
GF: w/day $80.00, w/end
$80.00
Carts: $Included

Three of the best courses in Arizona, if not the country! The Blue course is the shortest. The Gold course is the toughest, and the Red Course ends strong. The setting here is unsurpassed with mature landscaping.

--------------------------MESA--------------------------

Arizona GR
425 South Power Rd.,
85206
Ph: 602-832-1661

Yards: 6574, Holes: 18
Par: 71, USGA: 71.1
RP: Call for availability

Restaurant/Bar/Proshop
GF: w/day $20.00
Carts: $10.00

Arizona Golf Resort is unique, in that it is easy for the high handicapper and challenging for the low handicapper. There is out of bounds on both sides of every hole.

--------------------------MESA--------------------------

**Red Mountain Ranch
CC**
6425 East Teton, 85205
Ph: 602-985-0285

Yards: 6797, Holes: 18
Par: 72, USGA: 74.1
RP: 3 days maximum in
advance

Restaurant/Bar/Proshop
GF: w/day $79.00, w/end
$89.00
Carts: $Included

Red Mountain Ranch Country Club is located in the beautiful desert foothills of North East Mesa, Arizona. This Pete Dye designed championship course is a classic desert target design. Impeccably maintained, hand mown bentgrass greens.

--------------------------MESA--------------------------

**Superstition Springs
GC**
6542 E. Baseline Rd.,
85206
Ph: 602-890-9009

Yards: 7005, Holes: 18
Par: 72, USGA: 74.1
RP: Three days in
advance

Restaurant/Bar/Proshop
GF: w/day $90.00, w/end
$110.00
Carts: $Included

Nominated by Golf Digest magazine as one of the best new public courses in the country, Superstition Springs Golf Club features spectacular water holes and large white sand bunkers. Selected as a site for the 1992 and 1993 PGA Tour.

-------------------------- ORO VALLEY--------------------------

El Conquistador CC
10555 N La Canada,
85704
Ph: 602-742-6500

Yards: 6178, Holes: 36
Par: 72, USGA: 69.0
RP: Required

GF: w/day $25.00
Carts: $15.00

The course measures 6,715 from the blue tees, so it gives you plenty of room to really let your long ball fly. Hole #6 is a par 5573 yards from blue tee and 540 from the white. The hole has a slight dogleg and can keep you on your toes.

-------------------------- PARADISE VALLEY--------------------------

Stonecreek
4435 E Paradise
Village Pkwy S, 85032
Ph: 602-953-9110

Yards: 6839, Holes: 18
Par: 71, USGA: 73.5

Restaurant
GF: w/day $58.00
Carts: $Included

This course is considered one of the best 50 public courses. Set in rolling terrain, you can't always tell where the bunkers are, and the greens vary a great deal in size. This is a layout where accuracy is a must. Water, bunkers, creek beds, and mogels.

-------------------------- PARKER--------------------------

Emerald Canyon GC
72 Emerald Canyon
Dr., 85344
Ph: 602-667-3366

Yards: 6421, Holes: 18
Par: 72, USGA: 66.6
RP: Up to one week in
advance

Proshop
GF: w/day $16.00
Carts: $15.00

Located along the beautiful Colorado River, the course is nestled in the hills and canyons next to the river. Spectacular views are throughout the course. Our favorite hole is #5. A short par 3, 150 yards from an elevated tee.

────────────────PAYSON────────────────

Payson GC, Inc.
1504 West Country
Club Dr., 85541
Ph: 602-474-2273

Yards: 5854, Holes: 18
Par: 71, USGA: 66.1
RP: Up to 1 week in
advance

Restaurant/Bar/Proshop
GF: w/day $25.00, w/end
$28.00
Carts: $14.00

You can wander on the front nine but you better have it under control when you go to the backside. Never a dull moment.

────────────────PEARCE────────────────

Arizona Sunsites CC
Box 508, 85625
Ph: 602-826-3412

Yards: 6638, Holes: 18
Par: 72, USGA: 68.9
RP: Please call

Restaurant/Bar/Proshop
GF: w/day $16.70, w/end
$16.70
Carts: $14.00

Not crowded. 4300 feet elevation. Nice Summer temperatures. Suited for average player.

────────────────PHOENIX────────────────

Anasazi GC
4435 East Paradise
Village, 85032
Ph: 602-953-9110

Yards: 7113, Holes: 18
Par: 72, USGA: 70.1

This Scottish Links course was designed for the utmost in golfing pleasure. You'll take pleasure in the lush, emerald-green fairways and meticulously-maintained greens with just the right balance of hazards—all enhanced by a beautiful mountain view.

────────────────PHOENIX────────────────

Arizona Biltmore CC
24th St. & Missouri,
85016
Ph: 602-955-9655

Yards: 6400, Holes: 18
Par: 71, USGA: 72.2
RP: Up to 7 days with
credit card

Restaurant/Bar
GF: w/day $53.00
Carts: $Included

Golfers will want to play one or both of the PGA-rated championship courses. Try flat Adobe, built in 1930 with 6900 yards of tree-lined fairways, streams and lakes. Or play the long, narrow Links, with its unusual rolling terrain and five lakes.

────────────────PHOENIX────────────────

Cave Creek GC PC
15202 North 19th Ave.,
85023
Ph: 602-866-8076

Yards: 6290, Holes: 18
Par: 72, USGA: 68.8
RP: 2 days in advance

Restaurant/Bar/Proshop
GF: w/day $18.00
Carts: $12.80

Cave Creek wash works its way through the middle of the course. It is deep and wide. After three easy starting holes the wash comes into play on holes 4, 5, 6, 7, 8, 9, 11, 12 & 18. On holes 11 and 18 the drive must carry the wash.

────────────────PHOENIX────────────────

El Caro GC
2222 West Royal Palm
Rd., 85021
Ph: 602-995-3664

Yards: 3400, Holes: 18
Par: 60, USGA: 54.7

Restaurant/Bar
GF: w/day $8.00
Carts: $13.00

An executive style course right in Phoenix. The course abounds with doglegs, with a particularly good one on #18 for a really challenge of a finish.

---------------------------------PHOENIX---------------------------------

Papago GC   Yards: 7053, Holes: 18   Restaurant/Proshop
5595 E. Moreland Ave.,   Par: 72, USGA: 70.8   **GF:** w/day $18.00
85008   RP: 2 days in advance   **Carts:** $15.00
Ph: 602-275-8428

Site of the 1971 National Publinks Championship. Features large mature trees rolling fairways and undulating greens in a natural desert setting. Many sand traps and water hazards—ranked in the top 75 public golf courses by Golf Digest.

---------------------------------PHOENIX---------------------------------

Pointe GC on   Yards: 6630, Holes: 18   Restaurant/Bar/Proshop
Lookout Mountain   Par: 72, USGA: 71.7   **GF:** w/day $13.00
11111 N. 7th St., 85020   **Carts:** $12.00
Ph: 602-866-9816

Located in the Phoenix Mountain Preserve this course is very scenic and one of the favorites of the PGA Tour golfers. No. 9 is a tough par-3 with a hillside green. This is a difficult and memorable course.

---------------------------------PHOENIX---------------------------------

The Pointe on S.   Yards: 6400, Holes: 18   Restaurant/Bar/Proshop
Mountain   Par: 72, USGA: 69.9   **GF:** w/day $13.00
7777 South Pointe   RP: 2 days in advance   **Carts:** $12.00
Pkwy., 85044
Ph: 602-438-9000

This unique course offers pristine Sonoran desert terrain, rolling arroyos filled with saguaros and blossoming palo verde trees, with islands of manicured greens and tees—all placed before a spectacular backdrop of rugged mountains.

---------------------------------PHOENIX---------------------------------

Valley Club of Royal Yards: 2300, Holes: 9   Restaurant/Bar/Proshop
Palms Inn   Par: 36, USGA: 62.1   **GF:** w/day $8.00
5200 East Camelback   **Carts:** $12.00
Rd., 85018
Ph: 602-840-3610

A delightful nine hole (regulation nine) par 36 at the south slope of Camelback Mountain. Registered guests have complimentary golf.

--------------------------------SAN MANUEL--------------------------------

San Manuel GC   Yards: 3220, Holes: 9   Restaurant/Bar
Box 59, 85631   Par: 36, USGA: 69.7
Ph: 602-385-2224

Often the panoramic view of the surrounding mountains is quickly forgotten as one is astounded by the most treacherous bent grass greens in the Southwest. It is frequently said if you can chip and putt San Manuel, you can chip and putt the PGA Tour.

--------------------------------SCOTTSDALE--------------------------------

Camelback GC   Yards: 6486, Holes: 18   Restaurant/Bar
7847 N. Mockingbird   Par: 72, USGA: 70.9   **GF:** w/day $68.00
Ln., 85253   RP: Outside resident on   **Carts:** $Included
Ph: 602-948-6770   space available

The long and open Indian Bend Course lies within a verdant natural wash basin. Its links-type layout provides the golfer with stretches of gently-rolling terrain and incredible mountain vistas. The Padre course is short but tight.

————————————SCOTTSDALE————————————

Gainey Ranch GC
7600 Gainey Club Dr.,
85285
Ph: 602-951-0022

Yards: 6818, Holes: 27
Par: 72, USGA: 70.0
RP: Hyatt Regency
guest can play

Restaurant/Bar
GF: w/day $64.00
Carts: $Included

Three 9 holes courses make up a 27 hole championship course. Dunes is characterized by sand dunes amidst rolling greens. Golfers will find five lakes cropping up on the next nine, called the Lakes.

————————————SCOTTSDALE————————————

McCormick Ranch GC
7505 McCormick
Pkwy., 85258
Ph: 602-948-0260

Yards: 7021, Holes: 18
Par: 72, USGA: 68.8
RP: 2 days in advance

Restaurant/Bar/Proshop
GF: w/day $79.00
Carts: $Included

Home of the Arizona Open, the annual Arizona State University Golf Tournament, the Ping World Pro-Am. Surrounded by Scottsdale's most prominent hotels.

————————————SCOTTSDALE————————————

Mountain Shadows CC
5641 East Lincoln Dr.,
85253
Ph: 602-951-5427

Yards: 3000, Holes: 18
Par: 56, USGA: 51.7
Slope: 87
RP: Up to 7 days in
advance

Restaurant/Bar
GF: w/day $46.00, w/end
$46.00
Carts: $Included

Set near the Camelback Mountains, you'll enjoy the beauty of the setting. The greens are well bunkered and there's just enough water in play to make it interesting.

————————————SCOTTSDALE————————————

Orange Tree GC PC
10601 North 56th St.,
85254
Ph: 602-948-3730

Yards: 6762, Holes: 18
Par: 72, USGA: 69.6

Restaurant/Bar/Proshop
GF: w/day $49.00
Carts: $Included

Among the hazards on these tree-lined links are four lakes and 70 sand bunkers. The 403-yard par 4 finishing hole is a bogey-maker with water on the left and a green trapped with front-side bunkers. It's been featured by the USGA Golf Journal and ABC TV.

————————————SCOTTSDALE————————————

Phoenician GC
6000 E. Camelback
Rd., 85251
Ph: 602-423-2449

Yards: 6487, Holes: 18
Par: 71, USGA: 71.2
Slope: 134
RP: Up to 7 days in
advance

Restaurant/Bar
GF: w/day $125.00, w/end
$125.00
Carts: $Included

Some consider the course short, but the setting is choice and there's plenty of water. The resort itself is a Five-Star establishment, and not to be missed.

————————————SCOTTSDALE————————————

TPC Scottsdale
17020 North Hayden
Rd., 85255
Ph: 602-585-3600

Yards: 6992, Holes: 18
Par: 71, USGA: 68.9
RP: 7 days in advance

Restaurant/Bar
GF: w/day $106.00
Carts: $Included

The Stadium course was built specifically to be the host of the PGA Tour Phoenix open. Most dramatic Stadium course hole is #15 — the island green, a reachable par 5 with a lake on the left side of the fairway leading up to an island green.

──────────────SCOTTSDALE──────────────

Troon North GC
10370 E. Dynamite
Blvd., 85255
Ph: 602-585-7700

Yards: 6023, Holes: 18
Par: 72, USGA: 69.2
RP: 1 week in advance

Bar/Proshop
GF: w/day $105.00
Carts: $Included

Some steep drops what will eat your balls. The greens are often large but play true. There are plenty of long par-4s and very well placed bunkers. This course was rated very highly by Golf Digest, so you won't want to miss it.

──────────────SEDONA──────────────

Oakcreek CC
690 Bell Rock Blvd.,
86336
Ph: 602-284-1660

Yards: 6880, Holes: 18
Par: 72, USGA: 69.9
RP: 6 days in advance

Restaurant/Bar/Proshop
GF: w/day $45.00, w/end
$45.00
Carts: $Included

Oakcreek Country Club is located in Arizona's red rock country. Oakcreek for a number of years has been declared one of the ten courses to play while visiting Arizona. If you're looking for championship golf, breath-taking vistas, Sedona is for you.

──────────────SEDONA──────────────

**Poco Diablo Resort
GC**
1752 S Hwy 179, 86336
Ph: 602-282-7333

Yards: 781, Holes: 9
Par: 27

GF: w/day $7.00, w/end
$7.00

A nice resort setting offering a short pitch and putt type of course. If your short game has been troubling you, this is the place to come for much needed practice.

──────────────SEDONA──────────────

Sedona GC
7260 State Hwy 179,
86351
Ph: 520-284-9355

Yards: 6700, Holes: 18
Par: 71, USGA: 70.4
Slope: 121

Restaurant/Bar
GF: w/day $55.00
Carts: $Included

Some of the rocks on this course are truly a marvel, and will take your breath away. A top rated course, there's plenty of bunkers and water. A popular course for tournaments.

──────────────SHOW LOW──────────────

Show Low CC
860 N. 36th Dr., 85901
Ph: 602-537-4564

Yards: 5702, Holes: 18
Par: 71, USGA: 65.0
RP: 1 week in advance

Bar/Proshop
GF: w/day $14.00
Carts: $15.00

The front side was designed with accuracy in mind when cut out of beautiful ponderosa pines. No. 5 is a short and exacting par 4 that yields few birdies. The back is relatively open. Our course offers two different playing conditions.

──────────────SUN CITY WEST──────────────

Hillcrest GC
20002 Star Ridge Dr.,
85375
Ph: 602-975-1000

Yards: 6900, Holes: 18
Par: 72, USGA: 69.8

Restaurant/Bar
GF: w/day $46.00
Carts: $Included

A very scenic course, set on rolling land. There are elevated tees, and some holes that go uphill. Your short game is going to be very important on this course, and you're sure to get plenty of practice to perfect it.

─────────────── TEMPE ───────────────

Karsten GC at ASU
1125 E. Rio Salado
Pkwy., 85281
Ph: 602-921-8070

Yards: 7057, Holes: 18
Par: 72, USGA: 69.9

Restaurant
GF: w/day $56.00
Carts: $Included

A championship course that is sought-after for major tournaments. A typical Pete Dye course, with nasty water hazards and mounds. The layout has some of the most challenging holes of golf in the state.

─────────────── TEMPE ───────────────

Shalimar GC
2032 East Golf Ave.,
85282
Ph: 602-838-0488

Yards: 2134, Holes: 9
Par: 33, USGA: 60.0
RP: 2 days in advance

Restaurant/Bar/Proshop
GF: w/day $10.00, w/end $11.00
Carts: $5.00

Shalimar is a challenging par 33 9 hole golf course, featuring 6 par 4's and 3 par 3's. The 5th (100 yard par 3) and 9th (330 yard par 4) are the most memorable holes as the greens are virtually surrounded by water.

─────────────── TEMPE ───────────────

Tempe Rolling Hills GC
1415 North Mill Ave.,
85281
Ph: 602-350-5275

Yards: 3594, Holes: 18
Par: 62, USGA: 56.3
RP: 2 days in advance

Restaurant/Bar/Proshop
GF: w/day $5.00, w/end $9.00
Carts: $6.00

Two executive nines flow over hilly terrain amid the Papago Buttes. Challenging par 3's demand accuracy. Par 4's are mild in distance. #8 on south, a par 3 of 172 yards, compares to the best in the golf world.

─────────────── TUBAC ───────────────

Tubac Valley CC PC
Box 1358, 1 Oreta Rd.,
85646
Ph: 602-398-2211

Yards: 6592, Holes: 18
Par: 72, USGA: 70.4
Slope: 120

Restaurant/Bar
GF: w/day $36.00, w/end $36.00
Carts: $8.00

The trees are a big factor on this course and can come into play if you're not careful. Water isn't a big factor on most holes. The course resort offers swimming and tennis as well as golf.

─────────────── TUCSON ───────────────

El Conquistador PC
10000 N. Oracle, 85737
Ph: 602-297-0404

Yards: 7073, Holes: 18
Par: 72, USGA: 73.6
RP: 7 days in advance

Restaurant/Bar
GF: w/day $52.50
Carts: $Included

45 holes await the golfer staying at El Conquistador. Nine holes are at the resort itself. These are desert courses, with a spectacular backdrop of jagged mountain peaks and seemingly cloudless azure skies, gullies, dry washes, and a variety of cacti.

─────────────── TUCSON ───────────────

Fred Enke GC PC
8250 E. Irvington Rd.,
85730
Ph: 602-791-2539

Yards: 6363, Holes: 18
Par: 72, USGA: 70.5

GF: w/day $12.50
Carts: $7.00

A target type course with sand on greens as well as fairways. A challenging course with demands the best of your game.

────────────────────TUCSON────────────────────

La Paloma CC
3660 East Sunrise Dr., 85718
Ph: 602-299-1500

Yards: 7088, Holes: 27
Par: 72, USGA: 71.8
Slope: 140
RP: Hotel guests or members

Restaurant/Bar/Proshop
GF: w/day $95.00, w/end $95.00
Carts: $Included

27-holes of top rated golf await you here. The courses offer target type holes with the desert intruding on the fairways. The resort setting is also welcome if you have a companion who doesn't want to play golf.

────────────────────TUCSON────────────────────

Randolph Muni GC
600 S. Alveron Way, 85711
Ph: 602-325-2811

Yards: 6501, Holes: 18
Par: 72, USGA: 70.0

Restaurant/Bar
GF: w/day $13.50
Carts: $12.00

The course features water hazards on six holes, long fairways, and sports three rearranged holes that were reconstructed according to PGA recommendations to enhance the course and make it more challenging for the pros.

────────────────────TUCSON────────────────────

Randolph Municipal GC - South
600 S. Alveron Way, 85711
Ph: 602-325-2811

Yards: 5939, Holes: 18
Par: 70, USGA: 66.5

Restaurant/Bar
GF: w/day $12.50
Carts: $12.00

The South Course features tall trees and lush fairways. Most holes are straight away and the terrain is relatively flat and easy to walk, which makes it very popular with senior citizens.

────────────────────TUCSON────────────────────

Silverbell
3600 N. Silverbell Rd., 85745
Ph: 602-743-7284

Yards: 6500, Holes: 18
Par: 72, USGA: 69.4
RP: Can be made 7 days in advance

Restaurant/Bar
GF: w/day $12.50
Carts: $12.00

Silverbell Golf Course is built along the west bank of the Santa Cruz River. The course features nine lakes, but also offers spacious and grassy fairways and ample size greens. The course terrain is for the most part flat in nature.

────────────────────TUCSON────────────────────

Starr Pass
3645 W. 22nd St., 85745
Ph: 602-622-6060

Yards: 7010, Holes: 18
Par: 72, USGA: 74.9

Restaurant/Bar
GF: w/day $78.00
Carts: $Included

This course is in the mountains and has many elevation changes. Set in sand, the fairways and greens are jewel like. A long course that is a challenge to every level of golfer, you'll especially enjoy the large rolling greens.

────────────────────TUCSON────────────────────

Sun City Vistoso GC
1495A E. Rancho Vistoso Blvd., 85737
Ph: 602-297-2033

Yards: 6759, Holes: 18
Par: 72, USGA: 68.9
RP: Up to 3 days in advance

Restaurant/Bar/Proshop
GF: w/day $24.00
Carts: $8.00

Rolling desert course in the foothills of the Catalina Mountains. Many spectacular mountain views.

TUCSON

Tucson National Resort-Private 2727 W. Club Dr., 85741 Ph: 602-575-7540	Yards: 6550, Holes: 27 Par: 73, USGA: 71.0 RP: 30 days in advance	Restaurant/Bar/Proshop **GF:** w/day $99.00, w/end $99.00 **Carts:** $14.00

A host to some top rated tournaments, the course was rated #20 in Arizona by Golf Digest. You'll find a challenging round of golf awaits you. There are three nine hole courses that can be played in different combinations.

TUCSON

Ventana Canyon Golf & Racquet Club 6200 N. Clubhouse Lane, 85715 Ph: 602-577-1400	Yards: 6818, Holes: 18 Par: 72, USGA: 74.0 RP: 5 days in advance	Restaurant/Bar **GF:** w/day $55.00 **Carts:** $Included

The PGA Resort course leads pros and novices through rocky canyons, stony washes and crevasses of the foothills. The eighteenth hole is a smashing finish. This par 5 is a real challenge, with water to the right and behind the big green.

WHITE MOUNTAIN LAKE

Silver Creek GC P.O. Box 965, Silver Lake Blvd., 85912 Ph: 602-537-2744	Yards: 6813, Holes: 18 Par: 71, USGA: 70.0 RP: One day in advance	Restaurant/Bar/Proshop **GF:** w/day $24.50 **Carts:** $16.00

Teeing up on #17 is always a thrill for me. A tight driving hole for the long hitter, this straight away par four has everything imaginable including beauty. An approach shot that misses undulating bent grass green will find water right and sand bunker.

WICKENBURG

Los Caballeros GC PC P.O. Box QQ, Vulture Mine Rd., 85358 Ph: 602-684-2704	Yards: 6959, Holes: 18 Par: 72, USGA: 73.2 RP: Recommended	Restaurant/Bar/Proshop **GF:** w/day $50.00 **Carts:** $Included

Recently voted one on Top 75 Resort Courses in the U.S. (Golf Digest) Los Caballeros Golf Course offers many vista tees yet virtually every approach shot is uphill. Over 7000 yards from the back tees the course will give you all the golf you'll ever want.

YUMA

Cocopah Bend RV Resort 6800 Strand Ave., 85634 Ph: 602-343-1663	Yards: 5264, Holes: 18 Par: 70, USGA: 65.5 Slope: 100 RP: 2 days in advance	**GF:** w/day $18.00, w/end $18.00

A rolling, narrow fairwayed layout. The greens are level, but they offer a very small target.

Subscribe to our free newsletter, "Great Golf Gazette," and hear about the latest special golf vcation values.

ARKANSAS

---------BENTON---------

Longhills GC
Old Little Rock Hwy -
Hwy 5, 72015
Ph: 501-794-9907

Yards: 6300, Holes: 18
Par: 72, USGA: 68.9

Restaurant/Proshop
GF: w/day $7.00, w/end
$10.00
Carts: $12.00

Interesting layout. Not too difficult. Minutes from Interstate 30.

--------- BLYTHEVILLE---------

Blytheville Muni GC
1205 North Second,
72315
Ph: 501-762-5949

Yards: 6022, Holes: 9
Par: 72, USGA: 67.1

GF: w/day $5.00, w/end
$6.00
Carts: $10.00

Water can be reached from almost every tee box. A very deceptive course that requires accuracy. No. 6 will be an island by summer of 89. A fun course to play.

---------CHEROKEE VILLAGE---------

Cherokee Village GC
P.O. Box 840, 72525
Ph: 501-257-2555

Yards: 6515, Holes: 18
Par: 72, USGA: 70.0

Restaurant/Bar/Proshop
GF: w/day $16.00

Offers two spectacular golf courses. The South Course is a whopping 7,086 yards from the blue tees. All holes over well bunkered greens, and though you can really let 'er fly at times your shotmaking is very important too.

--------- FAIRFIELD BAY ---------

Mountain Ranch GC
P.O. Box 3008, 72088
Ph: 501-884-3333

Yards: 6780, Holes: 18
Par: 72, USGA: 71.8

Restaurant/Bar/Proshop
GF: w/day $25.00
Carts: $18.00

Rock outcroppings, rolling fairways, lots of mature trees, loads of well-placed bunkers, and a fair number of doglegs are some of the features of this course. And then don't forget the gorge Accuracy is a must on this course if you want to score well.

───────────────── FORREST CITY ─────────────────

Forrest City CC   Yards: 5697, Holes: 18   Restaurant/Bar/Proshop
922 E. Cross St., 72335   Par: 70, USGA: 65.5   **GF:** w/day $10.00
Ph: 501-633-3380   **Carts:** $15.00

*Located on Crowleys Ridge, the front nine is relatively open on rolling fairways
with greens protected with sand and two water holes. The back nine is cut from
timber land, fairways are narrow, tee shots must be controlled to score well.*

───────────────── FORT SMITH ─────────────────

Ben Geren GC   Yards: 6344, Holes: 18   **GF:** w/day $8.00
Box 3609, 7200 Zero,   Par: 72   **Carts:** $15.00
72913
Ph: 501-646-5301

*A very popular course where you're going to need a tee time in advance. The
course gives the appearance of being easy, but don't let that fool you.*

───────────────── HARRISON ─────────────────

Harrison CC   Yards: 5964, Holes: 18   Restaurant/Bar/Proshop
P.O. Box 113, 72602   Par: 70, USGA: 69.0   **GF:** w/day $10.00
Ph: 501-741-2443   **Carts:** $12.00

*Our course is relatively open but great for the beginners as well as for a good
golfer. You also want to lean back and let her fly.*

───────────────── HOLIDAY ISLAND ─────────────────

Table Rock GC   Holes: 27
95 Woodsdale Dr.,
72632
Ph: 501-253-7733

*Duffers and scratch players alike have a field day on our 18-hole course. Tree-
lined fairways and impeccable greens challenge every shot. There is also a nine-
hole executive golf course.*

───────────────── HOT SPRINGS ─────────────────

Belvedere CC   Yards: 6204, Holes: 18   Restaurant/Bar
Route 18 Box 115,   Par: 72   **GF:** w/day $15.00, w/end
71901 $20.00
Ph: 501-623-2305

*There are three holes here that have been rated Arkansas' three toughest con-
secutive holes. The doglegs are very nasty, and are going to give you a lot of
trouble.*

───────────────── LITTLE ROCK ─────────────────

Hindman Park GC   Yards: 6501, Holes: 18   Restaurant
60 Brookview Dr.,   Par: 72   **GF:** w/day $6.00, w/end
72209 $8.00
Ph: 501-565-6450   **Carts:** $14.00

*A very tough course that's seems to have nothing but doglegs and even more
doglegs.*

───────────────── LITTLE ROCK ─────────────────

Rebsamen Park GC   Yards: 6271, Holes: 27   Restaurant
210 Poinsetta, 72205   Par: 71   **GF:** w/day $6.00, w/end
Ph: 501-666-7965 $8.00
   Carts: $14.00

*A not too difficult course, there are no trees, and the terrain is flat. Only one
small pond.*

―――――――――――――― NORTH LITTLE ROCK ――――――――――――――

Burns Park GC   Yards: 5830, Holes: 27   **GF:** w/day $6.00, w/end
P.O. Box 973, 72114   Par: 71 $8.00
Ph: 501-758-5800   **Carts:** $14.00

Lost of bunkers are going to be your test of skill on this course.

―――――――――――――――――――― ROGERS ――――――――――――――――――――

Prairie Creek CC   Yards: 6574, Holes: 18   Restaurant/Proshop
P.O. Box 828, Hwy 12   Par: 72, USGA: 72.9   **GF:** w/day $10.00
East, 72757   **Carts:** $13.40
Ph: 501-925-2414

*Prairie Creek Country Club is a beautiful championship course located in the
Ozarks four miles from Rogers, Arkansas near Beaver Lake. It is a stiff challenge
with tree lined fairways, and a springfed creek comes into play on 8 holes of the
second 9.*

―――――――――――――――― SILOAM SPRINGS ――――――――――――――――

Dawn Hill GC   Yards: 6768, Holes: 18   Restaurant/Bar/Proshop
P.O. Box 296, Dawn   Par: 72, USGA: 70.7   **GF:** w/day $15.00
Hill Rd., 72761   RP: Call in advance   **Carts:** $15.00
Ph: 501-524-9321

*Set in the rustic Ozarks, the golf course is set in a valley surrounded by colorful
oaks and maples. Course is not tough, but demands accurate approach shots to
relatively small greens. A big hitter will score well here.*

**Please mention "Golf Courses―The Complete Guide" when you
reserve your tee time. Our goal is to provide as complete a
listing of golf courses open to the public as possible. If you
know of a course we don't list, please send us the name and
address on the form at the back of this guide.**

CALIFORNIA

Weed
McKinleyville
• Willow Creek
• Redding
• Paradise
• Graeagle
• Marysville
Bodega Bay
Santa Rosa
• Chino
Truckee
St. Helena
• Napa
Monte Rio
• Rodeo
• Arnold
San Rafael
Concord
Bonita
• Galt
Oakland Berkeley
• Walnut Creek
South San Francisco
• Livermore
Palo Alto
• Boulder Creek
Half Moon Bay
• Scotts Valley
Santa Cruz
• Watsonville
Carmel
• Monterey
Pebble Beach

• Oakhurst
• Kerman
Death Valley
• Avila Beach
• Bakersfield
• Arvin
Morro Bay
• Buellton
• Lancaster
Solvang
• Yucca Valley
• Lompoc
• Rancho Mirage
Goleta
• Ojai
Santa Barbara
Simi Valley
Palm Desert
San Dimas
Downey Fullerton • Indian Wells
• Anaheim
• Palm Springs
City of Industry Agoura • Santa Ana
• Banning
Rancho Santa Fe
So. Laguna
San Clemente
• Murrieta Temecula
Fallbrook
• Escondido
• Carlsbad Borrego Springs
• Lakeside
La Quinta
• Coronado • El Cajon
San Diego
Holtville

— 29 PALMS —

Combat Center GC   Ph: 619-368-6132   Yards: 6487, Holes: 18
Box X-11 Special   Par: 72, USGA: 70.4
Services Blvd., 92278

This course is all sidehill lies with nasty rough areas and lots of out-of-bounds. A real championship layout.

---------------------------------29 PALMS---------------------------------

Roadrunner Dunes GC
4733 Desert Knoll Ave., POB 204, 92277
Ph: 619-367-7610

Yards: 6259, Holes: 9
Par: 36, USGA: 68.8

GF: w/day $6.00, w/end $8.00
Carts: $11.00

Very little water here, but you won't miss it because you'll have plenty of other problems.

---------------------------------ACAMPO---------------------------------

Forest Lake GC
2450 E. Woodson Rd., 95220
Ph: 209-369-5451

Yards: 3675, Holes: 18
Par: 60, USGA: 55.1

GF: w/day $5.00, w/end $6.00
Carts: $10.00

The original nine holes on this course were opened in 1957, with the second nine being a fairly recent addition. A course that demands accuracy in your short game, you'll have to deal with lots of large trees and water.

---------------------------------AGOURA---------------------------------

Lake Lindero CC
5719 Lake Lindero Dr., 91301
Ph: 818-889-1158

Yards: 3338, Holes: 9
Par: 58, USGA: 56.5
RP: 1 week in advance

Bar/Proshop
GF: w/day $7.00, w/end $9.00

Difficult executive golf course. Rolling hills. Great for mid irons. Narrow fairways with two tough par 4's. Greens are small and tough to hit.

---------------------------------ALAMEDA---------------------------------

Alameda GC
One Memorial Dr., 94501
Ph: 510-522-4321

Yards: 5947, Holes: 18
Par: 71, USGA: 69.1

GF: w/day $2.00, w/end $10.00
Carts: $14.00

You must hit a straight ball here.

---------------------------------ALHAMBRA---------------------------------

Alhambra Muni GC
630 So. Almansor St., 91801
Ph: 818-570-5059

Yards: 5156, Holes: 18
Par: 70, USGA: 62.0
RP: 7 days in advance

GF: w/day $9.50, w/end $14.00
Carts: $16.00

There are beautiful mature eucalyptus and acacias to shade this rather short course. With three lakes and lots of bunkers. Accuracy is your best weapon on this one.

---------------------------------ALTURAS---------------------------------

Arrowhead GC
1901 N. Warner St., 96101
Ph: 916-233-3404

Yards: 6136, Holes: 9
Par: 70, USGA: 67.0

GF: w/day $4.00, w/end $8.00
Carts: $10.00

Watch out for the irrigation ditches on this one, as you'll see them everywhere. The fairways are fairly open and the greens are elevated. There are also some very long holes.

Please mention "Golf Courses—The Complete Guide" when you reserve your tee time. Our goal is to provide as complete a listing of golf courses open to the public as possible. If you know of a course we don't list, please send us the name and address on the form at the back of this guide.

──────────────ANAHEIM──────────────

Anaheim Hills CC Yards: 5966, Holes: 18 Restaurant/Bar/Proshop
6501 Nohl Ranch Rd., Par: 71, USGA: 68.4 **GF:** w/day $13.00, w/end
92807 RP: 1 week in advance $16.00
Ph: 714-748-8900 **Carts:** $17.00

*This challenging 18-hole championship course rests in the enchanting natural
terrain of the Santa Ana Canyons, full of valleys, slopes and stands of ancient
sycamores and oaks. Enjoy the country club atmosphere complete with modern
clubhouse and pro shop.*

──────────────ANAHEIM──────────────

H. G. "Dad" Miller Yards: 5811, Holes: 18 Restaurant/Bar/Proshop
Muni GC Par: 71, USGA: 66.2 **GF:** w/day $9.00, w/end
430 N. Gilbert St., RP: 1 week in advance $13.00
92804 **Carts:** $14.00
Ph: 714-991-5530

*This exceptionally well-kept course features a natural lake with lovely old trees
surrounding the fairways. The course is perfect for individual or tournament ·
play and offers the convenience of fine snack bar, restaurant and cocktail
lounge.*

──────────────ANTIOCH──────────────

Lone Tree GC Yards: 5970, Holes: 18 **GF:** w/day $6.50, w/end
4800 Lone Tree Way, Par: 73, USGA: 67.1 $9.00
P.O. Box 986, 94509 **Carts:** $14.00
Ph: 510-723-1025

A nice course for walking, the setting is rolling and open with plenty of trees.

──────────────APPLE VALLEY──────────────

Victorville Muni GC Yards: 6320, Holes: 18 **GF:** w/day $14.00, w/end
15200 Racherias Rd., Par: 72, USGA: 69.3 $17.00
PO Box 1045, 92307 **Carts:** $17.00
Ph: 619-242-3125

*Opened in 1949, you'll find a fairly long course considering the times. You can
walk the course here if you wish.*

──────────────APTOS──────────────

Aptos Par-3 GC Yards: 2100, Holes: 9 Proshop
2600 Mar Vista Dr., Par: 27 **GF:** w/day $4.00
95003
Ph: 408-688-5000

*A nice par-3 course to work on your short game. Not a difficult course, but
enjoyable nonetheless.*

──────────────APTOS──────────────

Aptos Seascape GC Yards: 6054, Holes: 18 **GF:** w/day $18.00, w/end
610 Clubhouse Dr., Par: 72, USGA: 69.0 $27.00
95003 **Carts:** $18.00
Ph: 408-688-3212

*Large Cypress trees line the fairways of this short but tight course. The club-
house sits atop a hill offering full view of the course. The front side is flat and the
back side is hilly.*

──────────────ARBUCKLE──────────────

Arbuckle GC Yards: 6460, Holes: 18 Proshop
P.O. Box 975, Hillgate Par: 72, USGA: 69.9 **GF:** w/day $10.00, w/end
Rd., 95912 $20.00
Ph: 916-476-2470 **Carts:** $16.00

A rolling, hilly course. Good greens help, but the doglegs can be tough.

───────────────ARCADIA───────────────

Arcadia Par-3 GC   Ph: 818-443-9367   Yards: 1898, Holes: 18
620 East Live Oak,   **GF:** w/day $6.50, w/end
91006 $8.00

*A good course for your short game. And you can play at night here. Check on
the evening and senior rates.*

───────────────ARCADIA───────────────

Santa Anita GC   Yards: 6823, Holes: 18   **GF:** w/day $11.00, w/end
405 S. Santa Anita   Par: 71, USGA: 70.2 $15.00
Ave., 91006   **Carts:** $17.00
Ph: 818-447-7156

*Small greens, narrow fairways and lots of bunkers are a feature of this long,
well-kept course. A very challenging round of golf.*

───────────────ARNOLD───────────────

Meadowmont GC   Yards: 2931, Holes: 9   Restaurant/Bar/Proshop
Hwy 4 & Country Club   Par: 36, USGA: 66.2   **GF:** w/day $12.00
Dr., 95223   **RP:** Starting times   **Carts:** $15.00
Ph: 209-795-1313   accepted

*Located in the Sierra Nevada mountains, our picturesque setting includes Raes
Creek which meanders thru the course and comes into play on 7 of the 9 holes.
This combined with the beautiful pine and poplar trees, makes for narrow
fairways and challenges.*

───────────────ARVIN───────────────

Sycamore Canyon   Yards: 6644, Holes: 18   Restaurant/Bar/Proshop
GC   Par: 72, USGA: 70.9   **GF:** w/day $8.00, w/end
Kenmar Ln., 93203   **RP:** 7 days in advance $10.00
Ph: 805-854-3163   **Carts:** $15.00

*Nestled among ancient sycamore groves this beautiful setting offers a challenge
to all levels of golfing.*

───────────────ATADENA───────────────

Altadena Town & CC   Yards: 5828, Holes: 18   **GF:** w/day $7.00, w/end
2290 Country Club Dr.,   Par: 72, USGA: 66.3 $9.00
91001   **Carts:** $10.00
Ph: 818-794-5792

*This rather flat course has the San Gabriel Mountains as a background. Some
sidehill lies and bunkers are the only problems here.*

───────────────ATASCADERO───────────────

Chalk Mountain GC   Yards: 6333, Holes: 18   Bar
10000 El Bordo Rd,   Par: 72, USGA: 70.6   **GF:** w/day $12.00, w/end
93422 $14.00
Ph: 805-466-8848   **Carts:** $16.00

*A truly challenging course. Set in the mountains you'll find many towering oak
groves, a really beautiful setting. But you'd better keep your eye on the ball,
because there's plenty of trouble ahead.*

**Our listings—supplied by the management—are as complete as
possible. Many of the courses have more features than we list.
Be sure to inquire when you book your tee time.**

─────────────────────ATWATER─────────────────────

Rancho Del Rey GC
5250 Green Sands
Ave., 95301
Ph: 209-358-7131

Yards: 6262, Holes: 18
Par: 72, USGA: 68.8

GF: w/day $12.00, w/end
$16.00
Carts: $14.00

This one will make you really think about what club to use. Sand and water will present some difficulty. Twilight rates begin at noon, so don't miss your chance.

─────────────────────AUBURN─────────────────────

Angus Hills GC
14520 Musso Rd.,
95603
Ph: 916-878-7818

Yards: 2378, Holes: 9
Par: 54, USGA: 51.7

GF: w/day $3.50, w/end
$6.00

Twilight tournaments are a feature of the club from spring to fall. Also hosts many annual tournaments. The course is a real challenge and the rates are quite affordable.

─────────────────────AUBURN─────────────────────

**Black Oak Women's
GC**
2455 Black Oak Rd.,
95603
Ph: 916-885-8315

Yards: 5240, Holes: 9
Par: 72, USGA: 69.8

GF: w/day $5.00, w/end
$9.00
Carts: $14.00

A hilly course with fast rolling greens. Watch out for the oaks, and bunkers. One of northern California's more challenging nine hole courses Junior and senior rates are available on weekdays.

─────────────────────AVALON─────────────────────

Catalina GC
#1 Country Club Rd.,
90704
Ph: 213-510-0530

Yards: 4203, Holes: 9
Par: 64, USGA: 58.0
RP: First come, first
served

GF: w/day $10.00
Carts: $20.00

A very demanding, old course. Narrow fairways and small greens that are well-trapped. A canyon setting that is very beautiful.

─────────────────────AVILA BEACH─────────────────────

San Luis Bay Club
Box 129; Box 487,
93424
Ph: 805-595-2307

Yards: 6544, Holes: 18
Par: 71, USGA: 68.4

Restaurant/Bar/Proshop
GF: w/day $13.00, w/end
$17.00
Carts: $16.00

The front nine has blind doglegs, elevated trees, ponds and creek with excessive sloping greens. The back nine is wide open, next to creek.

─────────────────────AZUSA─────────────────────

Azusa Greens CC
919 West Sierra Madre
Blvd., 91702
Ph: 818-969-1727

Yards: 6126, Holes: 18
Par: 70, USGA: 67.7
RP: 7 days

GF: w/day $16.00, w/end
$25.00
Carts: $Included

With the San Gabriels as a backdrop, you know this will be a very scenic layout. A flat course with lots of trees.

─────────────────────BAKERSFIELD─────────────────────

Kern River GC
Box 6339, 93386
Ph: 805-872-5128

Yards: 6258, Holes: 18
Par: 70, USGA: 68.8

GF: w/day $10.00, w/end
$15.00
Carts: $14.00

A tough course with a chance for some nasty lies. The greens here can be really tricky and some of the tree placements will give you a very hard time if you're not careful.

—————————————————— BAKERSFIELD ——————————————————

North Kern GC
17412 Quality Rd., PO
Box 80545, 93380
Ph: 805-399-0347

Yards: 6461, Holes: 18
Par: 72, USGA: 69.9
RP: Wednesday before
weekend

GF: w/day $7.50, w/end
$10.00
Carts: $15.00

Even though the fairways are wide here, the superabundance of trees and bunkers will still make a real challenge. Add to this the fact that the greens are small and wind can be an added negative factor. Many tournaments are hosted at this course.

—————————————————— BAKERSFIELD ——————————————————

Rio Bravo GC
11200 Lake Ming Rd.,
93306
Ph: 805-872-5000

Yards: 6960, Holes: 18
Par: 72, USGA: 70.1

Restaurant/Bar
GF: w/day $39.00
Carts: $Included

The front nine is flat and the back nine is hilly. The greens are big and undulating. #11 is a 600 yard par 5 uphill with a slope to the right fairway and the green is difficult.

—————————————————— BAKERSFIELD ——————————————————

Valle Grande GC
1119 Watts Dr., 93307
Ph: 805-832-2259

Yards: 5915, Holes: 18
Par: 72, USGA: 66.3

GF: w/day $7.00, w/end
$8.00
Carts: $14.00

This flat course has more trees and out-of-bounds on its narrow fairways than you'd care to see. There are going to be a lot of tricky water shots in your future too.

—————————————————— BANNING ——————————————————

Sun Lakes CC
850 South Country
Club Dr., 92220
Ph: 714-845-2135

Yards: 6997, Holes: 18
Par: 72, USGA: 70.4
RP: 4 days in advance

Restaurant/Bar/Proshop
GF: w/day $40.00, w/end
$50.00
Carts: $Included

The golf course appears innocent enough looking at it from the clubhouse, but the seven lakes, 111 sand traps, and small subtle greens affords only the golfer that hits accurate shots either to the pin or to a position that might allow a chip.

—————————————————— BARSTOW ——————————————————

Sun Valley CC
2781 Country Club Dr.,
92311
Ph: 619-253-5201

Yards: 6354, Holes: 9
Par: 72, USGA: 69.0

Proshop
GF: w/day $8.00, w/end
$11.00
Carts: $8.00

Designed by Ted Robinson in 1963, this course has many beautiful mature trees. Not a very difficult course, but a very pleasant round of golf.

—————————————————— BELL GARDENS ——————————————————

Ford Park GC
8000 Park Lane, 90201
Ph: 213-927-8811

Yards: 1017, Holes: 9
Par: 27

GF: w/day $3.50, w/end
$4.00

A par-3 layout that will test your skills with the irons A special senior rate is offered.

Our listings—supplied by the management—are as complete as possible. Many of the courses have more features than we list. Be sure to inquire when you book your tee time.

BELLFLOWER

Bellflower Muni GC
9030 E. Compton
Blvd., 90706
Ph: 213-920-8882

Yards: 1335, Holes: 9
Par: 27

GF: w/day $3.50, w/end
$4.00

A short par-3 to get some good iron practice. Your short game is sure to be an improvement here.

BERKELEY

Tilden Park GC
Gizzly Peak and
Shasta Rd., 94708
Ph: 510-848-7373

Yards: 7000, Holes: 18
Par: 70, USGA: 67.7

GF: w/day $9.00, w/end
$18.00
Carts: $9.00

The scenic course it set in the Berkeley hills. Wildlife abounds amid the parklike setting. A hilly course that doesn't let you get by with many mistakes. The greens are a real challenge, so you'd better practice on your putting.

BETHEL ISLAND

Bethel Island GC
3303 Gateway Rd., P.O.
Box 455, 94511
Ph: 510-684-2654

Yards: 6120, Holes: 18
Par: 72, USGA: 68.8

GF: w/day $3.75, w/end
$9.00
Carts: $14.00

An interesting island setting. A challenging course with wind, trees and water. And don't forget the sand traps.

BIG BEAR LAKE

Bear Mountain GC
43100 Goldmine Dr,
92315
Ph: 714-585-8002

Yards: 5218, Holes: 9
Par: 65

GF: w/day $10.00, w/end
$13.00
Carts: $11.00

Rolling hills, long par-3s and a lake will make this a challenging round of golf. Since the course is in the mountains, it has a short season.

BISHOP

Bishop CC
P.O. Box 1586,
Highway 395 S., 93514
Ph: 619-873-5828

Yards: 6072, Holes: 18
Par: 71, USGA: 67.1

Restaurant/Bar/Proshop
GF: w/day $14.00, w/end
$16.00
Carts: $14.00

Trees, water and bunkers make this course a difficult round of golf. Your shot making ability will definitely be called into play.

BLAIRSDEN

Feather River GC
Hwy 70, P.O. Box 67,
96103
Ph: 916-836-2722

Yards: 5760, Holes: 9
Par: 70, USGA: 66.2

GF: w/day $7.00, w/end
$8.50
Carts: $14.50

Plenty of trees here, but don't let the scenery take your mind off the narrow fairways. Open from April through October.

BLAIRSDEN

Feather River Park Resort GC
8339 Highway 89, PO
Box 37, 96103
Ph: 916-836-2328

Yards: 5164, Holes: 9
Par: 70

GF: w/day $11.00, w/end
$13.00

Feather River Park is only open from April to October. Near Truckee the winters can come on early. The course is a nice one to walk, and has marvelous scenery.

―――――――――――BLAIRSDEN―――――――――――

Plumas Pines CC　　Yards: 5843, Holes: 18　　**GF:** w/day $28.00
402 Poplar Valley Rd.,　Par: 72, USGA: 70.5　　**Carts:** $10.00
96103
Ph: 96103

A very hilly course in the Plumas National Forest, the fairways are narrow. The Feather River and an abundance of trees add their own woes for the unwary golfer. The course is only open from April through November, so plan ahead.

―――――――――――BLYTHE―――――――――――

Blythe GC　　　　Yards: 6567, Holes: 18　　**GF:** w/day $12.00
Route 1 Box 38A,　　Par: 72, USGA: 70.7　　**Carts:** $12.00
92226
Ph: 619-922-7272

Lots of hilly terrain at this course. Some trees will enhance the difficulty.

―――――――――――BODEGA BAY―――――――――――

Bodega Harbour GC　Yards: 6220, Holes: 18　　Restaurant/Bar/Proshop
21301 Heron Dr., 94923　Par: 70, USGA: 71.9　　**GF:** w/day $35.00, w/end
Ph: 707-875-3538　　RP: Can book 60 days in　$53.00
　　　　　　　　　advance　　　　　　**Carts:** $12.00

West of Scotland—north of Pebble Beach, Bodega Harbour Golf Links provides one of the finest golfing experiences in northern California. Sculpted along the rugged Sonoma coast, this Scottish links style course by Robert Trent Jones, Jr.

―――――――――――BONITA―――――――――――

Bonita GC　　　　Yards: 6287, Holes: 18　　Restaurant/Bar/Proshop
5540 Sweetwater Rd.,　Par: 71, USGA: 67.0　　**GF:** w/day $14.00, w/end
92002　　　　　　RP: 1 week in advance　$20.00
Ph: 619-267-1103　　　　　　　　　　**Carts:** $16.00

The course plays to a 4 hour average and all the holes are fair to all levels of skill. We are located in a river valley so most holes are flat, very nice course to walk and enjoy our coastal breeze.

―――――――――――BONITA―――――――――――

Chula Vista GC　　Yards: 6381, Holes: 18　　**GF:** w/day $13.00, w/end
Box 403 4475 Bonita　Par: 73, USGA: 69.9　　$17.00
Rd., 92002　　　　　　　　　　　　**Carts:** $19.00
Ph: 619-479-4141

Rolling fairways, with lots and lots of water. The greens are large. The course is great for walking.

―――――――――――BONSALL―――――――――――

San Luis Rey Downs　Yards: 6610, Holes: 18　Restaurant/Bar/Proshop
G&CC　　　　　Par: 72, USGA: 69.6　　**GF:** w/day $28.00, w/end
5772 Camino Del Rey,　RP: 7 days in advance　$35.00
92005　　　　　　　　　　　　　**Carts:** $Included
Ph: 619-758-9699

Narrow fairways, trees, quite a few lakes, and a river right though it are going to make this a memorable day of golf.

Enter your favorite resort in our "Golf Resort of The Year" contest (entry form is in the back of the book).

─────────────── BORREGO SPRINGS ───────────────

Rams Hill CC
1881 Rams Hill Rd.,
92004
Ph: 619-767-5124

Yards: 7076, Holes: 18
Par: 72, USGA: 69.9
RP: 5 days—hotel guest
at reservation of room

Restaurant
GF: w/day $50.00
Carts: $Included

A championship is the magnificent Anza-Borrego Desert State Park area. You can really let her fly on this one, 7,076 yards from the long tees. But watch out for the 52 traps and 4,000 trees along the way.

─────────────── BOULDER CREEK ───────────────

Boulder Creek GC
16901 Big Basin Hwy.,
95006
Ph: 408-338-2121

Yards: 4279, Holes: 18
Par: 65, USGA: 61.2
RP: Up to one week in
advance

Restaurant/Bar/Proshop
GF: w/day $16.00, w/end
$26.00
Carts: $16.00

This scenic course, set among the redwoods, lakes and creeks, offers golfers a challenging and memorable golf experience in an absolutely beautiful setting.

─────────────── BRAWLEY ───────────────

Del Rio CC
Box 38 102 East Del
Rio Rd., 92227
Ph: 619-344-0085

Yards: 5890, Holes: 18
Par: 70, USGA: 66.7

GF: w/day $25.00, w/end
$30.00
Carts: $Included

Accuracy is the byword on this course. Lots of small greens, tight fairways with doglegs and lots of trees will make it quite a round of golf.

─────────────── BREA ───────────────

Birch Hills GC
Box 1150, 2250 East
Birch St., 92621
Ph: 714-990-0201

Yards: 3521, Holes: 18
Par: 59, USGA: 54.0

GF: w/day $12.00, w/end
$16.00
Carts: $14.00

A short 18-hole course that has tricky greens and some sidehill lies.

─────────────── BREA ───────────────

Brea GC
501 West Fir, 92621
Ph: 714-529-3003

Yards: 1683, Holes: 9

GF: w/day $5.00, w/end
$6.00
Carts: $6.00

A flat with only a few trees.

─────────────── BREA ───────────────

Imperial GC
2200 E. Imperial Hwy.,
POB 1150, 92621
Ph: 714-529-3923

Yards: 5927, Holes: 18
Par: 72, USGA: 66.9

GF: w/day $15.00, w/end
$20.00
Carts: $20.00

A really tough round of golf awaits you here, you'll be challenged all the way. A good course to schedule your next tournament.

─────────────── BUELLTON ───────────────

Zaca Creek GC
223 Shadow Mountain
Dr., 93427
Ph: 805-688-2575

Yards: 1544, Holes: 9
Par: 29, USGA: 50.0
RP: 1 week in advance

Restaurant/Proshop
GF: w/day $5.00
Carts: $1.50

9 hole executive course where par is a challenge. Often narrow, with short, medium and long par 3s. The greens offer the biggest challenge, being fairly quick and undulating.

―――――――――――――――BURBANK――――――――――――――――

De Bell GC   Yards: 5813, Holes: 18   **GF:** w/day $13.00, w/end
1500 Walnut Ave,   Par: 71, USGA: 66.8 $16.00
91504   **Carts:** $16.00
Ph: 818-845-5052

A short, straight course with very little to surprise you.

―――――――――――――――BURLINGAME――――――――――――――――

Crystal Springs BC, Yards: 6321, Holes: 18   **GF:** w/day $20.00, w/end
Inc.   Par: 72, USGA: 69.9 $25.00
6650 Golf Course Dr.,   **Carts:** $19.00
94010
Ph: 415-342-0603

*A nice course for a weekday or twilight walk, even though hilly. Located in a
California Game Preserve, you should be able to see a lot of deer and foxes, not
to mention water birds. You'll need to pay attention to your game on this one.*

―――――――――――――――CALIFORNIA CITY――――――――――――――――

Tierra Del Sol GC   Yards: 6300, Holes: 18   Proshop
10300 North Loop   Par: 72, USGA: 69.6   **GF:** w/day $8.00, w/end
Blvd., 93505 $13.00
Ph: 619-373-2384   **Carts:** $15.00

*Two-thirds of the holes here have water coming into play. The course is a long
one with so many bunkers you can hardly count them all. The High Desert
Classic Pro-Am is only one of the tournaments that is regularly played here.*

―――――――――――――――CALIMESA――――――――――――――――

Calimesa CC   Yards: 5513, Holes: 18   **GF:** w/day $11.00, w/end
1300 South Third St.,   Par: 70, USGA: 65.5 $18.50
92320   **Carts:** $18.00
Ph: 714-795-2488

*A very hilly course, very beautiful views. The course will give you a run for your
money. The course is available for tournaments.*

―――――――――――――――CALISTOGA――――――――――――――――

Mount St. Helena GC Yards: 5510, Holes: 9   **GF:** w/day $6.00, w/end
Napa Couty   Par: 68, USGA: 64.9 $7.00
Fairgrounds, POB 344,   **Carts:** $12.00
94515
Ph: 707-942-9966

*Mount Saint Helena is a short course where you have to pick your clubs careful-
ly. A little water and narrow fairways will keep your game honest. If you're a
senior, be sure to ask about our special rates.*

―――――――――――――――CAMARILLO――――――――――――――――

Camarillo Springs   Yards: 5931, Holes: 18   **GF:** w/day $20.00, w/end
GC   Par: 71, USGA: 67.9 $40.00
791 Camarillo Springs   **Carts:** $Included
Rd., 93010
Ph: 805-484-1075

*A recently renovated course, so if you haven't been here for a while you'll find
that's it's completely different. Water comes into play on almost all the holes,
and lots of bunkers.*

-------------------------------CARLSBAD-------------------------------

Four Seasons Resort　Yards: 6054, Holes: 18　Restaurant/Bar/Proshop
Aviara GC　Par: 71, USGA: 68.7　**GF:** w/day $90.00
7447 Batiquitos Dr.,
92009
Ph: 619-929-0077

*Large greens, a high slope rating, wind, and water that comes into play over half
the course are features that make for a very challenging game of golf here. The
greens are large and tricky.*

-------------------------------CARLSBAD-------------------------------

Rancho Carlsbad CC　Yards: 2068, Holes: 18　**GF:** w/day $8.00
5200 El Camino Real,　Par: 56, USGA: 54.5
92008
Ph: 619-438-1772

*A layout with fast greens, tight fairways and lots of trees. A very unforgiving
course that will give you a very challenging round.*

-------------------------------CARLSBAD-------------------------------

Rancho La Costa GC　Yards: 6269, Holes: 36　Restaurant/Bar/Proshop
Costa del Mar Rd.,　Par: 72, USGA: 69.9　**GF:** w/day $80.00
92009　**Carts:** $40.00
Ph: 619-438-9111

*This Resort is annual host to the PGA Infinity Tournament of Champions and
Infinity Senior Tournament of Champions. A fabulous layout with lots and lots
of water. Wind can also be a real challenge to your scoring well on this round.*

-------------------------------CARMEL-------------------------------

Carmel Valley Ranch　Yards: 6005, Holes: 18　Restaurant/Bar
Resort GC　Par: 70, USGA: 69.6　**GF:** w/day $85.00, w/end
One Old Ranch Rd.,　RP: 10 days in advance　$85.00
93923　for guests　**Carts:** $Included
Ph: 408-626-2510

*Test your prowess on some of Dye's trademarks here—a layout dappled with
numerous deep sand and grass bunkers, undulating greens, and railroad ties
and telephone pole bulkheading. Five of the holes climb the mountainside
affording some incredible views.*

-------------------------------CARMEL-------------------------------

Rancho Canada GC -　Yards: 6113, Holes: 18　Restaurant/Bar/Proshop
East Course　Par: 71, USGA: 70.1　**GF:** w/day $45.00
Carmel Valley Rd.,　RP: Call the Proshop　**Carts:** $25.00
93922
Ph: 408-624-0111

*This scenic course in the heart of the Carmel Valley has 7 tricky hazard-lakes
and risky bunkered greens that leap over the Carmel River 5 times. A solid test
of golf for players of all levels.*

-------------------------------CARMEL-------------------------------

Rancho Canada GC -　Yards: 6299, Holes: 18　Restaurant/Bar/Proshop
West Course　Par: 72, USGA: 71.1　**GF:** w/day $65.00
Carmel Valley Rd.,　RP: Call the Proshop　**Carts:** $25.00
93922
Ph: 408-624-0111

*This Carmel Valley 18-hole champion course has 4 water-hazards and 3 skill-
testing shots across the Carmel River. The challenging back-nine is a solid test for
players of all levels, where a hook or a slice can spell trouble.*

34   California

─────────────────CARMICHAEL─────────────────

Ancil Hoffman Park GC
6700 Tarshes Dr., 95608
Ph: 916-482-5660

Yards: 6794, Holes: 18
Par: 72, USGA: 71.0
RP: One week in advance of day

GF: w/day $9.50, w/end $11.00
Carts: $8.00

A beautiful course set along the American River. A trademark here was the towering, magnificent old trees. Your shot off the tee is the most important, so try to place it well. The trees and bunkers here can give you a lot of trouble.

─────────────────CARSON─────────────────

Dominguez GC
19800 South Main St., 90745
Ph: 213-719-1942

Yards: 2070, Holes: 18
Par: 54, USGA: 51.7

GF: w/day $4.75, w/end $5.25

A short par-3 course, with lots of natural hazards and plenty of bunkers.

─────────────────CARSON─────────────────

Victoria GC
340 East 192nd St, 90746
Ph: 213-323-6981

Yards: 6558, Holes: 18
Par: 72, USGA: 69.5

GF: w/day $11.00, w/end $16.00
Carts: $16.00

Opened in 1966, this is a nicely matured course. The greens are well bunkered and the first hole is a killer.

─────────────────CASTRO VALLEY─────────────────

Willow Park GC
17007 Redwood Rd., 94546
Ph: 415-537-4733

Yards: 6070, Holes: 18
Par: 71, USGA: 67.2

GF: w/day $9.00, w/end $12.00
Carts: $14.00

The front nine is along a creek, and there is always a chance of seeing some wildlife. The fairways are narrow, and require some care in your choice of clubs.

─────────────────CATHEDRAL CITY─────────────────

De Anza Palm Springs CC
36-200 Date Palm Dr., 92234
Ph: 619-328-1315

Yards: 3085, Holes: 18
Par: 58, USGA: 51.4
RP: 24 hours in advance

GF: w/day $9.00
Carts: $10.00

Many towering trees and plenty of water make this a really beautiful course. A short course that truly lends itself to a nice walking game.

─────────────────CATHEDRAL CITY─────────────────

Lawrence Welk's Desert Oasis
34567 Cathedral Canyon Dr., 92234
Ph: 619-321-9000

Yards: 3196, Holes: 27
Par: 72, USGA: 71.6

GF: w/day $60.00, w/end $60.00
Carts: $Included

One of the valley's hardest and best kept golf courses. The greens are well guarded by bunkers, trees and water hazards, 23 lakes and over 90 bunkers. #16 best par 4 course in desert by golf pros, #14 voted best in desert by Palm Springs Life.

Plan ahead! Reserve tee time well in advance, and while you're doing so, confirm rates and services.

─────────── CHESTER ───────────

Alamanor West GC
111 Slim Dr., Lake
Almanor, 96020
Ph: 916-259-4555

Yards: 3135, Holes: 9
Par: 36, USGA: 34.8

Proshop
GF: w/day $10.00, w/end
$14.00
Carts: $16.00

*A beautiful mountain course with lots of evergreens lining the fairways. You can
see Mount Lassen in the distance.*

─────────── CHICO ───────────

Bidwell Park GC
Wildwood Ave., P.O.
Box 1341, 95927
Ph: 916-891-8417

Yards: 6163, Holes: 18
Par: 70, USGA: 68.1

GF: w/day $8.00, w/end
$10.00
Carts: $13.00

*Part of the course is on hilly terrain, but all of it has beautiful mature trees and
plenty of water. The rates are for all day, so you can play as long as you like.*

─────────── CHICO ───────────

Canyon Oaks GC
End of Yosemite Dr,
PO Box 7790, 95928
Ph: 916-345-1622

Yards: 6799, Holes: 18
Par: 72, USGA: 72.9

GF: w/day $18.00, w/end
$20.00
Carts: $16.00

*Undulating fairways that are narrow can cause you some rough shots. The
course has lots of trees and water. The course is available for outside tournaments.*

─────────── CHINO ───────────

El Prado GC
6555 Pine Ave., 91710
Ph: 714-597-1753

Yards: 6296, Holes: 18
Par: 72, USGA: 69.1

GF: w/day $15.00, w/end
$20.00
Carts: $20.00

*There are two 18-hole courses here. One is a particularly good course for the
beginner. The other is long, with water, rolling terrain and less forgiving to the
unwary.*

─────────── CHINO ───────────

Los Serranos GC CC
15656 Yorba Ave.,
91709
Ph: 714-597-1711

Yards: 6121, Holes: 18
Par: 71, USGA: 69.0
RP: One week in
advance

Restaurant/Bar/Proshop
GF: w/day $14.00, w/end
$16.00
Carts: $16.00

*Host to California State Open, L.A. Open Qualifying, So. Calif. Qualifying for
State Amateur Championship. One of the favorite holes on the North Course is
#15, a short 4-par, 329 yards, with a large lake in front of the green and 2 sand
traps.*

─────────── CHINO ───────────

**Los Serranos Golf &
CC - South**
15656 Yorba Ave.,
91709
Ph: 714-597-1711

Yards: 6559, Holes: 18
Par: 74, USGA: 70.9
RP: One week in
advance

Restaurant/Bar/Proshop
GF: w/day $14.00, w/end
$16.00
Carts: $16.00

*The only public course in North Carolina on I-95, Exit 150. You'll find the
fairways lined with tall Carolina pines. Water, sand traps, or trees come into play
on every hole. Excellent greens, along with Southern hospitality, makes Hickory
Meadows a must.*

─────────────CHULA VISTA─────────────

Eastlake CC
2375 Clubhouse Dr,
91914
Ph: 619-482-5757

Yards: 6225, Holes: 18
Par: 72, USGA: 68.7

GF: w/day $25.00, w/end
$40.00
Carts: $15.00

A Ted Robinson design that opened in 1991. There are trees everywhere with plenty of water.

─────────────CITY OF INDUSTRY─────────────

Industry Hill GC
1 Industry Hills Pkwy.,
91744
Ph: 818-965-0861

Yards: 6270, Holes: 18
Par: 72, USGA: 70.9
RP: Required

Restaurant
GF: w/day $42.00, w/end
$57.00
Carts: $Included

You can play the Babe Zaharias Course or the adjacent Eisenhower Course. The Eisenhower is a long, wide open course featuring high rough and plenty of hills. #2 is a par 4. You tee off on top of a hill.

─────────────CLAYTON─────────────

Oakhurst CC
8000 Clayton Rd.,
94517
Ph: 510-672-9737

Yards: 6275, Holes: 18
Par: 72, USGA: 70.9

GF: w/day $50.00, w/end
$70.00
Carts: $Included

Rolling fairways with difficult lies, hazards and out-of-bounds, you'll have plenty of challenge on this one.

─────────────COALINA─────────────

Polvadero G&CC
41605 Sutter Ave.,
93210
Ph: 209-935-3578

Yards: 3268, Holes: 9
Par: 36, USGA: 35.0

GF: w/day $5.00, w/end
$7.00
Carts: $6.00

A nice course to walk and enjoy a mildly challenging game of golf. Although hilly, it offers nice trees and a couple of lakes to please the eye.

─────────────COBB─────────────

Hobergs Forest Lake G&CC
P.O. Box 235, Hwy 175
& Golf Rd., 95436
Ph: 707-928-5276

Yards: 2246, Holes: 9
Par: 33, USGA: 30.1

Proshop
GF: w/day $7.00, w/end
$8.00
Carts: $15.00

A lovely mountain setting with lots of bunkers, pine trees, and its very own creek. A real challenge.

─────────────COLMA─────────────

Cypress Hills GC
2001 Hillside Blvd.,
94014
Ph: 415-922-5155

Yards: 3443, Holes: 9
Par: 37

Proshop
GF: w/day $7.00, w/end
$10.00
Carts: $8.00

A lake, trees and mostly par-4 holes make this an interesting round. Check about senior rates.

─────────────COLTON─────────────

Sunset Dunes GC
1901 Valley Blvd,
92324
Ph: 714-877-1712

Yards: 3095, Holes: 18
Par: 57

GF: w/day $11.00, w/end
$12.00
Carts: $10.00

A very short layout, but you will have an unparalleled opportunity to fine-tune your short game. The pros like this one too.

────────────────COLUSA────────────────

Colusa CC
P.O. Box 686, Highway
20 E, 95932
Ph: 916-458-5577

Yards: 3309, Holes: 9
Par: 36, USGA: 34.8

Proshop
GF: w/day $10.00, w/end
$15.00
Carts: $12.00

This is an older course with some recent renovations. Although the course is flat, you will find it a fairly challenging layout.

────────────────CONCORD────────────────

Buchanan Fields GC
3330 Concord Ave.,
94520
Ph: 415-682-1846

Yards: 5164, Holes: 9
Par: 68, USGA: 63.0

GF: w/day $5.50, w/end
$7.00
Carts: $16.00

There's plenty of water here. A flat course with rolling greens, your short game is going to get plenty of exercise. Senior rates are available on weekdays.

────────────────CONCORD────────────────

Diablo Creek GC
4050 Port Chicago
Hwy., 94520
Ph: 415-686-6262

Yards: 6344, Holes: 18
Par: 72, USGA: 69.5
RP: Call in advance

Restaurant/Bar/Proshop
GF: w/day $9.50, w/end
$11.50
Carts: $16.00

Course has an excellent view of Mt. Diablo, our tallest mountain in the area. The front nine starts out easy until we meet the third hole. 598 yards from white tees, 660 yards from blue tees. Hole is dogleg left with two large lakes in front.

────────────────CORONA────────────────

Cresta Verde GC
1295 Cresta Rd., 91719
Ph: 714-737-2255

Yards: 5390, Holes: 18
Par: 71, USGA: 64.9

GF: w/day $14.00, w/end
$20.00
Carts: $20.00

Believe it or not, this course was designed by Randolph Scott in 1927 Steep slopes, plenty of water, majestic trees and wandering fairways are all features here.

────────────────CORONA────────────────

Green River GC
5215 Green River Dr.,
91720
Ph: 714-970-8411

Yards: 6028, Holes: 18
Par: 71, USGA: 67.8

GF: w/day $15.00, w/end
$20.00
Carts: $20.00

Opened in 1958, these courses were designed by William Bell and Desmond Muirhead. A river runs through both courses. Many lakes and trees add spice to the sloping fairways.

────────────────CORONA────────────────

Mountain View CC
2121 Mountain View
Dr., 91720
Ph: 714-633-0282

Yards: 6157, Holes: 18
Par: 72, USGA: 69.0

GF: w/day $23.00, w/end
$33.00
Carts: $23.00

Very, very small greens, hills, and narrow fairways make your shot placement very important on this course. There is a senior rate on weekdays.

Enter your favorite resort in our "Golf Resort of The Year" contest (entry form is in the back of the book).

———————————————— CORONADO ————————————————

City of Coronado   Yards: 6446, Holes: 18   Restaurant/Bar/Proshop
Muni GC   Par: 72, USGA: 69.9   **GF:** w/day $13.00
2000 Visalia Row,   RP: 2 days in advance   **Carts:** $15.00
92118
Ph: 619-435-3121

Built along the shoreline of San Diego Bay, offering views of the Coronado Bay Bridge, downtown San Diego with the bay coming into play on several holes. A challenging course especially in p.m. when off shore breezes impact shotmaking on the back 9.

———————————————— COSTA MESA ————————————————

Costa Mesa Golf &   Yards: 6233, Holes: 18   **GF:** w/day $16.00, w/end
CC   Par: 72, USGA: 69.0 $29.00
Box 1829 1701 Golf   **Carts:** $20.00
Course Dr., 92626
Ph: 714-754-5267

This facility has 36 holes to choose from. One has lakes and trees in abundance. The other is noted for its undulating greens and is very well-trapped.

———————————————— COYOTE ————————————————

Riverside GC   Yards: 6504, Holes: 18   **GF:** w/day $7.50, w/end
P.O. Box 13128, 95013   Par: 72, USGA: 69.6 $15.00
Ph: 408-463-0622   **Carts:** $16.00

A long course that plays tough due the normal afternoon wind. The front side is wide open and long while the back side is narrow. A fun course where many birdies can be made.

———————————————— CRESCENT CITY ————————————————

Del Norte GC   Yards: 3000, Holes: 9   Proshop
130 Club Dr., 95531   Par: 36, USGA: 33.4   **GF:** w/day $10.00, w/end
Ph: 707-458-3214 $12.50
                                                         Carts: $12.00

Tree-lined fairways are the main feature of this course. There are some hazards, and one hole with a tight dogleg that can give you some difficulty.

———————————————— CRESCENT CITY ————————————————

Kings Valley GC   Yards: 2518, Holes: 9   **GF:** w/day $5.00, w/end
3030 Lesna Rd., 95531   Par: 56, USGA: 52.0 $6.00
Ph: 707-464-2886

You're going to have to walk this one as there are no carts.

———————————————— CUPERTINO ————————————————

Blackberry Farm GC   Yards: 3250, Holes: 9   **GF:** w/day $3.50, w/end
22100 Stevens Creek   Par: 58, USGA: 54.6 $6.00
Blvd., 95014
Ph: 408-253-9200

A nice one to walk due to its flat terrain. Although the course is short there are narrow fairways with mature trees and lots of water play.

———————————————— CUPERTINO ————————————————

Deep Cliff GC   Yards: 3365, Holes: 18   **GF:** w/day $8.50, w/end
10700 Clubhouse Ln.,   Par: 60, USGA: 54.4 $11.00
95014
Ph: 408-253-5359

This course has its own creek and you're going to see a lot of it. The course may be short, but with its very narrow fairways you have to be very accurate to score well.

─────────────────── DAVIS ───────────────────

Davis GC
P.O. Box 928, 95617
Ph: 916-756-4010

Yards: 4745, Holes: 18
Par: 66, USGA: 60.9

GF: w/day $4.00, w/end
$7.00
Carts: $12.00

Trees and out-of-bounds should keep your attention on the game. This short course features rolling greens, although it is otherwise flat.

─────────────────── DEATH VALLEY ───────────────────

Furnace Creek GC
Furnace Creek Box 1,
92328
Ph: 619-786-2301

Yards: 5759, Holes: 18
Par: 70, USGA: 66.3
RP: Weekends

Restaurant/Bar
GF: w/day $25.00
Carts: $18.00

Tamarisk trees and stands of date palms line the fairways. On the 5th hole you'll be putting 214 feet below sea level, and should you land in a bunker, you won't need your sand wedge, as all bunkers are grass. Water comes into play on several holes.

─────────────────── DELANO ───────────────────

Delano Public GC
PO Box 608 Memorial
Park, 93216
Ph: 805-725-7527

Yards: 4384, Holes: 9
Par: 64, USGA: 58.8

GF: w/day $6.50, w/end
$8.50

A long par-5 hole on this one is definitely a challenge.

─────────────────── DESERT CENTER ───────────────────

Lake Tamarisk GC
26-251 Parkview Dr,
PO Box 315, 92239
Ph: 619-227-3203

Yards: 3014, Holes: 9
Par: 35, USGA: 66.9

Proshop
GF: w/day $12.00
Carts: $12.00

A course which is set around lakes, palms abound here. The course isn't a long one, but challenging nevertheless.

─────────────────── DESERT HOT SPRINGS ───────────────────

Desert Dunes GC
19300 Palm Dr., 92240
Ph: 619-329-2941

Yards: 6876, Holes: 18
Par: 72, USGA: 74.1
RP: 7 days in advance

Restaurant/Bar/Proshop
GF: w/day $60.00, w/end
$70.00
Carts: $Included

Rated by Golf Digest as one of the top 75 public courses. Scenery, particularly the wildlife is fantastic. Depending on the tee you play from, all levels can enjoy it. Rolling terrain, well-trapped greens, mounds and moguls are just a few challenges.

─────────────────── DESERT HOT SPRINGS ───────────────────

Mission Lakes CC
8484 Clubhouse Dr.,
92240
Ph: 619-329-6481

Yards: 6396, Holes: 18
Par: 71, USGA: 70.2

GF: w/day $55.00, w/end
$60.00
Carts: $Included

A 1971 Ted Robinson design. Long par-3s, hills, wind, and fast greens are all going to make this a great round of golf.

Plan ahead! Reserve tee time well in advance, and while you're doing so, confirm rates and services.

─────────────── DESERT HOT SPRINGS ───────────────

Sands Mobile Home CC
15-500 Bubbling Wells Rd., 92240
Ph: 619-329-9333

Yards: 5254, Holes: 9
Par: 64, USGA: 57.5

GF: w/day $12.00

A short course, you shouldn't have much trouble with this one.

─────────────── DOWNEY ───────────────

Los Amigos City GC
7295 Quill Dr, 90242
Ph: 213-862-1717

Yards: 6006, Holes: 18
Par: 70, USGA: 66.4

GF: w/day $11.00, w/end $15.00

A long, well taken for course. The greens will give you more trouble than anything else. The course is available for outside tournaments.

─────────────── DOWNEY ───────────────

Rio Hondo CC
10627 Old River School Rd., 90241
Ph: 213-927-2420

Yards: 6003, Holes: 18
Par: 70, USGA: 67.3
RP: One week in advance

Restaurant/Bar/Proshop
GF: w/day $9.00, w/end $12.00
Carts: $14.00

Although a short golf course it is well lined with trees on all holes. Greens are on the small side and well bunkered par 3's toughest holes on course. Short game important to score well on our course.

─────────────── DURATE ───────────────

Rancho Duarte GC
1000 Las Lomas, 91010
Ph: 818-357-9981

Yards: 1800, Holes: 9
Par: 31

GF: w/day $6.00, w/end $8.00

A hilly, well-trapped course. Since the course is short your should get a work out on your irons.

─────────────── EL CAJON ───────────────

Rancho San Diego GC
3121 Willow Glen Rd., 92019
Ph: 619-442-9891

Yards: 6728, Holes: 18
Par: 73, USGA: 71.9
RP: 2 weeks in advance

GF: w/day $25.00, w/end $30.00
Carts: $19.00

Two 18-hole courses with a river, ponds and lakes. More than enough water Tight fairways and doglegs make for some really challenging holes. Senior rates are available during the week.

─────────────── EL CAJON ───────────────

Singing Hills CC
3007 Dehesa Rd., 92019
Ph: 619-442-3425

Yards: 6600, Holes: 18
Par: 72, USGA: 68.9
RP: 1 week in advance

Restaurant/Bar/Proshop
GF: w/day $25.00, w/end $30.00
Carts: $18.00

Favorite hole #5 Oak Glen Course, 395 yards—drive across river to narrow, rolling fairway sloping to river; mid iron into very long, narrow 3 level green protected on left by bunker and lateral water hazard; deep pit bunker fronts right entry to green.

─────────────── EL DORADO HILLS ───────────────

El Dorado Hills GC
3775 El Dorado Hills Blvd., 95630
Ph: 916-933-6552

Yards: 3920, Holes: 18
Par: 61, USGA: 59.0

GF: w/day $8.00, w/end $10.00
Carts: $12.00

A short course with only one-par five. Some hilly holes and there's enough water and trees to make it interesting. Ask about the twilight rates.

────────────── ELK GROVE ──────────────

Emerald Lakes GC
10651 East Stockton
Blvd., 95624
Ph: 916-685-4653

Yards: 4832, Holes: 9
Par: 66, USGA: 62.7

GF: w/day $6.00, w/end
$7.00
Carts: $8.00

You'll get lots of water on this one. The greens are tough and the fairways narrow. A driving range is available in the summer. The senior rates are quite affordable.

────────────── ELVERTA ──────────────

Cherry Island GC
2360 Elverta Rd, 95660
Ph: 916-991-0770

Yards: 6562, Holes: 18
Par: 72, USGA: 71.1

Restaurant/Bar
GF: w/day $11.50, w/end
$14.00

Designed in 1990 by Robert Muir Graves, there are narrow fairways and five lakes. There is water on over half the course, and you could have trouble with all of it. Plenty of bunkers too, with small greens.

────────────── ENCINO ──────────────

Sepulveda GC
16821 Burbank Blvd.,
91436
Ph: 818-986-4560

Yards: 6408, Holes: 36
Par: 72, USGA: 68.4

GF: w/day $11.00, w/end
$15.00
Carts: $16.00

Two 18-hole courses are at this location. One course is long and relatively open which the other, although long is much less forgiving. There are a lot of low trees, and well-trapped greens.

────────────── ESCALON ──────────────

Escalon GC
17051 So. Escalon
Bellota Rd., 95320
Ph: 209-838-1277

Yards: 3040, Holes: 9
Par: 62, USGA: 52.6

GF: w/day $3.75, w/end
$8.50

A nice walkable course without a great deal of difficulty. You might have to watch out for some of the trees.

────────────── ESCONDIDO ──────────────

Castle Creek CC
8797 Circle R Dr.,
92026
Ph: 619-749-2422

Yards: 6410, Holes: 18
Par: 72, USGA: 70.4
RP: 7 days in advance

Restaurant/Bar/Proshop
GF: w/day $18.00, w/end
$25.00
Carts: $20.00

No. 14, 350 and 340 long, you must carry your tee shot over Castle Creek, which is 170 yards away if you're dead straight, and close to 200 if you should fade your shot. Then you still have a demanding iron over lake that fronts green.

────────────── ESCONDIDO ──────────────

**Lawrence Welk
Resort Fountains**
8860 Lawrence Welk
Dr., 92026
Ph: 619-749-3225

Yards: 4002, Holes: 18
Par: 62, USGA: 54.6
RP: Resort guests any
time—1 week

Restaurant/Bar/Proshop
GF: w/day $20.00, w/end
$20.00
Carts: $10.00

Southern California's 1,000 acre Lawrence Welk Resort is the home of the beautiful 4,002 yard Fountains Executive Golf Course. Four spring-fed lakes are strategically located among the 10 par 3 and 8 par 4 holes, adding beauty and difficulty.

─────────────── ESCONDIDO ───────────────

Meadow Lake CC
10333 Meadow Glen
Way East, 92026
Ph: 619-749-1620

Yards: 6521, Holes: 18
Par: 72, USGA: 69.6
RP: Public - 1 week in
advance

Restaurant/Bar/Proshop
GF: w/day $24.00, w/end
$32.00
Carts: $12.00

Doglegs and sidehill lies meet you at every turn. A real tough game awaits you here. Course features narrow, tree-lined fairways with massive boulders and rock outcroppings everywhere.

─────────────── EUREKA ───────────────

Eureka GC
4750 Fairway Dr.,
95501
Ph: 707-443-4808

Yards: 5589, Holes: 18
Par: 70, USGA: 66.5

GF: w/day $6.50, w/end
$8.00
Carts: $12.00

The main feature of this course are the many water hazards. Otherwise the course is fairly flat with only a few trees. A twilight rate and senior rates make it an attractive bargain.

─────────────── FAIRFIELD ───────────────

Rancho Solano GC
3250 Rancho Solano
Pkwy., 94533
Ph: 707-429-4653

Yards: 6705, Holes: 18
Par: 72, USGA: 72.9

Restaurant/Bar
GF: w/day $15.00, w/end
$20.00

Set in rolling terrain, this course is well bunkered with large greens. Check into our twilight rates.

─────────────── FALL RIVER MILLS ───────────────

**Fall River Valley
G&CC**
Highway 299 E, P.O.
Box PAR, 96028
Ph: 916-336-5555

Yards: 6835, Holes: 18
Par: 72, USGA: 72.5

GF: w/day $5.00, w/end
$12.00
Carts: $14.00

A really difficult layout with water and trees causing a lot of the problems. The course is long with rolling fairways. The large green cause difficulties all their own. Very scenic with Mount Shasta and Mount Lassen as a backdrop.

─────────────── FALLBROOK ───────────────

Fallbrook GC
Box 2167, 2757 Gird
Rd., 92088
Ph: 619-728-8334

Yards: 6205, Holes: 18
Par: 72, USGA: 69.1
RP: 10 days in advance

Restaurant/Bar/Proshop
GF: w/day $22.00, w/end
$30.00
Carts: $18.00

Although our course is relatively short, golfers are still challenged by the natural hazards presented by Live Oak Creek (which runs the length of the course) and our beautiful, native live oak trees.

─────────────── FALLBROOK ───────────────

Pala Mesa Resort
2001 Old Hwy 395,
92028
Ph: 619-728-5881

Yards: 6472, Holes: 18
Par: 72, USGA: 69.5
RP: 3 days in advance

GF: w/day $45.00, w/end
$60.00
Carts: $Included

In a setting of majestic oaks, this is a course with some lovely views that will help you forget the tricky greens and tight fairways until it's too late.

Subscribe to our free newsletter, "Great Golf Gazette" and hear about the latest special golf vacation values.

—————————————— FILLMORE ——————————————

Elkins Ranch GC
Box 695 1386
Chambersburg Rd.,
93015
Ph: 805-524-1440

Yards: 6010, Holes: 18
Par: 71, USGA: 68.5

GF: w/day $11.00, w/end
$16.00
Carts: $17.00

A quiet country setting. There are elevated tees, plenty of water and lots of open country. The course has something to offer for everyone and you should enjoy your round of golf here.

———————————— FOUNTAIN VALLEY ————————————

Mile Square GC
10401 Warner Ave.,
92708
Ph: 714-968-4556

Yards: 6669, Holes: 18
Par: 72, USGA: 69.9
RP: Week days one
week in advance

GF: w/day $16.00, w/end
$20.00
Carts: $20.00

A flat course with a creek and beautifully treed. Water is the main problem to watch out for here.

—————————————— FREMONT ——————————————

Parkway GC
3400 Stevenson Blvd.,
94538

Ph: 415-656-6862

Yards: 4428, Holes: 18
Par: 54, USGA: 49.9
GF: w/day $9.50

You really need to make your shots carefully on this one, there's not much forgiveness. The many mature trees and water hazards really make it a championship course. Ask about the senior rates, both weekdays and weekends.

—————————————— FRESNO ——————————————

Fig Garden GC
7700 North Van Ness
Blvd., 93771
Ph: 209-439-2928

Yards: 6300, Holes: 18
Par: 72, USGA: 69.0

Proshop
GF: w/day $15.00, w/end
$20.00
Carts: $10.00

Fig Garden is a busy course that offers a fair test of your game. The landscape is flat and you are able to spray the ball off the tee without being penalized. A course you can score on.

—————————————— FRESNO ——————————————

Fresno Airways GC
5440 E. Shields Ave.,
93727
Ph: 209-291-6254

Yards: 5182, Holes: 18
Par: 68, USGA: 63.8

GF: w/day $4.50, w/end
$6.75
Carts: $12.00

Not the course for scratch players, but everyone else should enjoy it. The short, tree-filled layout is very well cared for.

—————————————— FRESNO ——————————————

Palm Lakes GC
5025 E. Dakota, 93727
Ph: 209-292-1144

Yards: 4262, Holes: 18
Par: 62, USGA: 57.9

GF: w/day $5.75, w/end
$6.75
Carts: $12.00

A nice course to walk, there is some danger from water, but otherwise an enjoyable, easy round. Check for senior and student rates.

Plan ahead! Reserve tee time well in advance, and while you're doing so, confirm rates and services.

---------------------------FRESNO--------------------------

Riverside GC
7672 N. Josephine
Ave., 93722
Ph: 209-275-5900

Yards: 6743, Holes: 18
Par: 72, USGA: 70.8

GF: w/day $8.00
Carts: $14.00

Riverside is a long course that is relatively wide open. Just tee the ball up high and give it a good rip. Have fun.

---------------------------FRESNO--------------------------

**Village Greens
G&CC**
222 South Clovis Ave,
93725
Ph: 209-255-2786

Yards: 3429, Holes: 9
Par: 60, USGA: 56.8

Proshop
GF: w/day $5.00, w/end
$6.00
Carts: $7.00

A well cared for course with numerous bunkers and a wealth of mature trees. Some very tricky holes, and you'll need to be very careful.

--------------------------FULLERTON-------------------------

Fullerton GC
2700 North Harbor
Blvd., 92635
Ph: 714-871-5141

Yards: 5380, Holes: 18
Par: 67, USGA: 63.8
RP: 1 week in advance

Restaurant/Bar/Proshop
GF: w/day $9.00, w/end
$12.50
Carts: $15.00

The course is nestled in a valley with a creek winding through 14 holes. The area is surrounded by a nice residential area in the heart of the Orange County, only 7 miles from Disneyland.

----------------------------GALT----------------------------

Dry Creek Ranch GC
809 Crystal Way, 95632
Ph: 209-745-2330

Yards: 6502, Holes: 18
Par: 72, USGA: 71.3
Slope: 126
RP: 2 weeks in advance

Restaurant/Bar/Proshop
GF: w/day $16.00, w/end
$26.00
Carts: $18.00

We are one of the best public courses in Northern California with beautiful and towering oak trees and lakes and creeks in the play. Slope 126 (White).

-------------------------GARBERVILLE------------------------

Benbow GC
7000 Benbow Dr.,
95440
Ph: 707-923-2777

Yards: 5098, Holes: 18
Par: 70, USGA: 64.1

GF: w/day $10.00, w/end
$12.00
Carts: $16.00

Very, very narrow fairways, with beautiful redwoods guarding them. A nice course to walk, with a very ethereal beauty.

----------------------------GILROY---------------------------

Gavilan GC
5055 Santa Teresa
Blvd., 95020
Ph: 408-848-1363

Yards: 3598, Holes: 9
Par: 62, USGA: 54.8

Bar/Proshop
GF: w/day $5.00, w/end
$8.00
Carts: $10.00

The greens on this short course are the main challenge. Senior rates are offered on weekdays.

----------------------------GILROY---------------------------

Gilroy GC
2695 Hecker Pass
Highway, 95020
Ph: 408-842-2501

Yards: 5934, Holes: 18
Par: 70, USGA: 67.4

Proshop
GF: w/day $8.00, w/end
$13.00
Carts: $15.00

This course opened in 1920 and offers you beautiful mature trees, small greens and lots of roll. Twilight, junior and senior rates offered.

————————————————GLENDORA————————————————

Glenoaks GC
200 West Dawson,
91740
Ph: 818-335-7565

Yards: 1020, Holes: 9
Par: 54

GF: w/day $3.25, w/end
$4.00

A very short, par-3 course that is a good test of your irons. We offer special junior, senior and women's rates.

————————————————GOLETA————————————————

Ocean Meadows GC
6925 Whittier Dr, 93117
Ph: 805-968-6814

Yards: 6392, Holes: 18
Par: 72, USGA: 70.0

Restaurant
GF: w/day $15.00, w/end
$20.00
Carts: $14.00

The bird life is varied and abundance on this course near the ocean. But you'll need to keep your eye on the ball, as this course can be a challenge. The course is available for outside tournaments.

————————————————GOLETA————————————————

Sandpiper GC
7925 Hollister Ave.,
93117
Ph: 805-968-1541

Yards: 7035, Holes: 18
Par: 72, USGA: 72.5
RP: 7 Days in advance

Restaurant/Bar/Proshop
GF: w/day $45.00, w/end
$65.00
Carts: $22.00

Sandpiper Golf Course presently ranks in the top 25 public golf courses in America. It is a championship public course situated in a spectacular coastal setting near scenic Santa Barbara. Large sweeping fairways and spacious greens.

————————————————GOLETA————————————————

Twin Lakes GC
6034 Hollister Ave.,
93117
Ph: 805-964-1414

Yards: 1400, Holes: 9
Par: 29, USGA: 49.0
RP: 1 week in advance

Restaurant/Bar/Proshop
GF: w/day $5.50

This course is a sleeper, with well bunkered, fast, sloping bent grass greens, Twin Lakes offers a challenge to all players. The par 4 360 yard 7th hole is as tight a driving hole as you will ever find. Tree line up on the right, O.B.

————————————————GRAEAGLE————————————————

**Graeagle Meadows
GC**
P.O. Box 68, 96103
Ph: 916-836-2323

Yards: 6655, Holes: 18
Par: 72, USGA: 70.7
RP: Call in advance

Restaurant/Bar/Proshop
GF: w/day $20.00
Carts: $18.00

Located in the Sierra's one hour north of Lake Tahoe Graeagle Meadows is built along the banks of the Feather River. The three pars are relatively short with longer four pars. The 6th hole is noted as one of the most picturesque in California.

————————————————GRANADA HILLS————————————————

Knollwood GC
12040 Balboa Blvd.,
91344
Ph: 818-368-5709

Yards: 6234, Holes: 18
Par: 72, USGA: 69.2

GF: w/day $11.00, w/end
$15.00
Carts: $17.00

Designed by William Bell in 1956, you'll find a well matured course here. There are many up hill shots and that can be very tough.

──────────── GRASS VALLEY ────────────

Alta Sierra G&CC
144 Tammy Way, 95949
Ph: 916-273-2010

Yards: 6342, Holes: y
Par: 18, USGA: 70.1

Proshop
GF: w/day $17.00, w/end
$20.00
Carts: $16.00

Wildlife is a definite attraction here, with views of the Sierra. The course is championship caliber and hosts numerous tournaments. Large greens are a feature of this hilly course.

──────────── GRASS VALLEY ────────────

Nevada County CC
1040 East Main St.,
95945
Ph: 916-273-6436

Yards: 2732, Holes: 9
Par: 34, USGA: 32.3

GF: w/day $8.00, w/end
$14.00
Carts: $7.00

A not too difficult course. Rolling terrain and tough greens abound.

──────────── GREENVILLE ────────────

Mount Huff
PO Box 569, 95947
Ph: 916-284-6204

Yards: 4375, Holes: 9
Par: 66, USGA: 60.2

GF: w/day $6.00, w/end
$7.00
Carts: $7.00

Water can made for some tough shots on this course. The fairways are fairly level, but you can still get into plenty of trouble.

──────────── GROVELAND ────────────

Pine Mountain Lake GC
P.O. Box PMLA,
Mueller Dr., 95321
Ph: 209-962-7783

Yards: 6106, Holes: 18
Par: 70, USGA: 68.4

GF: w/day $30.00
Carts: $20.00

Your best game will be put to the test here. A hilly course that has plenty of trees, and fairways that demand careful shots. Some interesting doglegs will keep your attention on the game.

──────────── GROVER CITY ────────────

Pismo State Beach GC
9 LeSage Drive, 93433
Ph: 805-481-5215

Yards: 2795, Holes: 9
Par: 54

GF: w/day $4.75, w/end
$5.25

No shortage of water here, with the ocean in view and water hazards on almost every hole. A windy course with evergreen lined fairways. Senior and twilight rates offered.

──────────── HALF MOON BAY ────────────

Half Moon Bay GC & GL
2000 Fairway Dr.,
94019
Ph: 415-726-4438

Yards: 7166, Holes: 18
Par: 72, USGA: 74.5

GF: w/day $68.00, w/end
$88.00
Carts: $Included

This beautiful 7116 yards of golf links designed by Francis Duane with Arnold Palmer as consultant capitalized on the picturesque setting of seascape and mountains. Here is a delightful test of golf–water holes, barrancas, and bluffs.

──────────── HAYWARD ────────────

Skywest GC
1401 Golf Course Rd.,
94541
Ph: 415-278-6188

Yards: 6540, Holes: 18
Par: 72, USGA: 69.4

GF: w/day $5.50, w/end
$12.00
Carts: $14.00

This is a nice test of your game. The course is fairly open but the greens are small. Beware of the planes that fly above because of the airport next door.

─────────────── HEALDSBURG ───────────────

Tayman Park GC
927 So. Fitch Mtn. Rd.,
POB 1193, 95448
Ph: 707-433-4275

Yards: 5304, Holes: 9
Par: 70, USGA: 64.8

GF: w/day $5.00, w/end
$7.00
Carts: $12.00

A small hilly course with plenty of trees. Seniors will enjoy the easy walk and the Senior rates.

─────────────── HEMET ───────────────

Echo Hills GC
545 E. Thornton, 92343
Ph: 714-652-2203

Yards: 4466, Holes: 9
Par: 35, USGA: 60.2
RP: 1 day ahead

GF: w/day $7.00
Carts: $8.00

A short course with large trees and narrow fairways.

─────────────── HEMET ───────────────

Seven Hills GC
1537 South Lyon Ave.,
92343
Ph: 714-925-4815

Yards: 6313, Holes: 18
Par: 72, USGA: 67.7

GF: w/day $16.00, w/end
$20.00
Carts: $9.00

Just a few bunkers and small greens, on this flat course, give you only a small picture of the conditions you'll find here. The course is available for outside tournaments.

─────────────── HESPERIA ───────────────

Hesperia G & CC
17970 Bangor Ave.,
92345
Ph: 619-244-9301

Yards: 6570, Holes: 18
Par: 72, USGA: 71.7

GF: w/day $15.00, w/end
$20.00
Carts: $18.00

The trees here are one of the most difficult features. A long course that will challenge you in every way. A championship course that has hosted many major tournaments in the past.

─────────────── HILMAR ───────────────

Poquito Lake G&CC
19920 First St., P.O.
Box 268, 95324
Ph: 209-668-2255

Yards: 5426, Holes: 9
Par: 58, USGA: 54.5

GF: w/day $6.00, w/end
$7.00

Recently renovated, but still retaining a great variety of mature trees. A beautifully maintained course with all the challenge you'll ever want. Check on the junior and senior rates.

─────────────── HOLLISTER ───────────────

Ridgemark GC
3800 Airline Hwy.,
95023
Ph: 408-637-1010

Yards: 6032, Holes: 36
Par: 72, USGA: 69.8

GF: w/day $15.00, w/end
$20.00
Carts: $16.00

A 36 hole layout with large greens. One course is very hilly and the other has lots of water. And you can always count on the wind here to give you problems. If you want to walk here, you have to wait until late afternoon.

─────────────── HOLTVILLE ───────────────

**Barbara Worth CC
and Inn**
2050 Country Club Dr.,
92250
Ph: 619-356-2806

Yards: 6239, Holes: 18
Par: 71, USGA: 68.6
RP: Reservations a
must

Restaurant/Bar/Proshop
GF: w/day $14.00, w/end
$16.00
Carts: $16.00

Huge tamarack (50-80 feet tall) close in most fairways—lots of water in our desert setting—lots of tall palm trees. Completely surrounded by vegetable fields—course completely manicured.

HUGHSON

River Oaks GC
3441 E. Hatch Rd.,
95326
Ph: 209-537-4653

Yards: 6000, Holes: 18
Par: 58, USGA: 52.7

GF: w/day $3.75, w/end
$8.00

Even though bordered by the Tuolumne River, this course doesn't present much difficulty. Lots of trees and a few ponds are the only other hazards. A nice easy game.

HUNTINGTON BEACH

Meadowlark GC
16782 Graham St.,
92647
Ph: 714-846-1364

Yards: 5761, Holes: 18
Par: 70, USGA: 66.1

GF: w/day $14.00, w/end
$19.00
Carts: $19.00

Some water hazards, narrow fairways and small greens are the main features of this course.

INDIAN WELLS

Indian Wells GR
44-500 Indian Wells
Ln., 92210
Ph: 619-346-4653

Yards: 6686, Holes: 18
Par: 72, USGA: 71.6
RP: 2 days in advance

Restaurant/Bar/Proshop
GF: w/day $100.00
Carts: $Included

The Resort's East and West golf courses offer beautiful greens, wide rolling fairways, splashes of water and fantastic panoramic views of the Santa Rosa Mountains. The courses feature an island green, an island fairway and world class golfing environment.

INDIO

Indian Palms GC
48-630 Monroe St.,
92201
Ph: 619-347-2326

Yards: 6709, Holes: 27
Par: 72, USGA: 72.7
RP: Call Golf Shop

Restaurant/Bar/Proshop
GF: w/day $40.00, w/end
$45.00
Carts: $Included

The home of the Senior Champions of Golf. A 27-hole championship golf course built on tradition and known throughout the desert for its tree-lined fairways and numerous lakes. Summer rates/twilight fees/golf packages available in our 59-room hotel.

INDIO

Indio Muni GC
83-040 Ave. 42, PO Box
X, 92202
Ph: 619-347-9156

Yards: 3004, Holes: 18
Par: 54, USGA: 49.1

GF: w/day $9.00
Carts: $9.00

A very long par-3 course, there is some water. Night golfing in offered here.

IRVINE

Newport Beach GC
3100 Irvine Ave.,
PO Box 18426, 92714
Ph: 714-852-8689

Yards: 3209, Holes: 18
Par: 59, USGA: 55.5

GF: w/day $8.50, w/end
$12.00

This course was opened in 1971, and designed by Robert Muir Graves. Bunkers and water will be difficult here, so you need to be on top of your game.

Enter your favorite resort in our "Golf Resort of The Year" contest (entry form is in the back of the book).

─────────────────── IRVINE ───────────────────

Rancho San Joaquin GC
One Sandburg Way, 92715
Ph: 714-786-5522

Yards: 6229, Holes: 18
Par: 72, USGA: 68.8

GF: w/day $15.00, w/end $30.00
Carts: $Included

A nice course for a weekday stroll.

─────────────────── JAMUL ───────────────────

Steele Canyon GC
3199 Stonefield Dr, 91935
Ph: 619-441-6900

Yards: 6220, Holes: 27
Par: 71, USGA: 69.1
RP: 7 days in advance

Bar/Proshop
GF: w/day $38.00, w/end $48.00
Carts: $Included

Designed by Gary Player, this course opened in 1991. A 27-hole layout with 3 sets of 9s that can be played in different combinations. The setting has many magnificent views. A stop well worth your time.

─────────────────── KELSEYVILLE ───────────────────

Buckingham G&CC
2855 Eastlake Dr., 95454
Ph: 707-279-4863

Yards: 6238, Holes: 18
Par: 72, USGA: 67.9
RP: Konocti Harbor Inn guests only

Proshop
GF: w/day $8.00, w/end $12.00
Carts: $12.00

There are some unusual hazards on this flat course.

─────────────────── KELSEYVILLE ───────────────────

Clear Lake Riviera GC
10200 Fairway Dr., 95451
Ph: 707-277-7129

Yards: 2819, Holes: 9
Par: 36, USGA: 33.8

Proshop
GF: w/day $9.00, w/end $10.00
Carts: $11.00

Located near the shores of Clear Lake. The course is hilly with many difficult lies. A real shot maker course.

─────────────────── KERMAN ───────────────────

Fresno West GC
23986 W. Whitebridge Rd., 93630
Ph: 209-846-8655

Yards: 6959, Holes: 18
Par: 72, USGA: 70.1
RP: Call in advance

Restaurant/Bar/Proshop
GF: w/day $10.00, w/end $12.00
Carts: $16.00

Our course is long and wide open, with big greens, plus seven lakes, our eighth hole the par 3 174 yard was regarded as one of the toughest 18 holes in the San Joaquin Valley according to Bruce Farris of the Fresno Bee.

─────────────────── KERNVILLE ───────────────────

Kern Valley GC & CC
9472 Burlando Rd., PO Box 888, 93238
Ph: 619-376-2828

Yards: 6061, Holes: 18
Par: 72, USGA: 67.2

GF: w/day $8.00, w/end $9.00
Carts: $12.00

This course has been maintained with loving care. Accuracy is important here, and your irons can get a workout.

─────────────────── KING CITY ───────────────────

King City GC
613 S. Vanderhurst, 93930
Ph: 408-385-4546

Yards: 5634, Holes: 9
Par: 70, USGA: 66.0

GF: w/day $7.00, w/end $8.00
Carts: $10.00

A creek and small greens are important considerations in how you play this one. Twilight rates are available.

———————————— KINGS BEACH ————————————

Woodvista GC　　　Yards: 3038, Holes: 9　　**GF:** w/day $15.00
P.O. Box 1269, 7900 N.　Par: 35, USGA: 34.9　　**Carts:** $10.00
Lake Rd., 95719
Ph: 916-546-9909

*Open from mid-April to November, this course has narrow-fairways which are
nicely tree-lined. A very scenic layout with a creek to add more difficulty.*

———————————— KLAMATH RIVER ————————————

Eagle Nest GC　　　Yards: 3634, Holes: 9　　**GF:** w/day $5.00, w/end
22112 Klamath River　Par: 64, USGA: 58.9　　$7.00
Rd., 96050
Ph: 916-465-9276

*Located near the Klamath River, Eagles Nest is loaded with trees. The fairways
are narrow, and this is the main challenge.*

———————————— LA GRANGE ————————————

Lake Don Pedro　　Yards: 6007, Holes: 18　**GF:** w/day $8.00, w/end
G&CC　　　　　　　Par: 70, USGA: 67.4　　$10.00
P.O. Box 193, Hayward　　　　　　　　　　　**Carts:** $16.00
Rd., 95329
Ph: 209-852-2242

*This course has a very hilly setting. There is some water, but not a lot. Available
for outside tournaments.*

———————————— LA MESA ————————————

Mission Trails　　　Yards: 6004, Holes: 18　Restaurant/Bar
7389 Golf Crest Pl,　　Par: 71, USGA: 68.6　　**GF:** w/day $15.00, w/end
92119　　　　　　　　　　　　　　　　　　$20.00
Ph: 619-460-5400　　　　　　　　　　　　　**Carts:** $19.00

*Set on a lake, Mission Trails offers many wonderful views and a pleasant walk if
you're in the mood. Plenty of trees and rolling fairways are the norm here.*

———————————— LA MESA ————————————

Sun Valley GC　　　Ph: 619-466-6102　　　Yards: 1080, Holes: 9
5080 Memorial Dr,　　　　　　　　　　　　Par: 27
92041　　　　　　　　　　　　　　　　　　**GF:** w/day $3.50

A very hilly par-3 course. A good workout for your irons.

———————————— LA MIRADA ————————————

La Mirada GC　　　Yards: 5700, Holes: 18　**GF:** w/day $11.00, w/end
15501 East Alicante　Par: 70, USGA: 66.6　　$15.00
Rd, 90638　　　　　　　　　　　　　　　　**Carts:** $17.00
Ph: 213-943-7123

A nice walkable course with only a few trees and traps.

———————————— LA QUINTA ————————————

Indian Springs CC　Yards: 6106, Holes: 18　**GF:** w/day $30.00, w/end
46080 Jefferson, 92253　Par: 71, USGA: 67.7　　$35.00
Ph: 619-347-0651　　　RP: Tee times　　　　**Carts:** $Included

Lots of sand on this mature course. The course is available for tournaments.

────────────────── LA QUINTA ──────────────────

La Quinta Hotel GC   Yards: 5775, Holes: 18   Restaurant/Bar
50-200 Ave. Vista   Par: 72, USGA: 68.7   **GF:** w/day $35.00, w/end
Bonita, 92253   RP: 1 week in advance $75.00
Ph: 619-346-2904   **Carts:** $Included

*Look for typical Dye touches such as railroad ties, big waste bunkers, elevation
changes, and mirror-smooth water hazards. #17 is one of the toughest 18 holes in
America according to pros. The acclaimed course hosted the 1985 World Cup
Pro-Am.*

────────────────── LA QUINTA ──────────────────

Palm Royale CC   Yards: 2118, Holes: 18   **GF:** w/day $12.00
78-259 Indigo Dr, 92253 Par: 54, USGA: 54.0
Ph: 619-345-9701

*A course that will let you use every iron you have, and there's water on at least
half the course. Twilight rates are offered.*

────────────────── LA QUINTA ──────────────────

The TPC Stadium   Yards: 6331, Holes: 18   **GF:** w/day $50.00, w/end
Course   Par: 72, USGA: 71.2 $100.00
Box 1578 55-900 PGA   **Carts:** $Included
Blvd., 92253
Ph: 619-564-7170

*Probably the toughest course in the country, Pete Dye's creation includes numer-
ous lakes, cavernous bunkers and undulating greens. The signature hole is the
par three, island green 17th, known as "Alcatraz". Trevino won the Skins Game
with a hole-in-one.*

────────────────── LA VERNE ──────────────────

Marshall Canyon GC   Yards: 5856, Holes: 18   **GF:** w/day $11.00, w/end
6100 North Stephens   Par: 71, USGA: 67.7 $15.00
Ranch Rd., 91750   **Carts:** $16.00
Ph: 714-593-6914

*This 1966 course is in a canyon with mountains overlooking it. Difficult greens
will give you a lot of trouble. Be sure to check the twilight and senior rates.*

────────────────── LAGUNA BEACH ──────────────────

Aliso Creek GC   Yards: 2200, Holes: 9   Restaurant/Bar
31106 S. Coast Hwy.,   USGA: 69.4   **GF:** w/day $11.00, w/end
92677   RP: 7 days in advance $18.00
Ph: 714-499-2271   **Carts:** $8.00

*The course is in a canyon setting, with a creek running down the middle, rolling
hills and sea breeze. There are 19 sand traps. The course is very narrow and
very challenging. Golf instruction, seminar and banquet facilities.*

────────────────── LAGUNA NIGUEL ──────────────────

The Links At   Yards: 5600, Holes: 27   **GF:** w/day $50.00, w/end
Monarch Beach   Par: 70, USGA: 67.2 $75.00
23841 Stonehill Dr.,   **Carts:** $Included
92677
Ph: 714-240-8247

*A lovely natural setting, with some definite creek problems. The ocean is not
only a scenic features, but a hazard as well.*

────────────────── LAKE ALMANOR ──────────────────

Lake Almanor CC
P.O. Box 3323, 951
Clifford Dr., 96137
Ph: 916-259-2868

Yards: 2937, Holes: 9
Par: 35, USGA: 33.5

GF: w/day $17.00
Carts: $16.00

Located in the mountains this course has many scenic wonders, one of which is Mount Lassen. Rolling greens make for interesting play and the wild life roams freely.

────────────────── LAKE ELIZABETH ──────────────────

Lake Elizabeth GC
42532 Ranch Club Rd,
93532
Ph: 805-724-1221

Yards: 5985, Holes: 18
Par: 70, USGA: 68.8
RP: Required on
weekends

GF: w/day $20.00, w/end
$26.00
Carts: $Included

Water, hills and small greens are a feature of this course. There is a particularly spectacular par-4 that you won't want to miss either.

────────────────── LAKE SAN MARCOS ──────────────────

Lake San Marcos GC
1750 San Pablo Dr.,
92069
Ph: 619-744-1310

Yards: 6214, Holes: 18
Par: 72, USGA: 68.8

GF: w/day $40.00
Carts: $Included

An 18-hole challenger that has small greens and tight fairways and an executive type course that will give your irons a workout. A junior rate is offered here.

────────────────── LAKESIDE ──────────────────

Willowbrook CC
11905 Riverside Dr.,
92040
Ph: 619-561-1061

Yards: 2983, Holes: 9
Par: 36, USGA: 67.1
RP: One week in
advance

Restaurant/Proshop
GF: w/day $9.00, w/end
$11.00
Carts: $10.00

You're inundated with array of lakes and strategically placed trees on this course. Since you play the course twice over, the lakes come into play on 19 holes. Large majestic sycamores force the player to hit either to one side of the fairway.

────────────────── LAKEWOOD ──────────────────

Lakewood County GC
3101 Carson St, 90712
Ph: 213-429-9711

Yards: 7058, Holes: 18
Par: 72, USGA: 71.6

GF: w/day $11.00, w/end
$15.00

This course has its very own lake, so it wouldn't hurt to bring a few extra balls. The course is popular so keep trying if you can get a tee time the first time you call.

────────────────── LANCASTER ──────────────────

Rancho Sierra GC
47205 60th Street East,
93535

Ph: 805-946-1080

Yards: 2431, Holes: 9
Par: 35, USGA: 62.2
GF: w/day $8.00

Relatively short and flat course. Water comes into play on 7 of the 9 holes. Narrow fairways reward precise shot making. Bent grass greens hold exceptionally and putt true.

Our listings—supplied by the management—are as complete as possible. Many of the courses have more features than we list. Be sure to inquire when you book your tee time.

──────────── LAWNDALE ────────────

Alondra Park GC Yards: 6292, Holes: 36 **GF:** w/day $11.00, w/end
16400 South Prairie, Par: 72, USGA: 67.7 $15.00
90260 **Carts:** $17.00
Ph: 213-217-9915

*This layout has two 18-hole courses, one an executive style course. Both are flat
courses with very few hazards.*

──────────── LEMOORE ────────────

Lemoore Muni GC Yards: 6134, Holes: 9 **GF:** w/day $7.00, w/end
350 West Ione, 93245 Par: 72, USGA: 68.3 $8.50
Ph: 209-924-9658 **Carts:** $14.00

*Recent course changes have increased the water hazards on this previously
water-filled course. Bring some extra balls just in case.*

──────────── LINDSAY ────────────

Lindsay Muni GC Yards: 2180, Holes: 9 **GF:** w/day $2.50, w/end
Tulare and Elmwood, Par: 54 $3.00
93221
Ph: 209-562-1144

*Located in a park, this course is in a pretty setting. The course is not very
demanding, but can be an enjoyable walking round.*

──────────── LITTLE RIVER ────────────

Little River Inn GC Yards: 2725, Holes: 9 **GF:** w/day $9.00, w/end
P.O. Box Drawer B, Par: 36, USGA: 33.0 $12.00
7750 N Hwy 1, 95456 **Carts:** $10.00
Ph: 707-937-5667

*Very tight and hilly fairways with the ocean in view. Lots of trees offer a home to
wildlife, and can often be seen.*

──────────── LIVERMORE ────────────

Las Positas GC Yards: 6540, Holes: 18 Bar/Proshop
909 Clubhouse Dr., Par: 72, USGA: 69.4 **GF:** w/day $9.00, w/end
94550 RP: One week in $15.00
Ph: 415-443-3122 advance **Carts:** $14.00

*Each of the 18-holes has its own strategy (green placement, water, tree lines and
traps). There are nine lakes on the course with a stream running through the
course. The golf course offers an executive nine holes at a par 31.*

──────────── LIVERMORE ────────────

Springtown GC Yards: 5468, Holes: 9 **GF:** w/day $5.50, w/end
939 Larkspur Dr., Par: 70, USGA: 65.4 $9.00
94550 **Carts:** $12.00
Ph: 415-449-9880

*A short, challenging course. Not too many hazards, but it will still demand your
best.*

──────────── LOC LOMOND ────────────

Adams Springs GC Yards: 5182, Holes: 9 **GF:** w/day $6.00, w/end
Hwy 175 at Snead Par: 70, USGA: 64.7 $10.00
Court, POB 2088, **Carts:** $12.00
95426
Ph: 707-928-9992

*Undulating, wide fairways are the fare on this extremely scenic course. Plenty of
water and plenty of wildlife. A very easy walking course for those who want
some exercise.*

─────────────────────LOMPOC─────────────────────

La Purisma GC
3455 State Hwy. 246,
93436
Ph: 805-735-8395

Yards: 7105, Holes: 18
Par: 72, USGA: 72.8
RP: 7 days in advance

Restaurant/Proshop
GF: w/day $35.00, w/end
$45.00
Carts: $22.00

La Purisma Golf Course is a championship public golf course situated on 300 acres of gently rolling hills bordering the beautiful Lompoc Valley in Santa Barbara County. Fairways and greens are surrounded by large stands of majestic oak trees.

─────────────────────LONE PINE─────────────────────

Mount Whitney GC
P.O. Box O, Highway
395, 93545
Ph: 619-876-5795

Yards: 3312, Holes: 9
Par: 36, USGA: 34.5

GF: w/day $8.00, w/end
$10.00
Carts: $8.00

Near Mount Whitney, you will find this a very scenic layout. The short game is very important here.

─────────────────────LONG BEACH─────────────────────

Bixby Village GC
6180 Bixby Village Dr,
90803
Ph: 213-498-7003

Yards: 1539, Holes: 9
Par: 29

GF: w/day $5.00, w/end
$6.00

A short course with a couple of par-4s and the rest 3s. The layout has some water and is hilly.

─────────────────────LONG BEACH─────────────────────

El Dorado GC
Box 15687 2400
Studebaker Rd., 90815
Ph: 213-430-5411

Yards: 6321, Holes: 18
Par: 72, USGA: 68.9

GF: w/day $15.50, w/end
$19.00
Carts: $17.00

Opened in 1955, you can expect to see some beautiful trees here. Some water and many doglegs are features here.

─────────────────────LONG BEACH─────────────────────

Heartwell GC
6700 East Carson St,
90808
Ph: 213-421-8855

Yards: 2153, Holes: 18
Par: 54, USGA: 50.1

GF: w/day $6.50, w/end
$6.75
Carts: $10.00

A par-3 18-holes course that is very well-maintained.

─────────────────────LONG BEACH─────────────────────

Recreation Park GC
5000 East 7th St, 90804
Ph: 213-494-5000

Yards: 6337, Holes: 9
Par: 64, USGA: 68.8

GF: w/day $15.50, w/end
$19.00

Narrow fairways, sloping terrain and rolling greens will all demand the best from your game if you want to score well.

─────────────────────LONG BEACH─────────────────────

Skylinks GC
4800 Wardlow Rd.,
90808
Ph: 213-429-0030

Yards: 6277, Holes: 18
Par: 72, USGA: 68.6

GF: w/day $16.00, w/end
$19.00
Carts: $17.00

A nice course to walk, but your shot-making better be working good because there are more doglegs than you usually see in one place.

──────────── LOOMIS ────────────

Indian Creek CC
4487 Barton Rd., PO
Box 303, 95650
Ph: 916-652-5546

Yards: 4164, Holes: 9
Par: 64, USGA: 59.2

GF: w/day $6.00, w/end
$7.00
Carts: $6.00

Lots of mature trees add to the beauty of this short course. There is a little water and some tricky greens. Ask about the senior rates.

──────────── LOS ANGELES ────────────

Chester Washington GC
1930 West 120th St,
90047
Ph: 213-756-6975

Yards: 6002, Holes: 18
Par: 70, USGA: 66.7

GF: w/day $11.00, w/end
$15.00

A long course, that is relatively worry-free.

──────────── LOS ANGELES ────────────

Griffith Park GC
4730 Crystal Springs
Dr., 90027
Ph: 213-664-2255

Yards: 6317, Holes: 36
Par: 72, USGA: 69.1

GF: w/day $10.50, w/end
$14.50
Carts: $16.00

Two 18-hole courses that are of championship caliber, what more can you ask? Plenty of trees and water, so you know where the troubles come from. Both courses are fairly long.

──────────── LOS ANGELES ────────────

Jack Thompson Par-3 GC
9637 South Western
Ave, 90047
Ph: 213-757-1650

Yards: 1008, Holes: 9
Par: 27

GF: w/day $3.50, w/end
$4.00

A short par-3 course. You can give your irons a real working over on this one.

──────────── LOS ANGELES ────────────

Rancho Park GC
10460 W. Pico Blvd.,
90064
Ph: 213-838-7373

Yards: 6216, Holes: 18
Par: 71, USGA: 68.9

GF: w/day $12.00, w/end
$15.00
Carts: $18.00

This course was the host to the Los Angeles Open and now hosts the Ceninela Classic, so you know that you're playing a championship quality course when you play here A very popular layout.

──────────── LOS ANGELES ────────────

Westchester GC
6900 West Manchester,
90045
Ph: 213-670-5110

Yards: 3470, Holes: 15
Par: 53

GF: w/day $8.00, w/end
$12.00
Carts: $15.00

The LA Airport took three of the holes here, so now we have 15 A good course to work on your short game.

──────────── LOS OSOS ────────────

Sea Pines GC
1945 Solano St., 93402
Ph: 805-528-1788

Yards: 2728, Holes: 9
Par: 28

GF: w/day $6.00, w/end
$7.00

Built in 1954, the trees here have had plenty of time to mature, and there are lots and lots of them.

──────────────── MADERA ────────────────

Madera Muni GC
Ave. 17 & Rd. 23, 93638
Ph: 209-675-3504

Yards: 6350, Holes: 18
Par: 72, USGA: 69.1

GF: w/day $9.00, w/end
$12.00
Carts: $16.00

With large well-trapped greens, lakes and fairway bunkers, you'll find that this course is not a pushover. Seniors can get reduced rates on carts as well as green fees.

──────────────── MAGALIA ────────────────

Paradise Pines GC
13917 S. Park Dr., 95954
Ph: 916-873-1111

Yards: 5200, Holes: 9
Par: 68, USGA: 64.6

GF: w/day $6.00, w/end
$8.00
Carts: $12.00

Paradise Pines is a course with narrow fairways. There are doglegs that are really hard to make a good shot on and plenty of bunkers in all the wrong places.

──────────────── MALIBU ────────────────

Malibu CC
901 Encinal Canyon
Rd., 90265
Ph: 818-889-6680

Yards: 6282, Holes: 18
Par: 72, USGA: 69.3

GF: w/day $45.00, w/end
$65.00
Carts: $Included

The course has more than enough water for anyone, be sure you have some extra balls just in case. Set in the Santa Monica Mountains, makes this a very scenic course.

──────────────── MAMMOTH LAKES ────────────────

**Snow Creek Resort
GC**
Old Mammoth Road,
PO Box 569, 93546
Ph: 619-934-6633

Yards: 6196, Holes: 9
Par: 70, USGA: 69.1

GF: w/day $20.00, w/end
$25.00
Carts: $7.00

The scenery could distract you here, but that would be a big mistake Water on almost all holes, large greens, and located at almost 8000 feet above sea level are sure to affect your round here. Open from the end of May through mid-October.

──────────────── MANTECA ────────────────

Manteca GC
305 N. Union Rd., P.O.
Box 611, 95336
Ph: 209-823-5945

Yards: 6281, Holes: 18
Par: 72, USGA: 69.2

GF: w/day $6.50, w/end
$8.50
Carts: $14.00

With small greens water and out-of-bounds, you'll have your work cut out for you. It will take all your skill to score well on this round.

──────────────── MARTINEZ ────────────────

Pine Meadows GC
451 Vine Hill Way,
94453
Ph: 415-372-9559

Yards: 2882, Holes: 9
Par: 27

GF: w/day $4.00, w/end
$5.00

A hilly course, with short par-3 holes. It sounds like an easy course, but don't be fooled, it isn't.

──────────────── MARYSVILLE ────────────────

Plumas Lake GC
1551 Country Club
Ave., 95901
Ph: 916-742-3201

Yards: 6500, Holes: 18
Par: 71, USGA: 71.0
RP: 1 weeks in advance

Restaurant/Bar/Proshop
GF: w/day $12.00, w/end
$15.00
Carts: $16.00

The course is level, small and tight fairways with small greens. There are a few parallel holes and plenty of oaks. #14 is a challenging, tight hole.

─────────────────── MCCLOUD ───────────────────

McCloud GC
1001 Squaw Valley Rd.,
PO Box 728, 96057
Ph: 916-964-2535

Yards: 6010, Holes: 9
Par: 72, USGA: 67.6

GF: w/day $6.00, w/end
$9.00
Carts: $14.00

This course is only open from April to November, as it is located in the mountains of northern California. There are some water hazards and sand traps to contend with.

─────────────────── MCKINLEYVILLE ───────────────────

Beau Pre GC
1777 Norton Rd., P.O.
Box 2278, 95521
Ph: 707-839-2342

Yards: 5762, Holes: 18
Par: 71, USGA: 67.6
RP: Call the Proshop

Restaurant/Bar/Proshop
GF: w/day $15.00, w/end
$20.00
Carts: $15.00

Pine and spruce trees line most of the fairways on both the mountainous and meadow portions of this course requiring precision placement shots. Water comes into play on nine holes and the sand traps are strategically placed.

─────────────────── MIDDLETOWN ───────────────────

**Hidden Valley Lake
G&CC**
P.O. Box 5130, #1
Hartman Rd., 95461
Ph: 707-987-3035

Yards: 6237, Holes: 18
Par: 71, USGA: 69.5

Proshop
GF: w/day $10.00, w/end
$17.00
Carts: $10.00

The front nine is long with 3 Par 4's over 400 yds. Although flat and open, the front 9 is challenging. The back 9 is very different.

─────────────────── MILL VALLEY ───────────────────

Mill Valley GC
280 Buena Vista Ave.,
94941
Ph: 415-388-9982

Yards: 4182, Holes: 9
Par: 65, USGA: 60.5

GF: w/day $5.00, w/end
$9.00
Carts: $12.00

A nine hole course that you can play twice by using a different set of tees. A short, hilly course that requires a well placed tee shot in order to negotiate the elevated greens and tree-lined fairways.

─────────────────── MILPITAS ───────────────────

Spring Valley GC
3441 E. Calaveras
Blvd., 95035
Ph: 408-262-1722

Yards: 6185, Holes: 18
Par: 71, USGA: 67.2

GF: w/day $9.00, w/end
$15.00
Carts: $16.00

The second hole is a par three that goes straight down hill. This is just one of many interesting shots that the golfer will find on this fun and challenging course.

─────────────────── MILPITAS ───────────────────

Summit Point GC
1500 Country Club Dr,
95035
Ph: 408-262-8813

Yards: 6400, Holes: 18
Par: 72, USGA: 70.3

Restaurant/Bar/Proshop
GF: w/day $17.00, w/end
$27.00

Summit Pointe has plenty of water so bring some extra balls.

Plan ahead! Reserve tee time well in advance, and while you're doing so, confirm rates and services.

———————————— MISSION VIEJO ————————————

Casta Del Sol GC
27601 Casta del Sol
Rd., 92692
Ph: 714-581-0940

Yards: 3868, Holes: 18
Par: 60, USGA: 58.8

GF: w/day $13.00, w/end
$17.00
Carts: $16.00

A short, tough course that will give your irons a real workout. Special afternoon rates are offered.

———————————— MODESTO ————————————

Dryden Park GC
920 So. Sunset Blvd.,
95351
Ph: 209-577-5359

Yards: 6140, Holes: 18
Par: 72, USGA: 68.3

GF: w/day $14.00
Carts: $7.00

You need to make your best shots here, trees and water present most of the difficulties here. A twilight rate is available. Outside tournaments are invited.

———————————— MODESTO ————————————

Modesto Creekside GC
701 Lincoln, 95353
Ph: 209-571-5123

Yards: 6021, Holes: 18
Par: 72, USGA: 68.5

GF: w/day $13.00, w/end
$15.00
Carts: $16.00

This course will become more difficult as it matures. Water is a big hazard on almost half the course. The course is available for outside tournaments.

———————————— MODESTO ————————————

Modesto Muni GC
921 Sunset, 95351
Ph: 209-577-5360

Yards: 6074, Holes: 9
Par: 70, USGA: 68.2

GF: w/day $9.00, w/end
$11.00
Carts: $8.00

Wavy greens and narrow fairways are a feature here. Some tight doglegs, large trees and strategically placed bunkers are some of the other difficulties. Wednesday is senior day and twilight rates are also available.

———————————— MOJAVE ————————————

Camelot Golf Club
3430 Camelot Blvd.,
93501
Ph: 805-824-4107

Yards: 6366, Holes: 9
Par: 72, USGA: 70.3
RP: First come, first
served

GF: w/day $7.50, w/end
$11.00
Carts: $14.00

The greens are the toughest part of this course, and that's saying a lot. A championship quality course that hosts an annual PGA tournament. Tight fairways and lots of mature trees will help to keep the round interesting.

———————————— MONTAGUE ————————————

Shasta Valley GC
500 Golf Course Rd.,
96064
Ph: 916-842-2302

Yards: 6130, Holes: 9
Par: 72, USGA: 67.9

GF: w/day $9.00, w/end
$10.00
Carts: $10.00

One of the nicer courses in the area, you are sure to enjoy playing here.

———————————— MONTE RIO ————————————

Northwood GC
19400 Hwy 116, 95462
Ph: 707-865-1116

Yards: 3000, Holes: 9
Par: 36, USGA: 69.0
RP: Advised

Restaurant/Bar/Proshop
GF: w/day $16.00, w/end
$20.00
Carts: $16.00

Nestled among majestic redwood trees and located near the famed Russian River between Guerneville and Monte Rio on Hwy. 116. Tee up on the 530 yard par 5 #9 rated toughest par 5 in Sonoma County.

---------------------------------MONTEREY---------------------------------

Laguna Seca GC	Yards: 6125, Holes: 18	Restaurant/Bar/Proshop
10520 York Rd., 93940	Par: 72, USGA: 70.4	**GF:** w/day $50.00
Ph: 408-373-3701	RP: Call the Proshop	**Carts:** $25.00

This Robert Trent Jones, Sr/Jr, designed course melds into its native countryside, weaving through clusters of oaks, winding uphill and down, providing a wonderful doubling of challenge and playing enjoyment.

---------------------------------MONTEREY---------------------------------

Old Del Monte GC	Yards: 6278, Holes: 18	**GF:** w/day $40.00, w/end
300 Sylvan Rd., 93940	Par: 72, USGA: 70.0	$45.00
Ph: 408-373-2436	RP: 60 days in advance	**Carts:** $12.00

The oldest golf course still in operation west of the Mississippi. Wide fairways bounded by strategically placed bunkers; greens are small and well-placed. Many large trees line the fairways.

------------------------------ MONTEREY PARK------------------------------

Monterey Park GC	Yards: 1400, Holes: 9	**GF:** w/day $4.50, w/end
3600 Ramona Blvd,	Par: 29	$5.00
91754		
Ph: 213-266-4632		

Night play is the main event here. There are also a driving range and practice green.

---------------------------------MORAGA---------------------------------

Moraga CC	Yards: 5718, Holes: 9	**GF:** w/day $10.00, w/end
1600 St. Andrews Dr.,	Par: 70, USGA: 68.8	$15.00
94556		**Carts:** $8.00
Ph: 510-376-2253		

A well bunkered, tight rolling course. You'll get to use most of your irons on this one.

---------------------------------MORENO---------------------------------

Palm Crest Resort &	Yards: 6868, Holes: 18	**GF:** w/day $10.00, w/end
CC	Par: 72, USGA: 70.4	$17.00
15960 Gilman Springs,	RP: 7 days in advance	**Carts:** $16.00
92355		
Ph: 714-654-2727		

Originally designed by Desmond Muirhead, this course was opened in 1969, and renovated in 1991. This course is highly rated and has been the host of many qualifiers.

------------------------------MORENO VALLEY------------------------------

General Old GC-	Yards: 6423, Holes: 18	**GF:** w/day $12.00, w/end
Military	Par: 72, USGA: 70.6	$15.00
Bldg 6104 Village W,		**Carts:** $14.00
March AFB, 92518		
Ph: 714-653-7913		

Water guards almost half the greens here, you bring plenty of balls if you usually have trouble with water Some hills, lots of bunkers and plenty of doglegs will complete the challenge.

Enter your favorite resort in our "Golf Resort of The Year" contest (entry form is in the back of the book).

─────────────────MORENO VALLEY─────────────────

Moreno Valley   Yards: 5907, Holes: 27
Ranch GC   Par: 72, USGA: 68.9
28095 John F.
Kennedy Avenue,
92360
Ph: 714-924-4444

Moreno Valley Ranch is a very difficult and demanding course.

──────────────────── MORGAN HILL ────────────────────

Hill Country GC   Yards: 3110, Holes: 18   Restaurant/Bar/Proshop
1590 Foothill Ave., P.O.   Par: 58, USGA: 52.0   **GF:** w/day $5.00, w/end
Box 999, 95037 $7.00
Ph: 408-779-4136   **Carts:** $8.50

*The greens are well guarded by water. A hilly course, your accuracy is very
important. Senior rates available.*

──────────────────── MORRO BAY ────────────────────

Morro Bay GC   Yards: 6116, Holes: 18   Restaurant/Bar/Proshop
State Park Rd., 93442   Par: 71, USGA: 68.2   **GF:** w/day $10.00, w/end
Ph: 805-772-4341   RP: 1-3 days ahead $12.00
                                                      Carts: $15.00

*Morro Bay Golf Course situated high up on knoll of Morro Bay State Park.
Beautiful views of the ocean can be seen from almost every tee. The course
proves to be interesting challenge for every golfer as the fairways & greens slope
every which way.*

──────────────────── MOUNTAIN VIEW ────────────────────

Shoreline GC   Yards: 6235, Holes: 18   **GF:** w/day $14.00, w/end
P.O. Box 1206, 94042   Par: 72, USGA: 69.0 $18.00
Ph: 415-969-2041   **Carts:** $15.00

*A course with rolling fairways and slick undulating greens. The course is located
on the marshlands of the San Francisco Bay. The wind usually picks up in the
afternoon making the course much tougher.*

──────────────────── MURPHYS ────────────────────

Forest Meadows GC   Yards: 4004, Holes: 18   **GF:** w/day $7.00, w/end
Box 70, 95247   Par: 60, USGA: 57.5 $13.00
Ph: 209-728-3439   **Carts:** $14.00

*Designed by Robert Trent Jones, Jr., the course opened in 1974. Mountainous
terrain and ravines will really test you. The greens are very tough here and the
course will definitely test you.*

──────────────────── MURRIETA ────────────────────

SCGA Members Club   Yards: 6900, Holes: 18   Restaurant/Bar/Proshop
Rancho California   Par: 72, USGA: 74.5   **GF:** w/day $45.00, w/end
38275 Murrieta Hot   RP: 7 days in advance $55.00
Springs, 92563   **Carts:** $Included
Ph: 909-677-7446

*The S.C.G.A. Members' Club at Rancho California is a Robert Trent Jones Sr.
masterpiece built on 190 acres of sprawling terrain. The 3rd hole is, as my 8-
year-old son says, "a rad hole." Elevated tee to tree-lined fairway, a pond fronts
the green.*

——————————————NAPA——————————————

Chardonnay GC   Holes: 9
2555 Jameson Canyon
Rd, 94559
Ph: 707-257-8950

This is a very scenic course in the Napa Valley. The course is new but it is starting to gain some serious recognition. The P.G.A. school has made this course an annual part of their rotation. The wind can blow which makes this course even tougher.

——————————————NAPA——————————————

Chimney Rock GC   Yards: 6772, Holes: 9   **GF:** w/day $8.00, w/end
5320 Silverado Trail,   Par: 72, USGA: 70.7 $13.00
94559   **Carts:** $15.00
Ph: 707-255-3363

Plenty of water on this course will be sure to give you a few bad moments. Senior rates with unlimited play on weekdays make this easy walking course particularly attractive.

——————————————NAPA——————————————

Napa Municipal GC   Yards: 6730, Holes: 18   Restaurant/Bar/Proshop
2295 Streblow Dr.,   Par: 72, USGA: 70.7   **GF:** w/day $11.00, w/end
94558   RP: 7 days prior $15.00
Ph: 707-255-4333   **Carts:** $15.00

This is a champion golf course that will play to over 7,000 yards with water hazards in play on 14 of the 18 holes.

——————————————NAPA——————————————

Silverado GC   Yards: 6620, Holes: 36   Restaurant/Bar
1600 Atlas Peak Rd.,   Par: 72, USGA: 73.9   **GF:** w/day $55.00
94558   RP: 2 days non guest   **Carts:** $Included
Ph: 707-257-5460

The South Course is a nicely contoured design with deceiving side-hill lies and over a dozen water crossings. The North Course stretches to 6700 yards and is occasionally more forgiving. Beautifully maintained.

——————————————NATIONAL CITY——————————————

National City GC   Yards: 4810, Holes: 9   **GF:** w/day $7.50, w/end
1439 Sweetwater Rd,   Par: 34, USGA: 60.5 $9.50
92050
Ph: 619-474-1400

Accuracy is your key on this course. The fairways are narrow and the out-of-bounds will be the biggest obstacle to a good score.

——————————————NEWPORT COAST——————————————

Pelican Hill GC   Yards: 5900, Holes: 18   Proshop
22653 Pelican Hill Rd., Par: 70, USGA: 68.4   **GF:** w/day $95.00, w/end
92660   RP: 6 days advance $125.00
Ph: 714-760-0707   with credit card   **Carts:** $Included

The Pacific Ocean is a beautiful backdrop to virtually the whole course. Thousands of trees have been planted here, so you know what's going to give you a tough game. The greens are very tricky, and are often elevated as well.

────────────────NIPOMO────────────────

Black Lake GC   Yards: 6427, Holes: 18   **GF:** w/day $14.00, w/end
1490 Golf Course Ln.,   Par: 72, USGA: 70.7 $20.00
93444   RP: 1 week advance   **Carts:** $16.00
Ph: 805-481-4204

If you're a John Madden fan, you might want to come here to see his Celebrity Golf Classic every June. A tough course with narrow tree-lined fairways and lots and lots of water. It's possible to walk this course.

────────────────NORWALK────────────────

Norwalk Golf Center   Yards: 970, Holes: 9   Snack Bar/Proshop
13717 S. Shoemaker   Par: 27   **GF:** w/day $3.25, w/end
Ave., 90650 $3.75
Ph: 310-921-6500

Almost a pitch-and-putt course, for beginners only.

────────────────NOVATO────────────────

Indian Valley GC   Yards: 5759, Holes: 18   **GF:** w/day $9.00, w/end
Stafford Lake-Novato   Par: 72, USGA: 67.4 $19.00
Blvd., 94948   **Carts:** $17.00
Ph: 415-897-1118

Home of the Hills Brothers Pro-Am, this is a hilly course. There's water on over half the holes, and an abundance of trees. The short game is the most important, so be sure to pick the right club.

────────────────OAKHURST────────────────

Sierra Sky Ranch GC   Yards: 5944, Holes: 9   Restaurant/Bar/Proshop
50556 Rd. 632, 93644   Par: 36, USGA: 68.0   **GF:** w/day $6.00
Ph: 209-683-7433   RP: 1 day in advance   **Carts:** $7.00

Our challenging regulation 9 hole golf course is surrounded by the serene beauty of the Sierras. Our climate affords year-round golfing with over 300 days of play.

────────────────OAKLAND────────────────

Lake Chabot GC   Yards: 6180, Holes: 27   **GF:** w/day $8.00, w/end
End of Golf Links Rd.,   Par: 72, USGA: 67.7 $11.00
94605   **Carts:** $14.00
Ph: 510-351-5812

A scenic course that offers spectacular views of the Bay Area on the 15th and 16th holes. The par five 18th hole measures an overwhelming 600 plus yards straight downhill back toward the clubhouse.

────────────────OAKLAND────────────────

Lew Galbraith GC   Yards: 6298, Holes: 18   Proshop
10505 Doolittle Dr.,   Par: 72, USGA: 69.9   **GF:** w/day $8.00, w/end
94603 $10.00
Ph: 510-569-9411   **Carts:** $14.00

Lew F. Galbraith Golf course is essentially flat. You can really let 'er fly here because you have plenty of length. Holes #5 and 16 are particularly challenging par-4s.

────────────────OAKLAND────────────────

Montclair GC   Yards: 1134, Holes: 9   **GF:** w/day $2.50, w/end
2477 Monterey Blvd,   Par: 27 $3.00
94611
Ph: 510-482-0422

A hilly, par-3 which is not a very challenging course. A good place to learn.

─────────────── OCEANSIDE ───────────────

Oceanside Center City Course
2323 Green Brier Dr.,
PO Box 1088, 92054
Ph: 619-433-8590

Yards: 5590, Holes: 18
Par: 71, USGA: 34.6

GF: w/day $5.00

A long nine-hole course. The fairways are long but unchallenging.

─────────────── OCEANSIDE ───────────────

Oceanside Muni GC
825 Douglas Dr., 92056
Ph: 619-433-1360

Yards: 6056, Holes: 18
Par: 72, USGA: 67.9

GF: w/day $10.00, w/end
$15.00
Carts: $16.00

Water is everywhere on this flat course. Towering trees and large greens are going to make the round even more difficult. The course is available for tournaments.

─────────────── OJAI ───────────────

Ojai Valley Inn and CC
Country Club Rd.,
93023
Ph: 805-646-5511

Yards: 6252, Holes: 18
Par: 70, USGA: 70.6
RP: Guests 90 days,
outside 1 day

Restaurant/Bar/Proshop
GF: w/day $76.00, w/end
$76.00
Carts: $14.00

The inn has a truly classic course that is the host to the PGA Senior Tour GTE Classic. It offers a variety of terrain through mature stands of California oaks. It is definitely a shotmaker's golf course requiring careful placement from tee to green.

─────────────── ONTARIO ───────────────

Ontario National GC
2525 Riverside Dr.,
91764
Ph: 714-947-3512

Yards: 6270, Holes: 18
Par: 72, USGA: 68.1

GF: w/day $13.00, w/end
$17.00
Carts: $16.00

The course is very open for the number of trees here.

─────────────── OROVILLE ───────────────

Kelly Ridge GL
36 Royal Oaks Dr.,
95966
Ph: 916-589-0777

Yards: 4207, Holes: 9
Par: 66, USGA: 61.8

GF: w/day $4.00, w/end
$7.00
Carts: $10.00

This course has greens with lots of protection. Located in the Sierras, you can expect to find a course with plenty of hills and many difficult lies.

─────────────── OROVILLE ───────────────

Table Mountain GC
2700 W Oro Dam Blvd,
PO Box 2767, 95965
Ph: 916-533-3924

Yards: 6472, Holes: 18
Par: 72, USGA: 70.1

GF: w/day $6.00, w/end
$8.00
Carts: $14.00

A very long and open course. Lots of water, and many mature trees. You really have to be on your toes at all times on this one. Senior, junior and twilight rates available.

─────────────── OXNARD ───────────────

River Ridge GC
2401 West Vineyard
Ave., 93030
Ph: 805-983-1756

Yards: 6111, Holes: 18
Par: 72, USGA: 68.7

GF: w/day $10.00, w/end
$13.00
Carts: $14.00

A tough course that requires a wise choice of club at all times. To say this course has a lot of water in an understatement. On some holes it can be a nightmare.

────────────── PACIFIC GROVE ──────────────

Pacific Grove Muni GC
77 Asilomar Blvd., 93950
Ph: 408-375-3456

Yards: 5553, Holes: 18
Par: 70, USGA: 66.3
RP: 1 week in advance

GF: w/day $12.00, w/end $14.00
Carts: $17.00

A course that has almost forested areas, sand dunes and winds will give you some unique challenges. Twilight rates are available.

────────────── PACIFICA ──────────────

Sharp Park GC
Sharp Park Hwy. #1, 94044
Ph: 415-586-2370

Yards: 6283, Holes: 18
Par: 72, USGA: 69.6

GF: w/day $6.50, w/end $12.00
Carts: $14.00

A seaside course that requires a solid tee shot as well as a good putting stroke. The course plays long due the cool San Francisco fog that hovers over the course in the summer.

────────────── PALM DESERT ──────────────

Desert Falls CC
1111 Desert Falls Pkwy., 92260
Ph: 619-340-5646

Yards: 6218, Holes: 18
Par: 72, USGA: 70.2

GF: w/day $40.00
Carts: $Included

Large greens, and very, very long. You'll really need your woods on this one.

────────────── PALM DESERT ──────────────

Emerald Desert CC
76-000 Frank Sinatra Dr, 92260
Ph: 619-345-4770

Yards: 3507, Holes: 9
Par: 62, USGA: 53.0

GF: w/day $15.00, w/end $20.00
Carts: $15.00

Accuracy is the keyword here. Lots of bunkers, tight fairways and lakes will also figure into your score.

────────────── PALM DESERT ──────────────

Ivey Ranch GC
74580 Varner Rd., 92276
Ph: 619-343-2013

Yards: 2611, Holes: 9
Par: 34, USGA: 64.0
RP: Phone for tee times

GF: w/day $20.00
Carts: $Included

Narrow fairways that are lightly treed and beautiful greens should make your game here enjoyable.

────────────── PALM DESERT ──────────────

Marrakesh CC
47-000 Marrakesh Dr., 92260
Ph: 619-568-2660

Yards: 3595, Holes: 18
Par: 60, USGA: 57.2

GF: w/day $25.00

This is an executive course that is always in great shape. The course winds through the housing development offering some interesting shots over roads and lakes. A good test for your iron game.

────────────── PALM DESERT ──────────────

Marriott's Desert Springs GC
74-855 Country Club Dr., 92260
Ph: 619-341-1756

Yards: 6679, Holes: 36
Par: 72, USGA: 68.5
RP: Resort guest 30 days

Restaurant/Bar/Proshop
GF: w/day $90.00
Carts: $Included

Palms Course–Signature course by Ted Robinson "King of the Waterscape"; 6800 yards of water, sand and breathtaking views. Valley Course–nominated best course/resort category by Golf Digest 1988. Tight fairways and small greens.

───────────PALM DESERT───────────

Oasis CC
42-330 Casbah Way,
92260
Ph: 619-345-2715

Yards: 3700, Holes: 18
Par: 60, USGA: 54.0
RP: 3 days in advance

Restaurant/Bar/Proshop
GF: w/day $23.00
Carts: $20.00

One of the finest executive course challenges in golf. Featuring 22 lakes to entertain the golfer while testing your ability upon our superbly manicured fairways and greens. The 18th hole par 4 dogleg back to the clubhouse offers a majestic views.

───────────PALM DESERT───────────

Palm Desert CC
77-200 California Dr.,
92260
Ph: 619-345-2525

Yards: 6273, Holes: 27
Par: 72, USGA: 67.9

GF: w/day $45.00, w/end $50.00
Carts: $Included

Three 9-hole course that have mature trees, and are very well designed. They can be played in different combinations with equal challenge.

───────────PALM DESERT───────────

Palm Desert Resort CC
77-333 Country Club Dr., 92260
Ph: 619-345-2791

Yards: 6241, Holes: 18
Par: 72, USGA: 68.8

GF: w/day $42.00, w/end $50.00
Carts: $Included

Many lakes here, so you're sure to have plenty of practice with water. Also featured are wide fairways and well-placed bunkers. The course is available for tournaments.

───────────PALM DESERT───────────

Palm Valley CC
76-200 Country Club Dr, 92260
Ph: 619-345-2742

Yards: 6545, Holes: 36
Par: 72, USGA: 71.1

Restaurant/Bar
GF: w/day $40.00

This facility consists of two 18-hole courses. You'll find both courses challenging. One has water on almost every hole and will offer a marvelous opportunity to practice your short game. The other is rolling.

───────────PALM DESERT───────────

Shadow Mountain GC
45-700 San Luis Rey Ave, 92260
Ph: 619-346-8242

Yards: 5418, Holes: 18
Par: 70, USGA: 65.5

Restaurant/Bar
GF: w/day $40.00

On this course you can really end up on the rocks.

───────────PALM DESERT───────────

Suncrest CC
73-450 Country Club Dr., 92260
Ph: 619-340-2467

Yards: 4886, Holes: 9
Par: 33, USGA: 60.0
RP: 2 days in advance

Restaurant/Bar/Proshop
GF: w/day $30.00

Best 9 hole course in desert which boast almost 100 courses. Sits on elevated knoll with panoramic view of desert area. Very challenging for a 9-hole executive course.

──────────────── PALM SPRINGS ────────────────

Canyon South GC
1097 Murray Canyon
Dr., 92264
Ph: 619-327-2019

Yards: 6205, Holes: 18
Par: 71, USGA: 68.6

Proshop
GF: w/day $50.00, w/end
$60.00
Carts: $Included

One of the most scenic courses in the area, but you'd better pay attention to your game if you don't want a high score.

──────────────── PALM SPRINGS ────────────────

**Fairchild's Bel-Air
Greens**
1001 S. El Cielo Rd.,
92262
Ph: 619-327-0332

Yards: 1670, Holes: 9
Par: 32

Restaurant/Bar
GF: w/day $10.00

Although this course was opened in 1975, it is so well tended that you will be surprised. Plenty of water and trees on this scenic layout.

──────────────── PALM SPRINGS ────────────────

Mesquite GC
2700 E. Mesquite Ave.,
92264
Ph: 619-323-9377

Yards: 5944, Holes: 18
Par: 72, USGA: 67.9
RP: 2 days in advance

GF: w/day $45.00, w/end
$55.00
Carts: $Included

Eight small lakes you bound to come into figuring your score. You'll need to be very accurate here. Although the course is flat, you'll find some beautiful mountain views. The course is available for tournaments.

──────────────── PALM SPRINGS ────────────────

Palm Springs CC
2500 Whitewater Club
Dr., 92262
Ph: 619-323-8625

Yards: 5714, Holes: 18
Par: 71, USGA: 66.5

GF: w/day $20.00, w/end
$30.00
Carts: $Included

Well bunkered greens with lots of mature trees will keep you on your toes here.

──────────────── PALM SPRINGS ────────────────

**Palm Springs Muni
GC**
1885 Gulf Club Dr.,
92264
Ph: 619-328-1956

Yards: 6460, Holes: 18
Par: 72, USGA: 69.6

GF: w/day $14.00
Carts: $18.00

This course is annually the host to the Palm Springs City Seniors tournament. The layout is well treed and has no traps.

──────────────── PALMDALE ────────────────

Desert Aire GC
3620 East Ave. P, 93550
Ph: 805-273-7778

Yards: 6195, Holes: 18
Par: 72, USGA: 68.1

GF: w/day $7.00, w/end
$10.00
Carts: $8.00

Tree-lined fairways, wind, desert heat, and bunkers are some of the things to contend with on this course. The course is available for tournaments.

──────────────── PALO ALTO ────────────────

Palo Alto Muni GC
1875 Embarcadero
Rd., 94303
Ph: 415-856-0881

Yards: 6525, Holes: 18
Par: 72, USGA: 70.1
RP: Weekdays - 1 week
in advance

Restaurant/Bar/Proshop
GF: w/day $10.00, w/end
$14.00
Carts: $16.00

#14 long par 3 usually against the wind. A right to left wind is most prevalent. Bunker placed to right of green. 216 yards from white tee and 232 from blue tee, requires a real solid wood shot from most players.

──────────────── PALOS VERDES ────────────────

Los Verdes G&CC   Yards: 6651, Holes: 18   Bar
7000 W Los Verdes Dr,   Par: 71, USGA: 71.1   **GF:** w/day $10.00, w/end
90274 $14.00
Ph: 213-377-7450   **Carts:** $17.00

Designed by William Bell in 1964, this is one of the most scenic courses in California. A beautifully maintained course that you will really enjoy.

──────────────── PALOS VERDES ESTATES ────────────────

Palos Verdes GC   Yards: 6206, Holes: 18   **GF:** w/day $85.00
3301 Via Campesina,   Par: 71, USGA: 70.5   **Carts:** $Included
90274
Ph: 213-375-2759

A course with lots of trees along the fairways and very tricky greens. The course opened in 1924 so you can count on nice mature trees.

──────────────── PARADISE ────────────────

Tall Pines GC   Yards: 4209, Holes: 9   Restaurant/Bar/Proshop
5325 Clark Rd., 95969   Par: 68, USGA: 62.2   **GF:** w/day $10.00
Ph: 916-877-5816   RP: On weekends   **Carts:** $16.00

At 1600 feet elevation Tall Pines is positioned above central valley fog below the snow line of the Sierra Nevada foothills affording it playability year round. Most challenging holes #1 at 340 yards, is a dogleg par 4 approaching elevated green.

──────────────── PASADENA ────────────────

Brookside GC   Yards: 6611, Holes: 36   **GF:** w/day $20.00, w/end
1133 Rosemont Ave.,   Par: 72, USGA: 71.6 $125.00
91103   **Carts:** $15.00
Ph: 818-796-8151

Lots of mature trees on these William Bell designed courses. The courses opened in 1928, for a total of 36-holes of championship golf. Lots of water and narrow fairways, and lots of irritatingly placed bunkers will give you a memorable round of golf.

──────────────── PASADENA ────────────────

Eaton Canyon GC   Yards: 2862, Holes: 9   **GF:** w/day $7.00, w/end
1150 North Sierra   Par: 70, USGA: 65.8 $9.00
Madre Villa Ave, 91107
Ph: 818-794-6773

A short course that has some hilly holes that is tree filled.

──────────────── PEBBLE BEACH ────────────────

Links at Spanish Bay Yards: 6195, Holes: 18   Restaurant/Bar
17-Mile Dr., 93953   Par: 72, USGA: 72.7   **GF:** w/day $75.00, w/end
Ph: 408-647-7495   RP: May be made with $90.00
                          hotel reservation   **Carts:** $30.00

A true seaside links course. A unique challenge of sand and soil, sea and foggy weather. The 13th, which turns the player back toward the Pacific and into the dunes, a 130-yard par 3 patterned after the "Postage Stamp" at Scotland's Royal Troon.

Enter your favorite resort in our "Golf Resort of The Year" contest (entry form is in the back of the book).

───────────────── PEBBLE BEACH ─────────────────

Pebble Beach GL
17-Mile Dr., 93953
Ph: 408-624-3811

Yards: 6357, Holes: 72
Par: 72, USGA: 72.7
RP: Call Golf Central
408-624-6611

Restaurant/Bar
GF: w/day $125.00, w/end
$225.00
Carts: $Included

A round of golf here is special because it's unusual for tournament-class courses to be available to the public. Pebble Beach course starts out along the ocean, then swings back and forth along the coast for holes 4 through 10. 11 through 16 are inland.

───────────────── PEBBLE BEACH ─────────────────

Peter Hay GC
P.O. Box 658, 17-Mile
Dr., 93953
Ph: 408-624-3811

Yards: 1570, Holes: 9
Par: 27

GF: w/day $6.00

Peter Hay is a short par three course that offers a test of your wedge game. The holes barely measure over one hundred yards but the greens are just tiny. It provides a nice warm-up for Pebble Beach which is just across the street.

───────────────── PEBBLE BEACH ─────────────────

Poppy Hills GC
3200 Lopez Rd., 93953
Ph: 408-625-2035

Yards: 6213, Holes: 18
Par: 72, USGA: 72.4
RP: 1 month in advance

Restaurant/Bar/Proshop
GF: w/day $95.00
Carts: $Included

The first course fully owned and operated by a regional golf association, the Northern California Golf Association. Poppy Hills requires both accuracy and length off the tee along with a proficient putting ability ... a true test of golf.

───────────────── PEBBLE BEACH ─────────────────

Spyglass Hill GC
Spyglass Hill Rd. &
Stevenson, 93953
Ph: 408-624-3811

Yards: 6810, Holes: 18
Par: 72, USGA: 73.1
RP: Call Golf Central
408-624-3811

GF: w/day $95.00
Carts: $Included

The course swings back and forth along the coast for holes 4 through 10, moves inland for the 11th through 16th, and returns to the rugged shoreline for the 17th and 18th. The 18th green is a strip of land running between the main building of the Lodge.

───────────────── PETALUMA ─────────────────

Adobe Creek GC
1901 Fates, 94954
Ph: 707-765-3000

Yards: 6900, Holes: 18
Par: 72, USGA: 72.6

Restaurant/Bar
GF: w/day $45.00, w/end
$55.00

Creeks, lakes and many, many bunkers make it important to pay careful attention to your shots. A long course with a great number of natural hazards.

───────────────── PETALUMA ─────────────────

Petaluma G&CC
P.O. Box 26, 1100
Country Club Dr,
94953
Ph: 707-762-7041

Yards: 2805, Holes: 9
Par: 35, USGA: 32.8

Proshop
GF: w/day $7.00, w/end
$10.00
Carts: $9.00

Lots of sidehill lies on this course, and throw in plenty of sand traps for good measure.

─────────── PIONEER ───────────

Mace Meadows GC Yards: 6054, Holes: 18 **GF:** w/day $10.00, w/end
26570 Fairway Dr., Par: 72, USGA: 68.4 $15.00
95666 **Carts:** $16.00
Ph: 209-295-7020

The course was design by Jack Fleming, and opened in 1966. A nice course to walk, with a lake for every other hole. Narrow fairways with plenty of trees make it more challenging.

─────────── PITTSBURGH ───────────

Delta Views GC Yards: 6359, Holes: 18 **GF:** w/day $9.00, w/end
2222 Golf Club Rd., Par: 72 $11.50
94565 **Carts:** $10.00
Ph: 510-427-4940

A windy layout that treasures the careful shot maker. Home of the Pittsburgh City Championships. A really very challenging course.

─────────── PLACERVILLE ───────────

Sierra GC Yards: 3348, Holes: 9 **GF:** w/day $7.00
1822 Country Club Dr., Par: 62, USGA: 56.0
95667
Ph: 916-622-0760

Beautiful old trees outline the fairways. The greens are very difficult. Has a very attractive junior rate.

─────────── PLEASANT HILL ───────────

Pleasant Hill G&CC Yards: 3051, Holes: 18 Restaurant/Bar/Proshop
1093 Grayson Rd., Par: 58, USGA: 52.5 **GF:** w/day $8.00, w/end
94523 $10.00
Ph: 415-932-0276 **Carts:** $5.00

The course was recently reopened after renovations.

─────────── PLEASANTON ───────────

Pleasanton Fairways Yards: 5020, Holes: 9 **GF:** w/day $4.50, w/end
GC Par: 60, USGA: 56.0 $9.50
P.O. Box 123, 94566
Ph: 415-462-4653

Since this course is located at the Alameda County Fairground, don't expect to play here during the County Fair in late June. The course is much more difficult then you would expect from the setting. This one calls for a lot of accuracy.

─────────── POMONA ───────────

Mountain Meadows Yards: 6146, Holes: 18 **GF:** w/day $11.00, w/end
GC Par: 72, USGA: 68.3 $15.00
1875 Ganesha Blvd., **Carts:** $18.00
91768
Ph: 714-629-1166

One of the most beautiful courses around.

─────────── POPE VALLEY ───────────

Aetna Springs GC Yards: 5372, Holes: 9 Proshop
1600 Aetna Springs Par: 70, USGA: 64.7 **GF:** w/day $3.00, w/end
Rd., 94567 $7.00
Ph: 707-965-2115

An old course set in the mountains. There are creeks here too. You can play all day, during the week, for the same price.

─────────────PORT HUENEME─────────────

Port Hueneme GC-   Yards: 6298, Holes: 18   **GF:** w/day $8.00, w/end
Military   Par: 72, USGA: 69.2 $10.00
Rec Svc Cod 32 Bldgs   **Carts:** $13.00
360, 93043
Ph: 805-982-2620

*This is a very unforgiving course, and you'll need to be careful of your shot
placement. Water, bunkers and wind are important challenges here.*

─────────────PORTERVILLE─────────────

Porterville GC   Yards: 5698, Holes: 9   **GF:** w/day $4.00, w/end
702 E. Isham, 93257   Par: 70, USGA: 65.6 $6.00
Ph: 209-784-9468   **Carts:** $12.00

*This course was opened in 1920 and shows the typical design of the period in its
small greens. Out-of-bounds are the main hazard to playing a good round.*

─────────────RAMONA─────────────

Mount Woodson CC   Yards: 6180, Holes: 18   Restaurant/Bar/Proshop
16302 North Woodson   Par: 70, USGA: 68.8   **GF:** w/day $40.00, w/end
Dr., 92065   RP: Call the Proshop $55.00
Ph: 619-788-3555   **Carts:** $Included

*Mt. Woodson CC is a magnificent "Landmark Signature" course with a private
atmosphere, but available for public play. Breathtaking layout plays through
ancient oaks and massive boulders in the quiet foothills and valleys below
majestic Mt. Woodson.*

─────────────RAMONA─────────────

San Vincente GC   Yards: 5595, Holes: 18   **GF:** w/day $35.00, w/end
24157 San Vincente   Par: 72, USGA: 66.3 $45.00
Rd., 92065   **Carts:** $Included
Ph: 619-789-3477

Lots of trees and an undulating setting should keep you on your toes here.

─────────────RANCHO MIRAGE─────────────

Rancho Las Palmas   Yards: 5716, Holes: 18
GC   Par: 71
42000 Bob Hope Dr.,
92270
Ph: 619-568-2727

*A beautiful course with well manicured fairways and plush greens. Tall palm
trees and a few lakes make this a challenging layout for any golfer.*

─────────────RANCHO MIRAGE─────────────

Westin Mission Hills   Yards: 6707, Holes: 18   Restaurant/Bar
Resort GC   Par: 70, USGA: 73.5   **GF:** w/day $45.00
71-501 Dinah Shore   RP: 2 days   **Carts:** $Included
Dr., 92270
Ph: 619-328-3198

*Guests have preferred tee times at the Westin Mission Hills Resort Course. A
gently rolling, tough layout designed by Pete Dye with his trademarks of large
lakes on five holes. Rancho Mirage offers some tremendous views of the nearby
San Jacinto Mtns.*

──────────────── RANCHO SANTA FE ────────────────

Rancho Santa Fe	Yards: 6497, Holes: 18	Restaurant
P.O. Box 869, 92067	Par: 72, USGA: 71.3	**GF:** w/day $50.00
Ph: 619-765-3094	RP: 5 daysin advance through Inn	**Carts:** $25.00

Inn guests play at private Rancho Santa Fe Golf Club, a rolling, wooded, challenge. The par 72 design claims #13 as its most noteworthy—no doubt due to a couple of small lakes to be carried.

──────────────── RANCHO SANTA FE ────────────────

Whispering Palms GC	Yards: 6343, Holes: 27	**GF:** w/day $23.00, w/end $28.00
4000 Concha De Golf, PO Box 3209, 92067	Par: 72, USGA: 69.2	**Carts:** $22.00
Ph: 619-756-3255		

A layout with 27 holes that can be played in three different combinations. The courses are nice for walking, with a river running through. The roughs are tall and the fairways narrow, so it should be an enjoyable round.

──────────────── RED BLUFF ────────────────

Oak Creek GC	Yards: 2500, Holes: 9	**GF:** w/day $7.00
2620 Montgomery Rd., 96080	Par: 70, USGA: 62.9	**Carts:** $12.00
Ph: 916-529-0674		

This course is the host of 5 different annual tournaments.

──────────────── REDDING ────────────────

Anderson-Tucker Oaks GC	Yards: 6346, Holes: 9	Restaurant/Bar
11411 Churn Creek Rd., 96001	Par: 72, USGA: 68.4	**GF:** w/day $5.00, w/end $9.00
Ph: 916-365-3350		**Carts:** $12.00

A course with many mature trees and more bunkers than you care to see.

──────────────── REDDING ────────────────

Churn Creek GC	Yards: 6203, Holes: 9	**GF:** w/day $5.00, w/end $9.00
8550 Churn Creek Rd., 96002	Par: 72, USGA: 68.6	**Carts:** $12.00
Ph: 916-222-6353		

Water, out-of-bounds, hazards, and small greens make this rather flat course more challenging than you would think.

──────────────── REDDING ────────────────

Gold Hills CC	Yards: 6603, Holes: 18	Restaurant/Bar/Proshop
1950 Gold Hills Dr., 96003	Par: 72, USGA: 69.5	**GF:** w/day $16.00, w/end $20.00
Ph: 916-246-7867	RP: Call in advance	**Carts:** $16.00

A tree lined shot maker's course with small greens that are always smooth and fast. Several creeks and lakes add to the natural beauty. During the round, views of both Mt. Shasta and Mt. Lasson abound.

──────────────── REDDING ────────────────

Lake Redding GC	Yards: 3756, Holes: 9	**GF:** w/day $6.50, w/end $7.50
1795 Benton Dr., 96003	Par: 62, USGA: 57.3	**Carts:** $9.00
Ph: 916-243-5531		

Lots of water and sand traps make this course very challenging. The fairways are narrow and there are plenty of trees. The course is short, but don't be fooled, it can be difficult. There are special rates for seniors Monday through Friday.

───────────────REDDING───────────────

River Bend G&CC   Ph: 916-246-9077   Yards: 4150, Holes: 9
5369 Indianwood   Par: 64, USGA: 59.0
Drive, 96003   **GF:** w/day $6.00

Water comes into play on five holes, so be very careful. Trees can also be a very important consideration on this course. A well designed course along the Sacramento River.

───────────────REDWOOD CITY───────────────

Emerald Hills GC   Yards: 2950, Holes: 9   **GF:** w/day $3.50, w/end
Wilmington Way, P.O.   Par: 58, USGA: 50.9 $5.50
Box 3, 94061
Ph: 415-368-7820

A difficult executive course that winds around the hillside. The first hole is a tight hole that requires a good tee shot. A fun course especially for a beginner.

───────────────RIALTO───────────────

El Rancho Verde CC   Yards: 6844, Holes: 18   **GF:** w/day $11.00, w/end
Foot of Country Club   Par: 72, USGA: 70.2 $21.00
Dr.,POB 1234, 92376   RP: Available one week   **Carts:** $16.00
Ph: 714-875-5346   prior

With the San Bernardino Mountains as a backdrop, you'll find this a scenic course if you can keep out of the orange groves. There are plenty of other trees too.

───────────────RICO RIVERA───────────────

Pico Rivera Muni GC   Yards: 1400, Holes: 9   **GF:** w/day $4.00, w/end
3260 Fairway Drive,   Par: 29 $5.00
90660
Ph: 213-692-9933

The lakes here made this an unusual course. A very nice setting, with elevated tees. Call for special rates.

───────────────RIVERSIDE───────────────

El Rivino CC   Yards: 6132, Holes: 18   **GF:** w/day $20.00, w/end
Box 3369 5530 El   Par: 72, USGA: 68.2 $26.00
Rivino Rd., 92519   **Carts:** $22.00
Ph: 714-684-8905

The first hole is almost enough to make you turn around and go home. And the fun has only begun. With large old trees and five lakes, you're sure to have a great day.

───────────────RIVERSIDE───────────────

Fairmont Park GC   Yards: 6165, Holes: 18   Bar/Proshop
2681 Dexter Dr., 92501   Par: 72, USGA: 68.5   **GF:** w/day $6.00, w/end
Ph: 714-683-9030 $8.00
                                                      Carts: $12.00

The first hole here has a particularly nasty tree placement, so your accuracy had better be in place. Lots of doglegs, mature trees and level fairways, so it's not all bad.

─────────────────RIVERSIDE─────────────────

Indian Hills CC
5700 Club House Dr.,
92509
Ph: 714-685-7443

Yards: 6099, Holes: 18
Par: 70, USGA: 66.5
RP: One week in
advance

GF: w/day $16.00, w/end
$23.00
Carts: $20.00

No parallel fairways here, so you can feel like the course is all your own. Tough greens, rolling terrain and a multitude of large trees will challenge you.

─────────────────RIVERSIDE─────────────────

Jurupa Hills CC
6161 Moraga Ave.,
92509
Ph: 714-685-7214

Yards: 6029, Holes: 18
Par: 70, USGA: 67.4
RP: Call in advance

GF: w/day $14.00, w/end
$21.00
Carts: $20.00

Designed by William Bell, the course opened in 1960. The trees are mature and the greens fast. Host of the SCPGA Senior's Championship annually. The course is available for outside tournaments.

─────────────────RIVERSIDE─────────────────

Paradise Knolls
9330 Limonite Ave,
92509
Ph: 714-685-7034

Yards: 6200, Holes: 18
Par: 72, USGA: 68.3

Restaurant/Bar
GF: w/day $10.50, w/end
$17.00
Carts: $19.00

Tree-lined fairways are the norm here. A level course with small green, you will often put your short game to the test. Check on the senior rates during the week.

─────────────────RIVERSIDE─────────────────

Riverside GC
1011 Orange St., 92501
Ph: 714-682-3748

Yards: 6252, Holes: 18
Par: 72, USGA: 67.3

Restaurant/Proshop
GF: w/day $9.00, w/end
$14.00
Carts: $16.00

A tree lined, level course with a lot of trees. Senior rates are offered here.

─────────────────RODEO─────────────────

Franklin Canyon GC
Hwy 4, 94572
Ph: 415-799-6191

Yards: 6202, Holes: 18
Par: 72, USGA: 69.3
RP: 7 days in advance

Restaurant/Bar/Proshop
GF: w/day $13.00, w/end
$19.00
Carts: $16.00

The course is quite challenging due to the canyon which you must cross seven times. Both the ninth and eighteenth finishing holes are par fives with water in front of the greens. You may go for it or lay up depending on how brave you are.

─────────────────ROHNERT PARK─────────────────

**Mountain Shadows
GC**
100 Golf Course Dr.,
94928
Ph: 707-584-7766

Yards: 6160, Holes: 18
Par: 72, USGA: 68.6

GF: w/day $7.00, w/end
$15.00
Carts: $14.00

A 36 hole layout, host to the Redwood Empire Championship-Golden State Tour and the Sonoma County Men's Amateur Championship. Undulating, tight fairways with large green make these courses a challenge to any level of golfer.

─────────────────ROSEMEAD─────────────────

Whittier Narrows GC
8640 East Rush St,
91770
Ph: 818-288-1044

Yards: 6490, Holes: 27
Par: 72, USGA: 69.3

GF: w/day $11.00, w/end
$15.00
Carts: $16.00

27-holes of golf all in one place.

-----------------------------ROSEVILLE-----------------------------

Diamond Oaks GC
349 Diamond Oakd
Rd., 95678
Ph: 916-783-4947

Yards: 6200, Holes: 18
Par: 72, USGA: 69.0

GF: w/day $5.50, w/end
$6.50
Carts: $12.00

An old course that is surrounded by large, magnificent oak trees. The course has tough par fours but relatively easy, reachable par fives. It is a very fair course that offers many birdie opportunities.

-----------------------------ROSEVILLE-----------------------------

**Roseville Rolling
Greens GC**
5572 Eureka Rd., 95661
Ph: 916-797-9986

Yards: 5980, Holes: 9
Par: 54, USGA: 53.5

GF: w/day $4.50

This course is a par-3 type, but don't be fooled, it can be really tough. A hilly location, for this popular course.

-----------------------------SACRAMENTO-----------------------------

Bing Maloney GC
6801 Freeport Blvd.,
95823
Ph: 916-428-9401

Yards: 6281, Holes: 18
Par: 71, USGA: 69.7

GF: w/day $8.00, w/end
$9.00
Carts: $15.00

A real shot maker course.

-----------------------------SACRAMENTO-----------------------------

**Campus Commons
GC**
#2 Cadillac Dr., 95825
Ph: 916-922-5861

Yards: 3346, Holes: 9
Par: 58, USGA: 54.0

GF: w/day $4.00
Carts: $5.00

A course with the American River as a natural hazard on several holes. A nice course for walking with a nice view of the river.

-----------------------------SACRAMENTO-----------------------------

Cordova GC
9425 Jackson Rd.,
95826
Ph: 916-362-1196

Yards: 4755, Holes: 18
Par: 63, USGA: 61.0

GF: w/day $5.00, w/end
$6.00
Carts: $10.00

With lakes, many bunkers and doglegs you'll be challenged all the time. Many trees add to your problems.

-----------------------------SACRAMENTO-----------------------------

Haggin Oaks GC
3645 Fulton Ave., P.O.
Box 137, 95853
Ph: 916-481-4507

Yards: 6254, Holes: 18
Par: 72, USGA: 67.6

GF: w/day $8.00, w/end
$10.00
Carts: $16.00

Get ready for one of your lowest scores ever.

-----------------------------SACRAMENTO-----------------------------

Hansen Dam GC
10400 Glen Oaks Blvd.,
91331
Ph: 818-899-2200

Yards: 6266, Holes: 18
Par: 72, USGA: 68.1

GF: w/day $10.50, w/end
$14.50
Carts: $16.00

The fairways are narrow here so watch out. Some elevated greens that are very small make your short game very important. The course is available for outside tournaments.

─────────────────SACRAMENTO─────────────────

**William Land Park
GC**
1701 Sutterville Rd.,
95822
Ph: 916-455-5014

Yards: 5100, Holes: 9
Par: 68, USGA: 63.5

GF: w/day $4.00, w/end
$4.50

*William Land Park boosts one of the most challenging holes of golf in northern
California. A beautifully treed course. Many natural hazards will make the
whole round an interesting one.*

─────────────────SALINAS─────────────────

Salinas Fairways GC
45 Skyway Blvd.,
93902
Ph: 408-758-7300

Yards: 6347, Holes: 18
Par: 72, USGA: 70.7

GF: w/day $6.00, w/end
$10.00
Carts: $13.00

*A good test of golf that will require the use of just about every club in your bag.
The front side is on one side of the road while the back side is on the other.
Watch out for the airplanes because the airport is right next door.*

─────────────────SALINAS─────────────────

**Sherwood Greens
GC**
1050 N. Main St., 93906
Ph: 408-758-7333

Yards: 5426, Holes: 9
Par: 56, USGA: 50.2

GF: w/day $3.50, w/end
$4.05

*Your short game expertise is a must here. Lots of trees come into play, so watch
out. A nice course for a walk.*

─────────────────SAN BERNARDINA─────────────────

Shandin Hills GC
3380 Littel Mountian
Dr., 92407
Ph: 714-886-0669

Yards: 6600, Holes: 18
Par: 72, USGA: 68.9

GF: w/day $15.00, w/end
$22.00
Carts: $10.00

*Tricky fairways, rolling terrain and tough roughs with more bunkers then you've
seen in a long time are only some of the problems to overcome.*

─────────────────SAN BERNARDINO─────────────────

San Bernardino GC
1494 S. Waterman
Ave., 92408
Ph: 714-885-2414

Yards: 5631, Holes: 18
Par: 69, USGA: 66.5

GF: w/day $11.00, w/end
$19.00
Carts: $16.00

*This course looks like a pushover with very little water and traps, but don't be
fooled–this is a challenging course.*

─────────────────SAN CLEMENTE─────────────────

San Clemente GC
150 East Magdalena,
92672
Ph: 714-492-3943

Yards: 6119, Holes: 18
Par: 72, USGA: 67.3
RP: One week in
advance

GF: w/day $14.00, w/end
$21.00
Carts: $16.00

*Designed by William Bell in 1928, this course has beautiful mature growth. Set
along the ocean, you'll have many spectacular views of the Pacific, but it can get
windy.*

─────────────────SAN CLEMENTE─────────────────

Shorecliffs GC
501 Avenida Vaquero,
92672
Ph: 714-492-1177

Yards: 6097, Holes: 18
Par: 71, USGA: 67.9
RP: One week in
advance

Restaurant/Bar/Proshop
GF: w/day $10.00, w/end
$17.00
Carts: $16.00

*It may be a short course but its very narrow and demanding. No. 11 is a tough
par 5. We straddle the freeway. Ocean on one side, (foggy maybe misty); on the
landward side sunshine and 80 degrees, it's like 2 different courses.*

─────────── SAN DIEGO ───────────

Balboa Park CG   Yards: 6058, Holes: 18   **GF:** w/day $33.00, w/end
Golf Course Dr., 92102   Par: 72, USGA: 68.1 $38.00
Ph: 619-239-1632   **Carts:** $18.00

Designed by William Bell, this facility has an 18-hole course and a 9-hole one as well. Small greens are a signature of these courses.

─────────── SAN DIEGO ───────────

Carmel Highland GC   Yards: 6112, Holes: 18   **GF:** w/day $30.00, w/end
14455 Penasquitos Dr.,   Par: 72, USGA: 68.9 $50.00
92129   **Carts:** $10.00
Ph: 619-672-2200

This course is championship caliber and is the host of many annual tournaments. The course is in impeccable condition with some difficult water holes and fantastic greens. You can walk the course on weekdays if you want.

─────────── SAN DIEGO ───────────

Carmel Mountain   Yards: 6241, Holes: 18   **GF:** w/day $45.00, w/end
Ranch GC   Par: 72, USGA: 70.6 $60.00
14151 Carmel Ridge   **Carts:** $Included
Rd., 92128
Ph: 619-487-9224

A hilly layout with lots of opportunity to work on sidehill lies.

─────────── SAN DIEGO ───────────

Colina GC   Yards: 1252, Holes: 18   **GF:** w/day $4.00
4085 52nd St, 92105   Par: 54
Ph: 619-582-4704

A short par-3 course that is set in very rolling terrain. Junior and senior rates are offered.

─────────── SAN DIEGO ───────────

De Anza-Mission Bay Yards: 3175, Holes: 18   **GF:** w/day $12.00, w/end
GC   Par: 58 $14.00
2702 N Mission Bay   **Carts:** $14.00
Dr, 92109
Ph: 619-490-3370

A short course that should give you lots of practice with your irons. A nice course for walking. Senior rates are offered 7 days a week.

─────────── SAN DIEGO ───────────

Miramar Memorial   Yards: 6600, Holes: 18   Restaurant/Bar
GC-Military   Par: 72, USGA: 72.1   **GF:** w/day $15.00
Miramar NAS, 92145   **Carts:** $15.00
Ph: 619-537-4155

Accuracy is a must here. Trees and bunkers are the main things to contend with on this long course.

─────────── SAN DIEGO ───────────

Oaks North GC   Yards: 3565, Holes: 27   **GF:** w/day $18.00, w/end
12602 Oaks North Dr.,   Par: 60, USGA: 57.8 $20.00
92128   **Carts:** $16.00
Ph: 619-487-3021

A layout with 27-holes of executive style courses that can be played in three different combinations. They all have narrow fairways and rolling greens. A good test of your short game.

--------------------------------- SAN DIEGO ---------------------------------

Presidio Hills GC
4136 Wallace St, PO
Box 10532, 92210
Ph: 619-295-9476

Yards: 1426, Holes: 18
Par: 54

GF: w/day $6.00

This course opened in 1932, and has majestic trees. The layout is short and can give you some great practice on your irons.

--------------------------------- SAN DIEGO ---------------------------------

**Rancho Bernardo
Inn GC**
17550 Bernardo Oaks
Dr., 92128
Ph: 619-487-1611

Yards: 6388, Holes: 18
Par: 72, USGA: 69.1
RP: 3 days in advance
or room register

Restaurant/Bar/Proshop
GF: w/day $44.00, w/end
$54.00
Carts: $11.00

The West Course unrolls from north to south down the valley like a great green ribbon ... stunning yet surprisingly deceptive. For here are 6700 yards that must be played with almost rifle like accuracy. Throughout are two lakes, a stream and doglegs.

--------------------------------- SAN DIEGO ---------------------------------

Stardust CC
950 N. Hotel Circle,
92108
Ph: 619-297-4796

Yards: 6686, Holes: 27
Par: 72, USGA: 72.4

Restaurant/Bar
GF: w/day $40.00
Carts: $Included

Three 9-hole courses that can be played in different combinations. The courses are flat and fairly long, but the greens are going to be the most difficult part of your game here if you want to score well.

--------------------------------- SAN DIEGO ---------------------------------

Torrey Pines GC
11480 N. Torrey Pines
Rd., 92109
Ph: 619-453-0380

Yards: 6706, Holes: 18
Par: 72, USGA: 72.3
RP: 2 days in advance

Restaurant/Bar/Proshop
GF: w/day $35.00, w/end
$40.00
Carts: $10.00

Two championship courses, rated by Golf Digest in its top 75 public courses year after year. Majestic trees and abundant wildlife make this a memorable round of golf. The greens are fast and not very large. The South Course is a little more difficult.

--------------------------------- SAN DIMAS ---------------------------------

**San Dimas Canyon
GC**
2100 Terrebonne Ave.,
91773
Ph: 714-599-2313

Yards: 6315, Holes: 18
Par: 72, USGA: 67.9
RP: 7 days in advance

Restaurant/Bar/Proshop
GF: w/day $13.00, w/end
$20.00
Carts: $19.00

San Dimas is a classic foothill golf course. Fairways are generous on some holes, and stingy on others. The short length is deceptive because it is not wise to hit a driver everywhere. Beautiful panorama of mountains, sky and water.

------------------------------- SAN FRANCISCO -------------------------------

**Gleneagles
International GC**
2100 Sunnydale Ave,
94134
Ph: 415-587-2425

Yards: 3211, Holes: 9
Par: 36, USGA: 35.5

Proshop
GF: w/day $7.00, w/end
$8.00
Carts: $9.00

Gleneagles is considered to be one of the toughest courses in the Bay Area that no one knows about. The course is very similar to the Olympic Club with its tall trees and small greens. There are two sets of tees that allow for a full eighteen holes.

──────────────SAN FRANCISCO──────────────

Golden Gate Park GC Yards: 1357, Holes: 9   Proshop
47th Ave. & Fulton St.,   Par: 27   **GF:** w/day $2.50, w/end
94117 $5.00
Ph: 415-751-8987   **Carts:** $8.00

The course, located by the ocean, gets plenty of wind. Narrow tree-lined fairways with lots of doglegs are a real challenge. You'll get to use all your irons on this one. A nice course to walk.

──────────────SAN FRANCISCO──────────────

Harding Park GC   Yards: 6400, Holes: 27   Restaurant/Bar
Harding Rd & Skyline   Par: 72   **GF:** w/day $15.00, w/end
Blvd, 94132 $20.00
Ph: 415-664-4690

Harding Park is among the busiest courses in the country. It is your typical San Francisco course that has tall pine and cypress trees and tiny greens. It is not very long but it is tough. The San Francisco City Championships are played here annually.

──────────────SAN FRANCISCO──────────────

Lincoln Park GC   Yards: 5149, Holes: 18   **GF:** w/day $6.00, w/end
3139 Clement St., 94121 Par: 68, USGA: 65.3 $11.00
Ph: 415-752-3422   **Carts:** $13.00

A short course with one of the most spectacular views in the game. The par three sixteenth offers a splendid view of the Golden Gate Bridge; however, do not get caught up in the view because this is a hole of 230 plus yards with a very tiny green.

──────────────SAN GERONIMO──────────────

San Geronimo Valley Yards: 6000, Holes: 18   **GF:** w/day $25.00, w/end
GC   Par: 72, USGA: 69.7 $35.00
P.O. Box 130, 5800   **Carts:** $20.00
Francis Drake, 94963
Ph: 415-488-4030

First opened in 1965, this course has recently seen a lot of renovations. There are lots more bunkers and water. A really challenging course.

──────────────SAN JACINTO──────────────

Soboba Springs CC   Yards: 6352, Holes: 18   **GF:** w/day $34.00, w/end
1020 Soboba Rd.,   Par: 73, USGA: 70.5 $40.00
92383   **Carts:** $Included
Ph: 714-654-9354

This course opened in 1967 and was designed by Desmond Muirhead. The terrain is flat. There is plenty of water, lots of trees, and a long playing layout.

──────────────SAN JOSE──────────────

Pleasant Hills GC   Yards: 6503, Holes: 36   Restaurant/Proshop
2050 South White Rd.,   Par: 72, USGA: 69.6   **GF:** w/day $10.00, w/end
95122 $14.00
Ph: 408-238-3485   **Carts:** $16.00

A flat course, this one boasts a very large number of trees. A twilight rate offered seven days a week.

──────────────SAN JOSE──────────────

San Jose Muni GC
1560 Oakland Road,
95131
Ph: 408-441-4653

Yards: 6362, Holes: 18
Par: 72, USGA: 68.7

GF: w/day $18.00, w/end
$25.00
Carts: $20.00

Rolling greens and doglegs are the major problems on this course. A well maintained course which offers a nice walking game if you wish.

──────────────SAN JOSE──────────────

Santa Teresa GC
260 Bernal Rd., 95150
Ph: 408-225-2650

Yards: 6373, Holes: 18
Par: 72, USGA: 69.6

GF: w/day $6.00, w/end
$14.00
Carts: $15.00

A nice test of one's game. The holes are medium in length but the greens are small. Santa Teresa is just a fun day of golf.

──────────────SAN JOSE──────────────

Thunderbird GC
221 South King Rd.,
95116
Ph: 408-259-3355

Yards: 4700, Holes: 18
Par: 64, USGA: 56.6

GF: w/day $12.00, w/end
$14.00
Carts: $15.00

A short, tree-lined course. Twilight rates are available as well as senior rates.

──────────────SAN JUAN CAPISTRANO──────────────

San Juan Hills GC
Box 1026 32120 San
Juan Creek, 92675
Ph: 714-493-1167

Yards: 5970, Holes: 18
Par: 71, USGA: 67.5

GF: w/day $16.00, w/end
$25.00
Carts: $16.00

This course starts out flat and civilized, then it becomes hilly with trees that will offer every chance to get in the way.

──────────────SAN LEANDRO──────────────

**Tony Lema GC -
Tomy Lema Cours**
13800 Neptune Dr.,
94577
Ph: 415-895-2162

Yards: 6044, Holes: 18
Par: 71, USGA: 67.1

GF: w/day $7.00, w/end
$10.00
Carts: $15.00

A par three course located alongside the bay. The course has small greens but there is a consistent afternoon breeze that makes the course play longer.

──────────────SAN MATEO──────────────

Bay Meadows GC
Delaware St., PO Box
5050, 94402
Ph: 415-341-7204

Yards: 2730, Holes: 9
Par: 56

GF: w/day $5.00

Definitely a beginner's course, but enjoyable nevertheless. It is located at Bay Meadows race track. During racing season it is best to check the hours.

──────────────SAN MATEO──────────────

San Mateo GC
Box 634, 94401
Ph: 415-347-1461

Yards: 5496, Holes: 18
Par: 70, USGA: 64.7

GF: w/day $8.00, w/end
$10.00
Carts: $12.00

A short course that offers many birdie chances. However, there is a consistent breeze which makes the course play tougher in the afternoon. Be careful of the drain canal that weaves its way through the back side.

——————————SAN RAFAEL——————————

Peacock Gap GC
333 Biscayne Dr.,
94901
Ph: 415-453-4940

Yards: 6284, Holes: 18
Par: 71, USGA: 67.9
RP: Thurs for wknds; 1
week wkdy

Restaurant/Bar/Proshop
GF: w/day $22.00, w/end
$27.00
Carts: $20.00

A creek runs through this long, flat layout. An easy course, with lots of trees.

——————————SAN RAMON——————————

Canyon Lakes GC
640 Bollinger Canyon
Way, 94583
Ph: 415-867-0600

Yards: 5975, Holes: 18
Par: 71, USGA: 68.2

GF: w/day $30.00, w/end
$35.00
Carts: $Included

A course with plenty of water holes, located in the foothills near Mount Diablo. The bunkers and trees should give you some second thoughts, as will the rolling greens.

——————————SAN RAMON——————————

**San Ramon Royal
Vista GC**
9430 Fircrest Ln.,
94583
Ph: 415-828-6100

Yards: 6300, Holes: 18
Par: 72, USGA: 69.3

GF: w/day $10.00, w/end
$16.00
Carts: $16.00

Early morning and twilight rates are available here. A lot of young growth, with large greens. A well maintained course.

——————————SANGER——————————

Sherwood Forest GC
79 N. Frankwood Ave.,
93657
Ph: 209-787-2611

Yards: 6160, Holes: 18
Par: 71, USGA: 68.4

GF: w/day $8.00, w/end
$10.00
Carts: $13.00

Sherwood Forest is a very fitting name for this course. Though it is not very long, the densely tree lined fairways make this a course for the straight driver.

——————————SANTA ANA——————————

River View GC
1800 West 22nd St.,
92706
Ph: 714-543-1115

Yards: 5600, Holes: 18
Par: 70, USGA: 66.1
RP: Recommended

Restaurant/Proshop
GF: w/day $10.00
Carts: $14.00

A sanctuary just minutes from Disneyland and Anaheim Stadium, located in the heart of Orange County, River View Golf offers a relaxing respite to the frenzied tourist. We proudly boast of our flawless putting greens and tight challenging fairways.

——————————SANTA ANA——————————

Willowwick GC
3017 West Fifth St.,
92703
Ph: 714-554-0672

Yards: 6013, Holes: 18
Par: 71, USGA: 67.2

GF: w/day $12.00, w/end
$19.00
Carts: $20.00

A nice level course to walk. The growth here is mature and sure to figure in your final score.

——————————SANTA BARBARA——————————

Hidden Oaks CC
4760 Calle Camarade,
93110
Ph: 805-967-3493

Yards: 1118, Holes: 9
Par: 27

GF: w/day $7.00, w/end
$9.00

Although this is a very short course, you may find it surprisingly difficult.

──────────── SANTA BARBARA ────────────

Montecito CC
920 Summit Rd, Box
1170, 93102
Ph: 805-969-0800

Yards: 6184, Holes: 18
Par: 71, USGA: 69.9

Restaurant/Bar
GF: w/day $45.00
Carts: $24.00

A Max Behr design, opened in 1922. The course plays long and is very unforgiving of mistakes. The 3rd and 18th holes are really tough, and will challenge you all the way to the hole.

──────────── SANTA BARBARA ────────────

**Santa Barbara
Community GC**
3500 McCaw Ave.,
93105
Ph: 805-687-7087

Yards: 6009, Holes: 18
Par: 70, USGA: 67.2
RP: Required

Restaurant/Bar/Proshop
GF: w/day $18.00, w/end
$20.00
Carts: $18.00

Extremely scenic view of mountain range along with a beautifully manicured golf course. Best hole on course is #12, a slight dogleg right 455 yards long with out of bounds on left and large trees on the right. A great par 4.

──────────── SANTA CLARA ────────────

Pruneridge GC
400 N. Saratoga Ave.,
95050
Ph: 408-248-4424

Yards: 3878, Holes: 9
Par: 62, USGA: 56.6

GF: w/day $5.00, w/end
$5.50

This is an executive course in which you play twice. The course is very penal as the out-of-bounds stakes are everywhere.

──────────── SANTA CLARA ────────────

Santa Clara GC
2501 Talluto Way,
95054
Ph: 408-980-9515

Yards: 6474, Holes: 18
Par: 72, USGA: 70.5

GF: w/day $12.00, w/end
$18.00
Carts: $16.00

This is a new course that is tough because of the usual wind that blows off the bay. The course offers a good mix of holes but you must take advantage of the downwind holes or you may be in for a long day.

──────────── SANTA CRUZ ────────────

De Laveaga GC
401 Upper Park Rd.,
Suite A, 95065
Ph: 408-423-7212

Yards: 6001, Holes: 18
Par: 72, USGA: 69.8

GF: w/day $15.75, w/end
$21.00
Carts: $18.00

This is a narrow course that requires a straight tee shot and a smooth putting stroke to handle the severe greens. Good shots are rewarded with birdies as the course weaves along a hillside in Santa Cruz.

──────────── SANTA CRUZ ────────────

Pasatiempo GC
18 Clubhouse Rd.,
95060
Ph: 408-426-3622

Yards: 6483, Holes: 18
Par: 71, USGA: 70.9
RP: Seven days in
advance

Restaurant/Bar/Proshop
GF: w/day $45.00, w/end
$55.00
Carts: $20.00

Each hole on this classic course requires shotmaking accuracy. After 18 holes here you'll find you've had to use every club in the bag. Watch out for the beautiful 16th hole with triple level green and tiny landing area.

──────────────SANTA MARIA──────────────

Rancho Maria GC
1950 Casmalia Rd.,
93455
Ph: 805-937-2019

Yards: 6114, Holes: 18
Par: 72, USGA: 68.7

GF: w/day $9.00, w/end
$12.00
Carts: $12.00

With a hill setting, you can expect to get some tough lies. The course has a par-4 which can really be murder on your overall score.

──────────────SANTA NELLA──────────────

Fore Bay GC
29500 Bayview Rd.,
Box 703, 95322
Ph: 209-826-3637

Yards: 6637, Holes: 9
Par: 72, USGA: 69.6

GF: w/day $7.50, w/end
$8.50
Carts: $12.00

Fore Bay has some water and a lot of young growth. An easily walkable course. Senior rates are available and there is also a special seniors day.

──────────────SANTA PAULA──────────────

Mountain View GC
16799 South Mountain
Rd., 93060
Ph: 805-525-1571

Yards: 5231, Holes: 18
Par: 69, USGA: 64.9

GF: w/day $7.00, w/end
$9.00
Carts: $12.00

A valley setting, with towering trees. An extremely short course that will demand your best.

──────────────SANTA ROSA──────────────

Bennett Valley GC
3330 Yulupa Ave.,
95405
Ph: 707-528-3673

Yards: 6221, Holes: 18
Par: 71, USGA: 68.6

GF: w/day $7.00, w/end
$10.00
Carts: $13.00

A nice course for a walk, with flat tree-lined fairways. A lot of water, since the course is endowed with its very own creek Senior rates available on weekdays.

──────────────SANTA ROSA──────────────

Fairgrounds GC
1350 Bennett Valley
Rd., 95404
Ph: 707-546-2469

Yards: 3296, Holes: 9
Par: 58, USGA: 54.6

GF: w/day $6.00, w/end
$7.00

This course is located on the Santa Rosa Fairgrounds race track. This is a flat course with very little hazard from water or bunkers. There are senior, junior and twilight rates, so be sure to ask.

──────────────SANTA ROSA──────────────

Fountaingrove CC
3555 Round Barn,
95403
Ph: 707-523-7555

Yards: 6800, Holes: 18
Par: 72, USGA: 72.9

Restaurant/Bar
GF: w/day $32.00, w/end
$55.00
Carts: $Included

The course makes good use of a wooded, hilly site. Challenging topography. Our favorite hole is #17, 218 yard par 3 over water.

──────────────SANTA ROSA──────────────

Oakmont GC
7025 Oakmont Dr.,
95409
Ph: 707-538-2454

Yards: 5000, Holes: 18
Par: 63, USGA: 58.6
RP: 1 day ahead— wknd
1 week ahead

GF: w/day $11.00, w/end
$13.00
Carts: $15.00

There are 36 holes of golf here.

———————————————————— SANTA ROSA ————————————————————

Wikiup GC
5001 Carriage Ln.,
95401
Ph: 707-546-8787

Yards: 3254, Holes: 9
Par: 58, USGA: 54.0

GF: w/day $4.50, w/end
$7.00
Carts: $10.00

Although this course is not long, don't let that fool you—there is still plenty to challenge you. The bunkers and water are all very well placed. A nice course to walk, and student and senior rates also make it attractive to many.

———————————————————— SANTEE ————————————————————

Carlton Oaks Lodge GC
9200 Inwood Dr., 92071
Ph: 619-448-8500

Yards: 6233, Holes: 18
Par: 72, USGA: 69.2

GF: w/day $65.00
Carts: $Included

A recently renovated course, you're going to find this one to be really long.

———————————————————— SATICOY ————————————————————

Saticoy Regional GC
1025 South Wells Rd.,
93004
Ph: 805-647-6678

Yards: 5423, Holes: 18
Par: 67, USGA: 64.8

GF: w/day $6.00, w/end
$8.00
Carts: $14.00

A hilly setting with tight fairways. The greens can give you a run for your money.

———————————————————— SCOTTS VALLEY ————————————————————

Valley Gardens GC
263 Mt. Hermon Rd.,
95066
Ph: 408-438-3058

Yards: 3666, Holes: 9
Par: 62, USGA: 54.1
RP: 1 week in advance

GF: w/day $8.00, w/end
$9.00
Carts: $1.50

This is a challenging 9 hole course nestled in the Santa Cruz Mountains. Water comes into play on several holes, especially the 175 yard par 3 8th hole. The gentle slope of the course makes it a perfect course to walk. It's ideal for the avid golfer.

———————————————————— SEA RANCH ————————————————————

Sea Ranch Golf Links
P.O. Box 10, Highway
1, 95497
Ph: 707-785-2468

Yards: 3138, Holes: 9
Par: 36, USGA: 34.9

GF: w/day $11.00, w/end
$15.00
Carts: $12.00

An open course with ocean views. Expect plenty of wind.

———————————————————— SEAL BEACH ————————————————————

Leisureworld GC
13580 Saint Andrews,
90740
Ph: 213-431-6586

Yards: 1800, Holes: 9
Par: 54

Over half this short, flat course offers some tricky water problems.

———————————————————— SEBASTOPOL ————————————————————

Sebastopol GC
2881 Scotts Right of
Way, 95472
Ph: 707-823-9852

Yards: 3242, Holes: 9
Par: 62, USGA: 52.1

GF: w/day $4.50, w/end
$7.00
Carts: $10.00

Not a long course, with only one water hole. Senior and student rates on weekdays.

SELMA

Selma Valley GC
12389 East Rose Ave., 93662
Ph: 209-896-2424

Yards: 5349, Holes: 18
Par: 69, USGA: 64.3

GF: w/day $7.00, w/end $9.00
Carts: $12.00

Designed by Robert Dean Putman in 1956, this is a nicely matured course. The doglegs here can be especially trying, so beware. The course is available for outside tournaments.

SEPULVEDA

Mission Hills Little League GC
PO Box 2642, 91343
Ph: 818-892-3019

Yards: 2254, Holes: 9
Par: 27

GF: w/day $3.25, w/end $4.00

A short par-3 course that is ideal for beginners. We offer a senior's and ladies' day and student rates.

SIMI

Sinaloa GC
980 Madera Rd., 93065
Ph: 805-581-2662

Yards: 903, Holes: 9
Par: 54

GF: w/day $3.25, w/end $4.00

This course has one of the most demanding short games of anywhere. You can give your irons a real workout.

SIMI VALLEY

Simi Hills GC
5031 Alamo St., 93063
Ph: 805-522-0803

Yards: 6509, Holes: 18
Par: 71, USGA: 67.9
RP: For weekends

Restaurant/Bar/Proshop
GF: w/day $10.00, w/end $16.00
Carts: $16.00

Course is a good public course in excellent condition with a friendly atmosphere.

SOLANA BEACH

Lomas Santa Fe Executive GC
1580 Sun Valley Rd., 92075
Ph: 619-755-0195

Yards: 2317, Holes: 18
Par: 56, USGA: 56.0

GF: w/day $12.00, w/end $15.00
Carts: $14.00

Eighteen holes of golf in a spectacular setting, and an executive course as well. You should call for special rates.

SOLVANG

Alisal Guest Ranch GC
1054 Alisal Rd., 93463
Ph: 805-688-6411

Yards: 6286, Holes: 18
Par: 72, USGA: 67.9
RP: Recommended

Restaurant/Bar
GF: w/day $24.00
Carts: $16.00

The Alisal blends ideally into the natural surroundings of the rolling terrain, dotted by 300 year old oak, sycamore and eucalyptus trees. The course, home of the 1986 South California Seniors, meanders along a seasonal creek; affords plenty of variety.

SONOMA

Los Arroyos GC
5000 Stage Gulch Rd., 95476
Ph: 707-938-8835

Yards: 3078, Holes: 9
Par: 58

GF: w/day $5.00, w/end $8.00

A flat course, with many trees. Has a particularly attractive all-day rate.

───────────── SONOMA ─────────────

Sonoma National GC
17700 Arnold Dr.,
95476
Ph: 707-996-0300

Yards: 6391, Holes: 18
Par: 72, USGA: 70.9

GF: w/day $6.50, w/end
$15.00
Carts: $16.00

Originally designed by Sam Whiting in 1926, 1991 saw major redesign by Robert Muir Graves. Lots of mature oaks and redwoods, and many doglegs. Considered one of the top courses in northern California.

───────────── SONORA ─────────────

Mountain Springs GC
1000 Championship Drive, 95370
Ph: 209-532-1000

Yards: 6198, Holes: 18
Par: 72, USGA: 70.2

GF: w/day $14.00, w/end
$22.00
Carts: $16.00

A very picturesque course, you'll be sure to enjoy the scenery. But be sure to watch out for the many lakes and bunkers, because their placement is really something.

───────────── SOUTH GATE ─────────────

South Gate Muni GC
9615 Pinehurst Ave,
90280
Ph: 213-564-1434

Holes: 9
Par: 27

GF: w/day $3.50, w/end
$4.00

A very demanding par-3 18-hole course, your short game will matter the most here.

───────────── SOUTH LAKE TAHOE ─────────────

Lake Tahoe CC
Hwy 50 West, PO Box
10406, 95702
Ph: 916-577-0802

Yards: 6244, Holes: 18
Par: 71, USGA: 67.9

GF: w/day $23.00
Carts: $15.00

The greens are one of the best points of this course. The Truckee River and several ponds make most of the holes water holes. A long course, but the short game is the most important thing here.

───────────── SOUTH PASADENA ─────────────

Arroyo Seco GC
1055 Lohman Lane,
91030
Ph: 213-255-1506

Yards: 2223, Holes: 18
Par: 54

GF: w/day $5.75, w/end
$6.50

A creek helps to make this short, flat course interesting. A par-3, 18-hole layout.

───────────── ST. HELENA ─────────────

Meadowood Resort GC
900 Meadowood Ln.,
94574
Ph: 707-963-3646

Yards: 4130, Holes: 9
Par: 62, USGA: 61.0
RP: 1 day in advance

Restaurant/Bar
GF: w/day $20.00

A nine-hole executive course. The layout winds around California Live Oak lined fairways which are tight, but demand accuracy. Players of all levels, genders and ages await the Century Pro-Am, a scratch best-ball 18-hole event, combined ages.

Enter your favorite resort in our "Golf Resort of The Year" contest (entry form is in the back of the book).

───────────────STOCKTON───────────────

Swenson Park GC
6803 Alexandria Pl.,
95207
Ph: 209-477-0774

Yards: 6479, Holes: 18
Par: 72, USGA: 70.1

GF: w/day $6.00, w/end
$7.00
Carts: $13.00

The Jack Fleming designed course was opened in 1952, so you can expect to find many mature trees. This course demands the best of your game for a good round.

───────────────STOCKTON───────────────

Van Buskirk GC
1740 Houston Ave.,
95206
Ph: 209-464-5629

Yards: 6541, Holes: 18
Par: 72, USGA: 69.2

GF: w/day $6.00, w/end
$7.00
Carts: $14.00

Some elevated greens, water everywhere and one par-5 that is really difficult. These are just some of the problems you will meet here.

───────────────STUDIO CITY───────────────

Studio City GC
4141 Whitsett Ave.,
91604
Ph: 818-761-3250

Yards: 975, Holes: 9
Par: 54

GF: w/day $5.00, w/end
$6.00

A par-3 course with very short holes. If your want to practice with your irons, this is the place to come. Or you can try to driving range.

───────────────SUN CITY───────────────

Cherry Hills GC
Box G 26583 Cherry
Hills Blvd., 92381
Ph: 714-679-1182

Yards: 6483, Holes: 18
Par: 72, USGA: 71.8

GF: w/day $20.00
Carts: $16.00

If it weren't for the very rough roughs and the doglegs, this flat course would be easy.

───────────────SUNNYVALE───────────────

Sunnyvale GC
605 Macara, 94086
Ph: 408-738-3666

Yards: 5744, Holes: 18
Par: 69, USGA: 67.0

GF: w/day $6.00, w/end
$13.00
Carts: $15.00

Get ready for a career day.

───────────────SUNOL───────────────

Sunol Valley GC
Interstate 680 at
Andrade Rd., 94586
Ph: 415-862-2404

Yards: 6195, Holes: 18
Par: 72, USGA: 69.5

GF: w/day $22.00
Carts: $20.00

Very popular tournament courses in the East Bay Hills, they offer many scenic holes. There are many opportunities for nasty sidehill lies and you have to watch out for the water and trees also.

───────────────SUSANVILLE───────────────

Emerson Lake GC
470-835 Wingfield Rd.
N, 96130
Ph: 916-257-6303

Yards: 6348, Holes: 9
Par: 72, USGA: 68.4

GF: w/day $9.00
Carts: $12.00

Plenty of water and mature evergreen trees dot this well maintained course. The course is available for outside tournaments.

---SUTTER---

Southridge GC
9413 South Butte Rd.,
95982
Ph: 916-755-4653

Yards: 6470, Holes: 18
Par: 72

GF: w/day $16.00, w/end
$20.00
Carts: $20.00

This course has a little bit of everything. Many sidehill lies on the front nine. There is water on six holes, and it affects the play on all of them A second nine is in the works. The course is available for outside tournaments.

---SYLMAR---

El Cariso GC
13100 Elridge Ave,
91342
Ph: 818-367-6157

Yards: 4065, Holes: 18
Par: 62, USGA: 58.3

GF: w/day $9.00, w/end
$13.00
Carts: $15.00

With five lakes, and well-trapped greens you'll really have your work cut out for you here. A real shot-makers course. Check on the senior and twilight rates.

---TAFT---

Buena Vista GC
Rt. 1 Box 115-C, 93268
Ph: 805-763-5124

Yards: 6656, Holes: 18
Par: 72, USGA: 69.0
RP: Required on

weekends
GF: w/day $6.50
Carts: $14.00

Set in the desert, this course will give you some unusual golfing experiences. Lots of palm trees add to the desert setting.

---TAHOE CITY---

Tahoe City GC
P.O. Box 226, 95730
Ph: 916-583-1516

Yards: 5251, Holes: 9
Par: 66, USGA: 63.4
RP: Not necessary but

good idea
GF: w/day $13.00
Carts: $10.00

A terrific place from which to view Lake Tahoe.

---TAHOE PARADISE---

Tahoe Paradise GC
Hwy 50, 95709
Ph: 916-577-2121

Yards: 4070, Holes: 18
Par: 66, USGA: 60.0

GF: w/day $16.00
Carts: $15.00

A hilly course with small greens. The fairways are narrow, so you'll need to pay attention. Senior and twilight rates are available.

---TEHACHAPI---

Deer Creek CC
22630 Woodford-
Tehachapi Rd., 93561
Ph: 805-822-9118

Yards: 6284, Holes: 9
Par: 72, USGA: 70.6

GF: w/day $7.00, w/end
$8.00
Carts: $16.00

The original nine here was designed by Ted Robinson in 1963, and the second nine was added in 1991. A lot of water and plenty of sidehill lies make this an interesting place to play.

---TEHACHAPI---

Horse Thief GC
Star RTE 1, Box 2931,
93561
Ph: 805-822-5581

Yards: 6317, Holes: 18
Par: 72, USGA: 70.1

GF: w/day $16.00, w/end
$26.00
Carts: $19.00

A beautiful mountain setting that has plenty of exposed rocks that you'll have to contend with. With the old oaks and water on other holes, you'll need to watch your shots to keep out of trouble.

──────────────── TEMECULA ────────────────

Red Hawk CC
45100 Red Hawk
Parkway, 92392
Ph: 714-695-1424

Yards: 6655, Holes: 18
Par: 72, USGA: 72.4

GF: w/day $45.00, w/end
$65.00
Carts: $Included

Opened in 1991, this is a narrow course with rolling, tricky greens and trees along the fairways.

──────────────── TEMECULA ────────────────

Temecula Creek Inn GC
44-501 Rainbow
Canyon Rd., 92390
Ph: 714-676-5631

Yards: 6380, Holes: 18
Par: 72, USGA: 69.4

Restaurant/Bar
GF: w/day $16.00, w/end
$21.00
Carts: $15.00

The course has played host to the U.S. Open Qualifying, U.S. Public Links Qualifying, and Golden State Tour events. There are rolling hills and tree lined fairways. The 13th hole has an elevated green with crosswind over the green.

──────────────── THOUSAND OAKS ────────────────

Los Robles GC
299 S. Moorpark Rd.,
91361
Ph: 805-495-6471

Yards: 5789, Holes: 18
Par: 70, USGA: 66.7

GF: w/day $9.00, w/end
$12.00
Carts: $13.00

Lots of trees along the fairways, hills and water are the main problems you run into on this course. There are some long par-3s too.

──────────────── THREE RIVERS ────────────────

Three Rivers GC
P.O. Box 202, 93271
Ph: 209-561-3133

Yards: 4950, Holes: 9
Par: 68, USGA: 64.8

GF: w/day $4.50, w/end
$7.50
Carts: $13.00

This is an easy walking course as it is in the main flat. A small amount of water and some slope are the main challenges to a round here.

──────────────── TORRANCE ────────────────

Sea Aire Park GC
22730 Lupine Dr, 90505
Ph: 213-316-9779

Yards: 618, Holes: 9
Par: 27

GF: w/day $4.00

A very short par-3 course. Mainly for beginners, but seniors can play here for only a dollar.

──────────────── TRES PINOS ────────────────

Bolado Park GC
P.O. Box 419, 95075
Ph: 408-628-9995

Yards: 5879, Holes: 9
Par: 70, USGA: 67.5

GF: w/day $6.00, w/end
$8.00
Carts: $12.00

A 1930's course which is well cared for and still considered a challenge.

──────────────── TRUCKEE ────────────────

Northstar GC
Hwy. 267 & Northstar.
P.O. Box 12, 95734
Ph: 916-562-1010

Yards: 6897, Holes: 18
Par: 72, USGA: 67.4

Restaurant/Bar/Proshop
GF: w/day $35.00
Carts: $10.00

This scenic mountain course offers views of the rugged Sierra Nevada and Martis Valley and a challenging 18 holes with water hazards on 14 of the holes, including the new lake on hole number 6. The front nine is fairly wide open.

──────────── TRUCKEE ────────────

Ponderosa GC
P.O. Box 729, 10962
Brockway, 95734
Ph: 916-587-3501

Yards: 3000, Holes: 9
Par: 36, USGA: 33.7

GF: w/day $11.00
Carts: $9.00

The course is only open from April to October, so be sure to make your plans accordingly A long playing course that is flat. Beautiful old evergreens are a feature of this layout.

──────────── TUJUNGA ────────────

Verdugo Hills GC
6433 LaTuna Canyon
Rd., 91042
Ph: 818-352-3161

Yards: 1805, Holes: 18
Par: 54

GF: w/day $7.00, w/end
$10.00

A nice short, hilly course that is easy walking. One of the best maintained courses in the south of the state. A driving range is also available for practicing on your woods.

──────────── TULARE ────────────

Tulare GC
5319 S. Laspina St.,
93274
Ph: 209-686-9839

Yards: 6534, Holes: 18
Par: 72, USGA: 69.5

Restaurant/Bar/Proshop
GF: w/day $6.00, w/end
$10.00
Carts: $12.00

Designed in 1956, this course believes in constant improvement. There are quite a few water holes, on a fairly flat terrain.

──────────── TULELAKE ────────────

Indian Camp GC
Route 1, Box 46-A,
96134

Ph: 916-667-2922

Yards: 1512, Holes: 9
Par: 28
GF: w/day $5.00

This course would be a par-3 course if it wasn't for its one par-4 hole Said to be an Indian camping area, this is the most northern course in the state. An all-day fee makes this scenic course even more attractive to the bargain hunter.

──────────── TURLOCK ────────────

Turlock G&CC
P.O. Box X, 10532 Golf
Links Rd., 95381
Ph: 209-634-4976

Yards: 6331, Holes: 18
Par: 72, USGA: 69.9

GF: w/day $25.00, w/end
$30.00
Carts: $16.00

You'll need to pay attention to your game here, accuracy is all important. The roughs are really rough. Water and doglegs will add to your fun.

──────────── TWAIN HARTE ────────────

Sierra Pines GC
P.O. Box 1013, 23736 S
Fork Rd., 95383
Ph: 209-586-2118

Yards: 2325, Holes: 9
Par: 33, USGA: 31.0

GF: w/day $9.00
Carts: $8.00

Set in the mountains, there will be plenty of opportunity to test your skills at sidehill lies. Your short game is very important here. A pleasant course to walk, and not too demanding. If you're looking for a pleasant day without too much hassle.

───────────────── TWAIN HARTE ─────────────────

Twain Harte G&CC
P.O. Box 333, 22909
Meadow Ln., 95383
Ph: 209-586-3131

Yards: 1715, Holes: 9
Par: 29, USGA: 29.0

GF: w/day $7.00
Carts: $57.10

The narrow fairways here will test your accuracy.

───────────────── UKIAH ─────────────────

Ukiah GC
599 Park Blvd., PO Box
364, 95482
Ph: 707-462-8857

Yards: 5612, Holes: 18
Par: 70, USGA: 66.5

GF: w/day $7.00, w/end
$9.00
Carts: $13.00

An extremely hilly course. The fairways are narrow, with a lot of difficult lies. The Ukiah Junior Open and the Mendocino County Men's Amateur tournaments are yearly events here.

───────────────── UPLAND ─────────────────

Upland Hills CC
1231 East 16th St.,
91786
Ph: 714-946-4711

Yards: 5700, Holes: 18
Par: 70, USGA: 66.0
RP: 3 days in advancae

GF: w/day $16.00, w/end
$23.00
Carts: $18.00

Designed by Ted Robinson, this course opened in 1983. The layout is short and easy to walk, but difficult to play 'cause it's tight too.

───────────────── VACAVILLE ─────────────────

**Cypress Lakes GC-
Military**
5601 Meridian Rd,
Travis AFB, 95687
Ph: 707-448-7186

Yards: 6796, Holes: 18
Par: 72, USGA: 72.6

Restaurant/Bar
GF: w/day $7.00, w/end
$19.00
Carts: $14.00

A nice course to walk, but keep out of the abundant water. A very windy course with plenty of trees.

───────────────── VACAVILLE ─────────────────

Green Tree GC
Leisure Town Rd., P.O.
Box 105, 95688
Ph: 707-448-1420

Yards: 5893, Holes: 27
Par: 72, USGA: 67.0

GF: w/day $6.00, w/end
$9.00
Carts: $12.00

Some water on this one can give you a hard time. A scenic golf course, well worth your time. There is a senior rate.

───────────────── VALENCIA ─────────────────

Vista Valencia GC
24700 Trevino Dr.,
91355
Ph: 805-255-4670

Yards: 4160, Holes: 18
Par: 61, USGA: 60.3

GF: w/day $14.00, w/end
$22.00
Carts: $18.00

Vista Valencia offers 27 holes of golf, an 18 hole course and a nine hole par-3 type. The 18 hole course has an island green, and plenty of water on the others holes as well, so you might want to bring a few extra balls with you.

───────────────── VALLEJO ─────────────────

Blue Rock Springs
Columbus Parkway,
PO Box 5207, 94589
Ph: 707-643-8476

Yards: 6091, Holes: 18
Par: 72, USGA: 68.2

Proshop
GF: w/day $8.00, w/end
$11.00
Carts: $14.00

A long course considering its 1938 design date. The layout will give you plenty of sidehill lies and more than enough trees. If you like doglegs this is a great course for you.

————————————— VALLEJO —————————————

Joe Mortara GC
815 Valle Vista Ave.,
94590
Ph: 707-642-5146

Yards: 1591, Holes: 9
Par: 28, USGA: 27.2

GF: w/day $2.50, w/end
$3.00

A nice course for walking, located on the race track at Solano County Fairgrounds. The short game is very important here.

————————————— VALLEY SPRINGS —————————————

La Contenta GC
1653 Hwy 26, 95252
Ph: 209-772-1081

Yards: 6501, Holes: 18
Par: 72, USGA: 71.3

Restaurant/Bar
GF: w/day $14.00, w/end
$24.00
Carts: $18.00

La Contenta is set in hilly country with some serious water hazards to eat up your golf balls. There are also some out-of-bounds that will test your accuracy. Twilight rates are available.

————————————— VAN NUYS —————————————

Van Nuys GC
6550 Odessa Ave,
91406
Ph: 818-785-8871

Yards: 2181, Holes: 27
Par: 54

GF: w/day $4.00, w/end
$4.25

A very short par-3 that can give your short game a real workout. The trees and lakes will add some spice to the round. A nice course to walk.

————————————— VAN NUYS —————————————

Woodley Lakes GC
6331 Woodley Ave.,
91406
Ph: 818-787-8163

Yards: 6545, Holes: 18
Par: 72, USGA: 69.8

GF: w/day $10.50, w/end
$14.50

Your woods should get a workout on this one.

————————————— VENICE —————————————

Penmar GC
1233 Rose Ave, 90291
Ph: 213-396-6228

Holes: 9
Par: 58

GF: w/day $5.50

This course is set in Venice, so you can expect to see just about anything.

————————————— VENTURA —————————————

Buena Ventura GC
5882 Olivas Park Dr,
93003
Ph: 805-642-2231

Holes: 18
Par: 70

GF: w/day $13.00, w/end
$16.00
Carts: $17.00

The greens are really fast here. Water is definitely a problem to the golfer here. Your short game will matter a great deal in your final score.

————————————— VENTURA —————————————

Olivas Park GC
3750 Olivas Park Dr,
93003
Ph: 805-485-5712

Yards: 6353, Holes: 18
Par: 72, USGA: 69.5

GF: w/day $13.00, w/end
$17.00
Carts: $17.00

A flat course with wind off the ocean. A championship course that annually hosts some important tournaments.

———————————————VISALIA———————————————

Oak Patch GC   Yards: 5200, Holes: 9   **GF:** w/day $3.50, w/end
30400 Road 158, 93291   Par: 56 $4.00
Ph: 209-733-5000

Oak Patch is set alongside the Kaweah River, and is very scenic. A course that isn't so terribly long, you could enjoy a walk.

———————————————VISALIA———————————————

Sierra View GC of   Yards: 6465, Holes: 18   Restaurant/Bar/Proshop
Visalia   Par: 72, USGA: 68.4   **GF:** w/day $6.50, w/end
12608 Ave. 264, 93277 $8.00
Ph: 209-732-2078   **Carts:** $12.00

The long hitters will really enjoy this course. But the greens are tricky and the bunkers and trees also play a part in a good score.

———————————————VISALIA———————————————

Valley Oaks GC, Inc. Yards: 6250, Holes: 18   Proshop
1800 So. Plaza Dr.,   Par: 72, USGA: 68.2   **GF:** w/day $5.00, w/end
93277 $9.00
Ph: 209-651-1441   **Carts:** $12.50

The main challenge here is the short game, lots of trees and water also. The course is available for outside tournaments.

———————————————VISTA———————————————

Shadow Ridge CC   Yards: 6859, Holes: 18   Restaurant/Bar
1980 Gateway Dr,   Par: 72, USGA: 73.3   **GF:** w/day $44.00
92082
Ph: 619-727-7706

Lots and lots of lakes on this undulating course that has large, mature eucalyptus trees.

———————————————WALNUT———————————————

Los Angeles Royal   Yards: 6300, Holes: 18   Restaurant/Bar/Proshop
Vista GC   Par: 71, USGA: 69.8   **GF:** w/day $12.00, w/end
20055 East Colima Rd.,   RP: 7 days in advance $23.00
91789   **Carts:** $18.00
Ph: 818-965-1634

A 27-hole layout in a hilly setting. Each nine-hole combination has different problems, so try them all for a good day of golf.

———————————————WALNUT CREEK———————————————

Boundary Oak GC   Yards: 6788, Holes: 18   Restaurant/Bar/Proshop
3800 Valley Vista Rd.,   Par: 72, USGA: 70.2   **GF:** w/day $10.00, w/end
94598   RP: Required $14.00
Ph: 415-934-6212   **Carts:** $18.00

One of the more challenging municipal courses in Northern California.

———————————————WALNUT CREEK———————————————

Diablo Hills GC   Yards: 4604, Holes: 9   **GF:** w/day $10.50, w/end
1551 Marchbanks Dr.,   Par: 68, USGA: 61.7 $15.00
94598   **Carts:** $16.00
Ph: 415-939-7372

A hilly course with lots of bunkers. The course is a fairly open one with a condominium setting.

───────────WARNER SPRINGS───────────

Warner Springs | Yards: 6701, Holes: 18 | Restaurant/Bar
Ranch GC | Par: 72, USGA: 71.7 | **GF:** w/day $35.00, w/end
Rt 79 Box 10, 92066 | | $45.00
Ph: 619-782-3555

Some water and hilly fairways will challenge you at Warner Springs Ranch.

───────────WASCO───────────

Wasco Valley Rose | Yards: 6230, Holes: 18 | **GF:** w/day $8.50, w/end
GC | Par: 72, USGA: 69.4 | $10.50
301 North Leonard | | **Carts:** $15.00
Ave, 93280
Ph: 805-758-8301

This relatively new course has elevated greens and tees. The fairways have a definite roll and are well bunkered with water and sand.

───────────WATSONVILLE───────────

Casserly Par-3 GC | Yards: 1158, Holes: 9 | Proshop
626 Casserly Rd., | Par: 27 | **GF:** w/day $4.00, w/end
95076 | | $4.00
Ph: 408-724-1654

Not a good course for the seasoned golfer, but the hills and water can cause a little difficulty. You'll have to walk this one as there are no power carts.

───────────WATSONVILLE───────────

Pajaro Valley GC | Yards: 6234, Holes: 18 | Restaurant/Bar/Proshop
967 Salinas Rd., 95076 | Par: 72, USGA: 70.0 | **GF:** w/day $50.00
Ph: 408-724-3851 | RP: Weekend 1 week; | **Carts:** $25.00
 | weekday 1 month

Serene and verdant Pajaro Valley provides an exquisite setting for this 18-hole course. Set amongst groves of Monterey Cypress trees, these meticulously groomed greens and fairways present a challenge for golfers of every level.

───────────WATSONVILLE───────────

Spring Hills GC | Yards: 6218, Holes: 18 | **GF:** w/day $9.50, w/end
31 Smith Rd., 95076 | Par: 71, USGA: 68.7 | $12.50
Ph: 408-724-1404 | | **Carts:** $18.00

Lots of doglegs and lots of trees on rolling terrain. Accuracy is very important here. Course is available for outside tournaments.

───────────WEAVERVILLE───────────

Trinity Alps G&CC | Yards: 1950, Holes: 9 | **GF:** w/day $5.50, w/end
P.O. Box 582, 111 | Par: 31, USGA: 29.5 | $6.50
Fairway Dr., 96093 | | **Carts:** $5.00
Ph: 916-623-5411

There is one hole where a tree comes into play if you're unlucky There is some water, but not a great deal. A very scenic course with views of the Trinity Alps. A nice walking course, if you want to get back to basics.

───────────WEED───────────

Lake Shastina GC | Yards: 6317, Holes: 18 | Restaurant/Bar/Proshop
5925 Country Club Dr., | Par: 72, USGA: 69.5 | **GF:** w/day $32.00
96094 | | **Carts:** $12.00
Ph: 916-938-3201

Four sets of strategically placed tees leading to broad fairways sculptured from native shrubland and pine forests, large undulating greens, well placed sand traps, a generous display of lakes and water hazards, are a tribute to Mr. Jones' ingenuity.

─────────────────────────WEED─────────────────────────

Weed GC   Yards: 2741, Holes: 9   **GF:** w/day $8.00, w/end
P.O. Box 204, 27730   Par: 35, USGA: 32.8 $10.00
Edgewood Rd., 96094   **Carts:** $15.00
Ph: 916-938-9971

Weed Golf Course hosts the Siskiyou Open Invitational. Water is a factor on quite a few holes, and the rolling fairways and trees add the rest. A very challenging first hole may make you wonder what is coming next. The course is enhanced by Mount Shasta.

─────────────────── WEST SACRAMENTO ───────────────────

Lighthouse GC   Yards: 4729, Holes: 18   Restaurant/Proshop
500 Douglas St., 95605 Par: 64, USGA: 63.7   **GF:** w/day $12.00, w/end
Ph: 915-372-0800 $14.00
                                                 Carts: $15.00

A course with mature trees and water on almost every hole. Although a new course, don't be surprised to find it tough.

─────────────────── WESTLAKE VILLAGE ───────────────────

Westlake Village GC Yards: 4973, Holes: 18   **GF:** w/day $13.00, w/end
Box 4216, 4812   Par: 67, USGA: 62.2 $20.00
Lakeview Canyon,   **Carts:** $16.00
91359
Ph: 818-889-0770

You'll find that the trees are the biggest hazard on this course, if you get off the fairways they'll try to keep you off. Good greens will help your game, and three lakes will try to get you in more trouble.

──────────────────────────WILLITS──────────────────────────

Brooktrails GC   Yards: 2718, Holes: 9   **GF:** w/day $6.50, w/end
24860 Birch St., P.O. Par: 56, USGA: 50.1 $7.50
Box 1003, 95490
Ph: 707-459-6761

A flat course with a creek for water hazards. There are many redwoods on this flat course.

─────────────────────── WILLOW CREEK ───────────────────────

Big Foot GC & CC   Yards: 5007, Holes: 9   Restaurant/Bar/Proshop
P.O. Box 836, 95573   Par: 70, USGA: 63.9   **GF:** w/day $12.00, w/end
Ph: 916-629-2977   RP: Call for weekends $14.00
                       & holidays   **Carts:** $14.00

The golf course is a true "gem." Surrounded by tree covered mountains. Warm to hot weather April thru September. Open year round.

──────────────────────────WILLOWS──────────────────────────

Glenn G&CC   Yards: 3258, Holes: 9   Proshop
R2 Box 172F, Bayliss Par: 36, USGA: 34.8   **GF:** w/day $9.00, w/end
Blue Gum, 95988 $12.00
Ph: 916-934-9918   **Carts:** $14.00

This course has some of the best greens in the area, and some of the toughest golf holes to go with them Many beautiful willows and eucalyptus make the course a beauty. Senior rates are available during the week.

---------------------------- WILMINGTON ----------------------------

Harbor Park GC   Yards: 6302, Holes: 9   **GF:** w/day $5.50, w/end
1235 North Figueroa,   Par: 72 $7.50
90744
Ph: 213-549-4953

Tricky greens and long holes makes this one a really challenging round.

---------------------------- WINDSOR ----------------------------

Windsor GC   Yards: 6169, Holes: 18   **GF:** w/day $19.00, w/end
6555 Skylane Blvd.,   Par: 72, USGA: 70.1 $29.00
95492   **Carts:** $10.00
Ph: 707-838-7888

*The Ben Hogan Tour has a tournament yearly on this course. There's more than
enough water to give you trouble, and on a couple of the holes it's a very big
factor in your score, so be very careful. Many large oaks and some small greens.*

---------------------- YOSEMITE NATIONAL PARK ----------------------

Wawona Hotel GC   Yards: 6969, Holes: 27   Restaurant/Bar
Highway 41, PO Box   Par: 72, USGA: 69.1   **GF:** w/day $34.00
2005, 95389   **Carts:** $20.00
Ph: 209-375-6572

*This course is set in Yosemite National Park, so you know the scenery can't be
surpassed. Plenty of wildlife will enliven your game. A short, well-maintained
course with numerous mature trees.*

---------------------------- YUBA CITY ----------------------------

Mallard Lake GC   Yards: 2637, Holes: 9   **GF:** w/day $5.00, w/end
4238 Sawtelle Ave,   Par: 35, USGA: 64.2 $6.00
95991   **Carts:** $8.00
Ph: 916-674-0475

*Mallard Lake is a water course, since you will find it everywhere. It is short and
flat, but don't be fooled, that won't help much.*

---------------------------- YUCCA VALLEY ----------------------------

Blue Skies CC   Yards: 6660, Holes: 18   Restaurant/Bar/Proshop
55-100 Martinez Trail,   Par: 71, USGA: 68.4   **GF:** w/day $15.00
92284   **Carts:** $15.00
Ph: 619-365-7694

*Back east beauty in a high desert setting over 400 hardwood trees make this
course exceptional for play and for relaxing beauty. The course plays at 80
degrees when lower desert courses around Palm Springs are over 100 degrees—
yet only 20 minutes away.*

COLORADO

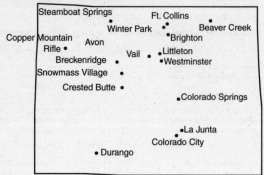

————————————ALAMOSA/MOSCA————————————

Great Sand Dunes CC
5303 Highway 150, 81146
Ph: 719-378-2357

Yards: 7000, Holes: 18
Par: 72, USGA: 68.0
RP: Call the Proshop

Restaurant/Bar/Proshop
GF: w/day $65.00, w/end $65.00
Carts: $Included

Spectacular views of Sangre de Cristo Mountains & Great Sand Dunes Nat'l Monument. Unique golf destination. Epic solitude. Design enhances natural beauty of area, provides wide range of conditions for all golfers.

————————————————AVON————————————————

Eagle Vail GC PC
Box 5660, 81620
Ph: 303-949-5267

Yards: 6819, Holes: 18
Par: 72, USGA: 68.4

Restaurant/Bar
GF: w/day $40.00
Carts: $20.00

Water comes into play on 10 holes, so you'd better be a good shotmaker or bring your wading boots Also plenty of trees just to keep it interesting. A very scenic course.

————————————BATTLEMENT MESA————————————

Battlement Mesa GC
3930 North Battlement Parkway, 81635
Ph: 303-285-7274

Yards: 6695, Holes: 18
Par: 72, USGA: 71.2

GF: w/day $25.00
Carts: $Included

The course has wonderful views of the Colorado River. Joe Finger and Ken Dye were the design team.

—————————————BEAVER CREEK—————————————

Beaver Creek GC
103 Offerson Rd., 81620
Ph: 303-949-7123

Yards: 6464, Holes: 18
Par: 70, USGA: 69.2
RP: 48 hours in advance

Restaurant/Bar
GF: w/day $50.00
Carts: $10.00

Beaver Creek is a world renowned Robert Trent Jones II course. A true mountain course with undulating fairways. Creeks run through the course.

─────────────── BRECKENRIDGE ───────────────

Breckenridge GC PC
200 Clubhouse Dr. P.O.
Box 7965, 80424
Ph: 303-453-9104

Yards: 7279, Holes: 18
Par: 72, USGA: 66.4
RP: Two days in
advance

Restaurant/Bar/Proshop
GF: w/day $40.00
Carts: $10.00

Jack Nicklaus designed, the course plays through mountains, valleys, forests and streams. Almost 7300 yards from the championship tees and approximately 6600 yards from the men's tee. Length of golf course is shortened by the 9300 plus feet of elevation.

─────────────── BRIGHTON ───────────────

Riverdale GC PC
13300 Riverdale Rd.,
80601
Ph: 303-659-6700

Yards: 7027, Holes: 18
Par: 72, USGA: 66.3
RP: 1 day in advance

Restaurant/Bar/Proshop
GF: w/day $23.00
Carts: $17.00

Scottish design, only Pete Dye public course west of Mississippi, so bigger landing areas than normal. Hole #5 429 yards from back tee, par 4 with big green, level, surrounded by grass swails and big depression undulating, can't see flag from it.

─────────────── CASTLE ROCK ───────────────

Plum Creek G&CC
331 Players Club Dr.,
80104
Ph: 303-668-2611

Yards: 5915, Holes: 18
Par: 72, USGA: 67.1
RP: Call up to 7 days in
adv.

Restaurant/Proshop
GF: w/day $45.00, w/end
$55.00
Carts: $Included

A Pete Dye design, there's lots of bunkers and small well-protected greens. Wind and water can add to the difficulties of this championship layout.

─────────────── COLORADO CITY ───────────────

Hollydot GC
#1 North Park Rd.,
81019
Ph: 303-676-3341

Yards: 7010, Holes: 27
Par: 72, USGA: 68.4

Restaurant/Bar/Proshop
GF: w/day $7.00, w/end
$10.00
Carts: $18.00

On this 27 hole championship course each 9 is unique. The first 9 is lush meadows with long par 4's, the Links nine is named appropriately as it links the 2 former 9 hole courses together in a Scottish style. The old course is tight with rolling fairways.

─────────────── COLORADO SPRINGS ───────────────

Pine Creek GC
9850 Divot Trail, 80920
Ph: 719-594-9999

Yards: 6980, Holes: 18
Par: 72, USGA: 72.1
RP: 3 days in advance

GF: w/day $16.00
Carts: $16.00

Generous fairways landing areas with subtle breaking greens ensure playability for all skill levels. Bunkers, trees, creeks and lakes, combined with elevation differences of the course are important features that create superb shot values.

─────────────── COPPER MOUNTAIN ───────────────

Copper Creek GC
170 and JNC. 91, P.O.
Box 3415, 80443
Ph: 303-968-2339

Yards: 6129, Holes: 18
Par: 70, USGA: 67.2
RP: 30 days resort
guest, 4 days otherwise

Restaurant/Bar/Proshop
GF: w/day $45.00
Carts: $Included

Magnificent panoramas of the snow-capped 13,000 foot peaks surround you while golfing at Copper Creek Golf Course. Copper Mountain's championship course, at an elevation of 9,700 feet, is the highest 18 hole golf course in America.

─────────────── CRESTED BUTTE ───────────────

Skyland Resort & CC   Yards: 6635, Holes: 18   Restaurant/Bar/Proshop
P.O. Box 879, 81225   Par: 72, USGA: 68.8   **GF:** w/day $45.00
Ph: 800-628-5496   **Carts:** $Included

Skyland Resort and Country Club earned top marks from the national press from the day it opened and was rated in the top one percent of all new golf courses in the country. The spectacular mountain backdrop offers a breathtaking distraction.

─────────────── DURANGO ───────────────

Tamarron Resort GC   Yards: 6885, Holes: 18   Restaurant
40292 U.S. Hwy 550 N.,   Par: 72, USGA: 69.9   **GF:** w/day $45.00
81301   RP: 1 day, if not on   **Carts:** $Included
Ph: 303-259-2000   package

Number 10 is one of Tamarron's more interesting holes. Try for about 210 yards on your drive. Any more and the ball and you will be in the rough of a steep embankment that drops far below the fairway's upper level.

─────────────── EDWARDS ───────────────

Singletree GC PC   Yards: 7059, Holes: 18   Restaurant/Bar/Proshop
P.O. Box AA, 81632   Par: 71, USGA: 72.7   **GF:** w/day $75.00
Ph: 303-926-3533   RP: Up to 48 hours in   **Carts:** $Included
                             advance

Lots of wind.

─────────────── FT. COLLINS ───────────────

Collindale GC PC   Yards: 7011, Holes: 18   Restaurant/Bar/Proshop
1441 E. Horsetooth   Par: 71, USGA: 68.8   **GF:** w/day $12.00, w/end
Rd., 80525   RP: Day before $12.00
Ph: 303-221-6651   **Carts:** $15.00

Easy walking course in very good shape. Tight fairways with fast-soft greens. #6 is par 5 with beautiful view of Rocky Mountains in background.

─────────────── HIGHLANDS RANCH ───────────────

The Links at   Yards: 4780, Holes: 18   Restaurant/Bar/Proshop
Highlands Ranch   Par: 62, USGA: 60.9   **GF:** w/day $16.00, w/end
5815 E. Gleneagles   RP: 1 week in advance $16.00
Village Park, 80126   **Carts:** $14.00
Ph: 303-470-9292

Standing on the first tee you have a panoramic view of the Rocky Mountains. Looking straight west on the first tee is a view of Mt. Evans. Although we are considered an executive golf course—each hole presents its own special challenge.

─────────────── KEYSTONE ───────────────

Keystone Ranch GC   Yards: 6521, Holes: 18   Restaurant/Proshop
P.O. Box 38, 80435   Par: 72, USGA: 69.9   **GF:** w/day $70.00
Ph: 303-468-4250   **Carts:** $Included

A championship courses set in the woods, with well-bunkered and rolling greens. Doglegs, water in the form of streams and a lake, and well-placed bunkers will also come into play. The high altitude is sure to help your ball carry further than usual.

──────────────── LA JUNTA ────────────────

La Junta GC PC   Yards: 6374, Holes: 18   Restaurant/Bar/Proshop
27696 Harris Rd., 81050   Par: 71, USGA: 69.0   **GF:** w/day $8.00, w/end
Ph: 719-384-7133 $10.00
                                                       Carts: $12.00

The course is relatively flat—no water holes. Blue grass fairways, bent grass greens. Very difficult rough. Tree lines fairways, small greens, narrow fairways. Tougher than it first appears.

──────────────── LITTLETON ────────────────

Arrowhead GC PC   Yards: 6682, Holes: 18   Restaurant/Bar/Proshop
10850 W. Sundown   Par: 70, USGA: 68.7   **GF:** w/day $45.00
Trail, 80125   RP: 7 days in advance   **Carts:** $Included
Ph: 303-973-4076

Very mountainous with some shots thru rock formations. There are 300 foot high rocks in fairway. There are elevated tees and fairways lined with pine, aspen and oak trees.

──────────────── PUEBLO ────────────────

Walking Stick GC   Yards: 6562, Holes: 18   Proshop
4301 Walkingstick   Par: 72   **GF:** w/day $13.00, w/end
Blvd., 81001 $15.00
Ph: 719-584-3400   **Carts:** $15.00

An Arthur Hills design, with all the design tricks that he usually displays.

──────────────── RIFLE ────────────────

Rifle Creek GC PC   Yards: 6250, Holes: 18   Restaurant/Bar/Proshop
3004 State Hwy. 325,   Par: 72, USGA: 67.0   **GF:** w/day $13.00, w/end
81650   RP: No more than 7 $16.00
Ph: 303-625-1093   days in advance   **Carts:** $16.00

You will enjoy the greatly contrasting nines—the front nine winding through the canyons and sandstone rock cliffs, the back nine meanders through the meadows and along the banks of sparkling clear Rifle Creek—both have a fabulous view of the Rocky Mtn.

──────────────── SNOWMASS VILLAGE ────────────────

Snowmass GC   Yards: 6900, Holes: 18   Restaurant/Bar/Proshop
P.O. Drawer G-2, 81615   Par: 71, USGA: 70.4   **GF:** w/day $52.00
Ph: 303-923-5600   **Carts:** $Included

Snowmass Golf Links is situated at the base of the valley, very Scottish links in appearance. It has nice elevation changes, and a substantial amount of water. Has hosted the Snowmass Club Invitational Pro-Am 1984-1987.

──────────────── STEAMBOAT SPRINGS ────────────────

Sheraton Steamboat   Yards: 6906, Holes: 18   Restaurant/Bar/Proshop
GC   Par: 72, USGA: 71.7   **GF:** w/day $52.00, w/end
P.O. Box 774808, 80477   RP: Given with room $52.00
Ph: 303-879-2220   reservation   **Carts:** $14.00

The course is characterized by some great water holes, large greens. Greens are bentgrass while fairways and tees are bluegrass. #10 is a par 5, requiring length and accuracy off the tee to reach the green in two. Lay up shot is generally recommended.

VAIL

Vail GC
1778 Vail Valley Dr.,
81657
Ph: 303-479-2260

Yards: 6282, Holes: 18
Par: 71, USGA: 68.0
RP: 48 hours in
advance

GF: w/day $65.00, w/end
$40.00
Carts: $14.00

The Vail Golf Club is an experience beyond description. The 7,100 yard championship course offers spectacular views of the magnificent Gore Range & is host to the annual Jerry Ford Invitational Golf Tournament.

WESTMINSTER

Hyland Hills GC
9650 N. Sheridan
Blvd., 80030
Ph: 303-428-6526

Yards: 7200, Holes: 18
Par: 72, USGA: 68.7
RP: Required

Restaurant/Bar/Proshop
GF: w/day $14.00
Carts: $16.00

The busiest course in Colorado. A tight hilly course with bent grass and big lakes. #7 is uphill 1st, par 4, downhill shot to a creek. #8 has an island green.

WINTER PARK

Pole Creek GC PC
P.O. Box 3348, 80482
Ph: 303-726-8847

Yards: 6882, Holes: 18
Par: 72, USGA: 69.6
RP: Up to 5 days ahead

Restaurant/Bar
GF: w/day $40.00, w/end
$45.00
Carts: $22.00

Voted best new public course of 1985 by Golf Digest. The flowing Pole Creek comes into play many times as it meanders through the course. Its four lakes, sand, elevated tees and greens makes each hole a unique and different experience.

CONNECTICUT

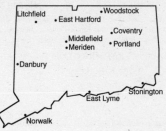

--------------------------BERLIN--------------------------

Timberlin GC
Southington Rd., Rte 364, 06037
Ph: 203-828-3228

Yards: 6342, Holes: 18
Par: 72

Restaurant/Bar
GF: w/day $15.00, w/end $18.00

Deigned by Al Zikorus, the features on this course are very large and tricky greens.

--------------------------COVENTRY--------------------------

Skungamaug River GC
104 Folly La., 06238
Ph: 203-742-9348

Yards: 6034, Holes: 18
Par: 70, USGA: 68.6
RP: One week in advance

Restaurant/Bar/Proshop
GF: w/day $15.00
Carts: $16.00

Very sporty course, not too long, but narrow, heavily wooded fairways and undulating greens make it a challenge for all handicaps. The course is named after the beautiful trout stream that comes into play on four holes.

--------------------------DANBURY--------------------------

Richter Park GC
100 Aunt Hack Rd., 06811
Ph: 203-792-2550

Yards: 6741, Holes: 18
Par: 72, USGA: 71.1
RP: Call the Pro

Restaurant/Bar/Proshop
GF: w/day $43.50, w/end $43.50
Carts: $22.00

13 holes have water. The front 9 has West Lake, back nine has forest of maple, oak, birch and dogwoods. #14 overlooks city with highest elevation. Rated in Top 25 Public GC's by Golf Digest.

--------------------------EAST HARTFORD--------------------------

East Hartford GC
130 Long Hill St., 06108
Ph: 203-528-5082

Yards: 6076, Holes: 18
Par: 71, USGA: 68.6
RP: On weekends & holidays

Restaurant/Bar/Proshop
GF: w/day $14.00, w/end $15.00
Carts: $8.50

"Looks are deceiving". Don't let yardage fool you. Course poses a challenge for everyone from beginner to club champion. One of the most heavily played golf courses in northeast.

---------------------------------EAST LYME---------------------------------

Cedar Ridge GC   Yards: 2959, Holes: 18   Proshop
18 Drabik Rd., 06333   Par: 54   GF: w/day $10.00, w/end
Ph: 203-739-8439 $13.00

The finest par 3 layout in Connecticut with rolling hills and water hazards makes this course a challenge for the serious and a pleasant 2-3 hours for the amateur. Ideal location for travelers and vacationers.

---------------------------------FARMINGTON---------------------------------

Tunxis Plantation   Yards: 6241, Holes: 36
GC   Par: 72
87 Town Farm Rd.,
06032
Ph: 203-677-1367

These two 18-holes courses that were designed by Al Zikorus have island greens and a large lake.

---------------------------------GROTON---------------------------------

Shennecossett GC   Yards: 6142, Holes: 18   Restaurant/Bar
Plant St., 06340   Par: 72   GF: w/day $13.00, w/end
Ph: 203-445-0262 $16.00

A flat course with abundant bunkers that are sure to give you lots of trouble. The designer here was Donald Ross.

---------------------------------HEBRON---------------------------------

Blackledge CC   Yards: 6416, Holes: 18   Restaurant/Bar
180 West St., 06248   Par: 72, USGA: 70.7   GF: w/day $18.00, w/end
Ph: 203-228-0250   RP: 5 to 7 days in $20.00
    advance

A course that makes the best use of its natural setting. Lots of water, lots and lots of trees, and hilly terrain make this an interesting round for everyone.

---------------------------------LITCHFIELD---------------------------------

Stonybrook GC   Yards: 5454, Holes: 9   Restaurant/Bar/Proshop
263 Milton Rd., 06759   Par: 68, USGA: 66.2   GF: w/day $11.00, w/end
Ph: 203-567-9977   RP: Call for starting $15.00
    times   **Carts:** $11.00

Demanding 9 hole course with small, undulating greens and rolling contour mowed fairways. Accuracy off the tee is a must and putting skills are tested.

---------------------------------MERIDEN---------------------------------

Hunter GC   Yards: 6400, Holes: 18   Restaurant/Bar/Proshop
680 Westfield Rd.,   Par: 71, USGA: 71.3   GF: w/day $12.00
06450   RP: Call in advance   **Carts:** $16.00
Ph: 203-634-3366

National Arbor Society recognizes the oak tree on 5th hole as oldest in state of Connecticut. The logo for golf course, also 610 yard par 5 10th hole longest in state of Connecticut. All new renovated in 1987 clubhouse and golf course.

---------------------------------MIDDLEFIELD---------------------------------

Lyman Meadow GC   Yards: 7011, Holes: 18   Restaurant/Bar/Proshop
Route 157, 06455   Par: 72, USGA: 73.5   GF: w/day $18.00, w/end
Ph: 203-349-8055   RP: Required $23.00
    Carts: $20.00

The front nine is more tree lined than the back. The back nine has water on 8 out of the 9 holes. The 12th hole is a great dogleg left par 5 with the gambler trying to cut off as much of the dogleg as possible. There is water on the left and right.

---MONROE---

Whitney Farms GC
175 Shelton Rd., Rte
110, 06468
Ph: 203-268-0707

Yards: 6262, Holes: 18
Par: 72

Restaurant/Bar
GF: w/day $30.00, w/end
$35.00

The large rolling greens are going to be a real test of your putting ability. Of course the fact that the course is hilly might give you a little trouble too.

---NORWALK---

Oak Hills GC
165 Fillow St., 06850
Ph: 203-838-0303

Yards: 6400, Holes: 18
Par: 71, USGA: 68.0
RP: Walk in or 1 week
in advance

Restaurant/Bar/Proshop
GF: w/day $16.00
Carts: $18.00

The first 7 holes are tight and hilly, while the remaining 11 holes appear to be more open and longer. The course in general is aesthetically pleasing and with the wooded area and random trees there's a feeling of being far removed from urban life.

---NORWICH---

Norwich GC
685 New London
Turnpike, 06360
Ph: 203-889-6973

Yards: 5927, Holes: 18
Par: 71

Restaurant/Bar
GF: w/day $15.00, w/end
$18.00

One course that won't give you much trouble with water, but it is very hilly, so you're likely to get a lot of sidehill lies.

---PORTLAND---

Portland GC West
Gospel Ln. (Rt 17),
06480
Ph: 203-342-4043

Yards: 4012, Holes: 18
Par: 60, USGA: 60.4
RP: Only needed for
weekends

Restaurant/Bar/Proshop
GF: w/day $17.50, w/end
$20.00
Carts: $17.00

18 hole par 60. A true test for any type of golfer.

---RIDGEFIELD---

Ridgefield GC
545 Ridgebury Rd.,
P.O. Box 59, 06877
Ph: 203-748-7008

Yards: 5919, Holes: 18
Par: 70, USGA: 68.1

GF: w/day $15.00, w/end
$20.00
Carts: $20.00

A very popular course on the weekends, you'll need a tee time. The front is open with the back nine much more difficult.

---STONINGTON---

Pequot GC
Wheeler Rd., Box
139A, 06378
Ph: 203-535-1898

Yards: 5903, Holes: 18
Par: 70, USGA: 67.2
RP: Tee times on
weekends

Restaurant/Bar/Proshop
GF: w/day $11.00, w/end
$15.00
Carts: $18.00

Pequot's par 70, 18 hole course is laid out over gently rolling terrain in a beautiful Connecticut country setting. A favorite golfing spot for summer visitors as well as year round residents.

DELAWARE

Smyrna

=========================SMYRNA=========================

Garrisons Lake GC
101 Fairways Circle, 19977
Ph: 302-653-6349

Yards: 7028, Holes: 18
Par: 72, USGA: 73.1
RP: Members only Sat & Sun

Restaurant/Bar/Proshop
GF: w/day $15.00, w/end $21.00
Carts: $9.00

The course is a tree lined championship course. Holes 5 and 8 were chosen as 2 of the best holes in Delaware. The back nine has 5 water holes. The course has been chosen by Golf Digest as one of the five best in the state.

=======================WILMINGTON=======================

Delcastle GC
801 Mc Kennans
Church Rd, 19808
Ph: 302-995-1990

Yards: 6335, Holes: 18
Par: 72, USGA: 70.4

Restaurant/Bar
GF: w/day $10.50, w/end $12.50

A course with some fairly difficult par-5s, hope your driver is working well. Otherwise the course is fairly open.

=======================WILMINGTON=======================

Ed Oliver GC
800 Dupont Rd, 19804
Ph: 302-571-9041

Yards: 5800, Holes: 18
Par: 69

Restaurant/Bar
GF: w/day $10.50, w/end $12.50

A short course that will give your irons a real workout. A beautifully maintained public course.

=======================WILMINGTON=======================

Rock Manor GC
202 Concord Pike, PO Box 7078, 19803
Ph: 302-652-4083

Yards: 5437, Holes: 18
Par: 69, USGA: 66.3

GF: w/day $10.50, w/end $12.50

A short course that plays very tough. Lots of trees, with water and very small greens.

=======================WILMINGTON=======================

Three Little Bakers CC
3542 Foxcroft Dr, 19808
Ph: 302-737-1877

Yards: 6165, Holes: 18
Par: 71, USGA: 71.8

GF: w/day $12.00, w/end $15.00

You're going to really challenged on your choice of clubs here. Alot of long holes which can be very challenging.

◄◄◄◄◄◄◄◄◄◄◄◄●►►►►►►►►►►►►►

DIST. OF COLUMBIA

──────WASHINGTON, D.C.──────

East Potomac Park GC
East Potomac Park SW, 20024
Ph: 202-554-7660

Yards: 6250, Holes: 36
Par: 72

Restaurant
GF: w/day $8.00, w/end $10.00

With an 18 hole course and two 9 hole layouts, there's something for everyone here. Close to downtown this course gets lots of play. The courses are open and flat with very few trees, but have a wonderful view of the Capital and monuments.

──────WASHINGTON, D.C.──────

Langston GC
2600 Benning Rd NE, 20002
Ph: 202-397-8638

Yards: 6340, Holes: 18
Par: 72

Restaurant
GF: w/day $9.00, w/end $10.00

This championship course is demanding right from the start with a tee shot over the river. There are plenty of bunkers, and a couple of really though par 4's.

──────WASHINGTON, D.C.──────

Rock Creek Park GC
16th & Rittenhouse Sts NW, 20011
Ph: 202-554-7660

Yards: 4719, Holes: 18
Par: 65

GF: w/day $10.00, w/end $12.00

This is a course that you'll need to use irons from the tee on some holes. Accuracy is important because of the small greens, and uneven ground, definitely hilly.

FLORIDA

──────────────AMELIA ISLAND──────────────

Summer Beach
Resort GC
4700 Amelia Island
Pkwy, 32034
Ph: 904-277-8015

Yards: 6119, Holes: 18
Par: 72, USGA: 69.1

Restaurant/Bar
GF: w/day $33.00, w/end
$39.00

Marshes dominate the front nine, and the back has an abundance of trees and water. Bunkers will offers some difficulty, but the water is the main hazard on this course.

──────────────BOCA RATON──────────────

Camino Del Mar CC
22689 Camino Del Mar
Dr., 33433
Ph: 407-392-7992

Yards: 6609, Holes: 18
Par: 71, USGA: 69.1
RP: Public 2 days in
advance

Proshop
GF: w/day $32.00, w/end
$32.00
Carts: $12.00

Offers the golfer an opportunity to test his/her strength, skill, and ingenuity on 18 holes of varying difficulty and complexity. Some holes are relatively simple, while others (like the 12th) will serve as barometers of one's ability to deal with dogleg.

──────────────BONIFAY──────────────

Dogwood's CC
Rt. 3, Box 954, 32425
Ph: 904-547-9381

Yards: 6583, Holes: 18
Par: 72, USGA: 71.4

Restaurant/Bar/Proshop
GF: w/day $9.00
Carts: $12.00

The Dogwood's is a gently rolling, tight fairways, water comes into play on 6 holes and all greens are well trapped. The Dogwood's is a beautiful setting and country club style. Very challenging well laid out course, the best kept secret in the panhandle.

Subscribe to our free newsletter, "Great Golf Gazette," and hear about the latest special golf vacation values.

─────────────BONITA SPRINGS─────────────

Pelican's Nest
4450 Bay Creek Dr.,
33923
Ph: 813-947-4600

Yards: 6908, Holes: 18
Par: 72, USGA: 70.8
RP: 2 days in advance

Restaurant/Bar/Proshop
GF: w/day $35.00
Carts: $Included

Designed for beauty, bordered by picturesque spring creek with venerable cypress and oak with views of forest. There are also pines, palm, meadow bushes & tropical swamp. #9 a par 5 is challenging with trees as obstacle, long shot into green over canyon.

─────────────BOYNTON BEACH─────────────

Boynton Beach Muni GC
8020 Jog Rd., 33437
Ph: 407-969-2200

Yards: 6032, Holes: 27
Par: 71, USGA: 68.5
RP: Call in advance

Restaurant/Bar/Proshop
GF: w/day $8.00
Carts: $6.00

Surrounded on three sides by major canals, and a farm to the west, this 156 acre 27 hole golf complex provides an isolated spot to play golf and commune with nature. Noted for its rolling terrain, numerous trees, and eight lakes.

─────────────BOYNTON BEACH─────────────

Cypress Creek CC
9400 Military Trail,
33436
Ph: 407-732-4202

Yards: 6369, Holes: 18
Par: 72, USGA: 70.0
RP: Required 24 hours
in advance

Restaurant/Bar/Proshop
GF: w/day $17.00
Carts: $Included

A relatively open golf course with water on 13 holes, not all of which come into play. The small greens have many interesting breaks for some different putting situations. Wide variety of par threes from 120 to 210 yards.

─────────────BROOKSVILLE─────────────

Seville G&CC
18200 Seville
Clubhouse Dr, 34614
Ph: 904-596-7888

Yards: 6163, Holes: 18
Par: 72, USGA: 70.5

GF: w/day $10.00

A course that is built to use the natural terrain to your disadvantage. The scenery on Seville will help to make you forget your troubles, but you'd better keep your eye on where your ball is going.

─────────────CAPE CORAL─────────────

Cape Coral G & RC
4003 Palm Tree Blvd.,
33904
Ph: 813-542-7879

Yards: 6771, Holes: 18
Par: 72, USGA: 69.3
RP: 48 hour
cancellation

Restaurant/Bar/Proshop
GF: w/day $7.00
Carts: $10.50

Features 113 sand traps and has water come into play on nine of the eighteen holes. Number nine, a par 5, is our character hole; the golfer starts out with trees and bunkers to the right and out of bounds to the left coming out of the shoot.

─────────────CAPE CORAL─────────────

Coral Oaks GC
1800 NW 28th Ave,
33909
Ph: 813-283-4100

Yards: 5579, Holes: 18
Par: 72

Restaurant/Bar
GF: w/day $30.00

An Arthur Hills design, there are majestic oaks and lots of palms on this somewhat hilly terrain.

─────────────────── CAPTIVA ───────────────────

South Seas   Yards: 3300, Holes: 9   Restaurant/Bar
Plantation GC   Par: 36   **GF:** w/day $14.00
P.O. Box 194, 33924   RP: 1 day in advance
Ph: 813-472-5111

*The course is flat with a couple of lakes and a pretty stretch of fairway bordering
the beach. This is the site of the annual South Seas Plantation Golf Traditional
Tournament benefiting the Big Brothers/Sisters of Lee County.*

─────────────────── COCOA BEACH ───────────────────

Cocoa Beach GC   Yards: 6600, Holes: 18   Restaurant/Bar/Proshop
Tom Warriner Blvd.,   Par: 72, USGA: 70.7   **GF:** w/day $13.75
POB 320280, 32932   RP: Weekends and   **Carts:** $14.00
Ph: 407-868-3351   holidays

*The front nine plays 1-2 shots easier than the back on this long open course set
by the Banana River. The back nine can be particularly brutal when winds come
up each afternoon. Being only 2 miles from the ocean provides comfortable
weather year round.*

─────────────────── CRESCENT CITY ───────────────────

Live Oak G&CC   Yards: 2800, Holes: 9
SR 309, Star Route 2   Par: 35, USGA: 33.5
Box 452, 32012
Ph: 904-467-2512

Near the St. Johns River.

─────────────────── CRYSTAL RIVER ───────────────────

Plantation Inn & GR   Yards: 6644, Holes: 27   Restaurant/Bar/Proshop
P.O. Box 1116, 32629   Par: 72   **GF:** w/day $25.00
Ph: 904-795-4211

*Home of the Florida Women's Open. Tropical vegetation, many natural lakes
and ponds, and strategically placed traps and bunkers offer a real test of your
game. We also have a marked driving range.*

─────────────────── DAYTONA BEACH ───────────────────

Daytona Beach G &   Yards: 5950, Holes: 18
CC   Par: 72, USGA: 68.6
600 Wilder Blvd.,
32014
Ph: 904-258-3119

*Two 18-hole courses, one has tight fairways that can be quite long, and has two
thirds of the course with water coming into play. The other has water on less
than half the course and has open fairways.*

─────────────────── DAYTONA BEACH ───────────────────

Indigo Lakes GC   Yards: 6176, Holes: 18   Restaurant/Bar/Proshop
312 Indigo Dr., 32120   Par: 72, USGA: 69.4
Ph: 904-254-3607

*Indigo Lakes is the site of the LPGA headquarters and qualifying school. That
will give you some idea of the quality of the course There are tree-lined fairways,
lots of lakes, and almost a hundred strategically placed bunkers.*

──────────────── DAYTONA BEACH ────────────────

Pelican Bay South G&CC
350 Pelican Bay Dr., 32014
Ph: 904-788-6496

Yards: 6100, Holes: 18
Par: 72

Proshop

An island green is featured here, but since 14 holes have water in play that shouldn't come as too big a surprise. The course was designed by Lloyd Clifton.

──────────────── DELAND ────────────────

Southridge GC
800 E Euclid Ave., 32724
Ph: 904-736-0560

Yards: 5855, Holes: 18
Par: 72, USGA: 67.4
RP: 2 days in advance

Bar/Proshop
GF: w/day $11.00
Carts: $18.00

Southridge is an interesting, well maintained, 18 hole course, built on rolling hills with lots of trees. A favorite of many people in Central Florida. People come here year after year. Once you play it, you'll see why.

──────────────── DELRAY BEACH ────────────────

Delray Beach GC
2200 Highland Ave., 33445
Ph: 407-243-7380

Yards: 6201, Holes: 18
Par: 72, USGA: 73.5

An older municipal course that was designed by Donald Ross.

──────────────── DELTONA ────────────────

Deltona Hills G&CC
1120 Elkcam Blvd., 32725
Ph: 904-789-3911

Yards: 6483, Holes: 18
Par: 72, USGA: 72.2

Restaurant/Bar/Proshop

A very hilly course with lots of sidehill lies.

──────────────── DESTIN ────────────────

Sandestin GC
Emerald Coast Pkwy., 32541
Ph: 904-267-8248

Yards: 5565, Holes: 18
Par: 72, USGA: 66.1
RP: Up to 24 hours in advance

Restaurant/Bar/Proshop
GF: w/day $25.00, w/end $39.00
Carts: $21.00

45 beautifully scenic holes—from the Links side course where 15 holes play around and through canals and levy to Baytowne where you can choose between The Dunes, The Harbor and The Troon 9's. Some of the most beautiful in Florida.

──────────────── DESTIN ────────────────

Santa Rosa GC & BC, Inc.
Rt 1, Box 3950, 32459
Ph: 904-267-2229

Yards: 6608, Holes: 18
Par: 72, USGA: 66.1
RP: 3 days in advance

Restaurant/Bar/Proshop
Carts: $20.00

Four sets of tees allow visiting players the opportunity to challenge their own abilities. The golf course plays through a mature seaside forest out to a scenic view of the Gulf of Mexico. Every club will be used in attempt to subdue and enjoy.

────────────────── DUNEDIN ──────────────────

Dunedin CC
1050 Palm Blvd., 34698
Ph: 813-733-7836

Yards: 6245, Holes: 18
Par: 72, USGA: 69.0
RP: Must stay in/live in
Dunedin

Restaurant/Bar/Proshop
GF: w/day $31.30
Carts: $Included

Formerly PGA National Golf Course from 1945 to 1962.

────────────────── ELKTON ──────────────────

St. Johns GC
4900 Cypress Land,
32084
Ph: 904-825-4900

Yards: 6575, Holes: 18
Par: 72

This layout is a long course with wide rolling terrain.

────────────────── FORT LAUDERDALE ──────────────────

**Bonaventure Hotel
GC**
250 Racquet Club Rd.,
33326
Ph: 305-389-3300

Yards: 6557, Holes: 18
Par: 72, USGA: 71.0

Restaurant/Bar
GF: w/day $25.75
Carts: $Included

Plenty of trees, water and bunkers on this course to make true shotmaking very important. The East Course at 7,011 from the blue tees, also give you plenty of opportunities to really cut loose. The 3rd hole of the East Course is a waterfall hole.

────────────────── FORT MYERS ──────────────────

Eastwood GC
4600 Bruce Herd Ln.,
33905
Ph: 813-275-4848

Yards: 6772, Holes: 18
Par: 72, USGA: 70.7
RP: Required—1 day in
advance

Restaurant/Bar/Proshop
GF: w/day $17.50
Carts: $22.05

Secluded park-like setting with no parallel holes. Front 9 short and tight; back is wider. #10 dogleg left par 4, carry water 200 yards, well bunkered gently sloping green.

────────────────── FORT MYERS ──────────────────

Gateway G&CC
11360 Championship
Dr., 33913
Ph: 813-561-1010

Yards: 6204, Holes: 18
Par: 72, USGA: 69.9

Restaurant/Bar/Proshop
GF: w/day $70.00
Carts: $Included

Water on over half the course is only one of the problems at this beautiful course. Large, fast and rolling greens, almost a hundred bunkers and winds will also be a factor in how you score on this round.

────────────────── FORT MYERS ──────────────────

**River's Edge Yacht &
CC**
14700 Portsmouth
Blvd. SW, 33908
Ph: 813-433-4211

Yards: 6896, Holes: 18
Par: 72, USGA: 67.9
RP: Two days in
advance

Proshop
GF: w/day $35.00
Carts: $Included

To warm up, the customer uses our beautiful aqua driving range. Our course is bordered by the beautiful Calooshatchee River in S.W. Fort Myers. Our golf course offers 4 sets of tees to accommodate all level of players.

─────────────────── FORT WALTON BEACH ───────────────────

Fort Walton Beach
Muni GC
Louis Turner Blvd,
P.O. Box 4090, 32549
Ph: 904-862-3314

Yards: 6083, Holes: 18
Par: 72, USGA: 67.7
RP: 2 days in advance

Restaurant/Proshop
GF: w/day $13.00
Carts: $10.00

There are four water holes, the tees are long, the greens large and the wide fairways are bordered by huge pines and live oaks. There are occasional fairway bunkers, but they are not too hard to avoid. The course is heavily played but is well handled.

─────────────────── GULF BREEZE ───────────────────

Tiger Point CC
1255 Country Club Dr.,
32561
Ph: 904-932-1333

Yards: 7033, Holes: 18
Par: 72, USGA: 69.8
RP: 2 days in advance

Restaurant/Bar/Proshop
GF: w/day $40.00
Carts: $18.00

The natural beauty & seaside scenery of the Tiger Point East and West course is a golfer's delight—offering memorable challenges in a picturesque setting. Pine trees and waterways line links type fairways. My favorite hole is the 4th hole on Tiger Point.

─────────────────── HERNANDO ───────────────────

Citrus Hills G & CC
500 E. Hartford St.,
32642
Ph: 904-746-4425

Yards: 6418, Holes: 36
Par: 70, USGA: 66.3
RP: 2 days in advance

Restaurant/Bar/Proshop
GF: w/day $18.00
Carts: $10.00

Citrus Hills offers a bit of New England in sunny Florida. The tree lined fairways traipse across gentle rolling hills. Water and sand bunkers abound aplenty.

─────────────────── HOLLYWOOD-BY-THE-SEA ───────────────────

Diplomat CC
3515 S. Ocean Dr.,
33019
Ph: 305-457-8111

Yards: 6625, Holes: 18
Par: 72, USGA: 70.6

Restaurant/Bar
GF: w/day $15.37
Carts: $Included

The Diplomat is a flat course with plenty of water hazards and bunkers.

─────────────────── HOWEY-IN-THE-HILLS ───────────────────

Mission Inn Golf &
Tennis Resort
10400 CR 48, 34737
Ph: 904-324-3101

Yards: 6770, Holes: 36
Par: 72, USGA: 70.9
RP: 1 week

Restaurant/Bar/Proshop
GF: w/day $50.00, w/end
$50.00
Carts: $Included

Mission Inn's picturesque 18 hole championship golf course boasts 85 foot elevation differences from tee to green, 13 holes with water, Scottish berms, well-placed traps, island greens and tree-lined fairways. New clubhouse.

─────────────────── HUTCHINSON ISLAND ───────────────────

Indian River
Plantation GC
385 NE Plantation Rd.,
33996
Ph: 407-225-3700

Yards: 4042, Holes: 18
Par: 61, USGA: 56.9
RP: 1 day in advance

Restaurant/Bar
GF: w/day $22.00
Carts: $24.00

The River Course, and Plantation Course are both relatively flat (everything is in these parts), have terrific bunkering, undulating greens, ocean breezes, and seem to have water everywhere.

─────────────────────INVERNESS─────────────────────

Point O' Woods GC   Yards: 1836, Holes: 9   Restaurant/Bar/Proshop
Gospel Island Rd.,   Par: 30, USGA: 29.5   **GF:** w/day $8.00
32650   **Carts:** $10.00
Ph: 904-726-3113

Easy walking executive 9 hole course, reasonable rates—friendly atmosphere.

─────────────────────JACKSONVILLE─────────────────────

Mill Cove GC   Yards: 6000, Holes: 18   Restaurant/Bar
1700 Monument Rd,   Par: 71   **GF:** w/day $25.00, w/end
32225 $30.00
Ph: 904-646-4653

*Arnold Palmer designed this course, which opened in 1990. There are wetlands
and lakes, you might want some extra balls just in case.*

─────────────────────JACKSONVILLE─────────────────────

Windsor Parke GC   Yards: 6043, Holes: 18   Restaurant/Bar/Proshop
4747 Hodges Blvd,   Par: 72, USGA: 68.7   **GF:** w/day $42.00, w/end
32224   RP: 3 days in advance $48.00
Ph: 904-223-4653   **Carts:** $Included

*Majestic trees, rolling terrain, water in play on half the holes and marshes make
this about as difficult round of golf as anyone can hope for. Many major tournaments are held here.*

─────────────────────JUPITER─────────────────────

Indian Creek GC   Yards: 6155, Holes: 18
1800 Central Blvd.,   Par: 70
33458
Ph: 407-747-6262

*A nice course for a leisurely game of golf, although there is some water to test
you a bit.*

─────────────────────KEY BISCAYNE─────────────────────

Key Biscayne GC   Yards: 7070, Holes: 18   Restaurant/Bar/Proshop
6700 Crandon Blvd.,   Par: 72, USGA: 71.0   **GF:** w/day $28.00, w/end
33149   RP: 2 days in advance $30.00
Ph: 305-361-9129   **Carts:** $Included

*Only course on an island, it's surrounded by mangrove swamps. On Biscayne
Bay, palm trees, alligators and birds abound. #3 in Golf Magazine in U.S. public
courses.*

─────────────────────KEY WEST─────────────────────

Key West Resort GC   Yards: 5843, Holes: 18   Restaurant/Bar/Proshop
6450 Junior College   Par: 70, USGA: 68.4   **GF:** w/day $18.00
Road, 33040   **Carts:** $9.00
Ph: 305-294-5232

A Rees Jones design, the course has narrow fairways with some water troubles.

─────────────────────KISSIMMEE─────────────────────

Poinciana GC   Yards: 6700, Holes: 18   Restaurant/Bar/Proshop
500 E. Cypress Pkwy.,   Par: 72, USGA: 69.1   **GF:** w/day $25.00
32759   RP: 7 days in advance   **Carts:** $Included
Ph: 407-933-5300

*Poinciana combines water on 13 holes, 69 bunkers and carves it's way through a
cypress forest. The result is one of Florida's top rated and best kept secrets. Hole
#7 is challenging, fun and beautiful. Your tee shot must carry the lake.*

---------------------LAKE BUENA VISTA----------------------

Walt Disney World Inn GC
1 Magnolia Palm Dr, 32830
Ph: 407-824-2288

Yards: 7190, Holes: 54
Par: 72, USGA: 73.9
RP: Resort 30 days else 7 days

Restaurant/Bar/Proshop
GF: w/day $70.00
Carts: $Included

99-holes of golf.

---------------------LAKE PLACID----------------------

Placid Lakes Inn CC
3601 Jefferson Ave., 33852
Ph: 813-465-4333

Yards: 6632, Holes: 18
Par: 72, USGA: 69.9
RP: 1 day in advance

Restaurant/Bar/Proshop
GF: w/day $14.00
Carts: $10.00

Our toughest hole is #18. This long, straightway par four measures 405 yards with water guarding both sides of the landing area. A tough finishing hole which usually plays into the wind.

---------------------LAKELAND----------------------

Big Cypress GC
10000 N. US Hwy 98 N, 33809

Ph: 813-859-6871

Yards: 6075, Holes: 18
Par: 71

This Ron Garl course is a championship layout that annually hosts the Florida Intercollegiate Golf Tournament.

---------------------LAKELAND----------------------

Sandpiper G&CC
6001 Sandpipers Dr., 33801
Ph: 813-859-5461

Yards: 5670, Holes: 18
Par: 70, USGA: 66.9

GF: w/day $10.00, w/end $12.00

You're likely to make the mistake of thinking that this open course with very little water is going to be a snap. Well guess again The sandtraps and very tricky greens are going to make your earn a good score.

---------------------LARGO----------------------

Bardmoor CC
7919 Bradmoor Blvd., 34647
Ph: 813-397-0483

Yards: 6484, Holes: 18
Par: 72, USGA: 70.4

This course is sure to be a true test of your accuracy. Of special importance will be your short game abilities since the greens are small.

---------------------LAUDERHILL----------------------

Inverrary CC
3840 Inverrary Blvd., 33319
Ph: 305-733-7550

Yards: 6621, Holes: 36
Par: 71, USGA: 71.5

Two 18-holes courses that have hosted many LPGA and PGA events. The large greens, tricky bunkering, and water on large portions of both layouts are going to be the most challenging parts of the game.

──────────────LEHIGH──────────────

Lehigh CC
225 East Joel Blvd.,
33936
Ph: 813-369-2121

Yards: 6115, Holes: 18
Par: 72, USGA: 68.8
RP: 24 hours before

Restaurant/Bar/Proshop
GF: w/day $20.00
Carts: $20.00

Number 9 on the North Course is the pro's favorite hole. The hole offers a dogleg right requiring an extremely long tee shot and a pin point accurate second shot onto a well bunkered green. The yardage on #5 at our South Course speaks for itself.

──────────────LONGBOAT KEY──────────────

Longboat Key GC
301 Gulf of Mexico Dr.,
34228
Ph: 813-383-8821

Yards: 6890, Holes: 45
Par: 72, USGA: 74.2
RP: Hotel guest-2-1/2
days advance

Restaurant/Bar
GF: w/day $100.00
Carts: $Included

Islandside, the "watery challenge" is an acknowledged 18-hole test of accuracy with long fairways threaded throughout lakes and lagoons. Harbourside is a longer 27-hole layout. The course is wrapped around Sarasota Bay.

──────────────MELBOURNE──────────────

Palm Gardens GC
2630 Minton Rd.,
32904
Ph: 407-723-3182

Yards: 1600, Holes: 9
Par: 31, USGA: 55.5

Restaurant/Bar/Proshop
GF: w/day $5.42
Carts: $5.19

Palm Gardens is a challenging nine hole executive golf course. It is an attractive course laid out with minimum alterations to the beautiful Florida landscape. Tees and greens are elevated, with water and traps in play often.

──────────────MIAMI──────────────

Doral Hotel GC
4400 NW 87th Ave.,
33178
Ph: 305-592-2000

Yards: 6597, Holes: 99
Par: 72, USGA: 70.4
RP: When you make
hotel reservation

Restaurant/Bar
GF: w/day $72.00, w/end
$72.00
Carts: $Included

The resort offers 99 holes of golf, including a par 3 executive course. The Blue Monster is a watery, sandy long expanse. The 18th hole here has been consistently ranked as one of the toughest on the PGA tour, a par 4 unless you're bunkering it.

──────────────MIAMI──────────────

Fountainbleau CC
9603 Fountainbleau
Blvd., 33172
Ph: 305-221-5181

Yards: 6107, Holes: 18
Par: 72

Two 18-holes courses, the East & West. The East, although the longer course, seems to play shorter than the West. The heavy use of water on the West may make the difference.

──────────────MIAMI──────────────

Kings Bay Resort CC
14401 SW 62nd Ave.,
33158
Ph: 305-235-7161

Yards: 6556, Holes: 18
Par: 73, USGA: 69.1

Restaurant/Bar
GF: w/day $15.00
Carts: $12.00

The rolling fairways, well-trapped greens and water hazards of the front nine contrast beautifully with the bayside back nine where both land and sea blend to provide the ultimate challenge.

─────────────── MIAMI ───────────────

Miami GC
6801 Miami Gardens
Dr., 33015
Ph: 305-826-4700

Yards: 6139, Holes: 54
Par: 72

Restaurant/Bar
GF: w/day $10.00, w/end
$20.00

Three 18-holes course that are all exceptionally well maintained. The West Course is the most difficult of the three, while the South Course is the shorter. There's something for every level of golfer here.

─────────────── MIAMI ───────────────

Miami Lakes GC
7601 NW Miami Lakes
Dr., 33014
Ph: 305-821-1150

Yards: 6512, Holes: 18
Par: 72, USGA: 70.5
RP: 24 hours

Restaurant/Bar
GF: w/day $15.00
Carts: $24.00

Beautiful course in a natural setting with tree lined fairways and wandering lakes. Our favorite is the 427 yard, par 4, 18th hole dogleg left over one of the largest lakes on the course.

─────────────── MIAMI ───────────────

Turnberry Isle CC
19735 Turnbury Way,
33180
Ph: 305-932-6200

Yards: 6985, Holes: 36
Par: 72, USGA: 72.9

Restaurant/Bar
GF: w/day $22.00
Carts: $22.00

Two of Robert Trent Jones' creations provide 36 challenging holes, featuring the largest triple green in the world. The South course has been the site of the Elizabeth Arden Classic, the PGA Senior Championship, and celebrity and private functions.

─────────────── MIAMI BEACH ───────────────

Bayshore GC
2301 Alton Rd., 33139
Ph: 305-532-3350

Yards: 6202, Holes: 18
Par: 72

Lakes come into play on two thirds of the course, and the elevated greens can be challenging too.

─────────────── MIDDLEBURG ───────────────

Ravines Golf & CC
2932 Ravines Rd.,
32068
Ph: 904-282-7800

Yards: 6132, Holes: 18
Par: 72, USGA: 72.2
RP: 2 days in advance

Restaurant/Bar/Proshop
GF: w/day $15.00
Carts: $10.00

Ravines Golf Course is without reservation or close competition the most dramatic natural course in Florida. More than 50 varieties of hardwood trees, rolling terrain, and deep ravines make it similar in character to the highland courses found in NC.

─────────────── NAPLES ───────────────

Lely Flamingo Island GC
8004 Lely Resort Blvd,
33963
Ph: 813-773-2223

Yards: 6527, Holes: 18
Par: 72, USGA: 70.9
RP: 3 days in advance

Restaurant/Bar/Proshop
GF: w/day $90.00
Carts: $Included

A very demanding layout with water in play on all but five holes. The large, well-bunkered greens, large trees, and rolling terrain will make it all the more difficult. Wind can also become a factor here, so be forewarned.

────────────────NAPLES────────────────

Marco Shores CC   Yards: 6368, Holes: 18   Restaurant/Bar
1450 Mainsail Blvd,   Par: 72, USGA: 70.7   **GF:** w/day $25.60
33961
Ph: 813-394-2581

A magical setting in the Everglades. The 120 bunkers here are likely to be a real test of your sand playing abilities if your accuracy is even a little bit off. There's also plenty of water on the course.

────────────────NAPLES────────────────

Naples Beach Hotel   Yards: 6101, Holes: 18   Restaurant/Bar
GC   Par: 72   **GF:** w/day $31.00
851 Gulf Shore Blvd.,
33940
Ph: 813-261-2222

Our golf course is a golfer's delight. Undulating greens, manicured fairways ... a superb layout where doglegs, water and sand combine to challenge every player's skill.

────────────────NAPLES────────────────

Palm River CC   Yards: 6426, Holes: 18   Restaurant/Bar/Proshop
Palm River Blvd.,   Par: 72, USGA: 71.3   **GF:** w/day $14.00
33942   **RP:** 48 hours in   **Carts:** $11.00
Ph: 813-597-3554   advance

One of Naples' oldest golf courses that proves challenging and enjoyable to golfers of all ability levels.

────────────────NAVARRE────────────────

Club at Hidden   Yards: 6266, Holes: 18   Restaurant/Bar
Creek GC   Par: 72, USGA: 70.8   **GF:** w/day $30.00
3070 PGA Blvd, 32566
Ph: 904-939-4604

An championship-caliber course with loads of towering trees and literally acres and acres of sand. The course also has a very high slope rating. This course will be a challenge to your golfing skills.

────────────────NICEVILLE────────────────

Country Club at Blue   Ph: 904-897-3613   Yards: 6888, Holes: 27
Water Bay   Par: 72, USGA: 70.4
P.O. Box 247, 32578   Restaurant/Bar

Golf on any combination of our three championship 9 hole Fazio designed courses is a beautiful, challenging experience. The heavily wooded course is enhanced by water, marsh and rolling terrain. The course is ranked among the top courses in the state.

────────────────NORTH FORT MYERS────────────────

Del Tura CC   Yards: 4102, Holes: 27   Restaurant/Bar/Proshop
18621 N. Tamiami Tr.,   Par: 61, USGA: 59.3   **GF:** w/day $15.00
33903   **RP:** 1 day in advance   **Carts:** $10.00
Ph: 813-731-5400

Don't let the term "executive" steer you clear of this golf course. The course record stands at 6 under par and this is through over 10 professional tournaments. This little tiger is very fair but no pussycat.

─────────────── NORTH FORT MYERS ───────────────

El Rio GC PC
1801 Skyline Dr., 33903
Ph: 813-995-2204

Yards: 2923, Holes: 18
Par: 60, USGA: 52.9
RP: May be made 7
days in advance

Restaurant/Bar/Proshop
GF: w/day $9.00
Carts: $4.50

El Rio is a sporty executive course where shot placement is more important than distance. Sand traps, lakes and trees blend to create a picturesque setting and add a challenging angle to the game.

─────────────── NORTH FORT MYERS ───────────────

Lochmoor CC
3911 Orange Grove
Blvd., 33903
Ph: 813-995-0501

Yards: 6940, Holes: 18
Par: 72, USGA: 70.6
RP: Two days in
advance

Restaurant/Bar/Proshop
GF: w/day $15.00
Carts: $12.00

Hundreds of existing and majestic Pines and Palms dot and shape the fairways and blend naturally with picturesque lakes as if they had been there for many years. Several lakes come directly into play, but are fairly situated.

─────────────── NORTH PALM BEACH ───────────────

**North Palm Beach
CC**
951 US Hwy 1, 33408
Ph: 407-626-4345

Yards: 5769, Holes: 18
Par: 72

There are fantastic views of the Intracoastal Waterway on this layout. The course is hilly and should give you a fairly good challenge.

─────────────── OCALA ───────────────

Golden Ocala GC
7300 US Highway 27,
32675
Ph: 904-662-0198

Yards: 6755, Holes: 18
Par: 72, USGA: 71.7

Proshop
GF: w/day $40.00
Carts: $Included

The course was designed with the intent to have a course that had replicas of the great golf course holes of the world. There are eight replica holes: Three from Augusta, two from St. Andrews, Baltusrol, Royal Troon, and Muirfield.

─────────────── OCALA ───────────────

Pine Oaks GC
2201 NW 21st St, 32675
Ph: 904-622-8558

Yards: 5762, Holes: 27
Par: 72, USGA: 67.5
RP: 2 days in advance

Restaurant/Bar/Proshop
GF: w/day $11.00
Carts: $6.00

The North nine begins with a short but tight par 4. Then opens up to give you a little breathing room. The last four holes are long and narrow with smaller greens. The East nine is very narrow with many large oak trees well placed.

─────────────── ORLANDO ───────────────

Bay Hill GC & Lodge
9000 Bay Hill Blvd.,
32819
Ph: 407-876-2429

Yards: 7114, Holes: 27
Par: 72, USGA: 71.8
RP: Lodge guests &
members only

Restaurant/Bar/Proshop
GF: w/day $100.00, w/end
$100.00
Carts: $12.00

Length is a must with some very demanding approach shots to greens. All eighteen greens were recently redesigned and renovated by Arnold Palmer. We are home to the Nestle Invitational and the 18th hole has been considered one of the toughest holes.

---ORLANDO---

Hunter's Creek
14401 Sports Club
Way, 32821
Ph: 407-240-4653

Yards: 6521, Holes: 18
Par: 72, USGA: 71.0
RP: 3 days in advance

Restaurant/Bar/Proshop
GF: w/day $33.00

Lots of bunkers here, with very tricky greens. A very long course that has water coming into play on every hole. One hole is over 600 yards long and has a double dogleg. A very challenging round of golf.

---ORLANDO---

Marriott's Orlando
World Center
One World Center Dr.,
32821
Ph: 407-239-5659

Yards: 6290, Holes: 18
Par: 71, USGA: 67.9
RP: One week in
advance

Restaurant/Bar/Proshop
GF: w/day $70.00, w/end
$70.00
Carts: $Included

Although this Joe Lee designed course is not long, water and sand make bogies out of errant shots. Our breathtaking hotel is in clear view from every hole. A prevailing wind from the east and elevated greens makes our 18th a difficult par.

---ORLANDO---

Metrowest CC
2100 S Hiawassee Rd,
32811
Ph: 407-299-1099

Yards: 5978, Holes: 18
Par: 72

Restaurant/Bar
GF: w/day $47.00, w/end
$55.00

This course was designed by Robert Trent Jones, Sr., and opened in 1987. Although the long game is the most important on this hilly course, your irons will still be important.

---ORLANDO---

Wedgefield GC CC
20550 Maxim Pkwy.,
32820
Ph: 407-568-2116

Yards: 6738, Holes: 18
Par: 72, USGA: 70.5
RP: 3 days in advance

Restaurant/Bar/Proshop
GF: w/day $21.00, w/end
$28.00

An interesting blend of short and long holes. Short holes placing a premium on accurate shotmaking. A very well manicured layout. The closing holes of Wedgefield are the makers or breakers of champions.

---ORMOND BEACH---

River Bend GL
730 Airport Rd., 32074
Ph: 800-334-8841

Yards: 6347, Holes: 18
Par: 72

A long, but enjoyable game can be had here. There isn't too much to give you difficulties except the length.

---ORMOND BEACH---

Riviera CC
500 Calle Grande Ave.,
32074
Ph: 904-677-2464

Yards: 6000, Holes: 18
Par: 71, USGA: 69.5

Riviera is considered the oldest course in the Ormond Beach area. A layout with wide fairways, it is a very popular tournament course.

─────────────── PALM BEACH ───────────────

Breakers Hotel GC
South County Rd.,
33480
Ph: 305-659-8470

Yards: 7101, Holes: 36
Par: 71, USGA: 70.1
RP: 2 days in advance

Restaurant/Bar
GF: w/day $24.00
Carts: $22.00

The Ocean Course is short with tight fairways and small, elevated greens. #14, a figure "S" hole uphill, has deep bunkers and small elevated green. The Breakers West's re-designed #9 has a distinct dog leg requiring a second water shot.

─────────────── PALM BEACH GARDENS ───────────────

PGA National Golf Club
1000 Ave. of the
Champions, 33418
Ph: 407-627-1800

Yards: 7022, Holes: 90
Par: 72, USGA: 74.4
RP: 1 year designated

Restaurant/Bar
GF: w/day $65.00
Carts: $16.00

There are five championship courses, including Jack Nicklaus redesigned Champion: host to P.G.A. Seniors' Championships, 1987 P.G.A. Championship, and 1983 Ryder Cup Matches. Health & Raquet Club w/ 19 Tennis Courts, Nautilus, Racquetball, Swimming Pools.

─────────────── PALM COAST ───────────────

Matanzas Woods GC
398 Lakeview Blvd.,
32151
Ph: 904-446-6330

Yards: 6514, Holes: 18
Par: 72, USGA: 71.0

Set in a pine forest, Matanzas Woods also features lakes, mounded fairways and large, large greens. The way the course is laid out you'll feel you're the only one playing here. A beautiful, championship course.

─────────────── PALM COAST ───────────────

Pine Lakes GC
400 Pine Lakes Pkwy.,
32037
Ph: 904-445-0852

Yards: 6122, Holes: 18
Par: 72, USGA: 69.7
RP: 6 days in advance

GF: w/day $18.00
Carts: $11.00

A popular course that was designed by Arnold Palmer.

─────────────── PANAMA CITY ───────────────

Majette Dunes G&CC
5304 Majette Tower
Rd., 32405
Ph: 904-769-4740

Yards: 6362, Holes: 18
Par: 72

Restaurant/Bar
GF: w/day $13.00

When you first see this course you're going to think it's easy because of the openness of the front nine, but beware. The back nine has water in play on almost all the holes.

─────────────── PENSACOLA ───────────────

Carriage Hills GC
2355 W. Michigan Ave.,
32506
Ph: 904-944-5497

Yards: 5530, Holes: 18
Par: 72, USGA: 65.3
RP: 2 days in advance

Restaurant/Bar/Proshop
GF: w/day $18.00
Carts: $14.00

Scenic course with creek running the entire length of the course. On several holes you have to make the decision of whether or not to lay up or "go for it". A real test of nerves.

---------------------------PENSACOLA---------------------------

Marcus Pointe GC Yards: 6095, Holes: 18
2500 Oak Pointe Dr, Par: 72
32503
Ph: 904-484-9770

Lots of large elevation changes, with extremely large and tricky greens are going to give you plenty to think about here.

---------------------------PENSACOLA---------------------------

Perdido Bay GC Yards: 7154, Holes: 18 Snack Bar/Bar/Proshop
1 Doug Ford Dr., 32507 Par: 72, USGA: 72.2 **GF:** w/day $34.00
Ph: 904-492-1223 RP: Call the Pro **Carts:** $Included

A challenging course that can give a great deal of difficulty. The scenery is magnificent, but the trees, well-placed bunkers and plenty of water will need all your attention.

---------------------------PLANTATION---------------------------

Jacaranda GC Yards: 6790, Holes: 36 Restaurant/Bar/Proshop
9200 W. Broward Par: 72, USGA: 70.3 **GF:** w/day $60.00, w/end
Blvd., 33324 RP: 7 days in advance— $65.00
Ph: 305-472-5836 resort **Carts:** $Included

Both golf courses are aesthetically appealing, providing a great challenge. Our East Course is open, comparatively speaking, to the West. Narrow fairways and small rolling greens on the West. The East Course stretches 7400 yards and the West 6700 yards.

---------------------------POMPANO BEACH---------------------------

Crystal Lake CC Yards: 6600, Holes: 18 Restaurant/Bar/Proshop
3800 Crystal Lake Dr., Par: 72, USGA: 72.0 **GF:** w/day $11.00, w/end
33064 RP: 2 days in advance $18.00
Ph: 305-943-2902 **Carts:** $12.00

Amen corner holes 4-5-6 are really good tests of golf. #18 on back requires 3 good shots just to reach the green. Plays 590 from back tees.

---------------------------POMPANO BEACH---------------------------

Palm Aire Spa Yards: 6371, Holes: 58 Restaurant/Bar
Resort Par: 72, USGA: 70.1 **GF:** w/day $36.00, w/end
2601 Palm Aire Dr. N., RP: 3 days in advance $36.00
33069 **Carts:** $11.00
Ph: 305-972-3300

This destination Resort has won the "Best of the South" award from Southern Links Magazine, as well as the Mobil Four Star and AAA Four Diamond Awards; it features two challenging 18-Hole Championship Courses—"the Palms" and "the Pines."

---------------------------PONTE VEDRA BEACH---------------------------

Marriott at Sawgrass- Yards: 5761, Holes: 99 Restaurant/Bar
TCP Stadium Par: 72, USGA: 70.6 **GF:** w/day $80.00
P.O. Box 600, 32082 RP: May be made with **Carts:** $15.00
Ph: 904-285-7777 room reservation

There are 99 holes of championship golf, including the famous par 3, 17th floating hole of the PGA TCP Stadium course. The new TPC Valley Course is rated as one of the all-time great courses. There's also Marsh Landing Course, Oceanside Course.

──────────────── PONTE VEDRA BEACH ────────────────

Ponte Vedra Inn -   Yards: 6066, Holes: 18   Restaurant/Bar
Ocean Course   Par: 72, USGA: 68.9   **GF:** w/day $35.00
200 Ponte Vedra Blvd,
32082
Ph: 904-285-1111

*Two 18-holes courses are set at Ponte Vedra, one of which opened to golfers in
1929. The other course has a lagoon on almost every hole. The winds on these
layouts can be a deciding factor at times on how your score will add up.*

──────────────── PORT LABELLE ────────────────

Port La Belle CC   Yards: 6400, Holes: 18
1 Oxbow Dr., 33935   Par: 72, USGA: 70.3
Ph: 813-675-4411

*A river view and majestic, towering oaks are important features on this lovely
course. There's water on all but two holes, and the fairways get more and more
narrow as you go along.*

──────────────── PORT ST. JOE ────────────────

St. Joseph's Bay CC   Yards: 6473, Holes: 18   Restaurant/Bar/Proshop
Route C-30 South, P.O.   Par: 72, USGA: 70.7   **GF:** w/day $12.00
Box 993, 32456   **Carts:** $6.50
Ph: 904-227-1751

*Warm up on our first five holes, then get ready for a challenge. Sixteen ponds
plus natural rough will test your ability. The par 3 twelfth hole is 180 yards plus
with a very narrow fairway. Green guarded by a pond on the right and a dense
woods on left.*

──────────────── PUNTA GORDA ────────────────

Marina GC at Burnt   Yards: 5809, Holes: 18   Restaurant/Bar
Store   Par: 60, USGA: 59.3   **GF:** w/day $10.00
3150 Matecumbe Key   RP: Call for tee times   **Carts:** $7.50
Rd., 33955
Ph: 813-637-1577

*An 18 hole par 60 executive course, it is a flat layout with plenty of water. A
second nine, par 29, was designed by Mark McCumber, also credited with Dunes
Country Club on neighboring Sanibel Island.*

──────────────── RIVERVIEW ────────────────

Summerfield GC   Yards: 5779, Holes: 18   Restaurant/Bar
13050 Summerfield   Par: 71   **GF:** w/day $15.90, w/end
Blvd, 33569 $26.50
Ph: 813-671-3311

A long course that should give you plenty of opportunities with your driver.

──────────────── ROCKLEDGE ────────────────

Turtle Creek GC   Yards: 6709, Holes: 18   Restaurant/Bar/Proshop
1278 Admiralty Blvd.,   Par: 72, USGA: 70.1   **GF:** w/day $37.00, w/end
32955   Slope: 129 $37.00
Ph: 407-632-2520   RP: 7 days in advance   **Carts:** $Included

*Blending the natural beauty of the terrain with the insight of the Arnold Palmer
Golf Management Company, the course features wooded fairways, meandering
creeks and strategic bunkers resulting in a splendid challenge for golfers of all
levels.*

─────────────── ROYAL PALM BEACH ───────────────

Royal Palm Beach CC
900 Royal Palm Beach Blvd., 33411
Ph: 407-798-6430

Yards: 7067, Holes: 18
Par: 72, USGA: 72.5

Restaurant/Bar/Proshop
GF: w/day $18.00
Carts: $Included

Old style Florida course featuring wide fairways bordered by impressive banyan trees. Well trapped with a moderate number of water hazards. Large, easily-accessible greens. Very fair for the average golfer using the white tees and an excellent challenge.

─────────────── SARASOTA ───────────────

Bobby Jones Golf Complex
1000 Azinger Way, 34232
Ph: 813-955-8041

Yards: 6468, Holes: 45
Par: 72, USGA: 69.2
RP: 3 days advance
(365-GOLF)

Restaurant/Bar/Proshop
GF: w/day $9.00
Carts: $9.00

This fine municipal facility was opened by Bobby Jones playing the inaugural match in 1927. Since that time many golf immortals such as Tommy Armour, Gene Saragen, Walter Hogen, Helen Hicks and Patty Berg have frequented the course.

─────────────── SARASOTA ───────────────

Foxfire GC
7200 Proctor Rd., 34241
Ph: 813-921-7757

Yards: 6000, Holes: 27
Par: 72, USGA: 69.1
RP: 2 days in advance

Restaurant/Proshop

Pretty course out in country. Pine 9—lots of trees, small well trapped greens. Pine 9—fairly open, links style, a bit longer than other 2 nines. Oak 9—pretty narrow, lots of trees, a bit of water, small, well trapped greens.

─────────────── SEBRING ───────────────

Harder Hall GC
3600 Golfview Dr., 33872
Ph: 813-382-0500

Yards: 6300, Holes: 18
Par: 72, USGA: 68.8
RP: 1 day in advance

Restaurant/Bar/Proshop
GF: w/day $6.00, w/end $6.00
Carts: $10.00

A charming course with character of the 50's. Carved in a southern slash pine forest, the course is especially a favorite with senior players, as it is very forgiving.

─────────────── SEBRING ───────────────

Spring Lake Golf & Tennis Resort
100 Clubhouse Lane, 33870
Ph: 813-665-0101

Yards: 6600, Holes: 18
Par: 72, USGA: 69.5
RP: Public 48 hours in advance

Restaurant/Bar/Proshop
GF: w/day $14.00
Carts: $16.00

Florida golfing at its classic best—come play and enjoy a game on a course designed by Bob Solomon. Nearby is Spring Lake Villas Hotel.

─────────────── SEBRING ───────────────

Sun 'n Lake G&CC
4101 Sun 'n Lake Blvd., 33872
Ph: 813-385-4830

Yards: 6430, Holes: 18
Par: 72, USGA: 72.2

Restaurant/Bar/Proshop

A course with wide fairways that are lined with mature trees. There are many lakes here that should makes this a difficult and memorable round of golf.

──────────────SEBRING──────────────

Sun'n Lake GC
4101 Sun 'n Lake Blvd.,
33872
Ph: 813-385-4830

Yards: 7024, Holes: 18
Par: 72, USGA: 72.1
RP: At time of room
reservation

Restaurant/Bar/Proshop
GF: w/day $10.00
Carts: $13.00

*Long, with very tough rough. Holes 6 through 12 are very demanding and 18 is
one of the longest par 5 holes in Central Florida.*

──────────────SEVEN SPRINGS──────────────

Seven Springs CC
7000 Country Club
Blvd., 33553
Ph: 813-376-0035

Yards: 6500, Holes: 18
Par: 72, USGA: 69.2
RP: Semi-private May-
Dec, Call

Restaurant/Bar/Proshop
GF: w/day $25.00
Carts: $12.50

*The courses place a premium on shot placement. Water comes into play on 16
of 18 holes on the championship course. The front nine offers opportunities for
the long hitter but the back is tight and tricky.*

──────────────SHALIMAR──────────────

Shalimar Pointe GC
2 Country Club Rd.,
P.O. Box 5, 32579
Ph: 904-651-1416

Yards: 6313, Holes: 18
Par: 72, USGA: 69.9

Bar/Proshop

*A course set along Choctawhatchee Bay, water comes into play quite often here.
Lots of sand is also strategically placed around the course. A layout that will test
you.*

──────────────SPRING HILL──────────────

Quail Ridge G&CC
1600 Shady Hills Rd.,
34610
Ph: 813-856-6064

Yards: 5600, Holes: 18
Par: 70, USGA: 69.0
RP: 2 days in advance

Restaurant/Bar/Proshop
Carts: $24.00

*Opens up with straightway par 4 in preparation for interesting double dogleg par
five with water down left side of fairway to just left of green. Second shot
requires pinpoint accuracy and correct club selection.*

──────────────ST. AUGUSTINE──────────────

Ponce De Leon GC
4000 US 1 North, P.O.
Box 98, 32085
Ph: 904-829-5314

Yards: 6698, Holes: 18
Par: 71, USGA: 69.3

Restaurant/Bar
GF: w/day $22.00
Carts: $10.00

*A Scottish link course. Very windy on certain fairways, marshlands do come into
play. The 14th hole, the "cyclops" named for the one eyed monster, with four sets
of tees offers all levels of golfers a challenge yet is a "playable" hole.*

──────────────ST. PETERSBURG──────────────

Mangrove Bay GC
875 - 62nd Ave. N.E.,
33702
Ph: 813-893-7800

Yards: 6113, Holes: 18
Par: 72, USGA: 68.4
RP: 7 days in advance
by Phone

Snack Bar/Proshop
GF: w/day $18.00, w/end
$18.00
Carts: $20.00

*One of the Top 50 Municipal golf courses in the United States, Golf Digest 1981.
Tee time phone: 813-893-7797.*

──────────STUART──────────

Golden Marsh at   Yards: 6785, Holes: 18   Restaurant/Bar
Harbour Ridge   Par: 72
P.O. Box 2451, 33495
Ph: 407-336-1800

*Every hole at Golden Marsh offers spectacular views of the lush surroundings.
From atop the elevated tees you look out on expanses of magnolia, myrtle,
fresh-water lakes and pine, to say nothing of the manicured fairways and speedy
putting greens.*

──────────SUN CITY CENTER──────────

Sun City Center GC   Yards: 6600, Holes: 90   Restaurant/Bar/Proshop
South Pebble Beach   Par: 72, USGA: 70.0   **GF:** w/day $20.00, w/end
Dr., 33573   RP: Resident of Sun $22.00
Ph: 813-634-3377   City only   **Carts:** $10.00

*Approximately one-third of Sun City Center's residents are active golfers, taking
daily advantage of the 108 holes of play available in the community. The golf
courses available to Sun City Center residents only.*

──────────SUNNY HILLS──────────

Sunny Hills CC   Yards: 6888, Holes: 18   Restaurant/Bar/Proshop
1150 Country Club   Par: 72, USGA: 70.3   **GF:** w/day $7.00
Blvd., 32428   RP: 2 days in advance   **Carts:** $12.00
Ph: 904-773-3619

*Sunny Hills has a slightly rolling terrain with wide, well maintained fairways.
Greens are Bermuda in summer and rye in winter. The course is well trapped
but has only one hole with water. A good challenge for expert and beginner
alike.*

──────────TALLAHASSEE──────────

Hilaman Park GC   Yards: 6364, Holes: 18   Restaurant/Bar/Proshop
2737 Blairstone Rd.,   Par: 72, USGA: 68.5   **GF:** w/day $7.80
32301   RP: Weekends one   **Carts:** $6.60
Ph: 904-878-5830   week in advance

*Although the course is short, it requires accuracy due to some tight fairways. The
entire back 9 can be seen from the 18th green.*

──────────TALLAHASSEE──────────

Killfarn Inn and CC   Yards: 6412, Holes: 27   **GF:** w/day $25.00, w/end
100 Tyron Circle,   Par: 72, USGA: 71.1 $30.00
32308   RP: Inn guests only or   **Carts:** $20.00
Ph: 904-893-2144   with member

*This 27-hole championship golf course in Tallahassee, Florida, is the home of
the PGA Central Classic. The fairways are lined with beautiful, mature trees, and
add to the beauty as well as the hazards.*

──────────TAMARAC──────────

Colony West CC   Yards: 7271, Holes: 18   Restaurant/Bar/Proshop
6800 NW 88th Ave.,   Par: 71, USGA: 71.8   **GF:** w/day $22.00, w/end
33321   RP: 3 days in advance $27.00
Ph: 305-726-8430   **Carts:** $15.00

*The course is level with fast greens. There are trees on every hill and 14 holes
have water. #12, a 452 yard par 4, is in a cypress forest. 2nd rated in Florida.*

─────────────────────TARPON SPRINGS─────────────────────

Tarpon Springs GC
PC
1310 S. Pinellas Ave.,
33590
Ph: 813-937-6906

Yards: 6211, Holes: 18
Par: 72

This course was opened in 1908, and has been in continuous play ever since. Beautiful old trees set on rolling terrain. There isn't a lot of water here.

─────────────────────TAVERES─────────────────────

Village Green GC
Shirley Shores Rd.,
POB 1226, 32778
Ph: 904-343-7770

Yards: 2620, Holes: 18
Par: 56

Proshop
GF: w/day $7.00
Carts: $1.00

A very challenging executive, easy to walk course available to the public all day, every day. Family owned and operated, impeccably maintained. Back nine overlooks beautiful lake. Quiet location out in the country.

─────────────────────TITUSVILLE─────────────────────

Royal Oak GC
2150 Country Club Dr.,
32780
Ph: 407-269-4500

Yards: 6709, Holes: 18
Par: 71, USGA: 70.1
RP: 24 hours in
advance

Restaurant/Bar/Proshop
GF: w/day $11.00, w/end
$11.00
Carts: $10.00

Owned and operated by the Canadian P.G.A., our beautiful 18 hole championship course is carved from rolling terrain, sprinkled with crystal clear lakes which provide a lot of water hazards and is considered a challenging test for all levels of ability.

─────────────────────VALRICO─────────────────────

Bloomingdale
Golfers Club
1802 Nature's Way
Blvd., 33594
Ph: 813-685-4105

Yards: 7165, Holes: 18
Par: 72, USGA: 70.2
RP: 9 days in advance

Restaurant/Bar/Proshop
GF: w/day $50.00
Carts: $Included

Our Golfers Only Club plays thru a setting of 100 year old oaks, towering pines, a marsh preserve and shimmering ponds. At the Golfers Club those around you, whether hacks, scratch golfers or visiting tour pros share your love of the game.

─────────────────────VENICE─────────────────────

Lake Venice GC
Harbor Dr. (P.O. Box
1385), 34285
Ph: 813-488-3948

Yards: 6862, Holes: 18
Par: 72, USGA: 70.7

Restaurant/Proshop
GF: w/day $15.00
Carts: $15.00

4 of the most difficult finishing holes.

─────────────────────VERO BEACH─────────────────────

Sandridge GC
5300 73rd St, 32967
Ph: 407-770-5000

Yards: 6100, Holes: 18
Par: 72

GF: w/day $16.50

Two 18-hole courses designed by Ron Garl. One third of the holes are located on a sand ridge. You should have a very interesting time here.

---------------------------------- VERO BEACH ----------------------------------

Vista Royale GC
100 Vista Royale Blvd.,
32962
Ph: 407-562-8110

Yards: 3000, Holes: 9
Par: 35, USGA: 33.4
RP: 2 days in advance

Restaurant/Bar/Proshop
GF: w/day $17.00
Carts: $16.00

A challenging par 70 golf course featuring the preservation of the flora of the property.

---------------------------------- W. PALM BEACH ----------------------------------

Boca Raton Hotel GC
501 El Camino Real,
33432
Ph: 407-395-3000

Yards: 6154, Holes: 36
Par: 71

Two 18-hole championship courses, this layout is host to the annual Chrysler National Long Drive Contest. The course is in the main flat and has an island green. There isn't too much water.

---------------------------------- W. PALM BEACH ----------------------------------

Palm Beach Lakes GC
1100 N. Congress Ave.,
33409
Ph: 407-683-2701

Yards: 5187, Holes: 18
Par: 70, USGA: 62.9

GF: w/day $9.00, w/end $12.00

Lots of water on this one. Narrow fairways too.

---------------------------------- W. PALM BEACH ----------------------------------

Palm Beach Polo & CC
13198 Forest Hill Blvd.,
33414
Ph: 407-798-7401

Yards: 5516, Holes: 45
Par: 72, USGA: 73.4
RP: Required 2 days in advance

Restaurant/Bar
GF: w/day $50.00
Carts: $Included

A championship course that has hosted the PGA's Chrysler Team Championship. Wide rolling fairways, with a wide variance in the size of the greens. Water on all but four holes will also add a little more fun to your round.

---------------------------------- WESLEY CHAPEL ----------------------------------

Saddlebrook GC
5700 Saddlebrook
Way, 33543
Ph: 813-973-1111

Yards: 6603, Holes: 18
Par: 70, USGA: 69.3
RP: 1 week in advance

Restaurant/Bar
GF: w/day $72.00, w/end $72.00
Carts: $18.00

The Saddlebrook Course features water on 13 holes, the greens are large, with open approaches and more than enough pine and cypress trees. The Palmer Course, completed in 1985, has undulating terrain; level lies are a rarity.

---------------------------------- WEST PALM BEACH ----------------------------------

Emerald Dunes GC
2100 Emerald Dunes
Dr, 33411
Ph: 407-687-1700

Yards: 6120, Holes: 18
Par: 72, USGA: 69.7

Restaurant/Bar
GF: w/day $32.50

This course is a truly unique experience in this essentially flat Florida location. The design artistry makes the course appear much more forbidding than it really is. A perfect layout for an enjoyable walk.

―――――――――― WEST PALM BEACH ――――――――――

West Palm Beach GC
7001 Parker Ave.,
33405
Ph: 305-582-2019

Yards: 6789, Holes: 18
Par: 72, USGA: 71.2
RP: Lottery system

Restaurant/Bar/Proshop
GF: w/day $25.00
Carts: $9.00

Mature flora, rolling terrain, large trees, dunes, wind, doglegs and well-placed bunkers are some of the problems you'll run into here. The 18th hole is a real monster, running 555 yards right into the wind with a well-trapped green.

―――――――――― WINTER HAVEN ――――――――――

Willowbrook GC
4200 Hwy. 544 N,
33881
Ph: 813-299-7889

Yards: 6328, Holes: 18
Par: 72
RP: 6 days in advance

Restaurant/Bar/Proshop
GF: w/day $9.00
Carts: $7.98

Willowbrook Golf Course is one of the finest municipal courses in central Florida. The course is challenging yet very playable, plenty of trees and water Our most challenging and rewarding hole is our par 5 #17, water comes into play with every shot.

―――――――――― WINTER SPRINGS ――――――――――

Winter Springs GC
900 State Rd. 434,
32708
Ph: 407-699-1833

Yards: 6551, Holes: 18
Par: 71, USGA: 70.4
RP: 2 days in advance

Restaurant/Bar/Proshop
GF: w/day $19.00, w/end
$23.00
Carts: $18.00

Course meanders through a scenic nature preserve featuring sparkling lakes and 2500-year-old cypress trees. You will face a challenging mixture of tree-lined fairways, such as the 583-yard sixth, and shots over and around water at Devil's Elbow.

―――――――――― ZEPHYRHILLS ――――――――――

Valle Oaks GC PC
6716 Old Wire Rd.,
34248
Ph: 813-788-4112

Yards: 5500, Holes: 18
Par: 70, USGA: 68.0
RP: 1 day in advance

Bar/Proshop
GF: w/day $9.54
Carts: $9.54

Open, rolling front 9 with minor hazards. Back 9 tight through giant live oaks with water on 5 holes. #10 #1 hole with water, trees and out of bounds. Great hole.

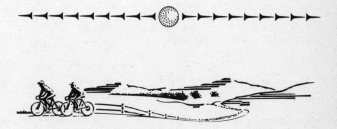

GEORGIA

---------------------------- ACWORTH ----------------------------

Centennial GC
5225 Woodstock Rd.,
30101
Ph: 404-974-8313

Yards: 6853, Holes: 18
Par: 72

Restaurant/Bar/Proshop
GF: w/day $21.00, w/end
$31.00
Carts: $11.50

One of the finest championship public courses in the South. From the back tees, the course is over 7,000 yards long. By the time you reach the 440 yard, par 4, 13th hole, you had better have your game in shape. #18 is a 450 yard, par 4.

---------------------------- AMERICUS ----------------------------

Brickyard Plantation GC
Hwy 280 E Rt 4, Box 360, 31709
Ph: 912-874-1234

Yards: 6114, Holes: 27
Par: 72, USGA: 69.1

Restaurant/Bar/Proshop
GF: w/day $12.00
Carts: $12.00

An intimidating par 3 is number 5. It is 205 yards all across water. The water is a large 8 acre lake and when the winds blow, especially in your face, this par 3 plays like 250 yards with no escape.

---------------------------- ATLANTA ----------------------------

Browns Mill GC
483 Cleveland Ave.,
30354
Ph: 404-366-3573

Yards: 6300, Holes: 18
Par: 72, USGA: 69.8

Proshop
GF: w/day $10.60, w/end
$12.72

A very accessible course as it is located in the middle of Atlanta.

---------------------------- ATLANTA ----------------------------

North Fulton GC
2115 W Wieuca Rd.,
30342
Ph: 404-255-0723

Yards: 6301, Holes: 18
Par: 71, USGA: 69.8

GF: w/day $14.00, w/end
$16.00
Carts: $19.08

This layout is unusually long for a municipal course.

─────────────────── AUGUSTA ───────────────────

Forest Hills GC   Yards: 6450, Holes: 18   Restaurant/Bar
1500 Comfort Rd,   Par: 72   **GF:** w/day $12.00, w/end
30909 $20.00
Ph: 706-736-8431

Located in the midst of Augusta, this is an easy course to get to. There's a little water, but length will be your biggest problem.

─────────────────── BLAIRSVILLE ───────────────────

Butternut Creek GC   Yards: 5862, Holes: 9   Proshop
P.O. Box 771, 30512   Par: 72, USGA: 67.8   **GF:** w/day $7.00, w/end
Ph: 404-745-4744 $8.00
                                                       Carts: $5.50

The 1st tee looks out on a panoramic view of the Tuylog Mountains. It is an easy par 4 if you can negotiate Butternut Creek, downhill and about a 180 yard carry. Water comes into play on 16 holes. The course is quite short if you can hit it straight.

─────────────────── BRASELTON ───────────────────

Chateau Elan GC   Yards: 7030, Holes: 18   Restaurant/Bar/Proshop
6060 Golf Club Dr.,   Par: 71, USGA: 73.5   **GF:** w/day $40.00, w/end
30517   RP: 3 days in advance $45.00
Ph: 800-233-9463   **Carts:** $15.00

The Chateau Elan Golf Club is a regional site for the Golf Digest Instructional Schools and has been nominated as the "Best New Public Course" for 1990 by Golf Digest. The course has two creeks, three lakes and 87 well placed bunkers.

─────────────────── CEDARTOWN ───────────────────

Cedar Valley CC   Yards: 6006, Holes: 9   Restaurant/Proshop
Hiway 27 South, 30125   Par: 72, USGA: 68.5   **GF:** w/day $5.00, w/end
Ph: 404-748-9671   RP: Call $7.00
                                                       Carts: $7.00

The #9 hole is a par 5. The green sits on a hill overlooking the fairway, the clubhouse has a view of the entire hole. Cedar Valley is in a valley of cedars. The course is really Cedar Valley.

─────────────────── CEDARTOWN ───────────────────

Meadow Lakes GC   Yards: 5987, Holes: 18   Restaurant/Proshop
Adams Rd, 30161   Par: 72, USGA: 69.4   **GF:** w/day $15.00
Ph: 404-748-4942   RP: Weekends only   **Carts:** $16.00

Meadow Lakes has twelve lakes and a winding creek, all of which comes into play on ten holes. Also has large, very undulated greens which may be the best putting surface in this area. Course is short enough to gamble, but tight enough for gambling.

─────────────────── CHATSWORTH ───────────────────

Magnolia Ridge GC   Yards: 6213, Holes: 18   Restaurant/Bar/Proshop
Route 6, Box 6181,   Par: 71, USGA: 69.8   **GF:** w/day $12.00, w/end
30705   RP: Call for weekend $17.00
Ph: 404-695-9300   times   **Carts:** $8.00

The course is located on 170 acres with lakes and mountains forming a picturesque backdrop. The 18-hole championship course covers 6213 yards and is a par 71. It has 5 lakes and lots of Georgia pines. A full view of the Blue Ridge Mountains.

---------------------------------CLEVELAND--------------------------------

Skitt Mountain GC   Yards: 6020, Holes: 18   Restaurant/Proshop
Route 2, Box 2131,   Par: 70, USGA: 67.4   **GF:** w/day $9.00, w/end
30528   RP: Weekends & $12.00
Ph: 404-865-2277   holidays   **Carts:** $14.00

*This beautifully maintained golf course is surrounded by mountains and running
streams. You can find delight in any season, but particularly our fall season
where you are tempted by the changing leaves. Also tempting, is the 17th hole,
long par 4.*

---------------------------------COLBERT--------------------------------

Whispering Pines   Yards: 6338, Holes: 18   Restaurant/Proshop
P.O. Box 315, 30628   Par: 72, USGA: 68.4   **GF:** w/day $9.25, w/end
Ph: 706-788-2720 $12.00

*A course set in hilly terrain, this course is a very scenic one. The majestic trees
will also add something to the challenge.*

---------------------------------COLUMBUS--------------------------------

Bull Creek GC   Yards: 6840, Holes: 36   Restaurant/Proshop
7333 Lynch, 31802   Par: 72, USGA: 71.3   **GF:** w/day $10.00, w/end
Ph: 706-561-1614   RP: Weekends & $12.00
                               holidays   **Carts:** $16.00

A scenic course with duck ponds, new red nine. Landscaping and upkeep great.

---------------------------------COMMERCE--------------------------------

Deer Trail CC   Yards: 6380, Holes: 9   Proshop
Hwy 15, 30529   Par: 72, USGA: 69.1   **GF:** w/day $8.50
Ph: 404-335-3987   RP: On weekends   **Carts:** $6.50

Our best hole is #9 425 yards uphill.

---------------------------------DOUGLASVILLE--------------------------------

West Pines GC   Yards: 6300, Holes: 18   Restaurant/Bar/Proshop
6606 Selman Dr., 30134   Par: 71, USGA: 69.4   **GF:** w/day $12.00, w/end
Ph: 404-949-7428   RP: Weekends $18.00
                                                          Carts: $7.00

*A scenic, hilly and sporty layout. Located one mile off Interstate 20, fifteen
minutes west of downtown Atlanta.*

---------------------------------EVANS--------------------------------

Jones Creek GC   Yards: 7008, Holes: 18   Restaurant/Bar/Proshop
4101 Hammonds Ferry,   Par: 72, USGA: 73.8   **GF:** w/day $30.00, w/end
30809 $40.00
Ph: 404-860-4228   **Carts:** $Included

*This course features large, rolling greens in a wooded setting. Some plays over
water on the front nine, but there's still lots more water on the back nine. A
beautifully maintained, championship layout. Well worth your time.*

---------------------------------FARGO--------------------------------

Fargo Recreation   Yards: 6300, Holes: 9   **GF:** w/day $10.00
Center   Par: 73, USGA: 69.8   **Carts:** $8.00
P.O. Box 218, Highway
441, 31631
Ph: 912-637-5218

*Course is located on banks of the Sawannee River and edge of the Okefenokee
Swamp. Camp Stephen Foster (Fargo entrance to Okefenokee) is nearby with
full camping facilities.*

──────────────── FLOWERY BRANCH ────────────────

Royal Lakes CC
4700 Royal Lakes Dr.,
30501
Ph: 404-382-3999

Yards: 6327, Holes: 18
Par: 72

Ranked as one of the top public courses in Georgia, you know this will be a championship-caliber course.

──────────────── GREENSBORO ────────────────

Port Armor Club-
Private
One Port Armor Dr.,
30642
Ph: 404-453-4561

Yards: 6924, Holes: 18
Par: 72, USGA: 73.6
RP: Guest of member,
or stay at Inn

Restaurant/Bar/Proshop
GF: w/day $35.00
Carts: $10.00

A redesign by Bob Cupp has lots of grassy mounds, sand, and water on at least half of the holes. Some elevated greens.

──────────────── HELEN ────────────────

Innsbruck Golf Club
of Helen
P.O. Box 580, 30545
Ph: 404-878-2100

Yards: 6220, Holes: 18
Par: 72, USGA: 70.0

Restaurant/Bar/Proshop
GF: w/day $35.00, w/end
$40.00
Carts: $Included

A mountain course built for playability—spectacular views. 150 foot drop par three is a challenge for the professional and fun for everyone. Rated 16th best in Georgia (Golf Digest).

──────────────── JEKYLL ISLAND ────────────────

Jekyll Island GC
Capt. Wylly Rd., 31520
Ph: 912-635-2368

Yards: 6596, Holes: 18
Par: 72, USGA: 69.3
RP: Call in advance

Restaurant/Bar/Proshop
GF: w/day $26.00
Carts: $26.00

Jekyll Island is Georgia's largest and leading public golf resort. Four courses with 63 holes have all the challenges you could want as you play along rolling fairways among stately oaks and pines. Winds from the Atlantic provide an extra challenge.

──────────────── JONESBORO ────────────────

Pebble Creek GC
9350 Thomas Rd.,
30246
Ph: 404-471-5455

Yards: 5815, Holes: 18
Par: 70, USGA: 65.7

Restaurant
GF: w/day $10.00, w/end
$15.00

A nicely treed course that has plenty of creeks to keep your attention. But you're in luck on one score, there's very little of it here.

──────────────── LAKE LANIER ISLAND ────────────────

Stouffer Pine Isle
Resort
Holiday Rd., 30518
Ph: 404-945-8921

Yards: 6003, Holes: 18
Par: 72, USGA: 69.8
RP: Non-hotel guest - 7
days

Restaurant/Bar
GF: w/day $32.00
Carts: $12.50

This course is very tight, with 8 holes calling for drives across sections of Lake Lanier. Hilly, rolling and pine-scented, with elevated tees. #5 is similar in design to Pebble Beach's 18th—a long drive over water.

─────────────── LAKE LANIER ISLANDS ───────────────

Lake Lanier Islands Hotel & GC
7000 Holiday Rd.,
30518
Ph: 404-945-8787

Yards: 6254, Holes: 18
Par: 72
RP: 1 week in advance

Restaurant/Bar/Proshop
GF: w/day $24.00
Carts: $10.00

Thirteen holes are on the banks of Lake Lanier. There are 85 bunkers. There are bent grass greens and no parallel fairways. You are challenged as a golfer, while you are tantalized by the views, the trees, and the rolling fairways.

─────────────── LAKE PARK ───────────────

Francis Lake Golf & CC
340 Golf Dr. South,
31636
Ph: 912-559-7961

Yards: 6200, Holes: 18
Par: 72, USGA: 67.5
RP: First come, first
served

Restaurant/Bar/Proshop
GF: w/day $8.00, w/end
$11.00
Carts: $12.00

Stay and play and shop.

─────────────── LITHONIA ───────────────

Metropolitan GC TC
3000 Fairington Pkwy.,
30038
Ph: 404-981-5325

Yards: 6930, Holes: 18
Par: 72, USGA: 70.5
RP: 2 days in advance

Restaurant/Bar/Proshop
GF: w/day $20.00, w/end
$30.00
Carts: $11.00

The Metropolitan Club has a championship golf course, which requires length off the tee and accuracy. It is a fair course which is enjoyable for all levels of players and is maintained in championship condition throughout the year.

─────────────── LITHONIA ───────────────

Mystery Valley Golf Association
6094 Shadow Rock Dr.,
30058
Ph: 404-469-6913

Yards: 6329, Holes: 18
Par: 72, USGA: 69.0

Restaurant
GF: w/day $16.00, w/end
$19.00

A pleasant round of golf located near Stone Mountain. You should enjoy this course.

─────────────── MILLEDGEVILLE ───────────────

Little Fishing Creek GC
Hwy 22 West, P.O. Box
607, 31061
Ph: 912-452-9072

Yards: 6650, Holes: 18
Par: 72, USGA: 71.1

Proshop
GF: w/day $6.00, w/end
$8.00
Carts: $13.00

My favorite hole is the 18th, a relatively short par 5 where accuracy is a must. Out of bounds lines the right side of the fairway from the tee, while a lake borders the left edge of your landing area. A deep bunker guards the front of the green.

─────────────── PINE MOUNTAIN ───────────────

Callaway Gardens GC
U.S. Highway 27, 31822
Ph: 404-663-2281

Yards: 6605, Holes: 18
Par: 72, USGA: 71.4
RP: Required

Restaurant/Bar
GF: w/day $26.00
Carts: $24.00

63-holes of golf are offered here.

─────────────────SAVANNAH─────────────────

Hunter GC-Military
Hunter Army Airfield,
31409
Ph: 912-925-5622

Yards: 6866, Holes: 18
Par: 72, USGA: 72.1
RP: 3 days in advance,
military

Proshop
GF: w/day $10.00, w/end
$15.00
Carts: $12.00

An excellent front nine with heavy trees and water on 5 holes. Picturesque and challenging even to top players. Second nine will compliment in kind. Considered one of the best layouts in the area; but limited to who can play. Military and their guests.

─────────────────SAVANNAH─────────────────

**Sheraton Savannah
Resort & GC**
612 Wilmington Island
Rd., 31410
Ph: 912-897-1612

Yards: 7000, Holes: 18
Par: 72, USGA: 70.3
RP: Strongly
recommended

Restaurant/Bar/Proshop
GF: w/day $28.00
Carts: $10.00

Four artificial lakes, a winding stream, live oaks, pine trees, and palm trees add to the scenic beauty of this exceptional island course. The course provides a very fine, fair test of golf; not overly difficult, but a real challenge. Contoured fairways.

─────────────────SAVANNAH─────────────────

Southbridge GC
415 Southbridge Bvld.,
31405
Ph: 912-651-5455

Yards: 6990, Holes: 18
Par: 72, USGA: 73.3
RP: Required

Restaurant/Bar/Proshop
GF: w/day $17.00, w/end
$23.00
Carts: $10.00

The golf course is extremely well trapped off the tee as well as near the greens. Each hole is like a private hole all to yourself. You don't see other golfers because of all the Georgia pines that cover both sides of the fairways.

─────────────────ST. MARY'S─────────────────

Osprey Cove GC
P.O. Box 878, 31558
Ph: 912-882-5555

Yards: 6791, Holes: 18
Par: 72, USGA: 72.8
RP: 1 week in advance

Restaurant/Bar/Proshop
GF: w/day $26.00, w/end
$31.00
Carts: $12.00

A wooded setting, with salt marshes, sloping fairways, rolling and tricky greens. The greens here are well bunkered, so you'll need to be on top of your short game to score well.

─────────────────ST. SIMON ISLAND─────────────────

Sea Island GC
100 Retreat Ave., 31522
Ph: 912-638-3611

Yards: 3185, Holes: 18
Par: 36, USGA: 34.7
RP: No more than 3 tee
times advance

Restaurant/Bar
GF: w/day $75.00
Carts: $13.00

All four nines include the beauty of moss draped oak trees, beautiful marshes and the Atlantic Ocean. "Seaside will leave you challenged and breathtaken. The seventh hole is 425 yds. long which includes a 185 yd. carry over an inland creek to narrow elev.

─────────────────ST. SIMONS ISLAND─────────────────

Sea Island GC
100 Retreat Avenue,
31522
Ph: 912-638-5118

Yards: 6322, Holes: 36
Par: 72, USGA: 39.7
RP: 24 hour advance
suggested

Restaurant/Bar/Proshop
GF: w/day $45.00
Carts: $13.00

Seaside Nine's #7, at 424 yards requires a powerful carry from the tee across 200 yards of tidal creek and marshes, then a tremendous bunker blocks a shorter drive to require a dogleg. Plantation Nine is characterized by sweeping fairways.

───────────────── ST. SIMONS ISLAND ─────────────────

Sea Palms GC	Yards: 6672, Holes: 27	Restaurant
5445 Frederica Rd.,	Par: 72, USGA: 69.8	**GF:** w/day $35.00, w/end
31522		$35.00
Ph: 912-638-3351		**Carts:** $13.00

The championship Sea Palms golf course winds its way through the live oaks and sparking ponds of the island landscape. The East Course is famous as the site of the Georgia PGA and Challenge Matches, and is ranked among the state's top 10 golf courses.

───────────────── ST. SIMONS ISLAND ─────────────────

St. Simon Island	Yards: 6114, Holes: 18	Proshop
Club	Par: 72, USGA: 69.9	**GF:** w/day $37.00
100 Kings Way, 31522		**Carts:** $13.00
Ph: 912-638-5130		

Designed by Joe Lee, this course opened in 1976. There's lots of marsh and a large number of lakes. As if that isn't enough, you'll also find 88 bunkers that are well-placed.

───────────────── STOCKBRIDGE ─────────────────

Southerness GC	Yards: 6350, Holes: 18
4871 Flatbridge Rd.,	Par: 72
Ph: 404-808-6000	

A Clyde Johnston designed course, it plays long and has a Scottish flavor.

───────────────── STONE MOUNTAIN ─────────────────

Stone Mountain Park	Yards: 6875, Holes: 36	Restaurant/Bar/Proshop
P.O. Box 778, 30086	Par: 72, USGA: 69.9	**GF:** w/day $38.00
Ph: 404-498-5715	RP: Weekend and	**Carts:** $Included
	holidays	

Rated one of 50 best public courses by Golf Digest. Hilly with Bermuda grass fairways and bent grass greens, heavily wooded with pines and maples, very narrow. Most tees are elevated. No holes are parallel. #11 has water, long & narrow par 4, 420 yards.

───────────────── VALDOSTA ─────────────────

Northlake Golf & CC	Yards: 4650, Holes: 18	Restaurant/Bar/Proshop
131 Northlake Dr.,	Par: 66, USGA: 63.5	**GF:** w/day $7.00
31602	RP: Weekends	**Carts:** $10.00
Ph: 912-247-8986		

Northlake is an executive length course. The front 9 holes are lighted for night play. The back nine is very challenging with water coming into play on 8 of the 9 holes. We have a driving range which is lighted, tennis courts, pool and fishing.

───────────────── WARNER ROBINS ─────────────────

Landings GC	Yards: 7010, Holes: 27	Restaurant/Bar
309 Statham's Way,	Par: 72, USGA: 69.7	**GF:** w/day $18.00, w/end
31088		$23.00
Ph: 912-923-5222		

3 9-holes courses that were the host to the Georgia State Amateur championship in 1993. These courses are going to be a real test of your game.

───────────────── WOODSTOCK ─────────────────

Eagle Watch	Yards: 6044, Holes: 18
3055 Eagle Watch Dr.,	Par: 72
30188	
Ph: 404-591-1000	

This fairly long course was designed by Arnold Palmer, and has beautifully maintained grounds.

HAWAII

AIEA, OAHU

Pearl GC
98-535 Kaonohi St.,
96701
Ph: 808-487-3802

Yards: 6750, Holes: 18
Par: 72
RP: Required, 1 month
in advance

Restaurant/Bar
GF: w/day $70.00, w/end
$75.00

A difficult and challenging course. Trees provide some very difficult choices with quite a few uphill shots, and the greens can be very tricky.

EWA BEACH

Ko Olina GC
92-1220 Aliinui Dr.,
96707
Ph: 808-676-5300

Yards: 6324, Holes: 18
Par: 72, USGA: 70.8

Restaurant/Bar/Proshop
GF: w/day $130.00
Carts: $Included

Wind and water can be a tough combination here.

EWA BEACH, OAHU

West Loch Muni GC
91-1126 Olepekeupe
Loop, 96706
Ph: 808-676-2210

Yards: 6070, Holes: 18
Par: 72
RP: One week in
advance

GF: w/day $20.00
Carts: $11.00

Hawaii's most challenging municipal course, there are plenty of water hazards here. Tight fairways and wind are some of the natural hazards. A water driving range is located here, a great place to get over your fear of water shots.

HAWAII VOLANCOES PARK

Volcano GC
Hwy. 11, P.O. Box 46,
96718
Ph: 808-967-7331

Yards: 5965, Holes: 18
Par: 72, USGA: 68.6
RP: Call for
reservations

Restaurant/Bar/Proshop
GF: w/day $50.00, w/end
$50.00
Carts: $Included

The most picturesque and challenging hole is the 15th, which is a dogleg left measuring 375 yards from the middle tees. During the winter months, both our majestic mountains, Mauna Loa and Mauna Kea seem to await your approach shot to an elevated green.

HILO

Hilo Muni GC
340 Haihai St., 96720
Ph: 808-959-7711

Yards: 6006, Holes: 18
Par: 71, USGA: 68.8
RP: 1 week in advance

GF: w/day $6.00, w/end
$8.00
Carts: $14.50

A nice playing course without a great deal of difficulty, great for a nice relaxing round. A lush Hawaiian setting with some amazing banyan trees. A very popular course.

---------------------HILO---------------------

Naniloa CC
120 Banyan Dr, 96720
Ph: 808-935-3000

Yards: 5285, Holes: 9
Par: 35, USGA: 65.8
RP: Required on
weekends & holiday

GF: w/day $25.00, w/end
$35.00
Carts: $14.00

*Small elevated greens, a multitude of trees, narrow fairways, are all features of
this short course. Accuracy is an important ingredient of your game here.*

---------------------HONOKAA---------------------

Hamakua CC
P.O. Box 751, 96727
Ph: 808-775-7380

Yards: 2520, Holes: 9
Par: 33, USGA: 63.8

GF: w/day $10.00

A short, tight course. A very green and lush setting, with marvelous ocean views.

---------------------HONOLULU---------------------

Ala Wai GC
404 Kapahulu Ave.,
96815
Ph: 808-296-4653

Yards: 6020, Holes: 18
Par: 70
RP: One week in
advance by phone

GF: w/day $18.00, w/end
$20.00
Carts: $10.00

One of the busiest courses in Hawaii.

---------------------HONOLULU---------------------

Hawaii Kai GC
8902 Kalanianaole
Hwy., 96825
Ph: 808-395-2358

Yards: 6350, Holes: 18
Par: 72, USGA: 70.3

GF: w/day $33.00, w/end
$35.00

*The par-3s are some of the most interesting challenges on this course. But one of
the par-4s has a very nasty dogleg. You can get into difficulty with water if you're
not careful.*

---------------------HONOLULU, OAHU---------------------

Moanalua GC
1250 Ala Aolani St.,
96819
Ph: 808-839-2411

Yards: 2972, Holes: 9
Par: 36, USGA: 67.8

Restaurant/Bar
GF: w/day $15.00, w/end
$25.00
Carts: $9.00

*The oldest course in Hawaii, your score here many be a very nasty surprise A lot
of tricky holes. Tiny greens and narrow fairways are the norm here. Not a great
course for beginners, with long grass and ragged greens.*

---------------------KAHUKU, OAHU---------------------

Kahuku GC
P.O. Box 417, 96731
Ph: 808-293-5842

Yards: 2699, Holes: 9
Par: 35, USGA: 65.4

GF: w/day $18.00

*The greens can really roll your ball, so you'll need to take that into account. On
the north tip of Oahu, there are some fantastic ocean views. The par-3s are the
most difficult holes.*

---------------------KAHUKU, OAHU---------------------

**Turtle Bay Hilton &
CC**
PO Box 187, 96731
Ph: 808-293-8574

Yards: 5871, Holes: 18
Par: 70, USGA: 68.0

Restaurant/Bar
GF: w/day $99.00

Lots of wind and sand here.

───────────────KAILUA, KONA───────────────

Kona GC
78-7000 Alii Dr., 96740
Ph: 808-322-2595

Yards: 6589, Holes: 27
Par: 72, USGA: 71.2

Restaurant/Bar/Proshop
GF: w/day $60.00

A setting with 36-holes of golf all in one place. One course has wide fairways and flat greens. A very scenic layout. The second course is much more of a challenge with fabulous views of the ocean. Lots of doglegs, hillside lies, water, and lava.

───────────────KAILUA, OAHU───────────────

Mid-Pacific CC
266 Kaelepulu Dr.,
96734
Ph: 808-261-9765

Yards: 6547, Holes: 18
Par: 72, USGA: 71.7

Restaurant/Bar
GF: w/day $150.00

A challenging course with many wonderful views.

───────────────KAILUA-KONA───────────────

Keauhou GC
78-7000 Alii Dr., 96740
Ph: 808-322-2595

Yards: 6800, Holes: 27
Par: 72

Proshop

27 holes of championship golf designed to call for every club in your bag. Play over and through ancient, rugged lava flows, on lush fairways, large manicured greens that are fast and rolling and true. At each hole a refreshing new vista.

───────────────KALAHEO, KAUAI───────────────

Kukuiolono GC
Paplina Rd., PO Box
1031, 96741
Ph: 808-332-9151

Yards: 6154, Holes: 9
Par: 36, USGA: 70.0

Proshop
GF: w/day $5.00, w/end
$10.00
Carts: $5.00

Lots and lots of trees here, in fact one of them has golf balls embedded in the trunk, you watch out for this hole. A nice relaxing, enjoyable round of golf.

───────────────KANEOHE───────────────

Bay View GC
45-285 Kaneohe Bay
Dr., 96744
Ph: 808-247-0451

Yards: 2234, Holes: 18
Par: 54
RP: Usually not
necessary

Proshop
GF: w/day $5.00
Carts: $2.00

Our 17th hole is long and tight. Don't hook it left or you're in grass 8 feet high, over the green is water. Keep it straight.

───────────────KANEOHE, OHAU───────────────

Pali GC
45-050 Kemehameha
Hwy., 96744
Ph: 808-296-7254

Yards: 6494, Holes: 18
Par: 70, USGA: 70.0

GF: w/day $18.00, w/end
$20.00

A hilly and rolling course, with much uneven terrain. A landscape rich in the foliage natural to the islands.

───────────────KAPALUA───────────────

Kapalua GC
300 Kapalua Dr.,
Kapalua, 96761
Ph: 808-669-8044

Yards: 6600, Holes: 18
Par: 72, USGA: 73.0
RP: One week in
advance

Restaurant/Bar
GF: w/day $110.00, w/end
$110.00
Carts: $Included

The Bay course's fifth is Kapalua's signature hole. The hole will vary in length depending on the tee used. While carrying the Pacific is first order of business, the green is well bunkered & offers varying pin placements. The Village Course climbs high.

─────────────── KIHEI ───────────────

Makena GC
5415 Makena Alanui,
96753
Ph: 808-879-3344

Yards: 6739, Holes: 18
Par: 72, USGA: 71.9
RP: Prior reservations
accepted

Restaurant/Bar/Proshop
GF: w/day $80.00
Carts: $20.00

Many have considered the 10th hole truly outstanding; a picture perfect "postcard" hole. The tee-shot heads straight downhill from the clubhouse toward the ocean falling from over 50 feet to a fairway bordered by water to its right.

─────────────── KIHEI ───────────────

Wailea GC
100 Wailea Golf Club
Dr., Wailea, 96753
Ph: 808-875-5111

Yards: 7070, Holes: 18
Par: 72, USGA: 73
RP: 2 days in advance

Restaurant/Bar/Proshop
GF: w/day $80.00, w/end
$80.00
Carts: $Included

Wailea Golf Course is a spectacular Robert Trent Jones, Jr., designed championship course featuring prehistoric lava rock walls, gardens of Hawaiian grasses, exposed lava outcroppings, and magnificent ocean and mountain views from virtually every hole.

─────────────── KIHEI, MANU ───────────────

Silversword GC
P.O. Box 1099, 1345
Piilani Hwy, 96753
Ph: 808-874-0777

Yards: 6404, Holes: 18
Par: 71, USGA: 70.6

GF: w/day $27.00, w/end
$60.00
Carts: $Included

A nasty water, hole, wind, and strategic bunkers can give you quite a time. But luckily the course is otherwise somewhat forgiving.

─────────────── KOHALA COAST ───────────────

**Francis H. I'I Brown
GC**
P.O. Box 4959, 96743
Ph: 808-885-6655

Yards: 6993, Holes: 18
Par: 72, USGA: 73.1
RP: Call ahead

Restaurant/Bar/Proshop
GF: w/day $80.00, w/end
$80.00
Carts: $Included

South Course—Fairways sculpted in ancient lava flows with ocean & mountain views & famous 15th hole crashing ocean surf. North Course—Built on lava bed much older than the Kaniku flow on which the South Course lies. Characterized by rolling terrain.

─────────────── KOHALA COAST ───────────────

Mauna Lani GC
P.O. Box 4959, 96743
Ph: 808-885-6655

Yards: 6370, Holes: 18
Par: 72

Restaurant/Bar
GF: w/day $65.00
Carts: $Included

Two 18-hole championship courses set in lava fields.

─────────────── KOHALA COAST ───────────────

Waikoloa Village GC
P.O. Box 383910, 96738
Ph: 808-883-9621

Yards: 6687, Holes: 18
Par: 72, USGA: 69.7
RP: 3 days in advance

Restaurant/Bar/Proshop
GF: w/day $65.00, w/end
$65.00
Carts: $Included

A golf challenge for all levels of golfing expertise. The pros believe this to be one of the 5 most challenging golf courses in Hawaii from the blue tees. Unsurpassed views of the Pacific Ocean and Mauna Kea from all fairways.

──────────────── KOHALA COAST, HAWAII ────────────────

Mauna Kea Beach GC   Yards: 7114, Holes: 18   Restaurant/Bar/Proshop
P.O. Box 218, 96743   Par: 72, USGA: 70.6   **GF:** w/day $60.00, w/end
Ph: 808-882-7222   RP: 1 day in advance $60.00
                                                         Carts: $40.00

It is love at first sight. When they created Mauna Kea, they combined a multitude of elements and built a course and a resort that is simply a pleasure to visit. Mauna Kea is ranked among "America's 100 Greatest" golf courses and as "Hawaii's Finest".

──────────────── KOLOA ────────────────

Kiahuna GC   Yards: 6353, Holes: 18   Restaurant/Bar/Proshop
2545 Kiahuna   Par: 70   **GF:** w/day $75.00, w/end
Plantation Dr., 96756   RP: Two weeks in $75.00
Ph: 808-742-9595   advance   **Carts:** $Included

Rolling fairways and undulating greens are a trademark at the Kiahuna Golf Club. Built in 1983 by world renowned golf course architect Robert Trent Jones Jr., Kiahuna lies on an ancient Hawaiian settlement with the lava rock walls and houses left.

──────────────── KOLOA, KAUAI ────────────────

Poipu Bay Resort GC   Yards: 5819, Holes: 18   **GF:** w/day $55.00
2250 Ainoko St., 96756   Par: 72   **Carts:** $Included
Ph: 808-742-8711

Rolling terrain and some very nasty greens will join the wind in making this a memorable round. Doglegs, mounds, bunkers all add to your troubles. A course that will mature nicely.

──────────────── KUALAPUU, MOLOKAI ────────────────

Ironwood Hills GC   Yards: 2816, Holes: 9   **GF:** w/day $10.00
Kalae Hwy, PO Box 8,   Par: 35, USGA: 33.8   **Carts:** $7.00
96757   RP: Anytime
Ph: 808-567-6000

A short course with very gritty sand traps, and wide fairways. The bunkers here will surely make your short game tough if you get into them.

──────────────── LAHAINA ────────────────

Royal Kaanapali GC   Yards: 6305, Holes: 18   Restaurant/Bar
Kaanapali Beach   Par: 72, USGA: 70.0   **GF:** w/day $70.00
Resorts, 96767   RP: 2 days in advance   **Carts:** $Included
Ph: 808-661-3691

The North Course has undulating elevated greens, and generous bunkers, difficult to par—but easy to boggie. The South Course can be even trickier, with narrow fairways and small greens.

──────────────── LANAI CITY ────────────────

Cavendish GC   Yards: 3071, Holes: 9   **GF:** w/day $5.00
P.O. Box 862, 96763   Par: 36

Rough greens and rough rough.

———————————————LANAI CITY———————————————

Experience at Koele GC
PO Box "L", 96763
Ph: 808-565-4653

Yards: 6628, Holes: 18
Par: 72

GF: w/day $75.00
Carts: $Included

A long and challenging course with the most spectacular scenery imaginable. The greens are fast and there's water and sand to watch out for.

———————————————LIHUE———————————————

Kauai Lagoons GC
Kalapaki Beach, 96766
Ph: 808-245-5063

Yards: 6942, Holes: 18
Par: 72

Restaurant/Bar/Proshop

The course, with its generous and gently rolling fairways, sandy waste areas, native grasses, and well contoured greens, is reminiscent of traditional Scottish links-type golf courses. A course where the players have plenty of room to hit the ball.

———————————————LIHUE———————————————

Wailua Muni GC
4444 Rice St. Rm. 230, 96766
Ph: 808-245-2163

Yards: 6585, Holes: 18
Par: 72, USGA: 71.9
RP: Up to one week in advance

Restaurant/Bar/Proshop
GF: w/day $18.00, w/end $20.00
Carts: $Included

This course is considered by some to be the best municipal course in the islands. This course was the site of the 1975 and 1985 USGA Amateur Public Links Championships. Set along the ocean, there are fast greens, doglegs, and large trees.

———————————————LIHUE———————————————

Westin Kauai
Kalapaki Beach, 96766
Ph: 808-246-5061

Yards: 6164, Holes: 36
Par: 72
RP: Guests up to a month in advance

Restaurant/Bar
GF: w/day $125.00
Carts: $Included

The Dunes is a Scottish style links course with treacherous pot bunkers, extensive mounding, grass traps and fairways full of swells and ripples. There's also Cypress Course by Pete and P.B. Dye. There's still another nine, the fabulous Fazio holes.

———————————MAUNALOA, MOLOKAI———————————

Kaluakoi GC
P.O. Box 26, 96770
Ph: 808-552-2739

Yards: 6564, Holes: 18
Par: 72, USGA: 70.4
RP: 1 month in advance

Restaurant/Bar/Proshop
GF: w/day $45.00
Carts: $15.00

We have five holes along the ocean and you can see the ocean from every hole, very scenic. Unspoiled beauty. The real Hawaii.

———————————————MILILANI TOWN———————————————

Mililani GC
95-176 Kuahelani Ave., 96789
Ph: 808-623-2222

Yards: 6360, Holes: 18
Par: 72, USGA: 70.4
RP: 3 months in advance

Restaurant/Bar/Proshop
GF: w/day $80.00, w/end $85.00
Carts: $Included

Mililani Golf Club is located in central Oahu. It is flanked by mountain ranges on both sides. The golf course has numerous trees and water to make your play challenging.

─────────── NAALEHU ───────────

Discovery Harbour   Yards: 6410, Holes: 18   **GF:** w/day $25.00
GC CC   Par: 72, USGA: 69.4   **Carts:** $Included
PO Box Q, 96772
Ph: 808-929-7353

The roughs are pretty rough and you'll have lots of hillside problems. The greens aren't in very good condition and will give you a lot of trouble.

─────────── PAHALA ───────────

Seamountain GC at   Yards: 6300, Holes: 18   Restaurant/Bar/Proshop
Punaluu   Par: 72, USGA: 69.7   **GF:** w/day $29.50
Hwy. 11, P.O. Box 85,   **Carts:** $11.50
96777
Ph: 808-928-6222

The golf course layout starts from sea level and eventually travels to 600 feet above sea level. Our signature hole is #17 with four lagoons and numerous monkey pod trees. Sea Mountain is known as the "Secret Golf Heaven" & is the home of the Rip Collin.

─────────── PAIA, MAUI ───────────

Maui CC   Yards: 6549, Holes: 18   **GF:** w/day $35.00
48 Nonohe Place,   Par: 72, USGA: 70.2   **Carts:** $Included
96779   RP: Tee times required
Ph: 808-877-0616

A course rich in foliage and wind.

─────────── PRINCEVILLE ───────────

Princeville Makai GC   Yards: 6778, Holes: 27   Restaurant/Bar
P.O. Box 3040, 96722   Par: 72, USGA: 72.3   **GF:** w/day $70.00, w/end
Ph: 808-826-3580   RP: Up to 1 year in $70.00
                               advance   **Carts:** $Included

Number 3 on the Ocean Course, a par 3, is world-renowned. Only 125 yards with dense grass on the left, a placid lake in front and a canyon beyond. Lake Course boasts ocean views and plenty of water. 16 years rated in America's 100 Greatest Golf Courses.

─────────── PUKALANI ───────────

Pukalani GC   Yards: 6494, Holes: 18   Restaurant/Bar/Proshop
360 Pukalani St., 96768   Par: 72, USGA: 70.6   **GF:** w/day $30.00
Ph: 808-572-1314   RP: 3 days in advance   **Carts:** $20.00

Set in the rolling hillsides of "upcountry" Maui, Pukalani Country Club actually has 19 holes (two greens on our 3rd hole - par 3). One green is across a gully and the other straight down.

─────────── WAHIAWA, OAHU ───────────

Hawaii CC   Yards: 5861, Holes: 18   Bar
98-1211 Kunia Rd., PO   Par: 72, USGA: 65.9   **GF:** w/day $60.00
Box 966, 96786   **Carts:** $Included
Ph: 808-621-5654

The trees definitely come into play here. Wind and water will come into play. Accuracy is very important here to avoid some very bad lies. The course offers a wonderful view of Pearl Harbor.

─────────────────WAIANAE─────────────────

Makaha Valley CC
84-627 Makaha Valley
Rd., 96792
Ph: 808-695-7111

Yards: 6091, Holes: 18
Par: 71, USGA: 67.6
RP: Recommended tee
times

Restaurant/Bar/Proshop
GF: w/day $50.00, w/end
$50.00
Carts: $Included

Sporty, well conditioned golf course in resort area. Great par 3s and tough finishing holes.

─────────────────WAIANAE─────────────────

**Sheraton Makaha
Resort**
84-626 Makaha Valley
Rd. Waianae, 96792
Ph: 808-695-9544

Yards: 7091, Holes: 18
Par: 72, USGA: 74.3
RP: 3 days in advance

Restaurant/Bar/Proshop
GF: w/day $75.00, w/end
$75.00
Carts: $Included

Our favorite hole is #18. Although not difficult in length it requires accuracy. Guarding the fairway are two bunkers and two ponds. Right of the fairway is best for all approaching shots. The green (like all of our greens) slopes towards the ocean.

─────────────────WAIKAPU, MAUI─────────────────

**Waikapu GC-
Sandalwood**
2500 Honoapiilani
Hwy., 96793
Ph: 808-242-7090

Yards: 5902, Holes: 18

Set with the mountains of Maui in the background, this is a beautiful course, with views of the ocean thrown in. The course is a real challenge.

─────────────────WAIKOLOA─────────────────

**Waikoloa GC - Kings'
Golf Course**
HCO2 Box 5575, 96743
Ph: 808-885-4647

Yards: 7074, Holes: 18
Par: 72, USGA: 75.0
RP: 1 day in advance

Restaurant/Bar/Proshop
GF: w/day $80.00, w/end
$80.00
Carts: $Included

The Kings' Course was designed by Tom Weiskopf and Jay Morrish. In Morrish's words, "The variety in the green design, the sophisticated bunker strategy, and the multiple tee placements all work together to create a course that can challenge.

─────────────────WAILUKU, MAUI─────────────────

Waiehu Muni GC
Box 507, 96796
Ph: 808-244-5934

Yards: 6330, Holes: 18
Par: 72, USGA: 69.8

Restaurant
GF: w/day $15.00, w/end
$25.00
Carts: $6.50

This course originally opened in 1930. The layout is along the ocean and can become very windy. The greens are well bunkered, sometimes surrounded in fact. Accuracy is a must on a few of the holes.

─────────────────WAIMANALO, OAHU─────────────────

Olomana Golf Links
41-1801 Kalanianaole
Hwy., 96795
Ph: 808-259-7926

Yards: 5887, Holes: 18
Par: 72, USGA: 67.2

GF: w/day $29.00
Carts: $Included

The front nine is hilly, with water on every hole on the back. If you do get into water here, forget about that ball forever. A very scenic course that is very representative of the beauty of Hawaii.

IDAHO

Sandpoint

Sun Valley

New Meadows

──────────────── BOISE ────────────────

Quail Hollow GC
4520 N 36th St, 83703
Ph: 208-344-7807

Yards: 5585, Holes: 18
Par: 71, USGA: 66.0
RP: 1 week in advance

Restaurant/Bar/Proshop
GF: w/day $14.00, w/end
$20.00
Carts: $Included

A hilly course, this championship layout features water, which comes into play on over half the course Some of the tees are really elevated.

──────────────── COUER D'ALENE ────────────────

**Couer d'Alene
Resort GC**
900 Floating Green Dr.,
83814
Ph: 208-765-4000

Yards: 6309, Holes: 18
Par: 71, USGA: 69.6

Bar/Proshop
GF: w/day $95.00
Carts: $Included

This course was designed to use the natural lay of the land and preserve the natural setting, set along a creek in a heavily wooded area. The is the home of the well-known floating green.

──────────────── EAGLE ────────────────

Eagle Hills GC
605 N Edgewood Ln,
83616
Ph: 208-939-0402

Yards: 6255, Holes: 18
Par: 72, USGA: 69.5

Restaurant/Bar
GF: w/day $10.00, w/end
$13.00

Lots of bunkers here so be prepared. The greens are tricky with a lot of roll, on this otherwise flat course.

──────────────── NEW MEADOWS ────────────────

**Kimberland
Meadows Resort**
PO Drawer C, Hwy 95,
83654
Ph: 208-347-2164

Yards: 6927, Holes: 18
Par: 72, USGA: 69.8
RP: 1 week for tee times

Restaurant/Bar/Proshop
GF: w/day $15.00, w/end
$18.00
Carts: $8.00

The course is set among mountains and pine trees. It's a demanding course from the championship tees and play fair from the whites. The fairways are tree lined and tight, the view in all directions is spectacular. Snow peaked mountains, etc.

─────────────── REXBURG ───────────────

Teton Lakes GC　　Yards: 5931, Holes: 18
Box 408, Rt 1 Hibbard　Par: 71, USGA: 67.8
Hwy, Ph: 208-359-3036

The back nine is heavily forested and has lots of water, but the front is flat.

─────────────── SANDPOINT ───────────────

Hidden Lakes CC　　Yards: 6155, Holes: 18　　Restaurant/Bar/Proshop
8838 Lower Pack　　　Par: 71, USGA: 69.1　　　**GF:** w/day $20.00, w/end
River, 83864　　　　　RP: 1 week in advance　$24.00
Ph: 208-263-1642　　　　　　　　　　　　　**Carts:** $20.00

Water, water, water. Truly a Florida golf course among the beautiful northwest evergreens. Water comes into play on 17 of the 18 holes ... 82 sand bunkers. Set in the Pack River Valley with the Pack River wandering through the golf course. Very scenic.

─────────────── SUN VALLEY ───────────────

Elkhorn GC　　　　Yards: 6575, Holes: 18　　Restaurant/Bar
P.O. Box 6009, 83354　Par: 72, USGA: 73.2　　　**GF:** w/day $40.00
Ph: 208-622-4511　　RP: May be made with　　**Carts:** $Included
　　　　　　　　　　reservations

This lengthy scenic treat nestled under majestic snow-capped peaks. Top rated course in Idaho. A very hilly course with a lot of water, antelope, fox, hare, and deer.

─────────────── SUN VALLEY ───────────────

Sun Valley Resort GC　Yards: 6057, Holes: 18　Restaurant/Bar
Sun Valley Rd., 83353　Par: 71, USGA: 71.1　　　**GF:** w/day $32.00
Ph: 208-622-4111　　RP: 7 days in advance　　**Carts:** $21.00

This is one of the west's truly beautiful mountain settings, and has hosted the Idaho Governor's Cup, Danny Thompson Memorial Celebrity Golf Tournament, and numerous others. The fifteenth hole, a 244 yard par 3 is singled out as a challenger.

─────────────── TWIN FALLS ───────────────

Canyon Springs GC　Yards: 6001, Holes: 18　　Restaurant/Bar/Proshop
PO Box 1032, 83303　Par: 72, USGA: 66.8
Ph: 208-734-7609

This course is set along the Snake River and has many beautiful poplars lining the fairways. There isn't much water or many bunkers to give you trouble.

Plan ahead! Reserve tee time well in advance, and while you're doing so, confirm rates and services.

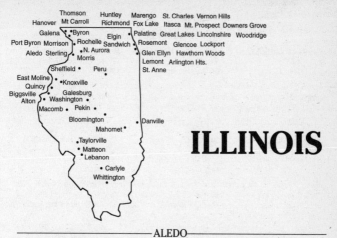

Thomson Huntley Marengo St. Charles Vernon Hills
Hanover Mt Carroll Richmond Fox Lake Mt. Prospect Downers Grove
Galena •Byron Elgin •Palatine Great Lakes Lincolnshire Woodridge
Port Byron Morrison •Rochelle Sandwich •Rosemont Glencoe Lockport
Aledo Sterling •N. Aurora •Glen Ellyn Hawthorn Woods
Morris Lemont Arlington Hts.
Sheffield • Peru St. Anne
East Moline •Knoxville
Quincy Galesburg
Biggsville • Washington •
Alton
Macomb • Pekin •
Bloomington •Danville
Mahomet •
•Taylorville
• Mattoon
•Lebanon
• Carlyle
Whittington

ILLINOIS

────────────────── ALEDO ──────────────────

Hawthorn Ridge GC	Yards: 6670, Holes: 18	Restaurant/Proshop
RR 2, SR-94, 61231	Par: 72, USGA: 69.9	**GF:** w/day $11.50
Ph: 309-582-5641	RP: Recommended	**Carts:** $15.50

Natural wooded setting, features plush watered fairways, large rolling greens and a very quiet setting abounding with wildlife, large oaks, ponds and streams. The par 4, #12 hole, with a fairway lined with huge oaks offers a striking shot across a pond.

────────────────── ALGONQUIN ──────────────────

Golf Club of Illinois	Yards: 7011, Holes: 18	Restaurant/Bar
1575 Edgewood Rd,	Par: 71, USGA: 71.8	**GF:** w/day $28.00
60102	RP: 1 week in advance	
Ph: 708-658-4400		

A unique course that is going to make you dream about prairie grass for many a moon. The winds here will add another dimension to an already challenging round. Golf Digest ranked this one of the top ten new public courses the year it opened.

────────────────── ALTON ──────────────────

Spencer T. Olin	Yards: 6945, Holes: 18	Restaurant/Bar/Proshop
Community GC	Par: 72, USGA: 70.3	**GF:** w/day $34.00, w/end
4701 College Ave., Box	RP: One week in	$40.00
1093, 62002	advance	**Carts:** $Included
Ph: 618-465-3111		

This Arnold Palmer designed and managed facility is first class from the word go. Already recognized as the finest public facility in the Midwest. Renowned for the standards of excellence exampled in the golf course and the service of its staff.

────────────────── ARLINGTON HTS. ──────────────────

Arlington Lakes GC	Yards: 5331, Holes: 18	Restaurant/Bar/Proshop
1211 S. New Wilke Rd.,	Par: 68, USGA: 64.6	**GF:** w/day $14.00, w/end
60005	RP: 5 days in advance	$16.00
Ph: 312-577-3030		**Carts:** $17.00

The course abounds with water hazards. And if that isn't enough the greens are well guarded by innumerable bunkers.

─────────────── BIGGSVILLE ───────────────

Hend-Co Hills CC
RR 1, 61418
Ph: 309-627-2779

Yards: 3235, Holes: 9
Par: 37, USGA: 70.6
RP: Weekends

Restaurant/Bar/Proshop
GF: w/day $6.00
Carts: $6.00

Hend-Co has golf, swimming pool, campgrounds, fishing. Golf lessons, driving range. This is pretty wide open course with 2 par threes one over water, the other with an uphill green 3 par 5's which are all over 500 yards.

─────────────── BLOOMINGTON ───────────────

Lakeside CC
1201 E. Croxton, 61701
Ph: 309-827-5402

Yards: 2900, Holes: 9
Par: 64, USGA: 62.9
RP: Call - usually can
walk on

Restaurant/Bar/Proshop
GF: w/day $12.00, w/end
$12.00
Carts: $13.00

Don't let the yardage fool you, this is an exceptionally challenging course. The greens are small and undulating. Fairways are extremely narrow and the long par 3's are mind boggling. My favorite hole is #6, only 290 yard par 4 but packed with excitement.

─────────────── BOURBONNAIS ───────────────

Bon Vivant CC
Career Center Road,
PO Box 67, 60914
Ph: 815-935-0403

Yards: 7400, Holes: 18
Par: 72, USGA: 75.8
RP: No more than 7
days in advance

Restaurant/Bar/Proshop
GF: w/day $12.00, w/end
$18.00
Carts: $14.00

The course is known for its elevated trees, length, large greens, and pesky water hazards.

─────────────── BYRON ───────────────

Prairie View GC
7993 River Rd., 61010
Ph: 815-234-GOLF

Yards: 6990, Holes: 18
Par: 72

Bar/Proshop
GF: w/day $14.00, w/end
$17.00
Carts: $10.00

Newest public course with unusual aesthetic additions of natural prairie, five tees per hole with challenging greens, traps and bunkers. Natural dolomite prairie with 600 acre Tonest Preserve adjacent to facility.

─────────────── CARLYLE ───────────────

Carlyle Lake GC
Rt. 127 South, 62231
Ph: 618-594-8812

Yards: 3295, Holes: 9
Par: 36, USGA: 35.5

Bar/Proshop
GF: w/day $5.00, w/end
$6.00
Carts: $14.00

Challenging 9 holes of golf. Course features multiple tees to challenge players of any level. Bermuda tees add to players enjoyment.

─────────────── CHICAGO ───────────────

Edgebrook GC
6100 North Central
Ave., 60646
Ph: 312-763-8320

Yards: 4626, Holes: 18
Par: 66

GF: w/day $6.00, w/end
$7.00

The main feature here is the greens which are not overly-large. Although the Chicago River goes through the course it isn't a problem on most holes.

Subscribe to our free newsletter, "Great Golf Gazette," and hear about the latest special golf vacation values.

─────────────── DANVILLE ───────────────

Harrison Park GC
W. Voorhees, 61832
Ph: 217-431-2266

Yards: 6066, Holes: 18
Par: 73, USGA: 69.0

Restaurant/Bar/Proshop
GF: w/day $7.50, w/end
$9.00
Carts: $14.00

You will enjoy newly watered fairways on this mature layout. Tree marred hills surround the course offering a beautiful backdrop sure to test your concentration. Keep focused on your golf shots and the opportunities will be there—most cannot.

─────────────── DOWNERS GROVE ───────────────

Downers Grove GC
2420 Haddow St.,
60515
Ph: 312-963-1306

Yards: 2900, Holes: 9
Par: 34, USGA: 33.4
RP: Weekends &
holidays

Restaurant
GF: w/day $7.50, w/end
$8.50
Carts: $9.00

Site of 1st 18 holes in USA now 9 holes. #7 Par 4, 375 yards tight fairway gradual rise to small tight green.

─────────────── EAST MOLINE ───────────────

Golfmohr GC
16724 Hubbard Rd.,
61244
Ph: 309-496-2434

Yards: 6543, Holes: 18
Par: 72, USGA: 69.8
RP: Recommended

Restaurant/Bar/Proshop
GF: w/day $10.00
Carts: $15.00

The course is surrounded by woods and a nature preserve. Lakes or ponds come into play on several holes, including the #2, par 4 hole, that in spite of its beauty claims 20,000 balls each year. Golfer survey rates Golfmohr #1 public course in the Quad Cities.

─────────────── EAST PEORIA ───────────────

Quail Meadows GC
2215 Centenial Dr,
61571
Ph: 309-694-3139

Yards: 6601, Holes: 18
Par: 72, USGA: 71.5

This is a very open course, with wide fairways. There's a lot here to challenge your long game.

─────────────── ELGIN ───────────────

Rolling Knolls GC
RR 1 Box 319,
Rohrssen Rd., 60120
Ph: 312-888-2888

Yards: 4300, Holes: 18
Par: 68
RP: Recommended

Bar/Proshop
GF: w/day $15.00
Carts: $16.00

An extremely challenging executive 18 hole golf course with fairways the width of airport runways and tees lining both sides. If the trees don't get you our water and traps will. A course you'll want to play again and again.

─────────────── FINDLAY ───────────────

Eagle Creek Resort GC
Eagle Creek State Park
Rd, 62534
Ph: 800-876-3245

Yards: 6908, Holes: 18
Par: 72, USGA: 73.5

Restaurant/Bar/Proshop
GF: w/day $35.00, w/end
$40.00
Carts: $Included

Ravines, water in the form of a lake, doglegs, and well-bunkered large greens are here in abundance. Accuracy is more important than usual here, because if you aren't, you're sure to be in some kind of trouble.

FOX LAKE

Fox Lake CC
7220 State Park Rd.,
60020
Ph: 312-587-6411

Yards: 6347, Holes: 18
Par: 72, USGA: 70.5
RP: Recommended

Restaurant/Bar/Proshop
GF: w/day $20.00, w/end
$25.00
Carts: $20.00

Fox Lake Country Club presents blind approach shots, difficult sidehill, downhill lies and deceptively fast greens. There is a fully stocked pro shop, driving range and snack shop. Banquet facility for up to 180 people. Golf outings welcome.

GALENA

**Eagle Ridge Inn &
Resort**
Box 777, 61036
Ph: 815-777-2444

Yards: 6836, Holes: 45
Par: 72, USGA: 73.4

Restaurant/Bar/Proshop
GF: w/day $68.00, w/end
$68.00
Carts: $22.00

Eagle Ridge has 45 holes set in the hills of the Mississippi River Valley. The North Course cuts through the highlands. It has many elevated tees and approach shots with spectacular views of the country side. The South Course is set in a valley.

GALESBURG

Bunker Links GKC
Lincoln Park, 61401
Ph: 309-344-1818

Yards: 6083, Holes: 18
Par: 71, USGA: 67.5
RP: Weekends &
holidays

Restaurant/Proshop
GF: w/day $6.00, w/end
$7.00
Carts: $13.00

#15 is a short par 3 picturesque hole guarded in front of green by a pond—sandtrap to left of green. Automatic water system on tees, greens, and fairways.

GLEN ELLYN

**Village Links of Glen
Ellyn**
485 Winchell Way,
60137
Ph: 708-469-8180

Yards: 6933, Holes: 27
Par: 71, USGA: 72.8
RP: 7 days in advance

Restaurant/Proshop
GF: w/day $25.00, w/end
$28.00
Carts: $20.00

Well placed drives and crisp iron shots will help avoid the 96 sand traps and 21 lakes strategically placed throughout the golf course. Every club in the bag will be used to successfully negotiate this championship layout.

GLEN ELLYN

Western Acres GC
21 W. 680 Butterfield
Rd., 60148
Ph: 312-469-6768

Yards: 3018, Holes: 9
Par: 35, USGA: 69.1
RP: Weekends only

Restaurant/Bar/Proshop
GF: w/day $6.00, w/end
$6.75
Carts: $6.50

No. 3 a 215 yard, par 3—The green is so near yet so far. You must clear the water and avoid the bunkers on each side. There is out of bounds on the left and a tree nursery on the right.

GLENCOE

Glencoe GC
621 Westley Rd., 60022
Ph: 312-835-0981

Yards: 6233, Holes: 18
Par: 72, USGA: 68.9
RP: Must be made in
person

Restaurant/Proshop
GF: w/day $15.00, w/end
$17.00
Carts: $18.00

Glencoe Golf Club is a very beautiful older golf course. We have 3 sets of tees to challenge the average or advanced golfer. Over 18 holes run through the woods and next to the Chicago Botanic Gardens. Our golf club is rated one of the top public.

───────────────── GODFREY ─────────────────

Rolling Hills GC
Route 2, Pierce Ln,
62035
Ph: 618-466-8363

Yards: 5239, Holes: 18
Par: 71

There's a lot of water on Rolling Hills. The terrain is somewhat rolling, and that can be a problem.

───────────────── HANOVER ─────────────────

Storybrook CC
2124 W. Storybrook
Rd., 61041
Ph: 815-591-2210

Yards: 3318, Holes: 9
Par: 36, USGA: 34.3
RP: 1 day ahead

Restaurant/Bar/Proshop
GF: w/day $11.00
Carts: $12.00

Storybrook is a fine 9 hole course site in the beautiful Jo Davies County of Illinois. A course where you cross water on every hole. The most spectacular view from the 5th tee box overlooks the whole course plus a large surrounding area.

───────────────── HAWTHORN WOODS ─────────────────

Kemper Lakes GC
Old McHenry Rd.,
60047
Ph: 312-540-3450

Yards: 7217, Holes: 18
Par: 72, USGA: 71.7
RP: One week in
advance

Restaurant/Bar/Proshop
GF: w/day $100.00
Carts: $Included

Heavily wooded course with lakes everywhere, #17 has an island green. Golf Shop Magazine rated the pro shop in the best 100 in the country.

───────────────── HUNTLEY ─────────────────

Pinecrest Golf & CC
11220 Algonquin Rd.,
60142
Ph: 312-669-3111

Yards: 6636, Holes: 18
Par: 72, USGA: 68.7
RP: 1 week in advance

Restaurant/Bar/Proshop
GF: w/day $15.00, w/end
$20.00
Carts: $20.00

Relatively open and gently rolling this public course is manicured like a private club to give the average golfer the best chance for a low score. A favorite hole is number 11, 161 yards over water to a peninsula green. It can make or break your back nine.

───────────────── ITASCA ─────────────────

Nordic Hills GC
Rohlwing & Nordic
Rds., 60143
Ph: 312-773-3510

Yards: 5897, Holes: 18
Par: 71, USGA: 68.9

Restaurant/Bar/Proshop

Recreation at Nordic Hills begins with a challenging 18-hole golf course, originally designed as a private country club by Scandinavian businessmen over 60 years ago. There is rolling terrain and century-old oaks.

───────────────── KNOXVILLE ─────────────────

Laurel Greens GC
RR 1 Box 115, 61448
Ph: 309-289-4146

Yards: 3100, Holes: 9
Par: 36

Restaurant/Bar/Proshop
GF: w/day $7.00
Carts: $12.00

A beautiful country setting with an outstanding 9 hole layout, manicured to perfect, 3100 yards, par 36. The additional new 9 holes is under construction. Keeping with the rustic setting, the clubhouse has been renovated from an old barn.

─────────────────────LEBANON─────────────────────

Locust Hills GC
1015 Belleville St.,
62254
Ph: 618-537-4590

Yards: 6005, Holes: 18
Par: 71, USGA: 67.2
RP: Weekends &
holidays

Restaurant/Bar/Proshop
GF: w/day $9.00, w/end
$11.00
Carts: $15.00

Located 20 minutes from downtown St. Louis—Locust Hills is an interesting course with the accent on accuracy. Water and trees abound the front nine with bunkers and rolling hills on the back nine. Area's finest greens. A true test of golf for beginners.

─────────────────────LEMONT─────────────────────

Cog Hill Golf & CC
12294 Archer Ave.,
60439
Ph: 708-257-5872

Yards: 6219, Holes: 72
Par: 71, USGA: 68.7
RP: Required, 6 days in
advance

Restaurant/Bar/Proshop
Carts: $24.00

With four different 18-hole courses, Cog Hill offers a quality round of golf to players of all handicaps. Courses 1 and 3 are medium length and medium difficulty. #2 is par 72 sporty, rolling and wooded, #4 is championship caliber, rated "Greatest 100".

─────────────────────LEMONT─────────────────────

Glen Eagles GC
123rd & Bell Ave.,
60439
Ph: 708-257-5466

Yards: 6090, Holes: 36
Par: 70, USGA: 68.6

Restaurant/Bar
GF: w/day $20.00, w/end
$24.00

Gleneagles has two 18-holes layouts. The terrain has many changes which will often challenge you.

─────────────────────LINCOLNSHIRE─────────────────────

Marriott's
Lincolnshire Resort
1 Marriott Dr., 60015
Ph: 312-634-1179

Yards: 6300, Holes: 18
Par: 70, USGA: 69.8
RP: Hotel guest 6
months, outside 1 week

Restaurant/Bar
GF: w/day $44.00, w/end
$48.00
Carts: $Included

Superlative, 18-hole course designed by George Fazio. Tee off and travel down pristine fairways edged by woodlands, around the shores of five shimmering lakes, over bunkers and onto immaculately-maintained greens. An inviting course.

─────────────────────LOCKPORT─────────────────────

Big Run GC
135th St., 60441
Ph: 815-838-1057

Yards: 6850, Holes: 18
Par: 72, USGA: 73.1
RP: 1 week in advance

Restaurant/Bar/Proshop
GF: w/day $30.00, w/end
$30.00
Carts: $12.00

Oak tress, hilly, exceptional par 5's and par 3's. Beautiful layout. 708-972-1652.

─────────────────────MACOMB─────────────────────

Western Illinois
Univ. GC
1215 Tower Rd., 61455
Ph: 309-837-3675

Yards: 3200, Holes: 9
Par: 36, USGA: 69.0
RP: 1 day in advance

Proshop
GF: w/day $7.00, w/end
$8.00
Carts: $6.00

Designed by Kilian and Nugent (Kemper Lakes), this 9 hole course is one of the best 9 hole facilities in Illinois. The rural setting and affordable price offers the avid golfer a different twist. The 196 yard par 3 8th hole will be one you won't forget.

———————————MAHOMET———————————

Lake of the Woods GC	Yards: 6503, Holes: 18	Restaurant/Bar/Proshop
Box 669 (1 mile N. of Mahomet), 61853	Par: 72, USGA: 69.8	**GF:** w/day $13.00, w/end $14.00
Ph: 217-586-2183	RP: Call Monday for weekend	**Carts:** $10.00

A rolling tree lined course with water on seven of the eighteen holes. Accuracy is rewarded more than length.

———————————MARENGO———————————

Marengo Ridge CC	Yards: 6500, Holes: 18	Restaurant/Bar/Proshop
9508 Harmony Hill Rd., 60152	Par: 72, USGA: 70.8	**GF:** w/day $14.00
Ph: 815-923-2332	RP: Required on weekends	**Carts:** $16.00

Marengo Ridge is gently rolling and rewards precision rather than power. Although 6800 yards from our championship tees, a golfer who uses his/her mind will outscore those who rely on muscle alone. Holes 6 and 15 reward the golfer with panoramic views.

———————————MATTOON———————————

Buck Grove Indian Trails GC	Yards: 3250, Holes: 9	Restaurant/Proshop
RR #3 Box 283A, 61938	Par: 36	**GF:** w/day $7.00
Ph: 217-258-PUTT	RP: Up to 1 week in advance	**Carts:** $7.00

9 holes opened July 1991, and all 18 holes opened July 1992. Big mounds, deep bunkers make the course very unique for this area.

———————————MT. CARROLL———————————

Oakville CC	Yards: 3111, Holes: 9	Restaurant/Bar/Proshop
RR 2, 61053	Par: 36, USGA: 69.7	**GF:** w/day $9.00, w/end $12.00
Ph: 815-684-5295	RP: Weekends & holidays	**Carts:** $13.00

A gently rolling course with many old trees with tight fairways. Water can come into play on 6 of the 9 holes. Greens are moderate to severely sloped making putting difficult. Hole #5 is the favorite hole, a short 114 yard par 3 going over a stream.

———————————MT. PROSPECT———————————

Old Orchard CC	Yards: 6010, Holes: 18	Restaurant/Bar/Proshop
700 W. Rand Rd., 60056	Par: 71, USGA: 68.3	**GF:** w/day $23.00, w/end $25.00
Ph: 312-255-2025	RP: 7 days in advance	**Carts:** $20.00

Old Orchard is one of the finest kept courses in the Chicago land area. The last 4 holes are a great chance to test your skills. The 17th hole is 230 yard par 3, all carry. It is the best par 3 in this whole area.

———————————MUNDELEIN———————————

Pine Meadow GC	Yards: 7129, Holes: 18	Restaurant/Bar/Proshop
1 Pine Meadow Ln., 60060	Par: 72, USGA: 69.5	**GF:** w/day $46.00
Ph: 312-566-4653	RP: Up to 6 days in advance	**Carts:** $24.00

A real championship layout.

─────────────── N. AURORA ───────────────

Valley Green GC
314 Kingswood Dr.,
60542
Ph: 312-897-3000

Yards: 3831, Holes: 18
Par: 60, USGA: 60.1
RP: Carts available by
appointment

Restaurant/Proshop
GF: w/day $9.00, w/end
$11.00
Carts: $12.00

This course is a very challenging "executive style" layout which puts more emphasis on accuracy than length off the tees. It is popular with both young and old as well as the novice and the low handicapper.

─────────────── NAPERVILLE ───────────────

Tamarack GC
24032 Royal
Worlington Dr, 60564
Ph: 708-904-4653

Yards: 6331, Holes: 18
Par: 70, USGA: 70.9

Restaurant/Bar
GF: w/day $40.00, w/end
$45.00

A flat, open course with water on all but three holes, and more sand traps than anyone wants to see in one place. This is a really challenging round of golf.

─────────────── NORMAL ───────────────

**Illinois State Univ.
GC**
Gregory St., 61761
Ph: 309-438-8065

Yards: 6205, Holes: 18
Par: 71, USGA: 69.7
RP: Call the proshop

Snack Bar/Proshop
GF: w/day $11.00, w/end
$11.00
Carts: $15.00

This fairly lengthy course is located at the State University, and is very well maintained.

─────────────── NORMAL ───────────────

Ironwood GC
1901 North Towanda,
60614
Ph: 309-454-9629

Yards: 6464, Holes: 18
Par: 72

The large greens here are a big feature with the protective bunkering and even an island green.

─────────────── OAK FOREST ───────────────

**Forest Preserve
National**
16300 163rd & Central
Ave., 60452
Ph: 312-429-6886

Yards: 7170, Holes: 18
Par: 72, USGA: 71.9
RP: First come, first
served

Restaurant/Proshop
GF: w/day $16.00
Carts: $16.00

The main features here are 8 lakes and 64 bunkers. The greens are large and fast. Set in the Cook County Forest Preserve, this is a very picturesque layout. This has been rated one of the best public courses in the country so don't miss it.

─────────────── ORLAND PARK ───────────────

Silver Lake CC
147th & 82nd Ave.,
60462
Ph: 708-349-6940

Yards: 6485, Holes: 45
Par: 72, USGA: 70.4
RP: Can be made 14
days in advance

Restaurant/Bar/Proshop
GF: w/day $21.00, w/end
$25.00
Carts: $22.00

Our favorite hole is the 8th on the South Course. An accurate and lengthy drive into a prevailing wind is required for a chance to reach the green in two. The second shot must carry over an expansive marsh to a steeply sloped elevated green.

─────────────OSWEGO─────────────

Fox Bend GC   Yards: 6360, Holes: 18   Restaurant/Bar/Proshop
State Rt. 34, Box 3,   Par: 71, USGA: 69.1   **GF:** w/day $20.00
60543   RP: 7 days in advance   **Carts:** $18.00
Ph: 708-554-3939

*This course is ranked among the top 10 in the Chicago area. Over half the
course has water that comes into play, and the greens are well guarded. A
challenging course that is beautifully maintained.*

─────────────PALATINE─────────────

Palatine Hills GC   Yards: 6500, Holes: 18   Restaurant/Bar/Proshop
512 W. NW Hwy., 250   Par: 72, USGA: 70.6   **GF:** w/day $18.75
E. Wood St., 60067   RP: 1 week in advance   **Carts:** $17.50
Ph: 312-359-4020   weekend, else 2

*Our golf course is a combination of hills and flat surfaces. Water comes into play
on several holes, both on the front nine and the back nine. Our golf course will
test the skills of all golfers, especially our 3 finishing holes which confuse
distance.*

─────────────PEKIN─────────────

Lick Creek GC   Yards: 6906, Holes: 18   Restaurant/Proshop
2210 Pkwy. Dr., 61554   Par: 72, USGA: 71.1   **GF:** w/day $8.00, w/end
Ph: 309-346-0077   RP: 1 week in advance $11.00
                                                   Carts: $13.50

*Very hilly course with tree-lined fairways. Front nine is the toughest. #6 is best
hole in Central Illinois, par 5, 533 yards. Big ravine 130 yards off tee. Tree-lined
fairway which drops 20 feet down.*

─────────────PEORIA─────────────

Kellogg CC   Yards: 6370, Holes: 18
7716 N Radnor Rd,   Par: 72, USGA: 68.4
61615
Ph: 309-691-0293

*This 27-holes layout was opened in 1971. The 18-hole course has lots of length,
so be sure your driver is working well.*

─────────────PEORIA─────────────

Newman GC   Yards: 6467, Holes: 18   Restaurant
2021 W. Nebraska,   Par: 71   **GF:** w/day $9.25, w/end
61604 $10.25
Ph: 309-674-1663

*The length of this course is going to be your main challenge. A few hills and
hardly any water.*

─────────────PERU─────────────

South Bluff CC   Yards: 2978, Holes: 9   Restaurant/Bar/Proshop
R.R. 1, 61354   Par: 36   **GF:** w/day $5.50, w/end
Ph: 815-223-0603 $7.00
                                                   Carts: $7.50

Sporty nine holes in the bluff overlooking LaSalle-Peru area.

─────────────PORT BYRON─────────────

Byron Hills GC   Yards: 6017, Holes: 18   Bar/Proshop
23316 94th Ave. North,   Par: 71, USGA: 69.1   **GF:** w/day $9.00
61275   RP: Weekends,   **Carts:** $14.00
Ph: 309-523-2664   weekday if large group

*A course blending old with new and a rolling terrain and a number of level lies
make this a course where all your clubs are used. My favorite hole is the 14th. A
dogleg par 4, you have a choice, over out of bounds or play safe.*

---RICHMOND---

Hunter CC
5419 Kenosha St.,
60071
Ph: 815-678-2631

Yards: 6405, Holes: 18
Par: 72, USGA: 71.2
RP: 1 week in advance

Restaurant/Bar/Proshop
GF: w/day $15.00
Carts: $16.00

Favorite hole is the 415 yard 9th. Your drive must be carefully positioned between out of bounds left and a creek that runs along the right side of the fairway and cuts across the fairway about 220 yards out. An exceptional drive can carry the creek.

---ROCKFORD---

Aldeen GC
1900 Reid Farm Road,
61107
Ph: 815-282-4653

Yards: 5736, Holes: 18
Par: 72

This fairly new course is a water paradise, with only 5 holes that it doesn't come into play. You might want to bring some extra balls to be sure you can finish.

---ROCKFORD---

Sinnissippi Park GC
1401 N 2nd St., 61107
Ph: 815-987-8838

Yards: 3230, Holes: 9
Par: 36

Ranked one of the five most challenging courses in the state, this is a real championship-caliber course. There are trees in some most unexpected places. You should really enjoy this round of golf.

---ROSEMONT---

**Ramada Htl O'Hare 9
Hole Par 3**
6600 N. Mannheim
Rd., 60018
Ph: 312-827-5131

Yards: 650, Holes: 9
Par: 27
RP: First come, first
served

Restaurant/Bar
GF: w/day $5.00

Our Course is perfect for the beginner yet tricky enough to challenge the best of players. Perhaps the most unique part about our par 3 nine hole is that we are lighted for night play.

---ROUND LAKE BEACH---

Renwood CC
1413 Hainesville Rd.,
60073
Ph: 708-546-8242

Yards: 6000, Holes: 18
Par: 72, USGA: 68.6
RP: Weekends &
holidays only

Restaurant/Bar/Proshop
GF: w/day $13.00, w/end
$16.00
Carts: $18.00

Although the course is not overly long, some small greens and a roving creek keep play very interesting.

---SANDWICH---

Edgebrook CC
RR 1 Box 1A, 60548
Ph: 815-786-3058

Yards: 6076, Holes: 18
Par: 72, USGA: 68.4
RP: Weekends &
holidays

Restaurant/Bar/Proshop
GF: w/day $18.00, w/end
$20.00
Carts: $9.50

The back nine is a little more wide open with undulating greens. The front nine is shorter but requires a little more planning. The fifth hole will tempt all golfers at all levels with water right and out of bounds left.

─────────────ST. ANNE─────────────

Shamrock GC
R #6 Box 255, 60964
Ph: 815-937-9355

Yards: 3600, Holes: 18
Par: 60, USGA: 60.0

Proshop
GF: w/day $7.50
Carts: $9.50

Shamrock is known as an executive course. We have only four par 4's—all the rest are par 3. The course is tight and calls for control. There are lots of trees and almost everyone is able to walk, which is what golfing is supposed to be all about.

─────────────ST. CHARLES─────────────

Pheasant Run GC
4051 East Main St.,
60174
Ph: 708-584-6300

Yards: 6100, Holes: 18
Par: 71, USGA: 70.0
RP: Recommended

Restaurant/Bar/Proshop
GF: w/day $25.00
Carts: $23.00

Our par 5's are our most thought provoking holes. Each is done so you may get home in two. However—failure is severe and keeping them 3 shot holes may be the smart thing to do.

─────────────STERLING─────────────

Lake View CC
23319 Hazel, 61081
Ph: 815-626-2886

Yards: 3010, Holes: 18
Par: 70, USGA: 68.7

Restaurant/Bar/Proshop
GF: w/day $8.50, w/end
$10.50
Carts: $14.00

In playing the back nine a player must cross water 6 times.

─────────────TAYLORVILLE─────────────

Lake Shore GC
316 N. Shumway, P.O.
Box 263, 62568
Ph: 217-824-5521

Yards: 6813, Holes: 18
Par: 72, USGA: 71.5
RP: 2 days in advance

Restaurant/Bar/Proshop
GF: w/day $11.00
Carts: $14.00

Bring every club in your bag.

─────────────THOMSON─────────────

Lynnwood Lynks
RR #1 Box 78, 61285
Ph: 815-259-8278

Yards: 2860, Holes: 9
Par: 36, USGA: 34.5
RP: Weekends &
holidays

Restaurant/Bar/Proshop
GF: w/day $6.00, w/end
$7.00
Carts: $7.00

A beautiful 9 hole completely watered fairway. Plenty of sandtraps. Beautiful pine trees line the fairways along with extraordinary houses. Our #9 is a long par 5 with a rolling green, that is sure to get even with the best putter.

─────────────VERNON HILLS─────────────

Vernon Hills GC
291 Evergreen Dr.,
60061
Ph: 312-680-9310

Yards: 2828, Holes: 9
Par: 34, USGA: 32.3
RP: Weekends &
holidays

Bar/Proshop
GF: w/day $7.00
Carts: $8.00

While the course is not long by most standards, water comes into play on 7 holes requiring all but the longest players to lay up, leaving longer irons into well protected greens. The fact the course record is 33 indicates the difficulty of the course.

───────────WASHINGTON───────────

Pine Lakes GC   Yards: 6132, Holes: 18   Bar/Proshop
RR # Schuck Rd.,   Par: 71, USGA: 68.8   **GF:** w/day $8.50, w/end
61571   RP: 1 day in advance $10.00
Ph: 309-745-9344   **Carts:** $12.00

*Front nine is totally different from back nine. Front has only one lake and is
generally flat and open. Back nine has more rolling hills with three water holes,
16, 17 and 18. Number 10 is very scenic, yet difficult — 413 yards. Tight.*

───────────WHEATON───────────

Arrowhead GC   Yards: 3240, Holes: 27
26 W. 151 Butterfield   Par: 35, USGA: 68.4
Rd., 60187
Ph: 312-653-5800

*Three 9-holes courses, only one of which is open in the winter. These courses
are very popular in the area.*

───────────WHEATON───────────

Cantigny GC TC   Yards: 6709, Holes: 27   Restaurant/Bar/Proshop
27 West 270 Mack Rd.,   Par: 72, USGA: 72.4   **GF:** w/day $50.00
60187   RP: 7 days in advance   **Carts:** $20.00
Ph: 708-668-3831

*Many varieties of mature, majestic trees encompass this course. The greens here
can be very tricky. Lots of water make your shot making abilities very important
to your score.*

───────────WHITTINGTON───────────

Rend Lake GC   Yards: 6426, Holes: 27   Restaurant/Bar/Proshop
RR 1, 62897   Par: 72, USGA: 69.2   **GF:** w/day $13.00, w/end
Ph: 618-629-2353   RP: Anytime in $13.00
                           advance   **Carts:** $16.00

*Championship course 6851 from blue tee but fun for players of all caliber from
6400 yard white tees. Large greens with combination of open holes and tree
lined overlooking beautiful Rend Lake.*

───────────WOODRIDGE───────────

Seven Bridges GC   Yards: 6293, Holes: 18
1 Mulligan Dr, 60532   Par: 72
Ph: 708-964-4653

*Part of the course is set in a heavily wooded terrain, and half has water protect-
ing the greens and fairways.*

───────────WOODRIDGE───────────

Village Greens of   Yards: 6290, Holes: 18   Restaurant/Bar/Proshop
Woodridge GC   Par: 72, USGA: 68.5   **GF:** w/day $20.00
1575 W. 75th St., 60517   **Carts:** $18.00
Ph: 312-985-8366

*Visit a spacious and colorful golf shop, that has been rated by Golf Digest as
being one of the top 100 golf shops of America. The 18 hole 6800 yard championship golf course occupies 116 acres of rolling greens and fairways with mature
trees.*

◄◄◄◄◄◄◄◄●►►►►►►►►►

INDIANA

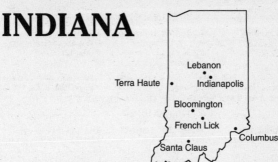

Lebanon
Terra Haute   Indianapolis
Bloomington
French Lick
Santa Claus   Columbus

---BLOOMINGTON---

Pointe GR
2250 E. Pointe Rd.,
47401
Ph: 812-824-4040

Yards: 6707, Holes: 18
Par: 71, USGA: 70.8
RP: 30 days in advance

Restaurant/Bar/Proshop
GF: w/day $27.00, w/end
$36.00
Carts: $Included

Large greens, very well bunkered, long par threes, a very demanding and fun resort golf course. Golf packages available.

---COLUMBUS---

Otter Creek GC
11522 E. 50 North,
47203
Ph: 812-579-5227

Yards: 7258, Holes: 18
Par: 72
RP: Weekdays as far
ahead as like

Restaurant/Bar/Proshop
GF: w/day $35.00, w/end
$44.00
Carts: $22.00

214 acres of rolling terrain bisected by creek. 2,000 ornamental trees, dogwood, crabapple, red bud, cherry. #11 is our most famous hole: Tee off a hill, 60 foot drop and over creek. 2nd shot over pond and 2 bunkers.

---EVANSVILLE---

Helfrich Hills GC
1550 Masker Dr., 47712
Ph: 812-428-0667

Yards: 6008, Holes: 18
Par: 71, USGA: 69.8
RP: For weekends only

GF: w/day $8.00
Carts: $14.00

This course is located in the city and gets lots of play. It's a fairly long, hilly layout.

---FRENCH LICK---

**French Lick Springs
CC**
Hwy 56, 47432
Ph: 812-935-9381

Yards: 6629, Holes: 36
Par: 70, USGA: 70.0
RP: Up to 6 months in
advance

Restaurant/Bar
GF: w/day $30.00, w/end
$30.00
Carts: $11.00

The Country Club Course is a Donald Ross design constructed in 1920. It was the site of the 1924 P.G.A. championship won by Walter Hagen. Two L.P.G.A. championship tournaments were held in the late 1950's. The Valley Course offers a milder challenge.

Our listings—supplied by the management—are as complete as possible. Many of the courses have more features than we list. Be sure to inquire when you book your tee time.

—————————————INDIANAPOLIS—————————————

Eagle Creek GC
8802 W. 56th St., 46234
Ph: 317-297-3366

Yards: 7154, Holes: 27
Par: 72, USGA: 73.4
RP: Required on
weekends

Restaurant/Bar/Proshop
GF: w/day $12.00
Carts: $21.00

Secluded course in a preserve like setting, with 2 ponds, blue grass and bent grass greens and tees. Very hilly with elevated tees and no parallel holes. #16 is a challenging par 4 split through 2 huge trees, drive onto a plateau.

—————————————LEBANON—————————————

GC of Indiana
6905 South 525 East,
46052
Ph: 317-769-6388

Yards: 7222, Holes: 18
Par: 72, USGA: 73.2
RP: at least 1 week in
advance

Restaurant/Bar/Proshop
GF: w/day $30.00, w/end
$35.00
Carts: $Included

Level course on a farm. There are 75 bunkers and 15 holes have water, little ponds and curving stream. Also bent grass, trees and very big greens. #12 a par 5 reached in two with creek and pond to carry on left.

—————————————SANTA CLAUS—————————————

Christmas Lake GC
Hwy. 245, 47579
Ph: 812-544-2271

Yards: 6515, Holes: 18
Par: 72, USGA: 71.4
RP: 7 days in advance

Restaurant/Bar/Proshop
GF: w/day $17.00, w/end
$26.00
Carts: $10.00

A player must decide to play the regular tees or challenge the championship tees at 7383 yards. Except for the first couple of holes, the front nine is relatively open. The back nine holes provide breathtaking scenery with doglegs carved through hill.

—————————————SPEEDWAY—————————————

Speedway GC
4400 W 16th St, 46222
Ph: 317-241-2500

Yards: 7179, Holes: 18
Par: 72

Restaurant/Bar
GF: w/day $13.00, w/end
$15.00

Reopened in 1993, Pete Dye has completely redesigned it. You should really enjoy the changes.

—————————————TERRE HAUTE—————————————

Hulman GC
Rt 32 Box 315, 47803
Ph: 812-877-2096

Yards: 7225, Holes: 18
Par: 72, USGA: 71.4
RP: 3 days in advance

Restaurant/Bar/Proshop
GF: w/day $15.00, w/end
$20.00
Carts: $16.00

Like Florida on front and Michigan on back. There are 130 sandtraps and bent grass greens. #18 has 2 ponds with a double dogleg par 5, 40 yards wide and U shaped sandtrap called "The Tunnel".

—————————————WEST HARRISON—————————————

Grand Oak GC
29755 Carolina Trace
Rd., 47060
Ph: 812-637-3943

Yards: 6100, Holes: 18
Par: 71

A target style course designed by Mike Hurdzan and opened in 1989. The terrain is somewhat rolling and hilly.

◄◄◄◄◄◄◄◄◄◄● ►►►►►►►►►►

IOWA

Milford
Spirit Lake

Milford

Garner • Clear Lake • Clarksville

Primghar •

• Webster City

Peosta

Dubuque

Ankeny

Iowa City • North Liberty

Boone •

Clinton

• Indianola   Wilton

• Atlantic

• Panora

─────────── AMANA ───────────

Amana Colonies GC
RR 1 Box 8500, 52203
Ph: 800-383-3636

Yards: 6824, Holes: 18
Par: 72, USGA: 73.3
RP: 30 days in advance,
with Card 1 year

Restaurant/Bar/Proshop
GF: w/day $38.50, w/end
$43.50
Carts: $25.50

*One of Iowa's top public courses, Amana Colonies is set in a forested area and
has lots of water, and traps. The fairways are narrow and tree-lined and rolling.*

─────────── ANKENY ───────────

Otter Creek GC
2388 NE 110th Ave.,
50021
Ph: 515-964-1729

Yards: 6479, Holes: 18
Par: 72, USGA: 70.0
RP: 1 week in advance

Restaurant/Bar/Proshop
GF: w/day $8.50, w/end
$10.00
Carts: $15.00

*One of two public courses in central Iowa having watered fairways, fast but
grass greens and a beautiful clubhouse.*

─────────── ATLANTIC ───────────

Atlantic Golf & CC
Box 363, 102 W. 29th
St., 50022
Ph: 712-243-3656

Yards: 5930, Holes: 18
Par: 69, USGA: 75.0

Restaurant/Bar/Proshop
GF: w/day $10.00, w/end
$12.00
Carts: $16.00

*Accuracy is important from the starting tee. Large oak trees surround every
fairway on the older front nine before moving to an entirely different look on the
back. The newer back nine is more open, lots of sand, with large, undulating
greens.*

─────────── CEDAR FALLS ───────────

St Andrews GC
1866 Blairs Fry Rd NE,
52402
Ph: 319-393-9915

Yards: 6354, Holes: 18
Par: 70

GF: w/day $7.50, w/end
$8.50

*St. Andrews is a very challenging course. The greens are fast and can be tricky,
and the finish is longer than the start.*

──────────────────CEDAR RAPIDS──────────────────

Ellis Park GC   Yards: 6410, Holes: 18   **GF:** w/day $7.25
1401 Zika Avenue NW,   Par: 72   **Carts:** $15.00
52405
Ph: 319-398-5384

A popular course with rolling terrain, water on only a few holes, and more than enough trees.

──────────────────CEDAR RAPIDS──────────────────

Twin Pines Muni GC   Yards: 5890, Holes: 18   **GF:** w/day $7.25
3800 42nd St NE, 52402   Par: 72   **Carts:** $15.00
Ph: 319-398-5183

One of the most popular courses in Cedar Rapids, there is lighted golfing on the back nine.

──────────────────CLARKSVILLE──────────────────

C.A.R.D. Inc.   Yards: 3126, Holes: 9   Bar/Proshop
Box 752, RR 1, 50619   Par: 36   **GF:** w/day $5.00, w/end
Ph: 319-278-4787 $7.00
                                                          Carts: $7.00

This quiet rural Iowa course offers a golfer some unexpected difficulties. For example our No. 6 hole, a par 4, 392 yards, has a pond that juts into the fairway on the right, out of bounds bordering the left, and a hungry creek cutting diagonally.

──────────────────CLEAR LAKE──────────────────

All Vets GC   Yards: 3061, Holes: 9   Restaurant/Bar/Proshop
2000 N. Shore Dr., P.O.   Par: 36, USGA: 66.4   **GF:** w/day $6.00, w/end
Box 3, 50428   RP: Weekends $9.00
Ph: 515-357-4457   **Carts:** $7.50

Challenging nine hole layout. Rolling terrain with manicured irrigated fairways. Well maintained course with a pleasant atmosphere. On the north shore of beautiful Clear Lake.

──────────────────CLINTON──────────────────

Valley Oaks GC   Yards: 6363, Holes: 18   Bar/Proshop
3330 Harts Mill Road,   Par: 72, USGA: 70.4   **GF:** w/day $8.00, w/end
52732   RP: In advance $11.00
Ph: 319-242-7221   **Carts:** $7.50

Beautiful challenging 18 hole course with lots of water and oak trees, two lakes on front 9, two lakes on back 9, with a creek winding through the course that comes into play on several holes.

──────────────────DES MOINES──────────────────

Waveland GC   Yards: 6519, Holes: 18   Restaurant/Bar
4908 University, 50311   Par: 72   **GF:** w/day $8.75, w/end
Ph: 515-242-2902 $11.75

The greens are elevated and the oaks are majestic on rolling terrain. This course is one of the oldest municipal courses in the country.

───────────────DUBUQUE───────────────

Bunker Hill GC
2200 Bunker Hill Rd.,
52001
Ph: 319-589-4261

Yards: 5316, Holes: 18
Par: 69, USGA: 65.0
RP: 1 week in advance

Proshop
GF: w/day $8.50, w/end
$9.00
Carts: $16.80

You may think the course looks short and easy, but the terrain is non-other like you have seen. Set in the rolling hills of the northern Mississippi River valley, it gives you the opportunity to hit every type of lie imaginable.

───────────────GARNER───────────────

Garner GC
205 Country Club Dr,
50438
Ph: 515-923-2819

Yards: 3015, Holes: 9
Par: 36, USGA: 68.9

Restaurant/Bar/Proshop
GF: w/day $8.75, w/end
$10.65
Carts: $12.00

With big greens, lots of traps and water, Garner Golf Club sets itself apart from many courses in north Iowa. Though the trees are young, they are becoming more of a hazard each year. Voted 9 hole course of the year in Iowa for 1987.

───────────────INDIANOLA───────────────

Indianola CC
Country Club Rd.,
50125
Ph: 515-961-3303

Yards: 2922, Holes: 9
Par: 35, USGA: 66.9

Bar/Proshop
GF: w/day $12.00
Carts: $10.00

Hilly with tree lined fairways, two ponds, creek bisects course opening hole par 5, 594 yards with creek coming into play on opening drive.

───────────────IOWA CITY───────────────

Finkbine GC
W. Melrose Ave., Univ.
of Iowa, 52242
Ph: 319-335-9556

Yards: 6850, Holes: 18
Par: 72, USGA: 72.1
RP: 7 days in advance

Proshop
GF: w/day $15.00
Carts: $17.00

Hole #13, 160 yards, par 3—from elevated tee to green surrounded by water.

───────────────MARION───────────────

Squaw Creek GC
Hwy 13, PO Box 365,
52302
Ph: 319-377-8433

Yards: 6289, Holes: 18
Par: 72

Proshop
GF: w/day $6.50

A municipal course with a few bunkers and plenty of water coming into play. There are lots of trees too.

───────────────MASON CITY───────────────

Highland Park GC
944 17th Street NE,
50401
Ph: 515-423-9693

Yards: 6202, Holes: 18
Par: 72

Restaurant
GF: w/day $8.00, w/end
$10.00

Some elevated greens, a long back nine, and lots of mature oaks. You're sure to have a memorable round.

───────────────MILFORD───────────────

Woodlyn Hills GC
RR 1-Box 169, 51351
Ph: 712-338-9898

Yards: 2660, Holes: 9
Par: 35

Restaurant
GF: w/day $5.00
Carts: $7.00

My favorite hole is #7, a par 3. The wind plays an important part at this hole as you must shoot across the water to reach it. People enjoy this course as it is not flat, yet can be walked with ease.

─────────────── NORTH LIBERTY ───────────────

Quail Creek GC
Highway 965, 52317
Ph: 319-626-2281

Yards: 3520, Holes: 9
Par: 36, USGA: 36.1

Restaurant/Bar/Proshop
GF: w/day $8.50, w/end
$10.00
Carts: $18.00

Quail Creek opens with 5 interesting and challenging holes: two par 5's, two par 4's and a par 3. If a low score is what you seek, you need to have it by the fifth green, for up next is our "Amen" corner. Holes 6 through 9 are all long.

─────────────── PANORA ───────────────

**Lake Panorama
National GC**
East Lake Panorama,
PO Box 625, 50216
Ph: 515-755-2024

Yards: 7001, Holes: 18
Par: 72, USGA: 73.3
RP: Tee times 1 week in
advance

Restaurant/Bar/Proshop
GF: w/day $30.00, w/end
$35.00
Carts: $Included

The front 9 is long and interesting to play. Most scenic hole is number 3 with a view of the course and lake. The back 9 is tight with #12 always the toughest. Beware of the big oak tree Come and enjoy Toll free #: 800-766-7013.

─────────────── PEOSTA ───────────────

Timberline GC
19804 E. Pleasant
Grove Rd., 52068
Ph: 319-876-3210

Yards: 6543, Holes: 18
Par: 72, USGA: 70.9
RP: Required - 5 days in
advance

Restaurant/Bar/Proshop
GF: w/day $10.00
Carts: $15.00

Carved out of native hardwood timber in the heartland of Iowa, Timberline offers a course that's "fun for all ages". #18, 368 yards downhill to a green completely fronted by a large pond, 4 lakes and a creek. Fall colors are fantastic. Come and enjoy.

─────────────── PRIMGHAR ───────────────

Primghar GC CC
2nd St. N.E., 51245
Ph: 712-757-6781

Yards: 3250, Holes: 9
Par: 36, USGA: 34.6
RP: First come, first
served

Restaurant/Bar/Proshop
GF: w/day $6.00
Carts: $6.00

It's hard to pick a favorite hole because they all offer a good challenge along with being aesthetically pleasing. A beautiful stream that winds its way through the course and two ponds bring water into play on five of the nine holes.

─────────────── SPIRIT LAKE ───────────────

Okoboji Vu GC
Hwy. 86 Box 412, 51360
Ph: 712-337-3372

Yards: 6051, Holes: 18
Par: 70, USGA: 68.3
RP: 1 day in advance

Restaurant/Bar/Proshop
GF: w/day $16.00
Carts: $16.00

Finest greens, watered fairways. 16 holes overlooking West Okoboji Lake, one of the seven true blue water lakes in the US.

─────────────── THORNTON ───────────────

Pleasant Valley GC
405 N. 1st., 50479
Ph: 515-998-2117

Yards: 3094, Holes: 9
Par: 36

GF: w/day $6.00, w/end
$8.00
Carts: $6.00

A nice course for a lot of practice with your short game, so get your irons ready.

———————— WATERLOO ————————

Byrnes Park GC
1000 Fletcher Ave.,
50701
Ph: 319-234-9271

Yards: 6268, Holes: 18
Par: 72, USGA: 68.2

Proshop
GF: w/day $8.50
Carts: $12.00

The course here opened in 1908. The trees here are mature and abundant, otherwise the course is short and in excellent condition.

———————— WEBSTER CITY ————————

Briggs Woods GC
2501 Briggs Woods
Trail, 50595
Ph: 515-832-9572

Yards: 6502, Holes: 18
Par: 72, USGA: 69.9
RP: Weekends and
holidays

Restaurant/Bar/Proshop
GF: w/day $9.00, w/end
$13.00
Carts: $15.00

The golf course is situated on rolling terrain with a beautiful view of a 70 acre lake and park. A new back 9 opened August 10, 1991, with a new clubhouse. Water, woods, sand traps and beautiful scenery enhances the golf outing.

———————— WILTON ————————

Wahkonsa CC
P.O. Box 701, Old Hwy
6, 52778
Ph: 319-785-6328

Yards: 3212, Holes: 9
Par: 36, USGA: 34.6

Restaurant/Bar/Proshop
GF: w/day $7.00, w/end
$11.00
Carts: $7.00

Hole #9 is a par 4 with a pond guarding the green, really a tough one.

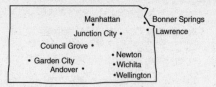

KANSAS

────────────── BONNER SPRINGS ──────────────

Sunflower Hills GC
122nd & Riverview,
66012
Ph: 913-721-2727

Yards: 7001, Holes: 18
Par: 72, USGA: 73.3
RP: 2 days in advance

Restaurant/Bar/Proshop
GF: w/day $11.50, w/end
$12.00
Carts: $18.00

Generally acknowledged as the best public golf course in the greater Kansas City area, Sunflower Hills best holes begin at #12 and finish on #17. If anyone shoots par on these holes they should end up with a great score.

────────────── COUNCIL GROVE ──────────────

Council Grove CC
830 Hays St., 66846
Ph: 316-767-5516

Yards: 2875, Holes: 9
Par: 36, USGA: 32.7

Proshop
GF: w/day $6.00, w/end
$10.00

A short but challenging course lying in the Flint Hills on the Santa Fe Trail. Challenge lies in negotiating the hilly terrain, blind shots and tricky greens. A large lake and meandering creek put water in play on seven holes.

────────────── DERBY ──────────────

Hidden Lakes GC
6020 S. Greenwich Rd.,
67037
Ph: 316-788-2855

Yards: 6269, Holes: 18
Par: 72, USGA: 69.4

Restaurant/Bar/Proshop
GF: w/day $9.00, w/end
$10.00

This course is set in hilly terrain. The course has a creek that gives plenty of water play, it should keep you on your toes to be accurate.

────────────── GARDEN CITY ──────────────

Buffalo Dunes GC
So. Star Route 83, Box
415, 67846
Ph: 316-275-1727

Yards: 6443, Holes: 18
Par: 72, USGA: 71.8
RP: 1 week in advance

Restaurant/Bar/Proshop
GF: w/day $6.50, w/end
$8.50
Carts: $14.00

Buffalo Dunes was nominated to be considered for the Top 100 Public Courses by Golf Digest. Home of Kansas' biggest and richest golf tournament—The Southwest Kansas Pro-Am. You will enjoy excellent blue grass fairways and will be challenged.

─────────────── JUNCTION CITY ───────────────

Rolling Meadows GC Yards: 6370, Holes: 18   Restaurant/Bar/Proshop
P.O. Box 287, 66441   Par: 72, USGA: 69.9   GF: w/day $8.50, w/end
Ph: 913-238-4303   RP: Call the Proshop $10.50
                                                  Carts: $16.00

*Consistently rated in Golf Digest as one of the top places to play golf in Kansas:
"Superb ... Beautifully maintained ... A hidden jewel ... Friendly staff ... Just a fun
course ... Easy to find 6 miles north of I-70 Exit 295."*

─────────────── LAWRENCE ───────────────

Alvamar GC   Yards: 7096, Holes: 18   Restaurant/Bar
1800 Crossgate Dr.,   Par: 72, USGA: 71.7   **GF:** w/day $14.50, w/end
66047   RP: 4 days in advance $18.00
Ph: 913-842-1907   **Carts:** $20.00

*The course is very hilly and has steep and long for par 3's. There are cotton-
woods, sweet-gums, walnuts, pines and silver maples lining the course. #14 has
trees, creek, dogleg left, right and left again, a par 4.*

─────────────── MANHATTAN ───────────────

Stagg Hill GC   Yards: 6427, Holes: 18   Restaurant/Proshop
4441 Ft. Riley Blvd.,   Par: 72, USGA: 70.3   **GF:** w/day $10.50
66502   RP: Weekends   **Carts:** $14.00
Ph: 913-539-1041

*Keeping your drives in play on tree lined fairways and accurate irons to small
greens will determine how well you score here. The par 3, 167 yard, 14th hole
across water to a small, elevated green is a beautiful challenging hole.*

─────────────── NEWTON ───────────────

Newton Public GC   Yards: 5662, Holes: 18   Bar/Proshop
622 E. 6th St., Jct I135 Par: 70, USGA: 66.4   **GF:** w/day $6.00, w/end
& K15, 67114   RP: Accepted $7.00
Ph: 313-283-4168   **Carts:** $13.00

*Elevated greens, two lakes and a creek running full length of course offers a
challenge to all golfers. Two par threes back to back, #6 and #7 are said to be the
toughest around. Our favorite is the 4th a long par 5 with a lake to carry and
double dogleg.*

─────────────── OLATHE ───────────────

Heritage Park GC   Yards: 6327, Holes: 18
16445 Lackman Rd.,   Par: 71
66202
Ph: 913-829-4653

*Heritage Park is bordered by three large lakes and has plenty of streams crossing
it also. The holes each have a definite personality all their own.*

─────────────── OVERLAND PARK ───────────────

Deer Creek GC   Yards: 6870, Holes: 18   Restaurant/Bar/Proshop
700 West 133rd St.,   Par: 72, USGA: 74.5   **GF:** w/day $35.00, w/end
66209   RP: 2 days in advance $42.00
Ph: 913-681-3100   **Carts:** $Included

All but 5 holes on this course have water coming into play.

─────────────────SALINA─────────────────

Salina Muni GC
2500 E. Crawford St.,
67401
Ph: 913-826-7450

Yards: 6212, Holes: 18
Par: 70, USGA: 67.4
RP: Call the Pro

Restaurant/Bar/Proshop
GF: w/day $8.00, w/end
$10.00
Carts: $10.00

A nice municipal course that won't give you too much trouble. Less than 5 minutes from I-35 & I-70 in Salinas. Ryegrass fairways, large bentgrass greens. Site of 1994 Kansas State Junior Championship.

─────────────────TOPEKA─────────────────

Lake Shawnee GC
4141 SE Eastedge Rd,
66609
Ph: 913-267-2295

Yards: 6113, Holes: 18
Par: 69, USGA: 68.9

Restaurant
GF: w/day $6.70, w/end
$7.95

A very popular course, you should enjoy this short course, it will give lots of practice with your irons.

─────────────────TOPEKA─────────────────

Western Hills GC
8533 SW 21st, 66615
Ph: 913-478-4000

Yards: 5524, Holes: 18
Par: 70, USGA: 66.8

Restaurant/Bar/Proshop
GF: w/day $9.90, w/end
$13.00
Carts: $16.68

There are lots of bunkers on the course, but with 12 lakes you may only get into the bunkers trying to avoid the water.

─────────────────WELLINGTON─────────────────

Wellington GC
1500 W. Harvey, P.O.
Box 117, 67152
Ph: 316-326-7904

Yards: 6201, Holes: 18
Par: 70, USGA: 66.6
RP: 1 week in advance

Restaurant/Bar/Proshop
GF: w/day $7.50, w/end
$9.00
Carts: $14.00

The Wellington Golf Club is a par 70 course, 6201 yards long, and has an average green size of 4,000 square feet. The hundreds of cedar, pine, oak, and elm trees, along with smallish greens will challenge most any golfer's game.

─────────────────WICHITA─────────────────

Pawnee Prairie GC
1931 S. Tyler, 67209
Ph: 316-722-6310

Yards: 6863, Holes: 18
Par: 72, USGA: 71.9

Restaurant/Bar
GF: w/day $12.00

This very long course has wide fairways with few trees and very tricky greens.

─────────────────WICHITA─────────────────

**Wichita State
University GC**
4201 E 21st St., 67208
Ph: 316-685-6601

Yards: 5944, Holes: 18
Par: 70, USGA: 69.8

GF: w/day $12.00, w/end
$12.00
Carts: $15.00

A beautiful course with majestic oaks lining the fairways.

KENTUCKY

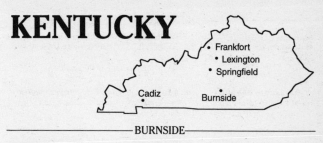

Frankfort
Lexington
Springfield
Cadiz
Burnside

―――――――――――BURNSIDE―――――――――――

General Burnside
State Park GC
P.O. Box 488, 42519
Ph: 606-561-4104

Yards: 5905, Holes: 18
Par: 71, USGA: 67.5

Proshop
GF: w/day $10.00
Carts: $15.75

Scenic gently rolling course on the shores of Lake Cumberland. Five holes run
along the shores of the lake.

――――――――――――CADIZ――――――――――――

Lake Barkley State
Resort Park
P.O. Box 790, 42211
Ph: 502-924-1131

Yards: 6417, Holes: 18
Par: 72, USGA: 70.1

Restaurant
GF: w/day $10.00
Carts: $15.75

Level 18 holes with a winding creek in a valley between the hills, the big blue
spring that supplies water for the course and winds twice across the 18th fair-
way.

―――――――――――FRANKFORT―――――――――――

Juniper Hills GC
800 Louisville Rd.,
40601
Ph: 502-875-8559

Yards: 6100, Holes: 18
Par: 70, USGA: 66.7
RP: Starters times 1st of
week

Proshop
GF: w/day $8.00, w/end
$8.00
Carts: $15.00

The course offers rolling fairways, small greens, tree lined fairways. Favorite
hole #13 with new lake and bridge is always in great shape with very courteous
personnel.

――――――――――GILBERTSVILLE――――――――――

Kentucky Dam
Village GC
Hwy. 641, 42044
Ph: 502-362-4271

Yards: 6307, Holes: 18
Par: 72

GF: w/day $10.00
Carts: $15.75

A very challenging course that has plenty of room for you to work on your wood
shots. Their are lots of pines and the layout is hilly.

―――――――――――LEXINGTON―――――――――――

Kearney Hills GC
3403 Kearney Rd.,
40511
Ph: 606-253-1918

Yards: 6501, Holes: 18
Par: 72, USGA: 70.5
RP: 7 days in advance

Proshop
GF: w/day $18.00
Carts: $7.00

A very well maintained course, with many, many strategically placed bunkers.
The greens are fast and tricky. You can also expect to find some very trying
doglegs. Accuracy is the key to a good score here. One of the best courses in
Kentucky.

———————————— LEXINGTON ————————————

Marriott's Griffin Gate Resort
1720 Newtown Pike, 40511
Ph: 606-254-4101

Yards: 6300, Holes: 18
Par: 72, USGA: 71.5
RP: Required

Restaurant/Bar
GF: w/day $42.00, w/end $47.00
Carts: $Included

A rambling, tree-lined layout with large rolling greens, long bluegrass fairways, more than 65 sand bunkers and water coming into play on twelve holes. Home for seven years of the Senior PGA Bank One Classic.

———————————— LOUISVILLE ————————————

Persimmon Ridge GC
72 Persimmon Ridge Dr., Ph: 502-241-0819

Yards: 6203, Holes: 18
Par: 72

Persimmon Ridge has been ranked the most difficult course in the state of Kentucky. A long course that offers plenty to challenge you.

———————————— OWENSBORO ————————————

Ben Hawes State Park GC
Box 761, 400 Booth Field Rd., 42302
Ph: 502-685-2011

Yards: 6372, Holes: 27
Par: 71

Proshop
GF: w/day $12.00
Carts: $16.00

A course with very open fairways, the front nine is flat and the back more rolling.

———————————— SPRINGFIELD ————————————

Lincoln Homestead St. Park GC
Rt. 1 Hwy. 528, 40069
Ph: 606-336-7461

Yards: 6359, Holes: 18
Par: 71
RP: Weekends

Proshop
GF: w/day $10.00
Carts: $15.00

Setting in a lovely wooded area. #15 is a particularly challenging par 5 with 2 large bunkers guarding either side of the fairway and 2 additional bunkers toward the front of the green, accuracy is a must.

◄—◄—◄—◄—◄—◄—◄—◄—◄—● ►—►—►—►—►—►—►—►—►—

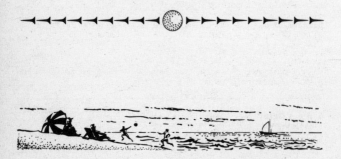

LOUISIANA

W. Monroe

Gretna • • Slidell

---------------------BATON ROUGE---------------------

Santa Maria GC
19301 Old Perkins Rd.,
Ph: 504-752-9667

Yards: 5758, Holes: 18
Par: 72

A long course where your short game is going to be called into action quite a bit.

---------------------GRETNA---------------------

Plantation G & CC
1001 Behrman Hwy.,
70053
Ph: 504-392-3363

Yards: 5780, Holes: 18
Par: 69
RP: 1 day ahead

Bar/Proshop
GF: w/day $5.00, w/end
$6.00
Carts: $10.00

The golf course is not too long but it is difficult to par the course. Course is not too crowded, you can always get a starting time. Due to small greens, the course is great to test your short game. Available for outings.

---------------------LA PLACE---------------------

Belle Terre CC
111 Fairway Dr, 70068
Ph: 504-652-5000

Yards: 6340, Holes: 18
Par: 72, USGA: 70.2

Restaurant/Bar
GF: w/day $35.00, w/end
$40.00

This course is an amphibian's delight, built around bayous, ponds and swamps. The last few holes will ruin your score if you don't keep your full attention on the game.

---------------------NEW IBERIA---------------------

Squirrel Run GC
500 Darby Ln, 70560
Ph: 318-367-7820

Yards: 6500, Holes: 18
Par: 72

Bar
GF: w/day $15.00, w/end
$20.00

The course has many huge trees that may give you a bit of trouble. A Joe Lee design.

---------------------SHREVEPORT---------------------

Huntington Park GC
8300 Pines Rd., 71129
Ph: 318-673-7765

Yards: 7295, Holes: 18
Par: 72, USGA: 71.4
RP: Required holidays
& weekends

Restaurant/Proshop
GF: w/day $8.60
Carts: $13.98

Water will give you difficulty on at least a third of the course. The fairways are wide and long, lots of driver skills here.

SLIDELL

Royal GC
201 Royal Dr., 70460
Ph: 504-643-3000

Yards: 6800, Holes: 18
Par: 72, USGA: 71.3
RP: Needed weekends
& holidays

Bar/Proshop
GF: w/day $10.00, w/end
$12.00
Carts: $15.00

We are located 45 minutes off Interstate Drive from downtown New Orleans. We have Tiff Dwarf greens, 419 Bermuda fairways and tees. Plenty of hardwoods, pines, and cypress.

ST. FRANCISVILLE

**Bluffs on Thompson
Creek GC**
Freeland Rd, PO Box
1220, 70775
Ph: 504-634-5551

Yards: 6522, Holes: 18
Par: 72, USGA: 70.5

Restaurant/Bar/Proshop
GF: w/day $40.00, w/end
$50.00
Carts: $Included

A beautiful natural setting in the woods. The course follows the natural lay of the land, using the elevation changes and natural hazards as much as possible. If you're not careful with your shots you'll probably land in the water, the woods or a bunker.

W. MONROE

Riverside Golf & CC
100 Arkansas Rd.,
71291
Ph: 318-322-0696

Yards: 6389, Holes: 9
Par: 72, USGA: 70.5

Restaurant/Bar/Proshop
GF: w/day $6.50, w/end
$8.00
Carts: $7.00

Enjoy the easy 108 yard par 3 #8—if you hit the green; if not, good luck. Water in front of green and three sand traps to front, right and left side can spell trouble for the weekend golfer.

MAINE

Island Falls ●

● Moose River

Carrabasset Valley ●

Carmel ●

Brooks ● Bangor ●

Rockport ●

●Bethel Rockland ● Trenton

Leeds ● Camden ●

Cumberland

Westbrook Hollis

─────────────BANGOR─────────────

Bangor Muni GC
278 Webster Ave.,
04401
Ph: 207-945-9226

Yards: 6400, Holes: 18
Par: 71

Restaurant/Proshop
GF: w/day $11.00
Carts: $12.00

1980 Golf Digest Top 50 Public.

─────────────BAR HARBOR─────────────

Kebo Valley GC
Eagle Lake Rd., 04609
Ph: 207-288-3000

Yards: 5926, Holes: 18
Par: 70

GF: w/day $25.00

The fairways are lined with trees and the greens are small. The course is very exacting, and will challenge you to be your very best.

─────────────BETHEL─────────────

Bethel Inn & CC
Village Common,
04217
Ph: 207-824-2175

Yards: 6663, Holes: 18
Par: 72

Restaurant/Bar/Proshop
GF: w/day $22.00, w/end
$27.00
Carts: $22.00

A classic New England resort offering traditional inn and luxury townhouse accommodations, fine dining, health center, and lake house. Geoffrey Cornish designed championship layout offers mountain vistas and a challenge for golfers of all levels.

─────────────BROOKS─────────────

Country View GC
Rt. 7, 04921
Ph: 207-722-3161

Yards: 2950, Holes: 9
Par: 36

Restaurant/Proshop
GF: w/day $12.00, w/end
$12.00
Carts: $16.00

This beautiful 9 hole layout is very unique as it sets on top of a hill with spectacular views from nearly every hole. No. 9 features a shot from the tee like you have never seen before.

CAMDEN

Goose River GC
Simonton Rd., Box
4820, 04843
Ph: 207-236-8488

Yards: 2910, Holes: 9
Par: 36, USGA: 34.0

Restaurant/Bar/Proshop
GF: w/day $10.00
Carts: $14.00

Tough par 5 to begin with hazard and woods on left off tee. Playing to right forces long carry over river with river again in play left of green. Goose River in play on 5 holes. Separate tees give entirely different look on back 9.

CARMEL

Carmel Valley GC
Rt. 2 Main Rd., P.O.
Box 133, 04419
Ph: 207-848-5237

Yards: 2416, Holes: 9
Par: 27, USGA: 55.7

Proshop
GF: w/day $5.00, w/end
$6.00
Carts: $8.00

Carmel Valley Golf Course is a true championship course for any level golfer. Each hole has its own character. The rewards can be enjoyed by all. The most interesting hole would be #6 miss and take six, 143 yards can give you a very unexpected surprise.

CARRABASSETT VALLEY

Sugarloaf GC
RR 1 Box 5000, 04947
Ph: 207-237-2000

Yards: 6902, Holes: 18
Par: 72
RP: 5 days in advance

Restaurant/Bar/Proshop
GF: w/day $32.00, w/end
$40.00
Carts: $13.00

Sugarloaf Golf Course is truly a wilderness course with spectacular vistas, picturesque views and abundant wildlife. Six holes on the back 9 play along or over the Carrabassett River, with the favorite being the 222 yard, par 3 eleventh.

CUMBERLAND

Val Halla GC
Val Halla Rd., 04021
Ph: 207-829-2225

Yards: 6324, Holes: 18
Par: 72, USGA: 70.6
RP: Call the Proshop

Restaurant/Bar/Proshop
GF: w/day $16.00, w/end
$22.00
Carts: $22.00

Our first nine is relatively open, conducive to good scoring but the back nine is carved out of woods and requires accurate tee shots. Our favorite hole would be the 18th, 398 yard dogleg right with out of bounds on the left.

GORHAM

Gorham CC
68 McLellan Rd., 04038
Ph: 207-839-3490

Yards: 6334, Holes: 18
Par: 71

GF: w/day $18.00

Gorham is set in rolling terrain with groves of pine trees that will definitely add a challenge.

HOLLIS

Salmon Falls Resort
Salmon Falls Rd. - off
Rt. 202, 04042
Ph: 207-929-5233

Yards: 6000, Holes: 18
Par: 72, USGA: 70.0
RP: Weekends &
holidays

Restaurant/Bar/Proshop
GF: w/day $15.00, w/end
$15.00
Carts: $18.00

Salmon Falls Country Club, restaurant, motel and golf course has a beautifully manicured course situated along the Saco River in Maine. Its subtle beauty is accentuated by Maine's scenic wonders that have made Maine one of the leading recreational spots.

──────────ISLAND FALLS──────────

Va-Jo-Wa GC
142 Walker Rd., 04747
Ph: 207-463-2128

Yards: 6203, Holes: 18
Par: 72
RP: Walk on—call for
res. times

Restaurant/Bar/Proshop
GF: w/day $15.00, w/end
$15.00
Carts: $18.00

The course features small greens which are well guarded by trees, traps and water. Approaches with accuracy are a must. The front nine is located in a valley on the shores of Pleasant Lake. The back nine, on a plateau, has panoramic views of Mt. Katahdin.

──────────LEEDS──────────

Springbrook GC
RR1, Box 2030, 04263
Ph: 207-946-5900

Yards: 6408, Holes: 18
Par: 71, USGA: 71.2
RP: Recommended

Restaurant/Bar/Proshop
GF: w/day $12.00
Carts: $16.00

Converted in 1966 from a farm, Springbrook offers a challenging championship course which has hosted the Maine Open in recent years. Known for excellent putting greens, Springbrook also offers a friendly, relaxing atmosphere in our unique clubhouse.

──────────MOOSE RIVER/JACKMAN──────────

Moose River GC
04945
Ph: 207-668-5331

Yards: 1976, Holes: 9
Par: 31

GF: w/day $7.00

We have 4 par 4 and 5 par 3. One water hole but very small greens. Open May 15, until November 1, or until snow flies. We also have a cemetery between #1 fairway and #3 hole.

──────────ORONO──────────

Penobscot Valley GC
356 Main Rd., 04473
Ph: 207-866-2423

Yards: 6301, Holes: 18
Par: 72, USGA: 69.6

Restaurant/Bar
GF: w/day $35.00

Penobscot is in a rural location with towering heavy stands of trees. The greens are small and the terrain is very hilly. The roughs and sandtraps will add another difficult dimension to this round of golf.

──────────RANGELEY──────────

Mingo Springs GC
off Rt 4 & Mingo Loop
Rd., 04970
Ph: 207-864-5021

Yards: 5923, Holes: 18
Par: 70

GF: w/day $19.00

Mingo Springs offers spectacular views of the Saddleback Mountains. The setting for the course is quite hilly.

──────────ROCKLAND──────────

Rockland GC, Inc.
Old County Rd., 04841
Ph: 207-594-9322

Yards: 6010, Holes: 18
Par: 70, USGA: 69.0
RP: Recommended

Restaurant/Bar/Proshop
GF: w/day $15.00
Carts: $18.00

Near Maine's beautiful coast, and a view of Chickawaukee Lake from the back nine. A wide open course, with few hazards, but wayward shots present many problems. The 595 yard par 5, 15th hole is a test for any golfer.

Our listings—supplied by the management—are as complete as possible. Many of the courses have more features than we list. Be sure to inquire when you book your tee time.

---ROCKPORT---

Samoset Resort GC
On the Ocean, 04856
Ph: 207-594-2511

Yards: 6362, Holes: 18
Par: 70, USGA: 68.9
RP: Tee times
recommended

Restaurant/Bar/Proshop
GF: w/day $25.00, w/end
$25.00
Carts: $22.00

The Samoset Resort Golf Club has been described as "the Pebble Beach of the East." With seven holes bordering the ocean and thirteen holes having ocean vistas the perfectly maintained golf course and beautiful gardens will make this a unique experience.

---SOUTH PORTLAND---

Sable Oaks GC
505 Country Club Dr,
04106
Ph: 207-775-6257

Yards: 6056, Holes: 18
Par: 72, USGA: 70.2

Proshop
GF: w/day $20.00, w/end
$25.00
Carts: $20.00

A course with heavily wooded fairways set on rolling terrain. There is a creek that you'll meet all too often. Winds off the ocean and the mature trees, and ponds and are the most challenging aspect of this course.

---TRENTON---

Bar Harbor GC
Jct. Rts. 3 & 204, 04605
Ph: 207-667-7505

Yards: 6621, Holes: 18
Par: 71, USGA: 69.5

Restaurant/Bar/Proshop
GF: w/day $15.00
Carts: $18.00

Playing alongside the Jordan River with the majestic mountains of Acadia National Park in the background, this course is one of the most picturesque in Maine. Save some strength for the 18th–no one has ever reached the green in two shots on the 620 yard.

---WATERVILLE---

Waterville CC
Country Club Rd., PO
Box 459, 04901
Ph: 207-465-9861

Yards: 6108, Holes: 18
Par: 73, USGA: 68.2
RP: Same day

Restaurant/Bar/Proshop
GF: w/day $30.00
Carts: $18.00

A beautiful course with a mountain backdrop, it is set in hilly terrain with majestic, abundant trees. A real championship layout that you won't want to miss.

---WESTBROOK---

River Meadow GC
216 Lincoln St., Box
1201, 04092
Ph: 207-854-1625

Holes: 9
Par: 70
RP: No tee times

Restaurant/Proshop
GF: w/day $8.00
Carts: $7.00

We have 9 holes not very long but interesting. It is easy to walk, follows close to the river with small streams running through the holes. #9 is a par 5 teeing from an island tee dogleg left out of the woods; small greens. We have land for 9 more holes.

MARYLAND

---ANNAPOLIS---

Annapolis CC
2638 Carrollton Rd., 21403
Ph: 301-263-6771

Yards: 3259, Holes: 9
Par: 36, USGA: 69.5

GF: w/day $7.00
Carts: $9.00

Located in the Bay Ridge area of Maryland, the course was formerly the Annapolis Country Club. Built in 1928, it features elevated greens with encircling deep grass bunkers. Recent redesign and plantings have given this course a new look.

---ARNOLD---

Bay Hills GC
545 Bay Hills Dr., 21012
Ph: 301-974-0669

Yards: 6057, Holes: 18
Par: 70, USGA: 68.5

Restaurant/Bar/Proshop
GF: w/day $20.00, w/end $25.00
Carts: $9.00

The character of this scenic course lies in the natural beauty of its wooded and gently rolling terrain. Six doglegs, fifty plus bunkers, and water coming into play on nine of the holes, all combine to place a premium on strategy and shot placement.

---BALTIMORE---

Clifton Park GC
2800 St. Lo Dr, 21213
Ph: 410-243-3500

Yards: 5583, Holes: 18
Par: 70

Bar
GF: w/day $7.50, w/end $8.50

A course that has a lot of forgiveness in it. But don't count on it all the time or the out-of-bounds will get you.

---BALTIMORE---

Mt. Pleasant GC
6001 Hillen Rd., 21239
Ph: 410-254-5100

Yards: 6395, Holes: 18
Par: 71

Restaurant
GF: w/day $9.50, w/end $11.00

A very hilly course that will give you a lot of sidehill problems. Not many trees, but that won't help you much.

---BERLIN---

Bay Club GC
9122 Libertytown Rd., 21811
Ph: 410-641-4081

Yards: 6033, Holes: 18
Par: 72

Restaurant/Bar
GF: w/day $25.00

The Bay Club has kept the best of its natural setting. You can't slice or hook here and expect to get away with it.

---------------------------------BERLIN---------------------------------

Pine Shore GC Yards: 3380, Holes: 27 Restaurant/Bar/Proshop
11285 Beauchamp Rd., Par: 60, USGA: 52.7 **GF:** w/day $9.00
21811   **Carts:** $12.10
Ph: 301-641-5100

There are three nine hole courses which rotate daily, so that you would get a different 18 every 3 days. The Dogwood is tight (wooded). The Pines and Willow have plenty of water. The greens and tees are regulation size so each hole could stand on its own.

---------------------------------BOWIE---------------------------------

Bowie G & CC Yards: 5840, Holes: 18 **GF:** w/day $16.00, w/end
P.O. Box 590, 20715 Par: 70, USGA: 69.7 $18.00
Ph: 301-262-8141

Narrow fairways with young trees give this course an open feeling. The back nine if hilly with water carry over three holes. There are also blind tee shots and sloped fairways to get you into a bit of trouble. The course is not long.

---------------------------------CHAPTICO---------------------------------

Wicomico Shores Yards: 6482, Holes: 18 Restaurant/Bar
Muni GC   Par: 71   **GF:** w/day $13.00, w/end
Rt. 234 & 236, 20621 $16.00
Ph: 301-884-4601

This course offers a lovely view of the Potomac River. Although the river is not in play, streams and ponds are, and the heavily bunkered greens can give you lots of challenge.

---------------------------------COLLEGE PARK---------------------------------

Paint Branch GC Holes: 9
4690 University Blvd.,
20740
Ph: 301-935-0330

The fairways are tree-lined, but very open. A flat course with water that usually doesn't cause a problem. A good course if you're looking for a relaxing game. A nice course for seniors.

---------------------------------CROWNSVILLE---------------------------------

Dwight D.   Yards: 6400, Holes: 18 Bar
Eisenhower GC Par: 71, USGA: 66.9 **GF:** w/day $13.00
Rt 178 General Hwy.,
21032
Ph: 301-222-7922

A hilly course with lots of water and dense woods. Water hazards occur on almost half the holes with wandering streams and a large pond. The green are well protected and the grounds are beautifully maintained.

---------------------------------DERWOOD---------------------------------

Needwood GC Yards: 6379, Holes: 27 Restaurant/Bar
6724 Needwood Rd., Par: 71   **GF:** w/day $13.50, w/end
20855 $15.00
Ph: 301-948-1075

An attractive and scenic course. The grounds offer some ornamental grasses which are well maintained. Nos. 16 and 18 are both very difficult holes. No. 18 gives you a terrific finish over a lot of water.

─────────────────DUNKIRK─────────────────

Twin Shields GC   Yards: 6284, Holes: 18   Restaurant/Bar/Proshop
2425 Roarty Rd., 20754   Par: 70, USGA: 68.0   **GF:** w/day $15.00, w/end
Ph: 301-855-8228 $18.00
                                                       Carts: $18.00

*Enjoy the beauty and personality of one of Southern Maryland's most scenic
courses. Gently rolling terrain and large undulating greens present a challenge
for even the most experienced golfers.*

───────────────── EASTON─────────────────

Hog Neck GC   Yards: 7018, Holes: 27   Restaurant/Proshop
10142 Old Cardove   Par: 72, USGA: 71.2   **GF:** w/day $18.00
Road, 21601   RP: 1 week in advance   **Carts:** $17.00
Ph: 410-822-6079

*Front nine wide open with sand and water 7 of 9 holes. The back nine is longer
and more scenic with pine trees.*

───────────────── ELKTON─────────────────

Brantwood GC   Yards: 6222, Holes: 18   Restaurant/Bar/Proshop
1190 Augustine   Par: 70, USGA: 68.9   **GF:** w/day $13.00, w/end
Herman Hwy., 21921   RP: 1 week in advance $16.00
Ph: 301-398-8848   **Carts:** $16.00

*Brantwood Golf Club is a fairly short track, but don't let that fool you, with water
coming into play on eight holes and trees capturing many errant shots, the
course is pleasantly surprising. It's easy to walk and not too crowded on weekdays.*

─────────────────FT. WASHINGTON─────────────────

Henson Creek GC   Holes: 9
7200 Sunnyside Ln.,
20744
Ph: 301-567-4646

*A long nine hole course with gently rolling fairways. The greens are well bun-
kered, with woods surrounding most holes. A very popular course with the
seniors.*

───────────────── GLENN DALE─────────────────

Glenn Dale GC   Yards: 6300, Holes: 18   Restaurant/Bar/Proshop
11501 Old Prospect   Par: 70, USGA: 67.5   **GF:** w/day $22.00, w/end
Hill Rd., 20769   RP: Call the Proshop $27.00
Ph: 301-262-1166   **Carts:** $10.00

*The course is open and flat on the front, and hilly and narrower on the back
nine. The 9th and 18th holes are the only ones with heavy bunkering.*

─────────────────HAGERSTOWN─────────────────

Beaver Creek CC   Yards: 6388, Holes: 18   Restaurant/Bar/Proshop
Route 9, Box 368 B,   Par: 72, USGA: 70.2   **GF:** w/day $16.00, w/end
21740   RP: Must call for $20.00
Ph: 301-733-5152   starting time   **Carts:** $16.00

*It's the kind of golf course you never get tired of playing. You always think you
should have done better. It has a good variety of holes. Fair but challenging.
"Form follows function."*

---ISSUE---

Swan Point GC   Ph: 301-259-2074   Yards: 6290, Holes: 18
1 Swan Point Rd,   Par: 72, USGA: 70.2
20645

*A beautifully treed layout on the Potomac River. Marshlands are the biggest
hazard on this challenging course. A must play.*

---LAUREL---

Gunpowder GC   Yards: 6000, Holes: 18   Restaurant/Bar
14300 Gunpowder Rd,   Par: 70, USGA: 69.0   **GF:** w/day $7.00, w/end
20707 $9.00
Ph: 301-725-4532

*A Scottish style course which follows the natural lay of the land. A really
challenging course with ravines and steep slops. Accuracy is much more important than power here. The grounds are not lush, but more rugged.*

---LAUREL---

Patuxent Greens GC   Yards: 6207, Holes: 18   Restaurant/Bar/Proshop
14415 Greenview Dr.,   Par: 71, USGA: 69.1   **GF:** w/day $12.00, w/end
20708   RP: Weekend $18.00
Ph: 301-776-5533   **Carts:** $18.00

*A huge clubhouse for a public course with fine dining and banquet rooms. The
golf course has a definite "Myrtle Beach" style with 16 water holes and many tall
trees, and bunkers. Back nine is very scenic.*

---LAYTONSVILLE---

Laytonsville GC   Yards: 6221, Holes: 18   **GF:** w/day $13.00, w/end
7130 Dorsey Rd., 20879   Par: 70 $15.00
Ph: 301-948-5288

*A hilly rolling course, with water running through many holes. A couple of
ponds also come into play. There are large green with few bunkers. A very
scenic course.*

---LEONARDTOWN---

Breton Bay G & CC   Yards: 6580, Holes: 18   Restaurant/Bar
Rt 3 Box 25-K L, 20650   Par: 72, USGA: 70.3   **GF:** w/day $15.00
Ph: 301-475-2300

*Features large greens and wide fairways, this course is quite long. Water hazards
occur on seven holes, some of them have more than one water hazard so you
might want to bring your hip boots. Spectacular views of the Potomac.*

---LUTHERVILLE---

Pine Ridge GC   Yards: 6390, Holes: 18   Restaurant
2101 Dulaney Valley   Par: 72   **GF:** w/day $10.50, w/end
Rd., 21093 $11.50
Ph: 410-252-1408

*A very scenic course with an abundance of wildlife. You'll find plenty to chal-
lenge you here.*

---MCHENRY---

Village Green at the   Yards: 6760, Holes: 18   Restaurant/Bar
WISP GC   Par: 72   **GF:** w/day $40.00
Marsh Hill Rd/PO Box
629, 21541
Ph: 301-387-4911

*This is one of the most difficult and challenging courses in Maryland. The
mountain setting will give you a terrific round of golf.*

─────────────────MITCHELLVILLE─────────────────

Enterprise GC   Yards: 6587, Holes: 18   **GF:** w/day $13.00, w/end
2002 Enterprise Rd.,   Par: 72, USGA: 69.4 $16.00
20716
Ph: 301-249-2040

A very scenic course located on the former farm and estate of Capt. Newton H. White, with protective covenants that protect the area. Particularly beautiful in the spring, when the course "blossoms."

─────────────────MITCHELLVILLE─────────────────

Lake Arbor Cc   Yards: 6406, Holes: 18   Restaurant/Bar
1401 Golf Course Dr,   Par: 71, USGA: 71.6   **GF:** w/day $12.00, w/end
20721 $16.00
Ph: 301-336-7771

Lots of water on this course with almost half of the holes having natural water hazards. The fairways have a gentle role and the greens are well bunkered. No. 18 is the most difficult hole, and can really do your score in.

──────────────────── POTOMAC ────────────────────

Falls Road GC   ·   Yards: 6257, Holes: 18   Bar
10800 Falls Rd., 20854   Par: 71, USGA: 68.0   **GF:** w/day $13.00, w/end
Ph: 301-299-5156 $15.00

The front nine is open and rolling while the back nine is in the woods. The course is lightly bunkered but on three holes a nasty slice can put you out of bounds.

───────────────────QUEENSTOWN───────────────────

Queenstown Harbor   Yards: 7110, Holes: 36   Restaurant/Bar/Proshop
GL   Par: 72, USGA: 70.0   **GF:** w/day $28.00, w/end
Rt 2 Box 54, 21658   RP: One week in $50.00
Ph: 800-827-5257   advance   **Carts:** $12.00

Both championship golf courses wander through woods and wetlands. Our man-made ponds and over 2 miles of shoreline, along with spectacles of wild geese and deer, make Queenstown Harbor an exciting experience. Our plush bent grass fairways are unsurpassed.

────────────────────ROCKVILLE────────────────────

Redgate Muni GC   Yards: 6120, Holes: 18
14500 Avery Rd., 20853   Par: 72, USGA: 68.9
Ph: 301-340-2404

Lots of blind tee shots and doglegs makes this an interesting course. Lots of bunkers guard the greens and water is a very big factor on half the course. A very well maintained course.

─────────────────── SILVER SPRING───────────────────

Sligo Creek Parkway   Yards: 2270, Holes: 9
GC   Par: 34, USGA: 64.0
9701 Sligo Creek
Pkwy., 20901
Ph: 301-585-6006

A short nine hole course with tree-lined fairways. There are few bunkers and some water on six of the holes. A good beginner's course.

UPPER MARLBORO

Marlboro CC
P.O. Box 29, 20772
Ph: 301-952-1350

Yards: 5701, Holes: 18
Par: 71, USGA: 67.5

Restaurant/Bar/Proshop
GF: w/day $17.00, w/end
$20.00

This course has so many bunkers you can hardly count them, so accuracy is very important. Water hazards also abound. The 15th hole has tee areas that reach out over the water. Annually hosts a charity tournament for the Children's Hospital.

WESTMINSTER

Wakefield Valley GC
1000 Fenby Farm Rd.,
21157
Ph: 301-876-6662

Yards: 6650, Holes: 27
Par: 72, USGA: 71.4

Restaurant/Bar/Proshop
GF: w/day $18.00, w/end
$20.00
Carts: $20.00

27 holes featuring beautiful Carroll County rolling countryside. All holes feature plenty of water and challenging shots from (4) sets of tees—best conditioned course in area.

WHEATON

Northwest Park GC
15711 Layhill Rd.,
20906
Ph: 301-598-6100

Yards: 7185, Holes: 27
Par: 72, USGA: 71.9
RP: 6 days in advance

Restaurant/Proshop
GF: w/day $13.50, w/end
$18.00
Carts: $17.00

Northwest Park Golf Course is one of the longest courses you will play. Off the blue tees you could play as long a 7,500 yards with par fours averaging 430 yards. Creeks border the course on the front and back nines as lateral water hazards.

WHITE PLAINS

White Plains GC
Box 68 Denmarr Rd.,
20695
Ph: 301-645-1300

Yards: 5943, Holes: 18
Par: 70, USGA: 67.5

Bar/Proshop
GF: w/day $9.50, w/end
$12.00

Doglegs abound on tight, tree-lined fairways. Large greens are well protected, with lots of water coming into play.

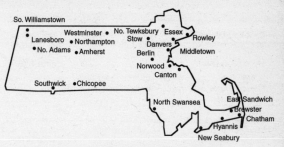

MASSACHUSETTS

───────────AMHERST───────────

Hickory Ridge CC
West Pomeroy Ln.,
01002
Ph: 413-253-9320

Yards: 6794, Holes: 18
Par: 72, USGA: 68.8
RP: 1 day in advance

Restaurant/Bar/Proshop
GF: w/day $20.00, w/end
$25.00
Carts: $18.00

Our favorite hole is the 18th, a 440 yard par four, a good drive from the elevated tee will leave you a solid iron to a large bunkered green, with the clubhouse as a background. Turn it loose.

───────────BERLIN───────────

Berlin CC
25 Carr Rd., 01503
Ph: 508-838-2733

Yards: 2313, Holes: 9
Par: 33, USGA: 62.9

Restaurant/Bar/Proshop
GF: w/day $8.00

Berlin Country Club provides a scenic view of the New England countryside. Although nestled in the small town of Berlin, it is only minutes away from major highways located in central Massachusetts.

───────────BREWSTER───────────

The Captains
1000 Free Man's Way,
02631
Ph: 508-896-5100

Yards: 6794, Holes: 18
Par: 72, USGA: 69.4
RP: 2 months in
advance

Restaurant/Bar/Proshop
GF: w/day $25.00
Carts: $21.00

Course is very gently sloping with lots of pine and oak trees. #13 is a par 4, 448 yard hole with tight drive into wind, lake and pond near 14, golf over it and lay up on 2nd shot.

───────────BREWSTER───────────

Ocean Edge GC
Route 6A, 832 Villages
Dr, 02631
Ph: 800-221-1837

Yards: 6700, Holes: 18
Par: 72

Restaurant/Bar
GF: w/day $46.00, w/end
$56.00

Our course is a true test of strategy and finesse. You'll tee off over a ravine, then over a cranberry bog. You'll chip over deep blue ponds and out of Scottish-style pot bunkers on your way to the sharply contoured greens.

─────────────────CANTON─────────────────

Brookmeadow CC
100 Everendon Rd.,
02021
Ph: 617-828-4444

Yards: 6750, Holes: 18
Par: 72, USGA: 69.4

Bar/Proshop
GF: w/day $15.00, w/end
$18.00
Carts: $20.00

*A full championship layout cut in wooded undulating land, large greens, lush
fairways, lined with trees, water holes and bunker hazards.*

─────────────────CHATHAM─────────────────

Chatham Bars Inn
Shore Rd., 02633
Ph: 508-945-0096

Yards: 2325, Holes: 9
Par: 34, USGA: 61.8

Restaurant/Bar
GF: w/day $6.00
Carts: $2.00

*Definitely short but quite challenging as the course winds through rolling terrain,
with views of the harbor and ocean from the 7th and 8th holes.*

─────────────────CHICOPEE─────────────────

Chicopee C
1290 Burnett Rd.,
01020
Ph: 413-592-4156

Yards: 7010, Holes: 18
Par: 72, USGA: 70.4
RP: Weekends

Restaurant/Bar/Proshop
GF: w/day $10.00
Carts: $15.00

*Golf course is tree lined with pine and oak and is considered a golf course for
golfers who can hook the ball. It's tight and we have on the front nine a double
green for #2 and #5 holes, the 2nd is a par 5 and the 5th holes is very narrow &
difficult.*

─────────────────DALTON─────────────────

Wahconah CC
Orchard St, PO Box 43,
01226
Ph: 413-684-1333

Yards: 6186, Holes: 18
Par: 71

Restaurant/Bar
GF: w/day $25.00, w/end
$35.00

*The front nine is open and the back tight. The nines are very different and will
require your abilities to shift to a different type of terrain.*

─────────────────DANVERS─────────────────

Tara Ferncroft GC
50 Ferncroft Rd., 01923
Ph: 617-777-2500

Yards: 6476, Holes: 18
Par: 72

Restaurant/Bar
GF: w/day $60.00

*Championship golf course, lots of mature trees, bunkers and water. Home of the
LPGA Boston Five Classic July 1987.*

─────────────────EAST SANDWICH─────────────────

Round Hill CC
Round Hill Rd., 02537
Ph: 508-888-3384

Yards: 6525, Holes: 18
Par: 72
RP: 1 day in advance

Restaurant/Bar/Proshop
GF: w/day $20.00, w/end
$22.00
Carts: $20.00

*Round Hill Country offers a unique setting with rolling fairways and a scenic
view of Cape Cod on the south side. The back 9 holes display a spectacular view
of Cape Cod Bay. Round Hill offers a challenge and the beauty of Cape Cod.*

─────────────────ESSEX─────────────────

Cape Ann GC
John Wise Ave (Rte.
133), 01929
Ph: 508-768-7544

Yards: 2950, Holes: 9
Par: 35, USGA: 70.0

Restaurant/Bar/Proshop
GF: w/day $8.00, w/end
$10.00
Carts: $9.00

*Most scenic course north of Boston. Panoramic view of salt marshes and beach-
es from 3rd hole to top of 4th tee.*

─────────────── HARVARD ───────────────

Shaker Hills GC   Ph: 508-772-2227   Yards: 5781, Holes: 18
Shaker Rd., PO Box   Par: 71
420, 01451

This course is quite long, and therein lies the challenge.

─────────────── HARWICH ───────────────

Cranberry Valley GC Ph: 508-432-4653   Yards: 6296, Holes: 18
P.O. Box 306, 183 Oak   Par: 72, USGA: 70.4
St., 02645   **GF:** w/day $27.50

Long considered one of the top fifty public courses in the country, Cranberry Valley is set in rolling terrain with lots of mature trees and marshlands. The bunkering here is very artful, and sure to be a great challenge.

─────────────── HYANNIS ───────────────

Hyannis GC   Yards: 6500, Holes: 18
Rte 132, 02601   Par: 72
Ph: 508-362-2606

A very tough course that challenges all levels of golfers. The greens are fairly large and the terrain is hilly.

─────────────── HYANNIS ───────────────

Tara Hyannis GC   Yards: 2600, Holes: 27   Restaurant/Bar/Proshop
West End Circel, 02601 Par: 9   **GF:** w/day $15.00
Ph: 508-775-7775   RP: 1 day in advance

Eight water holes, well bunkered, tree lined, excellent greens. Third hole, a difficult par 3 of 165 yards uphill, steep drop down the left side, right side guarded by a long bunker.

─────────────── LAKEVILLE ───────────────

Poquoy Brook CC   Yards: 6175, Holes: 18   Restaurant/Bar
20 Leonard St, 01347 Par: 72   **GF:** w/day $23.00
Ph: 508-947-5261

Accuracy is at a premium on this very challenging course. A beautifully maintained layout, that is considered one of the best public courses in the area.

─────────────── LANESBORO ───────────────

Skyline CC   Yards: 6517, Holes: 9   Restaurant/Bar/Proshop
405 S Main St, PO Box Par: 72, USGA: 70.4   **GF:** w/day $8.50, w/end
1485, 01257   RP: Weekends $11.50
Ph: 413-445-5584   **Carts:** $15.00

The fourth tee provides one of the best views in Berkshire County. You will be able to see Mt. Greylock, Pontoosie Lake and almost over the mountains into New York.

─────────────── METHUEN ───────────────

Hickory Hill   Yards: 5948, Holes: 18   Bar
200 N. Lowell St. Rt., Par: 71   **GF:** w/day $19.00, w/end
01844 $23.00
Ph: 617-686-0822

A course that is going to give you more of a challenge than you expect. You should enjoy your round here.

---------------------- MIDDLETON ----------------------

Middleton GC   Yards: 3215, Holes: 18   Restaurant/Bar/Proshop
Route 114, PO Box 400,   Par: 54   **GF:** w/day $20.00, w/end
01949 $20.00
Ph: 508-774-4075

Recognized as one of New England's finest par 3's. Middleton has holes that vary in length from 115 to 240 yards, with large modern tees and greens, and gently rolling fairways. The New England PGA annually plays a Pro-Lady Invitational on this course.

---------------------- NEW SEABURY ----------------------

Challenger   Yards: 5900, Holes: 18   Restaurant/Bar/Proshop
New Seabury Cape   Par: 70, USGA: 67.2   **GF:** w/day $20.00
Cod, P.O. Box B, 02649   **RP:** 1 day in advance   **Carts:** $12.00
Ph: 508-477-9111

New England's premier resort/residential community boasts the Blue Championship course, rated among the best in the nation. Together with the classic Green Challenger course, golfers are led past 36 holes of seascapes and salt marshes.

---------------------- NEW SEABURY ----------------------

New Seabury Cape   Yards: 6900, Holes: 18   Restaurant/Bar/Proshop
Cod GC   Par: 72, USGA: 70.8   **Carts:** $12.00
P.O. Box B, 02649   **RP:** 1 day in advance
Ph: 508-477-9110

New Seabury, New England's premier resort/residential community, boasts the magnificent Blue Championship course, rated among the best in the nation. Together with the classic Green Challenger course, golfers are led past 36 holes of dramatic seascapes.

---------------------- NORTH ADAMS ----------------------

North Adams CC   Yards: 5440, Holes: 9   Restaurant/Bar/Proshop
P.O. Box 241, 01247   Par: 72, USGA: 69.5   **GF:** w/day $7.00
Ph: 413-664-9011   **Carts:** $7.50

Old country course is popular, and in excellent condition. Some narrow fairways are a continuous challenge. Par 3, second hole may be reached in one, but is guarded ingeniously by traps. Par 5, 9th needs a mighty wallop to get over pond.

---------------------- NORTH FALMOUTH ----------------------

Ballymeade CC   Yards: 6500, Holes: 18   Restaurant/Bar/Proshop
145 Falmouth Woods   Par: 72, USGA: 70.0   **GF:** w/day $40.00, w/end
Rd., POB 367, 02556   **RP:** Call the Proshop $50.00
Ph: 508-540-4005   **Carts:** $Included

A great view of Buzzards Bay, an exceptionally well-maintained course that is beautifully treed, making for a great round of golf.

---------------------- NORTH FALMOUTH ----------------------

Cape Cod CC   Yards: 6018, Holes: 18   Bar
PO Box 876, Theater   Par: 71, USGA: 67.7   **GF:** w/day $20.00, w/end
Rd., 02556 $25.00
Ph: 508-563-9842

The course opened in the 1920s, so you know the trees are really going to be something to see. Tight fairways, small greens, and an abundance of bunkers make this a very challenging course.

NORTH QUINCY

Presidents GC
357 W. Squantum St.,
02171
Ph: 617-328-3444

Yards: 5055, Holes: 18
Par: 70

A short course that is going to make you use every iron you have. Much more difficulty here than meets the eye.

NORTH SWANSEA

Wampanoag GC
168 Old Providence
Rd., 02777
Ph: 508-379-9881

Yards: 3240, Holes: 9
Par: 35, USGA: 67.6

Restaurant/Bar/Proshop
GF: w/day $7.00, w/end
$9.00
Carts: $14.00

Located on Palmer River—Wampanoag Indians fought settlers here—8th hole par 3, 185-215 yards. Brook in front of green, well trapped. Least number of pars on this hole, cool breeze always.

NORTH TEWKSBURY

Trull Brook GC
170 River Rd., 01876
Ph: 508-851-6731

Yards: 6320, Holes: 18
Par: 72, USGA: 68.2
RP: Recommended

Restaurant/Proshop
GF: w/day $20.00
Carts: $18.00

Our 15th hole—a 195 yard par 3—has been featured in Golf Digest for being a beautiful example of New England golf architecture. From a hilltop tee carved out of the rocks, you hit to a large green, surrounded by 4 large bunkers, and the Merrimack River.

NORTHAMPTON

Pine Grove GC
254 Wilson Rd., 01060
Ph: 413-584-4570

Yards: 6115, Holes: 18
Par: 72, USGA: 70.6
RP: Weekends

Restaurant/Bar/Proshop
GF: w/day $9.50, w/end
$11.00
Carts: $14.00

A sporty and challenging picturesque 18 hole course, in a beautiful New England setting, if you stay in Northampton for business or pleasure, make your stay even more enjoyable, take time to play a round of golf, located just minutes from hotel.

NORTHBORO

Juniper Hill GC
202 Brigham St, 01532
Ph: 508-393-2444

Yards: 6140, Holes: 18
Par: 71

Restaurant
GF: w/day $15.00, w/end
$20.00

Two 18-holes courses, one has plenty of water and hills. The other is more open.

NORWOOD

**Norwood CC &
Resort**
400 Providence
Highway, 02062
Ph: 617-769-5880

Yards: 5942, Holes: 18
Par: 70, USGA: 67.6

Restaurant/Bar/Proshop
GF: w/day $14.00, w/end
$17.00
Carts: $20.00

The only hotel golf resort within greater Boston area. The course is flat, not long, but demands accuracy due to trees and water hazards. Hotel, tennis, 2 swimming pools, driving range are on the golf course. Lush fairways.

─────────────────OAK BLUFFS─────────────────

Farm Neck GC   Yards: 6269, Holes: 18   Restaurant/Bar
PO Box 1656, 02557   Par: 72, USGA: 69.6   **GF:** w/day $50.00
Ph: 508-693-3057

*Set along the ocean on Martha's Vineyard, there are many views of the ocean.
The front nine is narrow and has lots of traps, while the back nine is open and
long.*

─────────────────ROWLEY─────────────────

Rowley CC   Yards: 3055, Holes: 9   Restaurant/Bar/Proshop
Dodge Rd., 01969   Par: 36   **GF:** w/day $9.00, w/end
Ph: 508-948-2731   RP: Weekends & $12.00
                         holidays   **Carts:** $9.00

*Cross a covered bridge to the first green, view the many ponds that magnify the
beauty of this tight course. The 8th hole a long downhill par 5 meets a pond
crossing the fairway. Score well and you are playing good golf.*

─────────────────SOUTH WILLIAMSTOWN─────────────────

Waubeeka GL   Yards: 6296, Holes: 18   Restaurant/Bar/Proshop
137 New Ashford Rd.,   Par: 71, USGA: 69.5   **GF:** w/day $13.00, w/end
P.O. Box 511, 01267 $16.00
Ph: 413-458-8355   **Carts:** $18.00

*View from the third tee is outstanding, looking down the tight fairway the tee
shot must be well-placed. This should put you in position for a second shot
overlooking the green which is well-trapped behind and a small pond in front.
Very interesting.*

─────────────────SOUTHWICK─────────────────

Southwick CC   Yards: 6281, Holes: 18   Restaurant/Bar/Proshop
739 College Highway,   Par: 71, USGA: 67.0   **GF:** w/day $15.00
01077   RP: Call for tee times   **Carts:** $17.00
Ph: 413-569-0136

First hole, a par 4, is the toughest starting hole in Western Massachusetts.

─────────────────STOW─────────────────

Stow Acres CC   Yards: 6907, Holes: 36   Restaurant/Bar/Proshop
58 Randall Rd., 01775   Par: 72, USGA: 72.4   **GF:** w/day $27.00, w/end
Ph: 508-568-1100   RP: Call up to 5 days in $34.00
                         advance   **Carts:** $23.00

*Offers 36 well-maintained holes in quiet, rural setting. Voted "Best of Boston" by
Boston magazine. Hosting 1995 USGA Amateur Public Links Championship.
North Course (top-50 rating by Golf Digest) wanders through cathedral pines.*

─────────────────WAKEFIELD─────────────────

Colonial GC   Yards: 6175, Holes: 18
Audobon Rd., Rte. 128,   Par: 70
01880
Ph: 617-245-9300

*A flat course with water on over half the holes. Colonial is set in a rolling terrain
and has very fast and tricky greens.*

──────── WEST YARMOUTH ────────

Bayberry Hills GC
West Yarmouth Rd.,
02673
Ph: 508-394-5597

Yards: 6523, Holes: 18
Par: 72, USGA: 70.5
RP: 4 days in advance

A championship course that is very long and challenging A layout out with so many trees that you feel you're playing it all by yourself.

──────── WESTMINSTER ────────

Westminster CC
51 Ellis Rd., 01473
Ph: 508-874-5938

Yards: 6223, Holes: 18
Par: 71, USGA: 69.5
RP: Call in advance

Restaurant/Bar/Proshop
GF: w/day $20.00, w/end
$25.00
Carts: $20.00

The first ten holes are the warm up area of the golf course. The eleventh thru the sixteenth hole are the challenge. Length and accuracy are required to score these holes. Do that well, and you will be playing good golf.

──────── WILLIAMSTOWN ────────

Taconic GC
19 Meacham St., PO
Box 183, 01260
Ph: 413-458-3997

Yards: 6185, Holes: 18
Par: 71

Restaurant/Bar
GF: w/day $55.00

A Berkshires setting gives this course some spectacular views. The club was host to the Massachusetts State Open in 1992.

Enter your favorite resort in our "Golf Resort of The Year" contest (entry form is in the back of the book).

MICHIGAN

Ontonagon

Mackinac Island
Harbor Springs
Cedar • Gaylord
Bellaire • St. Helen
Empire • Grand Traverse Village
Thompsonville
Big Rapids • Cadillac • Greenbush   Hale
Houghton • Roscommon
Shelby   Frankenmuth
Pierson   Bridgeman • Bay City
Nunica   Grand Haven • Belmont Attica   Lexington
Hudsonville   Marne • Alto   Webberville   St. Clair   Washington
Grand Rapids   Clarkston   Pontiac   Romeo
Holland   Lansing • Battle Creek   Mt. Clemens   Plymouth
Saugatuck   Mason • Augusta   New Haven
Plainwell Dowagiac •   Jackson •   Brighton   Milford
Buchanan • •   Adrian Carleton   New Boston
New Buffalo   Coldwater   Monroe

ADRIAN

Woodlawn GC
4634 Treat Hwy., 49221
Ph: 517-263-3288

Yards: 6064, Holes: 18
Par: 71, USGA: 69.2
RP: 7 days in advance

Restaurant/Bar/Proshop
GF: w/day $11.00, w/end
$15.00
Carts: $18.00

Gently rolling fairways lined with a variety of mature trees. Sand traps and water hazards also enhance the scenic beauty. Small to medium sized contoured greens make shot-making necessary, especially the par 3's which are definite "skill testers".

ALTO

Tyler Creek GC
13495 92nd St., SE,
49302
Ph: 616-868-6751

Yards: 6055, Holes: 18
Par: 70, USGA: 68.4
RP: 1 week in advance

Restaurant/Proshop
GF: w/day $12.00, w/end
$12.00
Carts: $16.00

Creek winds through rolling hills amidst beautiful pine and hardwood forests. Water hazards, deep bunkers, and elevated greens will challenge you. Spectacular vacation packages. Campground and chalet available. Enjoy swimming, fishing and tubing.

ATLANTA

Elk Ridge GC
Hwy 33, Route 1, Box
28A, 49709
Ph: 517-785-2275

Yards: 7033, Holes: 18
Par: 72, USGA: 75.0
RP: Anytime in
advance

Restaurant/Bar/Proshop
GF: w/day $55.00
Carts: $Included

Set in a former hunting preserve, the woods are spectacular, with an abundance of wildlife. The well-bunkered greens are elevated. And there's the wetlands to be considered a most challenging layout.

ATTICA

Arcadia Hills GC
3801 Haines Rd., 48412
Ph: 313-724-6967

Yards: 2703, Holes: 9
Par: 36

Bar/Proshop
GF: w/day $5.00, w/end
$6.00
Carts: $7.00

Arcadia Hills is a short course good for beginners. But is also a challenge for the more avid golfer. The course is set in the middle of a wooded area. It makes for a good one-day getaway.

---------------------------------AUGUSTA---------------------------------

Gull Lake View GC-   Yards: 5820, Holes: 18   Restaurant/Bar/Proshop
East Course   Par: 70, USGA: 67.0   **GF:** w/day $17.00, w/end
7417 N. 38th St., 49012   RP: Required $19.00
Ph: 616-731-4148   **Carts:** $17.00

*The East Course, rated among Michigan's top ten public golf courses in 1986, is
not long but its par 70 is seldom matched. Bedford Valley has long holes, many
well placed bunkers, woods and big greens. Stonehedge is the newest course.*

-------------------------------BATTLE CREEK-------------------------------

Cedar Creek GC   Yards: 6225, Holes: 18   Bar/Proshop
14000 Renton Rd.,   Par: 72, USGA: 69.9   **GF:** w/day $9.00
49017   RP: Required   **Carts:** $15.00
Ph: 616-965-6423

*Water comes into play on six holes. The third hole a par 5 550 yard hole is
especially difficult with two ponds across the fairway. Accuracy is a definite must
or you're in trouble.*

---------------------------------BAY CITY---------------------------------

Bay Valley Inn GC   Yards: 6610, Holes: 18   Restaurant/Bar/Proshop
2470 Old Bridge Rd.,   Par: 71, USGA: 71.9
48706
Ph: 517-686-3500

*Begin with a few rounds of golf on the magnificent championship course de-
signed by Desmond Muirhead and Jack Nicklaus. The challenge of the "Heather
Hole" and the thirteen water holes awaits you.*

---------------------------------BELLAIRE---------------------------------

Shanty Creek-Schuss   Yards: 6394, Holes: 18   Restaurant/Bar
Mt. Resort   Par: 72, USGA: 71.5   **GF:** w/day $60.00
Box 355, 49615   RP: 2 months in   **Carts:** $Included
Ph: 616-533-6076   advance

*Arnold Palmer joined with his partner Ed Seay to create the outstanding "Leg-
end," one of his star creations. Playing the course is like walking solo in the
north woods. There are no parallel holes, and each fairway is framed by mature
pine and birch.*

---------------------------------BELMONT---------------------------------

Grand Island Golf   Yards: 6266, Holes: 18   Restaurant/Proshop
Ranch Inc.   Par: 72, USGA: 69.5   **GF:** w/day $10.00
6266 West River Dr.,   RP: Weekends &   **Carts:** $14.00
49306   holidays
Ph: 616-363-1262

*You ease off the first two par 4 holes with water behind the first green and water
in front of the 2nd tee. Then the fun begins by crossing a meandering creek on
#3, 4, 5 and 8 holes with a river behind #5 and 7 greens. The back 9 is long.*

--------------------------------BIG RAPIDS--------------------------------

Katke GC   Yards: 6683, Holes: 18   Restaurant/Bar/Proshop
Ferris State University,   Par: 72, USGA: 69.6   **GF:** w/day $18.00, w/end
M-20, 49307   RP: Two weeks in $20.00
Ph: 616-592-3765   advance   **Carts:** $20.00

*Located in the rolling hills of west central Michigan, Katke is one of the most
scenic and well-conditioned university courses in the country with large greens
and 5 par 5's and 5 par 3's. Variety for everyone. Enjoy a view of the whole
course.*

---------------------------- BOYNE FALLS ----------------------------

Boyne Mountain GC
Boyce Mountain Rd.,
49713
Ph: 616-549-2441

Yards: 7017, Holes: 18
Par: 72, USGA: 71.4

Restaurant/Bar
GF: w/day $50.00

Two championship-caliber 18-hole courses are offered here. One is very scenic and has very forgiving fairways. The other course is very demanding of your best game. There is also a 9-hole course.

---------------------------- BRIDGMAN ----------------------------

Pebblewood CC
9794 Jericho Rd.,
49106
Ph: 616-465-5611

Yards: 5576, Holes: 18
Par: 68, USGA: 62.0
RP: Weekends

Restaurant/Bar/Proshop
GF: w/day $11.00, w/end
$13.00
Carts: $12.00

Pebblewood is the oldest course in the area. This course has all new bent grass fairways, and trees. 3 new lakes, 100 new trees, the entire course has been rebuilt. Also, all new restaurant and lounge with an all glass view of the course.

---------------------------- BRIGHTON ----------------------------

**Huron Meadows
Metropark**
8765 Hammel Rd.,
48116
Ph: 313-227-2757

Yards: 6647, Holes: 18
Par: 72, USGA: 70.0
RP: 1 week in advance

Restaurant/Proshop
GF: w/day $11.00, w/end
$13.00
Carts: $15.00

Beautiful, wide, lush green fairways with a front nine spread over 200 acres. It's almost like playing your very own private course on each and every hole, with just enough challenge to bring you back again and again.

---------------------------- BUCHANAN ----------------------------

Brookwood GC
1339 Rynearson Rd.,
49107
Ph: 616-695-7818

Yards: 6540, Holes: 18
Par: 72, USGA: 72.0
RP: Weekends &
holidays

Restaurant/Bar/Proshop
GF: w/day $12.00, w/end
$16.00
Carts: $17.00

Brookwood's front nine calls upon your attention from the opening tee shot. The demand is shot placement off the tee to position your game for par numbers. Don't get greedy on this front nine that shares 7 out of 9 holes.

---------------------------- CADILLAC ----------------------------

**Lakewood on Green
GC**
128 Lakewood Dr.,
49601
Ph: 616-775-4763

Yards: 2931, Holes: 9
Par: 35, USGA: 75.0
RP: Required June,
July, August

Restaurant/Proshop
GF: w/day $7.00, w/end
$8.00

Scenic and relaxing to play—good test of golf—picked by N.G.F. as one of five golf courses in Michigan as most scenic and playable. Most favorite hole is #6. Placement of drive very important.

---------------------------- CADILLAC ----------------------------

**Mc Guire's
Evergreen**
7800 Mackinaw Trail,
49601
Ph: 616-775-9947

Yards: 6601, Holes: 27
Par: 71, USGA: 69.2

Restaurant/Bar
GF: w/day $35.00

27 holes of superb golf, but watch out for all those trees. #14 on the Spruce Course is a par 4, 352 yard straightway where you can really cut loose, if you're a shotmaker you'll stay out of the water guarding the large green.

─────────────────── CARLETON ───────────────────

Carleton Glen GC, Inc.
13470 Grafton Rd., 48117
Ph: 313-654-6201

Yards: 6307, Holes: 18
Par: 71, USGA: 71.0
RP: Required

Restaurant/Bar/Proshop
GF: w/day $15.00
Carts: $16.00

Eighteen holes of scenic delight and challenging golf, is the best way to describe Carleton Glen Golf Course. Every hole is completely different in yardage and scenery. Bring all your golf clubs. The variety of shots are a golfer's pleasure.

─────────────────── CEDAR ───────────────────

Sugar Loaf Resort GC
RTE 1, 49621
Ph: 616-228-5461

Yards: 6901, Holes: 18
Par: 72, USGA: 70.1
RP: Required

Restaurant/Bar/Proshop
GF: w/day $50.00, w/end $50.00
Carts: $Included

Golfers of all abilities will enjoy the challenge and the beauty of our 18-hole championship golf course. Jan Stephenson, LPGA, has chosen Sugar Loaf Resort to call home while visiting the Grand Traverse area. Please reserve tee-times in advance.

─────────────────── CHARLEVOIX ───────────────────

Belvedere GC
Ellsworth Rd., 49720
Ph: 616-547-2611

Yards: 6701, Holes: 18
Par: 72, USGA: 71.8

GF: w/day $45.00, w/end $50.00

The course was designed by William Watson and opened in 1971. The course has seen many major tournaments in its time.

─────────────────── CHARLEVOIX ───────────────────

Dunmaglas GC
09031 Boyne City Rd, 49720
Ph: 616-547-1022

Yards: 6487, Holes: 18
Par: 72

A well planned and executed design makes this a must see course. There are lots of scenery and plenty of trees.

─────────────────── CLARKSTON ───────────────────

Indian Springs Metropark
5100 Indian Trail, 48016
Ph: 313-625-7870

Yards: 6703, Holes: 18
Par: 72, USGA: 70.4
RP: 1 week in advance

Proshop
GF: w/day $11.00, w/end $13.00
Carts: $15.00

The front nine of this new course is open enough that the "everyday" golfer can warm up and enjoy the round. Beware—the back nine. The 13th hole is all of 600 yards and the 16th very short but treacherously surrounded by sand.

─────────────────── COLDWATER ───────────────────

Coldwater CC
42 Narrows Rd., Box 69, 49036
Ph: 517-278-4892

Yards: 6363, Holes: 18
Par: 72, USGA: 70.4
RP: 3 days advance for non-members

Restaurant/Bar/Proshop
GF: w/day $19.00
Carts: $18.00

Front nine is longer and relatively open, while the back nine features tight and rolling fairways. All situated on beautiful Morrison Lake.

DOWAGIAC

Hampshire CC
29592 Pokagon Hwy.,
49047
Ph: 616-782-7476

Yards: 7030, Holes: 18
Par: 72, USGA: 71.0
RP: Weekends &
holidays - 1 week

Restaurant/Bar/Proshop
GF: w/day $11.00, w/end
$14.00
Carts: $14.00

Just when you think you have mastered the front nine which is quite open, and you can spray the ball, and there are only 2 water holes—then you reach the back nine with its narrow, wooded fairways—a very different nine.

DRUMMOND ISLAND

**Rock at Woodmoor
GC**
Ph: 906-493-1006

Yards: 6837, Holes: 18
Par: 71, USGA: 74.9

GF: w/day $30.00, w/end
$30.00
Carts: $Included

A course that has been carved into its limestone setting. There's also a lot of wildlife to distract you.

EAST LANSING

Timber Ridge
16339 Park Lake Rd.,
48823
Ph: 517-339-8000

Yards: 6497, Holes: 18
Par: 72, USGA: 72.2
RP: Up to 1 week in
advance

Restaurant/Bar/Proshop
GF: w/day $30.00, w/end
$35.00
Carts: $20.00

The setting here is heavily wooded with a variety of trees that make it beautiful in any season of the year. Ranked one of the best public courses in America by Golf Digest, you won't want to miss this beauty.

EMPIRE

Dunes GC
M-72, 49630
Ph: 616-326-5390

Yards: 3277, Holes: 9
Par: 36

Proshop
GF: w/day $7.00
Carts: $7.00

The unique features are the roughs, have been left to nature but not hard to play out of. The favorite 5th hole par 5 has a hill in the center of the fairway, with a good roll to the right. A long straight drive off of tee is required.

FRANKENMUTH

Frankenmuth GC CC
950 Flint St., Box 304,
48734
Ph: 517-652-9229

Yards: 2960, Holes: 9
Par: 35, USGA: 68.5
RP: Recommended

Restaurant/Bar/Proshop
GF: w/day $13.50, w/end
$14.50
Carts: $9.00

The key holes are 6, 7, and 8. Hole #6 is a 130-160 yard par 5 island hole to a small green. Hole #7 is 560 yards, par 5 uphill and #8 is 435 yard par 4 uphill. If you can putt the fast sloping greens you'll do well.

GAYLORD

Hidden Valley GC
P.O. Box 556, 49735
Ph: 517-732-4653

Yards: 6305, Holes: 18
Par: 71

Restaurant/Bar/Proshop
GF: w/day $48.00

Hidden Valley Classic is acclaimed for impeccable maintenance and casually elegant setting. Carpet-like fairways and perfect but tough undulating greens combined with character-building tee shots out of the woods place demands on both accuracy and nerve.

GAYLORD

Michaywe Hills GC
1535 Opal Lake Rd.,
49735
Ph: 517-939-8911

Yards: 6835, Holes: 36
Par: 72, USGA: 71.4
RP: Begin taking tee
times in Jan.

Restaurant/Bar/Proshop
GF: w/day $40.00, w/end
$40.00
Carts: $10.00

All holes on the Pines Course are framed by large northern Michigan white pines and birches with large greens and strategic bunkering. The Lake Course features six "alpine" style holes, six holes of "Scottish" design, and six lakeside holes.

GAYLORD

**Treetops Sylvan
Resort GC**
3962 Wilkinson Rd.,
49731
Ph: 517-732-6711

Yards: 6399, Holes: 18
Par: 71, USGA: 72.6
RP: Call in advance

Restaurant/Bar/Proshop
GF: w/day $68.00
Carts: $Included

The Robert Trent Jones masterpiece covers over 400 glacier carved acres through the densely wooded Pigeon River valley. Treetops is bold but fair, the spectacular terrain offers you a variety of design features and breathtaking vistas.

GAYLORD

**Wilderness Valley/
Black Forest GC**
7519 Mancelona Rd.,
49735
Ph: 800-423-5949

Yards: 6985, Holes: 36
Par: 71, USGA: 68.4
RP: Recommended on
weekends

Restaurant/Bar/Proshop
GF: w/day $18.00, w/end
$23.00
Carts: $12.00

The Valley Course is carved from the forest. The front nine demands accurate tee shots over the water hazards and between the dense woods that border each fairway. Our new course, the Black Forest Course has spectacular bunkering and strategic holes.

GRAND HAVEN

Grand Haven GC
17000 Lincoln, 49417
Ph: 616-842-4040

Yards: 6789, Holes: 18
Par: 72, USGA: 69.2
RP: 1 week in advance
for weekends

Restaurant/Bar/Proshop
GF: w/day $26.00, w/end
$28.00
Carts: $20.00

Set in gentle hills, narrow and tight with no parallel holes. There are heavy pines and sand dunes with no water to carry. The course is oval in shape with no fairway bunkers.

GRAND RAPIDS

Gracewil CC
2597 Four Mile Rd NW,
49504
Ph: 616-784-2455

Yards: 5025, Holes: 18
Par: 72, USGA: 67.9
RP: Weekends &
holidays

Restaurant/Bar/Proshop
GF: w/day $8.50, w/end
$9.00
Carts: $14.00

Family owned/run business for 60 years. Carved thru an old apple orchard out in the country atmosphere minutes from Grand Rapids. We offer two 18 hole courses to choose from. Something for everyone.

GRAND TRAVERSE VILLAGE

**Grand Traverse
Resort Village**
Box 404, 49610
Ph: 616-938-1620

Yards: 440, Holes: 36
Par: 72, USGA: 75.8
RP: Guests - 2 weeks in
advance

Restaurant/Bar
GF: w/day $45.00
Carts: $10.00

The Bear is demanding #3, rated as one of the best holes in the state, is a picturesque par 5 at 529 yards. No two holes are similar. The Resort Course offers challenging versatility on a gently rolling landscape.

GREENBUSH

Greenbush GC
1981 US-23, 48738
Ph: 517-724-6356

Yards: 3005, Holes: 9
Par: 35

Restaurant/Bar/Proshop
GF: w/day $5.00
Carts: $8.00

We have redesigned 3 new holes for more interesting and testing play. The course overlooks beautiful Lake Huron and we call it the world's only air conditioned golf course.

HALE

Wicker Hills GC
7287 Wickert Rd.,
48739
Ph: 517-728-9971

Yards: 2975, Holes: 9
Par: 36, USGA: 33.8

Restaurant/Bar/Proshop
GF: w/day $6.00
Carts: $4.00

Scenic, hilly, situated and surrounded by the Huron National Forest in Northeast Lower Michigan.

HARBOR SPRINGS

Boyne Highlands GC
49740
Ph: 800-GO-BOYNE

Yards: 7210, Holes: 18
Par: 72, USGA: 74.0
RP: May be made with
room reservation

Restaurant/Bar/Proshop
GF: w/day $80.00, w/end
$80.00
Carts: $Included

The Heather course's greens are vast 7,000 to 10,000 sq. ft. It's heavily wooded with marshes & ponds dotting your scorecard. This is a toughie to par. The Moor plays a little longer with wide landing areas and fairways. New Donald Ross Mem. course.

HARBOR SPRINGS

Little Traverse Bay GC
995 Hideaway Valley

Dr., Ph: 616-526-6200

Yards: 6489, Holes: 18
Par: 72

This course has spectacular views of the bay, and is a quite long and challenging course. You'd better keep your eye on the ball or you'll get into trouble.

HOLLAND

Holland CC
51 Country Club Rd.,
49423
Ph: 616-392-1844

Yards: 5953, Holes: 18
Par: 70, USGA: 66.6
RP: 4 days in advance

Proshop
GF: w/day $15.00, w/end
$17.00
Carts: $15.00

This relatively short course will surprise you. Narrow tree lined fairways, small greens and the Macatawa River add to the beauty and the challenge of the beautiful course. Our favorite hole is the uphill 15th with the river, two ponds and two traps.

HOUGHTON

Portage Lake GC
US 41, 49931
Ph: 906-487-2641

Yards: 6300, Holes: 18
Par: 72, USGA: 69.7

Restaurant/Proshop
GF: w/day $10.00
Carts: $13.00

Scenic course borders the Pilgrim River and water comes into play on 5 holes. The most difficult is the 527 yard par 5 11th hole which has your tee shot over water, and bunkers to left front of green and one to the right—lots of luck.

───────────────HUDSONVILLE───────────────

Summergreen GC
3441 New Holland,
49426
Ph: 616-669-0950

Yards: 1947, Holes: 9
Par: 30

Proshop
GF: w/day $4.25, w/end
$5.00
Carts: $5.00

Our favorite hole is No. 4, a 347 yard par 4 with a deep ditch directly in front of the tee, 2 more ditches crossing the fairway. Condominiums lining the right rough, and dense trees lining the left rough.

───────────────JACKSON───────────────

Cascades GC
1992 Warren, 49203
Ph: 517-788-4323

Yards: 6614, Holes: 18
Par: 72, USGA: 70.8
RP: Weekends &
holidays

Restaurant/Proshop
GF: w/day $11.00
Carts: $16.00

Cascades is challenging, long by most standards, and features water and beautiful scenery. Number 17 is one hole golfers should take note of. It is one of the state's best according to the Michigan Travel Bureau.

───────────────LANSING───────────────

Royal Scot GC
4722 W. Grand River,
48906
Ph: 517-321-GOLF

Yards: 6606, Holes: 18
Par: 71, USGA: 68.9
RP: Call for tee times

Restaurant/Bar/Proshop
GF: w/day $16.00, w/end
$20.00
Carts: $21.00

Lansing's Michigan Capital Choice golf course. Scottish link golf course with undulating greens. Our favorite hole—so many to choose from ... you come out and let us know.

───────────────LEWISTON───────────────

Garland GC -
Monarch
County Rd. 489, 49756
Ph: 517-786-2211

Yards: 6056, Holes: 18
Par: 72, USGA: 68.4

Restaurant/Bar
GF: w/day $50.00

If you want lots of choices, you've come to the right place. Three 18-hole courses and a 9-hole one too. The layouts all offer different challenges, so you might just want to try them all.

───────────────LEXINGTON───────────────

Lakeview Hills CC
6560 E. Peck Rd.,
48450
Ph: 313-359-7333

Yards: 6206, Holes: 18
Par: 72, USGA: 69.3
RP: Required

Restaurant/Bar/Proshop
GF: w/day $15.00
Carts: $18.00

Lakeview Hills challenging course and scenic views of Lake Huron. From narrow tree lined fairways, to small carefully guarded greens. To a more generous fairway with spacious greens inviting you to hit away. A course that requires a variety of skills.

───────────────MACKINAC ISLAND───────────────

Grand Hotel GC
49757
Ph: 906-847-3331

Yards: 2335, Holes: 9
Par: 33
RP: Requested

Restaurant/Bar
GF: w/day $12.00
Carts: $10.00

A renovation program has made the nine-hole links more challenging, and much more enjoyable to play. The number seven green has been rebuilt as a peninsula out in the lake. Bunkers and sand traps have been added and/or enlarged.

─────────────────MACKINAC ISLAND─────────────────

Wawashkamo GC
British Landing Rd.,
49757
Ph: 906-847-3871

Yards: 3019, Holes: 9
Par: 36
RP: Recommended

Proshop
GF: w/day $12.00
Carts: $10.00

This course is a trip back in time. The Scottish links style 9 hole course was designed by Scot, Alex Smith in 1898 and remains basically unchanged. Tall heathery rough, hidden pot bunkers and beautiful wild flowers await you. Wawashkamo, rich in history.

─────────────────MARNE─────────────────

Li'l Acres GC
1831 Johnson Rd.,
49435
Ph: 616-677-3379

Yards: 1835, Holes: 9
Par: 30
RP: Tee times may be
reserved

Proshop
GF: w/day $3.00, w/end
$3.50

Short challenging course, excellent for beginners and senior citizens.

─────────────────MARNE─────────────────

Western Greens GC
2475 Johnson, 49435
Ph: 616-677-3677

Yards: 6400, Holes: 18
Par: 71, USGA: 68.5
RP: Preferred

Restaurant/Bar/Proshop
GF: w/day $10.00
Carts: $14.00

Being the highest point in Ottawa County the wind is always a factor. Course is rolling but not hilly. There now are 1500 trees but well placed.

─────────────────MASON─────────────────

Branson Bay GC
215 Branson Bay Dr.,
48854
Ph: 517-663-4144

Yards: 6111, Holes: 18
Par: 72, USGA: 69.8
RP: Not more than 1
week advance

Restaurant/Bar/Proshop
GF: w/day $12.00, w/end
$13.00
Carts: $14.50

#1 and #12 are ranked in the 18 most challenging holes in the Lansing golf market of over 40 courses. The back nine was carved out of mixed pines and hardwoods, with hills and ponds adding beauty and more concentration.

─────────────────MILFORD─────────────────

**Kensington
Metropark**
2240 W. Buno Rd.,
48042
Ph: 313-685-9332

Yards: 6436, Holes: 18
Par: 71, USGA: 70.8
RP: Recommended

Proshop
GF: w/day $11.00, w/end
$13.00
Carts: $15.00

Our well-manicured layout provides challenge for all golfers. However, the 382 yard 11th hole has both difficulty and beauty. An elevated, panoramic view of beautiful, sailboat-laden Kent Lake requires a precise tee shot.

─────────────────MONROE─────────────────

Raisin River GC
1500 N. Dixie Hwy,
48161
Ph: 313-289-3700

Yards: 6876, Holes: 36
Par: 71, USGA: 70.2
RP: 1 week in advance

Restaurant/Bar/Proshop
GF: w/day $15.00, w/end
$17.00
Carts: $18.00

Two championship layouts. The East Course has mammoth greens, wooded holes, lots of water and gently sloping watered fairways. The West Course is a compact beautifully designed course which demands expert shot placement. All greens trapped.

──────────────── MT. CLEMENS ────────────────

Bello Woods GC
23650 32 Mile Rd.,
48045
Ph: 313-949-1200

Yards: 6141, Holes: 18
Par: 72, USGA: 68.4
RP: Recommended

Restaurant/Bar/Proshop
GF: w/day $10.50
Carts: $15.00

Our Red Course has six holes where water comes into play. Our White Course has water on four holes and some tricky greens. The Gold, our newest nine, is cut through a beautiful woods with narrow fairways.

──────────────── MT. CLEMENS ────────────────

Partridge Creek GC
43843 Romeo Plank
Rd., 48044
Ph: 313-286-9822

Yards: 6405, Holes: 18
Par: 72, USGA: 70.2
RP: Required weekends
& holidays

Restaurant/Bar/Proshop
GF: w/day $11.50, w/end
$13.00
Carts: $17.00

Although there are no sand traps 2 meandering creeks and tree lined fairways make all 3 courses interesting and challenging.

──────────────── NEW BUFFALO ────────────────

**Whittaker Woods GC
& CC**
Wittaker Rd., 49117

Ph: 616-469-1313

Holes: 18

Whittaker Woods Golf and Country Club in New Buffalo, Michigan is presently under construction, designed by Ken Killian and developed by O'Brien Development Company. Plans include single family homes and maintenance free townhouses.

──────────────── NEW HAVEN ────────────────

Oak Ridge GC
35035 26 Mile Rd.,
48048
Ph: 313-749-5151

Yards: 6811, Holes: 18
Par: 72, USGA: 71.2
RP: 2 weeks for
weekends

Restaurant/Bar/Proshop
GF: w/day $12.00, w/end
$15.00
Carts: $17.00

Beautiful tree lined fairways make you want to play the course as soon as you see it. Service is number 1 at Oak Ridge, specializing in golf outing packages.

──────────────── NUNICA ────────────────

**Crockery Hills GC,
Inc.**
11741 Leonard Rd.,
49448
Ph: 616-837-8249

Yards: 6032, Holes: 18
Par: 70

Restaurant/Bar/Proshop
GF: w/day $7.50, w/end
$8.50
Carts: $14.00

If you like a challenge, if you like water in a beautiful setting, you'll enjoy your round at Crockery. Top it off at our bar for refreshments—and enjoy dinner at one of West Michigan's newest and finest restaurants—"Terra Verde."

──────────────── ONTONAGON ────────────────

Ontonagon GC
Parker Ave., P.O. Box
236, 49953
Ph: 906-884-4130

Yards: 2676, Holes: 9
Par: 35

Bar/Proshop
GF: w/day $7.00

We have trees, left and right doglegs, two holes for the long ball hitters, a blind approach to a green, and our famous numbers 8 and 9 with elevated tees, creeks, and elevated greens. Beautiful, challenging 9 hole course just 1 mile from Lake Superior.

OSCODA

Lake Wood Shores GC
7751 Cedar Lake Rd., 49750
Ph: 517-739-2075

Yards: 6528, Holes: 18
Par: 72, USGA: 72.9

Restaurant/Bar
GF: w/day $20.00, w/end $25.00

Two 18-holes layouts, and both of them are going to play long. A very challenging round of golf awaits you here.

PIERSON

Whitefish Lake GC
2241 Bass Lake Rd. N.W., 49339
Ph: 616-636-5260

Yards: 2200, Holes: 9
Par: 34
RP: Recommended

Proshop
GF: w/day $5.00, w/end $5.50
Carts: $6.00

You have to be accurate. It's a tight, challenging 9 holes. The greens are elevated so you don't want to be over. Our #3 is tough. It's a dogleg left par 4. You have to get the ball up quick and have distance to be over the trees or play it safe.

PLAINWELL

Lake Doster GC
136 Country Club Blvd., 49080
Ph: 616-685-5308

Yards: 6570, Holes: 18
Par: 72, USGA: 72.6

Restaurant/Bar/Proshop
GF: w/day $17.00, w/end $20.00
Carts: $10.00

Lake Doster is ranked as one of the top 25 courses in the state of Michigan. It is also the home of the PGA Super Seniors Pro-Am Golf outing. The number three hole is called the Little Monster—100 yards, green directly downhill.

PLYMOUTH

Fox Hills GC
8768 N. Territorial Rd., 48170
Ph: 313-453-7272

Yards: 3200, Holes: 9
Par: 35
RP: Weekends only, 7 days in advance

Restaurant/Bar/Proshop
GF: w/day $9.50, w/end $11.00
Carts: $10.00

Our favorite hole is #2 on the Lakes Course. A deceiving par 3, protected by four large bunkers. Hit your ball in these bunkers and you're history. If you do make the green, you're still not safe. It's just a great little hole. Try it.

PONTIAC

Pontiac Municipal GC
800 Golf Dr., 48053
Ph: 313-858-8990

Yards: 5700, Holes: 18
Par: 69, USGA: 66.8

Restaurant/Bar
GF: w/day $10.25
Carts: $14.00

With the par being only 69 you would think you could "burn" this little course up. Well, we have 6 par three holes each with the potential of tearing you up. Priced like a public course, condition like a private course.

PONTIAC

White Lake Oaks GC
991 Williams Lake Rd., 48386
Ph: 313-698-2700

Yards: 5572, Holes: 18
Par: 70, USGA: 67.0
RP: Weekends & holidays

Restaurant/Bar/Proshop
GF: w/day $13.00, w/end $16.00
Carts: $15.00

Built on fairly flat terrain, this gently rolling 18 holes is popular with every type of golfer. Easy to walk, relatively short, but challenging. Our favorite hole is the 13th, a tough par 4, dogleg right with the second shot over a pond.

---RIVERVIEW---

Riverview Highlands GC
15015 Sibley Rd., 48192
Ph: 313-479-2266

Yards: 6800, Holes: 27
Par: 72, USGA: 71.0
RP: Daily May thru
October

Restaurant/Bar/Proshop
GF: w/day $13.00
Carts: $15.00

The Gold 9 offers a good challenge to the novice as well as the low handicapper. The Red 9 features a number of water hazards along with numerous tree lots. The Blue 9, probably the most challenging of the 3 courses.

--- ROCHESTER HILLS---

Pine Trace GC
3600 Pine Trace Blvd.,
48309
Ph: 313-852-7100

Yards: 6347, Holes: 18
Par: 72

This course places a premium on a fast round of golf, it's very popular and you have to keep moving.

---ROMEO---

Pine Valley GC
16801 31 Mile Rd.,
48065
Ph: 313-752-9633

Yards: 6485, Holes: 27
Par: 72, USGA: 70.1
RP: 1 week in advance

Restaurant/Bar/Proshop
GF: w/day $16.00
Carts: $18.00

From an elevated 1st tee with water left and right, the challenging front nine offers 6 blind shots and tests your skill on the 470 yard par 4 ninth. The 13th, our signature hole, can be played several ways, any of which can result in a big score.

--- ROSCOMMON---

Ye Olde CC
904 W. Sunset, 48653
Ph: 517-275-5582

Yards: 3003, Holes: 9
Par: 35
RP: Recommended

Proshop
GF: w/day $8.00
Carts: $8.00

Challenging 9 holes that are beautifully maintained. The friendly staff and surroundings will make you glad you stopped. Watch the greens—they are small and tricky. We are five minutes away from beautiful Higgins Lake and the famous Au Sable River.

---SAUGATUCK---

Clearbrook GC
135th Ave. at 65th, P.O.
Box 66, 49453
Ph: 616-857-2000

Yards: 6439, Holes: 18
Par: 72, USGA: 69.8
RP: Recommended

Restaurant/Bar/Proshop
GF: w/day $22.00, w/end
$27.00
Carts: $20.00

Meandering across eight of the eighteen holes is the "clear brook" of the course's name and when combined with the small target size greens a stiff challenge to every golfer is provided. In addition, this fabulous golf course features rolling terrain.

---SHELBY---

Benona Shores GC
3410 Scenic Dr., 49455
Ph: 616-861-2098

Yards: 4200, Holes: 18
Par: 60, USGA: 58.2
RP: Required, July &
August

Proshop
GF: w/day $7.00
Carts: $12.00

A rolling 18 hole course which winds through hard woods, pines and fruit orchards.

ST. CLAIR

Rattle Run
7163 St. Clair Hwy.,
48079
Ph: 313-329-2070

Yards: 6891, Holes: 18
Par: 72, USGA: 73.4
RP: 1 week in advance

Restaurant/Bar/Proshop
GF: w/day $15.00, w/end
$40.00
Carts: $10.00

Rolling tree-lined fairways, many elevated tees and 95 sandtraps. #6 requires complete control of drive. From blue tees 418 yards, cross river twice. Shot up a hill elevated 20 feet.

ST. HELEN

**De Carlo's Birch
Pointe CC**
7071 Artesia Beach
Rd., 48656
Ph: 517-389-7009

Yards: 3200, Holes: 9
Par: 36
RP: Holiday weekends

Restaurant/Bar/Proshop
GF: w/day $7.00
Carts: $7.00

A true North Michigan layout. We offer rolling wooded fairways. Every hole features trees that come into play if your shot is not true. Our par 5 #7 hole has two water hazards plus woods on both sides, a real challenge and beauty.

THOMPSONVILLE

Crystal Mountain GC
M-115 @ Lindy Rd.,
49683
Ph: 616-378-2911

Yards: 6404, Holes: 18
Par: 72, USGA: 66.6

Restaurant/Bar/Proshop
GF: w/day $28.00
Carts: $20.00

This course was carved out of a hardwood and pine forest with very few fairways adjoining each other. In designing the course, great attention was given to preserving the natural landscape. Add to this the 13 ponds found on the back nine.

WASHINGTON

Stoney Creek GC
5140 Main Pkwy.,
48094
Ph: 313-781-9166

Yards: 6884, Holes: 18
Par: 72, USGA: 71.3
RP: 3 days in advance

Restaurant/Proshop
GF: w/day $12.00, w/end
$14.00
Carts: $16.00

This golf course is 15 miles from any major road. It's very quiet and nature is all around us. The course itself is very different from most others combining water, sand and out of bounds throughout the course.

WEBBERVILLE

Oak Lane GC
4875 N. Main, 48892
Ph: 517-521-3900

Yards: 6000, Holes: 18
Par: 70, USGA: 67.8
RP: Recommended

Restaurant/Bar/Proshop
GF: w/day $9.50, w/end
$11.00
Carts: $15.00

Water on course on 8, 10, and 11. Quiet surroundings and rolling and above average in trees but wide fairways. Good course for all players.

WILLIAMSBURG

High Pointe GC
5555 Arnold Road,
49690
Ph: 800-753-7888

Yards: 6849, Holes: 18
Par: 71, USGA: 72.9
RP: Anytime

Restaurant/Bar/Proshop
GF: w/day $30.00, w/end
$30.00
Carts: $14.00

Award-winning layout marked by distinctly different nines: an open-links course on the front and a tree-lined back-nine with lots of elevation change. Some holes patterned after great British holes—one of Golf Magazine's "100 Greatest US Courses."

MINNESOTA

Warroad •

Staples
Ely •

Pine River Longville •Virginia
Pequot Lakes East Grand Forks Garrison
Glyndon •Erskine •.•• Cloquet •.
Detroit Lakes •\Hawley
Glenwood Eagle Bend •Brainerd •Onamia Paynesville
Henning Elbow\Lake •Little Falls •Deerwood
Fergus\Falls • •Alexandria Coon Rapids Maplewood Pine City
Annandale • • Circle Pines Golden Valley Woodbury
Melrose Eagan •\ Richfield Hamel St. Paul
Tyler • Watertown
Fairfax • Minneota Shakopee • Rushford
Fairmont •.• Rochester
Albert Lea Austin
Mankato

────────────── ALBERT LEA ──────────────

Green Lea GC
101 Richway Dr., 56007
Ph: 507-373-1061

Yards: 6157, Holes: 18
Par: 73, USGA: 67.8
RP: Weekends

Restaurant/Bar/Proshop
GF: w/day $10.50
Carts: $14.00

Our favorite hole is the par 3 #6. It's a short 127 yards but accuracy is essential. Completely surrounded by tall oak trees except for a narrow opening in front, with elevated greens and prevailing winds to taunt every golfer.

────────────── ALEXANDRIA ──────────────

Lake Miltona GC
Hwy. 29N & Cty. Rd.5,
Box 207, 56308
Ph: 612-852-7078

Yards: 3102, Holes: 9
Par: 36, USGA: 33.7
RP: Recommended

Restaurant/Bar/Proshop
GF: w/day $9.00
Carts: $10.00

The first hole starts out through a chute of beautiful oaks and maples; with a dogleg left it opens to gently rolling terrain with a view of Lake Miltona. The ninth hole brings you back through the trees with a double dogleg par 5.

────────────── ANNANDALE ──────────────

Whispering Pines GC
County Rd. 6, P.O. Box 179, 55302
Ph: 612-274-8721

Yards: 3100, Holes: 9
Par: 35, USGA: 68.8
RP: Weekends

Restaurant/Bar/Proshop
GF: w/day $7.00
Carts: $8.00

Slightly rolling course with part of course with many mature trees. Large greens, some with two levels. #9 hole 210 par three 150 feet top to bottom greens with 2 levels great finishing hole. Has two holes with sharp dogleg right.

────────────── AUSTIN ──────────────

Ramsey GC
R.R. 1, 55912
Ph: 507-433-9098

Yards: 6034, Holes: 18
Par: 71, USGA: 68.2

Restaurant/Bar/Proshop
GF: w/day $9.00
Carts: $7.42

Our front nine is very sporty, back nine longer and more wide open. Play our tough par 3's well and you'll score well. Outstanding hole is No. 15 which measures 595 yards, one of the longest holes in state. Friendly atmosphere.

―――――――――――――BRAINERD―――――――――――――

Grand View Lodge
PC
Rt. 6 Box 22, 56401

Ph: 218-963-2234

Yards: 2300, Holes: 9
Par: 35, USGA: 64.0
Restaurant/Bar/Proshop

In the Minnesota Northwoods, our course is called by many the most beautiful course in the state. Thousands of flowers encircle the tree boxes while birch, oak, aspen and Norway Pines line the fairways.

―――――――――――――BRAINERD―――――――――――――

Madden's Pine
Beach
8001 Pine Beach, Box
387, 56401
Ph: 218-829-2811

Yards: 5900, Holes: 45
Par: 72, USGA: 67.2
RP: 1 day in advance

Restaurant/Bar/Proshop
Carts: $20.00

Maddens offers what no other Midwest resort can, the challenge and beauty of 45 holes of on premise golf. There are two 18 hole courses. Pine Beach East (with a par 6, 618 yard hole) and Pine Beach West. Maddens also has a par 3 executive 9 hole course.

―――――――――――――BROOKLYN PARK―――――――――――――

Edinburgh USA
8700 Edinbrook
Crossing, 55443
Ph: 612-424-7060

Yards: 6335, Holes: 18
Par: 72, USGA: 68.7
RP: Up to 4 days in
advance

Restaurant/Bar/Proshop
GF: w/day $26.00
Carts: $23.00

This course is ranked as one of the top 50 public courses in the US. The greens vary greatly in size, but they're all tricky. The course has many hazards in the form of tress, water and sand. Accuracy is a must if you want a good score.

―――――――――――――CIRCLE PINES―――――――――――――

KateHaven GC
8791 Lexington Ave.,
N.E., 55014
Ph: 612-786-2945

Yards: 2660, Holes: 9
Par: 30, USGA: 51.8
RP: Required

Restaurant/Proshop
GF: w/day $6.50, w/end
$7.50
Carts: $9.00

A challenging par 30 course with multiple tees which give choices to cross water or not. When standing on the par 4, 262 yard tee for the 5th hole you can barely see the flag and the creek is over the hill and out of sight.

―――――――――――――CLOQUET―――――――――――――

Big Lake GC
18 Cary Rd., 55720
Ph: 218-879-4221

Yards: 1565, Holes: 9
Par: 27, USGA: 79.0
RP: Call

Restaurant/Bar/Proshop
GF: w/day $7.00
Carts: $10.00

The toughest par 3 in Minnesota. In 20 years and a couple of million rounds of golf, has only been pared a couple of dozen times.

―――――――――――――COON RAPIDS―――――――――――――

Bunker Hills GC
12800 Bunker Prarie
Rd., 55433
Ph: 601-755-4140

Yards: 7030, Holes: 18
Par: 72, USGA: 71.9
RP: 3 days in advance

Restaurant/Bar/Proshop
GF: w/day $16.00
Carts: $19.00

A level course that is heavily wooded with pines and oaks. 3 lakes abut 7 of the holes. #15 (best 15th hole in state) is challenging with a narrow, tree-lined fairway.

─────────────────── COON RAPIDS ───────────────────

Coon Rapids-Bunker Hills GC
P.O. Box 33081, 55433
Ph: 612-755-4140

Yards: 7300, Holes: 27
Par: 72, USGA: 71.9
RP: 3 days in advance

Restaurant/Bar/Proshop
GF: w/day $16.00
Carts: $20.00

Site of 1976 USGA National Publinks Champ—Golf Digest Top 50 Public Courses. Annual site of National Open Championship.

─────────────────── DEERWOOD ───────────────────

Ruttgers Championship Lakes Course
Rt. 2, P.O. Box 400, 56444
Ph: 218-678-2885

Yards: 6485, Holes: 18
Par: 72, USGA: 71.0
RP: Call for tee times

Restaurant/Bar/Proshop
GF: w/day $22.00, w/end $25.00
Carts: $22.50

Ruttger's Championship Lakes Course is distinguished by a spectacular design skillfully meshed with the area's natural beauty. Hole lengths range from 130 to 550 yards. Natural hazards abound as the placid waters of Goose & Bass Lakes come into play.

─────────────────── DETROIT LAKES ───────────────────

Detroit CC
Rt 5, 56501
Ph: 218-847-5790

Yards: 5970, Holes: 36
Par: 71, USGA: 67.5
RP: 1 day in advance

Restaurant/Bar/Proshop
GF: w/day $16.00
Carts: $16.00

Hills, trees, sand, water and fast greens test all your golf skills. Home of the nationally known Pine to Palm amateur golf tournament.

─────────────────── EAGAN ───────────────────

Parkview GC PC
1310 Cliff Rd., 55123
Ph: 612-454-9884

Yards: 4568, Holes: 18
Par: 63, USGA: 60.8
RP: Recommended - up to 1 week

Restaurant/Bar/Proshop
GF: w/day $10.50
Carts: $15.00

An 18-hole executive golf course (par 63) that requires the use of all clubs. Can be played in close to three hours. A challenge to golfers of all skills. Many beautiful gardens, three fountains, bridge over rock causeway.

─────────────────── EAGLE BEND ───────────────────

Double Eagle GC PC
Cty Rd. #3, 56446
Ph: 218-738-5155

Yards: 6873, Holes: 18
Par: 73, USGA: 71.1

Restaurant/Bar/Proshop
GF: w/day $16.00
Carts: $15.00

Rated by M.G.A. as toughest 9 hole course in state. Lots of water and woods. Only Reversible golf course in U.S. Wrote up in June 1987 issue Golf Digest. 18 sets of tee boxes, reverses direction every other day.

─────────────────── EAST GRAND FORKS ───────────────────

Valley GC
1800 21st St. NW, 56721
Ph: 218-773-1207

Yards: 6001, Holes: 18
Par: 72, USGA: 68.9
RP: Weekends & holidays

Bar/Proshop
GF: w/day $10.00
Carts: $14.00

Narrow fairways, lots of trees, several doglegs, water on 7 holes, several elevated greens requiring lofted approach. Very scenic with several holes along the Rod River of the North.

───────────────EDINA───────────────

Braemar GC PC
6364 John Harris Dr.,
55439
Ph: 612-941-2072

Yards: 6368, Holes: 18
Par: 71, USGA: 70.6
RP: Spave avail. only in
person

Restaurant/Bar/Proshop
GF: w/day $18.00, w/end
$18.00
Carts: $20.00

A course with wide fairways and some rolling terrain. Some challenge, but all in all a pleasant round. Also two 9-hole executive type courses. Facility includes driving range and indoor dome.

───────────────ELBOW LAKE───────────────

Tipsinah Mounds CC
Grant County Rd. #24,
56531
Ph: 218-685-4271

Yards: 3055, Holes: 9
Par: 35, USGA: 68.8

Restaurant/Proshop
GF: w/day $7.00, w/end
$8.00
Carts: $7.00

Course built around Indian mounds used for hazards. Several mounds are formed in the shape of snakes to line edges of fairways, other animals for hazards and several peaks or mounds to protect greens. Holes 6 and 7 center around water.

───────────────ELY───────────────

Ely GC
901 S. Central Ave.,
Box 507, 55731
Ph: 218-365-5932

Yards: 4692, Holes: 9
Par: 36, USGA: 61.2

Proshop
GF: w/day $5.50
Carts: $7.00

Our course is a challenge—some hills and trees on most fairway borders. As we are under a large change now, I don't know which hole will be special. It was #8 below a hill and #9 across a valley.

───────────────ERSKINE───────────────

Win-E-Mac GC PC
Junction of Hwy. 2 &
59, 56535
Ph: 218-687-4653

Yards: 2620, Holes: 9
Par: 35, USGA: 32.3
RP: Only on weekends

GF: w/day $8.00
Carts: $8.00

A nice little 9 hole grass green country golf course, not very busy, rolling hills, fun to play. Watch out for moose strolling through the course.

───────────────FAIRFAX───────────────

Fort Ridgely GC
Rt 1, Box 65, 55332
Ph: 507-426-7840

Yards: 5514, Holes: 9
Par: 35, USGA: 64.2

GF: w/day $5.00, w/end
$7.00

This 60 year old course, located in Fort Ridgely State Park, features narrow, mature hardwood lined fairways and Mod-Sod artificial grass greens. The park also offers 39 campsites, hiking trails, and an historic site for non-golfing family members.

───────────────FAIRMONT───────────────

Rose Lake GC, Inc.
RR 2 Box 264-A, 56031
Ph: 507-235-9332

Yards: 6249, Holes: 18
Par: 71, USGA: 69.4
RP: Recommended

Restaurant/Bar/Proshop
GF: w/day $15.00, w/end
$15.00
Carts: $14.00

This natural setting with a lake, two large ponds, and a stream makes for a most picturesque and challenging golf course for any caliber golfer. We sincerely hope your experience here fulfills your desire to enjoy this game in the spirit intended.

──────────────── FERGUS FALLS ────────────────

Pebble Lake GC, Inc.
P.O. Box 772, 56537
Ph: 218-736-7404

Yards: 6342, Holes: 18
Par: 72, USGA: 69.6
RP: Call for tee times

Restaurant/Bar/Proshop
GF: w/day $14.00
Carts: $17.00

Front nine is wide open but there are fairway bunkers which come into play for the better than average golfer. The back nine is a hookers nightmare with some water and bunkers. An excellent course bordering Minnesota's lake country.

──────────────── GARRISON ────────────────

Mille Lacs Lake GC
Star Route, 56450
Ph: 612-682-4325

Yards: 5968, Holes: 18
Par: 71, USGA: 67.6

Restaurant/Bar/Proshop
GF: w/day $16.00, w/end
$20.00
Carts: $18.00

The course is located on the shores of Mille Lacs Lake and will delight you with its secluded, tree-lined fairways, and small beautifully maintained greens.

──────────────── GLENWOOD ────────────────

Minnewaska GC
Box 110, Golf Course
Rd., 56334
Ph: 612-634-3680

Yards: 6212, Holes: 18
Par: 72, USGA: 69.8
RP: 2 days in advance

Bar/Proshop
GF: w/day $8.00, w/end
$11.00
Carts: $11.00

Laid out on a bluff overlooking huge Lake Minnewaska, golfers are often hard pressed to keep their mind on the game because of the views. But don't be fooled. Gently rolling terrain seldom leaves you a flat lie and many greens break toward the lake.

──────────────── GLENWOOD ────────────────

Pezhekee National GC
Peters Sunset Beach
RR2 Box 118, 56334
Ph: 612-634-4501

Yards: 3000, Holes: 9
Par: 35, USGA: 68.5
RP: Resort guests have
priority

Restaurant/Bar/Proshop
GF: w/day $11.00, w/end
$15.00
Carts: $9.50

Heavily wooded 9 hole course requires accuracy more than distance except for the par 4 #7 hole. It requires a 190 yard drive to fly the creek. However, big hitters still must use a long iron to hit the long sloping green in regulation.

──────────────── GLYNDON ────────────────

Ponderosa GC
RR #2, 56547
Ph: 218-498-2201

Yards: 3073, Holes: 9
Par: 36, USGA: 72.0

Restaurant/Proshop
GF: w/day $5.00, w/end
$6.00
Carts: $7.50

First three holes are long and wide. #4 nice par 5, 255 to clear river elevated green, woods on all sides. No fairways running alongside one another. Lots of trees, river, water and sand traps. Lots of deer and small animals.

──────────────── GOLDEN VALLEY ────────────────

Brookview GC PC
200 Brookview
Parkway, 55426
Ph: 612-544-8446

Yards: 6369, Holes: 18
Par: 72, USGA: 69.0
RP: 2 days in advance

Restaurant/Proshop
GF: w/day $17.00, w/end
$17.00
Carts: $19.00

An exciting challenge with water coming into play on 13 out of 18 holes. 18 newly reconstructed greens are challenging target, with rolling hills and trees throughout the course. The 9th and 18th holes are challenging par 4's with water and traps.

───────────────HAM LAKE───────────────

Majestic Oaks GC
701 Bunker Lake Blvd.,
55304
Ph: 612-755-2142

Yards: 6337, Holes: 18
Par: 72, USGA: 70.4
RP: 4 days in advance

Restaurant/Bar/Proshop
GF: w/day $18.00, w/end
$20.00
Carts: $20.00

This course truly is the home of majestic oaks, and recent plantings will make the trees an even bigger problem in the future The greens are surrounded by bunkers. A layout where accuracy on your short game will be important.

───────────────HAMEL───────────────

Shamrock GC
19625 Lakin Rd., 55340
Ph: 612-478-9977

Yards: 6388, Holes: 18
Par: 72, USGA: 68.1
RP: Recommended

Restaurant/Proshop
GF: w/day $14.00, w/end
$16.00
Carts: $18.00

An easy course to walk, Shamrock is fairly flat. Fairways are spacious, with very few sand traps, so it's a great ego builder. Acres of rough separate fairways, making it a safe course too.

───────────────HENNING───────────────

Oakwood GC, Inc.
RR #1. Box 262 A,
56551
Ph: 218-583-2127

Yards: 2840, Holes: 9
Par: 36, USGA: 32.9

Restaurant/Bar/Proshop
GF: w/day $7.00
Carts: $8.00

A short but demanding course requiring driving accuracy and the small undulating greens require patience and skill. Rolling terrain, beautifully wooded with 100 year old white and red oak trees.

───────────────LITTLE FALLS───────────────

Little Falls GC
Golf Rd., 56345
Ph: 612-632-3584

Yards: 6051, Holes: 18
Par: 72, USGA: 68.4
RP: Suggested on
weekends

Restaurant/Bar/Proshop
GF: w/day $11.00
Carts: $12.00

The Little Falls Golf Course has 18 holes carved out of mature oaks and pines. The final three holes are situated along the Mississippi River. Par the 16th and 17th holes and you have a round to remember.

───────────────LONGVILLE───────────────

Erwin Hills GC
Route 1 Box 240, 56655
Ph: 218-363-2552

Yards: 3006, Holes: 9
Par: 36, USGA: 37.2
RP: Call for tee time

Restaurant/Proshop
GF: w/day $7.50
Carts: $10.00

Designed with beauty and challenge in mind, Erwin Hills meanders through 128 acres of rolling, northern Minnesota woods and lakes. Towering hardwoods lend an air of maturity to this new and exciting course. A 70-yard water carry of the 5th tee.

───────────────LUTSEN───────────────

**Superior National at
Lutsen GC**
Hwy 61, PO Box 177,
55612
Ph: 218-663-7195

Yards: 5990, Holes: 18
Par: 72, USGA: 69.3

Superior National is set on Lake Superior and has great views of the lake. But be sure to watch out for the many trees.

──────────────MANKATO──────────────

Terrace View GC Yards: 3093, Holes: 9 Restaurant/Proshop
Highway 22 South, Par: 36, USGA: 33.6 **GF:** w/day $6.75, w/end
P.O. Box 1203, 56001 $7.95
Ph: 507-387-2192 **Carts:** $8.00

*We have a challenging regulation nine hole course and a par 3 nine hole course
across the driveway. We also have a driving range and practice green. We host
numerous group events and tournaments. We have an extensive lesson program.*

──────────────MAPLEWOOD──────────────

Goodrich GC Yards: 6007, Holes: 18 Restaurant/Bar/Proshop
1820 N Van Dyke Ave., Par: 70, USGA: 67.8 **GF:** w/day $12.00
55109 RP: 4 days in advance **Carts:** $17.00
Ph: 612-777-7355

*Fairly open course except for oak woods surrounding holes 4, 5 and 6. Popular
course for seniors who are able to walk entire 18 holes. Noted for its exceptionally fine greens and manicured fairways.*

──────────────MARSHALL──────────────

Marshall GC Yards: 6222, Holes: 18
800 Country Club Dr, Par: 72, USGA: 70.0
PO Box 502, 56258
Ph: 507-537-1622

*A very challenging course with some very difficult water holes. Lots of trees, and
rolling terrain.*

──────────────MELROSE──────────────

Meadowlark CC Yards: 3135, Holes: 9 Bar/Proshop
837 S. 3rd Ave. W, Par: 36, USGA: 34.8 **GF:** w/day $7.75, w/end
56352 RP: Weekends and $9.00
Ph: 612-256-4989 holidays **Carts:** $10.00

*Hole 8, 475 yard par 5, fairway traps. Water to left and right of green, narrow
approach to green. Trees on right side of fairway, trap in left rough.*

──────────────MINNEOTA──────────────

Country Side GC Yards: 3340, Holes: 9 Bar/Proshop
E. Lyon St., 56264 Par: 36, USGA: 34.9 **GF:** w/day $6.00, w/end
Ph: 507-872-9925 RP: None $9.00
 Carts: $6.00

*Hole #8 is our favorite. It's only 345 yards but has tight out of bounds and water.
Must hit tee shot 240 to be safe.*

──────────────NISSWA──────────────

Birch Bay GC Yards: 2900, Holes: 9 Restaurant/Proshop
1771 Birch Dr. West, Par: 36, USGA: 34.7 **GF:** w/day $11.75, w/end
56468 RP: First come, first $11.75
Ph: 218-963-4488 served **Carts:** $12.00

*Tree-lined fairways & postage-stamp greens characterize this challenging 9-hole,
full-length, par-36 course near Gull Lake's west side. Maintained with pride by
our family for over 20 years. Watered fairways, bentgrass greens, level terrain ...
Lodging.*

───────────── NORTHFIELD ─────────────

Willinger GC Ph: 612-652-2500 Yards: 6255, Holes: 18
6900 Canby Trail, Par: 72, USGA: 68.5
55057

Set in an old trees nursery, the course uses this as a natural setting and hazard. A very challenging layout that is well maintained.

───────────── ONAMIA ─────────────

Izatys GC Yards: 6300, Holes: 18 Restaurant/Bar/Proshop
1 Izatys Rd., 56359 Par: 71, USGA: 68.5 **GF:** w/day $20.00
Ph: 612-532-3101 RP: Required 2 days in **Carts:** $20.00
  advance

Nestled amongst central Minnesota's scenic woodlands, Izatys demands precise shot-making and course strategy to overcome its numerous challenges which include sharp doglegs, pot bunkers, railroad ties, and countless water hazards.

───────────── PAYNESVILLE ─────────────

Koronis Hills GC Yards: 2990, Holes: 9 Restaurant/Proshop
Highway 23, P.O. Box Par: 36, USGA: 33.5 **GF:** w/day $6.00, w/end
55, 56362 RP: Required $7.00
Ph: 612-243-4111   **Carts:** $8.00

An old style course, with hundreds of oak trees. Position on drives more important than distance, not many flat areas on this tough little course. Our favorite hole is #9, lined with huge oaks to an elevated green 179 yards away, requires steady nerves.

───────────── PEQUOT LAKES ─────────────

Breezy Point GC Yards: 5192, Holes: 36 Restaurant/Bar
HCR-2 Box 70, 56472 Par: 68, USGA: 62.9 **GF:** w/day $18.50
Ph: 218-562-7166 RP: 3 days in advance **Carts:** $19.50

There are two courses here, the "original" nine holes, and a second course, referred to as Championship Nine, due to have an additional nine constructed. When players are queried as to what's memorable about golf here, the unanimous reply is "trees."

───────────── PEQUOT LAKES ─────────────

Whitefish GC Yards: 6407, Holes: 18 Restaurant/Bar/Proshop
Rt. 1 Box 111-B, 56472 Par: 72, USGA: 68.9 **GF:** w/day $13.00
Ph: 218-543-4900 RP: 1 day in advance **Carts:** $16.00

Whitefish Golf Course has been cut out of the north woods. It is surrounded by birch, oak and pine with a few attractive waterholes to add to its beauty.

───────────── PINE CITY ─────────────

Pine City CC PC Yards: 6348, Holes: 9
Rt 4 Box 6C, 55063 Par: 36, USGA: 68.3
Ph: 612-629-3848

Water covers 11 of the 18 holes. Many of the holes are cut through mighty oak trees that are characteristic of majestic oaks. Greens are very undulating and well protected by deep bunkers. The Minnesota Professional Golfers Association headquarters.

──────────────PINE RIVER──────────────

Irish Hills GC at
Piney Ridge
Rt. 1 Box 315, 56474
Ph: 218-587-2296

Yards: 3231, Holes: 9
Par: 36, USGA: 70.8

Restaurant/Bar/Proshop
GF: w/day $8.50
Carts: $9.00

Considered one of the finest new courses in Minnesota. Nationally featured in Golf Digest as well as Golf Traveler magazines. Carved out of a pine forest, Irish Hills rolls from ridge to ridge snuggling up against ponds, valleys and beautiful lakes.

──────────────RAMSEY──────────────

Rum River Hills GC
PC
16659 ST. Frances
Blvd., 55303
Ph: 612-753-3339

Yards: 6100, Holes: 18
Par: 71, USGA: 68.7
RP: 3 days in advance

Restaurant/Bar/Proshop
GF: w/day $13.00, w/end
$16.00
Carts: $20.00

Scenic views with water on 12 holes, the English/Scottish influence is evident on the course.

──────────────RICHFIELD──────────────

Rich Acres GC PC
2201 East 66th St.,
55423
Ph: 612-861-7145

Yards: 6606, Holes: 27
Par: 71, USGA: 69.2
RP: One day in advance

Restaurant/Bar/Proshop
GF: w/day $12.00, w/end
$13.00
Carts: $16.00

On the regulation course you will find 120 acres of beautiful undulating terrain. On the par-3 course there is an interesting variety of water hazards and sand traps set among the large rolling greens.

──────────────ROCHESTER──────────────

Maple Valley G&CC
RR 3, Box 165, 55904
Ph: 507-285-9100

Yards: 6106, Holes: 18
Par: 71, USGA: 67.4
RP: Tee Times

Restaurant/Bar
GF: w/day $14.00
Carts: $15.00

Located on Root River in hardwood forest of S.E. Minnesota. 18 hole scenic challenging. Open to public 7 days a week.

──────────────RUSHFORD──────────────

Ferndale CC
Hwy 16, 55971
Ph: 507-864-7626

Yards: 3228, Holes: 9
Par: 36, USGA: 69.8
RP: 1 week in advance

Bar/Proshop
GF: w/day $11.00, w/end
$12.00
Carts: $12.00

Situated in S.E. Minnesota's hardwood forest area just 2 miles from Rushford. The entire course can be viewed from the clubhouse area. A challenging and very beautiful 9-hole club where par is seldom broken.

──────────────SHAKOPEE──────────────

Stonebrooke GC
2693 Cty Rd 79, 55379
Ph: 612-496-3171

Yards: 6600, Holes: 18
Par: 71, USGA: 69.2
RP: 3 days in advance

Restaurant/Bar/Proshop
GF: w/day $21.00, w/end
$24.00
Carts: $20.00

Elevation changes and mature stands of native hardwoods allow for spectacular views and adventurous golf at Stonebrooke. Challenge the 13 great water holes and don't forget the relaxing ferry ride to your second shot on the famous par 4 8th hole.

─────────────────────ST. PAUL─────────────────────

Keller GC
2166 Maplewood Dr.,
55109
Ph: 612-484-3011

Yards: 6524, Holes: 18
Par: 72, USGA: 69.8
RP: 4 days in advance

Restaurant/Bar/Proshop
GF: w/day $16.00, w/end
$16.00
Carts: $19.00

Very scenic, gently rolling terrain that requires you to use all the clubs in your bag. Very interesting and challenging. Home of the St. Paul open 1930-1968, the National Pub-Links 1931, the National P.G.A. Championship 1932, 1954, the Western Open 1949.

─────────────────────STAPLES─────────────────────

Terrace GC PC
Box 26, 56479
Ph: 218-894-9907

Yards: 2945, Holes: 9
Par: 36, USGA: 33.7

Restaurant/Bar/Proshop
GF: w/day $8.00
Carts: $8.50

Located on the banks of the beautiful Crow Wing River, this course provides a new look for all 9 holes. Interesting layout.

─────────────────────TYLER─────────────────────

Tyler Community GC
County Rd 7, PO Box
447, 56178
Ph: 507-247-3242

Yards: 3184, Holes: 9
Par: 36, USGA: 67.8

Restaurant/Bar/Proshop
GF: w/day $7.00, w/end
$9.00
Carts: $7.00

Just a nine hole watered fairway course. Small greens, no sand, no water—but a real challenge.

─────────────────────VIRGINIA─────────────────────

Virginia Muni GC
9th Ave. North, 55792
Ph: 218-741-4366

Yards: 6131, Holes: 18
Par: 71, USGA: 68.7
RP: Call the Proshop

Restaurant/Bar/Proshop
GF: w/day $10.00, w/end
$15.00
Carts: $17.00

Course is situated on undulating hills dotted with mature pines. A challenging course. Recently reconstructed 60-year-old course.

─────────────────────WARROAD─────────────────────

WarRoad Estates GC
HCO-2 Box 30, 56763
Ph: 218-386-2025

Yards: 7101, Holes: 18
Par: 72, USGA: 70.7

Restaurant/Bar/Proshop
GF: w/day $10.75
Carts: $14.50

One of Minnesota's most challenging golf courses located near Canada, has an international flavor, on beautiful Lake of Woods known for its excellent fishing. Course has 11 holes of water hazards coming into play and several well-treed holes.

─────────────────────WATERTOWN─────────────────────

Timber Creek GC
9750 Co. Rd. 24, 55388
Ph: 612-446-1415

Yards: 6800, Holes: 18
Par: 72, USGA: 69.2
RP: Weekends

Restaurant/Proshop
GF: w/day $12.00
Carts: $16.00

Timber Creek is located in a beautiful rural setting; with two creeks, ponds, sandtraps and rolling wooded acres. The back tees challenge the low handicap golfer by locating many hazards in areas that will reward only the best of shots.

◄─◄─◄─◄─◄─◄─◄─◄─◄ ◉ ►─►─►─►─►─►─►─►─►

MISSISSIPPI

Pontotoc •
• Greenville
• Silver City

• Natchez

Ocean Springs
Biloxi •
Bay St. Louis

───────── BAY ST. LOUIS ─────────

Diamondhead CC   Ph: 601-255-2525   Yards: 6086, Holes: 18
7600 Country Club   Par: 72
Circle, 39520   Restaurant/Bar

*The Cardinal Course demands accuracy on its tight fairways flanked by deep
woods and features large, fast Tiftdorf green, ideal for winter play. The layout of
the Pine Course is wider fairways and smaller, slower greens.*

───────── BILOXI ─────────

Broadwater Beach   Yards: 6001, Holes: 18   Restaurant/Bar
2000 E Beach Blvd,   Par: 71, USGA: 69.0   **GF:** w/day $20.00
39533   RP: Guests 6-8 months,
Ph: 601-388-2211   others 2 days

*The Sea Course is a flat, tight layout on the Gulf. The Sun Course is more open,
but word has it that the pros quietly agree to play the middle tees so they can
save face. Fourteen of its holes traverse water.*

───────── BILOXI ─────────

Broadwater Beach -   Yards: 7200, Holes: 18   Restaurant/Bar
Sun Course   Par: 72, USGA: 69.0   **GF:** w/day $20.00
2000 E Beach Blvd,   RP: Guests 6-8 months,   **Carts:** $18.00
39533   others 2 days
Ph: 601-388-2211

*The Sea Course is a flat, tight layout, with a really big water hazard (called the
Gulf). The Sun Course is more open, but don't be lulled into thinking there's no
water. Word has it that the pros agree quietly to play the middle tees.*

───────── BRANDON ─────────

Bay Pointe CC   Yards: 6670, Holes: 18   Restaurant
800 Bay Pointe Dr,   Par: 72, USGA: 70.4   **GF:** w/day $15.00
39042
Ph: 601-829-1862

*A round of golf that is going to really test your skills. Lots of trees and more than
enough water.*

─────────────────────GAUTIER─────────────────────

Hickory Hills GC Yards: 6517, Holes: 18 Restaurant/Bar
900 Hickory Hill Dr., Par: 72 **GF:** w/day $21.50
38755
Ph: 601-497-5150

Water comes into play on at least two thirds of the course. And if that isn't enough the fairways have lots of very large trees. Your accuracy can become very important.

────────────────────GREENVILLE────────────────────

Greenville Yards: 6439, Holes: 18 Restaurant/Bar/Proshop
Municipal GC Par: 72 **GF:** w/day $5.00, w/end
Airbase Rd., 38755 $7.00
Ph: 601-332-4079 **Carts:** $12.00

Beautiful well designed course. Water involved on 10 of 18 holes. Former United States Air Force golf course now owned by City of Greenville. #3 one of toughest short par 3's anywhere. Out of bounds directly behind green. Deer Creek meanders to the edge.

────────────────────HATTIESBURG────────────────────

Timberton GC Yards: 6436, Holes: 18
PO Box 2002, 22 Par: 72, USGA: 70.5
Clubhouse Dr, 39403
Ph: 601-584-4653

Water is in play on two thirds of the course and the mature trees and rolling terrain are sure to add difficulties all their own.

──────────────────────LAUREL──────────────────────

Bear Creek GC Yards: 6179, Holes: 18
P.O. Box 2295, 39440 Par: 72, USGA: 70.7
Ph: 601-425-5670

The par-5s are considered very tough here. You're going to find a lot of water and the greens are bigger than a postage stamp, but just.

──────────────────────NATCHEZ──────────────────────

Duncan Park GC Yards: 6058, Holes: 9 Proshop
c/o Duncan Park, Par: 72, USGA: 68.4 **GF:** w/day $6.00
39120 **Carts:** $7.00
Ph: 601-442-5955

Duncan Park Golf Course is a very tricky old course built in 1925 on part of the grounds of the Antebellum Home Auburn. It is nestled among gigantic live oaks and pine trees, and it located almost in the heart of Natchez, oldest city on the Mississippi.

────────────────────OCEAN SPRINGS────────────────────

Pine Island GC Yards: 6001, Holes: 18 Restaurant/Bar/Proshop
Gulf Park Estates, P.O. Par: 71, USGA: 69.0 **GF:** w/day $14.00
Box 843, 39564 **RP:** Weekends **Carts:** $16.00
Ph: 601-875-1674

This course is built on 3 islands, beautiful serene setting, full of wildlife. Each hole has its own name, e.g., "The Secret Garden," all titles of books.

───────────────OCEAN SPRINGS───────────────

Royal Gulf Hills
Resort
13701 Paso Rd., 39564
Ph: 800-638-4902

Yards: 6200, Holes: 18
Par: 71, USGA: 70.4

Restaurant

Legendary Golfing — Country Inn setting. 65 years of tradition. Challenging, undulating greens. Must tee to appreciate.

───────────────PONTOTOC───────────────

Pontotoc CC
P.O. Box 390, 38863
Ph: 601-489-1962

Yards: 6400, Holes: 18
Par: 72, USGA: 68.5
RP: Call for tee times

Restaurant/Proshop
GF: w/day $15.00
Carts: $14.00

You get introduced with a relatively open front nine with rolling fairways overlooking the Natchez Trace State Park 2,100 acre lake. The back nine offers the golfer with challenging demanding shots with a 170 yard island par three.

───────────────SILVER CITY───────────────

Humphreys County
CC
P.O. Box 35, 39166
Ph: 601-247-3294

Yards: 6335, Holes: 9
Par: 72, USGA: 68.9

Restaurant/Bar/Proshop
GF: w/day $7.00, w/end
$10.00
Carts: $7.00

Best layout and most character of any course in the Mississippi delta. Requires length or accuracy on every tee shot, sometimes both. Don't let the levee intimidate you.

───────────────STARKVILLE───────────────

Mississippi State
Univ GC
PO Box 6070, 39762
Ph: 601-325-3028

Yards: 6940, Holes: 18
Par: 72, USGA: 73.5

Restaurant
GF: w/day $9.00, w/end
$12.00

This course was built by students of the University, they maintain it beautifully too. A must see layout that is well worth your time.

───────────────VICKSBURG───────────────

Clear Creek GC
Rt. 5 Box 322 C, 1556
Tiffentown, 39180

Ph: 601-638-9395

Yards: 6287, Holes: 18
Par: 72

A course that will give a challenge to everyone, and offers plenty of length to those who want it.

───────────────WIGGINS───────────────

Pine Burr CC
800 Pine Burr Dr,
39577

Ph: 601-928-4911

Yards: 6286, Holes: 18
Par: 72, USGA: 71.3

Pine Burr has long been considered a challenging course, and it just keeps getting better.

MISSOURI

• Excelsior Springs

Sullivan •

Lake Ozark •

• Osage Beach

Dexter •

────────── CRYSTAL CITY ──────────

Crystal Highlands GC
US Hwy 61 & Weaver

Rd, Ph: 314-933-3880

Yards: 6000, Holes: 18
Par: 72

Some of the greens are on more than one level, and they will surely challenge you. The course is in the foothills and is quite rolling.

────────── DEXTER ──────────

Hidden Trails CC
W. Grant St., P.O. Box 355, 63841
Ph: 314-624-3638

Yards: 6439, Holes: 18
Par: 72, USGA: 69.2
RP: Call for reservation

Restaurant/Bar/Proshop
GF: w/day $12.00, w/end $12.00
Carts: $13.00

A rolling course built atop Crowley Ridge. The front nine is relatively open and conducive to scoring. The back side is tight as it winds through a scenic subdivision of huge new homes. Straight tee shots are a premium.

────────── EXCELSIOR SPRINGS ──────────

Excelsior Springs GC
1201 E. Golf Hill, P.O. Box 417, 64024
Ph: 816-637-3731

Yards: 6464, Holes: 18
Par: 72, USGA: 70.3
RP: Required weekends & holidays

Restaurant/Bar/Proshop
GF: w/day $9.00, w/end $10.00
Carts: $16.00

Designed by world-famous architect, Tom Bendelow, often referred to as an "English-type: course, it is unique in that is has no bunkers, traps or other unpopular characteristics of the English course. The course is highly rated by top professionals.

────────── JACKSON ──────────

Bent Creek GC
Bent Creek Dr., 63755
Ph: 314-243-6060

Yards: 6444, Holes: 18
Par: 72

Restaurant/Bar
GF: w/day $14.00, w/end $16.00

A long and challenging course. Water and bunkers are going to be a problem. The rolling terrain can often test you too.

──────────────── KANSAS CITY ────────────────

Longview GC
11100 View High Dr,
64134
Ph: 816-761-9445

Yards: 6251, Holes: 18
Par: 72

GF: w/day $9.50, w/end
$11.00

Lots of large mounds and rolling terrain make this a very tough layout. The greens offer plenty of challenge to your putting game too.

──────────────── KANSAS CITY ────────────────

Swope Memorial GC
6900 Swope Memorial
Dr., 64132
Ph: 816-523-9081

Yards: 5780, Holes: 18
Par: 71

There are lots of trees and bunkers, but the many multi-level greens can be very tricky and will really test you.

──────────────── LAKE OZARK ────────────────

**Lodge of Four
Seasons GC**
P.O. Box 215, 65049
Ph: 314-365-8544

Yards: 6416, Holes: 45
Par: 72, USGA: 71.4
RP: Members/Lodge
Guest Only

Restaurant
GF: w/day $55.00, w/end
$60.00
Carts: $Included

Seasons Ridge Golf Club, a public championship golf course, is the Lodge Of Four Seasons newest addition to the existing 27-hole resort golf facilities. The 6416 par 72 course is one of the finest new golf facilities in the Midwest. Winding through hills.

──────────────── OAK GROVE ────────────────

Bent Oak GC
P.O. Box 537, 1300 SW
30th St, 64075
Ph: 816-625-3028

Yards: 6804, Holes: 18
Par: 72

Restaurant
GF: w/day $9.00, w/end
$11.00

Lots of long holes on Bent Oak. The setting is very rolling and offers a great round of golf.

──────────────── OSAGE BEACH ────────────────

**Best Western
Dogwood Hills GC**
Route 1, Box 1300,
65065
Ph: 314-348-3153

Yards: 6200, Holes: 18
Par: 71

Restaurant/Bar

One of the most picturesque holes is #17, a 357-yard hole dogleg right; you play uphill, past a lake and through the colorful trees. The fairways are wide with rolling hills, and the greens are undulated with smooth bent grass putting surfaces.

──────────────── OSAGE BEACH ────────────────

**Marriotts Tan-Tar-A
The Oaks**
State Route KK, 65065
Ph: 314-348-4163

Yards: 6465, Holes: 18
Par: 71, USGA: 72.1
RP: 7 days guests - 1
day non

Restaurant/Bar/Proshop
GF: w/day $40.00
Carts: $12.00

The Oaks plays 6465 yards from the blue tees. Small and well bunkered greens demand proper placement of tee shots as well as approach shots. Water comes into play on 11 of the 18 holes which are carved out of the natural oaks surroundings.

————————————SPRINGFIELD————————————

Deer Lake GC   Ph: 417-865-8888   Yards: 6454, Holes: 18
5544 W. Chestnut   Par: 72
Expressway, 65802

A well designed course that uses the lakes and rolling terrain. Lots of beautiful trees also.

————————————ST. LOUIS————————————

Normandie Park GC   Yards: 6258, Holes: 18   **GF:** w/day $14.00, w/end
7605 St. Charles Rock   Par: 71, USGA: 69.6 $18.00
Rd., 63133   **Carts:** $16.00
Ph: 314-862-4884

Designed by Robert Foulis, this course opened in 1901. It is thought to be the oldest course west of the Mississippi. The green are very small, and that can give you lots of work with your short game.

————————————ST. LOUIS————————————

Quail Creek GC   Yards: 6313, Holes: 18   Restaurant/Bar
6022 Wells Rd., 63128   Par: 72   **GF:** w/day $18.00, w/end
Ph: 314-487-1988 $24.00

The main difficulty on Quail Creek is the water. The many elevation changes can be tough too.

————————————SULLIVAN————————————

Sullivan CC   Yards: 3115, Holes: 9   Restaurant/Proshop
E. Vine St., 63080   Par: 36, USGA: 68.4   **GF:** w/day $12.00, w/end
Ph: 314-468-5803   RP: Out-of-towners only $12.00
                          on weekend   **Carts:** $12.00

Our 9-hole course is fun and very well manicured. Big oak trees scattered around course is our trademark. Keeping down the middle is a must to score well.

————————————WRIGHT CITY————————————

Innsbrook Estates   Yards: 6017, Holes: 18   Restaurant/Bar
CC   Par: 70   **GF:** w/day $16.00, w/end
One Innsbrook Estates $21.00
Dr., 63390
Ph: 314-928-3366

Lots of water and sandtraps that are easy to get into, but not so easy to get out of. The course is very hilly.

MONTANA

─────────────────BIG SKY─────────────────

Big Sky GC
P.O. Box 1, 59716
Ph: 406-995-4211

Yards: 6115, Holes: 18
Par: 72

Restaurant/Bar
GF: w/day $22.00
Carts: $16.00

The course sits in an alpine meadow at 6,500 feet. This is a relatively flat course, where you can't help but get the feeling of wide open spaces. The course meanders around the West Fork of the Gallitin River, with water coming into play on six holes.

─────────────────BIG TIMBER─────────────────

Overland GC
P.O. Box 1091, 59011
Ph: 406-932-4297

Yards: 6776, Holes: 9
Par: 36, USGA: 69.9
RP: Weekends

Proshop
GF: w/day $6.00, w/end
$7.00
Carts: $7.00

A beautifully maintained course with a spectacular view of the Yellowstone Valley and the Crazy Mountains. Play in a totally relaxed atmosphere, where it is not unusual to see deer on the course. The nine holes meander between babbling brooks.

─────────────────BIGFORK─────────────────

Eagle Bend GC
279 Eagle Bend Dr., PO
Box 960, 59911
Ph: 406-837-7300

Yards: 6237, Holes: 18
Par: 72, USGA: 69.6

Restaurant/Bar/Proshop
GF: w/day $35.00, w/end
$35.00
Carts: $10.00

Rated the #1 course in Montana and among America's top 50 public courses by Golf Digest. Located at the scenic north end of Flathead Lake. Meticulously manicured fairways and greens is complemented by the incomparable mountain and lake vistas.

─────────────────COLUMBIA FALLS─────────────────

Meadow Lake GC
1415 Tamarack Ln.,
59912
Ph: 406-892-7601

Yards: 6574, Holes: 18
Par: 71, USGA: 69.4
RP: 2 days in advance

Restaurant/Bar/Proshop
GF: w/day $15.00
Carts: $16.00

The course combines the best of Rocky Mountain golf—spectacular grandeur, lakes, streams and trees. A back nine that meanders among tall pines gives one a feeling of solitude and peacefulness.

---------------------------------FORSYTH---------------------------------

Forsyth CC, Inc.   Yards: 6140, Holes: 18   Restaurant/Bar/Proshop
Box 191, 59327   Par: 71, USGA: 67.9   **GF:** w/day $7.00
Ph: 406-356-7710   RP: Weekends &   **Carts:** $7.00
                      holidays

*You tee off on #1 to an elevated green which is trapped rising more than 40 feet
from the tee. The #2 hole sits on a needle requiring a well placed shot to hold the
green. The #3 hole is a long 560 yard hole as is #4 to be followed by a 235 yard
par 3.*

---------------------------------GLENDIVE---------------------------------

Cottonwood CC   Yards: 3130, Holes: 9   Restaurant/Bar/Proshop
P.O. Box 317, 59330   Par: 36, USGA: 69.5   **GF:** w/day $8.00, w/end
Ph: 406-365-8797 $10.00
                                              Carts: $6.00

*Good test for all playing levels, 9 holes with creeks, trees and sandtraps and
shrubs for hazards. Excellent small greens to challenge everyone. Friendly,
clean, new clubhouse with bar and proshop.*

---------------------------------KALISPELL---------------------------------

Buffalo Hill GC   Yards: 6247, Holes: 27   Restaurant/Bar/Proshop
N Main, P.O. Box 1116,   Par: 72, USGA: 70.2   **GF:** w/day $17.00
59903   RP: 2 days in advance   **Carts:** $16.00
Ph: 406-755-5902

*Montana's #1 ranked public golf course, redesigned in 1978 by Robert Muir
Graves, 27 holes of sheer pleasure. A shotmakers delight requiring a premium
on accuracy rather than power, until you get to #13, a demanding par 4 with
water, out of bounds.*

---------------------------------MISSOULA---------------------------------

Larchmont GC   Yards: 7118, Holes: 18   Restaurant/Bar/Proshop
3200 Old Fort Rd.,   Par: 72, USGA: 69.8   **GF:** w/day $12.00, w/end
59801   RP: 1 day in advance $14.00
Ph: 406-721-4416   **Carts:** $16.00

*This course is one of the longest in the area, but fairly wide open. Known for its
exemplary maintenance, the greens are fast, smooth, and firm, and surrounded
by deep Scottish style bunkers. Surrounded by the majestic Bitterroot Mountain
range.*

---------------------------------THREE FORKS---------------------------------

Headwaters GC   Yards: 3158, Holes: 9   Restaurant/Bar/Proshop
7th Ave. E, 59752   Par: 36, USGA: 67.1   **GF:** w/day $7.00
Ph: 406-285-3700   RP: Preferred   **Carts:** $7.00

*You will have many options to play the ball safe; however, there are water
hazards on 6 of our 9 holes. As our name implies, Three Forks is located at the
headwaters of the Missouri River. A superb vacation area.*

---------------------------------WEST GLACIER---------------------------------

Glacier View GC   Yards: 5105, Holes: 18   Restaurant/Bar/Proshop
Box 185, 59936   Par: 68, USGA: 63.9   **GF:** w/day $15.00
Ph: 406-888-5471   RP: Weekends   **Carts:** $14.00

*Glacier View Golf Club features unsurpassed views of Glacier National Park
from all 18 holes. Visitors are pleased to find a pro shop, bar and fine restaurant
all within the open beam ceilings of the clubhouse. Frequently seen wildlife.*

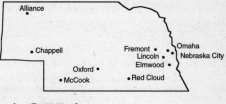

NEBRASKA

ALLIANCE

Skyview GC
RR 2, 69301
Ph: 308-762-1446

Yards: 6449, Holes: 18
Par: 72, USGA: 68.8

Bar/Proshop
GF: w/day $7.00, w/end
$8.50
Carts: $12.00

The 2nd hole is protected by two bunkers, one strategically placed midway on this par 3, 485 yard hole. The other bunker guards the green at the front right. Accuracy is everything.

CHAPPELL

Chappell GC
I-80 Exit, 69129
Ph: 308-874-9973

Yards: 6630, Holes: 9
Par: 72, USGA: 69.8
RP: Recommended

Proshop
GF: w/day $8.00
Carts: $10.00

You will not find better fairways and greens anywhere. User friendly course, not a lot of hazards, five small traps, water on two holes, flat and easy to walk if you desire.

ELMWOOD

Grandpa's Woods CC
Box 245, 68349
Ph: 402-994-3415

Yards: 1802, Holes: 9
Par: 31

GF: w/day $2.00

Grandpa's woods is a beautiful, challenging nine hole golf course located in a remote wooded area.

FREMONT

Valley View GC
Box 344, Rt. 2, 68025
Ph: 402-721-7772

Yards: 5232, Holes: 9
Par: 70, USGA: 64.1

Bar/Proshop
GF: w/day $7.50, w/end
$10.50
Carts: $8.50

The top nine offers a spectacular view of Fremont and the Platte River Valley. Back nine is more challenging with longer fairways and water. Hole #10 offers a huge elevation drop through a canyon.

GRAND ISLAND

Grand Island Muni GC
2803 Shady Bend Rd., 68802
Ph: 308-381-5340

Yards: 6752, Holes: 18
Par: 72

Restaurant
GF: w/day $6.50, w/end
$8.10

A real test of your skills if you're an average golfer, a piece of cake for the pro.

———————————————————LINCOLN———————————————————

Holmes Park GC Yards: 6805, Holes: 18 Bar
3701 S. 70th, 68506 Par: 72 **GF:** w/day $7.10, w/end
Ph: 402-471-8960 $8.15

The course is hilly with well protected greens. The par-3s can be long.

———————————————————LINCOLN———————————————————

Mahoney GC Yards: 6450, Holes: 18 Proshop
7900 Adams, 68507 Par: 71, USGA: 66.9 **GF:** w/day $7.15, w/end
Ph: 402-464-7542 RP: 1 week in advance $8.15
  Carts: $15.00

Flexibility of yardage is the greatest virtue of the golf course. The 6450 yards consist of undulating greens, rolling fairways and difficult roughs. 8th hole, slight dogleg left, 2nd shot across lake aiming at a small targeted 2 tiered green.

———————————————————LINCOLN———————————————————

Pioneers GC Yards: 6176, Holes: 18 Restaurant
Rt 1, 3403 W. Van Par: 71 **GF:** w/day $7.05, w/end
Dorn, 68502 $8.05
Ph: 402-471-8966

This is a very old course with grass bunkers. It has recently been renovated.

———————————————————MCCOOK———————————————————

Heritage Hills GC Yards: 6715, Holes: 18 **GF:** w/day $11.50, w/end
108 West D St., 69001 Par: 72, USGA: 68.3 $13.50
Ph: 308-345-5032 **Carts:** $14.00

A great course on undulating fairways. One of Golf Digest's Top 75 Public Golf Courses in America.

———————————————————NEBRASKA CITY———————————————————

Wildwood Muni GC Yards: 2831, Holes: 9 Proshop
Steinhart Park, Par: 36, USGA: 67.3 **GF:** w/day $5.00, w/end
Highway 2 W., 68410 $6.00
Ph: 402-873-3661

Enjoy this beautiful course adjacent to 2 major parks in Nebraska City which is also home of Arbor Day. This course is loaded with trees. Our fifth hole is on the Omaha World Herald's hall of fame by being surrounded by oaks and green.

———————————————————OMAHA———————————————————

Benson Park GC Yards: 6870, Holes: 18 **GF:** w/day $9.50
5333 N 72nd St., 68108 Par: 72
Ph: 402-444-4626

A very challenging course that will give you a real run for your money.

———————————————————OMAHA———————————————————

Eagle Run GC Yards: 2200, Holes: 9
3435 N. 132 St., 68164 Par: 32
Ph: 402-498-9900

A good place to work on your short game, and if you want some more there's also a pitch-and-putt type course here.

────────────────────OMAHA────────────────────

Knolls GC
11630 Sahler St., 68164
Ph: 402-493-1740

Yards: 5813, Holes: 18
Par: 71, USGA: 68.0

GF: w/day $10.00
Carts: $15.00

A well maintained course that is very pretty. Lots of water will demand your accuracy.

────────────────────OMAHA────────────────────

**Miracle Hill Golf &
Tennis Center**
1401 North 120th,
68154
Ph: 402-498-0220

Yards: 6412, Holes: 18
Par: 70, USGA: 70.0
RP: 7 days in advance

Proshop
GF: w/day $9.00, w/end
$10.00
Carts: $16.00

Miracle Hill holds the site of the Guiness Book of World Records for the Longest Straight Hole in One. Achieved by Bob Mitera on October 7, 1965 at age 21, his 444 yard ace on the par 4 #10 has yet to have been out done.

────────────────────OXFORD────────────────────

Oxford CC
101 Golf Course Rd.,
68967
Ph: 308-824-3296

Holes: 9
Par: 36

Restaurant/Bar
GF: w/day $10.00

Beautiful course winding around a creek in the rolling hills of southern Nebraska. The Republican River Valley lies just to the south. The course is known for the tough greens. You had better look twice when setting up a putt.

────────────────────RED CLOUD────────────────────

Red Cloud CC
Rt. 2 Box 17A, 68970
Ph: 402-746-2567

Yards: 3132, Holes: 9
Par: 36, USGA: 69.6

Bar/Proshop
GF: w/day $6.00
Carts: $7.00

Accuracy a must with our narrow-rolling fairways. Precision iron shots when approaching the small elevated greens will give you a good shot at a birdie, but if you miss, just getting on and staying on is the next challenge.

────────────────────SCOTTSBLUFF────────────────────

Riverview GC, Inc.
PO Box 700, W 20th
St., 69361
Ph: 308-635-1555

Yards: 6024, Holes: 18
Par: 70

Restaurant/Bar
GF: w/day $7.75, w/end
$8.75

An open back nine to give you an easy finish after all the trees on the front.

────────────────────VALENTINE────────────────────

Deer Park GC
HC 14 Box 68A, 69201
Ph: 402-376-1271

Yards: 5680, Holes: 18
Par: 70

Restaurant/Bar
GF: w/day $10.00

Set near a relatively rolling area, there is a creek that runs through. There's also abundant wildlife to make the day interesting.

────────────────────VALLEY────────────────────

The Pines CC
7516 N. 286th, 68064
Ph: 402-359-4311

Yards: 6655, Holes: 18
Par: 72, USGA: 68.8
RP: 1 day in advance

Restaurant/Bar/Proshop
GF: w/day $13.50, w/end
$15.00
Carts: $16.00

Wind and some tough short holes, with the added challenge of plenty of water. You're sure to get a workout on this one.

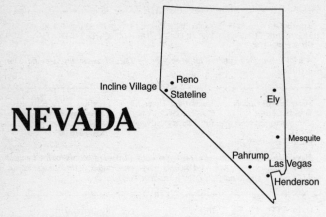

NEVADA

----------------------------------DAYTON----------------------------------

Dayton Valley GC
51 Palmer Dr., 89403
Ph: 702-246-7888

Yards: 5837, Holes: 18
Par: 72

An Arnold Palmer design, this layout has lots of water and will provide the usual Palmer challenges. A twilight rate is offered here.

----------------------------------ELKO----------------------------------

Spring Creek GC
451 E. Spring creek
Pwky, 89801
Ph: 702-753-6331

Yards: 6258, Holes: 18
Par: 71

GF: w/day $9.00
Carts: $14.00

Doglegs, water, and sandtraps in abundance are going to make this round a tough one.

----------------------------------ELY----------------------------------

White Pine GC
1 Burch Dr., 89301
Ph: 702-289-4095

Yards: 6489, Holes: 9
Par: 72, USGA: 69.2

Restaurant/Bar/Proshop
GF: w/day $8.00
Carts: $15.00

9 hole golf course with two sets of tees, flat terrain with small greens and very narrow fairways. Our favorite hole is #3, 441 yards dogleg left well bunkered both fairway and around the green. Small green to hit to and tough to putt.

----------------------------------HENDERSON----------------------------------

Indian Wells CC
1 Showboat Country
Club Dr., 89014
Ph: 702-451-2106

Yards: 6917, Holes: 18
Par: 71, USGA: 72.4
RP: 1 week, weekends 2
days

Restaurant/Bar/Proshop
GF: w/day $50.00, w/end
$50.00
Carts: $Included

The Indian Wells Country Club is a championship golf course on semi-flat desert terrain. The second hole is a 609 yard double dogleg par 5 that demands 3 good shots. The last 2 holes can either make or break a good round with length and out of bounds.

───────────────HENDERSON───────────────

Legacy GC @ Green Valley
130 Par Excellence Dr., 89016
Ph: 702-897-2200

Yards: 6211, Holes: 18
Par: 72, USGA: 69.1

Rolling fairways, roughs of varied depths, and mounds adorn this Scottish style course. 11, 12, and 13 are a few of the roughest holes that the game of golf offers. A truly challenging round.

───────────────HENDERSON───────────────

Royal Kenfield CC
Kenfield Club Dr., Ph: 702-434-9009

Yards: 5954, Holes: 18
Par: 72

A course with well-protected and rolling, small greens. And you have to watch out for the water too.

───────────────INCLINE VILLAGE───────────────

Incline Village Championship
955 Fairway Blvd., Box 7590, 89450
Ph: 702-832-1144

Yards: 7138, Holes: 36
Par: 72, USGA: 70.5
RP: May call in May for season

Restaurant/Bar/Proshop
GF: w/day $75.00, w/end $75.00
Carts: $Included

The championship course has recently been rated as one of the Top 50 public golf courses in the U.S. by Golf Digest. And the executive course has long been considered one of the Top 5 of its kind in the country. Both are a blend of beauty and difficulty.

───────────────LAS VEGAS───────────────

Angel Park GC
100 S. Rampart Blvd., 89128
Ph: 702-254-GOLF

Yards: 5751, Holes: 36
Par: 71, USGA: 67.8

Lots of lakes and bunkers, a double dogleg over drops, and a very tough par-5 are all going to try your luck. There is a magnificent view of the mountains and Las Vegas.

───────────────LAS VEGAS───────────────

Desert Inn CC
3145 Las Vegas Blvd. South, 89109
Ph: 702-733-4444

Yards: 7111, Holes: 18
Par: 72, USGA: 73.0
RP: Sat.-Sun. guests & member only

Restaurant/Bar/Proshop
GF: w/day $90.00
Carts: $10.00

The Desert Inn has a rich golf history, starting in 1953–1966 as the original home of PGA Tours "Tournament of Champions" and over the years played host to several LPGA Tour events. Presently the home of the "General Tire Las Vegas Classic."

───────────────LAS VEGAS───────────────

Desert Rose GC
5483 Clubhouse Dr., 89122
Ph: 702-431-4653

Yards: 6511, Holes: 18
Par: 71, USGA: 68.7
RP: Weekday-1 week; weekend-3 days

GF: w/day $19.50
Carts: $15.00

A spectacular setting in the Sunrise Mountain area. A course that will challenge the average golfer.

─────────────── LAS VEGAS ───────────────

Las Vegas GC
4349 Vegas Dr., 89114
Ph: 702-646-3003

Yards: 6700, Holes: 18
Par: 72

GF: w/day $10.00
Carts: $16.75

This course that opened in the 30s, has lots and lots of mature trees, and is otherwise fairly flat.

─────────────── LAS VEGAS ───────────────

Las Vegas Hilton CC
1911 East Desert Inn
Rd., 89109
Ph: 702-796-0013

Yards: 6418, Holes: 18
Par: 71, USGA: 70.2
Slope: 121
RP: Up to 7 days in
advance

Restaurant/Bar
GF: w/day $95.00, w/end
$95.00
Carts: $Included

A lovely, well-maintained older course with lakes and mature trees. Not your usual desert course, and well worth a visit.

─────────────── LAS VEGAS ───────────────

Mirage GC
3650 Las Vegas Blvd.,
89109
Ph: 702-737-4748

Yards: 6571, Holes: 18
Par: 72, USGA: 71.8

Bar/Proshop
GF: w/day $80.00, w/end
$90.00
Carts: $Included

There's water on one third of the course and the fairways don't have any roll. As if that isn't enough, 80 traps, large greens and trees are all going to add to the difficulty. A memorable layout.

─────────────── LAS VEGAS ───────────────

Painted Desert
5555 Painted Mirage
Dr., 89129
Ph: 702-645-2568

Yards: 6323, Holes: 18
Par: 72, USGA: 70.9
RP: 5 days in advance

A course that features dunes and rocks. There are an amazing number of bunkers. Considered a target course, and you'd better do your best to reach the target.

─────────────── LAS VEGAS ───────────────

Sahara GC
1911 E. Desert Inn Rd.,
89109
Ph: 702-796-0013

Yards: 6418, Holes: 18
Par: 71, USGA: 71.1
RP: For 2 or more - 21
days ahead

GF: w/day $55.00
Carts: $Included

Elevated and overly-protected greens, water on more than half the course, and the need for a very long drive on many, many holes will make this championship-caliber course a real workout.

─────────────── LAUGHLIN ───────────────

Emerald River GC
1155 W. Casino Dr.,
89029
Ph: 702-298-0061

Yards: 6809, Holes: 18
Par: 72, USGA: 70.7

A really challenging course with a very high slope rating. On some of the course there are views of the Colorado River. This is considered one of the best courses in Nevada, and there's a challenge for everyone here.

Enter your favorite resort in our "Golf Resort of The Year" contest (entry form is in the back of the book).

─────────────MESQUITE─────────────

Peppermill Palms GC
P.O. Box 360, 89024
Ph: 800-621-0187

Yards: 6096, Holes: 18
Par: 72, USGA: 70.9
RP: Hotel guest-1
month; else 1 week

Restaurant/Bar/Proshop
GF: w/day $23.00, w/end
$28.00
Carts: $12.00

The front nine is a typical resort type layout featuring numerous bunkers and palm trees as well as 26 acres of water. The back nine is a desert type course with several elevation changes. Number 14 is an exacting par 3 of 210 yards.

─────────────PAHRUMP─────────────

Calvada Executive GC
P.O. Box 220, 89041
Ph: 702-727-6388

Yards: 3587, Holes: 18
Par: 59, USGA: 56.9
RP: 3 days in advance

Restaurant/Bar/Proshop
GF: w/day $10.00

This course was designed for all players and presents a challenge to each level. For the beginner it allows the golfer to use all the clubs in their bag. For the low handicap player, this course offers a challenge of consistency.

─────────────PAHRUMP─────────────

Calvada GC
P.O. Box 220, 89041
Ph: 702-727-4653

Yards: 7036, Holes: 18
Par: 71, USGA: 74.6
RP: 3 days in advance

Restaurant/Bar/Proshop
GF: w/day $25.00
Carts: $Included

This course has 11 lakes and water comes into play on 13 holes, so watch out And just to make it interesting the back nine are carved out of a wooded area filled with mesquite, tamarisk and cottonwood trees. The greens average 8900 square feet.

─────────────RENO─────────────

Lakeridge GC
1200 Razorbank Rd.,
89505
Ph: 702-825-2200

Yards: 6717, Holes: 18
Par: 71
RP: One week in
advance

GF: w/day $38.00
Carts: $Included

A course that has a great view of the surrounding area near Reno. A layout that will give you an enjoyable round of golf.

─────────────RENO─────────────

Northgate GC
1111 Clubhouse Dr.,
89523
Ph: 702-747-7577

Yards: 6966, Holes: 18
Par: 72, USGA: 67.5
RP: 7 days in advance

Restaurant/Bar/Proshop
GF: w/day $20.00
Carts: $12.00

We have 37 sand bunkers and 144 grass bunkers. There are no holes that parallel one another. This is probably one of the finest 18 hole layouts without any trees. Hole #16 par 3, 216 yards from tiger tees.

─────────────RENO─────────────

Wildcreek GC
3500 Sullivan Ln.,
89431
Ph: 702-673-3100

Yards: 6200, Holes: 27
Par: 72, USGA: 69.1
RP: Taken one week in
advance

Restaurant/Bar/Proshop
GF: w/day $32.00
Carts: $Included

The course is on a rolling piece of ground, with a creek coming into play on 7 holes. There also are 9 lakes in play on several holes. Outstanding hole #17, 211 from gold tees—guarded on left by creek and in front by a lake. 9 hole par 3 course also.

NEW HAMPSHIRE

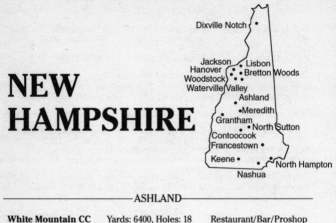

Dixville Notch

Jackson · Lisbon
Hanover · · Bretton Woods
Woodstock · ·
Waterville Valley
· Ashland
· Meredith
Grantham ·
· North Sutton
Contoocook
Francestown ·
Keene · · North Hampton
Nashua

----------ASHLAND----------

White Mountain CC N. Ashland Rd., P.O. Box 83, 03217 Ph: 603-536-2227	Yards: 6400, Holes: 18 Par: 71, USGA: 68.6 RP: Weekends	Restaurant/Bar/Proshop **GF:** w/day $16.00, w/end $18.00 **Carts:** $18.00

The first hole starts you off with a spectacular view of Stinson Mountain and the Pemi-Baker River Valley. A solid front nine is a must because the back nine is where every club in the bag comes out. With its narrow fairways and two tough finishes.

----------BETHLEHEM----------

Bethlehem CC Main St., 03574 Ph: 603-869-5745	Yards: 5756, Holes: 18 Par: 70, USGA: 66.7	Bar/Proshop **GF:** w/day $12.00, w/end $15.00 **Carts:** $16.00

A very old course set in the mountains. This is a beautifully maintained course. A must see.

----------BETHLEHEM----------

Maplewood CC Rt. 302 Box 238, 03574 Ph: 603-869-2113	Yards: 6001, Holes: 18 Par: 72

A Donald Ross design that has a hole over 600 yards long. You've got to see this one.

----------BRETTON WOODS----------

Mt. Washington CC Rt. 302, 03575 Ph: 603-278-1000	Yards: 6638, Holes: 18 Par: 71, USGA: 70.1 RP: 1 day in advance	Restaurant/Bar/Proshop **GF:** w/day $20.00, w/end $24.00 **Carts:** $20.00

Original 18-hole course is early 1900s Donald Ross layout, on the grounds of the majestic Mt. Washington Hotel. Spectacular views of Presidential Mountain Range from almost everywhere on the course, including 2 holes requiring a drive across the Ammonoosu

─────────────────CONTOOCOOK─────────────────

Duston CC Yards: 2109, Holes: 9 Bar/Proshop
Rte. 3, Box 400, 03229 Par: 32, USGA: 59.5 **GF:** w/day $7.00, w/end
Ph: 603-746-4234 RP: Weekends only $10.00
 Carts: $8.00

Duston Country Club is a relatively short course, with four par threes and five par fours. Duston requires a premium on shotmaking, rather than a long ball, because of its postage stamp size greens.

─────────────────DIXVILLE NOTCH─────────────────

Balsams Grand Yards: 6804, Holes: 27 Restaurant/Bar/Proshop
Resort Hotel Par: 72, USGA: 71.4 **GF:** w/day $30.00
Rte 26, 03576 RP: 24 hour notice—no **Carts:** $22.00
Ph: 603-255-4961 charge to hotel guest

The Panorama Course is a spectacular Donald Ross layout built high on the side of Keyser Mountain. From the first tee scan a 30 mile horizon overlooking Vermont and Canada. This classic course is rated "toughest" in the state because of mountainside lies.

─────────────────FRANCESTOWN─────────────────

Tory Pines GC Yards: 5818, Holes: 18 Restaurant/Bar/Proshop
RTE 47, 03043 Par: 71 **GF:** w/day $10.00, w/end
Ph: 603-588-2923 $12.00

Tory Pines' Hall of Fame Golf Course is patterned after 18 great holes from across the world. Beautiful mountain vistas and numerous flower gardens will enhance your golfing pleasure. Careful placement and a keen putting touch is necessary to excel.

─────────────────GRANTHAM─────────────────

Eastman Golf Links Yards: 6338, Holes: 18 Restaurant/Bar/Proshop
Clubhouse Ln., 03753 Par: 71, USGA: 71.5 **GF:** w/day $27.00
Ph: 603-863-4500 RP: 2 days in advance **Carts:** $24.00

Rated by Golf Digest as one of top courses in New Hampshire. Each hole cut through forests of pine and birch. No parallel fairways. 9th hole is long uphill par 4. The green is guarded by three traps. Rated most difficult on course.

─────────────────GREENLAND─────────────────

Portsmouth CC Yards: 6609, Holes: 18 Bar/Proshop
Country Club Ln., P.O. Par: 72, USGA: 71.5 **GF:** w/day $35.00
Box 87, 03840 RP: Up to 24 hours in **Carts:** $20.00
Ph: 603-436-9719 advance

The longest course in New Hampshire, it is set along Great Bay with half the course on a peninsula. The greens are well-trapped, large and rolling. There are also marshlands that play as water hazards. Definitely the course to play in New Hampshire.

─────────────────HANOVER─────────────────

Hanover CC Yards: 6015, Holes: 18 Restaurant/Bar/Proshop
Rope Ferry Rd., 03755 Par: 70, USGA: 67.2 **GF:** w/day $25.00, w/end
Ph: 603-646-2000 RP: 4 days in advance $25.00
 Carts: $20.00

A lush New England antique in process of being updated by Nicklaus "Golforce" group. Home of Dartmouth Men's and Women's Collegiate Golf Teams.

──────────────HOLLIS──────────────

Overlook at Hollis GC
5 Overlook Dr, Rte 111, 03049
Ph: 603-465-2909

Yards: 6051, Holes: 18
Par: 71, USGA: 69.0

This scenic course has a very leisurely feel to it. It's set on the Nashua River.

──────────────JACKSON──────────────

Wentworth Resort GC
Rte 16A, 03846
Ph: 603-383-9700

Yards: 5360, Holes: 18
Par: 69, USGA: 64.5
RP: One week in advance

Restaurant/Bar/Proshop
GF: w/day $16.00, w/end $18.00
Carts: $18.00

The course is surrounded by the breathtaking mountains and forests of the White Mountain National Forest.

──────────────JAFFREY──────────────

Shattuck Inn GC
28 Dublin Rd., 03452
Ph: 603-532-4300

Yards: 6077, Holes: 18
Par: 71, USGA: 71.0
RP: 7 days in advance

Proshop
GF: w/day $30.00
Carts: $22.00

A course with a very high slope rating, this one will be a real challenge. The abundance of wildlife and the many bridges make this a visually pleasing layout. Only two holes are not affected by water or wetlands, so you may want to bring extra balls.

──────────────KEENE──────────────

Bretwood GC
E. Surry Rd., 03431
Ph: 603-352-7626

Yards: 6852, Holes: 27
Par: 72, USGA: 71.6
RP: Weekends only

Restaurant/Proshop
GF: w/day $20.00, w/end $22.00
Carts: $18.00

Rated one of the finest 18-hole courses in New Hampshire by Golf Digest. Our gentle, rolling, irrigated fairways are always plush and green. The large Penncross greens are guarded by interesting bunkers and mounds. Water hazards include several ponds.

──────────────LISBON──────────────

Lisbon Village CC
P.O. Box 3 Bishop Rd., 03585
Ph: 603-838-6004

Yards: 6000, Holes: 9
Par: 72

Restaurant/Bar/Proshop
GF: w/day $8.00, w/end $10.00
Carts: $10.00

Play begins on lower portion of course with five holes along the Ammonoosuc River. An extremely challenging fifth (par 3, 212) brings play to a tight shotmakers upper four. These include breathtaking views of Mt. Lafayette in the Franconia Range.

──────────────MEREDITH──────────────

Waukewan GC
P.O. Box 403, 03253
Ph: 603-279-6661

Yards: 5735, Holes: 18
Par: 71, USGA: 67.0
RP: Open Time

Restaurant/Bar/Proshop
GF: w/day $20.00, w/end $20.00
Carts: $20.00

18 individual holes in natural setting of New Hampshire terrain. Spectacular panoramic view of White Mountains. Shotmaking is the premium, yet enough length exists to challenge the long hitter. Golf cars available, but not mandatory.

---------------------NASHUA---------------------

Sky Meadow CC
Sky Meadow Dr.,
03062
Ph: 603-888-9000

Yards: 6036, Holes: 18
Par: 72, USGA: 70.8
RP: Call in advance for
tee times

Proshop
GF: w/day $56.00, w/end
$61.00
Carts: $Included

Rated the best course in the state by Golf Digest, you'll surely want to give this challenging course your best. A course where accuracy and a good short game are the keys to a good score.

------------------- NORTH CONWAY-------------------

Hale's Location CC
Box 1580, West Side
Rd, 03818
Ph: 603-356-7100

Yards: 2816, Holes: 9
Par: 36, USGA: 68.0

Set in a heavily treed area, you'll find many breathtaking views on this course.

------------------- NORTH CONWAY-------------------

North Conway CC
Norcross Circle, Box
555, 03860
Ph: 603-356-9391

Yards: 6659, Holes: 18
Par: 71, USGA: 69.9
RP: 5 days in advance

GF: w/day $18.00, w/end
$22.00
Carts: $18.00

An easy appearing course, there are some blind shots here that can really get you.

-------------------NORTH HAMPTON-------------------

**Sagamore-Hampton
GC**
101 North Rd., 03862
Ph: 603-964-5341

Yards: 6489, Holes: 18
Par: 71, USGA: 67.1
RP: Call ahead

Restaurant/Bar/Proshop
GF: w/day $23.00, w/end
$23.00
Carts: $2.00

Two courses in one with the first nine a wide open par 35 (blue rating 34.2) with a minimum of hazards, while the back nine is a longer, narrower par 36 (blue rating 36.3) requiring the use of all 14 clubs and a fair share of strategy.

-------------------NORTH SUTTON-------------------

**Country Club New
Hampshire**
P.O. Box 142, 03026
Ph: 603-927-4246

Yards: 6727, Holes: 18
Par: 72, USGA: 69.6
RP: Taken 1 week in
advance

Proshop
GF: w/day $20.00, w/end
$22.00
Carts: $20.00

The course is backed up against the Kearsarge Mountains. Very hilly and heavily wooded with pines and birch. Back side has narrow fairways. Many holes are parallel, many elevated tees.

------------------- OSSIPPE-------------------

Indian Mound GC
Old Rte 16B, 03814
Ph: 603-539-7733

Yards: 3215, Holes: 18
Par: 36, USGA: 68.2

GF: w/day $14.00
Carts: $15.00

Indian Mound is now operational with 18 holes. Winding through the White Mountains of New Hampshire, the newly-designed holes offer a challenge as well as wonderful vistas.

WATERVILLE VALLEY

Waterville Valley GC
Rte 49, 03223
Ph: 603-236-8666

Yards: 2407, Holes: 9
Par: 32

Restaurant/Bar
GF: w/day $10.00
Carts: $10.00

Located on the valley floor of the resort, surrounded by mountain peaks. The 7th hole, par 4, is elevated. Very small green, over the road.

WOLFEBORO

Kingswood CC
Main St., 03894
Ph: 603-569-3569

Yards: 5800, Holes: 18
Par: 71, USGA: 67.5

GF: w/day $20.00, w/end
$25.00

A beautiful setting among three lakes. Only a little water comes into play on this rolling course.

WOODSTOCK

Jack O'Lantern
Rte. 3, 03293
Ph: 603-745-8121

Yards: 5820, Holes: 18
Par: 70, USGA: 68.2
RP: Required until 1
p.m.

Restaurant/Bar/Proshop
GF: w/day $20.00
Carts: $19.00

Surrounded by the White Mountain National Forest and bordered for over a mile by the Pemigewasset River, this testing layout lies on gently rolling valley terrain in a virtually undisturbed setting. The golf course is very good; experience unforgettable.

NEW JERSEY

---ABSECON---

Marriott CC
Route Nine, 08201
Ph: 609-652-1800

Yards: 6417, Holes: 36
Par: 71, USGA: 70.9
RP: Guests 7 days in
advance

Restaurant/Bar
GF: w/day $40.00
Carts: $13.00

The Bay Course features windswept bunkers and panoramic seaside views. As with most layouts subjected to buffeting winds, it is relatively short in yardage. The newer, more demanding Pines course, lined with 100 year old pines and oaks.

---COLTS NECK---

Hominy Hill GC
Mercer Rd., 07722
Ph: 908-462-9222

Yards: 7059, Holes: 18
Par: 72, USGA: 71.7
RP: First come, first
served

Restaurant/Proshop
GF: w/day $27.00, w/end
$29.00
Carts: $24.00

110 sand traps.

---FARMINGDALE---

Howell Park GC
Preventorium Road,
07727
Ph: 201-938-4771

Yards: 6869, Holes: 18
Par: 72, USGA: 70.0
RP: First come, first
served

Restaurant/Proshop
GF: w/day $20.50
Carts: $20.00

Level course which circles around. Fairways wide open and lined with trees and little meandering creeks. #7 cuts off the corner and has a big trap.

---FLANDERS VALLEY---

Flanders Valley GC
Pleasant Hill Rd.,
07836
Ph: 201-584-8964

Yards: 6765, Holes: 18
Par: 72, USGA: 71.4

Restaurant/Bar/Proshop
GF: w/day $14.00, w/end
$20.00
Carts: $20.00

On the White Course #5 has water on left, tree-lined par 4, dogleg right. Course has lots of traps. On the Blue #5 is a dogleg left around water, longer, elevated green. The Blue Course is more challenging with more doglegs, only 3 straight holes.

————————————————HAMBURG————————————————

Crystal Springs GC   Yards: 5955, Holes: 18
123 Crystal Springs   Par: 72
Rd, Ph: 201-827-1444

Crystal Springs is a Robert von Hagge design. The setting is very rocky.

————————————————MCAFEE————————————————

Great Gorge CC   Yards: 6819, Holes: 27   Restaurant/Bar/Proshop
Route 517, P.O. Box   Par: 71, USGA: 73.3   **GF:** w/day $34.00, w/end
1140, 07428   RP: 1 month in advance $50.00
Ph: 201-827-5757   **Carts:** $14.00

The golf course is located in an area which is unlike anything in New Jersey. It sits in a valley between the tallest mountains in the state northwest corner. The views combine with 3 different nines here make this one of NJ's best public/resort courses.

————————————————MOUNT LAUREL————————————————

Ramblewood CC   Yards: 6498, Holes: 27   Restaurant/Bar/Proshop
Country Club Pkwy.,   Par: 72, USGA: 71.1   **GF:** w/day $20.00, w/end
08054 $25.00
Ph: 609-235-2119   **Carts:** $20.00

Our golf course is very playable.

————————————————NESHANIC STATION————————————————

Hillsborough GC CC   Yards: 6100, Holes: 18   Restaurant/Bar/Proshop
Wertsville Rd., P.O.   Par: 70, USGA: 68.7   **GF:** w/day $15.00, w/end
Box 365, 08853   RP: Weekends $20.00
Ph: 201-369-3322   **Carts:** $20.00

Arguably the nicest view in the state. Front side relatively open, our back side tight and hilly. Favorite hole #8, 190 yard par 3 tight left, traps right, narrow green. Good luck.

————————————————PISCATAWAY————————————————

Rutgers University   Yards: 5890, Holes: 18   Proshop
GC   Par: 71, USGA: 68.2
777 Hoes Ln., 08854   RP: Weekends &
Ph: 201-932-2631   holidays

All of our holes are named after trees. Our favorite is the Sour Gum at hole #11 which is delight to see especially during the fall when the colors are red, gold, and yellow and the curving branches give it character.

————————————————SOMERS POINT————————————————

Greate Bay CC   Yards: 6370, Holes: 18   Restaurant
901 Mayslanding Rd,   Par: 71   **GF:** w/day $40.00, w/end
08244 $40.00
Ph: 609-927-0066

This course hosts the LPGA ShopRite Classic. The pines here are majestic and guard most of the course.

Plan ahead! Reserve tee time well in advance, and while you're doing so, confirm rates and services.

──────────── TUCKERTON ────────────

Atlantis GC
Country Club Rd.,
08087
Ph: 609-296-2444

Yards: 6313, Holes: 18
Par: 72, USGA: 69.7

Restaurant/Bar
GF: w/day $15.00, w/end
$18.00

One of the most beautiful and challenging courses in Southern New Jersey. Fairways are well maintained to ensure a good lie to your ball. Greens receive tender loving care and your first putt will show the difference.

──────────── WASHINGTON ────────────

Fairway Valley GC
Box 219A, Minehill
Rd., 07882
Ph: 201-689-1530

Yards: 3006, Holes: 9
Par: 70, USGA: 69.9

Restaurant/Bar/Proshop
GF: w/day $7.00, w/end
$8.00
Carts: $17.00

Located in the "Valley of the Hawk", lies Fairway Valley Golf Club. Known for its beauty in all seasons, the club boasts a track to challenge the low handicapper and novice alike, in a setting where nature and wildlife galley for pleasure.

──────────── WOODBURY ────────────

Westwood GC
850 Kings Highway,
08096
Ph: 609-845-2000

Yards: 5931, Holes: 18
Par: 71, USGA: 67.9
RP: Suggested on
weekends

Restaurant/Bar/Proshop
GF: w/day $14.00, w/end
$18.00
Carts: $20.00

Our par 3, 11th hole is definitely a challenge with a "slight" northern downhill slope to it.

NEW MEXICO

---------------ALBUQUERQUE---------------

Ladera GC
3401 Ladera Dr. NW,
87120
Ph: 505-836-4449

Yards: 6618, Holes: 27
Par: 72, USGA: 69.9

Restaurant
GF: w/day $12.50

A nice public course that plays very long and is well cared for.

---------------ALBUQUERQUE---------------

Los Altos GC
9717 Cooper Ave NE,
87123
Ph: 505-298-1897

Yards: 6180, Holes: 18
Par: 71

Restaurant
GF: w/day $9.50

A nice day in the sun, but this flat layout won't be much of a challenge to the average golfer.

---------------ALBUQUERQUE---------------

University of New Mexico GC
Univ. Blvd. SE., 87131
Ph: 505-277-4546

Yards: 6480, Holes: 36
Par: 72, USGA: 70.8
RP: 3 players to reserve
weekend

Restaurant/Proshop
GF: w/day $14.00
Carts: $16.00

University of New Mexico South is one of Golf Digest's Top 25 public courses in America. The course features rolling fairways and desert terrain which present many challenging shots into large, undulating, well-bunkered greens, and views of Albuquerque.

---------------ANGEL FIRE---------------

Angel Fire GC
Drawer B
Hwy 434, 88710
Ph: 505-377-3055

Yards: 6275, Holes: 18
Par: 72, USGA: 69.0
RP: Reservations are
advised

Restaurant/Bar
GF: w/day $43.00
Carts: $Included

Angel Fire is in a beautiful forest setting, you'll probably see more of the trees than you want.

---------------------------------BERNALILLO---------------------------------

Valle Grande GC
288 Prairie Star Rd,
87004
Ph: 505-867-9464

Yards: 5870, Holes: 27
Par: 71, USGA: 66.7
RP: 3 days in advance

Restaurant/Bar/Proshop
GF: w/day $14.00, w/end
$18.00
Carts: $9.00

The course is set along the Rio Grande and has spectacular mountains as a backdrop. There are 27-holes that can be played in different combinations of 9-hole courses. There are eight lakes set among the different 9s, so you'll see plenty of water here.

---------------------------------CLOUDCROFT---------------------------------

Lodge GC
Corona Ave., P.O. Box
182, 88317
Ph: 505-682-2098

Yards: 2451, Holes: 9
Par: 34, USGA: 63.0
RP: 7 days ahead with
credit card

Restaurant/Bar/Proshop
GF: w/day $9.00, w/end
$12.00
Carts: $10.00

Established in 1899 near its present location. For many years this was the highest golf course in the world at 9200 feet. Our double tee and double pin layout makes for an interesting 18 hole game. Rolling mountain greens.

--------------------------------- COCHITI LAKE---------------------------------

Cochiti Lake GC
Box 125, 87083
Ph: 505-465-2239

Yards: 6450, Holes: 18
Par: 72, USGA: 68.5
RP: 7 days in advance

Restaurant/Proshop
GF: w/day $16.00, w/end
$18.00
Carts: $18.00

A Robert Trent Jones design at the foot of Jemez Mountains. Tree-lined with a mix of cedar and ponderosa pines. Hole #13 one of top 50 holes in country. Rated as one of top 25 Public courses in America.

---------------------------------DEMING---------------------------------

Rio Mimbres GC
Rt. 2, P.O. Box 110,
88030
Ph: 505-546-9481

Yards: 6188, Holes: 9
Par: 71, USGA: 68.6

Restaurant/Bar/Proshop
GF: w/day $10.00, w/end
$11.00
Carts: $11.00

Our golf course is flat and relatively short. The strength of Rio Mimbres Country Club is the greens. They're small, undulated and difficult to approach to and putt on.

---------------------------------FARMINGTON---------------------------------

Pinon Hills GC
2101 Sunrise Parkway,
87401
Ph: 505-326-6066

Yards: 6239, Holes: 18
Par: 72, USGA: 69.5
RP: 1 week in advance

Proshop
GF: w/day $11.00, w/end
$13.00
Carts: $14.00

Rated by Golf Digest as the best golf course in New Mexico, this course is a challenging one. Set in the high desert, there is very little water on the course. The fact that a ball carries further at this altitude can make it more difficult to judge.

---------------------------------LOS ALAMOS---------------------------------

Los Alamos GC
4250 Diamond Dr.,
87544
Ph: 505-662-8139

Yards: 6440, Holes: 18
Par: 71, USGA: 69.8
RP: Weekends &
holidays

Restaurant/Bar/Proshop
GF: w/day $10.00, w/end
$12.00
Carts: $14.50

Beautiful mountain setting 7500 feet altitude, 35 miles north of Santa Fe. Tree lined fairways, ponderosa pines and cottonwoods. Average playing season April through November.

NEW YORK

Loon Lake
Lake Placid
Clayton
East Amhearst
Ellicottville
LeRoy • Rochester
Lima   Shortsville
• Locke
• Clymer
Catskill   New Paltz
South Fallsburg   Ellenville   Accord   Greenport
Kiamesha Lake   Brewster
Montgomery   Montauk
Suffern   Middle Island
Hauppauge
Long Island

ACCORD

Rondout CC
P.O. Box 194, Whitfield
Rd., 12404
Ph: 914-626-2513

Yards: 7035, Holes: 9
Par: 35, USGA: 68.5

Restaurant/Bar/Proshop
GF: w/day $6.00
Carts: $9.00

No trick holes with yardage markers every 25 yards from 200 yards out from the center of the greens. Our reputation for excellent greens and also being very quick is consistent year after year. Our favorite hole is one of our shortest par 4s with water.

ADLER CREEK

Alder Creek GC
Rt 12, Box 5, 13301
Ph: 315-831-5222

Yards: 3178, Holes: 9
Par: 36, USGA: 70.2

Restaurant/Proshop

The greens are very, very large and well bunkered. The terrain is rolling and well treed with some water.

BOLTON LANDING

Sagamore GC
110 Sagamore Dr, 12814
Ph: 518-644-9400

Yards: 6706, Holes: 18
Par: 70, USGA: 72.9
RP: Guests at
reservation time

Restaurant/Bar/Proshop
GF: w/day $50.00
Carts: $16.00

This is a scenic course set in the mountains above Lake George. This course will demand accuracy. Majestic pine and birch line the fairways and small greens will be your final targets. Lots of very deep bunkers and rolling terrain.

BREWSTER

Vails Grove GC
RFD #2, Peach Lake,
10509
Ph: 914-669-5721

Yards: 4300, Holes: 9
Par: 66, USGA: 58.5

Proshop
GF: w/day $15.00, w/end
$15.00
Carts: $18.00

Picturesque, challenging. Friendly atmosphere.

————————————CANANDAIGUA————————————

Bristol Harbour GC
5500 Seneca Point Rd,
14424
Ph: 716-396-2460

Yards: 6095, Holes: 18
Par: 72, USGA: 69.6

Restaurant/Bar/Proshop
GF: w/day $30.00, w/end
$35.00

A course with breathtaking views of a lake and hills. The front nine are more open, with tighter fairways on the back nine. With lots of bunkers, your accuracy will be put to the test.

————————————CATSKILL————————————

Catskill GC
27 Brooks Ln., 12414
Ph: 518-943-2390

Yards: 6286, Holes: 9
Par: 72, USGA: 69.5

Restaurant/Bar/Proshop
GF: w/day $15.00
Carts: $18.00

Fairly wide fairways with tiny greens. 7 different tees on back nine completely change 7 of the 9 holes. Totally irrigated and always in top condition. Par 5 3rd hole, at 560 yards, with water fronting the green is a classic, natural beauty.

————————————CLAYTON————————————

C-Way GC
37093 NY State Rte 12,
13624
Ph: 315-686-4562

Yards: 6102, Holes: 18
Par: 72, USGA: 68.0
RP: 1 day in advance

Restaurant/Bar/Proshop
GF: w/day $15.00, w/end
$15.00
Carts: $16.00

C-Way Golf Club is in the heart of the 1000 islands. Partially wooded course complete with sand traps and water hazards to test your skills.

————————————CLYMER————————————

Peek'n Peak GC
1405 Ye Olde Rd.,
14724
Ph: 716-355-4141

Yards: 6260, Holes: 18
Par: 72, USGA: 69.8
RP: Call anytime for
starting time

Restaurant/Bar/Proshop
GF: w/day $19.00, w/end
$27.00
Carts: $20.00

Ponds and streams interspersed within tree-lined fairways create an unparalleled golfing experience. Roland Stafford School at Peek's Peak provides intense personalized golf training. Additional 9-hole opened Spring '93.

————————————COOPERSTOWN————————————

Leatherstockings GC
Highway 80, 13326
Ph: 607-547-9853

Yards: 6383, Holes: 18
Par: 72, USGA: 71.0
RP: Call anytime

Restaurant/Bar/Proshop
GF: w/day $35.00, w/end
$45.00
Carts: $24.00

Water, wind, and over 100 sand bunkers adorn this challenging course. The greens are tricky, and you'll find that your short game here is going to be a big factor in how you score.

————————————EAST AMHEARST————————————

Glen Oak
711 Smith, 14051
Ph: 716-688-5454

Yards: 6730, Holes: 18
Par: 72, USGA: 71.9
RP: 3 days in advance

Restaurant/Bar/Proshop
GF: w/day $21.00, w/end
$30.00
Carts: $Included

Course is level with small rolling hills and many creeks and ponds. Many elevated tees with oaks and evergreens lining the fairways. #18 choose easy or hard route; tough one over a pond.

————————————————ELLENVILLE————————————————

Fallsview Hotel & CC
12428
Ph: 914-647-5100

Yards: 3173, Holes: 9
Par: 35, USGA: 70.4
RP: One day in advance

Restaurant/Bar/Proshop
GF: w/day $9.00, w/end
$11.00
Carts: $11.00

Best 9 holes course in the area.

————————————————ELLENVILLE————————————————

Nevele CC
Rte 209, 12428
Ph: 914-647-6000

Yards: 6200, Holes: 18
Par: 71, USGA: 69.4

Restaurant/Bar/Proshop
GF: w/day $25.00

A course with the green as an island, and lots of water on the rest of the course. Rolling, forested terrain is the feature here.

————————————————ELLENVILLE————————————————

The Nevele GC
12428
Ph: 914-647-6000

Yards: 6500, Holes: 18
Par: 70, USGA: 69.4
RP: Guests 2 weeks;
non guest 1 week

Restaurant/Bar/Proshop
GF: w/day $20.00
Carts: $20.00

The entire course is fair yet quite challenging for all caliber of golfers. Keep plenty of balls around for the devilish 16th hole. A carry across water to a green almost surrounded by water makes for some exciting shotmaking.

————————————————ELLICOTTVILLE————————————————

Holiday Valley Resort
PO Box 370, Holiday
Valley Rd., 14731
Ph: 716-699-2346

Yards: 6555, Holes: 18
Par: 72, USGA: 70.9
RP: Call the Proshop

Restaurant/Bar/Proshop
GF: w/day $25.00, w/end
$25.00
Carts: $20.00

Holiday Valley Resort is best known as a great ski area. The ponds used for snowmaking provide watery graves for many golf balls and the tree lined ski slopes produce tight fairways. Hit it straight and score well.

————————————————ELMA————————————————

Elma Meadows GC
1711 Girdle Rd., 14059
Ph: 716-652-2022

Yards: 6415, Holes: 18
Par: 70, USGA: 70.0
RP: First come, first
served

Restaurant/Proshop
GF: w/day $8.00, w/end
$10.00
Carts: $16.00

18 holes with rolling fairways which are almost all tree lined. 1st tee shot off a huge hill is just a start of 18 uniquely different golf holes.

————————————————ENDICOTT————————————————

En-Joie GC
722 W Main St, 13760
Ph: 607-785-1661

Yards: 6088, Holes: 18
Par: 72

Restaurant/Bar/Proshop
GF: w/day $14.00

The host course to the PGA B.C. Open, this is a championship layout from start to finish. Beautiful trees and lots of water that's sure to become a problem.

————————————————FARMINGDALE————————————————

Bethpage State Park
Round Swamp Rd.,
11735
Ph: 516-249-0700

Yards: 7065, Holes: 90
Par: 71, USGA: 70.5

Restaurant/Bar/Proshop
GF: w/day $14.00, w/end
$10.00
Carts: $20.00

One of the highest ranked course in the country, whether private or public A course with smaller greens in a hilly setting. Doglegs are going to be a major problem here, as will be the elevated greens.

———————————— GOLTON LANDING ————————————

The Sagamore GC　　Yards: 6810, Holes: 18　　Restaurant/Bar
On Lake George, 12814　Par: 70, USGA: 71.5
Ph: 518-644-9400　　　RP: With Reservation

The thirteenth hole is considered by many to be the most breathtaking, but also the most difficult. It's a very tight driving hole with water right and in front of the green. The second shot is uphill to "one undulating mass."

———————————————— GRAND ISLAND ————————————————

River Oaks GC　　　Yards: 6588, Holes: 18　　Restaurant/Bar/Proshop
201 Whitehaven Rd.,　Par: 72, USGA: 71.0　　**GF:** w/day $10.00, w/end
14072　　　　　　　 RP: 3 days prior　　　　 $17.00
Ph: 716-773-3336　　　　　　　　　　　　　 **Carts:** $15.00

A challenging course that will really test you. It runs along the Niagara River and has majestic, mature oaks and maples. If the creeks and lakes don't get you into trouble the bunkers and rough will.

———————————————— GREENPORT ————————————————

Island's End Golf &　Yards: 6639, Holes: 18　　Restaurant/Bar/Proshop
CC　　　　　　　　 Par: 72, USGA: 68.9　　**GF:** w/day $10.00, w/end
Box 39 Rte 25, 11944　RP: Recommended　　　 $25.00
Ph: 516-477-9457　　　　　　　　　　　　　 **Carts:** $20.00

Relatively flat. 700' Long Island Sound selected one of the top 18 holes in metropolitan area in 1968. Hole #16 par 3, 220 yards over a ravine and out of bounds to Sound side.

———————————————— GROSSINGER ————————————————

Grossinger GC　　　Yards: 6406, Holes: 27　　Restaurant/Bar/Proshop
Golf Course Ln, 12734　Par: 71, USGA: 71.0　　**GF:** w/day $25.00
Ph: 914-292-1450　　　　　　　　　　　　　 **Carts:** $20.00

A scenic and demanding course set in the Catskills. There are mature trees along the fairways, elevated tees, elevation drops, and lots and lots of water, a very challenging round. There is also a 9-hole course.

———————————————— HAMILTON ————————————————

Seven Oaks GC　　　Yards: 6423, Holes: 18　　Restaurant/Bar/Proshop
East Lake Rd & Payne　Par: 72, USGA: 71.4　　**GF:** w/day $28.00
St, 11346　　　　　　　　　　　　　　　　 **Carts:** $21.00
Ph: 315-824-1432

Towering trees, rolling fairways and large tough greens are all featured here. Water comes into play on two thirds of the holes. A truly challenging round of golf.

———————————————— HAUPPAUGE ————————————————

Hauppauge CC　　　Yards: 6280, Holes: 18　　Restaurant/Bar/Proshop
Veterans Memorial　　Par: 72, USGA: 70.4　　**GF:** w/day $20.00
Hwy, Box 237, 11788　　　　　　　　　　　 **Carts:** $22.00
Ph: 516-724-7500

A very challenging course where water comes into play on seven of the eighteen holes. The 17th hole is a 370 yard par 4 with a large pond guarding the front of the green and three bunkers nestled at the rear of green. Accuracy is a must.

———————————HAUPPAUGE———————————

Marriott's GC at Windwatch
1717 Vanderbilt Motor Pkwy., 11788
Ph: 516-232-9850

Yards: 6405, Holes: 18
Par: 71
RP: Hotel guests 7 days; public 3

Restaurant/Bar/Proshop
GF: w/day $46.00, w/end $52.00
Carts: $13.00

Perhaps Gene Sazazan says it best, "Joe Lee, course architect has a graceful ability to combine the pleasures of a golf course for the average player with the strategy concept of a championship test without getting out of a balance in either direction."

———————————KERHONKSON———————————

Granit GC
Lower Granit Rd., 12446
Ph: 914-626-3141

Yards: 5828, Holes: 18
Par: 71

Restaurant/Bar/Proshop
GF: w/day $12.00
Carts: $18.00

A lovely course set near the Catskills. A very scenic area for the mildly challenging course.

———————————KIAMESHA LAKE———————————

Concord Hotel GC
12751
Ph: 914-794-4000

Yards: 7205, Holes: 45
Par: 72, USGA: 76.0
RP: 7 months in advance

Restaurant/Bar
GF: w/day $60.00
Carts: $Included

Concord's 45 holes include its infamous "Monster," a 6,793 yard by Joe Finger, wizard of Cedar Ridge in Oklahoma. This par 72 heavily wooded rolling course has hosted many tournaments.

———————————KINGS PARK———————————

Sunken Meadow State Park
P.O. Box 716, 11754
Ph: 516-269-4333

Yards: 3060, Holes: 9
Par: 35

Restaurant/Proshop
GF: w/day $7.00, w/end $8.00

Sunken Meadow is three-nine hole courses located on the rolling hills of the north shore of Long Island. The Red and Blue courses are heavily wooded and the Blue has many doglegs. The Green course is more wide open with back to back par 5s.

———————————LAKE PLACID———————————

Whiteface Inn Resort & CC
Whiteface Inn Rd., 12946
Ph: 518-523-2551

Yards: 6490, Holes: 18
Par: 72, USGA: 70.6
RP: Required for all play

Restaurant/Bar/Proshop
GF: w/day $19.00
Carts: $24.00

One of golf's great par 3's is the 14th hole at Whiteface. Over 200 yards in length, the tee shot over a pond with trees bordering closely on each side must be well struck to land on the tiered green. Hole 6 is the signature hole for the resort.

———————————LE ROY———————————

Le Roy CC
7759 East Main Road, 14482
Ph: 716-768-7330

Yards: 6400, Holes: 18
Par: 71, USGA: 67.6
RP: Starting times 24 hours in advance

Restaurant/Bar/Proshop
GF: w/day $11.00, w/end $13.00
Carts: $18.00

Front fairly short—gives the golfer a chance to warm up before playing a much longer back nine which includes from the blues, a 555 yard part 5, 470 yard par 4 and a 227 yard par 3.

─────────────── LIDO BEACH ───────────────

Lido GC
Lido Dr., 11561
Ph: 516-431-8778

Yards: 6387, Holes: 18
Par: 71

The wind can really play havoc with your drives.

─────────────── LIMA ───────────────

Lima Golf & CC
2681 Plank Rd., 14485
Ph: 716-624-1490

Yards: 6372, Holes: 18
Par: 72, USGA: 72.3
RP: Required weekends

Restaurant/Bar/Proshop
GF: w/day $12.00, w/end
$13.50
Carts: $16.00

Play some of the finest greens anywhere. Our fast greens hold well. Eighteen, a good finishing hole, where you lay up short of pond with a 200 yard tee shot. Then hit a middle iron to a two-tiered green, trapped on left.

─────────────── LOCKE ───────────────

Fillmore GC
RD 1 Box 409, 13092
Ph: 315-497-3145

Yards: 5523, Holes: 18
Par: 71, USGA: 67.1

Restaurant/Bar/Proshop
GF: w/day $8.00, w/end
$9.00
Carts: $14.00

This 18 hole course, named in honor of the 13th President of the USA, sets on a hill overlooking the beautiful Owasco Lake and valley. The front nine is designed for the amateur golfer while the back nine offers a challenge to the more ardent golfer.

─────────────── LOON LAKE ───────────────

Loon Lake GC
Rt 99, 12968
Ph: 518-891-3249

Yards: 5400, Holes: 18
Par: 70

Restaurant/Bar/Proshop
GF: w/day $8.00
Carts: $12.00

If you want to see what America's earliest courses looked like, Loon Lake is worth the stop. The holes are short; the greens, especially on the front nine, tiny. You'll need your ace wedge game. The back nine, built in 1894, is treed and curvy.

─────────────── MIDDLE ISLAND ───────────────

Spring Lake GC
Bartlett Rd., Rt.25,
11953
Ph: 516-924-5115

Yards: 7048, Holes: 27
Par: 72, USGA: 71.0

Restaurant/Bar/Proshop
GF: w/day $17.00, w/end
$20.00
Carts: $23.00

With 27 holes available, you can play a picturesque 9 hole course on the shore of Spring Lake or the tree lined, manicured, 18 hole championship course. Hosts of the 1989 Met Public Links Championship which plays from 5732 yards to 7048 yards.

─────────────── MONTAUK ───────────────

Montauk Downs GC
P.O. Box 735 off
Westlake Dr., 11954
Ph: 516-668-5000

Yards: 6762, Holes: 18
Par: 72, USGA: 70.5
RP: None

Restaurant/Bar/Proshop
GF: w/day $14.00, w/end
$16.00
Carts: $20.00

75 percent of the fairways are narrow, first few are parallel. Course is wooded with rolling hills, big ponds and lakes. #18 is a challenging par 4, 417 yard hole.

───────────────MONTGOMERY───────────────

Stony Ford GC
Rd #3, Box 100, Rt. 416,
12549
Ph: 914-457-3000

Yards: 6200, Holes: 18
Par: 72, USGA: 69.2
RP: One no more than 1
week ahead

Restaurant/Bar/Proshop
GF: w/day $10.00, w/end
$20.00
Carts: $15.00

A scenic, well-landscaped course with hilly terrain, numerous water hazards, and wooded fringe. The front nine requires good positioning due to the many hazards and doglegs on five of the holes. On the back nine, the par 4 15th offers the challenge.

───────────────MONTICELLO───────────────

Kutsher's CC
Kutsher Rd., 12701
Ph: 914-794-6000

Yards: 6638, Holes: 18
Par: 72, USGA: 71.2

Restaurant/Bar/Proshop
GF: w/day $10.00

A tough course set in the mountains. The course is not treed, it is forested. The fairways are tight, and the greens are tricky.

───────────────NEW PALTZ───────────────

Mohonk GC
Mountain Rest Rd.,
12561
Ph: 914-255-1000

Yards: 2569, Holes: 9
Par: 35

Restaurant/Proshop
GF: w/day $5.50, w/end
$6.50
Carts: $8.00

This course, set on a mountain ridge, was opened in 1897. A very hilly layout that you should see.

───────────────NEW PALTZ───────────────

New Paltz GC
215 Huguenot St.,
12561
Ph: 914-255-8282

Yards: 3610, Holes: 9
Par: 36, USGA: 70.0
RP: None

Restaurant/Bar/Proshop
GF: w/day $6.00, w/end
$8.00
Carts: $8.00

Clearly one of New York's finest 9 hole layouts. Tee shots that drift can find water on 5 of the well designed 9 holes. Throughout the challenge there is a feeling of peacefulness when playing this course. The contrast of the thick woods, marshes, water.

───────────────ROCHESTER───────────────

Durand Eastman GC
1200 Kings Hwy.
North, 14617
Ph: 716-266-8364

Yards: 6089, Holes: 18
Par: 70, USGA: 68.8
RP: First come

Proshop
GF: w/day $8.00, w/end
$9.00
Carts: $16.00

My favorite hole is the 17th, 146 yards, rolling fairway that look over Lake Ontario. It is often called the mountain goat course and is said to be one of the sportiest, if not the sportiest and most scenic in the land.

───────────────SARANAC INN───────────────

Saranac Inn GC
PO Box 1030, 12982
Ph: 518-891-1402

Yards: 6453, Holes: 18
Par: 72, USGA: 70.6
RP: Anytime

Restaurant/Bar/Proshop
GF: w/day $45.00

A course with fast, rolling greens, bunkers, and rolling terrain. Set along Upper Saranac Lake, the setting is breathtaking. This setting will be sure to capture your heart, you'll want to play this one again and again.

─────────────SARATOGA SPRINGS─────────────

Saratoga Spa GC
Box W Saratoga Spr St
Pk, 12866
Ph: 518-584-2006

Yards: 7025, Holes: 18
Par: 72, USGA: 74.0

Restaurant/Bar/Proshop
GF: w/day $10.00, w/end
$12.00
Carts: $17.00

Well placed bunkers, large, slow, sloping greens and lots of mature trees are the main attractions. Some very tight holes that will challenge you and lots of length too.

─────────────SHORTSVILLE─────────────

Winged Pheasant GL
1475 Sand Hill Rd.,
14548
Ph: 716-289-8846

Yards: 6345, Holes: 18
Par: 70, USGA: 69.0

Restaurant/Bar/Proshop
GF: w/day $13.00, w/end
$15.00
Carts: $14.00

Opening hole is a dog right par 5. The course on the front nine demands a careful positioning of shots and water must be contended with. Our par threes are rated 3.2. The course has several holes that are outlined with trees.

─────────────SOUTH FALLSBURG─────────────

Tarry Brae GC
Pleasant Valley Rd.,
12779
Ph: 914-434-9782

Yards: 6800, Holes: 18
Par: 72, USGA: 70.0
RP: Only taken for
afternoon

Restaurant/Bar/Proshop
GF: w/day $13.00
Carts: $20.00

Tarry Brae is a hilly course with many tree lined fairways. There are several panoramic views of mountains and valleys. There are several excellent courses in the Catskill Mountains and Tarry Brae is one of them.

─────────────SUFFERN─────────────

Spook Rock GC
Spook Rock Rd., 10952
Ph: 914-357-6466

Yards: 6894, Holes: 18
Par: 72, USGA: 70.9
RP: Required

Restaurant/Bar/Proshop
GF: w/day $20.00, w/end
$27.00
Carts: $19.00

All fairways are narrow and tree-lined. The course is heavily wooded with maple and pine and water on 5 holes. The tees are elevated.

─────────────SWAN LAKE─────────────

Swan Lake GC
PO Box 455, Mt. Hope
Rd., 12783
Ph: 914-292-0748

Yards: 6300, Holes: 18
Par: 71

Restaurant/Bar/Proshop
GF: w/day $13.00, w/end
$19.00
Carts: $26.00

A scenic mountain course. If it weren't for the water, the length and the bunkers this layout would be easy.

NORTH CAROLINA

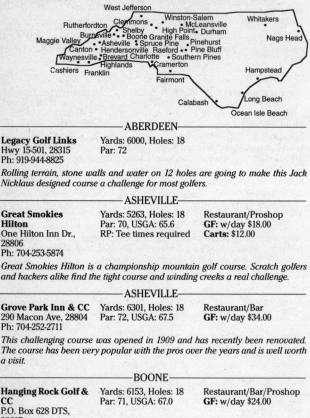

------ ABERDEEN ------

Legacy Golf Links
Hwy 15-501, 28315
Ph: 919-944-8825

Yards: 6000, Holes: 18
Par: 72

Rolling terrain, stone walls and water on 12 holes are going to make this Jack Nicklaus designed course a challenge for most golfers.

------ ASHEVILLE ------

Great Smokies Hilton
One Hilton Inn Dr., 28806
Ph: 704-253-5874

Yards: 5263, Holes: 18
Par: 70, USGA: 65.6
RP: Tee times required

Restaurant/Proshop
GF: w/day $18.00
Carts: $12.00

Great Smokies Hilton is a championship mountain golf course. Scratch golfers and hackers alike find the tight course and winding creeks a real challenge.

------ ASHEVILLE ------

Grove Park Inn & CC
290 Macon Ave, 28804
Ph: 704-252-2711

Yards: 6301, Holes: 18
Par: 72, USGA: 67.5

Restaurant/Bar
GF: w/day $34.00

This challenging course was opened in 1909 and has recently been renovated. The course has been very popular with the pros over the years and is well worth a visit.

------ BOONE ------

Hanging Rock Golf & CC
P.O. Box 628 DTS, 28607
Ph: 704-963-6565

Yards: 6153, Holes: 18
Par: 71, USGA: 67.0

Restaurant/Bar/Proshop
GF: w/day $24.00

Our fairways wind themselves through the many cuts, runs, and ridges that are common to mountain terrain. And around every turn is a strategically placed green, manicured and groomed to our high standards, with a variety of hazards.

------ BROWN SUMMIT ------

Bryan Park GC
6275 Bryan Park Rd., 27214
Ph: 919-621-4256

Yards: 7183, Holes: 36
Par: 72, USGA: 74.0
RP: 2 months/weekday, prior Wed weekend

Proshop
GF: w/day $23.00

Two 18-hole courses that offer very different challenges. The Players course is open with difficult par-3s. It also has shorter par-5s. The Champions Course has lots of water, plenty of bunkers, and is heavily treed, with many varieties of trees.

———————————————BURNSVILLE———————————————

Mount Mitchell GC
7590 Highway 80
South, 28714
Ph: 704-675-5454

Yards: 6475, Holes: 18
Par: 72, USGA: 68.0
RP: 1 week in advance

Restaurant/Proshop
GF: w/day $25.00
Carts: $10.00

This mountain course lies in a valley at 3000 feet elevation with 15 flat holes. The back nine follows the Southtoe River which comes into play on 2 holes. The par 4, 450 yard 14th hole requires a second shot over the river to a well bunkered green.

———————————————CALABASH———————————————

Marsh Harbour GL
P.O. Box 65, North
Mrytle Beach, 28597
Ph: 803-249-3449

Yards: 6970, Holes: 18
Par: 71, USGA: 70.1
RP: 9 months in
advance

Restaurant/Bar/Proshop
GF: w/day $47.00
Carts: $Included

The course has a lot of marsh grass and sand with big shady oak trees everywhere. 7 closing holes are by the marsh. #18 has logo tree; #17, par 5, has 3 island landing areas.

———————————————CALABASH———————————————

Ocean Harbour GL
10301 Sommerset Dr.,
28459
Ph: 919-579-3588

Yards: 6148, Holes: 18
Par: 72, USGA: 70.4

Restaurant/Bar
GF: w/day $15.00

This course is surrounded by water as it is set on the Intercostal Waterway and the Calabash River. And you can count on the water to come into play on most holes. The greens are tricky. A true challenge to your game.

———————————————CALABASH———————————————

Pearl Golf Links
Route 8, Sunset Lakes
Blvd., 28459
Ph: 919-579-8132

Yards: 6749, Holes: 18
Par: 72
RP: Call for starting
times

Restaurant/Bar/Proshop
GF: w/day $39.00
Carts: $11.00

Start off on a Scottish links, then play into a Pinehurst look, then finish along the scenic coastal marsh land. Extensive manicuring and landscaping, magnificent clubhouse facility, this world class masterpiece awaits you with a warm welcome.

———————————————CALABASH———————————————

**Sandpiper Bay
G&CC**
6660 Sandpiper Bay
Dr., 28459
Ph: 800-356-5827

Yards: 6420, Holes: 18
Par: 71, USGA: 69.0

A very scenic course with forgiving fairways. Set in a wildlife sanctuary, you're going to have an opportunity to see a lot of different creatures. A delightful round of golf that offers very wonderful water views.

———————————————CANTON———————————————

Springdale CC
Rt.2 Box 271, 28716
Ph: 800-553-3027

Yards: 6437, Holes: 18
Par: 72, USGA: 70.7
RP: Recommended

Restaurant/Bar/Proshop
GF: w/day $22.00, w/end
$22.00
Carts: $13.00

Despite large penncross bent greens, Springdale places a premium on accuracy. The front 9 is long, hilly and well trapped. And there's a mountain stream you'll get to know. The back 9 is shorter and flatter with wider fairways.

---CASHIERS---

High Hampton Inn & CC	Yards: 6012, Holes: 18	Restaurant/Proshop
P.O. Box 338, Hwy. 107, South, 28717	Par: 71	**GF:** w/day $29.00
Ph: 704-743-2411	RP: 1 day in advance	**Carts:** $21.00

High Hampton Inn & Country Club is a golfer's Mecca. The par 3, 137-yard famed 8th hole (upon which Golf Digest bestowed the title "One of America's Great Golf Holes") is rivaled by 17 others, each one equally beautiful and equally challenging.

---CHARLOTTE---

Pawtuckett GC	Yards: 6510, Holes: 18	Restaurant/Bar/Proshop
1 Pauwtuckett Rd., 28214	Par: 70, USGA: 68.5	**GF:** w/day $19.00, w/end $24.00
Ph: 704-394-5890	RP: 1 day in advance	**Carts:** $5.00

The rolling hills and beautiful countryside setting will make Pawtuckett a golf course you will love to play.

---CLEMMONS---

Tanglewood Park GC	Yards: 6710, Holes: 18	Restaurant/Bar/Proshop
Tanglewood Park, 27012	Par: 72, USGA: 68.5	**GF:** w/day $20.00
Ph: 919-766-0591	RP: 2 weeks in advance	**Carts:** $10.00

Two courses as different as night and day, both bent greens and Bermudas. #5 Champ, par 4, 435 yards across water, 200 yard carry, fairway slope. #18 Rey, very hilly, 430 yards uphill, lake with sandtrap 30 yards from landing area.

---CRAMERTON---

Lakewood GL	Yards: 5907, Holes: 18	Proshop
25 Lakewood Rd., 28032	Par: 71, USGA: 67.1	**GF:** w/day $8.00
Ph: 704-825-2852	RP: Weekends only	**Carts:** $6.00

Front 9 wide open with small bent grass greens. Back 9 tight, #15 long par 4 dogleg right.

---DURHAM---

Duke University GC	Yards: 7003, Holes: 18	Restaurant/Bar/Proshop
Route 751 & Science Dr., 27706	Par: 72, USGA: 70.3	**GF:** w/day $13.00, w/end $18.00
Ph: 919-684-2817		**Carts:** $18.00

Opened in 1957, this typically outstanding Jones creation will offer you a memorable golf outing. On the course, we feature hole after hole of lush Bermuda fairways and fast bent grass greens.

---DURHAM---

Hillandale GC	Yards: 6350, Holes: 18	Proshop
P.O. Box 2786, Hillandale Rd., 27705	Par: 71, USGA: 69.5	**GF:** w/day $12.00, w/end $13.00
Ph: 919-286-4211	RP: For weekends - 7-14 days advance	**Carts:** $15.00

Located in the heart of Durham, Hillandale encompasses a variety of situations. The front side is relatively flat terrain with the Ellerbee Creek meandering through 7 of the nine holes. The back side becomes rolling and entails three holes.

---------------------------------DURHAM---------------------------------

Lakeshore GC   Yards: 5829, Holes: 18   Proshop
4621 Lumley Rd.,   Par: 71, USGA: 67.3   **GF:** w/day $8.00, w/end
27703   RP: Weekends $10.50
Ph: 919-596-2401   **Carts:** $14.00

This course is laid out around a 25 acre lake and it is very picturesque.

---------------------------------FAIRMONT---------------------------------

Flag Tree GC   Yards: 6183, Holes: 18   Bar/Proshop
Golf Course Rd., 28340 Par: 72, USGA: 69.5   **GF:** w/day $8.00, w/end
Ph: 919-628-9933   RP: Weekends $10.00
                                                    Carts: $8.00

*Enjoy a fairly open front nine in preparation for the Flat Tree "Amen Corner."
The 12th through the 15th wrap around a series of old irrigation ponds requiring
a number of challenging shots. It's quality golf in a serene country setting.*

---------------------------------FRANKLIN---------------------------------

Holly Springs GR   Yards: 6000, Holes: 18   Restaurant/Bar/Proshop
110 Holly Springs Golf Par: 72   **GF:** w/day $12.00
Village, 28734   **Carts:** $16.00
Ph: 704-524-7561

*A beautiful mountain challenge with 13 water hazard holes. You experience
unsurpassed mountain views from every fairway and tee. Hole #1 is a ninety
yard chip across a lake. From the elevated tee #14 you can view mountain
ranges 10 to 15 miles away.*

---------------------------------GRANITE FALLS---------------------------------

Tri-County GC, Inc. Yards: 6094, Holes: 18   Bar/Proshop
Rt. 2, Box 281, 28630   Par: 72   **GF:** w/day $9.00, w/end
Ph: 704-728-3560   RP: Required weekends $12.00
                         & holidays   **Carts:** $9.00

*Set in the foothills of the Appalachian Mountains, the rolling terrain gives golfers
a true test of golf skills. The front nine offers a wide variety of golf shots, while
the back nine reward you if you deserve it.*

---------------------------------HAMPSTEAD---------------------------------

Belvedere Plantation Yards: 6500, Holes: 18   Restaurant/Bar/Proshop
Box 999, 28443   Par: 72   **GF:** w/day $15.00, w/end
Ph: 919-270-2703 $20.00

*Elevated greens on most holes, surrounded by steeply sloping mounds which
can severely penalize the errant approach shot. Getting the ball up and down
demands shotmaking at its best.*

---------------------------------HENDERSONVILLE---------------------------------

Etowah Valley   Yards: 6880, Holes: 27   **GF:** w/day $25.00
P.O. Box 2150, 28793   Par: 72, USGA: 70.0   **Carts:** $12.00
Ph: 704-891-7022   RP: 2 days in advance

*The bent grass greens are probably some of the largest in the south—some as
large as 9,000 feet, as the course winds through rolling valleys. The course is
designed to eliminate ball crossover from one fairway to another, insuring
uninterrupted play.*

HERTFORD

Sound GL   Yards: 6504, Holes: 18
Albermarle Plantation,   Par: 72
Cbhouse Dr, 27944
Ph: 919-426-5555

Beautiful groves of trees are a real hazard.

HIGH POINT

Blair Park GC   Yards: 6449, Holes: 18   Restaurant/Proshop
1901 S. Main St., 27260   Par: 72, USGA: 67.4   **GF:** w/day $6.00
Ph: 919-883-3497   RP: Weekends &   **Carts:** $8.00
                        holidays

*Newly renovated bent grass greens are relatively small. There are few bunkers,
many tall pine trees and a creek that runs throughout the course which comes
into play on 10 holes. Hole #14 is 400 yards; 2nd shot is 175 yards.*

HIGH POINT

Oak Hollow GC   Yards: 6429, Holes: 18   Restaurant/Proshop
1400 Oakview Rd.,   Par: 72, USGA: 67.9   **GF:** w/day $10.00, w/end
27260   RP: 2 days in advance $13.00
Ph: 919-869-4014   **Carts:** $16.00

*This Pete Dye designed course, which follows the shoreline of the lake to a large
extent, has Bermuda fairways and bent grass greens. Some of Dye's design
features include sand bunkers lined with pilings, and an island tee.*

JEFFERSON

Jefferson Landing   Yards: 6389, Holes: 18
GC   Par: 72, USGA: 69.4
Hwy 16/88, 28640
Ph: 919-246-4653

*A scenic course set along Naked Creek and the New River. There is a breathtak-
ing view of mountains as a backdrop. There is also an abundance of ponds here
in addition to the creek, so bring your hip boots.*

LONG BEACH

Oak Island GC CC   Yards: 6608, Holes: 18   Restaurant/Bar/Proshop
P.O. Box 789, 28465   Par: 72, USGA: 69.6   **GF:** w/day $20.00
Ph: 919-278-5275   RP: 1 week in advance   **Carts:** $10.00

*#18 par 5—The fairway is lined with gnarled oak trees from a steady ocean wind.
You are hitting 2 good shots into the ocean wind, which will leave you 150 yards
carry over water that sometimes has alligators in it.*

MAGGIE VALLEY

Maggie Valley Resort Yards: 6284, Holes: 18   Restaurant/Bar/Proshop
P.O. Box 99, 340   Par: 71, USGA: 68.5   **GF:** w/day $25.00, w/end
Country Club Rd.,   RP: Call for tee time $25.00
27851   same day   **Carts:** $12.50
Ph: 800-438-3861

*Maggie's 18-hole, par 71 championship course is scenically beautiful, with the
mountain setting of Blue Ridge and Smokies, the front nine begins in the valley
with the back nine built into the mountains. The elevation changes gradually
from 2,600 to 3,500*

MCLEANSVILLE

Cedar Crest GC
340 Birch Creek Rd.,
27301
Ph: 919-697-8251

Yards: 5682, Holes: 18
Par: 70, USGA: 66.0

Proshop
GF: w/day $7.50, w/end
$9.00
Carts: $7.50

The course is relatively short by some standards, rolling with the land, yet designed for pleasure. Our favorite hole is No. 3 with short par 5 and all uphill. The penalty is the large oak tree in the center of the fairway at 210 yards.

NAGS HEAD

Nags Head Golf Links
P.O. Box 1719, Hwy.
158,Mi Ps 15, 27959
Ph: 919-441-8073

Yards: 6240, Holes: 18
Par: 71, USGA: 68.9
RP: Reserve through
year

Restaurant/Bar/Proshop
GF: w/day $40.00, w/end
$40.00
Carts: $10.00

A visit to Scottish golf lies here on the Outer Banks of North Carolina. Sandy lies, love grass and sea oats await the errant shot with prevailing winds always a factor. Selected to "Top 50 in the Southeast" by Golf Week Magazine.

OCEAN ISLE BEACH

Brick Landing Plantation GC
Route 2, 28459
Ph: 919-754-4373

Yards: 6482, Holes: 18
Par: 72, USGA: 69.4

Restaurant/Bar/Proshop
GF: w/day $22.00, w/end
$35.00
Carts: $10.00

Once again Brick Landing has been selected by Golfweek magazine as one of the Top 50 resort developments in the Southeast. "The Amateur," a new national men's amateur tournament is contested here every July. "The Amateur" brings 120 top players together.

PINEBLUFF

Pines Golf Resort
US Hwy. 1 S., P.O. Box
427, 28373
Ph: 919-281-3165

Yards: 6610, Holes: 18
Par: 72, USGA: 68.5
RP: Call for tee times

Restaurant/Bar/Proshop
GF: w/day $10.00
Carts: $10.00

The Pines Golf Resort course is situated on 250 acres in the beautiful sandhills (Pinehurst) area. The course is on rolling terrain through stands of longleaf and lollolly pine and is punctuated by several lakes. A challenging and fun course for golfers.

PINEHURST

Foxfire Resort & CC
P.O. Box 711, 28374
Ph: 919-295-5555

Yards: 6286, Holes: 18
Par: 72, USGA: 69.7

Restaurant/Bar/Proshop
GF: w/day $40.00, w/end
$40.00
Carts: $14.00

The original West Course follows the gentle slopes along the shores of Lake Mackenzie and the large Foxfire ponds. The newer East Course winds through the hillier section surrounding wide Lake Forest.

PINEHURST

Longleaf CC
Midland Rd., 28374
Ph: 919-692-6100

Yards: 6073, Holes: 18
Par: 71, USGA: 67.3

Restaurant/Bar
GF: w/day $34.00

A course that features elevation changes, lots of trees and hedges, and a small lake. An terrific course to play the whole year.

──────────────── PINEHURST ────────────────

Pinehurst Hotel CC
P.O. Box 4000, 28374
Ph: 919-295-6811

Yards: 7020, Holes: 18
Par: 72, USGA: 73.5
RP: Hotel or resort
guests only

Restaurant/Bar/Proshop
GF: w/day $50.00, w/end
$50.00
Carts: $13.00

It's impossible to describe one hole at Pinehurst. With seven championship courses, Pinehurst is affectionately known as the "Golf Capital of the World." The world renowned #2 Course is considered Donald Ross's great masterpiece.

──────────────── PINEHURST ────────────────

**Pinewild CC of
Pinehurst**
801 Linden Rd, RTE
211, 28374
Ph: 919-295-5145

Yards: 6216, Holes: 27
Par: 72

Abundant bunkers and heavy stands of trees are going to cause the most difficulty here. A championship-caliber course that also has very tricky greens.

──────────────── PINEHURST ────────────────

The Pit
P.O. Box 3006
Macintire Sta., 28374
Ph: 919-944-1600

Yards: 6455, Holes: 18
Par: 71, USGA: 69.3

Restaurant/Bar/Proshop
GF: w/day $42.00
Carts: $Included

#8 is in the top 50 U.S. holes

──────────────── RAEFORD ────────────────

Arabia GC
Rt 2 Box 151, Golf
Course Rd., 28376
Ph: 919-875-3524

Yards: 6013, Holes: 27
Par: 71, USGA: 68.8
RP: 1 day in advance

Proshop
GF: w/day $12.00, w/end
$21.00
Carts: $Included

Family oriented semi-private course about 30 miles from Pinehurt. Our favorite hole is the No. 2, par 3. Water from tee to green splashing over a dam demands deep concentration to avoid penalties.

──────────────── RUTHERFORDTON ────────────────

**Cleghorn Plantation
GC**
Rt 4 Box 69 Cleghorn
Mill Rd., 28139
Ph: 704-286-9117

Yards: 6313, Holes: 18
Par: 72, USGA: 70.5
RP: 1 week in advance

Restaurant/Proshop
GF: w/day $8.00, w/end
$15.00
Carts: $10.00

Truly great George Cobb design. Rolling hills and flowing streams. Bent grass greens, laid out around Civil War battleground and burial grounds. Very historic.

──────────────── RUTHERFORDTON ────────────────

Meadowbrook GC
Rt. 4, Box 185-B, 28139
Ph: 704-863-2690

Yards: 6348, Holes: 18
Par: 72, USGA: 69.4

Proshop
GF: w/day $11.00
Carts: $14.00

Nice rolling terrain with bent grass greens, water on six holes.

──────────────── SHELBY ────────────────

Challenger 3 GC
1650 N. Post Rd., 28150
Ph: 704-482-5061

Yards: 2600, Holes: 18
Par: 54

Proshop
GF: w/day $4.50

We think this is the south's finest par 3 golf course. We have bent greens, excellent lighting for night play. Holes up to 160 yards. Greens average 3400 square feet.

──────────────SOUTHERN PINES──────────────

Mid Pines Resort
1010 Midland Rd.,
28387
Ph: 919-692-2114

Yards: 6500, Holes: 18
Par: 72, USGA: 71.4
RP: Advised to book
well ahead

Restaurant
GF: w/day $40.00, w/end
$40.00
Carts: $14.00

A narrow, tree-lined course with small undulating greens. Mid Pines isn't particularly long or strenuous, but often the subtle undulations are difficult to read. The course has played host to several national championships, including 1988's Womens East.

──────────────SOUTHERN PINES──────────────

Southern Pines CC
Country Club Dr., P.O.
Box 1180, 28387
Ph: 919-692-6551

Yards: 6250, Holes: 27
Par: 71, USGA: 70.0
RP: May be made
anytime

Restaurant/Bar/Proshop
GF: w/day $18.00
Carts: $12.00

Southern Pines Country Club is a classic 80 year old Donald Ross course. No 2 holes are similar, with many doglegs, hills and beautiful surroundings of dogwood and pine trees. A great test for the low handicapper and most enjoyable for the high.

──────────────SOUTHERN PINES──────────────

Talamore GC
1595 Midland Rd,
28374
Ph: 919-692-5884

Yards: 6393, Holes: 18
Par: 72

The elevation changes are very marked on this hilly layout. There is abundant bunkering and some very nasty water holes.

──────────────SPRUCE PINE──────────────

Grassy Creek G&CC
101 Golf Course Rd.,
28777
Ph: 704-765-7436

Yards: 6277, Holes: 18
Par: 72, USGA: 70.0
RP: Tee times are
required

Restaurant/Proshop
GF: w/day $20.00
Carts: $10.00

Cool mountain weather, a chance to escape the heat of the lowlands. #15 is a 514 yard par 5, the drive will take a 200 yard carry over a creek to a small landing area. Then you are uphill the rest of the way to a small tucked away green.

──────────────SUNSET BEACH──────────────

Oyster Bay GC
Lakeshore Dr. PO Box
2035, 28459
Ph: 803-272-6399

Yards: 6435, Holes: 18
Par: 70, USGA: 70.2
RP: Call in advance

Restaurant/Bar/Proshop
GF: w/day $70.00
Carts: $Included

Marshlands and water are going to be your main problems here A truly championship course, there are greens that are on the small side and well-placed bunkers. This course will demand the best from your game.

──────────────SUNSET BEACH──────────────

Sea Trails GL
651 Clubhouse Rd.,
28468
Ph: 919-579-4350

Yards: 6332, Holes: 54
Par: 72, USGA: 71.9

Restaurant/Bar
GF: w/day $29.00

Three championship-caliber 18-holes courses to choose from at this location. The area is heavily treed and the terrain is rolling. With three different layouts you'll find some of everything on these courses.

─────────────────────────VASS─────────────────────────

Woodlake GC
P.O. Box 648, 150
Woodlake Blvd., 28394
Ph: 919-245-4686

Yards: 7003, Holes: 28
Par: 72, USGA: 73.4

Restaurant/Bar
GF: w/day $12.00, w/end
$38.00

Three nine-hole courses with a practice hole to boot.

────────────────────WAYNESVILLE────────────────────

Lake Junaluska GC
19 Golf Course Rd.,
28786
Ph: 704-456-5777

Yards: 2872, Holes: 9
Par: 35, USGA: 34.7
RP: Call for tee times

Restaurant/Proshop
GF: w/day $8.00
Carts: $16.00

*Lake Junaluska is a beautiful nine hole course set in the Smokey Mountains of
North Carolina. The lake itself is a beautiful background for the second hole.
Number six is our strongest hole requiring a very accurate drive with out of
bounds on the left.*

────────────────────WAYNESVILLE────────────────────

Waynesville CC Inn
Box 390, 28786
Ph: 704-456-3551

Yards: 6080, Holes: 27
Par: 70
RP: Tee times required

Restaurant/Proshop
GF: w/day $23.00
Carts: $12.00

*The 18-hole course has certain subtleties that demand a well placed shot. No
matter what hole you're playing, you'll find the bent grass greens painstakingly
perfect, the fairways lush and quiet and the views unparalleled.*

────────────────────WEST JEFFERSON────────────────────

Mountain Aire GC
Rt. 3, Golf Course Rd.,
28694
Ph: 919-877-4716

Yards: 3240, Holes: 9
Par: 36, USGA: 68.0
RP: Call for tee time

Proshop
GF: w/day $5.00, w/end
$10.00
Carts: $10.00

*A beautiful course in an unsurpassed setting in the Blue Ridge Mountains.
Spectacular views from holes 2, 4, 8 and 9. 3500 feet elevation. A second nine
holes are under construction.*

────────────────────WILLOW SPRINGS────────────────────

Hidden Valley GC
Rt. 2 Box 7900, 27592
Ph: 919-639-4071

Yards: 6174, Holes: 18
Par: 72, USGA: 69.0
RP: Taken on weekends
only

Restaurant/Proshop
GF: w/day $8.00, w/end
$11.00
Carts: $8.00

*The course is wide open on most holes on the front side, with very few sand
traps. But the most treacherous thing about the course is the greens. They are
small bentgrass greens with a lot of funny breaks to them. My favorite hole is a
490 yard par 5.*

────────────────────WILMINGTON────────────────────

Cape GC
535 The Cape Blvd.,
28412
Ph: 910-799-3110

Yards: 6800, Holes: 18
Par: 72, USGA: 73.5
RP: Call the Proshop

Restaurant/Bar/Proshop
GF: w/day $15.00, w/end
$20.00
Carts: $13.00

*The Cape is nestled on the peninsula between the Cape Fear River and the
Atlantic Ocean. You'll never forget the beauty of the signature double green on
15 and 17, or the challenge of avoiding the 24 lakes and ponds that guard the
fairways and greens.*

◄◄◄◄◄◄◄◄◄●►►►►►►►►►

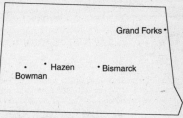

NORTH DAKOTA

―――――――――――――――BISMARCK――――――――――――――――

Apple Creek CC
E of Bismarck Hwy 10,
58501
Ph: 701-258-5234

Yards: 6129, Holes: 18
Par: 72

Restaurant/Bar
GF: w/day $25.00

Apple creek has forested, hilly terrain on half the course, and the rest is more level. There's a creek coming into play at most of the holes.

―――――――――――――――BISMARCK――――――――――――――――

Riverwood
Box 2063, 58501
Ph: 701-223-9915

Yards: 6900, Holes: 18
Par: 72, USGA: 69.8
RP: 1 day in advance

Restaurant/Proshop
GF: w/day $9.00
Carts: $13.00

Riverwood is a tree lined golf course. The 60 foot cottonwood trees also create an ideal habitat for much wildlife: deer, wild turkey, wild ducks. So while you enjoy your round of golf you can also enjoy the wildlife.

―――――――――――――――BOWMAN――――――――――――――――

Sweetwater GC
P.O. Box 1182,
Highway 85 S, 58623
Ph: 701-523-5800

Yards: 2985, Holes: 9
Par: 36, USGA: 64.8

Bar/Proshop
GF: w/day $8.00
Carts: $10.00

This short but difficult par nine golf course features water hazards on six of the nine holes. The conservative golfer who concentrates on shot placement will walk away with bragging rights while the ego busting type of golfer might hang his head.

―――――――――――――――FARGO――――――――――――――――

Edgewood GC
North Elm St., Box
1845, 58107
Ph: 701-232-2824

Yards: 6045, Holes: 18
Par: 71, USGA: 66.6
RP: 3 days in advance

Restaurant/Bar/Proshop
GF: w/day $10.00, w/end
$12.00
Carts: $15.00

The greens are well-trapped, the greens are large and fast, and the trees are fantastic. What more could you ask for a terrific round of golf?

Our listings—supplied by the management—are as complete as possible. Many of the courses have more features than we list. Be sure to inquire when you book your tee time.

GRAND FORKS

Ray Richards GC
De Mers W, Box 8275
Univ. Sta., 58202
Ph: 701-777-4340

Yards: 3165, Holes: 9
Par: 36, USGA: 34.6

Proshop
GF: w/day $4.75, w/end
$4.80
Carts: $6.50

A young course with a bright future. Located next to the University of North Dakota within the city of Grand Forks. Our favorite hole is the 9th, a par 4 with water on the left and an elevated green protected by a large bunker in the front.

HAZEN

Hazen GC
Highway 200, east 1/2
mile, 58545
Ph: 701-748-2011

Yards: 2664, Holes: 9
Par: 35, USGA: 64.0

Restaurant/Bar/Proshop
GF: w/day $6.00, w/end
$8.00
Carts: $7.50

The most challenging hole is the 5th, a medium to long par 3, playing from 180 to 230 yards. With out of bounds right, trees left, water in front, and an elevated green, it has often been called "the shortest par 5 in North Dakota".

MINOT

Minot GC
1 Minot Country Club
Rd., Box 250, 58722
Ph: 701-839-6169

Yards: 6235, Holes: 18
Par: 72, USGA: 69.6
RP: 24 hours in
advance

Restaurant/Bar/Proshop
GF: w/day $25.00, w/end
$30.00
Carts: $8.00

Originally opened as a nine hole course in the 1920s, there are now 18-holes of superb golf. This course is rated one of the best in North Dakota and hosts the Western North Dakota Charity Pro-Am.

MINOT

Souris Valley GC
Box 101 Burdick
Expresswy, 58701
Ph: 701-838-4112

Yards: 6532, Holes: 18
Par: 72

Restaurant/Bar
GF: w/day $8.48

The fairways are wide and fairly open. There's water on six holes, but this layout shouldn't be much of a problem for the average golfer.

OHIO

-----------------------------AKRON-----------------------------

Valley View GC
1212 Cuyahoga St.,
44313
Ph: 216-928-9034

Yards: 5440, Holes: 27
Par: 72

GF: w/day $11.00, w/end
$13.00

Three 9-holes courses. One course is very forgiving, one is very narrow, has lots of water and is a real test of your short game. The third has a fair bit of water.

-----------------------------BOARDMAN-----------------------------

Mill Creek Park GC
West Golf Dr., 44512
Ph: 216-740-7112

Yards: 6302, Holes: 36
Par: 70, USGA: 70.8
RP: Weekends &
holidays only

Proshop

The par 70 North Course is played on gently rolling terrain through majestic trees. The South Course, also par 70, is laid out on nearly level land with tree lined fairways. Numerous sand bunkers and occasional creeks on both courses challenge.

-----------------------------CALEDONIA-----------------------------

Whetstone GC
5211 Marion Mt. Gilead
Rd., 43314
Ph: 614-389-4343

Yards: 6371, Holes: 18
Par: 72, USGA: 69.5
RP: Weekends

Restaurant/Bar/Proshop
GF: w/day $10.00
Carts: $14.00

Whetstone offers a challenge to all golfers with water, sand and tight greens in a rural country setting.

-----------------------------CANTON-----------------------------

**Tam O'Shanter GC
PC**
5055 Hills and Dales
Rd. NW, 44708
Ph: 800-462-9964

Yards: 6249, Holes: 36
Par: 70, USGA: 107
RP: Anytime with major
credit card

Restaurant/Bar/Proshop
GF: w/day $20.00, w/end
$20.00
Carts: $16.00

Designed in the 1920's by a disciple of Donald Ross, both Tam O'Shanter courses are traditional layouts shaped by glaciers, not bulldozers. Rolling terrain, mature trees, lush fairways, wall-to-wall irrigation; an atmosphere reminiscent of a first-class.

――――――――――CHESTERLAND――――――――――

Fowler's Mill GC   Yards: 6623, Holes: 27   Bar
13095 Rockhaven Rd.,   Par: 72   **GF:** w/day $17.00, w/end
44026 $23.00
Ph: 216-286-9545

One of the better courses in the area, you'll find plenty to test your game. The
greens are large, and the course has lots of length.

――――――――――CINCINNATI――――――――――

Blue Ash GC   Yards: 6211, Holes: 18   Restaurant/Proshop
4040 Cooper Rd.,   Par: 72, USGA: 70.3   **GF:** w/day $12.00
45241   RP: 5 days in advance   **Carts:** $17.00
Ph: 513-745-8577

The rolling terrain, lakes and a meandering creek make Blue Ash a beautiful as
well as a challenging layout. The condition of the course is second to none and
the numerous teeing areas make playing enjoyable for golfers of all ability
levels.

――――――――――CINCINNATI――――――――――

Vineyards GC   Yards: 6789, Holes: 18   Restaurant/Bar/Proshop
600 Nordyke Rd, 45255   Par: 71, USGA: 73.0   **GF:** w/day $20.00
Ph: 513-474-3007   RP: 5 days in advance   **Carts:** $29.00

Greens here are surrounded by small lakes and sand traps. The greens are tough
and will challenge your putting abilities. The course gets increasingly difficult as
you go along, so don't be fooled if you have an easy start.

――――――――――CLYDE――――――――――

Green Hills GC   Yards: 5800, Holes: 27   Restaurant/Bar/Proshop
1959 S. Main St., 43410   Par: 70, USGA: 65.6   **GF:** w/day $10.00
Ph: 419-547-9996   RP: 1 week in advance   **Carts:** $15.00

This 18 hole golf course is one you will never tire of playing. Each hole is a
totally different hole, with hills, trees, traps, lakes, and creeks. A course you will
want to play again and again.

――――――――――COLUMBUS――――――――――

Airport GC   Yards: 5901, Holes: 18   Restaurant/Bar
900 N Hamilton Rd,   Par: 70, USGA: 66.6   **GF:** w/day $11.00, w/end
43219   RP: First come, first $13.00
Ph: 614-645-3127   served   **Carts:** $9.00

Planes land over the course, flat, three lakes, lots of trees, modern course.

――――――――――COLUMBUS――――――――――

Minerva Lake GC   Yards: 5600, Holes: 18   Restaurant/Proshop
2955 Minerva Lake Rd,   Par: 69, USGA: 67.8   **GF:** w/day $10.50, w/end
43231   RP: First come, first $12.00
Ph: 614-882-9988   served   **Carts:** $17.00

Small greens, rolling terrain, old style, flat with large trees. Creek runs through
the middle of the course, no lakes.

――――――――――COLUMBUS――――――――――

Turnbury GC   Yards: 6085, Holes: 18   Restaurant/Bar/Proshop
901 West Broad St.,   Par: 72, USGA: 68.8   **GF:** w/day $12.00, w/end
43147   RP: 7 days in advance $13.00
Ph: 614-645-2582   **Carts:** $9.25

Link style course, elevated greens, undulated. Scottish links fairly flat and open.
Wildlife areas, creek lining most of the course, three lakes.

---CONCORD---

Quail Hollow GC
11080 Concord-
Hambden Rd., 44077
Ph: 216-352-6201

Holes: 18
Par: 72, USGA: 71.6

Restaurant/Bar/Proshop
GF: w/day $33.00, w/end
$38.00
Carts: $12.69

In the warmer months, enjoy the challenging 18-hole, par 72 golf course designed and planned by Bruce Devlin and Robert Von Hagge. Also a driving range and putting green.

---CORTLAND---

Tamer Win G&CC
2940 Niles Cortland
Rd. N.E., 44410
Ph: 216-637-2881

Yards: 6275, Holes: 18
Par: 71, USGA: 68.8
RP: Weekend needed,
Call for daily

Restaurant/Bar/Proshop
GF: w/day $15.00, w/end
$17.00
Carts: $16.00

A family owned golf course, we take pride in our condition of the course. It will challenge you and give you a great feel of the out doors.

---DAYTON---

Kittyhawk GC
3383 Chuck Wagon Ln,
45414
Ph: 513-237-5424

Yards: 6619, Holes: 54
Par: 72

Restaurant/Bar
GF: w/day $9.00, w/end
$18.00

54-holes of golf.

---DELLROY---

Atwood Resort GC
2650 Lodge Rd., 44620
Ph: 216-735-2630

Yards: 6057, Holes: 18
Par: 70, USGA: 68.0
RP: Tee times 1 year in
advance

Restaurant
GF: w/day $12.00, w/end
$13.00
Carts: $19.00

The 18-hole golf course is challenging, playable and always meticulously maintained. The lighted par-three is in top shape for quick rounds or casual family golf and to polish your game, a practice range.

---FINDLAY---

Findlay Hillcrest GC
800 W. Bigelow, 45840
Ph: 419-423-7211

Yards: 6981, Holes: 18
Par: 72, USGA: 69.4

Restaurant/Bar/Proshop
GF: w/day $11.00, w/end
$12.00
Carts: $19.00

Plenty of length. The front nine is fairly tight. Lots of trees. Back is more open but longer than the front. Two lakes on each nine. Favorite hole #16. You hit through a chute of large oak trees out of bounds left.

---GALENA---

Blackhawk GC
8830 Dustin Rd., 43021
Ph: 614-965-1042

Yards: 6524, Holes: 18
Par: 71, USGA: 70.6
RP: First come, first
served

Restaurant/Proshop
GF: w/day $14.00, w/end
$14.00
Carts: $10.00

Rolling with trees, creek runs through the course, several small lakes, nice view of Hoover Reservoir. 22 years old, mature trees, modern course.

—————————————GALLOWAY—————————————

Thornapple CC
1051 Alton-Darby
Creek Rd, 43119
Ph: 614-878-7703

Yards: 6824, Holes: 18
Par: 72

Bar
GF: w/day $11.00, w/end
$12.00

Water comes into play on over half the holes. A few tricky greens, but all-in-all, it's going to be the water that's the most problem.

—————————————HINCKLEY—————————————

Hinckley Hills GC
300 State Rd., 44233
Ph: 216-278-4861

Yards: 6248, Holes: 18
Par: 72, USGA: 70.9
RP: Weekends

Restaurant/Bar/Proshop
GF: w/day $16.00
Carts: $16.00

This scenic 18 holes of golf offers the ultimate in golf. With its long, rolling and challenge it offers a beautiful view of the area. One of the nicest in our area.

—————————————HINCKLEY—————————————

Pine Hills GC
433 W. 130th St., 44233
Ph: 216-225-4477

Yards: 6300, Holes: 18
Par: 72
RP: Necessary on
weekends

Restaurant/Bar/Proshop
GF: w/day $15.00
Carts: $15.00

Pine Hills is hilly, filled with traps, trees and doglegs, and water, not to mention slick greens. It has a par of 72, slope rating 124. It plays tough, but it's fair. Gather your courage and play—you may even spot one of Hinckley's famous buzzards.

—————————————HURON—————————————

Sawmill Creek GC
2401 Cleveland Rd.,
P.O. Box 358, 44839
Ph: 419-433-3789

Yards: 6378, Holes: 18
Par: 71, USGA: 70.3

Restaurant/Bar
GF: w/day $35.00

This course is set along Lake Erie and offers some fabulous scenery. An open, rather flat course, you might make the mistake of thinking round of golf is going to be easy. Water is everywhere, and the wind won't help you a bit.

—————————————KINGS ISLAND—————————————

**Jack Nicklaus Sports
Center**
3565 Kings Mill Rd.,
45034
Ph: 513-398-5200

Yards: 6250, Holes: 18
Par: 71, USGA: 69.6
RP: Seven days in
advance

Restaurant/Bar/Proshop
GF: w/day $21.00, w/end
$27.00
Carts: $8.75

The most challenging hole on our course is the par 5 18th, the "Grizzly". Don't let the length of 546 yards scare you, there's also out of bounds left and a creek down the right. The green is well guarded by a lake and 3 sand traps.

—————————————MEDINA—————————————

Bunker Hill GC
3060 Pearl Rd., 44256
Ph: 216-722-4174

Yards: 5805, Holes: 18
Par: 70, USGA: 67.1
RP: Tee times
weekends & holidays

Bar/Proshop
GF: w/day $17.00, w/end
$19.00
Carts: $18.00

Bunker Hill is the oldest and most beautiful course in Medina County, Ohio. Featuring rolling hills, elevated tees and greens on several holes, this is a testy and scenic joy for most any level of golfer. Our favorite hole is #18.

MIDDLETOWN

Weatherwax
5401 Mosiman, 45042
Ph: 513-425-7886

Yards: 7174, Holes: 36
Par: 72, USGA: 71.0
RP: Weekends &
holidays

Restaurant/Bar
GF: w/day $10.00
Carts: $16.00

4 sets of 9 holes, making 6 combinations possible for your play. Water runs along side of most holes, hills and big mature woods line courses. 2 long ones, wider open, more parallel and other 2 shorter with lots of sand and tighter.

RAVENA

Windmill Lakes GC
6544 State Route 14,
44266
Ph: 216-297-0440

Yards: 6861, Holes: 18
Par: 70

Restaurant/Bar
GF: w/day $14.00, w/end
$20.00

A long course with abundant bunkers and large greens. A real test of your accuracy.

SANDUSKY

Woussickett GC
6311 Mason Rd., 44870
Ph: 419-359-1141

Yards: 5963, Holes: 18
Par: 70, USGA: 67.0
RP: Daily tee times

Restaurant/Bar/Proshop
GF: w/day $10.00
Carts: $15.00

The 18th hole is one of the most scenic and demanding holes in the area. The creek splits the fairway that runs in front of this large double green with trees on both sides. A beautiful view from the clubhouse.

SOUTH MADISON

Thunder Hill CC
7050 Griswold Rd.,
44957
Ph: 216-298-3474

Yards: 6700, Holes: 18
Par: 72

Bar
GF: w/day $20.00, w/end
$25.00

Some very long holes, and lots of water, in fact there's water everywhere, are going to really test your accuracy.

SUNBURY

Bent Tree GC
350 Bent Tree Rd.,
43074

Ph: 614-965-5140

Yards: 6800, Holes: 18
Par: 72

65 sand traps, if you're not careful you'll get lots of practice in them The course is beautifully maintained and will offer a truly memorable round of golf.

UPPER SANDUSKY

Lincoln Hills GC
5377 U.S. 30, 43351
Ph: 419-294-3037

Yards: 3084, Holes: 9
Par: 36, USGA: 68.3

Restaurant/Bar/Proshop
GF: w/day $9.00
Carts: $14.00

Postage stamp greens and hilly terrain make Lincoln Hills unique in Northwest Ohio.

VAN WERT

The Woods GC
12083 SR 127 S, 45891
Ph: 419-238-0441

Yards: 6775, Holes: 18
Par: 72, USGA: 69.5
RP: Weekends &
holidays

Restaurant/Bar/Proshop
GF: w/day $8.75, w/end
$10.00
Carts: $14.00

Water hazards on 10 of the 18 holes provide some rough going. #4 is a toughy, par 3 160 yards almost completely over water #11 is a sharp dogleg par 4 that should really keep you on your toes.

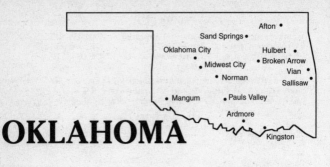

OKLAHOMA

―――――――――――――――AFTON―――――――――――――――

Shangri-La GC
Rte 3, Highway 125,
74331
Ph: 918-257-4204

Yards: 6500, Holes: 18
Par: 72, USGA: 70.3
RP: In advance

GF: w/day $35.00
Carts: $Included

36 holes of challenging golf with lush fairways, polished bent-grass greens and tree-studded roughs in a one-of-a-kind natural landscape. This home course of touring pro Bruce Lietzke includes a practice tee and driving range, a putting green.

―――――――――――――――AFTON―――――――――――――――

Shangri-La GC
Rt 3, Hwy 125, 74331
Ph: 918-257-4204

Yards: 5500, Holes: 18
Par: 70, USGA: 66.3
RP: Call ahead

GF: w/day $35.00
Carts: $Included

36 holes of challenging golf with lush fairways, polished bent-grass greens and tree-studded roughs in a one-of-a-kind natural landscape. This home course of touring pro Bruce Lietzke includes a practice tee and driving range, and a putting green.

―――――――――――――――ARDMORE―――――――――――――――

Ardmore Muni GC
3905 N. Commerce,
P.O. Box 249, 73402
Ph: 405-223-4260

Yards: 6367, Holes: 18
Par: 70, USGA: 68.0
RP: 1 day in advance
for weekends

Restaurant/Proshop
GF: w/day $7.00
Carts: $13.00

The golf course meanders through rolling hills, and pine trees with Lake Meadow bordering several holes on each nine. The short but challenging layout provides fun for all levels of ability.

―――――――――――――――BROKEN ARROW―――――――――――――――

Forest Ridge GC
7501 E. Kenosha, 74014
Ph: 918-357-2282

Yards: 7069, Holes: 18
Par: 71, USGA: 74.0
RP: 7 days with card,
else 4 days

Restaurant/Bar/Proshop
GF: w/day $50.00, w/end
$50.00
Carts: $Included

Each hole has its own individual personality and playing characteristics. The signature hole is the sixteenth which typifies the uniqueness and beauty of Forest Ridge. The drive from elevated tees must carry a native area with a creek to the fairway.

──────────────── HULBERT ────────────────

Sequoyah State Park GC
Western Hills Rt 1-Box 201, 74441
Ph: 918-772-2297

Yards: 5860, Holes: 18
Par: 70, USGA: 66.7

Restaurant/Bar
GF: w/day $7.00
Carts: $13.00

#9 is our favorite hole. It looks easy. Pine trees line both sides of the fairway; it doglegs to the right. There is an open slot in trees on right side, encouraging an attempt to cut dogleg but, very difficult to make it back into fairway.

──────────────── KINGSTON ────────────────

Lake Texoma GC
E on SH-32, PO Box 279, 73439
Ph: 405-564-3333

Yards: 6128, Holes: 18
Par: 71, USGA: 67.8

Restaurant/Bar/Proshop
GF: w/day $7.00
Carts: $13.00

Low undulating fairways with large bent grass greens, long open front nine and shorter tight back nine. #12, 475 yard par 5, 230 yards to 90 degree dogleg right between tree lines, 30 yard fairway, 225 yards to green with tree hazard to left and trees.

──────────────── MANGUM ────────────────

Mangum Muni GC
West of Intersect Hwy 9-Hwy 34, 73554
Ph: 405-782-3676

Yards: 5558, Holes: 9
Par: 70, USGA: 32.0

Proshop
GF: w/day $5.00, w/end $6.00
Carts: $6.00

One of the best bent grass greens in the State of Oklahoma. Irrigated fairways and sand traps on all par 3's. Driving range and tee markers that show the layout of the hole with hazards. Very unusual to catch a day when the wind doesn't blow.

──────────────── MIDWEST CITY ────────────────

John Conrad GC
711 S. Douglas Blvd., 73130
Ph: 405-732-2209

Yards: 6854, Holes: 18
Par: 36, USGA: 70.1
RP: 24 hrs. weekday-7 day weekend

Restaurant/Proshop
GF: w/day $8.56
Carts: $13.91

Heavily treed, winding fairways with particularly demanding par threes. The last four holes, 15, 16, 17 and 18, provides a challenge to the best of players.

──────────────── MIDWEST CITY ────────────────

Midwest City GC
3210 Belaire Dr., 73110
Ph: 405-732-9021

Yards: 1937, Holes: 9
Par: 30, USGA: 29.0

Bar/Proshop
GF: w/day $3.75
Carts: $6.42

Midwest City Golf Club has the distinction of being the only executive course in the state of Oklahoma. Our scenic course offers fairways lined with a variety of beautiful trees. With a par of thirty, the course has 6 par threes and 3 par fours.

──────────────── NORMAN ────────────────

Univ. of Oklahoma GC
One Par Dr., 73019
Ph: 405-325-6716

Yards: 6251, Holes: 18
Par: 72, USGA: 69.0
RP: Required on weekends

Restaurant/Proshop
GF: w/day $9.00, w/end $9.00
Carts: $14.00

A typical Maxwell design with small greens and rolling fairways. "Dog Out" Creek provides an extra challenge on 10 holes. Front nine open and long, back nine short and tight.

NORMAN

Westwood Park GC
2400 Westport Dr.,
73069
Ph: 405-321-0433

Yards: 6015, Holes: 18
Par: 70, USGA: 66.4
RP: Weekends &
holidays

Restaurant/Bar/Proshop
GF: w/day $10.00
Carts: $15.00

My favorite hole is the 14th a short par 4 demanding an accurate tee shot, hookers go home, and a delicate approach to a postage stamp unforgiving green.

OKLAHOMA CITY

Earlywine Park GC
115 & So. Portland,
P.O. Box 2086, 73156
Ph: 405-691-1727

Yards: 6295, Holes: 18
Par: 71, USGA: 69.1
RP: Recommended

Restaurant/Proshop
GF: w/day $10.00
Carts: $15.00

Cohansy bent grass. The first putting surface presented by Jim Broughton, C.G.C.S. From the first hole past Howard's tree to the sun-setting backdrop of the eighteenth green, golfers of all levels enjoy the game of golf.

OKLAHOMA CITY

Lake Hefner GC
4491 S. Lake Hefner
Dr., 73132
Ph: 405-843-1565

Yards: 6305, Holes: 18
Par: 70, USGA: 67.0
RP: Weekends-1 week;
else 1 day

Restaurant/Proshop
GF: w/day $10.00, w/end
$10.00
Carts: $15.00

South course is diverse with doglegs, rolling terrain and ending with one of the greatest finishing holes. North course places a premium on the shot into the green as well as a bonus of a view of Lake Hefner throughout your round.

PAULS VALLEY

Pauls Valley GC
Airport Rd.. P.O. Box
578, 73035
Ph: 405-238-7462

Yards: 3177, Holes: 9
Par: 36, USGA: 68.5

Proshop
GF: w/day $6.05, w/end
$7.55
Carts: $6.00

We're proud to offer golfers a clean, quiet "Country" golf course. Nothing fancy—just small town friendliness. Greens small and elevated, bent grass.

SALLISAW

Shadow Creek CC
27 Club View, 74955
Ph: 918-775-6997

Yards: 5655, Holes: 18
Par: 71, USGA: 66.5

Proshop
GF: w/day $8.00, w/end
$10.00
Carts: $14.00

The course lays flat with 2 meandering creeks, beautifully green with lots of trees. Distance is no great accomplishment, but accuracy and ball control is a must for good scores. All holes are different and very interesting.

SAND SPRINGS

Sand Springs GC
1801 N. McKinley,
74063
Ph: 918-245-7551

Yards: 6113, Holes: 18
Par: 71, USGA: 66.8
RP: Weekends &
holidays

Restaurant/Proshop
GF: w/day $7.00, w/end
$8.00
Carts: $14.00

Narrow fairways, doglegs, and uphill or downhill lies make the course play longer than the card reads. The breathtaking view of the Tulsa skyline from the 185 foot drop-off of the par 3 12th tee will leave a lasting impression in any golfers memory.

OREGON

Gerhart
Portland   Wilsonville
Gleneden Beach
Waldport   McMinnville   Weiches
Newport   Warm Springs
Neskowin   Redmond
Eugene   Blue River   Sunriver
Springfield   Cottage Grove
Creswell

Medford
Gold Hill   Klamath Falls

BLACK BUTTE RANCH

Lodge at Black Butte Rch-Glaze PO Box 8000, 97759 Ph: 503-595-6689	Yards: 6600, Holes: 36 Par: 72, USGA: 68.0 RP: Call for starting time	Restaurant/Bar **GF:** w/day $28.00 **Carts:** $10.00

Golfers love it here—no outside events are held on the two 18 hole course, Big Meadow and Glaze Meadow. They're gently rolling as they zigzag through tall pines, and aspen, and across water. You'll have ample time to gaze upward for a glimpse of geese.

BLUE RIVER

Tokatee GC 54947 McKenzie Hwy, 97413 Ph: 503-882-3220	Yards: 6817, Holes: 18 Par: 72, USGA: 69.7 RP: 2 weeks in advance	Restaurant/Bar/Proshop **GF:** w/day $22.00 **Carts:** $18.00

The course blends with area, looks like nature made it. Offers a great view of the 3 Sisters in the Cascades. Very secluded, with 5 lakes and no parallel holes. Firs line the fairways.

CORNELIUS

Pumpkin Ridge GC (Ghost) 12930 Old Pumpkin Ridge Rd., 97113 Ph: 503-647-4747	Yards: 6010, Holes: 18 Par: 71

This layout is set in the wetlands, and they will come into play on lots of the holes.

COTTAGE GROVE

Hidden Valley GC 775 N. River Rd., 97424 Ph: 503-942-3046	Yards: 5644, Holes: 9 Par: 70	Restaurant/Bar/Proshop **GF:** w/day $7.00 **Carts:** $7.00

Tucked away in the northwest hills of Cottage Grove, you'll find a delightful old fashioned Scottish style golf course with oak lined fairways.

―――――――――――――CRESWELL―――――――――――――

Emerald Valley GC
83293 Dale Kuni Rd.,
97426
Ph: 503-895-2174

Yards: 6873, Holes: 18
Par: 72, USGA: 71.4
RP: 1 week in advance

Restaurant/Bar/Proshop
GF: w/day $18.00, w/end
$20.00
Carts: $15.00

Setting just 10 miles south of Eugene just off Interstate 5 along the coast fork of the Willamette River, Emerald Valley is a championship golf course that is always in excellent condition. Year-round golf, driving range, RV park, and residential homes.

――――――――――――――EUGENE――――――――――――――

Laurelwood GC
2700 Columbia, 97403
Ph: 503-687-5321

Yards: 6000, Holes: 9
Par: 70
RP: One day in advance

Restaurant/Bar/Proshop
GF: w/day $13.00, w/end
$14.00
Carts: $17.00

Number 1 hole par 5 is rated as one of the most difficult in the state. 595 blues, 565 white dogleg left, out of bounds left, water hazard right.

―――――――――――――GEARHART―――――――――――――

Gearhart GL
N. Marion, P.O. Box
2758, 97138
Ph: 503-738-3538

Yards: 6089, Holes: 18
Par: 72, USGA: 68.5
RP: Call the Proshop

Restaurant/Bar/Proshop
GF: w/day $20.00, w/end
$20.00
Carts: $20.00

Gearhart Golf Links, oldest golf course in Oregon or Washington. Established 1892, located by the ocean 12 miles south of Astoria which is the oldest settlement in Oregon. Originally 9 holes, extended to 18 holes in 1913.

――――――――――――GLENEDEN BEACH――――――――――――

Salishan Lodge GL
Hwy. 101, 97388
Ph: 503-764-3632

Yards: 6439, Holes: 18
Par: 72, USGA: 71.5
RP: 2 weeks in advance

Restaurant
GF: w/day $36.00, w/end
$36.00
Carts: $26.00

Players who prefer to carry their clubs love to play here, carts aren't mandatory. Number 13, a 402 yard par 4, will take a straight drive between the troublesome dunes on both right and left. The green is guarded by a gargantuan H-shaped trap.

―――――――――――――GOLD HILL―――――――――――――

Laurel Hill GC
9450 Old Stage Rd.,
P.O. Box 167, 97525
Ph: 503-855-7965

Yards: 1905, Holes: 9
Par: 31
RP: Recommended on
weekends

Restaurant/Bar/Proshop
GF: w/day $4.00, w/end
$5.00

The course meanders through a dense forest of oak, fir, and madrone trees, some of them several hundred years old. The dogleg par-fours and narrow (avg. 40 yards) fairways make this a highly challenging irons course despite its modest length.

―――――――――――――KLAMATH FALLS―――――――――――――

Round Lake GC
4000 Round Lake Rd.,
97601
Ph: 503-884-2520

Yards: 1554, Holes: 9
Par: 29

GF: w/day $5.00

We also have a mobile home park and welcome RVs. Complete hook-up and showers available. Reduced golf rates and swimming pool for tenants only.

─────────────────── MEDFORD ───────────────────

Cedar Links GC
3155 Cedar Links Dr.,
97504
Ph: 503-773-4373

Yards: 5893, Holes: 18
Par: 70, USGA: 67.7
RP: 1 week in advance

Restaurant/Bar/Proshop
GF: w/day $16.00, w/end
$17.00
Carts: $18.00

*The front nine at Cedar Links is rolling with four water hazards and some
smaller greens with breaking putts. From the back nine, which is newer, you
have a beautiful view of the Rogue Valley, with larger less contoured greens.*

─────────────────── NESKOWIN ───────────────────

Neskowin Beach GC
#1 Hawk Ave., P.O. Box
839, 97149
Ph: 503-392-3377

Yards: 2616, Holes: 9
Par: 35, USGA: 65.3
RP: Recommended

Restaurant/Bar/Proshop
GF: w/day $7.50
Carts: $8.00

*Very relaxing golf course as it is very flat but built on lush turf with two streams
wandering through most holes. Small but beautiful greens and many trees add to
difficulty. Number 7 hole will bring you back.*

─────────────────── NEWPORT ───────────────────

Agate Beach GC
4100 N Coast Hwy.,
97365
Ph: 503-265-7331

Yards: 3002, Holes: 9
Par: 36, USGA: 65.8

Restaurant/Bar/Proshop
GF: w/day $16.00
Carts: $16.00

*Beautiful, well-kept golf course, somewhat rolling but easy to walk. Enjoyable
and relaxing. Influenced by the breezes off the Pacific Ocean but always in great
shape with manicured greens which putt moderately and very true. Trees are a
major factor.*

─────────────────── PORTLAND ───────────────────

Eastmoreland GC
2425 SE Bybee Blvd.,
97202
Ph: 503-775-2900

Yards: 6508, Holes: 18
Par: 72, USGA: 69.8
RP: 6 days in advance

Restaurant/Bar/Proshop
GF: w/day $11.00, w/end
$13.00
Carts: $18.00

*A level course, very green and beautiful with many flowers around every hole.
Wide creek winds through a couple of times. #13 is a long par 5 with canyon to
go over.*

─────────────────── PORTLAND ───────────────────

Heron Lakes GC
P.O. Box 17375, 97208
Ph: 503-289-1818

Yards: 6579, Holes: 36
Par: 72, USGA: 71.4
RP: 6 days in advance

Restaurant/Bar/Proshop
GF: w/day $12.00, w/end
$14.00
Carts: $20.00

*Two 18-hole courses of championship caliber. One course has large, fast greens,
lots of water hazards and plenty of wind. The second course has three very
tough finishing holes. A couple of rounds of golf that you'll never forget.*

─────────────────── REDMOND ───────────────────

Juniper GC
139 S. E. Sisters Ave.,
97756
Ph: 503-548-3121

Yards: 6525, Holes: 18
Par: 72, USGA: 69.8
RP: Call for tee times

Restaurant/Bar/Proshop
GF: w/day $18.00
Carts: $15.00

*Course wanders through lava rocks and juniper trees to give one a true central
Oregon high desert experience. Small greens, four ponds, and difficult roughs
make for a fine challenge of golf.*

─────────────── SPRINGFIELD ───────────────

McKenzie River GC
41723 Madrone, 97478
Ph: 503-896-3454

Yards: 2800, Holes: 9
Par: 35, USGA: 64.8
RP: 1 week out

Bar/Proshop
GF: w/day $8.00
Carts: $8.00

Immaculately groomed course that is nestled right on the beautiful McKenzie River. Parts of five holes nudge right along the river. The par 3 uphill 9th at 137 yards requires accuracy as a huge maple guards the left, with a creek and steep bank in front.

─────────────── SUNRIVER ───────────────

Sunriver Lodge & Resort
P.O. Box 3609, 97707
Ph: 800-962-1769

Yards: 6880, Holes: 18
Par: 72, USGA: 70.2
RP: Guest - at
reservation

Restaurant/Bar/Proshop
GF: w/day $55.00, w/end $55.00
Carts: $28.00

The South Course offers wonderful views of Mt. Bachelor, particularly the 16th hole which is a 192 yard par-3 playing directly toward the mountain. Designed by Robert Trent Jones, II, the North Course offers golfers of any caliber fun and challenge.

─────────────── WALDPORT ───────────────

Crestview Hills GC
1680 Crestline Dr., 97394
Ph: 503-563-3020

Yards: 2800, Holes: 9
Par: 36

Restaurant/Proshop
GF: w/day $6.00
Carts: $6.00

This beautiful hilltop golf course offers rolling hills and the sound of the ocean. Due to our location of 1.5 miles from the ocean, you can enjoy a view of the ocean from the 8th fairway yet escape the wind and fog.

─────────────── WARM SPRINGS ───────────────

Kah-Nee-Ta Resort
P.O. Box K, 97761
Ph: 503-553-1112

Yards: 6288, Holes: 18
Par: 72, USGA: 69.7
RP: 2 week advance
notice

Restaurant/Proshop
GF: w/day $21.00
Carts: $20.00

Kah-Nee-Ta offers exciting adventures on a golf course, set upon an ancient natural Indian reservation. The golfer has a chance to test his or her skills by attempting to cross the Warm Springs River on the 17th hole.

─────────────── WELCHES ───────────────

The Resort at the Mountain
68010 E. Fairway Ave., 97067
Ph: 503-622-3151

Holes: 27
Par: 72, USGA: 70.0

Restaurant/Bar/Proshop
GF: w/day $22.00, w/end $25.00
Carts: $20.00

Rippling River Resort is located 60 miles east of Portland at the foot of Mt. Hood. We have 27 holes of golf that play through big fir trees and along the Salmon River. We're nestled in a big valley. The #8 hole West ranks as one of the most difficult.

─────────────── WILSONVILLE ───────────────

Charbonneau GC
32020 Charbonneau Dr., 97070
Ph: 503-694-1246

Yards: 2200, Holes: 27
Par: 31, USGA: 59.3

Restaurant/Bar/Proshop
GF: w/day $12.00, w/end $14.00
Carts: $15.00

This course is in the executive class, even though it has difficult par 3's, 150–250 yards scoring par 4's for the long hitters (good driving targets) a strong test for low handicap players (but high handicap players can play 18 holes in 3 hours).

PENNSYLVANIA

Tunkhannock •   Buck Hill •
Mount Pocono • Pocono Manor
White Haven • •
   E. Stroudsburg   • Bushkill
Shawnee-on-Delaware • / Delaware Water Gap
Elizabeth   • State College
•   • Champion   • Hershey
   Downington •
• Bedford   • Fairfield   Lancaster •
Millersville

BEDFORD

Bedford Springs Hotel GC
Rt 6, 15522
Ph: 814-623-6121

Yards: 7000, Holes: 18
Par: 74

Restaurant

7000 yards of golf course.

BENSALEM

Bensalem CC
2000 Brown Rd, 19020
Ph: 215-639-5556

Yards: 6200, Holes: 18
Par: 70

Restaurant/Bar
GF: w/day $25.00, w/end $30.00

Rolling narrow fairways with lots of trees will make this a tougher round than you expected. The greens are tricky and large.

BOLIVAR

Champion Lakes GC
RD 1, Box 285, 15923
Ph: 412-238-5440

Yards: 6205, Holes: 18
Par: 71
RP: Anytime in advance

Restaurant/Bar/Proshop
GF: w/day $17.00, w/end $23.00
Carts: $18.00

A course that will give your long irons a real test.

BUCK HILL

Buck Hill GC
PO Box 393, 18323
Ph: 717-595-7441

Yards: 6800, Holes: 27
Par: 71

Restaurant/Bar/Proshop
GF: w/day $27.00

The brooks and woodlands make this one of the most scenic courses imaginable. Postage-stamp greens, narrow fairways, seven holes with water coming into play, and each hole's personality demanding thought on the part of the player, makes for exciting golf.

BUSHKILL

Fernwood GC
PO Box 447, 18324
Ph: 717-588-6661

Yards: 6208, Holes: 18
Par: 72

Restaurant/Bar/Proshop
GF: w/day $20.00, w/end $25.00

On our 600 yard sixth hole, you'll need a cannon, but on the next twelve holes you'll need all your golfing finesse. Two lakes and many streams wind through the back nine holes. The tenth hole doglegs to the left; crosses Fawn Lake.

───────BUTLER───────

Conley Inn GC
740 Pittsburg Rd. - Rte.
8, 16001
Ph: 412-586-7711

Yards: 6200, Holes: 18
Par: 72, USGA: 69.5
RP: Tee times on
weekends

Restaurant/Proshop
GF: w/day $12.00, w/end
$15.00
Carts: $9.00

This course has a really tough 18th hole. There's plenty of water and rolling hills too.

───────BUTLER───────

Lake Vue North GC
691 Pittsburgh Rd., Rte
8, 16001
Ph: 412-586-7097

Yards: 6355, Holes: 18
Par: 72

Restaurant/Bar/Proshop
GF: w/day $28.00, w/end
$36.00

The front nine will make you think this course isn't so tough. But when you get to the back you'll find it much more rolling, and a couple of water holes are going to be tough too.

─────CAMBRIDGE SPRINGS─────

Riverside GC
RD 2, Box 281, 16403
Ph: 814-398-4692

Yards: 6113, Holes: 18
Par: 70, USGA: 69.3
RP: Call the Proshop

Restaurant/Bar/Proshop
GF: w/day $19.00, w/end
$23.00
Carts: $11.00

"A comfortable challenge" best describes this lush 18-hole course. Spacious dining & banquet facilities with picturesque views of the golf course for banquet, business meeting, dinner or luncheon. Our golf shop provides top sportswear and golf items.

───────CARLISLE───────

Mayapple Village GC
1 Mayapple Dr., 17013
Ph: 717-258-4088

Yards: 6650, Holes: 18
Par: 71

Restaurant/Bar
GF: w/day $20.00, w/end
$25.00

A rather lengthy and challenging course loaded with pot bunkers. There are a few elevated greens to add to the difficulty.

───────CHAMPION───────

**Seven Springs
Mountain Resort**
RD. 1, 15622
Ph: 814-352-7777

Yards: 6360, Holes: 18
Par: 71, USGA: 69.5
RP: Required

Restaurant/Bar/Proshop
GF: w/day $35.00, w/end
$36.00
Carts: $12.72

The course sits amid breathtaking scenery of the Laurel Highland Mountains of Western Pennsylvania. While the front nine offers the opportunity to score well, the back nine features rolling hills elevated tees and more yardage ... beware of #11.

───────CRESSON───────

Summit CC
Country Club Rd,
16630
Ph: 814-886-9985

Yards: 6349, Holes: 18
Par: 72

Bar
GF: w/day $15.00, w/end
$20.00

Large rolling greens are going to give your putting a lot of practice. A beautiful setting in the woods.

---------------------------------DAWSON---------------------------------

Linden Hall GR
RD 1, 15428
Ph: 412-529-7543

Yards: 6405, Holes: 18
Par: 72

GF: w/day $13.00, w/end
$16.00
Carts: $16.50

A little water, rolling fairways and lots of beautiful scenery.

-------------------------DELAWARE WATER GAP-------------------------

Water Gap CC
Mountain Rd., P.O.
Box 188, 18327
Ph: 717-476-0200

Yards: 6186, Holes: 18
Par: 72, USGA: 68.7
RP: 5 days in advance

Restaurant/Bar/Proshop
GF: w/day $16.00, w/end
$24.00
Carts: $32.00

The championship layout offers a rare challenge to the golfer ... capitalizing on the natural features of some of the Pocono's most picturesque terrain to present a truly challenging course.

---------------------------------DOWNINGTON---------------------------------

Downingtown CC
Rt 30 Drawer J, 19335
Ph: 215-269-2000

Yards: 6585, Holes: 18
Par: 72, USGA: 69.6

Restaurant/Bar/Proshop
GF: w/day $15.00, w/end
$29.50

You can really let 'er fly on #11, 425 yards, but be careful of the bunkers to the right of the fairway and guarding the green, not to mention the out of bounds at the rear of the green.

---------------------------------DRUMS---------------------------------

**Edgewood in the
Pines GC**
Edgewood Rd, 18222
Ph: 717-788-1101

Yards: 6218, Holes: 18
Par: 72

Restaurant/Bar
GF: w/day $19.00, w/end
$23.00

Set in the Pocono Mountains, Edgewood has water in play on more than half the course, and the greens are well bunkered.

---------------------------EAST STROUDSBURG---------------------------

Skytop GC
RTE 390, 18357
Ph: 717-595-7401

Yards: 6220, Holes: 18
USGA: 69.1

Restaurant/Bar
GF: w/day $20.00
Carts: $20.00

The course is relatively flat, water in play on two hole, and the greens are small. #18 has narrow landing area, with water coming in play before an elevated green.

---------------------------------ELIZABETH---------------------------------

Butler's GC
800 Rock Run Rd.,
15037
Ph: 412-751-9121

Yards: 6398, Holes: 27
Par: 72, USGA: 69.2
RP: Required

Restaurant/Bar/Proshop
GF: w/day $17.50, w/end
$23.00
Carts: $10.00

Butler's is one of the oldest public courses in western Pennsylvania. It is challenging yet still fun to play. Probably the most scenic hole is #13. From its elevated tee there is an outstanding view of the Youghiogheny River and valley.

Please mention "Golf Courses—The Complete Guide" when you reserve your tee time. Our goal is to provide as complete a listing of golf courses open to the public as possible. If you know of a course we don't list, please send us the name and address on the form at the back of this guide.

─────────────────── FAIRFIELD ───────────────────

Carrol Valley GC
Rt 116, Sanders Rd.,
P.O. Box T, 17320
Ph: 717-642-8211

Yards: 6425, Holes: 36
Par: 71, USGA: 70.4
RP: Mandatory, 7 days
in advance

Restaurant/Bar/Proshop
GF: w/day $15.00, w/end
$19.00
Carts: $19.00

*Eight holes have water hazards to cross which can cause extreme trouble.
Number 4 is a par 5 measuring 580 yards. The area is very scenic with mountain
ranges surrounding the golf course. The back nine is the more demanding to
shoot par due to a par 3.*

─────────────────── HARRISBURG ───────────────────

Blue Mountain GC
511 Lakewood Dr,
17112
Ph: 717-599-5028

Yards: 6053, Holes: 18
Par: 71

Bar
GF: w/day $35.00

*Set in the mountains, this course has very narrow fairways with lots and lots of
trees. You'll have quite a round.*

─────────────────── HERSHEY ───────────────────

Hershey CC
1000 E. Derry Rd.,
17033
Ph: 717-533-2360

Yards: 6480, Holes: 36
Par: 73, USGA: 71.7
RP: Must be guest of
Hershey Hotel

Restaurant
GF: w/day $50.00
Carts: $13.50

*Play a game of golf on the historic West Course which dates back to 1930, for
years listed as one of America's top 100 courses, or the new East Course which is
dotted with three man-made lakes and 100 traps.*

─────────────────── HERSHEY ───────────────────

Hershey Parkview
600 West Derry Rd.,
17033
Ph: 717-534-3450

Yards: 6146, Holes: 18
Par: 71, USGA: 68.6
RP: Times taken on
weekends

Restaurant/Bar/Proshop
GF: w/day $12.50, w/end
$16.00
Carts: $9.50

*There are only 2 parallel holes here and 1/2 elevated tees. Course is pretty hilly
with lots of obstacles and hazards: meandering creek runs through. There are
many blind shots and the fairways are narrow and lined with dogwood, oak and
pines.*

─────────────────── HIDDEN VALLEY ───────────────────

Hidden Valley GC
One Craighead Drive,
15502
Ph: 800-458-0175

Yards: 6071, Holes: 18
Par: 72, USGA: 69.0

GF: w/day $42.00, w/end
$52.00

*Highly ranked by Golf Digest, this course is set in the mountains and plays very
hilly. The layout is heavily forested. A course that most golfers can score well on.*

─────────────────── LANCASTER ───────────────────

Lancaster GC
2300 Lincoln Hwy E,
17601
Ph: 717-299-5500

Yards: 6604, Holes: 27
Par: 70

Restaurant/Bar
GF: w/day $40.00

*Three 9-hole courses. One is a beginners course. The other two will be quite
challenging with lots of trees, water, rolling greens, and some narrow fairways.*

LANCASTER

Sheraton Host Golf Resort
2300 Lincoln Hwy. E., 17602
Ph: 717-397-7756

Yards: 6859, Holes: 27
Par: 72

Restaurant/Bar/Proshop
GF: w/day $28.00, w/end $28.00
Carts: $23.00

Gently rolling slopes with water holes surrounded by weeping willow trees. The course's most famous aspects are the challenging water holes with mature willow trees and surrounding rolling countryside.

LEWISBURG

Bucknell University GC
Smoketown Rd, RD 2, 17837
Ph: 717-523-8193

Yards: 6268, Holes: 18
Par: 70

Restaurant/Bar
GF: w/day $17.00, w/end $22.00

A course set in a heavily treed area, with lots of rolling hills. A nice round of golf.

MIDWAY

Quicksilver GC
Rt 980, PO Box 5895, 15060
Ph: 412-796-1811

Yards: 6411, Holes: 18
Par: 72, USGA: 71.5
RP: 5 days in advance

Restaurant/Bar/Proshop
GF: w/day $40.00
Carts: $10.00

The rough areas are cut at different lengths here, so it can be difficult to judge them correctly. A very scenic course that offers many memorable and challenging holes.

MIFFLINVILLE

Arnolds GC
18631
Ph: 717-752-7022

Yards: 5134, Holes: 18
Par: 70

Proshop

Lots of water and trees will put your irons to the test on this short course.

MILLERSVILLE

Crossgate CC
17551
Ph: 717-872-7415

Yards: 6200, Holes: 18
Par: 70

Restaurant/Bar/Proshop

The course is under development with a residential community. When completed, there will be 6 holes along the creek. The 11th. tee is perched to make you hope you've held up so you can enjoy the view. This course will ensure that you will use every club.

MOUNT POCONO

Mt.Airy/Pocono Garden
18344
Ph: 717-839-8811

Yards: 7200, Holes: 18
Par: 72

Restaurant/Bar/Proshop
GF: w/day $30.00, w/end $45.00

The name of the golf course is "18 Best". The original design came from Sports Illustrated's 18 best holes some years ago. Water comes into play on 10 holes and there are 95 sandtraps to keep the game interesting. The high handicapper can score decently.

─────────────── PHILADELPHIA ───────────────

Cobbs Creek GC
72nd St & Lansdowne
Ave., 19131
Ph: 215-877-8707

Yards: 6130, Holes: 27
Par: 70
RP: Required weekends
& holidays

Restaurant/Proshop
GF: w/day $6.00, w/end
$8.00

Two 18-hole layouts. On one the small greens may give you some tough moments. The other is longer and has a bit of water.

─────────────── POCONO MANOR ───────────────

Pocono Manor GC
PO 7 Manor Rd., 18349
Ph: 717-839-7111

Yards: 6675, Holes: 36
Par: 72, USGA: 71.0

Restaurant/Bar/Proshop
GF: w/day $28.00, w/end
$35.00

With two championship courses to conquer, you can spend a day playing golf and never play the same hole twice. The West Course has plenty of length and if you're a long hitter you can really cut loose.

─────────────── RUSSELL ───────────────

Blueberry Hill GC
RD 1, Box 1740, 16345
Ph: 814-757-8620

Yards: 6428, Holes: 18
Par: 72

Restaurant/Bar
GF: w/day $14.00

A peaceful setting with tight rolling fairways with lots of trees.

─────────────── SHAWNEE-ON-DELAWARE ───────────────

Shawnee Inn CC
18356
Ph: 717-421-1500

Yards: 6636, Holes: 27
Par: 72, USGA: 72.4
RP: 7 days in advance

Restaurant/Bar
GF: w/day $20.00, w/end
$40.00
Carts: $15.00

#7 of the blue nine is a 152 yard par 3 stretch—you tee off from the island to a green across the river. As you try to stay clear of the water and bunkers, bear in mind that it was here that many avid golfers chipped & probably prayed to carry the same.

─────────────── STATE COLLEGE ───────────────

Toftrees Lodge GC
1 Country Club Ln.,
16803
Ph: 814-238-7600

Yards: 7018, Holes: 18
Par: 72, USGA: 71.6

Restaurant
GF: w/day $48.00, w/end
$54.00
Carts: $Included

Enjoy pampered greens and perfectly manicured bent-grass fairways that gently weave through magnificently wooded hillsides. The course stretches a challenging 7,018 yards from back tees. Site of the annual Pennsylvania PGA Golf Tournament.

─────────────── TAMIMENT ───────────────

Tamiment GC
18371
Ph: 717-588-6652

Yards: 6599, Holes: 18
Par: 72, USGA: 71.4

Restaurant/Bar/Proshop

A Robert Trent Jones, Sr. design that has some breathtaking scenery. A nice, enjoyable round of golf that offers a pleasant walk if you have the time.

─────────────── TOBYHANNA ───────────────

Pocono Farms GC
7000 Lake Rd, 18466
Ph: 717-894-8441

Yards: 6219, Holes: 18
Par: 72

Restaurant/Bar/Proshop
GF: w/day $20.00, w/end
$25.00

Very fast greens and only a part of the difficulties here. Lots of sidehill lies, narrow fairways and towering trees.

RHODE ISLAND

---CRANSTON---

Cranston CC	Yards: 6710, Holes: 18	Restaurant/Bar/Proshop
69 Burlingame Rd.,	Par: 72, USGA: 71.4	**GF:** w/day $14.00, w/end
02921	RP: Recommended	$17.50
Ph: 401-826-1683		**Carts:** $18.00

*Each hole is challenging in a different way. You will use every club in your bag.
The greens are large and kept in excellent condition. The country location is
home to many kinds of wildlife and wildflowers. It is really beautiful.*

---DAVISVILLE---

North Kingstown	Yards: 3196, Holes: 18	Restaurant/Bar/Proshop
Muni GC	Par: 70, USGA: 67.4	**GF:** w/day $12.00, w/end
Bldg. D.S. 69, 02854	RP: First come, first	$15.00
Ph: 401-294-4051	served	**Carts:** $16.00

*This scenic former military course is fun to play. The course is not long, includes
5 par 3s, but is a good test of golf. The ever present wind and the tough back
nine down by Narragansett Bay make this course one of the most scenic public
courses.*

---EXETER---

Exeter CC	Yards: 6390, Holes: 18	Restaurant/Bar
Victory Highway,	Par: 72	**GF:** w/day $11.00, w/end
02822		$14.00
Ph: 401-295-1178		

A very challenging course that will test your driver on all the holes.

---HARMONY---

Melody Hill CC	Yards: 6185, Holes: 18	Restaurant/Bar/Proshop
PO Box 369/Melody	Par: 71, USGA: 69.0	**GF:** w/day $11.00, w/end
Hill Rd., 02829		$14.00
Ph: 401-949-9851		**Carts:** $9.00

*Course is laid out for the average golfer. You cannot take out your driver on all
of the long holes. A placement course. Back 9 all doglegs but 2 short holes.*

————————————HOPE VALLEY————————————

Richmond CC   Yards: 6724, Holes: 18
Sandy Pond Rd., 02832   Par: 71
Ph: 401-364-9200

Lots and lots of magnificent trees. A beautiful course that you won't want to miss.

————————————JAMESTOWN————————————

Jamestown CC   Yards: 2999, Holes: 9   GF: w/day $7.00, w/end
245 Conanicus Dr,   Par: 36 $8.00
02835
Ph: 401-423-9930

This course is over a hundred years old.

————————————NORTH KINGSTOWN————————————

Rolling Greens   Yards: 3069, Holes: 9   GF: w/day $5.50, w/end
1625 Ten Rod Rd.,   Par: 36 $6.50
02852
Ph: 401-294-9859

Just one set of tees, and you're still going to be challenged. The course is tight and very hilly.

————————————PORTSMOUTH————————————

Green Valley CC   Yards: 6674, Holes: 18   Restaurant/Bar
371 Union St., 02871   Par: 71   **GF:** w/day $12.00, w/end
Ph: 401-849-2162 $16.00

Green Valley has tight fairways that demand your best shot making abilities. The course is considered one of the most difficult in the state.

————————————PROVIDENCE————————————

Triggs Memorial GC Yards: 6619, Holes: 18   GF: w/day $11.00, w/end
1533 Chalkstone Ave., Par: 72 $14.00
02908   RP: Recommend   **Carts:** $16.00
Ph: 401-272-GOLF   weekend reservations

95 bunkers.

————————————WARWICK————————————

Goddard Memorial   Yards: 3021, Holes: 9   GF: w/day $2.50, w/end
State Park GC   Par: 36 $3.00
Ives Rd., 02818
Ph: 401-884-9834

No reservations are required here, so just come on out. A nice course to walk.

————————————WESTERLY————————————

Pond View CC   Yards: 3162, Holes: 9   GF: w/day $6.00, w/end
265 Shore Rd, 02891   Par: 36 $9.00
Ph: 401-322-7870

This one starts out easy and gets harder and harder as it goes along. A very scenic layout set along its own pond.

————————————WYOMING————————————

Meadow Brook GC   Yards: 6075, Holes: 18   Proshop
Rte. 138, 02898   Par: 71   **GF:** w/day $12.00, w/end
Ph: 401-539-8491 $15.00
                             Carts: $15.00

Most of the course winds through large white pine and oak woods. The 18th hole is a 140 yard par 3 over a pond and the small green has sand traps on either side. A well placed tee shot makes this an easy hole but it causes many to have a lot of trouble.

SOUTH CAROLINA

Gramling
Fountain Inn
Easley
Hartsville
Aynor
Little River
McCormick
Saluda
Johnsonville
Columbia
No. Myrtle Beach
Myrtle Beach
St. Stephen
Pawleys Island
Georgetown
Mt. Pleasant
Isle of Palms
Charleston
Hilton Head Island
Edisto Island
Beaufort

───────────────── AYNOR ─────────────────

Rolling Hills GC
Hwy. 501 West, P.O.
Box 607, 29511
Ph: 800-633-2380

Yards: 6255, Holes: 18
Par: 72, USGA: 68.6
RP: Call toll free for tee
times

Restaurant/Bar/Proshop
GF: w/day $12.00
Carts: $8.00

The front 9 has an appearance of openness with many links type holes, while the back 9 holes are justly being recognized as 9 of the best holes in Holly County. Come play "OUR" Amen corner and our famed hole number 13.

───────────────── BAMBERG ─────────────────

Pawpaw CC
Old Charleston
August, 29003
Ph: 803-245-4171

Yards: 6723, Holes: 18
Par: 72, USGA: 72.2

Restaurant/Bar/Proshop
GF: w/day $16.00, w/end
$20.00

Golf Week considers this one of the most underrated golf courses in South Carolina. An enjoyable course for players of all skill levels.

───────────────── BEAUFORT ─────────────────

Golf Professional's Club
93 Francis Marion
Circle, 29902
Ph: 803-524-3635

Yards: 6700, Holes: 36
Par: 72, USGA: 71.4
RP: 1 day in advance

Restaurant/Bar/Proshop
GF: w/day $14.00, w/end
$14.00
Carts: $22.00

The course meanders through majestic oaks, peaceful lakes, saltwater lagoons, and placid marsh lands all filled with an abundance of wildlife. The huge lightning fast greens are well protected by 57 bunkers and make the course exciting.

───────────────── BISHOPVILLE ─────────────────

Bishopville CC
Hwy 15 S Box 362,
29010
Ph: 803-428-3675

Yards: 3400, Holes: 9
Par: 36, USGA: 72.0

Bar
GF: w/day $5.25, w/end
$7.50

With lots of water, bunkers, and 7 doglegs included with rolling fairways, you should really enjoy this course. Oh, we shouldn't forget to mention there are also lots and lots of trees.

───────────────── BLUFFTON ─────────────────

Old South GL
50 Buckingham
Plantation Dr, Ph: 803-
785-5353

Yards: 6354, Holes: 18
Par: 72

This course makes use of the natural lay of the land without disturbing it. Marshes, and heavy groves of trees are the main features.

─────────────── CALABASH ───────────────

Ocean Harbor GL   Yards: 6148, Holes: 18
10301 Sommersett Dr.,   Par: 72
Ph: 919-579-3588

The course was designed by Clyde Johnston and opened in 1989. The course is set in the Calabash River. You're sure to enjoy your round here.

─────────────── COLUMBIA ───────────────

Northwoods GC   Yards: 6800, Holes: 18   Restaurant/Bar/Proshop
201 Powell Rd., 29203   Par: 72, USGA: 70.4   **GF:** w/day $19.25, w/end
Ph: 803-786-9242   RP: One week ahead $23.50
                                                        Carts: $10.50

Our favorite hole is the 14th, a short 313 yard par 4 that plays along a large lake. The hole features the famous Dye railroad ties and a variety of tees, mounds, and bunkers. It's a gamblers delight, go for the green or play it smart and dry.

─────────────── COLUMBIA ───────────────

Oak Hills GC   Holes: 18
7629 Fairfield Rd.,
29203
Ph: 803-735-9830

The course is under development with a residential community. When completed, there will be six holes along the creek (river). The 11th tee is perched to make you hope you're held up so you can enjoy the view looking over southern Lancaster County.

─────────────── CONWAY ───────────────

Witch GC   Yards: 6011, Holes: 18   Bar
1900 Hwy 544, 29526   Par: 71, USGA: 68.3   **GF:** w/day $35.00
Ph: 803-448-1300

A golf course that is held together by bridges.

─────────────── EASLEY ───────────────

Rolling Green GC   Yards: 6102, Holes: 18   Restaurant/Proshop
Rt. 2 Box 449, 29640   Par: 72, USGA: 69.9   **GF:** w/day $10.00, w/end
Ph: 803-859-7716   RP: Weekends $12.00
                                                        Carts: $6.00

Rolling Green Golf Club is named after the large rolling, bent grass greens which challenge even the best putters.

─────────────── EDISTO ISLAND ───────────────

Fairfield's CC at   Yards: 6300, Holes: 18   Restaurant/Bar/Proshop
Edisto   Par: 71, USGA: 69.5   **GF:** w/day $29.00
1 King Cotton Rd., Box   RP: 24 hours in   **Carts:** $Included
27, 29438   advance
Ph: 803-869-2561

Our championship 18-hole course is fully equipped with 59 sand traps, water on 14 holes, and wildlife spectators (among them a resident alligator).

─────────────── FLORENCE ───────────────

Traces GC   Yards: 5566, Holes: 18
4322 West   Par: 72, USGA: 65.1
Southborough Rd.,
29501
Ph: 803-662-7775

A real championship layout with rolling terrain and large greens. Many beautiful mature trees.

─────────────FOUNTAIN INN─────────────

Carolina Springs
G&CC
1680 Scuffletown Rd.,
29644
Ph: 803-862-3551

Yards: 7036, Holes: 27
Par: 72
RP: Required

Restaurant/Bar/Proshop
GF: w/day $12.00, w/end
$17.00
Carts: $10.00

Carolina Springs is a semi-private 27 hole facility with bent grass greens, masi IV irrigation system, 5 sets of tees, driving range, fully stocked pro shop and snack bar. Hole #3 on the Cedars 9 is outstanding, closely resembling Augusta National.

───────────── FRIPP ISLAND─────────────

Ocean Point GC
250 Ocean Point Dr.,
29920
Ph: 803-838-2309

Yards: 6060, Holes: 18
Par: 72, USGA: 69.4
RP: Resort guests &
members

Restaurant/Bar
GF: w/day $13.00

With the Atlantic and many lagoons you're sure to see lots of water come into play. The course is flat, but has had mounds added to increase the challenge.

─────────────GEORGETOWN─────────────

Wedgefield
Plantation GC
100 Manor Dr., 29440
Ph: 803-546-8585

Yards: 7077, Holes: 18
Par: 72, USGA: 70.0
RP: Required

Restaurant/Bar/Proshop
GF: w/day $17.00
Carts: $12.00

Ranked the 15th best in S.C. and among the top 50 in the S.E. by "Golfweek". Set within natural vistas, massive 400 year old moss covered oaks and magnolias provide a suitable backdrop for "Gone With The Wind" and are part of the character and charm.

─────────────GRAMLING─────────────

Village Greens CC
P.O. Box 76, 29348
Ph: 803-472-2411

Yards: 6372, Holes: 18
Par: 72, USGA: 69.0
RP: Required weekends
& holidays

Proshop
GF: w/day $9.00, w/end
$12.00
Carts: $6.00

Lots of water problems as there are ten holes with water hazards. And added to this there are also 46 bunkers to contend with.

─────────────GREENWOOD─────────────

Stoney Point GC
709 Swingabout, 29646
Ph: 803-942-0900

Yards: 6175, Holes: 18
Par: 72

A Tom Jackson design, this course offers golf with every hole a different challenge all its own.

─────────────HARTSVILLE─────────────

Hartsville CC
116 Golf Course Rd.,
29550
Ph: 803-332-1441

Yards: 6200, Holes: 18
Par: 72

Restaurant/Bar/Proshop
GF: w/day $15.00
Carts: $7.35

Holes 5-7 represent our "Amen Corner." 3 of the 4 par 3s on the course are over 185 yards long, they are difficult. The greens are very difficult to read. The members of the club play the hole as it lies from June through September.

─────────────HILTON HEAD─────────────

Indigo Run GC   Yards: 6251, Holes: 18
100 Indigo Run Dr.,   Par: 72
29926
Ph: 803-689-2200

This is a very challenging course. The design was by Jack Nicklaus Golf Services, so you know it's going to be a good course.

───────────── HILTON HEAD ISLAND ─────────────

Harbour Town GL   Yards: 5824, Holes: 18   Restaurant/Bar/Proshop
11 Lighthouse Ln., P.O.   Par: 71, USGA: 70.0   **GF:** w/day $65.00
Box 7000, 29938   RP: Sea Pines guest 90   **Carts:** $11.00
Ph: 803-671-2446   days, 14 day

The legendary Harbour Town Golf Links, one of the top 25 courses in America is home of the MCI Heritage Classic. In 1989, Harbour Town will host the Nabisco Championships, the richest event in the history of the PGA.

───────────── HILTON HEAD ISLAND ─────────────

Hilton Head   Yards: 6260, Holes: 18   Restaurant/Bar
National GC   Par: 72, USGA: 69.9   **GF:** w/day $42.00
P.O. Box 5597, 29910
Ph: 803-842-5900

A course that offers a gentle challenge, and is one of the most popular layouts on the island. The trees are thick and there are mounds and lots of tall grass. A typical Gary Player design.

───────────── HILTON HEAD ISLAND ─────────────

Palmetto Dunes   Yards: 6122, Holes: 18   Restaurant/Bar
P.O. Box 5606, 29938   Par: 72, USGA: 69.3   **GF:** w/day $67.00
Ph: 803-785-1138   RP: 2 months in   **Carts:** $12.00
                           advance

The Robert Trent Jones's #10 is a long par 5, with green sitting on the Atlantic's edge. The George Fazio course's 16th hole features a few of the course's yawning fairways and greenside bunkers. The Arthur Hills course is characterized by palmettos.

───────────── HILTON HEAD ISLAND ─────────────

Palmetto Hall   Yards: 6257, Holes: 18
Plantation GC   Par: 72
108 Fort Howell Dr.,
29938
Ph: 803-689-4100

Lots of sand on hilly land, with some wetlands, to increase the difficulty.

───────────── HILTON HEAD ISLAND ─────────────

Port Royal Resort GC   Yards: 6009, Holes: 54   Restaurant/Bar
PO Box 7000/Coggins   Par: 72, USGA: 70.6   **GF:** w/day $62.55
Point, 29928
Ph: 800-277-5588

Three 18-hole courses are set here. They were designed by Williard Byrd and George Cobb. They are in a lagoon setting with magnificent oaks and magnolias. A truly beautiful setting with loads of challenge.

──────────────── HILTON HEAD ISLAND ────────────────

Shipyard GC
130 Shipyard Dr.,
29928
Ph: 803-785-2402

Yards: 3035, Holes: 9
Par: 36, USGA: 34.5
RP: 2 weeks in advance

Restaurant/Bar
GF: w/day $53.50
Carts: $Included

Shipyard Golf Club is the home of the Hilton Head Seniors International, and numerous Senior PGA events. It's a narrow 27 hole course with water hazards on 25 holes. You'll wander through tall pines, magnolias and moss-draped oaks, and over lagoons.

──────────────── HILTON HEAD ISLAND ────────────────

Westin Resort
135 S. Port Royal Dr.,
29928
Ph: 803-681-3671

Yards: 6038, Holes: 54
Par: 72, USGA: 68.7
RP: Recommended

Restaurant/Bar
GF: w/day $50.00
Carts: $29.60

Barony has small greens that are well protected by deep bunkers, lagoons and Bermuda rough that require accurate approach shots. Robber's Course is on the marsh side atop what was once Civil War Grounds. Planter's Row hosted the 1985 Hilton Head Seniors.

──────────────── HILTON HEAD PLANTATION ────────────────

Oyster Reef GC
High Bluff Rd., P.O.
Box 2419, 29926
Ph: 803-681-7717

Yards: 6961, Holes: 18
Par: 72, USGA: 70.0
RP: Taken for the
calender year

GF: w/day $20.00
Carts: $11.55

Set on Hilton Head, this course offers magnificent views of the other islands in the area. But you'd better try to pay attention to business as this is a very demanding course.

──────────────── HOLLYWOOD ────────────────

**Links at Stono Ferry
GC**
5365 Forest Oak Dr,
29449
Ph: 803-763-1817

Yards: 6085, Holes: 18
Par: 72

Restaurant/Bar
GF: w/day $15.00, w/end
$30.00

Lots of trees that guard the front nine. There's also water bordering some holes that's sure to come into play.

──────────────── IRMO ────────────────

Coldstream CC
PO Box 288, 29063
Ph: 803-781-0114

Yards: 5733, Holes: 18
Par: 71, USGA: 67.9

Hilly fairways and small greens make accuracy very important. A very popular course that is beautifully treed.

──────────────── ISLE OF PALMS ────────────────

Wild Dunes GC
5757 Palm Blvd., 29402
Ph: 803-886-6000

Yards: 6108, Holes: 18
Par: 72, USGA: 70.3
RP: Required-limited
public access

Proshop
GF: w/day $58.00
Carts: $12.00

Links Course—Finishing holes on the beach some of the best in the world. Harbor Course—beautiful, along the intercostal waterway.

────────────── JOHNS ISLAND ──────────────

Seabrook Island GC
1002 Landfall Way,
29455
Ph: 803-768-2529

Yards: 6832, Holes: 36
Par: 72, USGA: 73.2
Slope: 117

Restaurant/Bar
GF: w/day $65.00, w/end
$65.00
Carts: $Included

This resort has two regulation 18-hole courses. One course demands your accuracy more than the other, and wind can be a factor too. The other course has lots of water, is well bunkered and has very small greens.

────────────── JOHNSONVILLE ──────────────

Wellman Club GC
P.O. Drawer 188, 29555
Ph: 803-386-2521

Yards: 7028, Holes: 18
Par: 72, USGA: 70.2
RP: 2 days in advance

Restaurant/Bar/Proshop
GF: w/day $12.00
Carts: $8.50

The Wellman Club is set amid gentle rolling hills and in a relaxed country setting. Opened in 1967, it has quickly become one of the state's finest island golf courses. A lot of fun to play, but definitely not a pushover by any means.

────────────── KAIWAH ISLAND ──────────────

Kiawah Island GC
12 Kiawah Beach Dr.,
29412
Ph: 803-768-2121

Yards: 5968, Holes: 18
Par: 72, USGA: 68.8
Slope: 118
RP: Call for times

Restaurant/Bar
GF: w/day $94.00, w/end
$94.00
Carts: $Included

The Marsh Course has water on 13 holes and small greens. The Ocean was a best new resort course pick in 1991. The Osprey is a Fazio classic, and Turtle Point considered one of Nicklaus' best. How can you go wrong at this resort?

────────────── KINGSTREE ──────────────

Swamp Fox GC
Hwy 261, 29556
Ph: 803-382-3436

Yards: 6000, Holes: 18
Par: 72, USGA: 67.2

The fairways are narrow here and well tended with lots of trees and water.

────────────── LITTLE RIVER ──────────────

**River Hills Golf &
CC**
P.O. Box 1049, 29566
Ph: 803-249-8833

Yards: 6873, Holes: 18
Par: 72, USGA: 70.6
RP: Required

Restaurant/Bar/Proshop
GF: w/day $18.00
Carts: $11.00

18 hole championship, signature course designed by Tom Jackson. Non-parallel fairways, designed to challenge golfers at all levels of skill. Four sets of tees on each hole allow you to play according to your own ability. 13 character holes (beautiful).

────────────── LONGS ──────────────

**Buck Creek Golf
Plantation GC**
701 Buck's Trail, 29568
Ph: 803-249-5996

Yards: 6751, Holes: 27
Par: 72

Bar
GF: w/day $11.00, w/end
$13.00

Highly rated by Golf Digest, these three 9-hole courses are set in wetlands. Abundant bunkers, rolling greens and elevated tees, as well as plenty of water, will give your skills a real test.

———————————————LONGS———————————————

Long Bay Club GC
Hwy 9, PO Box 330,
29568
Ph: 803-399-2222

Yards: 7020, Holes: 18
Par: 72, USGA: 74.3
RP: Anytime

Restaurant/Bar/Proshop
GF: w/day $75.00
Carts: $Included

*Lots of bunkers on the fairways and around the greens, all well placed to give
the maximum difficulty. A rough course to score well because of all the hazards.
You'll have your work cut out for you on this course.*

———————————————LYDIA———————————————

Fox Creek GC
Hwy 15, PO Box 240,
29079
Ph: 803-332-0613

Yards: 6493, Holes: 18
Par: 72, USGA: 70.1

Restaurant
GF: w/day $8.00, w/end
$12.00

*The natural setting of this course is one of its strong points. You'll probably need
to bring your full set of clubs to do this one justice.*

———————————————MANNING———————————————

Clarendon G & CC
PO Box 322, 29102
Ph: 803-435-8752

Yards: 6624, Holes: 18
Par: 72, USGA: 71.3

Bar/Proshop
GF: w/day $7.35, w/end
$14.35

You need to be a real shot-maker to score well.

———————————————MANNING———————————————

Players GC
300 Players Course
Dr., 29102
Ph: 803-478-2500

Yards: 6069, Holes: 18
Par: 72

*A long, rolling layout of championship caliber. Featured are large greens, ma-
ture trees, water and mounds. You need to be on top of your game when you
play here.*

———————————————MARION———————————————

Dusty Hills CC
Country Club Rd, PO
Box 1001, 29571
Ph: 803-423-2721

Yards: 6120, Holes: 18
Par: 72

Bar/Proshop
GF: w/day $9.00, w/end
$11.00

*A very popular course for tournaments in the past, this course has small greens
and short holes, so your short game will definitely come into play.*

———————————————MAYESVILLE———————————————

**Pineland Plantation
GC**
Rt 1 Box 54-C, 29104
Ph: 803-495-3550

Yards: 7080, Holes: 18
Par: 72, USGA: 73.0

Restaurant/Bar/Proshop
GF: w/day $10.00, w/end
$12.00

Course has been featured in Golf Digest twice.

———————————————MCCORMICK———————————————

**Hickory Knob State
Park GC**
Route 1 Box 199-B,
29835
Ph: 803-443-2151

Yards: 6560, Holes: 18
Par: 72
RP: Required

Restaurant/Bar/Proshop
GF: w/day $10.00, w/end
$12.00
Carts: $8.00

*Our championship 18-hole course challenges even the experts with a 72.1 PGA
rating. The course is unique for its placement among woodlands, water, dogwoods and azaleas. A full-service pro shop and clubhouse adds the final touch
to your pleasant golfing.*

────────────── MOUNT PLEASANT ──────────────

Dunes West GC
3535 Wando
Plantation Way, 29464
Ph: 803-856-9000

Yards: 6871, Holes: 18
Par: 72, USGA: 70.7
RP: Call the Proshop

Restaurant/Bar/Proshop
GF: w/day $49.00, w/end
$59.00
Carts: $Included

A course with water coming into play on a third of the holes, it has rolling terrain and large tricky greens. The finishing hole here is a dogleg guarded by majestic oaks.

────────────── MT. PLEASANT ──────────────

Patriot's Point Links
P.O. Box 438, 29464
Ph: 803-881-0042

Yards: 6575, Holes: 18
Par: 72, USGA: 71.6
RP: Call for
reservations

Bar/Proshop
GF: w/day $17.00, w/end
$19.00
Carts: $9.50

Our course is located on the Charleston Harbor and it has a great view of ocean and coastal waters. 5 holes play along ocean water.

────────────── MURRELLS INLET ──────────────

Blackmoor GC
Hwy 707, 29576
Ph: 803-650-5555

Yards: 6217, Holes: 18
Par: 72, USGA: 69.3

A Gary Player designed course, the flora is very abundant. The back nine is the more difficult, and one hole on the front nine has two different paths to the green.

────────────── MURRELLS INLET ──────────────

Indigo Creek GC
9480 Hwy 17 Bypass,
29587
Ph: 803-650-0381

Yards: 6167, Holes: 18
Par: 72, USGA: 69.1

A nice course to walk, as the setting is lush and scenic, with lots of wildlife. Towering trees, and lots of water are going to be the main challenges here.

────────────── MYRTLE BEACH ──────────────

Arcadian Shores GC
701 Hilton Rd., 29577
Ph: 803-449-5217

Yards: 5974, Holes: 18
Par: 72, USGA: 68.8
RP: Up to 1 year ahead

Restaurant
GF: w/day $37.00
Carts: $11.00

Natural lakes weaving in and out of the fairways, sixty-four white sand bunkers, a variety of trees, and the salty breezes off the Atlantic offer plenty of challenge. When you make your reservation, you'll be able to choose from a slew of nearby courses.

────────────── MYRTLE BEACH ──────────────

Cane Patch Par 3 GC
72nd Ave. N. & Old
Kings Hwy., 29577
Ph: 803-449-6085

Yards: 2023, Holes: 27
Par: 81

Proshop
GF: w/day $7.00

Enjoy 27 holes of par 3 golf amidst the splendor of tall pines and oaks on rolling acreage situated just two blocks from the Atlantic Ocean. An abundance of flowering dogwood, azaleas, magnolias, and crape myrtles dot the landscape in spring.

--------------------MYRTLE BEACH--------------------

Deertrack GC	Yards: 6428, Holes: 18	Bar
P.O. Box 14430 Hwy 17	Par: 72, USGA: 70.7	**GF:** w/day $54.00, w/end
South, 29587	Slope: 121	$54.00
Ph: 803-650-2146	RP: A year in advance	**Carts:** $Included

The South course has very, very difficult greens. The North course gets the most play and both courses get more than their share of wind.

--------------------MYRTLE BEACH--------------------

Island Green CC	Yards: 3047, Holes: 27	Restaurant/Bar/Proshop
P.O. Box 14747, 29587	Par: 36, USGA: 66.3	
Ph: 803-650-2186		

Design of the course carefully utilizes the landscape with its rolling terrain, streams of spring water, native white dogwoods, wild flowers, and stately old oaks. A string of lakes are strewn throughout the ravines and are brought into play.

--------------------MYRTLE BEACH--------------------

Myrtle Beach Natl. GC	Yards: 6759, Holes: 54	Restaurant/Bar
Hwy. 501, P.O. Box	Par: 72	**GF:** w/day $28.00
1936, 29578		
Ph: 800-344-5590		

The greens are tricky, and there's water along a third of the course.

--------------------NORTH MYRTLE BEACH--------------------

Bay Tree Golf Plantation	Yards: 6363, Holes: 18	
Rt 2, Hwy 9, 29582	Par: 72, USGA: 70.0	
Ph: 800-845-6191		

Bay Tree has three 18-hole courses. The Gold Course is considered the most difficult, but you'll want to try them all.

--------------------NORTH MYRTLE BEACH--------------------

Heather Glen GL	Yards: 6325, Holes: 27	Restaurant/Bar/Proshop
P.O. Box 297, 29597	Par: 72, USGA: 70.0	**GF:** w/day $52.00
Ph: 803-249-9000	RP: Call anytime in advance	**Carts:** $14.00

Set among hundred year old evergreens, there are also a beautiful variety of other trees. 3 9-hole courses can be played in any combination. There are unusual bunkers, plenty of water hazards, and lots of dunes. A memorable day of golf.

--------------------NORTH MYRTLE BEACH--------------------

Legends Golf Complex	Yards: 6190, Holes: 54	Restaurant/Bar/Proshop
P.O. Box 65, 29597	Par: 71, USGA: 72.0	**GF:** w/day $75.00
Ph: 803-236-9318	RP: Up to one year in advance	**Carts:** $Included

The Legends offers three separate 18-hole courses.

--------------------NORTH MYRTLE BEACH--------------------

Marsh Harbour GL	Yards: 6695, Holes: 18	Restaurant/Bar/Proshop
P.O. Box 65, Sunset	Par: 70, USGA: 70.2	**GF:** w/day $25.00
Beach, 29597	RP: 9 months in advance	**Carts:** $12.00
Ph: 803-249-3449		

Surrounded by water and greens made out of oyster shells. A tight course with narrow fairways. #13 is "picture hole", short and challenging.

──────────────NORTH MYRTLE BEACH──────────────

Tidewater GC
4901 Little River Neck
Rd, 29582
Ph: 314-965-8787

Yards: 7020, Holes: 18
Par: 72, USGA: 73.7
RP: Up to 13 months in
advance

Bar/Proshop
GF: w/day $80.00
Carts: $Included

The greens are very large, and will provide a lot of practice in putting. With the wind and water on thirteen holes there will be more than enough here to challenge every level of golfer.

──────────────PAGELAND──────────────

White Plains
PO Box 508, 29728
Ph: 803-672-7200

Yards: 6596, Holes: 18
Par: 72, USGA: 69.4

Restaurant/Bar
GF: w/day $13.00, w/end
$20.00

A relaxed atmosphere with winding fairways. Seniors really love this course.

──────────────PAWLEYS ISLAND──────────────

Heritage Club
P.O. Box 1885, 29585
Ph: 803-237-3424

Yards: 6599, Holes: 18
Par: 71, USGA: 72.0
RP: Up to 1 year in
advance

Restaurant/Bar/Proshop
GF: w/day $55.00
Carts: $15.00

Many old and majestic trees grace this setting. There are large rolling greens, water on almost half the course, and plays every bit as long as the score card says it will. Heritage is rated by Golf Digest as one of the best public courses in the country.

──────────────PAWLEYS ISLAND──────────────

Litchfield CC
P.O. Box 320, 29585
Ph: 803-237-3411

Yards: 6320, Holes: 36
Par: 72, USGA: 69.9

Restaurant/Bar
GF: w/day $35.00

Litchfield Country Club and River Club are recognized as two of the Carolinas' top courses, with exquisite Southern Plantation surroundings, brilliant design, meticulous grooming, offers superb golf every season of the year.

──────────────PAWLEYS ISLAND──────────────

**Litchfield's
Willbrook
Plantation**
Hwy 17, PO Box 379,
29585
Ph: 803-237-4900

Yards: 6674, Holes: 18
Par: 72, USGA: 71.8
Slope: 125
RP: A year in advance

GF: w/day $47.00, w/end
$47.00
Carts: $16.00

Set on an old plantation, you can still see some of the ruins. The bunkers can be a big problem on this one. The resort offers swimming, tennis and a fitness center.

──────────────PAWLEYS ISLAND──────────────

Pawley's Plantation
PO Box 2070 Hwy 17 S,
29585
Ph: 803-237-1736

Yards: 6522, Holes: 18
Par: 72, USGA: 71.5
Slope: 127
RP: A year in advance

Restaurant/Bar
GF: w/day $63.00
Carts: $16.00

The fairways are often narrow, and the course will give you a real work-out. Not to be missed, one of the best in the south, this course was highly rated by Golf Digest.

---------------------------------PAWLEYS ISLAND---------------------------------

River Club   Yards: 6283, Holes: 18   Restaurant/Bar
P.O. Box 1885, 29585   Par: 72, USGA: 69.0   **GF:** w/day $35.00
Ph: 803-237-8755

*Set in a mature forested area, the large bunkers here are very well placed and
over half of the course has water in play. The greens are large enough to give
your putting some challenges.*

-------------------------------------SALUDA-------------------------------------

Persimmon Hill GC   Yards: 6405, Holes: 18   Restaurant/Bar/Proshop
Rt 3 Box 364, 29138   Par: 72, USGA: 70.2   **GF:** w/day $15.00
Ph: 803-275-3522   RP: Required weekends   **Carts:** $9.00
                        & holidays

*We advertise the largest greens & widest fairways on the eastern shore. We have
been in the resort business for over 20 years, so we know how to cater to your
golfing needs. If you break 70 you can play, but if you shoot 90 at home you can
shoot 90 here.*

-------------------------------------SANTEE-------------------------------------

Lake Marion GC   Yards: 6223, Holes: 18   Restaurant/Bar/Proshop
Santee Cooper Resort,   Par: 72, USGA: 69.8   **GF:** w/day $17.00
29142   **Carts:** $8.00
Ph: 803-854-2554

*Rolling fairways with lots of trees are the trademark of the championship
course. The greens are well tended and large.*

-------------------------------------SANTEE-------------------------------------

Santee National GC Yards: 6125, Holes: 18
P.O. Drawer 190, 29142 Par: 72, USGA: 68.7
Ph: 800-448-0152

*The grass is the thing on this course, with bent grass on the greens and Bermuda
fairways. A challenging course.*

-----------------------------------ST. MATTHEWS-----------------------------------

Calhoun CC   Yards: 6482, Holes: 18   Bar/Proshop
1 Box 36, PO Box 96,   Par: 71, USGA: 70.9   **GF:** w/day $7.00, w/end
29135 $12.00
Ph: 803-823-2465

*Extremely scenic course set in the rolling hills of South Carolina. Bermuda grass
is used throughout. The par 3 7th hole is considered to be most challenging.*

-----------------------------------ST. STEPHEN-----------------------------------

St. Stephen GC   Yards: 3198, Holes: 9   Restaurant/Proshop
River Rd., P.O. Box   Par: 36, USGA: 68.9   **GF:** w/day $4.00
1382, 29479   **Carts:** $4.00
Ph: 803-567-3263

*You can start by hitting some practice shots on a nice practice area, and then
take off for a fun but challenging nine holes carved out of a natural habitat,
consisting of water, sand and trees. Wildlife abounds here and lends to a good
golf challenge.*

─────────────SUMMERTON─────────────

Foxboro GC
Interstate 95, Exit 108,
29148
Ph: 803-478-7000

Yards: 6300, Holes: 18
Par: 72, USGA: 68.4

A very scenic course, water comes into play on all but one hole. Bring some extra balls or your game may be over sooner than you'd planned.

─────────────SUMTER─────────────

Beech Creek GC
1800 Sam Gillespie,
29153
Ph: 803-499-4653

Yards: 6805, Holes: 18
Par: 72, USGA: 71.8

GF: w/day $8.00, w/end
$12.00

Beautiful scenery and rolling fairways make this a wonderful golfing experience. The front 9 is open, while the back makes you watch your step. Four tees make this inviting to every level of golfer.

─────────────SUMTER─────────────

Crystal Lakes GC
1305 Clara Louise
Kellogg Dr, 29150
Ph: 803-775-1902

Yards: 5870, Holes: 9
Par: 72

A great course to practice your short game.

─────────────SUMTER─────────────

Lakewood Links GC
3600 Greenview Hwy
15 S, 29154
Ph: 803-481-5700

Yards: 6525, Holes: 18
Par: 72, USGA: 71.0

Restaurant/Bar
GF: w/day $16.00

Breathtaking scenery and water on over half the holes. Very difficult. Site of the 1991, 1992 and 1993 T. C. Jordan Professional Golf Tour.

─────────────SUMTER─────────────

Pocalla Springs GC
1700 Hwy. 15 S., 29150
Ph: 803-481-8322

Yards: 5442, Holes: 18
Par: 72, USGA: 65.4

Restaurant
GF: w/day $6.50, w/end
$8.00
Carts: $6.00

Lots of bunkers and trees. The course hosts Annual Pro-Am. Also featured in Golf Week '91.

─────────────TEGA CAY─────────────

Tega Cay CC
One Molokai Dr.,
29715
Ph: 803-548-2918

Yards: 6352, Holes: 18
Par: 72, USGA: 69.1
RP: 5 days in advance
for weekends

Restaurant/Bar/Proshop
GF: w/day $14.00, w/end
$18.00
Carts: $8.00

Rolling hills and valleys encompass the entire layout. Tega Cay requires premium accuracy but rewards good shot placement. Our favorite hole is the par four fifth. The long tee shot is not needed at this hole, but the second shot is most difficult.

─────────────WEST COLUMBIA─────────────

Charwood CC
4082 Bachman Rd.,
29169
Ph: 803-755-2000

Yards: 6314, Holes: 18
Par: 72

Proshop
GF: w/day $18.00, w/end
$22.00

A 27-holes layout. One 9 is tight and short, another is more of a challenge, and the third 9 is a bit of everything.

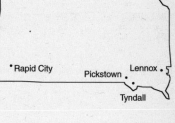

SOUTH DAKOTA

———LENNOX———

Lenkota CC
W. Hwy 44, 57064
Ph: 605-647-5335

Yards: 3113, Holes: 9
Par: 36, USGA: 33.2

Restaurant/Bar/Proshop
GF: w/day $6.00
Carts: $6.00

An open course with relatively few hazards and a creek which winds its way across four of the nine holes. Number nine offers the choice of threading it through the opening in the cottonwoods 80 yards away or blasting it over the top.

———PICKSTOWN———

Randall Hills CC
White Swan, 57367
Ph: 605-487-7884

Yards: 6550, Holes: 18
Par: 72, USGA: 67.9

Restaurant/Bar/Proshop
GF: w/day $6.00, w/end
$12.00
Carts: $10.00

The golf course is located just 1/2 mile from the Missouri River and the Fort Randall Dam and the beautiful Lake Francis Case. Both fishing and water sports abound both above and below the dam. There are lovely, modern camping sites.

———RAPID CITY———

Meadowbrook GC
3625 Jackson Blvd.,
57702
Ph: 605-394-4191

Yards: 7054, Holes: 18
Par: 72, USGA: 70.7
RP: One day in advance

Restaurant/Bar/Proshop
GF: w/day $15.40, w/end
$16.65
Carts: $15.90

Meadowbrook is a very challenging public golf course currently ranked in the top 50 in Golf Digest's America's Best Public Golf Courses.

———SIOUX FALLS———

Willow Run GC
RR 2 Box 211, 57104
Ph: 605-335-5900

Yards: 6510, Holes: 18
Par: 71, USGA: 69.2
RP: 1 week in advance

Bar/Proshop
GF: w/day $13.25, w/end
$15.50
Carts: $17.00

One of the best courses in South Dakota, with a creek that comes into play on almost every hole. Plenty of mature trees that will make accuracy an important aspect of your game.

---------------------------- TYNDALL ----------------------------

Bon Homme CC
Hwy 50, 57066
Ph: 605-589-3186

Yards: 2930, Holes: 9
Par: 36, USGA: 33.3

Restaurant/Bar/Proshop
GF: w/day $7.00, w/end
$8.00
Carts: $6.00

Course has a creek running through the entire course. It comes into play 8 of 9 holes.

---------------------------- YANKTON ----------------------------

Hillcrest G&CC
2206 Mulberry, 57078
Ph: 605-665-4621

Yards: 6530, Holes: 18
Par: 72, USGA: 70.6
RP: 1 week in advance

Restaurant/Bar/Proshop
GF: w/day $20.00, w/end
$20.00
Carts: $16.00

Beautifully manicured fairways and greens that are well guarded by strategically placed trees and bunkers. The third ranked course in the state of South Dakota. "If you can par the 8th or 17th hole, you can par any hole."

Enter your favorite resort in our "Golf Resort of The Year" contest (entry form is in the back of the book).

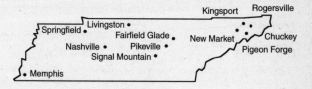

TENNESSEE

BUCHANAN

Paris Landing GC
RTE. 1, 38222
Ph: 901-644-1332

Yards: 6479, Holes: 18
Par: 72, USGA: 71.6
Slope: 124
RP: Weekends and
holidays

Restaurant
GF: w/day $16.00, w/end
$16.00
Carts: $18.0

Set on a lake, the course is heavily treed, hilly and has small greens.

CHATTANOOGA

Brainerd GC
5203 Old Mission Rd.,
37411
Ph: 615-855-2692

Yards: 6112, Holes: 18
Par: 72

Restaurant/Bar
GF: w/day $7.00, w/end
$9.00

*Brainerd features small greens set in a wooded area. One nine is rolling and the
other is flat.*

CHUCKEY

Graysburg Hills GC
Rt 1, Box 1415, 37641
Ph: 615-234-8061

Yards: 6341, Holes: 18
Par: 72, USGA: 70.4
RP: Required

Restaurant/Bar/Proshop
GF: w/day $13.00, w/end
$15.00
Carts: $8.00

*Nationally known course designer Rees Jones combined the site's beautiful
topography with strategic design to create a challenging, yet enjoyable, course
suited to all playing skills.*

CRAB ORCHARD

**Cumberland
Gardens Resort GC**
Mt. Laurel Pkwy, 37723
Ph: 615-484-5285

Yards: 6341, Holes: 18
Par: 72, USGA: 72.3
Slope: 128
RP: A year in advance

GF: w/day $30.00, w/end
$36.00
Carts: $Included

*Water, hilly terrain and trees are going to give you nightmares on this course.
Not a course you'll soon forget.*

CROSSVILLE

Thunder Hollow GC
815 Tennessee Ave,
38557
Ph: 615-484-9566

Yards: 6109, Holes: 18
Par: 72
Slope: 120

Restaurant/Bar
GF: w/day $22.00, w/end
$22.00
Carts: $8.00

*An island green, trees everywhere and much too much water to make it easy.
This one should offer some real challenges.*

─────────── FAIRFIELD GLADE ───────────

Fairfield Glade's
Dorchester GC
Westchester Dr., 38555
Ph: 615-484-3709

Yards: 5817, Holes: 18
Par: 72, USGA: 68.2
Slope: 119

Restaurant/Bar
GF: w/day $25.00, w/end
$25.00
Carts: $9.00

The course is in a quiet country setting, so some wild life may entertain you.
Bunkers can cause difficulties here, as well as the narrow fairways.

─────────── FAIRFIELD GLADE ───────────

Stonehenge GC
Peevine, P.O. Box
1500, 38555
Ph: 615-484-3731

Yards: 6549, Holes: 18
Par: 72, USGA: 71.8
Slope: 131
RP: Must be staying at
resort

Restaurant/Bar/Proshop
GF: w/day $50.00, w/end
$50.00
Carts: $Included

One of the top rated courses in the country. The course plays long, with a
stunning back nine. The greens are very fast and there are plenty of trees. The
course has been host to The Tennessee State Open for a number of years.

─────────── GATLINBURG ───────────

Bent Creek GR
3919 E. Parkway, 37738
Ph: 615-436-3947

Yards: 6182, Holes: 18
Par: 72, USGA: 70.3

Restaurant/Bar/Proshop
GF: w/day $28.00, w/end
$28.00
Carts: $13.00

Bent Creek Golf Resort is a Gary Player design located 15 min. from Gatlinburg.
The 18-hole par-72 course plays up to 6182 yards with lots of trees, water and
sand. Bent Creek offers a variety of accommodations with golf packages and a
restaurant.

─────────── GREENEVILLE ───────────

Andrew Johnson GC
Rt.2 Box 9A Lick
Hollow Rd., 37743
Ph: 615-636-1476

Yards: 6103, Holes: 18
Par: 70, USGA: 66.1
RP: Tee times
recommended

Restaurant/Bar/Proshop
GF: w/day $11.00, w/end
$13.00
Carts: $9.00

The opening 9 holes are picturesque and tough. The front and back nines are
different enough to be two different courses. My favorite hole is the thirteenth—
the last and toughest par 3 on the course.

─────────── JAMESTOWN ───────────

Big South Fork CC
Allardt-Tinchtown Rd.,
38504
Ph: 615-879-8197

Yards: 6587, Holes: 18
Par: 71
RP: 1 day in advance

Restaurant/Bar
GF: w/day $15.00, w/end
$15.00
Carts: $10.00

A very hilly course with canyons and difficult lies. There is a green here that is
so large you'll have to see it to believe it! A very scenic course with water on
over half the course, and yes, it does come into play.

─────────── KINGSPORT ───────────

Warriors Path St. Pk.
P.O. Box 5026, 37663
Ph: 615-323-4990

Yards: 6581, Holes: 18
Par: 72, USGA: 68.6
RP: Required weekends
& holidays

Bar/Proshop
GF: w/day $12.00
Carts: $14.00

Northeast Tennessee offers this scenic bluegrass course. Its rolling hills and well
trapped bent grass greens offer an interesting challenge. Especially enjoyable is
the downhill 5th, a short par 4 whose tee overlooks Patrick Henry Lake.

─────────────MEMPHIS─────────────

Audubon GC
4160 Park Ave., 38117
Ph: 901-683-6941

Yards: 6345, Holes: 18
Par: 70, USGA: 69.8
RP: 2 days in advance
for weekend

Restaurant/Proshop
GF: w/day $9.00
Carts: $14.00

*Locally referred to as Sawgrass North, our favorite hole is the 434 yard par 4
fourth. Trees lining the right and wasteland left demand an accurate tee shot.
Into the prevailing wind, a long iron second to a small green hidden behind a
giant oak.*

─────────────MEMPHIS─────────────

T.O. Fuller State Park
3269 Boxtown Rd.,
38109
Ph: 901-785-7260

Yards: 5986, Holes: 18
Par: 71
RP: Call for tee times

Restaurant/Proshop
GF: w/day $7.00, w/end
$12.00
Carts: $14.00

*The most difficult hole on the front is the number four hole, located on a plateau
with only a 5800 square foot green to reach on this 196 yard par three. If you
miss the green to either side you have to go back up hill with a blind shot.*

─────────────MILLINGTON─────────────

Orgill Park GC
9080 Bethuel Rd.,
38053
Ph: 901-872-3610

Yards: 6400, Holes: 18
Par: 71, USGA: 66.8
RP: 2 days in advance
for weekends

Restaurant/Proshop
GF: w/day $11.00
Carts: $7.50

*Rolling hills around 82 acre lake, listed in Golf Digest as public course to play in
Tennessee, best fairways in mid-south, Bermuda greens.*

─────────────MOUNTAIN CITY─────────────

Roan Valley
PO Box 1338, 37683
Ph: 615-727-7931

Yards: 6078, Holes: 18
Par: 72, USGA: 68.9

GF: w/day $30.00, w/end
$35.00
Carts: $Included

*A beautiful manicuring, this course which has views of the Blue Ridge Moun-
tains is spectacular. The holes each have a personality of their own, and will
offer a wide variety of challenges.*

─────────────NASHVILLE─────────────

Nashboro Village GC
2250 Murfreesboro
Rd., 37217
Ph: 615-367-2311

Yards: 6784, Holes: 18
Par: 72, USGA: 71.0
RP: Make in advance -
recommended

Restaurant/Bar/Proshop
GF: w/day $15.00
Carts: $8.00

*The ninth hole is particularly beautiful when viewed from the elevated tee with
a tight landing area. This 370 yard par four dogleg right has water hazards left
and right the entire length of the hole. A creek in front of the green and a water
hazard.*

─────────────NASHVILLE─────────────

Springhouse GC
18 Springhouse Rd.,
Ph: 615-871-7759

Yards: 6185, Holes: 18
Par: 72

*There are seven lakes in this property, some of them will make you take care so
you won't loose your shot.*

NEW MARKET

Lost Creek GC
Rt #3 Box 7, 37820
Ph: 615-475-9661

Yards: 5523, Holes: 18
Par: 71, USGA: 65.4

Restaurant/Bar/Proshop
GF: w/day $5.00, w/end
$7.00
Carts: $14.00

Front nine surrounds course—fairly rolling—heavily wooded, large bent grass greens. Back nine less rolling but can still cause trouble. Considered sporty course.

PIGEON FORGE

Gatlinburg CC
Dollywood Ln., P.O.
Box 1170, 37863
Ph: 615-453-3912

Yards: 6235, Holes: 18
Par: 72, USGA: 69.9

Restaurant/Bar/Proshop
GF: w/day $20.00
Carts: $24.00

The course, designed by William Langford, is set in a tranquil wooded setting surrounded by breathtaking panoramic views of nearby mountains. Gatlinburg's hole number 12, affectionately known as "Sky Hi," is one of the most dramatic in the country.

PIKEVILLE

Fall Creek Falls GC
St. Hwy. 30 RT. 3,
37367
Ph: 615-881-3706

Yards: 6706, Holes: 18
Par: 72, USGA: 70.8
RP: Recommended

Restaurant/Proshop
GF: w/day $12.00
Carts: $14.00

Level, narrow fairways lined with oak, hickory and pines. There are over 70 sand traps but no water to carry. #15 curves to left and is surrounded by trees.

ROGERSVILLE

Camelot GC
Rt 9 Box 376 Hwy 94,
37857
Ph: 615-272-7499

Yards: 6844, Holes: 18
Par: 73, USGA: 69.7
RP: Suggested

Restaurant/Proshop
GF: w/day $9.50
Carts: $7.00

Camelot Golf Course is nestled in a beautiful valley with a historical background. It was the home of Pressman's Union for 50 years. The front nine challenges the golfer in length par 37 3,640 yards while the back nine around mountainous terrain.

Our listings—supplied by the management—are as complete as possible. Many of the courses have more features than we list. Be sure to inquire when you book your tee time.

TEXAS

---ABILENE---

Maxwell Muni GC
1002 S. 32nd, 79602
Ph: 915-692-2737

Yards: 6125, Holes: 18
Par: 71

GF: w/day $8.08, w/end
$10.22

A very old course that is beautifully maintained. There are some difficulties here, but in the main a very playable course.

---ALEDO---

Lost Creek GC
4101 Lost Creek Blvd.,
76008
Ph: 817-244-3312

Yards: 6388, Holes: 18
Par: 71, USGA: 69.2
RP: Two days in
advance

Restaurant/Bar/Proshop
GF: w/day $15.00, w/end
$21.50
Carts: $18.00

The peaceful countryside atmosphere will test even the best of golfers. An accurate iron and wood play as well as good club selection is a must.

---ALPINE---

Alpine CC
Bos 985 Loop Rd.,
79831
Ph: 915-837-2752

Yards: 2960, Holes: 9
Par: 35, USGA: 66.4

GF: w/day $7.50, w/end
$10.00

A short course with small greens that will require all your short game abilities to get on. There's also lots of water and tree-lined fairways.

---ARLINGTON---

Lake Arlington Muni GC
P.O. Box 13215, 1516
Green Oaks, 76013
Ph: 817-451-6101

Yards: 6204, Holes: 18
Par: 71

GF: w/day $10.00, w/end
$12.00

Small greens and hundreds of trees that look like more, are going to be the main hazards here, as there is no sand.

─────────────────────AUSTIN─────────────────────

Barton Creek CC
8212 Barton Club Dr,
78735
Ph: 512-329-4001

Yards: 6956, Holes: 72
Par: 72, USGA: 72.2
RP: Must be a resort
guest

Restaurant/Bar/Proshop
GF: w/day $100.00, w/end
$120.00
Carts: $11.00

36-holes of championship golf onsite and another championship 18-holes near-by. The Fazio Course has been rated very high in popularity in Texas.

─────────────────────AUSTIN─────────────────────

Morris Williams GC
4305 Manor Rd., 78723
Ph: 512-926-1298

Yards: 6249, Holes: 18
Par: 72, USGA: 69.3
RP: 4 somes only - 1
day in advance

Restaurant/Bar/Proshop
GF: w/day $9.00
Carts: $14.00

A tree lined course that is rolling and has target greens. Site of two intercolle-giate tournaments sponsored by the University of Texas.

─────────────────────BOERNE─────────────────────

**Tapatio Springs
Resort & CC**
P.O. Box 550, 78006
Ph: 512-537-4197

Yards: 6472, Holes: 27
Par: 72, USGA: 67.6

Restaurant/Bar

10 of our holes offer water hazards on the 18-hole course and 5 holes of water on our 9-hole course. #2 is a par 4 with water along the left of fairway with a dogleg right before the green. Over shoot the green and you're in water.

─────────────────────BRIDGEPORT─────────────────────

Bay G&CC
400 Half Moon Way,
76026
Ph: 817-575-2228

Yards: 6291, Holes: 18
Par: 71

Restaurant/Bar
GF: w/day $22.00

Some of the fairways are very tight and have lots of trees guarding them. There are a couple of long holes that can give your some real problems with water.

─────────────────────CARROLLTON─────────────────────

Indian Creek GC
1650 Frankford Rd.,
75011
Ph: 214-492-3620

Yards: 7234, Holes: 18
Par: 72, USGA: 74.7
RP: 3 days in advance

Restaurant/Proshop
GF: w/day $12.00, w/end
$16.00
Carts: $14.00

The Creeks Course built in 1984, travels in and around the Trinity River and Indian Creek itself. Beautiful wooded fairways and Bermuda greens are mostly bunkered to create a very challenging and light course.

─────────────────────COMANCHE─────────────────────

Par Country GC
Rt. 1, P.O. Box 12,
76442
Ph: 817-879-2296

Yards: 6068, Holes: 18
Par: 72, USGA: 67.9

Restaurant/Bar/Proshop
GF: w/day $8.00, w/end
$15.00
Carts: $12.00

Located on Lake Procter.

─────────────────────COPPELL─────────────────────

Riverchase GC
700 Riverchase Dr.,
75019
Ph: 214-462-8281

Yards: 6041, Holes: 18
Par: 71, USGA: 68.4

Eight lakes and a river will certainly add some challenge to this layout Although the water doesn't come into play on most holes (or at least it shouldn't), it's always there. There are also elevated tees and lots of mounds.

─────────────────── CORPUS CHRISTI ───────────────────

Oso Beach Muni GC
P.O. Box 8335, 5600 S
Alameda, 78412
Ph: 512-991-5351

Yards: 6179, Holes: 18
Par: 70

Restaurant/Bar
GF: w/day $6.00, w/end
$7.25

*Water is going to be your main difficulty on this course. The fairways are wide
and forgiving.*

─────────────────── DFW AIRPORT ───────────────────

Hyatt Bear Creek GC
P.O. Box 619014, 75261
Ph: 214-615-6800

Yards: 6677, Holes: 36
Par: 72, USGA: 72.7

Restaurant/Bar
GF: w/day $32.00, w/end
$42.00
Carts: $11.00

*Two 18-hole golf courses, driving range and 2 putting greens. #5 East Course is a
picturesque par-4 that's not long, but requires 2 perfectly placed shots over water
to reach the bentgrass green.*

─────────────────── DALLAS ───────────────────

Tenison GC
3501 Samuel Blvd.,
75223
Ph: 214-670-1402

Yards: 6516, Holes: 36
Par: 71

GF: w/day $10.00, w/end
$12.00

*Two 18-hole courses. You'll know the caliber of the layout when you hear that
the 1968 US Public Links tournament was played here. There's a challenge for
every level of golfer here.*

─────────────────── EL PASO ───────────────────

Painted Dunes GC
12000 McCombs, Ph:
915-821-2122

Yards: 6479, Holes: 18
Par: 72

*A desert course with all the natural desert hazards. The well protected greens
are multi-leveled. This is a championship-caliber course.*

─────────────────── ENNIS ───────────────────

**Summit at Eagle's
View GC**
102 Crescent View,
75119
Ph: 214-875-9756

Yards: 6801, Holes: 18
Par: 72, USGA: 71.7
RP: Three days in
advance

Proshop
GF: w/day $10.00, w/end
$15.00
Carts: $16.00

*Native foliage, meandering creeks, and bent grass greens join to accent the
summit at Eagle's View. Combining six links style holes, an island par three and
a variety of contemporary golf holes, the Summit is without question a championship layout.*

─────────────────── FORT WORTH ───────────────────

Lost Creek GC
Box 26417, 4101 Lost
Creek Blvd, 76116
Ph: 817-244-3312

Yards: 6388, Holes: 18
Par: 71

Restaurant/Bar
GF: w/day $15.00, w/end
$21.50

*The fairways are heavily guarded by trees, and the course seems to have its own
creek all over the place.*

***Our listings—supplied by the management—are as complete as
possible. Many of the courses have more features than we list.
Be sure to inquire when you book your tee time.***

──────────── FORT WORTH ────────────

Marriott's GC at Fossil Creek
3401 Clubgate Dr., 76137
Ph: 817-847-1900

Yards: 6457, Holes: 18
Par: 72, USGA: 71.1

Restaurant/Bar
GF: w/day $36.00, w/end $45.00

An Arnold Palmer designed championship-caliber course. As if cliffs and ravines aren't enough, all but three holes have lakes and creeks to contend with and the greens are small.

──────────── FORT WORTH ────────────

Timber View GC
4508 E. Enon Rd., 76140
Ph: 817-478-3601

Yards: 6345, Holes: 18
Par: 71, USGA: 69.7
RP: Do not accept tee times at all

Proshop
GF: w/day $6.00, w/end $9.00
Carts: $14.00

The course is a relatively flat open layout, but with a generous supply of large trees strategically located particularly around several of the greens. A significant number of small ponds add up to a real challenge for any golfer.

──────────── FREEPORT ────────────

Freeport Muni GC
830 Slaughter Rd., 77541
Ph: 409-233-8311

Yards: 6437, Holes: 18
Par: 71

GF: w/day $6.50, w/end $9.00

Part of the course is set along a river, and you're going to get lots of practice with water shots.

──────────── FRISCO ────────────

Plantation Resort GC
P.O. Box 1696, 4701 Plantation Ln, 75034
Ph: 214-335-4653

Yards: 5945, Holes: 18
Par: 72

A course set in the midst of majestic oaks. Lots of water and some bunkers. A beautiful, natural setting.

──────────── GALVESTON ────────────

Pirates Galveston Muni GC
1700 Sydnor Ln., P.O. Box 778, 77551
Ph: 409-744-2366

Yards: 6739, Holes: 18
Par: 72

Restaurant/Bar

Water on every hole.

──────────── GARLAND ────────────

Firewheel Golf Park GC
P.O. Box 462074, 600 W Blackburn, 75046
Ph: 214-205-2795

Yards: 6255, Holes: 36
Par: 72

Restaurant/Bar
GF: w/day $15.00, w/end $20.00

Two 18-hole championship layouts. The Old Course is considered one of the best courses in Texas, it's very open and long. The Lake Course is shorter with lots of water, and has narrow fairways.

──────────── GRAND PRAIRIE ────────────

Grand Prairie Muni GC
3203 S.E. 14th St., 75051
Ph: 214-263-0661

Yards: 6478, Holes: 27
Par: 72

GF: w/day $11.00, w/end $13.00

3-sets of nine holes that can be played in different combinations. There's plenty of water and mesquite here, so beware.

─────────────── GRAND PRAIRIE ───────────────

Riverside GC
3000 Riverside Pkwy.,
75050
Ph: 817-640-7800

Yards: 7025, Holes: 18
Par: 72, USGA: 69.2
RP: 4 days in advance
for weekends

Proshop
GF: w/day $22.00, w/end
$32.00
Carts: $22.00

Rated in the top 20 public courses in Texas, Riverside offers golfers of all abilities a challenge on every hole. Our motto is "Just rip it."

─────────────── GRAPEVINE ───────────────

Grapevine Muni GC
3800 Fairway Dr.,
76051
Ph: 817-481-0421

Yards: 6369, Holes: 18
Par: 72, USGA: 69.5
RP: 3 days prior

GF: w/day $10.00, w/end
$12.00
Carts: $12.50

Lots of well-placed bunkers, plenty of trees, and a creek. There's water on most of the holes, a real challenge.

─────────────── HEMPSTEAD ───────────────

Fox Creek GC
Route 3, Box 128F,
77445
Ph: 409-826-2131

Yards: 5277, Holes: 18
Par: 70

Each nine has a very different personality. Rolled all in one, there's water and lots of trees. It's a very pleasant game of golf.

─────────────── HORSESHOE BAY ───────────────

Horseshoe Bay CC
Ranch Rd 2147, Box
7766, 78654
Ph: 512-598-2561

Yards: 6999, Holes: 54
Par: 72, USGA: 73.9
RP: 7 days in advance

Restaurant/Bar/Proshop
GF: w/day $90.00, w/end
$100.00
Carts: $20.00

Three 18-holes courses, all designed by Robert Trent Jones, Sr. over a 12-year period. What more can a serious golfer ask of a resort? The staff has 15 PGA professionals to give all the help with your game that you could possibly want. Terrific layout.

─────────────── HOUSTON ───────────────

Bear Creek Golf World
16001 Clay Rd., 77084
Ph: 713-859-8188

Yards: 7048, Holes: 54
Par: 72, USGA: 71.7
RP: 7 days in advance

Restaurant/Bar/Proshop
GF: w/day $27.00, w/end
$38.00
Carts: $22.00

The Masters course is rated in the top 50 public courses in the country and especially the 18th will prove why. No. 18 is among the top 5 finishing holes within country just behind Pebble Beach's #18.

─────────────── HOUSTON ───────────────

Clear Creek GC
3902 Fellows Rd.,
77047
Ph: 713-738-8000

Yards: 6110, Holes: 18
Par: 72

Restaurant/Bar
GF: w/day $10.00, w/end
$18.00

Water in play on some holes, not an easy course. There are sure to be plenty of surprises.

─────────────── HOUSTON ───────────────

Melrose GC
401 Canino Rd., 77076
Ph: 713-847-1214

Yards: 2187, Holes: 18
Par: 57, USGA: 59.2
RP: Weekends only

Proshop
GF: w/day $5.50, w/end
$6.50

Melrose is centrally located to both the downtown business center and intercontinental airport. We feature Houston's finest 18 hole par 3 golf course and practice facility, with nine holes completely lighted for play after dark. Rental clubs available.

---HOUSTON---

Pasadena Muni GC
1000 Duffer Ln., 77034
Ph: 713-481-0834

Yards: 6235, Holes: 18
Par: 72, USGA: 69.7
RP: Weekends

Proshop
GF: w/day $6.00, w/end
$8.75
Carts: $13.00

You start out on a relatively easy par 5. As you look out over the course you get the feeling that it is wide open. But as you find out on #1 water comes into play on all but one hole. And we never say anything about the wind, which always blows (hard).

---HUNTSVILLE---

Waterwood Natl. GC
Waterwood Box One,
77340
Ph: 509-891-5211

Yards: 6258, Holes: 18
Par: 71, USGA: 69.7
RP: Required

Restaurant/Bar
GF: w/day $25.00, w/end
$35.00
Carts: $9.00

You need to be in control of your game, because accuracy is the key to a good score at the end. The par-4s are going to be particularly difficult. With a slope rating of 142, this is a very difficult and challenging course.

---LA PORTE---

Bay Forest GC
201 Bay Forest Dr.,
77571
Ph: 713-471-4653

Yards: 6235, Holes: 18
Par: 72

Bay Forest has water on all but 2 holes.

---LANCASTER---

Lancaster's Country View GC
240 West Beltline Rd.,
75146
Ph: 214-227-0995

Yards: 6097, Holes: 18
Par: 71

Even though the large greens can be difficult, it's the water on most holes that's going to be the biggest challenge.

---LUBBOCK---

Elm Grove GC
3202 Milwaukee, 79407
Ph: 806-799-7801

Yards: 6390, Holes: 18
Par: 71

Bar
GF: w/day $7.00, w/end
$8.00

A course with heavy trees guarding the fairways, so be sure to keep it straight down the middle.

--- MCKINNEY---

Ranch CC
5901 Glen Oaks Dr.,
75070
Ph: 214-540-2200

Yards: 7087, Holes: 18
Par: 72, USGA: 73.8
RP: 3 days in advance

Restaurant/Bar/Proshop
GF: w/day $27.00, w/end
$40.00
Carts: $11.00

Sandtraps, grass bunkers, mounds, water on almost half the course, large, fast greens and a long course—there's going to be plenty to challenge you here.

---MONTGOMERY---

Del Lago Resort GC
500 La Costa Dr., 77356
Ph: 409-582-6100

Yards: 6825, Holes: 18
Par: 71, USGA: 69.1
RP: 1 week in advance

Restaurant/Bar/Proshop
GF: w/day $20.00, w/end
$25.00
Carts: $20.00

Most of the fairways are tree lined and the greens well bunkered. Water comes into play on 11 holes. Hole #9 requires a long and accurate tee shot. Your second shot will be with a long iron to a long narrow green that has water on left and 3 bunkers.

─────────────────MONTGOMERY─────────────────

Walden on Lake Conroe
14001 Walden Rd., 77356
Ph: 409-582-6441

Yards: 6146, Holes: 18
Par: 72
RP: 1 week in advance

Restaurant/Bar
GF: w/day $30.00
Carts: $20.00

Course winds through Texas timberland where everything seems to be bigger than life. #11 is a monster where double-digit scores are common—a double dogleg par 5 that winds its way up to a peninsula bordered by Lake Conroe.

─────────────────NACOGDOCHES─────────────────

Woodland Hills GC
319 Woodland Hills Dr., 75961
Ph: 409-564-2762

Yards: 6178, Holes: 18
Par: 72

Proshop
GF: w/day $12.00, w/end $14.00
Carts: $16.00

A course set in the hills, the fairways are not tree-lined, they're forested.

─────────────────NEW BRAUNFELS─────────────────

Landa Park Muni GC
Golf Course Dr, 78132
Ph: 512-625-3225

Yards: 6103, Holes: 18
Par: 72

GF: w/day $8.00, w/end $10.00

A flat course that has some difficulty, but is forgiving.

─────────────────ODESSA─────────────────

Ratliff Ranch GL
P.O. Box 12580, 7500 N Grandview, 79768
Ph: 915-368-4653

Yards: 6263, Holes: 18
Par: 72

GF: w/day $9.00, w/end $13.00

Moguls and grass bunkers are a trademark here. The greens are fast and tricky. This is considered one of the best courses in the country.

─────────────────PLANO─────────────────

Plano Muni GC
4501 E.14th, 75074
Ph: 214-423-5444

Yards: 6879, Holes: 18
Par: 72, USGA: 70.1
RP: required for weekends

Proshop
GF: w/day $10.00, w/end $12.00
Carts: $14.00

Plano Municipal is an enjoyable yet challenging golf course for all levels of golfers. From the 6900 yard blue tees to the 550 yard red tees, this pecan, tree lined course is scenic and fun. Our final three finishing holes are our trademark.

─────────────────POTTSBORO─────────────────

Tanglewood Texoma GC
P.O. Box 265, 75076
Ph: 214-786-2968

Yards: 7332, Holes: 18
Par: 72, USGA: 67.0

Restaurant/Bar
GF: w/day $17.50, w/end $22.50
Carts: $7.50

Relatively open with grass and sand bunkers, 3 water holes, bent grass greens. #18 is a dogleg right, par 5 with water two-thirds of the way down on right side. Good change in elevations from tee to green.

─────────────────RANCHO VIEJO─────────────────

Rancho Viejo CC
1 Rancho Viejo Dr., 78575
Ph: 800-531-7400

Yards: 6213, Holes: 18
USGA: 69.8
RP: Resort guests & members only

GF: w/day $25.00
Carts: $20.00

Typical of the beauty and challenge every golfer enjoys is the 224 yard par 3 16th of El Diablo. The 120 yard carry over water, out-of-bounds left and right and a large well bunkered green make an exciting addition to the golfer's round.

──────── RICHARDSON ────────

Sherrill Park Muni GC	Yards: 6511, Holes: 36	**GF:** w/day $10.00, w/end
2001 Lookout Dr., 75080	Par: 72	$12.00
Ph: 214-234-1416		

Two 18-hole courses. One course is quite long and is a very challenging layout that demands accuracy on your drives, and your short game.

──────── RICHMOND ────────

Old Orchard CC	Yards: 3226, Holes: 27
13134 FM 1464, P.O. Box 1950, 77469	Par: 36
Ph: 713-277-3300	

Three sets of 9-hole course, you can play them in whatever order you wish. There's plenty of challenge, something for any level of golfer.

──────── ROUND ROCK ────────

Forest Creek GC	Yards: 6405, Holes: 18
99 Twin Ridge Pkwy,	Par: 72
Ph: 512-388-2874	

A Dick Phelps designed course which opened in 1990. Doglegs and water makes this one of the championship-caliber courses in the state.

──────── SALADO ────────

Mill Creek GC	Yards: 6052, Holes: 18	Restaurant/Bar
Old Mill Rd., PO Box 67, 76571	Par: 71, USGA: 69.3	**GF:** w/day $28.00, w/end $38.00
Ph: 817-947-5141	RP: Can play if staying at resort	**Carts:** $17.00

If it isn't water, it's sand. Both things are going to be a problem here if your short game is not accurate, or if you choose the wrong club.

──────── SAN ANTONIO ────────

Cedar Creek GC	Yards: 6660, Holes: 18
8250 Vista Collina, 78255	Par: 72, USGA: 71.6
Ph: 210-695-5050	

A tree-lined course that is very scenic. You're sure to enjoy your round here.

──────── SAN ANTONIO ────────

Historic Brackenridge Park GC	Yards: 6400, Holes: 18	Restaurant/Proshop
2315 Ave. B, 78215	Par: 72, USGA: 67.0	**GF:** w/day $8.00, w/end $9.00
Ph: 512-226-5612	RP: 1 day notice in person	**Carts:** $8.75

Several world records are held here—Mike Souchek's 27 under par in 1955 Texas Open. The PGA Tour started here in 1922. Very old oak and pecan trees line the fairways. One is 93 feet tall. The famous San Antonio River runs through the entire course.

──────── SAN ANTONIO ────────

Pecan Valley	Yards: 7163, Holes: 18	Restaurant/Bar/Proshop
4700 Pecan Valley Dr., 78223	Par: 72, USGA: 71.0	**GF:** w/day $17.00, w/end $22.00
Ph: 512-333-9018	RP: Weekdays 1 week in advance	**Carts:** $18.00

All Bermuda grass and level course with many layup shots. Narrow fairways are lined with oaks and pecans. #18 par 5, carry 240 yards to clear creek. In 1968 P.G.A. Championship, Arnold Palmer missed 1st birdie putt.

──────────SAN ANTONIO──────────

Riverside Muni GC
203 McDonald, 78210
Ph: 210-533-8371

Yards: 6186, Holes: 27
Par: 72, USGA: 70.0

The back nine is a little easier here, what with all the lakes on the front. But water comes into play on both sides of the course.

──────────SPRING──────────

Cypresswood GC
21602 Cypresswood
Dr., 77373
Ph: 713-821-6300

Yards: 6906, Holes: 18
Par: 72, USGA: 69.2
RP: Required on
weekends & holiday

Restaurant/Bar/Proshop
GF: w/day $15.00
Carts: $17.00

Cypresswood Golf Club, Houston's finest 36 hole public golf facility, features rolling terrain, meandering creeks carved from a heavily wooded tract. Cypresswood employs PGA golf professionals to teach individuals by appointment on its 17 acre range.

──────────THE WOODLANDS──────────

**The Woodlands Inn
& CC**
2301 North Millbend
Rd., 77380
Ph: 713-367-1100

Yards: 6387, Holes: 54
Par: 72
RP: Resort guests have
priority

Restaurant/Bar/Proshop
GF: w/day $60.00
Carts: $Included

The highlight of the resort is the championship TPC Course, one of eight currently used in the United States, and open to the public. #17 is a stickler with a lake guarding the green. North Course is open for Inn guests.

──────────TOMBALL──────────

Treeline GC, Inc.
17505 N. Eldridge
Pkwy., 77375
Ph: 713-376-1542

Yards: 5400, Holes: 18
Par: 68, USGA: 66.1
RP: 7 days in advance

Restaurant/Bar/Proshop
GF: w/day $16.00, w/end
$20.00
Carts: $9.50

This golf course is well liked by all ages and calibers. Senior play is plentiful because of length and design. Seven par 3's make for a challenge for anyone's iron play. Located in the heavily populated area of North Houston. Piney woods and water.

──────────WINBERLEY──────────

Woodcreek Resort
1 Pro. Ln., 78676
Ph: 512-847-9700

Yards: 5973, Holes: 18
Par: 72, USGA: 68.8
RP: Recommended

Restaurant/Proshop
GF: w/day $16.00
Carts: $16.00

Located in Wimberley, heart of the Texas hill country, Woodcreek golf course twists and bends through this residential community. Driving accuracy off the tee is a premium where distance is lacking. Undulating greens test any golfers' shot-making skills.

◄◄◄◄◄◄◄◄◄◄●►►►►►►►►►►

UTAH

---------------------------------- AMERICAN FORK ----------------------------------

Tri City GC
1400 North 200 East,
84003
Ph: 801-756-3594

Yards: 6710, Holes: 18
Par: 72, USGA: 71.4
RP: Required

Narrow fairways make this course very challenging. The grounds are meticulously tended.

---------------------------------- BEAVER ----------------------------------

Canyon Breeze GC
East Canyon Rd.,
84713
Ph: 801-438-9601

Yards: 2847, Holes: 9
Par: 34, USGA: 65.2

One of the holes on this course runs through a horse racing track, but you won't have time to stop and make a bet.

---------------------------------- BLOOMINGTON ----------------------------------

Bloomington CC
3174 E Bloomington
Dr, Ph: 801-673-2029

Yards: 6948, Holes: 18
Par: 72

Great course for any time of the year. Terrific greens, considered one of Utah's best courses.

---------------------------------- BOUNTIFUL ----------------------------------

Bountiful City GC
2430 S. Bountiful
Blvd., 84010
Ph: 801-298-6040

Yards: 6461, Holes: 18
Par: 71, USGA: 67.3
RP: 1 day in advance

Restaurant/Proshop
GF: w/day $10.00
Carts: $14.00

Situated on Wasatch Front, the course provides a breathtaking mountain setting as well as a spectacular view of the Salt Lake valley. The course offers long rolling fairways as well as large undulating greens. The open front combined with the tight back.

---------------------------------- BRIGHAM CITY ----------------------------------

Eagle Mountain GC
700 S. 780 East, 84302
Ph: 801-723-3212

Yards: 6769, Holes: 18
Par: 71

Restaurant
GF: w/day $12.00

This is a fairly new course with a very challenging finishing hole.

─────────────────CEDAR CITY─────────────────

Cedar Ridge GC   Yards: 3225, Holes: 9   Proshop
1000 East 800 North,   Par: 36, USGA: 68.2
84720
Ph: 801-586-2970

A John Evans designed course.

─────────────────DELTA─────────────────

Sunset View GC   Yards: 3362, Holes: 9   Proshop
North Highway #6,   Par: 36, USGA: 68.2
84624
Ph: 801-864-2508

*This course is on the route to Great Basin National Park. Which makes it all the
more surprising that it has an unhurried atmosphere.*

─────────────────DUGWAY─────────────────

Dugway GC   Yards: 3314, Holes: 9
334 B Coyote Cove,   Par: 36, USGA: 69.4
84022
Ph: 801-831-2305

An interesting 9 hole course.

─────────────────EDEN─────────────────

Wolf Creek CC   Yards: 6459, Holes: 18   Restaurant/Proshop
3900 N. Wolf Creek Dr., Par: 72, USGA: 70.5
84310
Ph: 801-745-3365

*This course has many hazards to overcome, from bunkers to tight tree-lined
fairways.*

─────────────────FERRON─────────────────

Millsite GC   Yards: 2989, Holes: 9
84523   Par: 36
Ph: 801-384-2350

*Located in a state park, many other attractive activities are also available after
your game of golf.*

─────────────────FIELDING─────────────────

Belmont Springs   Yards: 6400, Holes: 18   **GF:** w/day $6.00
Park GC   Par: 72
Box 36, 84311
Ph: 801-458-3200

This is a very hilly course with quite a few long holes.

─────────────────FRUIT HEIGHTS─────────────────

Davis Park GC   Yards: 5929, Holes: 18
1074 E. Nichols Rd.,   Par: 71, USGA: 67.4
84037
Ph: 801-546-4154

Not very long, but very demanding. Fairways have lots of rolling terrain.

***Plan ahead! Reserve tee time well in advance, and while you're
doing so, confirm rates and services.***

————————————HELPER————————————

Carbon CC
Hwy 6 Price-Helper,
84526
Ph: 801-637-9949

Yards: 3167, Holes: 9
Par: 35, USGA: 69.3
RP: Required

Restaurant/Bar/Proshop

Set in a river bottom, this course runs along the Price river.

————————————HIGHLAND————————————

Alpine CC
P.O. Box 220, 84003
Ph: 801-322-3971

Yards: 6492, Holes: 18
Par: 72, USGA: 70.0

Well known for its greens, this is a challenging course with a very trying back 9.

————————————KANAB————————————

Coral Cliffs GC
700 East Highway 89,
84741
Ph: 801-644-5005

Yards: 3350, Holes: 9
Par: 36, USGA: 69.4
RP: 2 weeks in advance

Proshop
GF: w/day $6.00
Carts: $7.00

Unquestionably the prettiest course in the southern half of Utah. Play this undiscovered gem before they make it a state park. Watch the ball hang against towering red cliffs. So quiet you can hear your shots spin and land on the green.

————————————LAYTON————————————

Valley View GC
2501 East Gentile,
84040
Ph: 801-546-1630

Yards: 7110, Holes: 18
Par: 72, USGA: 69.2
RP: 1 day in advance

Restaurant/Bar/Proshop
GF: w/day $10.00
Carts: $14.00

Mountainous and hilly, unusual terrain with hillside overlooking many elevated tees. 10 ponds and 40 sandtraps. #12 is a par 3 elevated to green bordered by reservoir, bunkered on left side 166 from white tee.

————————————LOGAN————————————

Sherwood Hills GC
Sardine Canyon, US
Hwy 80 & 91, 84404
Ph: 801-245-6055

Yards: 3125, Holes: 9
Par: 36, USGA: 68.5
RP: Required

Restaurant/Proshop

A beautiful mountain course near Brigham City.

————————————MANTL————————————

**Palisade State Park
GC**
Palisade Park Rd.,
84642
Ph: 801-835-4653

Yards: 6068, Holes: 9
Par: 36, USGA: 66.9
RP: Required

Great greens, surrounded by wonderful scenery.

————————————MIDWAY————————————

Homestead GC
700 N. Homestead Dr.,
84049
Ph: 801-654-1901

Yards: 6250, Holes: 18
Par: 72

The course offers a panoramic view of the valley below. The area abounds with wildlife. A real championship layout.

─────────────────────MIDWAY─────────────────────

Wasatch Mountain   Yards: 6322, Holes: 27   Restaurant/Proshop
State Park GC   Par: 72, USGA: 69.2   **GF:** w/day $12.00
P.O. Box 138, 84049   RP: Recommended   **Carts:** $14.00
Ph: 801-654-1901

The entire course is in a beautiful mountain setting with abundant wildlife to
break up the monotony of your game. There are streams and lakes and some
rolling fairways which will tax your patience yet give you a definite feeling of
accomplishment.

─────────────────────MOAB─────────────────────

Moab GC   Yards: 5502, Holes: 18   Bar/Proshop
2705 S.E. Bench Rd.,   Par: 72, USGA: 67.0
84532
Ph: 801-259-6488

Located in the sandstone bluffs, this makes for an unusual course.

─────────────────────MONTICELLO─────────────────────

San Juan GC   Yards: 5404, Holes: 9   Proshop
549 South Main, 84535   Par: 70, USGA: 63.4   **GF:** w/day $5.00
Ph: 801-587-2468   **Carts:** $13.50

The course is located at the foot of the Blue Mountains. At 7,000 foot elevation
summer temperature average is about 85 degrees with cool evenings. RV park
across the street from the pro shop.

─────────────────────MORGAN─────────────────────

Round Valley GC   Yards: 3173, Holes: 9   Restaurant/Proshop
1875 E. Round Valley   Par: 36, USGA: 68.5
Dr., 84050   RP: Required
Ph: 801-829-3796

A course that is becoming more and more popular. Be sure to give us a try.

─────────────────────MT. CARMEL─────────────────────

Thunderbird GC   Yards: 2146, Holes: 9   Restaurant/Bar/Proshop
PO Box 36, 84755   Par: 34, USGA: 62.0
Ph: 801-648-2262

A challenging course with a beautiful mountain setting.

─────────────────────MURRAY─────────────────────

Fore Lakes GC   Yards: 3635, Holes: 18
1285 West 4700 South,   Par: 52, USGA: 59.1
84123
Ph: 801-266-8621

A 9 hole par 3 combined with an executive 9 hole course. Water comes into play
on many holes.

─────────────────────MURRAY─────────────────────

Mick Riley GC   Yards: 3100, Holes: 9
421 East Vine St., 84107 Par: 27, USGA: 67.4
Ph: 801-266-8185   RP: Required

Lots and lots of lakes make this par 3 interesting. The course has wide fairways.

——————————————MURRAY——————————————

Murray Parkway GC
6345 S. Riverside Dr.,
84123
Ph: 801-262-4653

Yards: 6369, Holes: 18
Par: 72, USGA: 69.2
RP: Call for tee times

Restaurant/Proshop
GF: w/day $12.00
Carts: $14.00

Nestled at the foot of the Wasatch Mountains Murray Parkway combines rolling fairways, streams and lakes, and over forty bunkers to provide golfers with a scenic and enjoyable test of golf. Score well on key holes throughout the course.

——————————————NEPHI——————————————

Canyon Hills Park GC
1200 E. 100 N, 84648
Ph: 801-623-9930

Yards: 3100, Holes: 9
Par: 36, USGA: 68.8

Proshop

A nice course to play, very relaxed and no rushing.

——————————————OGDEN——————————————

Ben Lomond GC
1600 North 500 West,
84404
Ph: 801-782-7754

Yards: 5778, Holes: 18
Par: 72, USGA: 65.6
RP: Required

The par 4 are short, but the par 3's are tough. Also enjoy the mountain in the background, very scenic.

——————————————OGDEN——————————————

El Monte GC
1300 Valley Dr., 84401
Ph: 801-399-8333

Yards: 2950, Holes: 9
Par: 35, USGA: 66.2
RP: Required

Rolling hills and old-style grass make this a very interesting course. Give it a try.

——————————————OGDEN——————————————

Golf City GC
1400 E. 5600 South,
84403
Ph: 801-479-3410

Yards: 1200, Holes: 9
Par: 28

Something for the whole family: lit for night range, mini-golf and baseball and softball cage use at night.

——————————————OGDEN——————————————

Hubbard Memorial GC-Military
Bldg. #720, Hill Air
Force Base, 84406
Ph: 801-777-3272

Yards: 6560, Holes: 18
Par: 72, USGA: 70.3
RP: Required

GF: w/day $12.00
Carts: $14.00

We have the longest greens in the state. This course gives the long hitter some room.

——————————————OGDEN——————————————

Mt. Ogden GC
3000 Taylor Ave.,
84403
Ph: 801-399-8700

Yards: 5850, Holes: 18
Par: 71, USGA: 67.5
RP: Required

This course lies on the side of a mountain and has really tough greens. Definitely a challenge.

OGDEN

Mulligans GC
1690 W 400 N, 84404
Ph: 801-392-4653

Yards: 1093, Holes: 9
Par: 27

Offers the best lit range in U.S.

OGDEN

Ogden G&CC
4197 Washington
Blvd., 84402
Ph: 801-745-0135

Yards: 6439, Holes: 18
Par: 73, USGA: 70.2
RP: Required

Proshop

Set in the center of the beautiful Weber Valley.

OGDEN

Schneiters Riverside GC
5460 So. Weber Dr.,
84405
Ph: 801-399-4636

Yards: 6225, Holes: 18
Par: 71, USGA: 66.5
RP: 1 day in advance

Restaurant/Proshop
GF: w/day $10.00, w/end
$12.00
Carts: $14.00

Beautiful 18 holes situated along the Weber River with a magnificent view of the Wasatch Mountain range. The front 9 framed by large cottonwoods and evergreens. The back 9 more open but water keeps your interest. #17 being the most exciting hole.

OREM

Cascade Fairways GC
1313 East 800 North,
84057
Ph: 801-226-6677

Yards: 4522, Holes: 9
Par: 35, USGA: 65.0
RP: Required

Restaurant/Proshop

A difficult course with an easy to reach location in the center of the city.

PARK CITY

Jeremy Ranch
8770 N. Jeremy Rd.,
84060
Ph: 801-531-9000

Yards: 7025, Holes: 18
Par: 72, USGA: 69.3
RP: Required

GF: w/day $39.00, w/end
$44.00
Carts: $Included

An Arnold Palmer designed course, it is home of the Senior PGA Tour Showdown Classic.

PARK CITY

Park City GC
Lower Park Ave., P.O.
Box 2067, 84060
Ph: 801-521-2135

Yards: 6800, Holes: 18
Par: 72, USGA: 69.7
RP: 7 days in advance

Restaurant/Bar/Proshop
GF: w/day $20.00
Carts: $8.00

We have water on 16 of our holes. Mountain streams and lakes make it exciting getting to the toughest greens in Utah. The course plays short at 7000 feet elevation, but is difficult to score.

PARK CITY

Park Meadows CC
2000 Meadows Dr.,
84060
Ph: 801-649-2460

Yards: 7338, Holes: 18
Par: 72, USGA: 70.6

GF: w/day $27.00
Carts: $Included

Lots of bunkers and water, a Jack Nicklaus design.

────────────── PARLEYS CANYON ──────────────

Mountain Dell GC   Yards: 6322, Holes: 18   Restaurant
E Canyon Exit, 84109   Par: 70   **GF:** w/day $10.00
Ph: 801-582-3812

18 new holes have been added, you should come and give them a try.

──────────────── PAYSON ────────────────

Gladstan GC   Yards: 5548, Holes: 18
#1 Gladstan Dr., 84651   Par: 70, USGA: 60.5
Ph: 800-634-3009

The front 9 has rolling terrain, and a mountainous back 9.

──────────────── PROVO ────────────────

East Bay GC   Yards: 6262, Holes: 27
1860 S. East Bay Blvd.,   Par: 71, USGA: 66.0
84601   RP: Required
Ph: 801-373-0111

Beautiful area with lakes and a fantastic view.

──────────────── RICHFIELD ────────────────

Cove View GC   Yards: 5976, Holes: 9
South Airport Rd.,   Par: 36, USGA: 68.2
84701
Ph: 801-896-9987

A long, well maintained 9 hole course.

──────────────── ROOSEVELT ────────────────

Roosevelt GC   Yards: 3531, Holes: 9
1155 Clubhouse Dr.,   Par: 36, USGA: 70.7
84066
Ph: 801-722-9644

Many hazards. This one will be a real challenge for any golfer.

──────────────── ROY ────────────────

Royal Greens GC   Yards: 3162, Holes: 9
5200 S. 2885 W., 84067   Par: 36, USGA: 68.5
Ph: 801-825-3467   RP: Required

Near Ogden, this is a beautifully kept course, definitely worth a visit.

──────────────── SALT LAKE CITY ────────────────

Rose Park GC   Yards: 6397, Holes: 18
1385 N. Redwood Rd.,   Par: 72, USGA: 67.7
84116   RP: Required
Ph: 801-596-5030

A flat course made more challenging by the including of several doglegs.

──────────────── SALT LAKE CITY ────────────────

Bonneville GC   Yards: 6553, Holes: 18
954 Connor St., 84108   Par: 72, USGA: 69.0
Ph: 801-596-5044   RP: Required

A scenic and hilly course. This one has a tough finish over a ravine with a creek.

———————————————SALT LAKE CITY———————————————

Forest Dale GC
2375 South 900 East,
84106
Ph: 801-483-5420

Yards: 2970, Holes: 9
Par: 36, USGA: 67.7
RP: Required

An historic course that has been redesigned. Many huge trees and plenty of water.

———————————————SALT LAKE CITY———————————————

Glendale GC
1630 W. 2100 South,
84119
Ph: 801-974-2403

Yards: 6470, Holes: 18
Par: 72, USGA: 69.3
RP: Required

A very popular Salt Lake City public course.

———————————————SALT LAKE CITY———————————————

Jordan River GC
1200 N. Redwood Rd.,
Ph: 801-533-4496

Yards: 1170, Holes: 9
Par: 27
RP: Required

Near the airport, this par 3 can help to while away the wait between flights.

———————————————SALT LAKE CITY———————————————

Meadowbrook GC
4197 S. 1300 W., 84123
Ph: 801-266-0971

Yards: 6125, Holes: 18
Par: 72, USGA: 67.0
RP: Required

Six ponds and the Jordan River should keep you hopping.

———————————————SALT LAKE CITY———————————————

Nibley Park GC
2780 S. 700 East, 84106
Ph: 801-483-5418

Yards: 2900, Holes: 9
Par: 34, USGA: 65.0

Hazards make this historic redesigned course a very difficult one indeed.

———————————————SALT LAKE CITY———————————————

**University of Utah
GC**
100 S. 1900 East, 84109
Ph: 801-581-6511

Yards: 2621, Holes: 9
Par: 34, USGA: 63.6

Former home of the Ft. Douglas Country Club.

———————————————SALT LAKE CITY———————————————

Wingpointe GC
1965 West 500 South,
84115
Ph: 801-972-7800

Yards: 7200, Holes: 18
Par: 72

An Arthur Hills designed course that borders the Jordan River.

———————————————SANDY———————————————

**Schneiter's Pebble
Brook**
8968 South 1300 East,
84070
Ph: 801-566-2181

Yards: 4800, Holes: 18
Par: 68, USGA: 58.7

Rolling terrain and lots and lots of hazards make this short more challenging than you would expect.

———————————————SANDY———————————————

Willow Creek CC   Yards: 6556, Holes: 18
8300 So. 2700 East,   Par: 72, USGA: 71.0
84092
Ph: 801-942-1621

Scenic views of the surrounding mountains, this rolling course is the site of the Utah Open.

———————————————SMITHFIELD———————————————

Birch Creek GC   Yards: 6770, Holes: 18   Proshop
600 East Center St.,   Par: 72, USGA: 70.0
84335   RP: Required
Ph: 801-563-6825

If you're in a hurry, this is the course to play. Very fast paced.

———————————————SOUTH JORDAN———————————————

Glenmoor GC   Yards: 6428, Holes: 18
9800 South 4800 West,   Par: 72, USGA: 69.3
84065   RP: Required
Ph: 801-255-1742

Almost continual wind makes it very difficult to figure your shots, a real challenge.

———————————————SPANISH FORK———————————————

Spanish Oaks GC   Yards: 5850, Holes: 18   Bar/Proshop
2400 E. Powerhouse   Par: 72, USGA: 67.2
Rd., 84660   RP: Required
Ph: 801-798-9816

This course is an exciting play because of its very difficult greens.

———————————————SPRINGVILLE———————————————

Hobble Creek GC   Yards: 5950, Holes: 18
Canyon Dr./Hobble   Par: 71, USGA: 67.1
Creek Canyon, 84663   RP: Required
Ph: 801-489-6297

This course has a perfect natural setting, must be seen to be believed.

———————————————ST. GEORGE———————————————

Dixie Red Hills GC   Yards: 2564, Holes: 9
1000 North 700 West,   Par: 34, USGA: 65.5
84770   RP: Required
Ph: 801-634-5852

One of the top 9 holes courses in the state, it was built in 1965.

———————————————ST. GEORGE———————————————

Green Valley GC   Yards: 1050, Holes: 9   Proshop
1200 S. Dixie Downs   Par: 27, USGA: 50.3
Rd., 84770
Ph: 801-628-3778

An unusual par 3 executive course, each hole is very different.

Plan ahead! Reserve tee time well in advance, and while you're doing so, confirm rates and services.

———————————————ST. GEORGE———————————————

Southgate GC
1975 S. Tonaquint Dr.,
84770
Ph: 801-628-0000

Yards: 6141, Holes: 18
Par: 69, USGA: 66.0
RP: One week in
advance

Restaurant/Proshop
GF: w/day $12.00
Carts: $12.00

The redesign on this course has greatly improved the weaker holes.

———————————————ST. GEORGE———————————————

St. George GC
2190 South 1400 East,
84770
Ph: 801-634-5854

Yards: 6728, Holes: 18
Par: 73, USGA: 67.0
RP: Required

Restaurant/Proshop

One of St. George's most played courses.

———————————————ST. GEORGE———————————————

Sun Brook GC
2240 Sunbrook Dr,
84770
Ph: 801-634-5866

Yards: 6411, Holes: 18
Par: 72

A hilly course that has a bit of water and trees to provide an interesting round of golf.

———————————————ST. GEORGE———————————————

Twin Lakes
660 N. Twin Lakes Dr.,
84770
Ph: 801-673-4441

Yards: 1001, Holes: 9
Par: 27, USGA: 46.9
RP: Required

Restaurant/Bar/Proshop

This is the city's only lighted course. The elevation is different on every hole.

———————————————STANSBURY PARK———————————————

Stansbury Park GC
#1 Country Club,
84074
Ph: 801-882-4162

Yards: 6432, Holes: 18
Par: 72, USGA: 69.8
RP: Required

This course has lots of water for you, 22 water hazards in all. Let 'er fly, and hope its a good straight shot.

———————————————TOOELE———————————————

Oquirrh Hills GC
7th & Edgemont,
84074
Ph: 801-882-4220

Yards: 3005, Holes: 9
Par: 35, USGA: 67.7
RP: Required

Set by the Great Salt Lake, this course offers many interesting views.

———————————————TREMONTON———————————————

Skyway GC
450 N. Country Club
Dr., 84337
Ph: 801-257-5706

Yards: 2704, Holes: 9
Par: 34, USGA: 64.7
RP: Required

Proshop

A short course with lots of hazards to help keep you on your toes.

———————————————VERNAL———————————————

Dinaland GC
675 South 2000 East,
84078
Ph: 801-781-1428

Yards: 3200, Holes: 9
Par: 36, USGA: 68.7
RP: Required

This course, designed by Bill Johnston, is located in the area of many dinosaur finds.

WASHINGTON

Green Spring GC
588 North Green
Spring Dr., 84780
Ph: 801-673-7888

Yards: 6717, Holes: 18
Par: 71, USGA: 69.3
RP: Monday for
following, Mon-Sun

Restaurant/Proshop
GF: w/day $20.00, w/end
$20.00
Carts: $14.00

Nestled in the Red Desert of southern Utah, Green Springs Golf Course is a golfing oasis. This challenging Gene Bates design matches unique surroundings with a magically sculptured layout to form one of the west's most spectacular golfing facilities.

WEST JORDAN

Mountain View GC
2400 West on 8660
South, 84088
Ph: 801-255-9211

Yards: 6280, Holes: 18
Par: 72, USGA: 66.0

The large number of water holes and bunkers make up for the generally flat terrain of this course.

WEST VALLEY CITY

Westridge GC
5055 S. West Ridge
Blvd, 84119
Ph: 801-966-4653

Yards: 5857, Holes: 18
Par: 71

A municipal course that is quite challenging. You will be surprised at the level of difficulty here.

WOODS CROSS

**West Bountiful City
GC**
1201 North 1100 West,
84087
Ph: 801-295-1019

Yards: 2744, Holes: 9
Par: 36, USGA: 65.1

A scenic course that all golfers should enjoy.

VERMONT

──────────────BOMOSEEN──────────────

Bomoseen GC
Vt Rt #30, P.O. Box 90,
05732
Ph: 802-468-5581

Yards: 5185, Holes: 9
Par: 35, USGA: 64.0

Restaurant/Bar/Proshop
GF: w/day $11.00, w/end
$13.00
Carts: $8.00

A resort course on the shore of Lake Bomoseen offering visitors a golf package with meals and lodging.

──────────────FAIRLEE──────────────

Lake Morey CC
Lake Morey Rd., 05045
Ph: 802-333-4800

Yards: 6024, Holes: 18
Par: 70

Restaurant/Bar/Proshop
GF: w/day $20.00

A narrow layout with well-protected greens. There are lots of trees, and water in all the wrong places.

──────────────FERRISBURG──────────────

Basin Harbor GC
Basin Harbor Rd.,
05456
Ph: 802-475-2311

Yards: 6232, Holes: 18
Par: 72

Restaurant/Bar/Proshop
GF: w/day $16.00
Carts: $18.00

On the eastern shores of Lake Champlain, Basin Harbor's 6400-yard course is challenging yet enjoyable no matter what your level of play. Also a practice fairway and putting green.

──────────────JERICHO──────────────

West Bolton GC
P.O. Box 305 West
Bolton, 05465
Ph: 802-434-4321

Yards: 5432, Holes: 18
Par: 69, USGA: 65.6

Bar/Proshop
GF: w/day $11.00, w/end
$13.00
Carts: $16.00

"One of the prettiest golf courses ever walked by man or deer..." Franklin County Courier. Early morning golfers can share the course with deer, fox, ducks, and even an occasional moose.

—————————————KILLINGTON—————————————

Killington GC
Killington Rd., 05751
Ph: 802-422-3333

Yards: 6500, Holes: 18
Par: 72, USGA: 71.5
RP: 2 days in advance

Restaurant/Bar/Proshop
GF: w/day $34.00, w/end
$34.00
Carts: $26.00

Beautiful mountain course located in Green Mountains of Vermont. Narrow tree lined fairways, large greens, spectacular views.

—————————————LUDLOW—————————————

Fox Run GC
Fox Ln., RFD #1 Box
123, 05149
Ph: 802-228-8871

Yards: 2547, Holes: 9
Par: 36, USGA: 65.6
RP: 2 days in advance

Restaurant/Bar/Proshop
GF: w/day $8.00
Carts: $10.00

A short but tight golf course. Be careful.

—————————————MANCHESTER—————————————

Manchester CC, Inc.
P.O. Box 947, Beech
St., 05255
Ph: 802-362-2233

Yards: 6164, Holes: 18
Par: 72

Restaurant/Bar/Proshop
GF: w/day $45.00

Half the course is forested and the other half is open. There's a little water but not too much.

—————————————MANCHESTER VILLAGE—————————————

Equinox CC
Box 618, Historic Rte
7A, 05254
Ph: 802-362-3223

Yards: 6069, Holes: 18
Par: 71

Restaurant/Bar/Proshop
GF: w/day $65.00

A very scenic course, set in rolling terrain. There's water on a third of the course that can present some difficulties.

—————————————RUTLAND—————————————

Rutland CC
P.O. Box 195, 05701
Ph: 802-773-3254

Yards: 5701, Holes: 18
Par: 70, USGA: 69.1
RP: Same day

Restaurant/Bar/Proshop
GF: w/day $37.00
Carts: $27.00

Golf Digest rates this course as #3 in Vermont. You're going to have a most challenging round of golf. This is a course that you'll be able to play a better second round than a first. Your short game is going to be very important.

—————————————SHELBURNE—————————————

Kwiniaska GC
Spear St., P.O. Box 129,
05482
Ph: 802-985-3672

Yards: 6796, Holes: 18
Par: 72, USGA: 71.4

Restaurant/Bar/Proshop
GF: w/day $12.00, w/end
$15.00
Carts: $15.00

The front is quite open and flat. The second nine is more rolling with a stream crossing four holes. Beautiful views of the Green Mountains and the Adirondacks.

—————————————STOWE—————————————

Stowe GC
Cape Cod Rd., 05672
Ph: 802-253-4893

Yards: 6163, Holes: 18
Par: 72, USGA: 68.9
RP: Tee times
requested

Restaurant/Bar/Proshop
GF: w/day $30.00
Carts: $12.50

Golf course offers spectacular views of the Green Mountains with enough challenge to satisfy all golfers.

---------------------------- STRATTON MT. ----------------------------

Stratton Mt. CC
05155
Ph: 802-297-1880

Yards: 6400, Holes: 27
Par: 72, USGA: 69.8
RP: Public play 1 week,
1 day weekend

Restaurant/Bar/Proshop
GF: w/day $50.00
Carts: $26.00

*Stratton Mountain Country Club is a delightful mixture of long and short holes,
played at the base of the famous Strattonski resort. Straight, well placed tee
shots are required here to avoid the numerous mountain brooks that wander
through the course.*

---------------------------- VERGENNES ----------------------------

**Basin Harbor Club
GC**
RR #3, 05491
Ph: 802-475-2309

Yards: 6513, Holes: 18
Par: 72, USGA: 70.4
RP: 2 days in advance

Restaurant/Bar/Proshop
GF: w/day $26.00, w/end
$26.00
Carts: $20.00

*The front nine require precision, and the long back nine demand concentration.
The course is surrounded by native wild areas, with some frontage on Lake
Champlain. The Adirondacks and Green Mountains frame the sweeping vistas.*

---------------------------- WARREN ----------------------------

Sugarbush Inn
Sugarbush Access Rd.,
05674
Ph: 802-583-2722

Yards: 6524, Holes: 18
Par: 72, USGA: 71.7
RP: Call for availability

Restaurant/Bar/Proshop
GF: w/day $24.00, w/end
$28.00
Carts: $22.00

*Designed by Rob. Trent Jones, Jr, the course here is dramatic. With mountains
that top four thousand feet looming in the background. You won't have a lot of
level lies; the old timers will tell you to just play from one landing area to the
next.*

---------------------------- WEST DOVER ----------------------------

Mount Snow CC
Mount Snow Resort,
05356
Ph: 802-464-5642

Yards: 6443, Holes: 18
Par: 72, USGA: 70.3
RP: Required

Restaurant/Bar/Proshop
GF: w/day $28.00
Carts: $26.00

*The par-4 fourth hole, named by Travel Weekly magazine as one of the 100
prettiest holes in North America, features a downhill approach to a green bordered by a marsh and two sand traps. With a spectacular view of the Green
Mountains in the background.*

---------------------------- WILMINGTON ----------------------------

Haystack GC
RR #1, Box 173, Mann
Rd., 05363
Ph: 802-464-8301

Yards: 6164, Holes: 18
Par: 72, USGA: 69.8
RP: Nonmembers 48
hours in advance

Restaurant/Bar/Proshop

*This course in set in the mountains, and should give you plenty of practice on
sidehill lies. A very difficult round of golf.*

---------------------------- WOODSTOCK ----------------------------

**Woodstock Inn &
Resort**
Fourteen the Green,
05091
Ph: 802-457-2114

Yards: 6001, Holes: 18
Par: 69, USGA: 67.0
RP: Same day

Restaurant/Bar/Proshop
GF: w/day $46.00, w/end
$46.00
Carts: $13.50

*Most golfers will find more than enough trouble on this 6001 yard course. The
Kedron Brook comes into play on all but six of the eighteen holes coupled with
more than eighty bunkers throughout the beautiful Kedron Valley. Golf packages
available.*

VIRGINIA

New Market
Leesburg
Herndon
Wintergreen Basye
Staunton
Fredericksburg
Hot Springs
Charlottesville
Callao
Bastian
Irvington
Virginia Beach
Roanoke
Williamsburg
Newport News
Norfolk

ALEXANDRIA

Greendale GC
6900 Telegraph Rd,
22307
Ph: 703-971-3788

Yards: 6363, Holes: 18
Par: 70, USGA: 70.2

Restaurant/Bar
GF: w/day $15.00, w/end
$17.00

A flat course with few bunkers on the fairways. The trees also present little problem. The 17th hole is very difficult, with a marked loped to the right. The hole also offers a terrific view of the whole layout.

BASTIAN

Wolf Creek GC CC
Rt 1 Box 421, 24314
Ph: 703-688-4610

Yards: 6079, Holes: 18
Par: 71, USGA: 68.7
RP: 1 week in advance

Restaurant/Proshop
GF: w/day $13.00, w/end
$15.00
Carts: $15.00

This course has water on 6 of the first 9 holes and all nine on the back. It is surrounded by the beautiful Jefferson National Forest. The 16th hole is a par 3 which has water on three sides and sand in front.

BASYE

Bryce Resort
P.O. Box 3, 22810
Ph: 703-856-2124

Yards: 6175, Holes: 18
Par: 71, USGA: 68.7

Restaurant/Bar/Proshop
GF: w/day $8.00, w/end
$25.00
Carts: $24.00

The golf course is a relatively flat mountain valley course. A wandering creek, strategically placed bunkers and plentiful trees make every hole a demanding test. Views of the mountains add to the attractiveness of the course. Swimming facilities.

CALLAO

Village Green GC
P.O. Box 247, 22435
Ph: 804-529-6332

Yards: 6000, Holes: 9
Par: 72, USGA: 68.0

Restaurant/Bar/Proshop
GF: w/day $11.00
Carts: $13.00

Enjoy our beautifully landscaped 9 holes in the Old Northern Neck. You won't putt on more lush greens anywhere in Virginia. After a challenging round relax in our restaurant overlooking the 9th hole.

Plan ahead! Reserve tee time well in advance, and while you're doing so, confirm rates and services.

─────────────CHARLOTTESVILLE─────────────

Birdwood GC (Univ. Virginia)
Rt. 250 West, P.O. Box 5126, 22905
Ph: 804-293-4653

Yards: 6821, Holes: 72
Par: 18, USGA: 70.4

Restaurant/Bar

A really tough course with water on nine holes. #14, a 158 yard par 3 is really something, all carry as the green is on an island in the middle of a pond. You've got to have your shotmaking together for this one.

─────────────CHESTER─────────────

River's Bend CC
22700 Hogan's Alley Dr., 23831
Ph: 804-530-1000

Yards: 6200, Holes: 18
Par: 71, USGA: 69.3

Set in a heavily wooded area, part of the course is on the bank of the James River. Don't let the wonderful views distract you here, you'll need all your attention on the ball.

─────────────CLIFTON─────────────

Twin Lakes GC
6100 Clifton Rd, 22024
Ph: 703-631-9099

Yards: 7010, Holes: 18
Par: 73, USGA: 73.0

Restaurant/Bar
GF: w/day $13.00, w/end $15.00

Definitely a long and challenging course, with rolling to hilly setting. Water and bunkers are lightly sprinkled through the course, but the need for long approach shots make them very effective. A course you can walk anytime.

─────────────FAIRFAX─────────────

Penderbrook GC
3700 Golf Trail Ln, 22033
Ph: 703-385-3700

Yards: 6152, Holes: 18
Par: 71, USGA: 71.2

Restaurant/Bar
GF: w/day $15.00, w/end $20.00

This course is set in dense woods and is very rolling. Well bunkered throughout with water hazards on over half the holes. Four tees have a long carry over water. No. 12 calls for all the accuracy your game will give.

─────────────FREDERICKSBURG─────────────

Shannon Green GC
I-95 & Virginia Rt. 3, 22401
Ph: 703-786-8385

Yards: 7155, Holes: 18
Par: 72, USGA: 72.7
RP: Required

Restaurant/Bar/Proshop
GF: w/day $24.00
Carts: $22.00

You warm up on a relatively open front nine with a view of the rolling meadows of what used to be dairy farm. Several lakes have to be negotiated to shoot a decent round. The back nine offers a little reprieve for those who stray from the fairway.

─────────────GLEN ALLEN─────────────

Crossings GC
800 Virginia Center Pkwy, 23060
Ph: 804-266-2254

Yards: 6229, Holes: 18
Par: 72

GF: w/day $33.00, w/end $38.00

A very challenging, championship-caliber course. Very large greens and 13 holes where water can come into play. You'll really enjoy this round.

HERNDON

Herndon Centennial GC
909 Ferndale Ave., 22070
Ph: 703-471-5769

Yards: 6445, Holes: 18
Par: 71

GF: w/day $14.00, w/end $18.00

The 27-hole championship course has been called one of New England's best by Golf Digest Magazine. You'll love its spectacular views of mountains, valleys and Stratton Lake as the course challenges you at every turn. A must for every golfer.

HOT SPRINGS

Cascades GC
US 220, 24445
Ph: 703-839-5600

Yards: 6566, Holes: 18
Par: 70, USGA: 72.9
RP: Call in advance

Restaurant/Bar/Proshop
GF: w/day $75.00
Carts: $Included

A rolling course which has a tendency to give you some nasty and unusual fairway lies. There are plenty of mature trees and the greens are well protected. You'll get plenty of chances to see if you can pick the right club on this one.

HOT SPRINGS

Lower Cascades GC
US 220, 24445
Ph: 703-839-5600

Yards: 6619, Holes: 18
Par: 72, USGA: 72.2
RP: Call in advance

Restaurant/Bar/Proshop
GF: w/day $65.00
Carts: $Included

The course was host to the 1988 U.S. Amateur, and is a wonderful championship layout. The traps here are numerous and very large. Your accuracy and placement are going to make the difference between a good score and a bad one.

HOT SPRINGS

The Homestead
24445
Ph: 703-839-5500

Yards: 6282, Holes: 54
Par: 70, USGA: 70.0
RP: Required, 1 week in advance

Restaurant
GF: w/day $75.00, w/end $75.00
Carts: $28.00

Considered by many to be the best mountain course, Cascades Upper is hilly and demanding, requiring a variety of shots. Lower Cascades has heavily-trapped large greens and long tees. The Homestead Course claims the oldest first tee in continuous use.

IRVINGTON

Golden Eagle GC
Rt. 646, 22480
Ph: 804-438-5501

Yards: 6943, Holes: 27
Par: 72, USGA: 68.2
RP: Hotel guest as far as wished

Restaurant/Bar/Proshop
GF: w/day $42.00, w/end $42.00
Carts: $26.00

The Golden Eagle GC of the Tides Inn has been voted among the top three courses in the state of Virginia. We are rarely crowded and wish to allow our golfing guests a leisurely and unhurried round of golf.

IRVINGTYON

Tides Lodge Tartan GC
PO Box 309, 22480
Ph: 804-438-6200

Yards: 6586, Holes: 18
Par: 72, USGA: 69.2
RP: Call the Pro

Restaurant/Bar/Proshop
GF: w/day $35.00, w/end $40.00
Carts: $30.00

Narrow fairways and majestic trees are featured here, but you should also pay attention to the creek. Your long game can be very important on this course.

──────────────── LAUREL FORK ────────────────

Olde Mill Golf Club   Yards: 6185, Holes: 18   Restaurant/Bar/Proshop
Route 1, Box 84, 24352   Par: 72, USGA: 69.5   **GF:** w/day $15.00, w/end
Ph: 703-398-2638 $18.00
                                                         Carts: $10.00

Set in a heavily wooded area the Olde Mill is a very scenic course. A large lake, ponds, and lots of creeks are going to give your a difficult test, you may want to bring a few extra golf balls for your round here.

──────────────── LEESBURG ────────────────

Goose Creek GC   Yards: 6100, Holes: 18   Restaurant/Bar
Rt 1 Box 392, 22075   Par: 72   **GF:** w/day $14.00, w/end
Ph: 703-729-2500 $18.00

Here the greens are very small and require your shotmaking abilities to come into play. A creek wanders through over half of the course giving plenty of water hazard experience. The course is not long, but has some really difficult par 3 holes.

──────────────── LEESBURG ────────────────

Landscowne GC   Yards: 5954, Holes: 18   Restaurant/Bar/Proshop
44050 Woodridge   Par: 72, USGA: 68.6   **GF:** w/day $81.00, w/end
Parkway, 22075 $91.00
Ph: 703-729-8400   **Carts:** $Included

The front and back nines are very different on this course. The front has open fairways lined by mature trees, whereas the back is through the woods with plenty of water.

──────────────── LEESBURG ────────────────

Westpark Hotel &   Yards: 6300, Holes: 18   Restaurant/Bar/Proshop
GC   Par: 71, USGA: 71.5   **GF:** w/day $14.00, w/end
59 Clubhouse Dr. SW, $20.00
22075
Ph: 703-777-7023

Water on eleven holes, get out your hip boots if your shotmaking goes bad. #7 dogleg, par 4, 417 yards with water running through the fairway and when you get past that there are bunkers on the right and left of the green.

──────────────── LORTON ────────────────

Pohick Bay GC   Yards: 5927, Holes: 18
10301 Gunston Rd.,   Par: 72
22079
Ph: 703-339-8585

A beautiful, scenic course with plenty of wildlife. With heavy woods and hilly, you may not always want to use your driver.

──────────────── NEW MARKET ────────────────

Shenvalee GR   Yards: 6337, Holes: 18   Restaurant/Bar
P.O. Box 930, 22844   Par: 70, USGA: 65.7   **GF:** w/day $16.50, w/end
Ph: 703-740-3181 $19.00
                                                         Carts: $18.00

Plenty of course to pull out all the stops on your long ball. Our #17 is a challenging par 5, 507 yard hole with water and sand guarding the green, so get your shotmaking skills ready for this one.

───────────── NEWPORT NEWS ─────────────

Deer Run GC
13564 Jefferson Ave.,
23603
Ph: 804-886-2848

Yards: 6680, Holes: 36
Par: 72, USGA: 72.4

Restaurant/Proshop
GF: w/day $8.00, w/end
$10.00
Carts: $13.59

Our scenic 36 holes offer both a bucolic haven and a friendly challenge to golfers of all skill levels. In addition to many outstandingly designed holes, one will see hundreds of deer who make their home in the adjoining woods.

───────────── NOKESVILLE ─────────────

**Prince William
Public GC**
14631 Vint Hill Rd,
22123
Ph: 703-754-7111

Yards: 6453, Holes: 18
Par: 72, USGA: 70.1

Restaurant
GF: w/day $13.00, w/end
$17.00

Water can cause you a lot of trouble on at least half the course. A very scenic setting, with rolling, open countryside.

───────────── NORFOLK ─────────────

Lake Wright GC
North Hampton Blvd.,
23502
Ph: 804-461-2246

Yards: 6174, Holes: 18
Par: 70

Restaurant/Bar/Proshop

Silky, smooth putting greens are combined with tough sand traps, water hazards and roughs to challenge even the best golfer on this Lake Wright championship course. The greens are bent grass, and there's also a driving range and two putting greens.

───────────── RESTON ─────────────

Hidden Creek CC
11599 North Shore Dr,
22090
Ph: 703-437-4222

Yards: 6450, Holes: 18
Par: 71, USGA: 71.6

Restaurant/Bar
GF: w/day $20.00, w/end
$35.00

A hilly course with some blind shots. The fairways are tree-lined, with water hazards on 11 holes. A challenging course.

───────────── RESTON ─────────────

Reston GC
11875 Sunrise Valley
Dr, 22091
Ph: 703-620-9333

Yards: 6480, Holes: 18
Par: 71, USGA: 71.2

Restaurant
GF: w/day $14.00, w/end
$18.00

Large, heavily bunkered greens are a feature of this course. Open fairways bordered by trees make this a nice setting. Plenty of fairway bunkers will call your accuracy into play.

───────────── ROANOKE ─────────────

Countryside GC
1 Countryside Rd.,
24017
Ph: 703-563-0391

Yards: 6861, Holes: 18
Par: 71, USGA: 68.5
RP: 1 day in advance

Restaurant/Proshop
GF: w/day $12.00, w/end
$15.00
Carts: $18.00

Countryside is located in the beautiful Roanoke Valley surrounded by the Blue Ridge Mountains. The course has four sets of tees. The five par 3 holes are demanding for tee shot. There is a spacious driving range, with practice sand trap, chip, and putt.

─────────────────SALEM─────────────────

Hanging Rock GC Yards: 6216, Holes: 18   Grill
1500 Red Lane, 24153 Par: 73, USGA: 70.0   **GF:** w/day $18.00, w/end
Ph: 703-389-7275   RP: Call the Pro $21.00
                                                Carts: $11.50

Come play challenging golf and enjoy nature's beauty at one of Virginia's finest public courses. Various features compliment Hanging Rock GC's complete golf experiences. Outing packages available.

─────────────────STAUNTON─────────────────

Country Club of   Yards: 6342, Holes: 18   Restaurant/Bar
Staunton   Par: 71, USGA: 71.6   **GF:** w/day $40.00
P.O. Box3209, 24401   RP: 1 day in advance
Ph: 704-248-6020

The Country Club of Staunton is the home of the 1988 Virginia PGA Championship, and numerous tournaments. Beautiful rolling fairways and classic greens, some sloped, all under the watchful eye of the mountains. Not too much water.

─────────────────STERLING─────────────────

Algokian GC   Yards: 6720, Holes: 18   Restaurant
1600 Potomac View   Par: 72   **GF:** w/day $14.00, w/end
Rd., 22170 $18.00
Ph: 703-450-4655

The course is very popular, with an annual play in the area of 70,000 rounds a year. The front nine is open and somewhat flat, while the back nine has narrower fairway with lots of trees. The green are well protected by bunkers. A very scenic course.

─────────────────SUFFOLK─────────────────

Sleepy Hole GC   Yards: 6215, Holes: 18
4700 Sleepy Hole Rd, Par: 72
Box 5010, 23435
Ph: 804-393-5050

An open course despite the water. The fairways are flat and the greens raised.

─────────────────VIRGINIA BEACH─────────────────

Hells Point GC   Yards: 6030, Holes: 18   Restaurant
2700 Atwood Town   Par: 72, USGA: 67.6   **GF:** w/day $25.00, w/end
Rd, 23456 $27.50
Ph: 804-721-3400

This is rated one of the best-designed courses in the country, so you'll definitely want to try it. Set in a forest, there are plenty of well-placed bunkers, but the water is almost everywhere. A challenging round for every golfer.

─────────────────VIRGINIA BEACH─────────────────

Red Wing Lake GC Yards: 7250, Holes: 18   **GF:** w/day $12.00
1080 Prosperity Rd., Par: 72, USGA: 70.0   **Carts:** $14.00
23451   RP: Weekends only
Ph: 804-437-4845

Lots of trees and plenty of water on this George Cobb designed course.

Our listings—supplied by the management—are as complete as possible. Many of the courses have more features than we list. Be sure to inquire when you book your tee time.

─────────────────VIRGINIA BEACH─────────────────

Stumpy Lake GC
4797 E. Indian River
Rd., 23456
Ph: 804-467-6119

Yards: 6347, Holes: 18
Par: 72, USGA: 70.1
RP: Required on
weekends

Restaurant/Bar/Proshop
GF: w/day $10.50, w/end
$12.00
Carts: $14.00

Surrounded on three sides by an elegant cypress-filled lake, Stumpy Lake is the quietest golf course in the area. Wildlife from the surrounding woods often add to an 18-hole round. Natural water hazards and placed bunkers intersect the fairway.

─────────────────WEST LURAY─────────────────

Caverns CC Resort
P.O. Box 749, Hwy 211
Bypass, 22835
Ph: 703-743-6551

Yards: 6299, Holes: 18
Par: 72

A very hilly course where the hills are a definite factor in your play. There are also a lot of trees along the fairways the narrow fairways. You'll need all your accuracy.

─────────────────WILLIAMSBURG─────────────────

Ford's Colony CC
240 Ford's Colony
Drive, 23188
Ph: 804-565-4130

Yards: 3371, Holes: 27
Par: 72, USGA: 72.3
RP: 30 days in advance

Restaurant/Bar
GF: w/day $61.00, w/end
$69.00
Carts: $8.00

The Dan Maples designed golf courses provide challenges for all caliber of golfers. Each hole is distinctive with rolling Bermuda grass fairways, speckled with sand and water, and lined with trees. Undulating bentgrass greens provide inviting targets.

─────────────────WILLIAMSBURG─────────────────

**Golden Horseshoe
GC**
Williamsburg Inn,
S.England St, 23185
Ph: 804-229-1000

Yards: 6750, Holes: 36
Par: 71, USGA: 71.0
RP: Required

Restaurant/Bar/Proshop
GF: w/day $58.00, w/end
$58.00
Carts: $32.00

One of the top 12 resort golf courses in United States as picked by Golf Magazine in 1988. Narrow fairways, tree lined, lots of water with four of the finest par three holes on any one given golf course. Our sixteenth hole is an island hole of 165 yards.

─────────────────WILLIAMSBURG─────────────────

Kingsmill GC
100 Golf Club Rd.,
23185
Ph: 804-253-3906

Yards: 6587, Holes: 36
Par: 72, USGA: 70.0

Restaurant/Bar

Home of the Anheuser-Busch Golf Classic. Kingsmill's 36 holes offer challenge and excitement for golfers at all skill levels. You'll play around lakes, ponds, trees and 350 years of history in a beautiful setting overlooking the James River.

─────────────────WILLIAMSBURG─────────────────

Kingsmill Resort
1010 Kingsmill Rd.,
23105
Ph: 809-253-1703

Yards: 6776, Holes: 36
Par: 71, USGA: 74.5
RP: May be made with
room reservation

Restaurant/Bar
GF: w/day $45.00
Carts: $13.00

The River Course is home of the PGA Anheuser Bucsh Golf Classic. Plenty of big rolls and swells on the greens. The Plantation Course, around ponds, lakes and river views. The Golf Shop heads the list of "friendliest and most helpful anywhere."

WASHINGTON

---BELLINGHAM---

Lake Padden GC
4004 Samish Way,
98226
Ph: 206-676-6989

Yards: 6406, Holes: 18
Par: 72

Restaurant/Proshop
GF: w/day $10.00
Carts: $15.00

Recognized as one of the finest municipal golf courses in the Pacific Northwest, the Lake Padden course is carved out of a second growth forest and has the capability of being a 6700 yard championship course.

---BELLINGHAM---

Sudden Valley GC
399 Sudden Valley,
98226
Ph: 206-734-6435

Yards: 6553, Holes: 18
Par: 72, USGA: 70.0
RP: 7 days in advance

Restaurant/Bar/Proshop
GF: w/day $25.00, w/end
$35.00
Carts: $23.00

The golf course is located on the shores on Lake Whatcom and is surrounded by the natural beauty of the Pacific northwest. Austin Creek winds its way through the front nine while the tight back nine offers a beautiful view over the lake.

---BINGEN---

**Museum Hills G &
CC**
Box 266, 98605
Ph: 509-493-1211

Yards: 2500, Holes: 9
Par: 35, USGA: 67.0
RP: Weekends &
holidays

Restaurant/Bar/Proshop
GF: w/day $11.00, w/end
$18.00
Carts: $7.00

Museum Hills is nestled between Mt. Hood and Mt. Adams near the Columbia River Gorge. The course is well kept with No. 5 a par 3 the toughest par 3 in the Mid Columbia.

---BIRCH BAY---

Sea Links GC
7878 Birch Bay Dr.,
98230
Ph: 206-371-7933

Yards: 2320, Holes: 18
Par: 54, USGA: 50.7
RP: Required weekends
& holidays

Restaurant/Bar/Proshop
GF: w/day $10.00
Carts: $13.00

The length and rating of Sea Links is deceiving. Each hole is unique and offers sand bunkers and water for beauty, definition and challenge. The amateur records are 53 for men and 59 for women. Greens are seaside bent & highly rated; terrain is moderate.

---------------------------------BLAINE--------------------------------

Semiahmoo Golf &   Yards: 7005, Holes: 18   Restaurant/Bar/Proshop
CC   Par: 72, USGA: 71.6   **GF:** w/day $55.00, w/end
8720 Semiahmoo Pky.,   RP: 24 hours in $60.00
98230   advance   **Carts:** $13.00
Ph: 206-371-7005

The 11th and 12th holes are the most difficult here, but you'll find plenty to occupy you on the others. A Palmer and Seay design, this is a beautiful and challenging course.

-------------------------------BRIDGEPORT-------------------------------

Lake Woods GC   Yards: 5471, Holes: 9   Restaurant/Proshop
240 State Park Rd., Box   Par: 70, USGA: 63.8   **GF:** w/day $7.00, w/end
427, 98813 $10.00
Ph: 509-686-2901   **Carts:** $12.00

Lake Woods golf course is located on the beautiful Columbia River. Fairways are narrow with small fast greens to challenge anyone's ability. For the traveler we have a very nice State Park with full hook ups within walking distance.

------------------------------BRUSH PRAIRIE------------------------------

Cedar's GC   Yards: 6021, Holes: 18   Restaurant/Bar/Proshop
15001 NE 181st St.,   Par: 72, USGA: 69.2   **GF:** w/day $17.00, w/end
98606   RP: Desired but not $19.00
Ph: 206-687-4322   demanded   **Carts:** $20.00

A resort course at half the price and half the distance. Only 30 minutes from Downtown Portland. A charming course with Salmon Creek passing through. Lovely cedar trees that make it breathtaking as well as interesting. A must see golf course.

-------------------------------BURLINGTON-------------------------------

Avalon GC   Yards: 3205, Holes: 27
1717 Kelleher Rd.,   Par: 36
98233
Ph: 206-757-1900

Three 9-holes courses designed by Robert Muir Graves, a very scenic layout with views of the Cascade Mountains.

---------------------------------COLFAX---------------------------------

Colfax GC   Yards: 5476, Holes: 9   Bar/Proshop
Rt 1 Box 46A, 99111   Par: 70, USGA: 67.5   **GF:** w/day $6.00, w/end
Ph: 509-397-2122   RP: Weekends & $7.00
   holidays   **Carts:** $15.00

We get a great deal of favorable comments from strangers because of the relatively easy play of the course. It is fairly flat and has two holes on it which are considered birdie holes by the average golfer.

-------------------------------DESERT AIRE-------------------------------

Desert Aire GC   Yards: 6223, Holes: 9   Proshop
3 Club House Way,   Par: 36, USGA: 68.9   w/end $8.00
99344   RP: Suggested   **Carts:** $15.00
Ph: 509-932-4439   weekends & holidays

Desert Aire Golf Course is located in eastern Washington's desert area on the Columbia River. It offers one of the longest playing seasons in this area, it is a challenging course and very interesting to play.

——————————————ELLENSBURG——————————————

Ellensburg GC
Route 1 Box 411,
Thorp Rd., 98926
Ph: 509-962-2984

Yards: 6093, Holes: 9
Par: 70, USGA: 68.6
RP: Recommended

Restaurant/Bar/Proshop
GF: w/day $6.00
Carts: $7.00

This 9 hole golf course plays relatively flat for all 9 holes with the scenic Yakima River coming into play on holes #4 and #5. The wind, which often times blows in our Kittitas Valley, comes out of the northwest and will take many shots out of bounds.

——————————————FALL CITY——————————————

Snoqualmie Falls GC
35109 S.E. Fish
Hatchery Rd., 98024
Ph: 206-222-5244

Yards: 5427, Holes: 18
Par: 71, USGA: 65.2
RP: 6 days in advance

Restaurant/Proshop
GF: w/day $14.00, w/end
$16.00
Carts: $18.00

Don't slice on holes 1 through 5 and don't hook on holes 10 through 15. Other than that you should have no problems on this well manicured course. The fairly flat terrain is easy to walk and the view of Mt. Si is beautiful.

——————————————GOLDENDALE——————————————

Goldendale CC
1901 N. Columbus,
98620
Ph: 509-773-4705

Yards: 5610, Holes: 9
Par: 72, USGA: 66.2

Proshop
GF: w/day $7.00, w/end
$8.00
Carts: $8.00

Looks easy but it pays to think your way around. Both par threes go over Bloodgood Creek. Good views of snow capped mountains. Big hitters can score well here if they are accurate too.

——————————————KENNEWICK——————————————

Canyon Lakes GC
3700 Canyon Lakes
Dr., 99337
Ph: 509-582-3736

Yards: 6950, Holes: 18
Par: 72, USGA: 69.6
RP: Call Tuesdays for
following wk

Restaurant/Proshop
GF: w/day $12.00, w/end
$18.00
Carts: $16.00

In 1980 Canyon Lakes was rated by Business Week magazine one of the top 50 new courses in the nation. In 1986 Canyon Lakes was rated the best public course in the state of Washington by the Washington Golf Assoc.

——————————————KENT——————————————

Riverbend GC
2019 W. Meeker, 98032
Ph: 206-854-3673

Yards: 6156, Holes: 27
Par: 72

Lots of water and sand on this otherwise flat, open course. A 9-hole course is also available at this facility.

——————————————LONGVIEW——————————————

Mint Valley GC
4002 Pennsylvania,
98632
Ph: 206-577-3395

Yards: 6304, Holes: 18
Par: 71, USGA: 67.9

Restaurant/Proshop
GF: w/day $11.00
Carts: $16.00

38 bunkers and water hazards on nine holes.

Our listings—supplied by the management—are as complete as possible. Many of the courses have more features than we list. Be sure to inquire when you book your tee time.

─────────────────── MARYSVILLE ───────────────────

Cedarcrest GC
6810 84th Street NE,
98270
Ph: 206-659-3566

Yards: 5474, Holes: 18
Par: 70
RP: One day ahead

GF: w/day $10.00
Carts: $10.00

Some trees and a bit of water on this hilly course.

─────────────────── MONROE ───────────────────

Monroe GC
22110 Old Owens Rd.,
98272
Ph: 206-794-8498

Yards: 4902, Holes: 9
Par: 33, USGA: 62.2
RP: Recommended

Restaurant/Proshop
GF: w/day $9.00, w/end
$10.00
Carts: $6.00

#6 begins with a check of the fairway ahead through the periscope. You'll see heavy rough and 180 foot firs left and steep slope right. Your 2nd shot is to a narrow green elevated 30 feet and ringed with grass bunkers.

─────────────────── MOUNTLAKE TERRACE ───────────────────

Ballinger Park GC
23000 Lakeview Dr.,
98043
Ph: 206-775-6467

Yards: 2718, Holes: 9
Par: 34, USGA: 64.6
RP: Recommended - 1
week in advance

Restaurant/Proshop
GF: w/day $6.00, w/end
$6.75

Easy-walking 9 holes; challenges golfer with Hall's Creek traversing 4 fairways and our famous "lake" hole, a 500 yard par 5, bordered entirely by the north shore of Lake Ballinger.

─────────────────── MUKILTEO ───────────────────

Harbour Pointe GC
11817 Harbour Pointe
Blvd., 98204
Ph: 206-355-6060

Yards: 6052, Holes: 18
Par: 72, USGA: 70.4
RP: Up to 5 days in
advance

Restaurant/Bar/Proshop
GF: w/day $35.00, w/end
$40.00
Carts: $25.00

The front nine is set on wetlands, the back is heavily treed and more hilly. There are some very difficult and memorable holes on this course.

─────────────────── NORTH BEND ───────────────────

Cascade GC
14303 436th Ave SE,
98045
Ph: 206-888-2044

Yards: 2275, Holes: 9
Par: 34, USGA: 60.2

Restaurant/Proshop
GF: w/day $6.00, w/end
$7.00
Carts: $8.60

A flat wooded course surrounded by the beautiful Cascade Mountains and foothills. Located off I-90 at exit 32 with quick easy access. Snoqualmil Pass is 25 miles to the east and Snoqualmil Falls is 6 miles to the west.

─────────────────── NORTH BONNEVILLE ───────────────────

Beacon Rock GC
P.O. Box 162, MP 37,
Hwy 14, 98639
Ph: 509-427-5730

Yards: 5580, Holes: 9
Par: 72, USGA: 67.5
RP: Call for starting
times

Restaurant/Bar/Proshop
GF: w/day $6.00, w/end
$10.00

The golf course is located in the heart of the Columbia River scenic area and offers the golfers spectacular views to enjoy while playing a tight and tricky 9 hole layout.

Plan ahead! Reserve tee time well in advance, and while you're doing so, confirm rates and services.

─────────────── OCEAN SHORES ───────────────

Ocean Shores GC P.O. Box 369, 98569 Ph: 206-289-3357	Yards: 6100, Holes: 18 Par: 71, USGA: 69.0	Restaurant/Bar/Proshop **GF:** w/day $15.00, w/end $20.00 **Carts:** $22.00

The front nine is open and close to the ocean while the back nine gets into some large spruce trees. It is a great contrast between nines, with many fine holes on both.

─────────────── ODESSA ───────────────

Odessa GC Hwy 28, P.O. Box 621, 99159 Ph: 509-982-0093	Yards: 6300, Holes: 9 Par: 72, USGA: 69.5	Restaurant/Bar/Proshop **GF:** w/day $7.00 **Carts:** $8.00

Play here on a plush, uncrowded course in a peaceful small town. R.V. spaces available at the course.

─────────────── OLYMPIA ───────────────

Delphi GC 6340 Neylon Dr. SW, 98502 Ph: 206-357-6437	Yards: 2060, Holes: 9 Par: 32 RP: 1 week in advance	Proshop **GF:** w/day $6.00, w/end $6.50 **Carts:** $10.00

Narrow, tree-lined fairways in a residential setting. Don't let the short yardage fool you; small, undulating greens and treacherous pin settings make par an elusive number. Delphi is a serious test of position golf and putting.

─────────────── OLYMPIA ───────────────

Scott Lake GC 11746 Scott Creek Dr. S.W., 98506 Ph: 206-352-4838	Yards: 4878, Holes: 9 Par: 70, USGA: 63.4	Restaurant/Proshop **GF:** w/day $6.00, w/end $7.50 **Carts:** $9.00

Nine hole course with separate tee boxes. Flat good walking with 2 ponds. Water hazards come into play on 5 holes. Lots of trees with few bunkers. Number 1 borders Scott Lake—#2, tough dogleg left over pond—#6, tee box on island. Grass tees, immaculate.

─────────────── OROVILLE ───────────────

Oroville GC Route 1, Box G-20, 98844 Ph: 509-476-2390	Yards: 5880, Holes: 9 Par: 36, USGA: 68.5	Proshop **GF:** w/day $10.00, w/end $12.50 **Carts:** $15.00

The first hole is a 458 yard, par 5 to a small green surrounded on three sides by rock outcroppings. A river or canal is in view from most tees but you don't have to shoot over them. A real challenge for the avid golfer.

─────────────── ORTING ───────────────

High Cedars GC P.O. Box 490, 98360 Ph: 206-893-3171	Yards: 6043, Holes: 18 Par: 72, USGA: 68.5 RP: Recommended	Restaurant/Proshop **GF:** w/day $16.00, w/end $27.00 **Carts:** $17.00

A very relaxing, well conditioned golf course with a panoramic view of Mt. Rainer. The course has a beautiful creek (Clover Creek) that meanders through the course. Our #13 hole is a great par 5 with a testy shot thru the trees to an elevated green.

────────────────── PORT LUDLOW ──────────────────

Port Ludlow GC
9483 Oak Bay Rd.,
98365
Ph: 206-437-2222

Yards: 6262, Holes: 18
Par: 72, USGA: 71.6
RP: 1 week unless
resort guest

Restaurant/Bar/Proshop
GF: w/day $20.00, w/end
$25.00
Carts: $25.00

Rated in the top 1% in the nation by the Golf Course Architects Society of America, and ranked as one of the 25 best resort courses in the country, Port Ludlow offers the ultimate golf experience. The fee includes a small bucket of balls, no cart.

────────────────── PORT ORCHARD ──────────────────

McCormick Woods
5155 McCormick
Woods Dr. SW, 98366
Ph: 206-895-0130

Yards: 6155, Holes: 18
Par: 72, USGA: 69.8
RP: Up to 5 days in
advance

Proshop
GF: w/day $32.25, w/end
$43.00
Carts: $20.00

All the hazards on this course are strategically placed.

────────────────── SEQUIM ──────────────────

**Dungeness Golf &
CC**
491-A Woodcock Rd.,
98382
Ph: 206-683-6344

Yards: 6400, Holes: 18
Par: 72, USGA: 68.8
RP: As far ahead as
needed

Restaurant/Bar/Proshop
GF: w/day $18.00, w/end
$22.00
Carts: $20.00

Excellent dry course, our rainfall is only 17 inches per year. Fun course for all types of golfers. Approximately 58 bunkers and scenic water through the whole course. Beautiful view of the mountains from most of the holes.

────────────────── SEQUIM ──────────────────

Sunland Golf & CC
109 Hilltop Dr., 98382
Ph: 206-683-6800

Yards: 6051, Holes: 18
Par: 72, USGA: 69.0
RP: Required

Proshop
GF: w/day $14.00, w/end
$18.00
Carts: $18.00

Located in the beautiful Sequim-Dungeness Valley, SunLand is a beautiful, well conditioned and sporty golf course. While the front nine is relatively flat, the back nine is undulating. Although the course is very tight, there are no parallel fairways.

────────────────── SPOKANE ──────────────────

**Indian Canyon Muni
GC**
4304 West Dr., 99204
Ph: 509-747-5353

Yards: 6296, Holes: 18
Par: 70, USGA: 68.9
RP: 1 day in advance

Restaurant/Bar/Proshop
GF: w/day $18.00

Course has rolling hills and every fairway is lined by evergreen trees. #14 in Sports Illustrated in '82.

────────────────── STANWOOD ──────────────────

Kayak Point GC
15711 Marine Dr.,
98292
Ph: 206-652-9676

Yards: 6731, Holes: 18
Par: 72, USGA: 70.2
RP: 1 week in advance

Restaurant/Bar/Proshop
Carts: $20.00

Back Nine magazine lists Kayak Point as the number one public golf course in Washington, number two in the entire region. In addition, Kayak is the only Western Washington course named to Golf Digest's list of America's 75 Best Public Golf Courses.

─────────────────SUMNER─────────────────

Tapps Island GC
20818 Island Pkwy.
East, 98390
Ph: 206-862-6616

Yards: 2683, Holes: 9
Par: 35, USGA: 33.0
RP: No more than 7
days in advance

Restaurant/Proshop
GF: w/day $6.50, w/end
$8.50

In the shadow of the Pacific Northwest's tallest peak, 14,111 foot Mount Rainier, this meticulously maintained course, with narrow contoured fairways, challenging greens, ample white-sand bunkers, and water hazards on seven of nine holes.

─────────────────TACOMA─────────────────

Fort Steilacoom GC
8202 87th Ave S.W.,
98498
Ph: 206-588-0613

Yards: 5000, Holes: 9
Par: 68, USGA: 62.7
RP: Required weekends
& holidays

Proshop
GF: w/day $6.00
Carts: $6.00

Very flat easy walking–great for seniors. Despite low course rating course can be difficult to score on due to small greens and numerous out of bounds holes. Favorite hole #7 dogleg left, out of bounds left and fairway tree lined on the right.

─────────────────TACOMA─────────────────

Meadow Park GC
7108 Lakewodd Dr. W.,
98467
Ph: 206-473-3033

Yards: 5640, Holes: 18
Par: 71

A very pleasant setting with rolling terrain and lots of trees. An executive-type 9-hole course is also offered here.

─────────────────TUMWATER─────────────────

Tumwater Valley GC
4611 Tumwater Valley
Dr., 98501
Ph: 206-943-9500

Yards: 6531, Holes: 18
Par: 72, USGA: 70.5
RP: Required - can do 8
days ahead

Restaurant/Bar/Proshop
GF: w/day $13.00, w/end
$16.00
Carts: $17.00

Tumwater Valley poses a challenge to good players but is a fair test for golfers of all levels. Players enjoy beautiful views of Mt. Rainier to the east. Another exceptional feature is the player's choice on two of the par threes of the hole he wishes.

─────────────────UNION─────────────────

Alderbrook GC
E 7101 Hwy. 106, 98592
Ph: 206-898-2200

Yards: 6133, Holes: 18
Par: 72, USGA: 69.8

Restaurant/Bar/Proshop
GF: w/day $18.08
Carts: $17.00

No fairways border each other and fir trees line each hole. #8 has a double dogleg and par 5. #18 has a view of the Olympic Mountains and Hood Canal.

─────────────────VANCOUVER─────────────────

Bowyer's Par 3 GC
11608 N. E. 119th,
98662
Ph: 206-892-3808

Yards: 1020, Holes: 9
Par: 27

Proshop
GF: w/day $4.00

View of Mt. St. Helens (volcano).

─────────────────WALLA WALLA─────────────────

**Veterans Memorial
GC**
201 E Rees, 99362
Ph: 509-527-4507

Yards: 6311, Holes: 18
Par: 72

Restaurant/Bar
GF: w/day $9.75, w/end
$10.50

A scenic course located near the Blue Mountains. The layout is hilly but walkable.

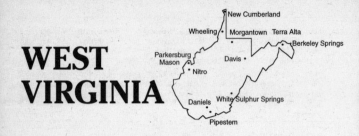

WEST VIRGINIA

---BERKELEY SPRINGS---

Cacapon Resort State Park
Rt.1, 25411
Ph: 304-258-1022

Yards: 6940, Holes: 18
Par: 72, USGA: 70.0
RP: Required March thru November

Restaurant/Bar/Proshop
GF: w/day $16.00
Carts: $16.00

The course is located on a 6,100 acre state park. The front nine plays in a valley with the back nine more in the hills. You will spot many forms of wildlife; deers, squirrels, woodpeckers, etc. as you play the course. Rated as one of the best in W. VA.

---DAVIS---

Canaan Valley State Park GC
Rt. 1, Box 330, 26260
Ph: 304-866-4121

Yards: 6982, Holes: 18
Par: 72

Restaurant/Bar
GF: w/day $20.00, w/end $20.00
Carts: $20.00

Canaan Valley Resort's 18 hole championship golf course is relaxing and yet challenging. Surrounded by magnificent mountain vistas and situated in a gently rolling valley.

---MASON---

Riverside GC
Rt. 1 Box 35, 25260
Ph: 304-773-9527

Yards: 6022, Holes: 18
Par: 70, USGA: 68.7
RP: Weekends

Restaurant/Proshop
GF: w/day $11.00
Carts: $8.00

#6 a par 5 of 510 yards number 1 handicap hole. A dogleg right with out of bounds left and hazard right. Large trap in front of green and 3 pot bunkers in rear. A long tee shot over lateral hazards and long second shot may reach green.

---MORGANTOWN---

Lakeview Inn G&CC
Highway 6, Box 88A, 26505
Ph: 304-594-2001

Yards: 6357, Holes: 36
Par: 72, USGA: 72.8
RP: 7 days in advance

Restaurant/Bar/Proshop
GF: w/day $30.00, w/end $35.00
Carts: $24.00

There are lots of elevation changes, fast, tricky greens, well-placed bunkers and narrow fairways. The fairways don't have much give, you're going to have to earn everything you get.

---------------------------MORGANTOWN--------------------------

Sheraton Lakeview GC
Rte 6, Box 88A, 26505
Ph: 304-594-1111

Yards: 6357, Holes: 18
Par: 72, USGA: 70.9

Restaurant/Bar

The legend and heritage surrounding Lakeview, the original, 18-hole course, is reason enough for professionals and duffers alike to journey to Cheat Lake. Now add the lure of the new Mountainview Golf Course.

-------------------------NEW CUMBERLAND-------------------------

Woodview GC
RD 1 Box 6,
Ballentyne Rd., 26047
Ph: 304-564-5765

Yards: 6570, Holes: 18
Par: 71, USGA: 69.0
RP: 1 day in advance

Bar/Proshop
GF: w/day $8.50
Carts: $7.50

Set in majestic West Virginia hills, our course offers greens which are comparable to those of the finest golf courses anywhere. The 190 yard par 3 number 15 leaves no room to escape, with out of bounds behind the green and water short and left.

-----------------------------NITRO-----------------------------

Scarlet Oaks CC
P.O. Box 425, 25143
Ph: 304-755-0408

Yards: 6575, Holes: 18
Par: 72, USGA: 71.7
RP: Required

Restaurant/Bar/Proshop
GF: w/day $18.00
Carts: $10.00

Set among the hills, Scarlet Oaks offers West Virginia's top rated championship golf course with sculptured greens and multiple tee placements. #17 is one of the most challenging holes.

--------------------------PARKERSBURG--------------------------

Willow Brook GC
Gihon Rd., P.O. Box 3008, 26103
Ph: 304-422-8381

Yards: 6103, Holes: 18
Par: 72, USGA: 69.6

Restaurant/Bar/Proshop
GF: w/day $10.00, w/end $12.00
Carts: $8.00

Willowbrook golf club is owned and operated by two PGA professionals, who pride themselves, to give the golfer the most challenging, best maintained golf facility in the area. The course is a challenge from the white tees.

--------------------------PARKERSBURG--------------------------

Worthington GC
3414 Roseland Ave., 26104
Ph: 304-428-4297

Yards: 5810, Holes: 18
Par: 71, USGA: 67.1

Restaurant/Bar/Proshop
GF: w/day $8.75, w/end $9.50
Carts: $7.00

Flat terrain with creek passing through both nines—lots of trees, but fairways are not generally tight—a few sand bunkers.

----------------------------PIPESTEM----------------------------

Pipestem State Park GC
25979
Ph: 304-466-1800

Yards: 6884, Holes: 18
Par: 72, USGA: 69.8

Restaurant

An 18-hole championship course carved out of a wooded area. A long 6,884 yard from the blue tees, you'll get plenty of practice with those long shots. There is also a 9-hole par three miniature golf course.

Plan ahead! Reserve tee time well in advance, and while you're doing so, confirm rates and services.

―――――――――――――TERRA ALTA―――――――――――――

Alpine Lake Resort
Rt. 2, Box 99 D-2, 26764
Ph: 304-789-2481

Yards: 5772, Holes: 18
Par: 71, USGA: 67.3
RP: Recommended

Restaurant/Bar/Proshop
GF: w/day $9.00, w/end
$14.00
Carts: $12.00

Our beautiful and challenging mountain course is sure to provide you with an exhilarating round of golf. Our clean, fresh mountain air is sure to invigorate your spirit. And our greens fees are low enough to be a delight to any golfer's budget.

―――――――――――――WHEELING―――――――――――――

Crispin GC
Route 88, North, 26003
Ph: 800-752-9436

Yards: 6985, Holes: 36
Par: 71, USGA: 69.0
RP: 60 days in advance

Restaurant/Bar/Proshop
GF: w/day $18.00, w/end
$18.00
Carts: $21.00

One of the best courses in West Virginia, this layout has large greens and equally large bunkers. Uneven lies and lots of trees are some of the others problems to be overcome. Wind and water will also cause the occasional problem.

―――――――――――――WHEELING―――――――――――――

Speidel GC
Oglebay Park, 26003
Ph: 800-752-9436

Yards: 7000, Holes: 18
Par: 71, USGA: 69.0
RP: Up to one year

Restaurant/Bar/Proshop
GF: w/day $30.00, w/end
$30.00
Carts: $23.50

You begin a front 9 that is very difficult with water holes and tree lined fairways. Landing areas are flat. Back 9 is more open but long. Favorite hole #13 par 3 across a large lake. Course has bent greens, tee and fairway and very lush. Rated top 75.

――――――――――― WHITE SULPHUR SPRINGS―――――――――――

The Greenbrier
24986
Ph: 304-536-1110

Yards: 6311, Holes: 18
Par: 72, USGA: 71.7
RP: May be made with
hotel

Restaurant/Bar/Proshop
GF: w/day $80.00, w/end
$80.00
Carts: $34.00

Lakeside opened in 1910. Old White was next, designed in 1914. Jack Nicklaus redesigned what had been a somewhat flat Greenbrier course in 1976. He added a lake, redid greens so now they're tiered and increased the size of many traps.

WISCONSIN

---ANTIGO---

Riverview CC & GC
W11817 Highland Rd.,
54409
Ph: 715-623-2663

Yards: 3120, Holes: 9
Par: 36, USGA: 68.9

Restaurant/Bar/Proshop
GF: w/day $7.00
Carts: $15.00

A scenic and challenging 9 hole layout, which crosses the winding Eau Claire River several times, and features an island green on #4 and a unique par 3 at #8. The 155 yard hole requires a very accurate tee shot over the river to a small, tree.

---BAILEYS HARBOR---

Maxwelton Braes GC
Bonnie Brae Rd.,
54202
Ph: 414-839-2321

Yards: 6070, Holes: 18
Par: 71, USGA: 68.2

Restaurant/Bar/Proshop
GF: w/day $14.00
Carts: $14.00

The Scottish brae links are rolling with open fairways dotted with bunkers. Green are bent grass. Club rentals are available.

---BERLIN---

Mascoutin CC
RTE. 2, P.O. Box 125,
54923
Ph: 414-361-2365

Yards: 6448, Holes: 18
Par: 72, USGA: 70.5
RP: $50.00 1 month
prior tee time

Restaurant/Bar/Proshop
GF: w/day $16.00, w/end
$19.00
Carts: $19.00

Mascoutin is recognized as one of the top ten courses in the state and is the site of the Gene Edwards Greater Green Lake Pro-Am Tournament. Mascoutin's large, undulating greens, 60 sand traps and water on the 15th, 16th and 17th, and 18th holes.

---BIG BEND---

Edgewood GC
W240 S10050 Castle
Rd., 53103
Ph: 414-662-2738

Yards: 6424, Holes: 27
Par: 72, USGA: 70.2
RP: 1 week in advance

Restaurant/Bar/Proshop
GF: w/day $17.00, w/end
$21.00
Carts: $20.00

Rolling fairways meandering between lakes and woods that overlook the Fox River.

BRISTOL

Bristol Oaks CC
16801 75th St., 53104
Ph: 414-857-2302

Yards: 5933, Holes: 18
Par: 72, USGA: 67.8
RP: 2 weeks in advance

Restaurant/Bar/Proshop
GF: w/day $10.50, w/end
$14.75
Carts: $17.50

Green grass, blue sky, rolling hills and valleys of the beautiful Wisconsin countryside are all part of the experience of golfing at Bristol Oaks Country Club. The scenic course will delight as well as challenge both the professional and novice golfer.

DELAVAN

Lake Lawn Lodge GC
Hwy. 50 E., 53115
Ph: 414-728-5511

Yards: 6173, Holes: 18
Par: 70, USGA: 67.3
RP: Tee times
recommended

Restaurant/Bar/Proshop
GF: w/day $38.00, w/end
$38.00
Carts: $12.00

Scenic course on the shore of Delavan Lake, beautiful mature trees. Number 13, a par 4,301 yard hole where your tee shot is over water, then a fairway bunker on the left side and your shot into the green with trees backing the green.

DURAND

Durand GC
1324 3rd Ave. West,
54736
Ph: 715-672-8139

Yards: 3274, Holes: 9
Par: 36, USGA: 34.0
RP: 1 days in advance

Restaurant/Bar/Proshop
GF: w/day $7.00
Carts: $7.00

A member of the CUGS this demanding 9 hole course puts a premium on accuracy. Starting with a very difficult par 3 of 205 yards and ending with a 400 yard par 4 with out of bounds right and tree lined on the right.

EAGLE RIVER

Eagle River Muni GC
527 McKinley
Blvd.,P.O. Box 39,
54521
Ph: 715-479-8111

Yards: 6075, Holes: 18
Par: 70, USGA: 68.0
RP: First come, first
served

Restaurant/Bar/Proshop
GF: w/day $12.00
Carts: $12.00

Formerly a 9 hole course, our newly redesigned 18 hole golf course features 12 new holes. Holes 1 thru 8 wind through the northwoods forest and hole 9's elevated tee offers a view of Eagle River which connects to a chain of 28 lakes.

EAU CLAIRE

Mill Run
3905 Kane Rd., 54703
Ph: 715-834-1766

Yards: 6027, Holes: 18
Par: 71, USGA: 65.1
RP: Recommended

Restaurant/Bar/Proshop
GF: w/day $14.50, w/end
$14.50
Carts: $14.00

Gently rolling terrain with lush fairways. Five ponds and a cattail filled creek that catches balls that go. A fun course that is landscaped with thousands and thousands of flowers throughout the course. Clubhouse with patio area with outdoor grill.

EDGERTON

Coachman's Inn CC
984 County Trunk A,
53534
Ph: 608-884-8484

Yards: 6184, Holes: 18
Par: 71, USGA: 68.7
RP: Suggested

Restaurant/Bar/Proshop
GF: w/day $11.50, w/end
$12.50
Carts: $22.00

The longest hole is 503 yards, the shortest 180 yards. Located on gentle rolling land, slightly wooded, with several water hazards, it is a sporty and challenging course for all golfers.

───────────────── EGG HARBOR ─────────────────

Alpine GC
County Trunk G, P.O.
Box 200, 54209
Ph: 414-868-3232

Yards: 6047, Holes: 27
Par: 70, USGA: 69.4
RP: 1-2 days in advance

Restaurant/Bar
GF: w/day $12.50
Carts: $14.00

We have a tram that takes the golfer up a bluff from the white to the blue nine ... our 9th hole on the Blue nine was written up in Golf Digest as the most scenic hole in Wisconsin.

───────────────── EVANSVILLE ─────────────────

Evansville C
Route 1, Cemetery
Rd., 53536
Ph: 608-882-6524

Yards: 6300, Holes: 9
Par: 36, USGA: 34.5
RP: 1 week in advance

Restaurant/Bar/Proshop
GF: w/day $5.50, w/end
$6.50
Carts: $8.00

One of the finest 9 hole courses in the Midwest. A very picturesque course with water coming in to play on four holes and somewhat rolling terrain throughout the course. Our No. 7 and No. 9 holes have been sources of beautiful pictures for scorecard.

───────────────── FISH CREEK ─────────────────

**Peninsula State Park
GC**
P.O. Box 218, 54212
Ph: 414-868-5791

Yards: 6211, Holes: 18
Par: 71, USGA: 67.5
RP: 7 days in advance

Restaurant/Proshop
GF: w/day $12.00
Carts: $16.00

Peninsula's challenging and very wooded 18 holes are interspersed with varying views of the water of Green Bay and outlying islands. A most memorable hole is the big dogleg on number 12 where golfers approach an elevated hillside green.

───────────────── FOND DU LAC ─────────────────

Ledgewood GC
W4430 Golf Course
Dr., 54935
Ph: 414-921-8053

Yards: 3094, Holes: 9
Par: 36, USGA: 68.6
RP: 30 days in advance

Restaurant/Bar/Proshop
GF: w/day $6.25
Carts: $7.50

A sporty nine hole course located on the Ledge called the Niagra escarpment. The course overlooks the city of Fon Du Lac and the Lake Winnebago. Hilly terrain with woods bordering 6 out of 9 holes.

───────────────── FONTANA ─────────────────

Abbey Springs GC
Route 1, Box K, So
Lake Dr., 53125
Ph: 414-275-6111

Yards: 6342, Holes: 18
Par: 72, USGA: 69.8
RP: 2 weeks in advance

Restaurant/Bar/Proshop
GF: w/day $28.00
Carts: $12.00

Scenic beauty with spectacular views of Geneva Lake are the hallmark of this course. Oak woods line many of the fairways making accuracy of shots important as reflected in the 129 slope rating. Beautiful flower plantings and undulating greens.

───────────────── FORT ATKINSON ─────────────────

**Koshkonong Mounds
CC**
R.R. 3 Koshkonong
Mounds Rd., 53538
Ph: 414-563-2823

Yards: 6259, Holes: 18
Par: 71, USGA: 69.3
RP: Recommended

Restaurant/Bar/Proshop
GF: w/day $13.00
Carts: $18.00

Between 700 A.D. and 1,000 A.D., Indians built burial grounds around a 10,000 acre natural lake. You will see 23 of these mounds on the course and finish on #18 which overlooks many of these mounds as well as scenic Lake Koshkonong.

---------------------------------GREEN LAKE---------------------------------

Lawsonia GC
Hwy. 23 RTE. 1, 54941
Ph: 414-294-3320

Yards: 6764, Holes: 36
Par: 72, USGA: 72.8
RP: Starting Jan 1 for all
year

Restaurant/Proshop
GF: w/day $28.00, w/end
$28.00
Carts: $12.00

Two 18 hole courses to choose from. Links is ranked by Golf Digest as one of the top 75 public courses. Woodlands—wooded contrast features holes such as 165 yard-par 3 bluff next to lake surrounded by woods 65 foot drop to green. Beautiful surroundings.

---------------------------------HARSHAW---------------------------------

Pinewood CC
4705 Lakewood Rd.,
54529
Ph: 715-282-5500

Yards: 6085, Holes: 18
Par: 71, USGA: 74.9
RP: Reservations
required

Restaurant/Bar/Proshop
GF: w/day $18.00, w/end
$18.00
Carts: $18.00

Shorter and open front nine with Bearskin Creek wandering through the course. The back nine is long, hilly with #15 offering a tough golf hole with pines near the landing area. The back nine is cut right through the woods with no parallel holes.

---------------------------------HAYWARD---------------------------------

Hayward GC TC
P.O. Box 1079, 54843
Ph: 715-634-2760

Yards: 6550, Holes: 18
Par: 72, USGA: 69.7
RP: Strongly advised

Restaurant/Bar/Proshop
GF: w/day $12.00, w/end
$13.00
Carts: $8.00

Our golf course features 10 doglegs lined with spruce and Norway pine. The front nine is fairly wide open although well bunkered, while our back nine is noted for smaller greens and tighter fairways.

---------------------------------HOLMAN---------------------------------

**Drugan's Castle
Mound GC**
W7765 Sylvester Rd.,
54636
Ph: 608-526-3225

Yards: 6150, Holes: 18
Par: 72, USGA: 66.9
RP: Suggested

Restaurant/Bar/Proshop
GF: w/day $10.25, w/end
$11.25
Carts: $13.00

The tight front nine challenges even the best golfers, with tree-lined fairways and undulating valleys. Nature surrounds you as you nestle among the "hidden holes." You can "open up" on the lengthier back nine, but caution still lingers.

---------------------------------HORICON---------------------------------

Rock River Hills GC
Main St. Rd., 53032
Ph: 414-485-4990

Yards: 5945, Holes: 18
Par: 70, USGA: 68.7
RP: Call for tee times

Restaurant/Bar/Proshop
GF: w/day $9.00, w/end
$12.00
Carts: $15.00

Located on the beautiful Rock River just south of the famous Horicon Marsh Wildlife Area. The panoramic view with migrating geese make for a most enjoyable round of golf. A superb restaurant coupled with a friendly 19th hole tops off the day.

---------------------------------JANESVILLE---------------------------------

Riverside GC
City Route Hwy 14,
53545
Ph: 608-754-9085

Yards: 6322, Holes: 18
Par: 71
RP: Weekends

Restaurant/Bar/Proshop
GF: w/day $11.43, w/end
$13.33
Carts: $11.00

Three holes are bordered by the Rock River. The third hole is bordered by a ravine, so you'd better make a good shot or you're in trouble.

──────────KENOSHA──────────

**Petrifying Springs
GC**
4909 7th St., 53142
Ph: 414-552-9052

Yards: 5970, Holes: 18
Par: 71, USGA: 67.5
RP: 12 days in advance

Restaurant/Bar/Proshop
GF: w/day $14.75, w/end
$15.50
Carts: $15.00

*Very pretty course. Cut out of natural forest. Trees a definite factor on all but two
of the holes, accuracy a must.*

──────────KIELER──────────

Birchwood GC Inc
P.O. Box 72, 53812
Ph: 608-748-4743

Yards: 3171, Holes: 9
Par: 36

Restaurant/Bar/Proshop
GF: w/day $7.00
Carts: $8.00

*The landing areas are narrow and sloped. #2 is a 359 yard par 4 that doglegs to
the left, and slopes severely from right to left. Land your drive on the right edge
of the fairway and it's likely to bounce down to the left edge of the rough.*

──────────KOHLER──────────

Black Wolf Run GC
1111 West Riverside
Dr, 53044
Ph: 414-457-4446

Yards: 7142, Holes: 36
Par: 72, USGA: 74.8
RP: Up to 30 days in
advance

Restaurant/Bar/Proshop
GF: w/day $70.00
Carts: $Included

*Two 18-hole courses designed by Pete Dye that are set in a wildlife sanctuary.
The courses are separated by a river, and are totally different. Both will be a real
challenge, as well as scenic.*

──────────KOHLER──────────

Blackwolf Run GC
111 West Riverside Dr.,
53044
Ph: 414-457-4446

Yards: 6068, Holes: 36
Par: 72, USGA: 70.7
RP: 1 month in advance

Restaurant/Bar/Proshop
GF: w/day $85.00, w/end
$62.00
Carts: $13.00

*Selected as best new public course for 1988 by Golf Digest magazine. With its
Penncross Creeping Bent grass fairways, fescue roughs, prairie grass mounds
and wild flowers which border many of the playing areas. It is a course to be
played over and over.*

──────────LADYSMITH──────────

Tee-A-Way GC
1401 E. 11th St. No.,
54848
Ph: 715-532-3766

Yards: 2946, Holes: 9
Par: 35, USGA: 67.3
RP: Call ahead

Restaurant/Bar/Proshop
GF: w/day $7.50
Carts: $8.50

*Beautiful rolling course, lots of large trees that come into play, greens are fast
and undulating. Number 9 hole is a tough par 4 with the Flambeau River a
lateral hazard the entire length of the hole.*

──────────LAKE GENEVA──────────

**Americana Lake
Geneva**
Hwy 50 & U.S. 12,
53147
Ph: 414-248-8811

Yards: 7250, Holes: 18
Par: 72, USGA: 74.5
RP: The earlier, the
better

Restaurant/Bar/Proshop
GF: w/day $37.50
Carts: $12.50

*The Briar Patch is typical Scottish style with small greens, (some double), deep
rough, and little rolling hills. The aptly-named Brute, with a rating of 74.5, is a
longer course, with water on twelve holes, and typically American in design.*

─────────────── LAKE GENEVA ───────────────

Geneva National GC   Yards: 7193, Holes: 36
1221 Geneva National   Par: 72
Ave S, 53147
Ph: 414-245-7010

Two championship 18-hole courses, one designed by Arnold Palmer and the other by Lee Trevino. One course is heavily treed, and has lots of water. The other course is more forgiving and can offer a challenge to any level of player.

─────────────── LUXEMBURG ───────────────

NorthBrook CC   Yards: 6110, Holes: 18   Restaurant/Bar/Proshop
P.O. Box 238, 407   Par: 71, USGA: 68.3   **GF:** w/day $15.00, w/end
North Brook Dr., 54217   RP: Required $15.00
Ph: 414-845-2383   **Carts:** $18.00

NorthBrook Country Club has become a standard to the Green Bay area and northeast Wisconsin for its excellent golf and fine food since 1970. Our favorite hole is the 10th, a long par 4 with beautiful trees dissected by a picturesque, rock-ledged brook.

─────────────── MENASHA ───────────────

High Cliff GC   Yards: 5931, Holes: 18   Proshop
5055 Golf Course Rd.,   Par: 71, USGA: 67.3   w/end $11.50
54952
Ph: 414-989-1045

An open back nine, but the front is heavily wooded and demands your best game.

─────────────── MENOMONIE ───────────────

Rainbow Ridge GC   Yards: 3088, Holes: 9   Restaurant/Bar/Proshop
2200 Crestwood Dr.,   Par: 36, USGA: 33.6   **GF:** w/day $5.50, w/end
54751 $6.00
Ph: 715-235-9808   **Carts:** $7.00

A good test of golf for all skill level players featuring beautifully rolling terrain and mature trees to challenge the golfer. Clubhouse overlooks most of course enabling golfers to relive memorable shots in the cozy comfort of the 19th hole.

─────────────── MEQUON ───────────────

Mee-Kwon Park GC   Yards: 6185, Holes: 18   Restaurant/Bar/Proshop
6333 W. Bonniwell Rd.,   Par: 69, USGA: 69.2   **GF:** w/day $11.50
53092   RP: 3 days in advance   **Carts:** $16.00
Ph: 414-242-1310

Run by the county park system, the course abounds in beautiful trees, which also add to the challenge of the course. #13 has two bunkers guarding the green and a water hazard on the right side of the fairway which extends to the middle of same.

─────────────── MERRIMAC, ───────────────

Devil's Head GC   Yards: 6336, Holes: 18   Restaurant/Bar/Proshop
S6330 Bluff Rd., 53561   Par: 73, USGA: 69.8   **GF:** w/day $20.00
Ph: 608-493-2251   **Carts:** $20.00

Devil's Head well manicured greens and sloping fairways will provide any golfer a challenging 18 holes of golf. The course meanders through acres upon acres of lush forest and rolling countryside thriving with oaks, ash and fruit trees.

────────────────────MILTON────────────────────

Oak Ridge GC
1280 Bowers Lake Rd.,
53563
Ph: 608-868-4353

Yards: 5949, Holes: 18
Par: 70, USGA: 68.3
RP: 1 day in advance

Restaurant/Bar/Proshop
GF: w/day $12.00
Carts: $8.40

Very attractive, sporty, well maintained course with numerous sandtraps and fully watered tees, greens and fairways. Although, a short course, the greens are very challenging with tricky undulations.

────────────────────MILWAUKEE────────────────────

Brown Deer Park GC
7835 N. Green Bay Rd.,
53209
Ph: 414-352-8080

Yards: 6470, Holes: 18
Par: 71, USGA: 71.0
RP: Milw. County
resident only

GF: w/day $9.00
Carts: $15.00

A George Hansen design, this course opened in 1929. A lengthy and challenging layout.

────────────────────MINERAL POINT────────────────────

Ludden Lake GC
Rt 3 Box 100, 53565
Ph: 608-987-2888

Yards: 2500, Holes: 9
Par: 34
RP: 1 day in advance
for weekends

Restaurant/Bar/Proshop
GF: w/day $6.50
Carts: $8.00

Dedicated in the memory of Allen Ludden, popular T.V. game show host of Password. A sporty 9 hole course with rolling terrain and hilltop views of beautiful Ludden Lake.

────────────────────MONTELLO────────────────────

White Lake GR
R.R. 2 Box 274, 53949
Ph: 608-297-2255

Yards: 6516, Holes: 9
Par: 72, USGA: 70.4

Restaurant/Bar/Proshop
GF: w/day $10.95
Carts: $8.00

Rolling hills, elevated greens and wood lined fairways make this a scenic course and a challenge to the average golfer. Hole #3—152 yards long, you have to shoot over a water hazard to the green which is 35 feet in elevation above the tee.

────────────────────NEKOOSA────────────────────

Lake Arrowhead GC
1195 Apache Ln.,
54457
Ph: 715-325-2929

Yards: 6624, Holes: 18
Par: 72, USGA: 70.2
RP: 2 weeks ahead

Restaurant/Bar/Proshop
GF: w/day $20.00, w/end
$24.00
Carts: $20.00

Course is heavily wooded and bunkered with bent grass all the way. #9 is a par 5 towards clubhouse, bunker of rock wall, water to carry, pond out of bounds down right, green to right.

────────────────────NEW FRANKEN────────────────────

Royal Scot CC
4831 Church Rd.,
54229
Ph: 414-866-2356

Yards: 6572, Holes: 18
Par: 72, USGA: 70.0
RP: 5 days in advance

Restaurant/Bar/Proshop
GF: w/day $9.80, w/end
$11.90
Carts: $16.00

Royal Scot boasts about its huge greens, fast greens, and soft greens. Along with the best greens in northeast Wisconsin Royal Scot has 44 large sand bunkers, and water holes coming into play 10 out of the 18 championship holes.

NEW LISBON

Castle Rock GC
W6285 Welch Prairie
Rd., 53950
Ph: 608-847-4658

Yards: 6184, Holes: 18
Par: 72, USGA: 71.1
RP: 1 week in advance

Restaurant/Bar/Proshop
GF: w/day $14.00, w/end
$15.00
Carts: $18.00

Located 2.5 miles north of Mouston nestled among a well developed forest. The course is tight and very well manicured. Our favorite hole is the 3rd hole. It is a par 5, 485 yards. You tee off over a creek. The hole is a dogleg right with a pond guarding.

OCONOMOWOC

Olympia Resort GC
1350 Royale Mile Rd.,
53066
Ph: 414-567-0311

Yards: 6567, Holes: 18
Par: 72, USGA: 71.0
RP: Resort guests have
priority

Restaurant/Bar
GF: w/day $17.85
Carts: $20.00

This course, most of which is level or gently rolling with many crisscrossing small lakes and streams, plays longer than the yardage indicates. Both nines are very different, with the front characterized by long, narrow holes and tree–lined fairways.

OCONTO

Oconto GC
532 Jefferson St., 54153
Ph: 414-834-3139

Yards: 3030, Holes: 9
Par: 36, USGA: 64.1
RP: 1st come, 1st
served

Restaurant/Bar/Proshop
GF: w/day $5.00, w/end
$6.00
Carts: $7.00

If you're a bird lover, the par 4, number 5 is the hole for you. As the crow flies, the 370 yard dogleg left can be shortened if you're not afraid to challenge the three possible water hazards along the left side of the fairway.

ONEIDA

Brown County GC
897 Riverdale Dr.,
54155
Ph: 414-497-1731

Yards: 6729, Holes: 18
Par: 72, USGA: 70.2
RP: 1 day in advance

Restaurant/Bar/Proshop
GF: w/day $16.00, w/end
$16.00
Carts: $18.00

The course is 5 miles out in the country. Has rolling terrain and is heavily wooded with hickory, oak, elm and pines. It's curvy and tight with creeks and ponds.

OSHKOSH

Lake Shore GC
2175 Punhoqua Dr.,
54901
Ph: 414-236-5090

Yards: 6030, Holes: 18
Par: 70, USGA: 66.9
RP: One week in
advance

Restaurant/Bar/Proshop
GF: w/day $8.50
Carts: $15.00

The front 9 starts off with a difficult par 4 going to back to back par 5's centered around beautiful Lake Butte des Morts. The back 9 is shorter in length but plays between 100 year old oak trees with tight fairways. Club house is conveniently located.

PRAIRIE DU SAC

Lake Wisconsin CC
N1076 Golf Rd., 53578
Ph: 608-643-2405

Yards: 5690, Holes: 18
Par: 70, USGA: 67.2
RP: 1 day in advance

Restaurant/Bar/Proshop
GF: w/day $14.00, w/end
$17.00
Carts: $15.00

Distances are deceiving, basically a short course with some tight fairways. Back nine plays along both Lake Wisconsin and Wisconsin River. The most unique hole on the course is the twelfth, which play from an island tee.

RHINELANDER

Northwoods GC
6301 Hwy 8 W, 54501
Ph: 715-282-6565

Yards: 5863, Holes: 18
Par: 71, USGA: 68.9

Rolling hills and lots of heavily wooded terrain is going to make this a very challenging round of golf.

RIVER FALLS

Clifton Hollow GC
Route #3, P.O. Box 260,
54022
Ph: 715-425-9781

Yards: 5950, Holes: 27
Par: 72, USGA: 67.7
RP: Recommended on
weekends

Restaurant/Bar/Proshop
GF: w/day $10.00, w/end
$14.00
Carts: $14.50

18 holes of championship golf, a fun par 3 course and a spacious driving range make Clifton Hollow a complete golf experience located in the St. Croix River Valley Clifton Hollow Golf Club is 30 minutes from the Twin Cities Metro area.

SAUKVILLE

Hawthorne Hills GC
4720 County Trunk I,
53080
Ph: 414-692-2151

Yards: 6403, Holes: 18
Par: 71, USGA: 69.6
RP: 3 days in advance

Restaurant/Bar/Proshop
GF: w/day $11.50
Carts: $16.00

Fairways are lined with beautiful, mature trees. The first hole, a 357 yard par 3 is a great opening hole. It's a sharp dogleg over water with water behind the green. Accuracy is a must for this one.

SEYMOUR

Crystal Springs GC
French Rd., P.O. Box
185, 54165
Ph: 414-833-6348

Yards: 6236, Holes: 18
Par: 72, USGA: 68.9
RP: 1 week in advance
only

Restaurant/Bar/Proshop
GF: w/day $11.00, w/end
$12.25
Carts: $16.00

Opening and finishing holes on each side are very good par 5's. Hole #10, 560 yards.

SHAWANO

Shalagoco CC
1233 Lake Dr., 54166
Ph: 715-524-4890

Yards: 6201, Holes: 18
Par: 71, USGA: 67.9

Restaurant/Bar/Proshop
w/end $11.00
Carts: $16.00

Both nines very challenging, fairways lined with trees, six water holes, numerous bunkers and elevated greens. A scenic course with each hole different.

SISTER BAY

Bay Ridge GC
1116 Little Sister Rd.,
54234
Ph: 414-854-4085

Yards: 2934, Holes: 9
Par: 35
RP: Do not take

Proshop
GF: w/day $12.00, w/end
$16.00
Carts: $17.00

Very clean, neat and well kept golf course with two different tees for each hole. An abundance of flowers make Bay Ridge a very special place.

SPOONER

Spooner GC
Rt 1, 54801
Ph: 715-635-3580

Yards: 6407, Holes: 18
Par: 71, USGA: 68.0
RP: Call for tee times

Restaurant/Bar/Proshop
w/end $11.00
Carts: $15.00

With 36 bunkers, 4 water holes and fast greens, Spooner Golf Club is a links style course developed on rolling farm terrain intermixed with numerous white pine. The 18th hole requires two demanding shots over water and is one of the best finishing holes.

―――――――――――――――SPRING GREEN―――――――――――――――

Springs GC
Route 3 Golf Course
Rd., 53588
Ph: 608-588-7707

Yards: 6603, Holes: 18
Par: 72, USGA: 68.9
RP: Can phone at
beginning season

Restaurant/Bar/Proshop
GF: w/day $14.00
Carts: $15.00

Course is a well-kept secret. Magnificently secluded with beautiful oak, birch, poplar and black walnut. Set in a valley shaped like a bow tie, back nine with streams, springs and ponds. Course is level and walkable with lots of water to carry.

―――――――――――――――STEVENS POINT―――――――――――――――

Sentry World GC
601 N. Michigan Ave.,
54481
Ph: 715-345-1600

Yards: 7055, Holes: 18
Par: 72, USGA: 69.8
RP: March 1 beginning
of booking

Restaurant/Bar/Proshop
GF: w/day $55.00
Carts: $Included

A flat course with 35 acres of water, four big lakes. #5 is a challenge with water down the full left side. #16 is our flower hole with 90–100,000 flowers Multi-colored flowers change every year.

―――――――――――――――STURGEON BAY―――――――――――――――

Cherry Hills GC
5905 Dunn Rd., 54235
Ph: 414-743-3240

Yards: 6163, Holes: 18
Par: 72, USGA: 68.6
RP: Pass, 7 days, Lodge,
1 year

Restaurant/Bar/Proshop
GF: w/day $17.00, w/end
$19.00
Carts: $19.00

Great view of pastoral Wisconsin farmland vistas. Each nine different—front open and expansive suggestive of a Scottish links course and the back surrounded by native birch and cedar tress combined with Door County rock cliffs.

―――――――――――――――STURTEVANT―――――――――――――――

**Ives Grove Golf
Links**
14101 Washington
Ave., 53177
Ph: 414-878-3714

Yards: 6915, Holes: 18
Par: 72, USGA: 70.3
RP: 1 week in advance

Restaurant/Bar/Proshop
GF: w/day $13.50
Carts: $14.50

The sweeping winds at Ives Grove provide an ever changing personality to this outstanding public course. Large well trapped greens, watered fairways and our bent grass tees await all golfers. Strategy and skill needed to finish the 18th.

―――――――――――――――SUN PRAIRIE―――――――――――――――

Sun Prairie CC
Box 1, Happy Valley
Rd., 53590
Ph: 608-837-6211

Yards: 6487, Holes: 18
Par: 72, USGA: 69.1
RP: Call ahead

Bar/Proshop
GF: w/day $10.00
Carts: $14.00

The course is known for having some of the largest greens in the state. Enjoy the peaceful countryside setting.

―――――――――――――――SUPERIOR―――――――――――――――

Nemadji GC
N. 58th St. & Hill Ave.,
54880
Ph: 715-394-9022

Yards: 6058, Holes: 36
Par: 72, USGA: 71.4
RP: 1 day M-F; Wknds:
prior Wend.

Restaurant/Bar/Proshop
GF: w/day $8.00, w/end
$8.00
Carts: $7.50

On May 20, 1992 Nemadji Golf Course became a 36-hole facility. The Old Course features open fairways, lush greens, and a level terrain. The New Course plays to rolling hills, large bunkers, undulating greens and 6 lagoons.

────────────VERONA────────────

University Ridge GC   Yards: 6402, Holes: 18
7120 County Trunk   Par: 72
PD, Ph: 608-845-7700

The course is set in very hilly terrain, with the back of the course filled with trees.

────────────WHITEHALL────────────

Whitehall CC   Yards: 6080, Holes: 9   Restaurant/Bar/Proshop
West & Creamery Sts.,   Par: 70, USGA: 68.4   **GF:** w/day $5.00, w/end
54773 $7.00
Ph: 715-538-4800   **Carts:** $7.00

You start out on #1 (par 4) with a tree lined dogleg right termed the toughest starting hole in the state by CUGA President. The course has rolling terrain which causes many (up, down, and side) hill stances. Our favorite #2 (dogleg right) par 4.

────────────WISCONSIN DELLS────────────

Christmas Mountain   Yards: 6589, Holes: 18   Restaurant/Bar/Proshop
Village   Par: 71, USGA: 72.1   **GF:** w/day $22.00, w/end
S. 944 Christmas Mt.   Slope: 129 $22.00
Rd.,Hwy H, 53965   RP: Requested   **Carts:** $20.00
Ph: 608-253-1000

Relax among the rolling fairways flanked by stands of pines and oaks. The front nine is challenging but somewhat forgiving. The back nine, cut from the wooded hills is more than a walk in the park, requiring both accuracy and distance.

────────────WISCONSIN DELLS────────────

Cold Water Canyon   Yards: 2444, Holes: 9   Restaurant/Bar/Proshop
GC   Par: 33, USGA: 63.4   **GF:** w/day $9.00
4065 River Rd., Box 64,   RP: Recommended   **Carts:** $9.00
53965
Ph: 608-254-8489

With natural hazards, along the famous canyons of the Upper Dells, the beauty of this course far exceeds others in the area. For instance, though relatively short, Coldwater provides challenge to all levels of golfers. Hole #5 is a 296 yard (par 3).

────────────WISCONSIN RAPIDS────────────

Ridges GC   Yards: 6322, Holes: 18   Restaurant/Bar/Proshop
2311 Griffith Ave.,   Par: 72, USGA: 69.6   **GF:** w/day $5.00, w/end
54494   RP: Suggested $20.00
Ph: 715-424-1111   **Carts:** $20.00

The golf course is an 18 hole championship caliber layout winding through woods, a river, and hills.

────────────WOODRUFF────────────

Trout Lake G & CC   Yards: 6175, Holes: 18   Restaurant/Bar/Proshop
AV 3800 Hwy. 51   Par: 72, USGA: 69.6   **GF:** w/day $10.00
North, 54568   RP: Recommended   **Carts:** $18.00
Ph: 715-385-2189

This is a challenging, 18-hole course carved out of the beautiful forests of northern Wisconsin. Huge oak, maple, birch, and pine trees line the fairways as the Trout River wends its way through the course and comes into play on many of the hole.

WYOMING

• Jackson Hole

Cheyenne •

CHEYENNE

Cheyenne Airport GC
4801 Central Ave.,
82009
Ph: 307-637-6418

Yards: 6121, Holes: 18
Par: 70

Restaurant/Bar
GF: w/day $9.00, w/end
$18.00

This is a course of contrasts with the front narrow and tree filled, the back is longer and more wide open.

CHEYENNE

Holding's Little America GC
P.O. Box 1529, 82003
Ph: 307-634-2771

Yards: 2080, Holes: 9
Par: 30

Restaurant/Bar
GF: w/day $8.00

Enjoy golf on our 9-hole executive course surrounding the hotel, but look out for sandtraps, lakes, and a stray antelope or two.

CODY

Olive Glenn G&CC
802 Meadow Ln., 82414
Ph: 307-587-5551

Yards: 6887, Holes: 18
Par: 72, USGA: 71.6
RP: Call anytime in advance

Restaurant/Bar/Proshop
GF: w/day $20.00
Carts: $18.00

This course has a very dramatic setting on the edge of the prairie. The first hole and the last three holes are the most memorable. A course well worth you time.

GILLETTE

Bell Nob GC
4600 Overdale Dr., Ph:
307-686-7069

Yards: 6428, Holes: 18
Par: 72

This long course was designed by Frank Hummel. The wildlife may come into play here, as it is quite abundant.

JACKSON

Teton Pines CC
3450 Clubhouse Dr.,
83001
Ph: 307-733-1733

Yards: 7401, Holes: 18
Par: 72, USGA: 74.2
RP: Beginning in April
for season

Restaurant/Bar
GF: w/day $75.00, w/end
$75.00
Carts: $13.00

Water comes into play on nearly every hole of the meadow-type course, which is well-bunkered with contoured greens. Players rave about the par three #12 (221 yards) with its "over the water" tee shot set dramatically at mountain's base.

JACKSON HOLE

Jackson Hole Golf & | Yards: 7168, Holes: 18 | Restaurant/Bar/Proshop
Tennis Club | Par: 72, USGA: 70.3 | **GF:** w/day $28.00
5200 Spring Gulch Rd., | | **Carts:** $21.00
83001
Ph: 307-733-3111

Scattered lakes and streams provide interesting and challenging hazards. The course is rated among the 65 "Best Designed" golf courses in the country built prior to 1962 by American Society of Golf Course Architects.

LARAMIE

Laramie CC | Yards: 3209, Holes: 9
Hwy 130, Ph: 307-745- | Par: 36
8490

A nice, easy round with only small trees, and not a great deal of water.

ROCK SPRINGS

White Mountain GC | Yards: 6741, Holes: 18 | Restaurant/Bar
625 Ganett, 82901 | Par: 72 | **GF:** w/day $9.00, w/end
Ph: 307-382-5030 | | $10.00

A popular municipal course, that has some water holes.

SHERIDAN

Kendrick GC | Yards: 6532, Holes: 18 | **GF:** w/day $11.00, w/end
Box 6145, Big Goose | Par: 72, USGA: 69.8 | $12.00
Rd, 82801 | | **Carts:** $14.00
Ph: 307-674-8148

An older course that is one of the most challenging courses in the state. A scenic course that's set with views of the Big Horn Mountains.

TORRINGTON

Cottonwood CC | Yards: 6272, Holes: 18
W 15th St., Ph: 307-532- | Par: 72
3868

A course with lots of trees, set in hilly, rolling terrain. You should enjoy this round of golf.

WORLAND

Green Hills GC | Yards: 6052, Holes: 18 | Restaurant/Bar
1455 Airport Rd, 82401 | Par: 72 | **GF:** w/day $10.00, w/end
Ph: 307-347-8972 | | $11.00

A course that is quite flat, it's heavily treed, some water, and the greens are small.